Praise for *Philip & Elizabeth*

Gyles Brandreth:
'The writer who got closest to the human truth about our long-serving senior royals.'
Libby Purves, *The Times*

'*Philip & Elizabeth* boldly goes where other royal biographers have previously feared to tread . . . The book is exceptionally hard to put down.'
Humphrey Carpenter, *Sunday Times*

'Probably the most revealing portrait ever of the Queen.'
Marian Finucane, *RTE*

'The most insightful portrait of Prince Philip written to date.'
Robert Lacey, *Sunday Times*

'Wonderfully entertaining . . . impressive . . . compelling.'
John-Paul Flintoff, *Financial Times*

'Thoroughly entertaining . . . Filled with insights . . . He has had enviable access and he has used it well.'
Penny Junor, *Daily Telegraph*

'Cheeky, gossipy, often highly amusing . . . A most engagingly intimate volume.'
Peter Mackay, *Evening Standard*

'A joy . . . thoughtful . . . outrageous . . . sympathetic, wholly original, often hilarious, occasionally profound and unfailingly interesting . . . I came away with the strong feeling that I had glimpsed the Queen and Prince Philip for the first time as they really are.'
Craig Brown, *Mail On Sunday*

'*Philip & Elizabeth* is a unique biography. It is a powerful and revealing portrait of a remarkable partnership, told with authority and insight, and illustrated with photographs from the couple's collections.'
Ingrid Seward, *Majesty*

Blair: The First Centenary

Philip: The Final Portrait

Also by Gyles Brandreth

Biography
Dan Leno: The Funniest Man on Earth
John Gielgud: An Actor's Life
Brief Encounters: Meetings with Remarkable People
Philip & Elizabeth: Portrait of a Marriage
Charles & Camilla: Portrait of a Love Affair

Autobiography
Under the Jumper
Breaking the Code: Westminster Diaries
Something Sensational to Read in the Train: The Diary of a Lifetime

Novels
Who Is Nick Saint?
Venice Midnight

Murder Mysteries
Oscar Wilde and the Candlelight Murders
Oscar Wilde and the Ring of Death
Oscar Wilde and the Dead Man's Smile
Oscar Wilde and the Nest of Vipers
Oscar Wilde and the Vatican Murders
Oscar Wilde and the Murders at Reading Gaol
Jack the Ripper: Case Closed

Selected Non-fiction
Created in Captivity
I Scream for Ice Cream: Pearls from the Pantomime
Yaroo! The World of Frank Richards
The 7 Secrets of Happiness
Word Play

Children's fiction
The Ghost at Number Thirteen and sequels
The Slippers That Talked and sequels
Nattie & Nuffin
Max: The Boy Who Made a Million
Maisie: The Girl Who Lost Her Head

Theatre
Lewis Carroll Through the Looking-Glass
Dear Ladies (with Hinge & Bracket)
Now We Are Sixty (with Julian Slade)
Zipp! 100 Musicals for the Price of One
Wonderland (with Susannah Pearse)

Philip: The Final Portrait

Elizabeth, their Marriage and their Dynasty

GYLES BRANDRETH

CORONET

First published as *Philip & Elizabeth: Portrait of a Marriage*
Copyright © Gyles Brandreth 2004

1

Revised and updated edition
Copyright © Gyles Brandreth 2021

The right of Gyles Brandreth to be identified as the Author of
the Work has been asserted by him in accordance with
the Copyright, Designs and Patents Act 1988.

A CIP catalogue record for this title
is available from the British Library

Hardback ISBN: 978 1 444 76957 9
Trade Paperback ISBN: 978 1 444 76958 6

Typeset in Bembo by Palimpsest Book Production Limited,
Falkirk, Stirlingshire

Printed and bound in Great Britain by Clays Ltd, Elcograf S.p.A.

Hodder & Stoughton policy is to use papers that are natural,
renewable and recyclable products and made from wood grown
in sustainable forests. The logging and manufacturing processes
are expected to conform to the environmental
regulations of the country of origin.

Hodder & Stoughton Ltd
Carmelite House
50 Victoria Embankment
London EC4Y 0DZ

www.hodder.co.uk

Contents

Harold: You agree that a successful marriage is the greatest of human benefits?

Vita: Yes.

Harold: And that it must be based on love guided by intelligence?

Vita: Yes.

Harold: That an essential condition is a common sense of values?

Vita: Yes.

Harold: That the only things that will stave off marital nerves are modesty, good humour and, above all, occupation?

Vita: Yes.

Harold: And give and take?

Vita: And give and take.

Harold: And mutual esteem. I do not believe in the permanence of any love which is based on pity, or the protective or maternal instincts. It must be based on respect.

Vita: Yes, I agree. The caveman plus sweet-little-thing theory is long past. It was a theory insulting to the best qualities of both.

Harold Nicolson and Vita Sackville-West discussing marriage on BBC radio in 1929, quoted in *Portrait of a Marriage* by their son Nigel Nicolson, 1973

Introduction

'People who write books ought to be shut up,' said King George V.

'This is Gyles Brandreth,' said the Duke of Edinburgh, introducing me to Queen Elizabeth II.

Her Majesty proffered me a tightly gloved hand and murmured an almost inaudible, 'How do you do?' Her consort continued cheerily, 'Apparently, he's writing about you.' The Duke paused and leant towards his wife's ear: 'Be warned. He's going to cut you into pieces.'

The Queen looked startled. The Duke chuckled. I smiled.

I knew the Duke of Edinburgh over a period of more than forty years. I was accustomed to his sense of humour. I liked it. I liked him. I admired him as much as any man I have known. It was knowing him as I did that led me to write this book about him, and his wife, and their remarkable marriage – the longest-lasting marriage of any sovereign and consort in history.

I first met Prince Philip in the 1970s, when he was in his fifties and I was in my twenties, and I became involved in the work of the National Playing Fields Association. The Association is the National Trust of recreational space: it protects playing fields and playgrounds, and aims to enhance opportunities for competitive sport and creative play, especially for young people and those with disabilities. It is a good cause, if a touch unglamorous. The charity, now known as Fields in Trust, was founded in the 1920s, with Elizabeth II's father, then a young Duke of York, as its first president. Prince Philip, as a young Duke of Edinburgh, took on the presidency in 1948, soon after he married Princess Elizabeth. It was the first national charity in which he became involved. He remained its president until the week of his ninety-second birthday in June 2013, when he handed over the reins to his grandson, Prince William.

As the President of the NPFA Prince Philip was impressive: informed, committed, personally involved. He took the responsibilities of his office seriously. He was an effective fund-raiser. 'The fund-raising never stops!' he used to sigh. He was an intelligent and persuasive leader, with an unnerving eye for detail (and for flannel and flimflam), who was at his best when given a problem to solve, a difficult meeting to chair, an internal row requiring resolution. He liked to be given something specific to do. He welcomed detail. I accompanied him to the opening of a youth centre on Merseyside. His debriefing note to me was devoted to how best to relocate the lavatories and showers so as to maximise the space available for the sports facilities. 'Yes,' he said, 'I am practical. I like to help make things work.' He wanted to make a difference where others, often, only make a noise. He wasn't one for honeyed words and empty gestures. He did not give his wife bunches of flowers or cards inscribed with sentimental messages: he gave her pieces of jewelry he had designed and made himself.

I liked his style. I admired his achievement. I enjoyed his company. Having observed it at close quarters, I thought his manner with people was delightful and the more unassuming the people the friendlier he was. I recall coming down the back stairs with him after some lunchtime function at a club in central London. We passed the kitchen. The Duke stopped, turned back and marched in, unannounced, to meet the chefs and dish-washers. There was laughter, back-slapping, joshing: an enviable display of people skills and unselfconscious charm. The only time I have seen it quite as well done was recently – by Prince William.

What the Duke of Edinburgh made of me, if anything, I cannot tell you.[1] He called me 'Gyles'. I called him 'Sir'. His last letter to

---

1 The writer Craig Brown thinks he knows. Here is Brown's parody of an entry from Brandreth's 'royal diary': 'January 22. To Buckingham Palace to attend an investiture. Prince Philip greets me with his usual affectionate male banter. "What the hell are you doing here?" he jests. "I thought I told them to keep you away!" I roar with infectious laughter as he turns on his heel – but with perfect timing I catch him just as he reaches the door. "You are an irrepressible old character, sir!" I congratulate him. "A national treasure, forsooth!" At this point, the Prince raises a good-natured fist and socks me in the mouth. "Marvellous, sir!" I enthuse, picking up my front teeth from the beautifully polished floor.'

me, written from Windsor Castle, was full of characteristic dry humour and his trademark double exclamation marks (!!); it was signed 'Yours ever'. But I am mindful of the former Prime Minister James Callaghan's observation: 'What senior royalty offer you is friendliness, not friendship. There is a difference.'

There were times when I felt quite close to Prince Philip – like a proper friend, or as much of a friend as you can be with a man who is thirty years your senior and the husband of the head of state. Sitting alone with him in his library at Buckingham Palace, sharing a drink, he was the best company: completely unstuffy, easy to talk to – and happy to talk about anything.

We talked about life. 'Has it been fun?' I asked him once.

'Fun?' he snorted. 'I don't think I think much about "fun". Do you think much about fun?'

'Yes,' I said. 'Now and again.'

'*Really*? I suppose the polo was fun,' he conceded. 'Playing cricket was fun, in the old days. The carriage driving is fun – when you don't fall off the box seat. Then it's just bloody painful.'

'Has it been enjoyable?'

'My life? Enjoyable?' He screwed up his eyes. 'I enjoyed flying. I enjoyed flying very much. I sometimes think I should have joined the air force instead of the navy.'

'Is that one of your regrets?'

'Regrets are a waste of energy. There's no point in having regrets.'

'Has it been a good life?' I persisted. 'Worthwhile?'

He shrugged. 'I don't know about that. I've kept myself busy. I've tried to make myself useful. I hope I've helped keep the show on the road. That's about it, really.'

We talked about death. 'Death is part of life,' he said. 'You've got to face it. You've got to accept it – with a good grace.' He laughed. 'When you get to my age, there's a lot of it about.'

Death was part of Prince Philip's life from the beginning. His grandfather, King George I of Greece, was assassinated a few years before he was born. His favourite sister, Cécile, was killed in an aeroplane accident when he was still a teenager. His favourite uncle (and his guardian at the time), George Milford Haven, died of cancer soon after. His father, Prince Andrew of Greece, died when Philip was just twenty-three. His other favourite uncle, Earl Mountbatten of Burma, was murdered by the IRA in 1979. 'I'm quite ready to die,' the Duke said to me. 'It's what happens – sooner or later.'

'Later rather than sooner, we hope,' I said.

He looked at me, smiling. 'I certainly don't want to hang on until I am a hundred like Queen Elizabeth [the Queen Mother]. I can't imagine anything worse. I'm already falling to pieces as it is. Bits keeps dropping off. I have absolutely no desire to cling on to life unnecessarily. Ghastly prospect.'

I think that when he died, he died happy. In the last ten years of his life he seemed a more settled soul than once upon a time. He could still be cantankerous and tetchy – he was wilful and contrary to the last – but, overall, he appeared to me to be more contented in late life than he had been in middle age, more at ease with himself, with his family, and with the world. I believe he recognised, finally, that people recognised his contribution and, though he made light of it, that pleased him very much.

On Monday, 4 June 2012, six days before his ninety-first birthday, he should have been at the Queen's side at the Diamond Jubilee concert that was staged in her honour in front of Buckingham Palace. He wasn't there because the day before, as part of the Jubilee River Pageant, for several hours he had stood at the Queen's side in a boat on the Thames in driving rain and had exacerbated a pre-existing bladder infection. He stood because the Queen stood – and the Queen stood because neither of them wanted to be seen seated on the grandiose thrones the pageant organisers had provided for them. 'We'd have looked like Mr and Mrs Beckham, wouldn't we?' said the Duke. 'You've got to draw the line somewhere.' And because the Queen remained on deck, standing in the rain, the Duke remained there, too. It would not have occurred to him to be anywhere else.

Having spent Sunday in the rain, Prince Philip was admitted to hospital on Monday. That night, at the end of the Jubilee concert, the Prince of Wales stood next to the Queen and gave a short speech, saluting his mother and thanking those who had performed during the evening. The speech was warm, witty, and well judged. The crowd cheered almost every phrase, but they cheered loudest by far when Prince Charles asked them to cheer for the one person who was conspicuous by his absence: his father, Prince Philip. In the Mall on that wet and windy Monday night in June 2012, a quarter of a million people stood in the cold chanting, 'Philip, Philip, Philip!'

A mile away, in his hospital bed, the Duke of Edinburgh watched the scene on television – and was touched by what he saw and heard.

I know (because he told me) that Prince Philip was disappointed that his doctors' orders obliged him to miss some of the celebrations for the Queen's Diamond Jubilee. In truth, perhaps not the pop concert outside Buckingham Palace (the Duke felt that he had endured more than his fair share of Elton John down the years), but certainly the Service of Thanksgiving at St Paul's Cathedral on the following day. 'I was sad not to be there,' he said to me. He had wanted to be there, at the Queen's side. That's why, a year later, he was so determined to be at Westminster for the service marking the sixtieth anniversary of the Queen's Coronation. It was, after all, what his life had been about.

'That's what you do,' I said to him. 'You support the Queen.'

'Yes.'

'It is who you are.'

He smiled. 'It is a family business.'

In 1897 the Duke's mother, aged twelve, was there for Queen Victoria's Diamond Jubilee. Princess Alice was born at Windsor Castle, the daughter of Princess Victoria, one of Queen Victoria's favourite granddaughters. And the Duke's father's father, King George I of Greece, was an ADC to Queen Victoria – and, later, to Edward VII (who married Philip's great-aunt Alexandra) and, later still, to George V (whose granddaughter Philip married.) By birth, Prince Philip was twice as royal as Elizabeth II. The Queen's father was a king, but her mother was a commoner. The Duke of Edinburgh was royal to the marrow – related through each of his parents to kings, queens, emperors, kaisers, tsars.

In the summer of 2012, the Duke was touched, too, and surprised, by the Diamond Jubilee television film made by Prince Charles and broadcast at the start of the Jubilee weekend. The film was essentially a personal tribute by Charles to his mother, illustrated with 'home movies' from the early years of his parents' marriage.

Once upon a time Prince Charles was in the habit of complaining about his childhood – plaintively and to almost anyone who would listen. In the early 1990s, when he cooperated with the broadcaster Jonathan Dimbleby to produce a documentary and a book about his life, the Prince of Wales made it clear to all the world that, as a boy, he had felt neglected at home and abandoned at school. His parents did not cherish him, or understand him, in the way that his grandmother, Queen Elizabeth the Queen Mother, did. Twenty years on, in 2012, it became clear from the Prince's Jubilee broadcast that his view had changed. Charles spoke of both his parents with unfeigned affection. And rightly so. It was evident from those old family films – as it always had been from the accounts of those who had been there at the time – that the Queen and Prince Philip had been loving parents: caring, concerned, and, given the style of parenting of those of their class and generation and the restrictions imposed on them by their official duties, remarkably hands-on.

When Prince Philip talked to me about Prince Charles in the 1980s and 1990s there was invariably a touch of exasperation in his tone – and often, too, a note of sarcasm. The Duke gave the impression that he would have liked his son to be more robust, less fey. The father did little to disguise his feelings about the son. In the summer of 1986, for example, at a meeting of the officers of the Playing Fields Association, we presented our president with what we hoped would be a welcome birthday present: three pairs of carriage-driving gloves. He unwrapped the parcel and inspected our gift. The first pair of gloves were a light tan colour. The Duke sniffed approvingly. The second pair were dark tan. 'Thank you very much,' he said. The third pair were a pale lilac colour. He held them up disdainfully between his thumb and forefinger and said, 'I think we'll give these to the Prince of Wales.'

There was a time when the Duke of Edinburgh regarded the Prince of Wales as 'precious, extravagant, and lacking in the dedication necessary to make a good king' – and said so. I don't believe that is what he felt at the time of his death, but it was certainly what he felt in the aftermath of the death of Diana, Princess of Wales.

The Duke's disdain for his eldest son was the more shocking because of the way he made little or no attempt to hide it. Once, boldly, I challenged him about it. I told Prince Philip that, having met him and his son, I was struck, not by their differences, but by their similarities. Their gait, their body language, the joshing humour, the moments of pig-headedness each displayed, the shared enthusiasms (nature conservancy, painting, poetry, comparative religion). I said, 'You're clearly peas from the same pod, you're so similar.' He interrupted me: 'Yes, but with one great difference. He's a Romantic – and I'm a pragmatist. That means we do see things differently. And because I don't see things as a Romantic would, I'm *unfeeling*.'

Prince Charles was not alone in sometimes thinking his father 'unfeeling'. As I researched this book, I encountered a number of people – including some who had known Prince Philip for some years, including members of his wife's family – who, unprompted, described him to me as 'cool', 'cold', 'hard', 'distant', and 'unfeeling'. In my experience of him, while he could be distant and forbidding – even frightening – when he chose, he was not unfeeling. That said, he did reflect the attitudes of his generation – much as Charles reflects his. Prince Philip was born in 1921 and brought up in the age when introspection equalled self-indulgence and a stiff upper lip was a virtue, not a disability. He made his marriage work, both because he wanted to and because, in his day, that's what you did. 'You've made your bed, now lie on it.' As the Queen's consort, whatever the frustrations, the Duke of Edinburgh knuckled down to the job in hand, because in his day that was what was expected. He was not one to brood about the past or talk to the flowers, because in his day you didn't.

Prince Philip and Prince Charles both had unusual childhoods, but, by any standards, Philip's was the more challenging. When Philip was a baby his father was put on trial and then sent into exile. When Philip was nine, his parents separated. His father left the family home in Paris and floated down to Monte Carlo, where he became something of a boulevardier, with a fondness for the ladies and the bottle. Philip's mother suffered a mental breakdown and was sent away for treatment to a Swiss sanatorium. From the age of nine, and throughout his adolescence, Philip had no parental home. In the school holidays he travelled, without complaint, between the homes of assorted relations.

From first to last, Philip resolutely refused to accept that any of this affected him adversely. When I first wrote an account of his life, I sent my draft to him. By return, he sent me a memorandum correcting facts, dates, and usage with customary briskness ('In the Navy you serve IN a ship, not on a ship. Rather like living in a house not on a house'), but he did not quibble with any of my personal observations – except when it came to his upbringing.

With regard to what I had written about his father, the Duke protested:'I am not sure what you mean by "floated" down to Monte Carlo. He was in exile with no home and very little money. It was a lot cheaper than living in Paris. He had a very small flat there and spent a lot of time visiting his daughters.' With regard to what I had said about his peripatetic school holidays, the Duke questioned my turns of phrase: 'Why "without complaint"? What did I have to complain about? Why "assorted" relations? They were my sisters and their in-laws.'

Prince Philip would not – did not – complain about any aspect of his childhood. In my experience he did not complain about any aspect of his life – except, perhaps, the way in which he and the Royal Family were treated by the press. Certainly, if you suggested that he might have been personally frustrated that the Queen's accession to the throne in 1952 had brought his naval career to a premature close, he would deny it. 'You have to make compromises,' he said to me. 'That's life. I accepted it. I tried to make the best of it.'

'Try to make the best of it' was what he counselled each of his three elder children to do when their marriages began to falter. As you will discover in Chapter 12, in his practical, pragmatic way he made heroic attempts to help Charles and Diana as their marriage failed. 'I did my best,' he told me. 'We did our best.'

'Did they do their best?' I asked.

He didn't answer.

'Anne did her best,' he said. When Princess Anne's first marriage foundered, the Queen and Prince Philip were saddened, of course, but as the Duke put it to me, 'What can you do? It isn't easy. She tried to make it work. She really did.' A few years later, when Anne had remarried, the Duke told me that she and her new husband were having a 'rocky patch – you're married, you know how it is?'

'I do,' I said.

'I don't know what to do to help,' he said. He shook his head. He made no attempt to hide his distress and concern. It clearly weighed on him quite heavily. It must have done because this conversation was taking place in public: at a charity fund-raising lunch in the Cabinet War Rooms. We had only just taken our places: food was being served. I was seated one place away from the Duke. He turned to the middle-aged woman who was seated between us. 'As a rule, I try to keep out of these things,' he explained.

'But you want to help,' said the woman, who had married children of her own.

'Yes,' said the Duke, contemplating his starter, 'but I don't know what to say – except, "Keep going, it will work out. With good will on both sides, it usually does."' He sighed. 'Children.'

On the whole, he was reasonably circumspect when talking about his children and their relationships – except in the case of Prince Andrew and Sarah Ferguson. He spoke with real affection of their daughters, the Princesses Beatrice and Eugenie, but he made no secret of the fact that he regarded Sarah, Duchess of York, as 'simply beyond the pale'. That Andrew and Sarah appeared to remain friends after their separation – and that they shared a home even after their divorce – seemed to him 'truly bizarre'. 'I don't pretend to understand it,' he said.

'But you won't even see her,' I said to him. 'She is the mother of your granddaughters. Why won't you see Sarah?'

'I am not vindictive,' he said, looking directly at me. 'I am not vindictive,' he repeated emphatically, 'but I don't see the point.'

When, one day in the summer of 1992, photographs appeared in a daily newspaper of Sarah, topless, having her toes sucked by a lover in the south of France, the Duke of Edinburgh decided that, as far as he was concerned, 'enough was enough'. He did not want – or need – to have anything more to do with her.

A few years later, in the spring of 2001, when a Sunday newspaper ran a different embarrassing story about another of his daughters-in-law, the Duke was more sympathetic. Sophie, Countess of Wessex, wife of the youngest of the royal children, was the victim of a 'sting' set up by the *News of the World*. Her reported remarks were unfortunate, but her parents-in-law immediately forgave her. Why? 'She was "set up" by Murdoch and his merry men,' said the Duke. 'It was entrapment.'

Sophie's husband, Prince Edward, seemingly a bit wet and a tad irritating to the rest of us, was always his parents' favourite. That became apparent in 1987 when Edward, aged twenty-two, opted out of the Royal Marines when he was just a third of the way through his twelve-month basic training course. To the surprise of some, Prince Philip (Captain-General of the Royal Marines) did not come down on his son like a ton of bricks. He accepted that the Marines 'wasn't right for Edward' – and to this day Edward is grateful for that.

Edward was always close to his father. At the time of the Queen's Diamond Jubilee, when Prince Philip was taken into hospital, it wasn't a surprise to see that it was Edward and Sophie (the parents of the only ones of the royal grandchildren to carry the surname Mountbatten-Windsor) who were the first to visit the Duke. And Edward and Sophie were there, in pride of place, in a wedding photo on the sideboard behind the Queen, when Her Majesty made her Thank You broadcast to the nation at the end of the jubilee celebrations. And now that Prince Philip is dead, it is Prince Edward who will be recreated as the next Duke of Edinburgh.

'I tried to be a good father,' said Prince Philip. 'I did my best.' That he was an outstanding grandfather has never been in dispute. From youth to old age, he was always good with very small children, and with William and Harry, who lost their mother when they were only fifteen and twelve years of age, he was – in William's phrase – 'a tower of strength and understanding'. At the time of the Queen's Diamond Jubilee Prince Harry managed to capture both Prince Philip's elusive quality and his indispensability to the Queen in the same revealing sentence: 'Regardless of whether my grandfather seems to be doing his own thing, sort of wandering off like a fish down the river, the fact that he's there – personally, I don't think that she could do it without him, especially when they're both at this age.'

What was remarkable about the Duke of Edinburgh was that he managed, across seven decades, to be both a pivotal figure at the centre of the British Royal Family and, at the same time, something of a loner, an outsider, his own man: a face familiar to all and yet an individual who remained a touch unknowable, even to those who knew him well.

To me, sometimes he seemed like a proper friend, sometimes almost like a father (I was born in the same year as Prince Charles), but in my experience you could never be entirely sure where you were with him: the easy intimacy of one meeting might be replaced by a definite formality at the next. For the most part, when others were present he treated me as though, somehow, I had joined his staff by mistake, that I shouldn't really be there, but since I was, I might as well stay. He seemed gently amused by me, if a little wary. He knew that I was fundamentally 'on side' – I was the chairman of one of his pet charities; I wrote and broadcast about him sympathetically – but he also never forgot that I was a journalist and, with good reason, he was very suspicious of journalists.

Over the years I spent many hours with him – at breakfasts, lunches, dinners, in meetings, formal and informal, on sundry visits and official tours – and I never found him anything but agreeable: occasionally impatient, but always tolerant. When I accompanied him to a charity pantomime one Christmas, he hissed the villain as required and chorused, 'He's behind you!' on cue. When I asked him if I could bring a parade of clowns and stilt-walkers into the forecourt of Buckingham Palace as part of a fund-raising event, he raised a doubtful eyebrow but agreed.

In the early 1980s, when I was a presenter with TV-am, Britain's first commercial breakfast television station, I told Prince Philip one day that I happened to have had breakfast with 'Blake Carrington' from *Dynasty*. His Royal Highness looked at me, bemused. 'I haven't the first idea what you're talking about,' he said. 'I had breakfast with the Queen.' When I told him there was now breakfast television on both BBC and ITV, he seemed utterly appalled. 'Every day?' he asked, incredulous. In those days he watched very little TV – *A Question of Sport* and the *Nine O'Clock News*, that was about it. On another occasion I was at Buckingham Palace, in attendance, while he presented the Playing Fields Association's 'President's Certificates' to assorted supporters of the cause. I arrived a little late for the ceremony and explained that I had been delayed because I had been judging a charity Knit-a-Teddy-Bear competition and there had been 1,300 entries. The Duke looked at me pityingly. 'And I thought I had to do some damned stupid things,' he said. Then he handed out the President's Certificates, as planned, shook hands with the recipients, chatted amiably, and, duty done, nodded to the assembled company and wandered on his way. He had seven similar engagements that day. 'I think I'm with the clockmakers next,' he said to me as I walked with him to the door. 'I like to be a bit on the late side for them.' He was a funny man. He liked to laugh – and to make others laugh.

And now he's gone, I miss him. What do I miss most?

I miss his energy.

Even in old age, Prince Philip crackled with energy. In 2011, the year he turned ninety, he undertook 330 official engagements. The following year he managed 347. In his prime, he was a dynamo. At sixty-five, the age at which most men retire, the Duke of Edinburgh was the active founder, fellow, patron, president, chairman, or member of at least 837 organisations – as well as a Colonel or Colonel-in-Chief, Field Marshal, Admiral, and Air Commodore forty-two times over. During his long life he endured more than sixty-five years of royal flummery: parades, processions, receptions, launches, lunches, dinners – upwards of 25,000 official engagements. He made speeches, he unveiled plaques, he handed out certificates. He measured out his life in handshakes and small talk. And to maintain his sanity, alongside the surface stuff, the meeting and the greeting, the waving and saluting, ('It's necessary, unavoidable,' he said. 'I know that'), he got 'stuck into' a range of particular projects where in-depth involvement gave him the satisfaction of achievement. The Duke of Edinburgh's Award Scheme, as just one example, has touched the lives of millions of young people around the world in a multiplicity of positive ways. He did not just turn up, he made things happen.

I will miss his sense of humour. Even in his nineties the banter did not stop. On the last two occasions when he and I were speakers at fund-raising events at Buckingham Palace, throughout each of my speeches His Royal Highness kept up a barrage of barracking designed to disconcert me and entertain the crowd. 'Get on with it,' he'd call out. 'We've heard this story before – and it isn't true. Don't believe a word he says. What on earth's he going on about now?'

The Duke's reputation for curmudgeonliness came about not simply because of the kind of banter that sometimes came my way, but also, and more so, because, in conversation, he was deliberately challenging. He questioned, he argued, he played devil's advocate, he answered back. Whatever you'd say, his automatic response was, 'Yes, but—' He did it, I believe, both to show an interest and to maintain his own interest. When you meet scores of people in a day (and some days he met hundreds) it would be easy to let everything that's said wash over you. However briefly, the Duke of Edinburgh tried to become engaged in whatever he was doing. He had an enquiring mind. 'I suppose I challenge things to stimulate myself,' he told me once, 'and to be stimulating. You don't have to agree with everyone all the time. It would be a dull world if you did.'

He was more thoughtful and much kinder than the common caricature of him would suggest. For example, when I told him that I hoped to become a Member of Parliament but had never attended the State Opening of Parliament, he sent me tickets. When I told him I had found a constituency where I hoped to be the candidate, he gave me useful advice on how to make small talk with all and sundry. He offered the question 'What's keeping you busy these days?' as an all-purpose opening gambit. (The ingenuity of the phrasing comes into its own when the person you are addressing is someone you have met before but have wholly forgotten.) When, in 1992, I was elected as MP for the City of Chester and the Queen and the Duke happened to pay an official visit to my constituency (for the Queen to distribute the Royal Maundy in Chester Cathedral), His Royal Highness broke away from the formal procession – abandoning the Queen and the Lord Mayor – to say hello to me. The effect on those around me was noticeable – and gratifying.

Prince Philip went out of his way to perform small kindnesses – and to put people at their ease. He knew that he was portrayed in the press as 'a cantankerous old sod' (his phrase, not mine), but protested: 'I don't think I have ever got up to make a speech of any kind, anywhere, ever, and not made the audience laugh at least once. You arrive somewhere and you go down that receiving line . . . I get two or three of them to laugh. Always.'

Meeting royalty is not a comfortable experience. It's oddly nerve-racking. Prince Philip would make a crack to break the ice. But Michael Seward, when canon treasurer at St Paul's Cathedral, was one of those who complained about the Duke's manner. 'You never know if it will be a snort, a snub, or a merry laugh,' he said. I think it was only ever banter. Prince Philip knew he must say *something*, because if he stayed silent that would have been interpreted as him being surly. He couldn't win.

From my limited experience as an MP, I reckon one of the most wearisome aspects of public life is the requirement to be genial all the time. If you are the Queen's consort, you will not remember everyone you meet, but everybody you meet will remember you, and how you seem, and what you say. The Duke admitted this much: 'Occasionally I get fed up, going to visit a factory, when I'm being shown round by the chairman who clearly hasn't got a clue, and I try to get hold of the factory manager but I can't because the chairman wants to make sure he's the one in all the photographs.'

I know I pleased him once by saying to him, 'You've got a reputation for not suffering fools gladly, but in fact you've been suffering fools willingly for more than fifty years.' He grinned at me, nodded, and said, slowly and quietly, 'I have suffered fools . . . with . . . patience.'

But he could be impatient. He could be irascible. He could be grumpy. Once I saw him bark sharply at a footman in Buckingham Palace. It was not a pretty sight. And the footman, of course, could not answer back.

When it came to unflattering and inaccurate stories about him in the press, Prince Philip could not answer back either. This he found frustrating. What exasperated him in particular, he told me, was that so much of the coverage of the Royal Family had become 'so unremittingly negative'. Once upon a time, royalties (as they were called) could take a discreet and deferential press for granted. Not any more. I asked Prince Philip when he thought it started to go wrong. He said, without hesitation, 'After [Rupert] Murdoch bought the *Today* newspaper from Eddie Shah [in 1987]. Day after day there was a derogatory story about one member of the family or another.'

It rankled. Prince Philip gave the impression of having a hide like a rhinoceros. It was an impression he cultivated. As I discovered, the impression belied the truth. The man was much more sensitive than he appeared.

When, once, I told him that I had made a list of the popular myths that existed about him, he asked immediately, 'Tactless overseas? Is that on your list?' He glanced at the notebook I was holding in my hand, saw the words 'slitty eyes', and sighed.

On 16 October 1986, in Beijing, when the Queen and the Duke were on a state visit to China, Prince Philip met a group of British students studying at the North West University in Xian. The Duke was particularly interested in the students because they came from Edinburgh University (he was Chancellor of four universities: Edinburgh from 1952) and chatting to them informally (with neither Chinese nor press present) he expressed surprise when he discovered that they were spending a whole year in China – long enough 'to go native and come home slit-eyed'.

It was a joke, a bit of badinage, but, because one of the students later gave a friendly account of the conversation to a journalist, an inconsequential private aside was turned into banner headlines around the world. 'The great wally of China,' said the *Mirror*; 'The Duke gets it wong,' said the *Sun*. As well as depicting the Duke as gaffe-prone, there was the unpleasant implication that he was an old-school casual racist. Certainly, Prince Philip was no disciple of the politically correct, but in forty years I never detected a hint of racism in him. Indeed, he told me that two of his best friends at his first school in Paris, when he was a little boy of six or seven, were Chinese: the Koo brothers, Freeman and Wellington, sons of the Chinese Ambassador to Paris, V.K. Wellington Koo. At the school, Philip recalled that he was known as 'the boy who had no surname' and young Wellington Koo was known as 'Ching Ching Chinaman'. 'That's just the way it was,' he said to me. He was a man of his era. 'If I did use the phrase "slit-eyed",' he protested, 'I certainly didn't use it offensively. Why would I?'

I was once with him at a private lunch party where, across the table, he stopped someone mid-sentence because they were attempting to tell a joke with a mildly racist overtone. Prince Philip was not a racist, but nor was he a disciple of political correctness. He would speak his mind, regardless of the consequences. When upbraided for making a comment about a fuse box that had so many wires hanging out 'that it looked as if it had been put together by an Indian', he retorted, 'Have you ever been to India and looked at a fuse box there?'

'How do you keep the natives off the booze long enough to get them through the test?' the Duke of Edinburgh allegedly asked a driving instructor in Oban, Scotland, in 1995. 'You managed not to get eaten, then?' he said, in 1998, to a student who had been trekking in Papua New Guinea. To a Briton he met in Budapest,

Hungary, in 1993, he remarked, 'You can't have been here that long – you haven't got a pot belly.' In Australia in 2002, at an Aboriginal cultural display, he enquired of his host, 'Do you still throw spears at each other?' The Duke knew that his so-called 'gaffes' would feature prominently in his obituaries and accepted that there was nothing much he could do about it – except growl in private.

In May 1999 he was particularly incensed when he was accused of mocking some deaf children at a pop concert in south Wales. He was reported to have jeered at them, 'Deaf? No wonder you are deaf, listening to this row.' A few days after the event, on 4 June, he wrote to me from Buckingham Palace: 'You may have noticed that the tabloids were quick to suggest that I had made another 'gaffe' and 'insulted' some deaf children at Cardiff recently. Needless to say, the story is largely invention. It so happens that my mother was quite seriously deaf and I have been Patron of the Royal National Institute for the Deaf for ages, so it's hardly likely that I would do any such thing. Quite apart from that, I have no recollection of meeting a group of deaf children at the event for the Prince's Trust in the grounds of Cardiff Castle. There were young people milling all over the place and there may well have been a group of deaf children amongst them. What I do remember is that the noise from various stages and bands was quite deafening and I may well have said at some point something to the effect that if anyone were to sit too close to the loud speakers they would certainly be in danger of going deaf.'

But the gaffes weren't the worst of it. Over the years, he was distressed as well as infuriated by the steady stream of newspaper and magazine stories about his supposed extramarital love life. Around the world, over many years, journalists and publishers – and documentary film-makers and book writers – peddled unsubstantiated tittle-tattle about him and, mostly, got away with it because what, realistically, could he do about it? As he saw it, suing was not the answer: 'It's a cumbersome and costly process and gives more coverage to the libel. "Queen's husband in court" – oh, yes? No smoke without fire . . .'

In 1994, when I was an MP, I was the victim of a tabloid 'sting'. A prostitute told a Sunday newspaper that I had visited a 'massage parlour' in my constituency. I had done no such thing and I resented the suggestion that I had. Happily, because there was no truth in the story, it was not published, but the experience of being pursued by the newspaper (and being told that the newspaper had secured 'signed affidavits' from the prostitute) was a nasty one and I decided to clear the air by writing an article for the *Daily Telegraph* describing the experience.

My article prompted a letter to me from Prince Philip. He typed it himself. The letter illustrates his feelings about, and his experience of, the modern media, and the way in which, when faced with a problem, the Duke always tried to come up with a solution.

BUCKINGHAM PALACE
18 May 1994

Dear Gyles,

I enjoyed your article in the DT this morning. It is about time that something was said about this particular form of harassment by the tabloids. However, it is not the only way in which journalists enjoy venting their spleen on those in the public eye. I have had fairly extensive experience of that sort of treatment over the years! For the last few years, it is regularly predicted that Kitty Kelley is writing a book about me.

It is a relatively new phenomenon. I don't think any newspaper – tabloid or broadsheet – was quite as vicious or carping 40 years ago as they have become today. There are probably many reasons for this, but I would like to suggest three: –

1. The introduction by Murdoch of Australian tabloid standards. I was out in Australia during the war and I well remember being struck by the sheer viciousness of their tabloids such as 'Truth'.

2. The development of TV has meant that newspapers are no longer the purveyors of news. Whatever they print is bound to be out of date. Therefore – apart from the sports pages – they have to compete as entertainers and there is no doubt – whatever anyone says – that ordinary people love gossip and they seem to love reading disparaging things about public figures that give them a glow of self-righteousness.

3. All journalists have a very high regard for themselves, even

if others do not have to share that view. I suspect that being rude about public figures, or making them look ridiculous, makes them feel more important – it boosts their egos . . . 'look at me, I have just spat in this important person's eye and he is too frightened of me to do anything about it.'

You suggest that there is nothing that should be done about this except to invite them to change their attitude. I rather doubt whether anything will change while the present circulation war continues in a declining market. Indeed, I think it will become even more desperate as circulations drop still further.

I would like to put forward just one idea. At the moment any paper can print stories as rumours and they can print what they claim are quotations, very often in inverted commas which imply that the words were actually uttered by the person concerned. The victim is then left to deny the rumour of the quotation, but the damage has been done while the journalist merely claims that it came from an impeccable source. It seems to me that the 'boot should be on the other foot'. It should be up to the journalist to produce proof that the story – even if it is said to be a rumour – has a basis in fact, or some convincing evidence that a statement was actually made by the victim. In other words, it would give the victim the right to say 'prove it, or pay up'.

Incidentally the tabloids are not alone in this sleazy business. Not long ago I was interviewed for one of the broadsheet magazines. It may interest you to know that, among several questions, the interviewer told me that it was commonly believed, and wanted me to say whether, I had any illegitimate children, my second son was fathered by someone else and I had a homosexual relationship with Giscard D'Estaing!!

Yours sincerely,
Philip

Kitty Kelley's book, when it appeared in 1997, was called *The Royals* and did not devote very many of its seven hundred and fifty pages to Prince Philip and his alleged peccadilloes. However, it did carry an account of the interview His Royal Highness had given to Fiammetta Rocco for the *Independent on Sunday*. She was the journalist who had asked him whether his second son had been fathered by someone else. He greeted the question with an uncompromising silence. According to Kitty Kelley, 'he sat as impassive as stone'. However, when Ms Rocco put it to the Duke that he had once enjoyed an affair with the former French president, Valéry Giscard D'Estaing, Prince Philip apparently responded with a laugh, 'Oh, Giscard is a delightful old boy, but I never stayed at the Elysée Palace when he was president. I would stay there when [Vincent] Auriol was president [1947–54], and he was a frightful buggerer.'

A few days later, a message came to Fiammetta Rocco from Prince Philip: 'Do not use the Auriol anecdote on your tape.' She didn't. According to Kitty Kelley: 'Afterward, Philip said he would never give another interview to a British reporter. But by then his personal life, once off limits to the press, had become vulnerable. The *Independent on Sunday* reported that he and the Queen slept in separate bedrooms. *Vanity Fair* said he kept a mistress. The *New Yorker* said it was a "succession of actress-mistresses who regularly appeared on television, prompting viewers in the know to smile and say, 'She's one of his.'" For those not in the know, the *Tatler* published "The Royal Collection", which provided the names, biographies, and photographs of thirteen women described as the "Duke of Edinburgh's fan club".'

Whatever was the truth about Prince Philip's alleged extramarital relationships – and in Chapter 11 I will tackle the issue in full and head-on – what no one is going to deny is that the Queen's husband enjoyed the company of intelligent, articulate, and attractive women. Indeed, to mark his seventieth birthday, I organised a 'ladies only' lunch in his honour at the Savoy Hotel. The room was filled with good-looking younger women – and several were actresses. The actress Jane Asher baked the birthday cake. I placed another attractive actress, Joanna Lumley, and my own beautiful wife, Michèle Brown, either side of His Royal Highness. By several accounts (I was not there: it really was ladies only, apart from the Prince) a happy time was had by all.

Prince Philip was attractive to women. He had the gifts of the charmer: he listened to you, he looked into your eyes, he took you seriously, he made you feel he wanted your company. He never glanced over your shoulder to see if someone more interesting was coming along. Dame Norma Major – who, as the Prime Minister's wife in the 1990s, often found herself in conversation with the Queen's husband, and whose own husband, John Major, is no slouch himself in the charmer stakes – told me, 'I am a huge fan and have always enjoyed his company on the numerous occasions I have been privileged to sit beside him at dinner.' Joanna Lumley said to me, 'Prince Philip is just the best dinner companion, the *best*.'

This book came about because, having got to know Prince Philip, and admiring him, liking him, and respecting him as I did and do, I felt he deserved to be better understood. My first thought was simply to write his biography. In 2002, as part of the official celebration at the Royal Albert Hall in honour of his eightieth birthday, with his approval and involvement, I wrote a short account of his life. Researching it, and talking with him, I was particularly fascinated by his family history, his unusual childhood, and his impressive wartime career in the Royal Navy, but, looking at his story overall, I had to accept that, since 1947, he had only led the life he had because he married the woman he married. In our world, even in the twenty-first century, few men's lives are defined by their wives' roles. Prince Philip as an individual is interesting because he was an interesting and unusual man. He is doubly interesting because he was the Queen's consort – and the longest-serving consort in the thousand-year history of the British monarchy.

Over a number of years in a number of roles – as chairman of a national charity of which the Queen is patron and the Duke of Edinburgh was president, as an MP and government whip, and as a journalist and broadcaster – I have been able to observe the Queen and the Duke at close range. Watching the pair of them – two sharply contrasting characters, with wholly different natures – I decided to write a biography of them both. I called it *Philip & Elizabeth: Portrait of a Marriage* and this book is based in large part on it.

The phrase 'portrait of a marriage' was used by the writer Nigel Nicolson as the title for his moving and revelatory account of his own parents' relationship – and relationships. Vita Sackville-West and Harold Nicolson led unusual and, to some extent, exotic lives. The Queen and Prince Philip, also, led lives that are and were, by any standard, out of the ordinary.

Different marriages work (or fail) in different ways, and different people (and generations and classes) will have different expectations of what marriage has to offer. To begin to understand this particular royal marriage, we need – obviously – to understand the natures of the couple in question: what they are and were like as individuals, and how consequently they related to each other as they did. Much of this book concentrates on the background and childhood of Prince Philip and the Queen because where they came from tells us so much about what they became. As the novelist Angela Carter put it, 'The destination of all journeys is their beginning.'

Some will regard aspects of the book as unnecessary and intrusive. Prince Philip complained to me more than once, 'The media have turned us into a soap opera.' It was ever thus. As Shakespeare reminds us at the beginning of *Twelfth Night* (first performed before Elizabeth I more than four hundred years ago), 'What great ones do, the less will prattle of.' Prince Philip said much the same to me in that letter from Windsor Castle: 'Ordinary people love gossip.'

In 1947, the year in which Philip and Elizabeth were married, Henry 'Chips' Channon, Member of Parliament and diarist, witnessed the royal unveiling of a statue of George V, who had died eleven years before. 'The ceremony itself was over in twenty minutes,' Channon noted, 'but then followed that interminable pause whilst the Royalties greeted each other, interkissed and chatted. It is only in England that a crowd of several thousands can stand happily in the rain and watch one family gossip.' We are especially fascinated by this one family, not only because its story has all the essential romantic and melodramatic ingredients of a soap opera, but also, and principally, because the central characters are royal.

The hold of royalty on the public imagination is extraordinary. Several million cheering people filled the streets to salute Elizabeth II on the occasion of her Diamond and Golden jubilees. They did not know her personally – and yet they had known her all their lives. She was part and parcel of the fabric of their lives. As one of her private secretaries said to me, 'The Queen represents the very best of Britain, of its values and its heritage. In many ways, she represents the soul of the nation.'

When Prince Philip died many in Britain were surprised by how much they felt his passing. He had always been there – and now he wasn't. And in the immediate aftermath of his death, and watching his funeral on television, millions sensed the Queen's loss and were suddenly moved by the realisation of how much her husband had meant to her and how lonely for her the rest of her reign would be.

It is not really surprising that a royal death touches us in the way it does. Members of the Royal Family feature in our newspapers and on our television screens almost daily, but our relationship with royalty is neither fleeting nor superficial. The Queen is on our postage stamps and coins and banknotes. But she is more than head of state: she is at the heart of our national identity – and for a reason. Elizabeth II – from 10 September 2015 the longest-reigning monarch in our history – is the latest in a line of sovereigns that links her directly to King Edgar, Richard III, Henry VIII, George IV, Queen Victoria. She is the embodiment of our nation's story. Her presence links us to our past.

Elizabeth II is living history – and more besides. The Queen and her family have something that even the greatest celebrities of the age do not have. The Queen was a beautiful princess who married a handsome prince. Their children and grandchildren are princes and princesses too. They live in palaces and castles. These people are the stuff of fairy tale.

Marilyn Monroe, Elvis Presley, David Beckham may have fame, fortune, and talent, may even, eventually, join the ranks of the great immortals (they are heroic figures: perhaps the image of Marilyn will outlive the name of Helen of Troy?), but they are not royal. Elizabeth was born a princess. Philip was born a prince. It is wholly absurd, of course, but that makes them different. And, somehow, extra-special.

To a few, Prince Philip was more than a man. To members of the Yaohnanen tribe living on the island of Tanna in Vanuatu in the South Pacific, he was a divine being – the pale-skinned son of one of their mountain spirits who had travelled across the seas to a distant land and married a powerful woman. In the 1950s the Yaohnanen tribal folk observed the respect accorded to Elizabeth II by the island's colonial administrators and concluded that her husband must be the pale-skinned son of their legends. The Duke of Edinburgh did not encourage their cult, but when a group of them travelled to England in 2007 he agreed to meet them behind closed doors. He told me that he was 'embararrased by their attention', but was ready to respect their tradition. He gave them his photograph, but did not want to be photographed with them or 'the whole thing will be turned into a media circus'.

To me, Prince Philip was no god, but he was a fascinating man, who became more interesting (and surprising) the better I got to know him. His interests were so varied, ranging from the scientific to the spiritual, from pharmacology and farming to poetry and painting ('I prefer oils. Charles does the watercolours.') He was interested in history and acutely aware of his own heritage, but to the very end of his days he was ready to explore the new and the experimental. At Sandringham he installed some of the first solar panels in the country. In London he drove around first in an electric-powered van and then in a gas-powered taxi, years before such green initiatives were fashionable. One year, when he was in his late eighties, he took his staff to the Fat Duck restaurant at Bray for a Christmas outing to check out Heston Blumenthal's experimental menu. He was intrigued – and amused – by the notion of a Christmas dinner of snail porridge and egg-and-bacon ice cream. As a rule, he was a modest eater and, while he enjoyed a beer and an occasional gin and tonic, he was not a heavy drinker. He was remarkably self-disciplined. He kept himself fit. He remained as active as possible to the end of his days. No other prince has ever lived so long a life.

I am a royalist. I believe that the ever-evolving institution of the monarchy has served the United Kingdom well and can – and will – continue to do so. I believe, too, that the Queen, over more than six decades, has fulfilled her destiny with considerable skill and matchless dedication. And I reckon that the Duke of Edinburgh played the bizarre hand that life dealt him pretty flawlessly. His commitment to his role as the Queen's consort and his staying power were extraordinary.

As I say, my first thought was simply to write a biography of the Duke of Edinburgh. But there was a particular moment when I realised that it would be wrong to write about him in isolation. It was on a November evening several years ago when I accompanied the Queen and the Duke to the Royal Variety Performance at the Dominion Theatre in London's West End.

I remember the evening well. One of the highlights of the

entertainment was an excerpt from *The Full Monty*, the stage version of the film about a group of unemployed steel-workers who decide to form a male striptease troupe, like the Chippendales. Prince Philip looked at the programme and mused, '*The Full Monty*? Will it be a tribute to Field Marshal Montgomery and the Battle of El-Alamein, do you think?' I told him what *The Full Monty* was about. He shook his head in disbelief. 'At the end of their big routine,' I explained, 'all their kit comes off.' I looked anxiously in the direction of the Queen. 'Don't worry,' smiled the Duke. 'She's been to Papua New Guinea. She's seen it all before.'

During the interval, in the mezzanine bar, drinks were served and the Queen and her husband did what they had done countless times before: they worked the room. He took one end, she took the other, and, for half an hour, the royal couple mingled, shaking hands with smiling strangers, nodding, chatting, then moving on. I stood at the edge of the crowd, watching Her Majesty and His Royal Highness as they went about their business. What they were doing, they did well. Not surprisingly. They had had a lifetime of practice. To a seasoned royal-watcher, the scene was entirely predictable. And then came the moment that took me by surprise. I witnessed it quite by chance. I happened to be looking in the right direction, that's all, when I saw Philip catch Elizabeth's eye across the crowded room. He simply smiled at her and gently raised his glass. She smiled back and, almost imperceptibly, raised hers. And the moment was over.

But in that moment I sensed that I was seeing something I had not known about before. These two were allies engaged in a mutual conspiracy that sustained them over more than seventy years.

I realised, there and then, that I wanted to know more. This couple was famous – world famous, *so* famous, and famous for so long – and yet, in many ways, what did we know of them? Who were they? What were they really like? What I saw that night, in that moment in the bar at the Dominion Theatre, seemed at odds with so much that I had heard about them before. I had heard that they led very separate lives. Could it be true? I had heard that Philip had other women. Could that be true? Was this ever a love story? Was it still? What was the truth about Philip and Elizabeth? Who were these people? What was their secret? Could I crack the code? Could I unravel the enigma? I decided to try. And this is the result of my endeavour: a final portrait of Prince Philip, but a portrait of Elizabeth, too, and a portrait of a partnership that has been part of our lives for as long as almost any of us can remember.

PHILIP

Chapter One

'Uneasy lies the head that wears a crown.'
William Shakespeare (1564–1616), *Henry IV Part II*

In 1953, the Queen's Coronation year, a book was published called *Manifest Destiny*. It was a handsome volume designed as a celebration of the unique genius of the Mountbatten family. When invited by an equerry to sign a copy of the book, the Duke of Edinburgh obliged, adding, above his signature on the title page, two words: 'Manifest Bunkum!'

Prince Philip was wary of biographers, particularly those who came bearing purple prose and vivid imaginations. If his story had to be told he would prefer it to be done without exaggeration or speculation. If we could stick to the facts, and present them simply, chronologically, and accurately, he would be obliged.

I shall do my best. It will not be easy. In talking about his early life, Prince Philip did not give a lot away. And, perversely, with a shrug of his shoulders, and a quizzical raised eyebrow, he liked to dismiss what, to us, seems a quite extraordinary start in life – lurid, disturbing, amazing: a grandfather assassinated, a father imprisoned, a peripatetic childhood with, from the age of nine, both parents absent, one in an asylum, the other with his mistress at Monte Carlo – as, somehow, almost normal, certainly unremarkable.

Royals are different from us: they have more relations. Prince Philip could claim kinship with the whole compass of European royalty: kings, emperors, kaisers, tsars. Include his sisters and his cousins and his aunts (princesses, admirals, grand duchesses) and it was the cast of a comic opera. (They even had the costumes.) Look at the story of the extended family over a century and a half and you have the plot of a comic opera as well: unlikely and confusing.

To understand Prince Philip you need to know his family. To keep things simple, and as a reminder that almost all the people who feature in the pages that follow are related one to another, let us begin with Queen Victoria. We know where we are with her.

Queen Victoria had nine children. Her third child, and second daughter, was Princess Alice, who, in 1862, at Osborne House on the Isle of Wight, married Prince Louis of Hesse-Darmstadt, later Grand Duke Louis IV of Hesse and by Rhine, one of the pocket principalities that made up much of Germany before unification. (We really are in comic opera country.[2]) Alice and Louis had seven children, including a future Princess of Prussia, who lived to see the Coronation of Elizabeth II in 1953, and the last Tsarina of Russia, who was less fortunate. They named their eldest Victoria and she became a favourite grandchild of the great Queen Empress.

In April 1884, as she turned twenty-one, in Darmstadt, in the presence of Queen Victoria, Victoria of Hesse married her cousin, Louis of Battenberg, son of Prince Alexander of Hesse and grandson of Grand Duke Louis II of Hesse – or, possibly, in fact, grandson of the Grand Duchess's charismatic chamberlain, Baron Augustus Senarclens von Grancy. (There were rumours . . . There so often are.)

Louis was nearing thirty and, though thoroughly German (Queen Victoria called him Ludwig), a rising star in the British Royal Navy. He had connections, but he was also able and intelligent: conscientious yet outgoing, ambitious yet popular. There were rumours about him, too. In his bachelor days he had a self-confessed eye for the girls,[3] and he was noted for his virility, energy, charm, and fondness

2   The Grand Ducal family lived in some two dozen assorted *Schlösser* in and around Darmstadt, a small town with a population, in the 1860s, of only a few thousand. In 1944, heavy Allied bombing of Darmstadt destroyed most of the inner city, killed 12,300 people and left 70,000 homeless. Today Darmstadt is thriving, with a population of around 150,000.

3   As a protégé of the then Prince of Wales, Louis was introduced to the Prince's occasional mistress, the actress and noted beauty Lillie Langtry. Louis believed himself to be the father of the daughter born to Mrs Langtry in the spring of 1881. His legitimate younger son, Louis Mountbatten, believed it too, but it now seems not to have been the case. Given the scope of Mrs Langtry's conquests it is difficult to be sure, but the latest evidence lays the paternity suit at the feet of one Arthur Jones, one of Lord Ranelagh's litter of bastards. (He had at least seven.) Film producers in search of a subject offering royalty, lust and adventure in equal

for uniforms. Like his younger son, Louis Mountbatten, and, to a degree, his younger grandson, Prince Philip, Louis of Battenberg enjoyed dressing up. He had a variety of uniforms and an array of medals and, in public and in private, he relished parading in both. He also had an extravagant tattoo of a rampant dragon emblazoned across his chest and trailing down his legs. He lived life to the full.

Queen Victoria liked Louis and she loved her granddaughter and, consequently, she insisted that their first child be born not in one of their homes (they had two: one, of course, in Darmstadt; the other just outside Chichester in Sussex) but in one of hers. Princess Victoria of Hesse gave birth to the first of her four children in the Tapestry Room at Windsor Castle on 25 February 1885. The Queen recorded the event in her diary: 'Woke before 7. Hearing that Victoria had a bad night, I got up & went over to see her. She was very suffering. I had some breakfast, & then went back remaining with dear Victoria on & off, till at length, at 20m to 5 in the afternoon, the child, a little girl, was born. The relief was great for poor Victoria had had such a long hard time, which always makes me anxious. How strange and indeed affecting, it was, to see her lying in the same room, & in the same bed, in which she herself was born. Good Ludwig was most helpful & attentive, hardly leaving Victoria for a moment. The Baby is very small, thin & dark. I held it for a few moments in my arms.'

Princess Victoria's mother, Princess Alice, had died of diphtheria, aged only thirty-five, in 1878. The new baby was named after her. This Princess Alice was eventually to become Princess Andrew of Greece, mother of Prince Philip, and a most unusual woman: striking, strange, and, in her own way, heroic.

---

measure could do worse than make their way to the Hartley Library at the University of Southampton and dip into the early pages of Prince Louis of Battenberg's memoirs, kept with the Mountbatten papers there. Here can be found amazing tales of youthful conquests across several continents. The cast includes bold English princes, blushing American heiresses, willing Indian princesses, and memorable encounters with, among others, 'a young native girl in transparent white garments' and Thakumbow, the cannibal king of Fiji, who 'could not deny that he had occasional yearnings for babies' legs, which he said were the best dish in the world'. According to Prince Philip's archivist, Dame Anne Griffiths, although pronounced Thakumbow the correct spelling is Cakobau.

Princess Victoria was a pretty child and a handsome woman: reserved but direct, straightforward, unspoilt, and, by several accounts, somewhat masculine in her manner. Her daughter Alice was simply beautiful: a gorgeous baby, a lovely girl, a fine woman. The Prince of Wales is said to have declared, 'No throne in Europe is too good for her.'

She did, however, have one defect. She was hard of hearing. When she was four, her mother reported to Queen Victoria, 'The child has grown very much since you last saw her, is very lively & quick with her fingers, but decidedly backward of speech, using all sorts of self-invented words & pronouncing others very indistinctly, so that strangers find it difficult to understand her.'

Alice was taken to ear specialists in Darmstadt and London: there was nothing to be done[4] and, for better or worse, her family decided to make no special concessions to her problem. Although, over time, she became a skilful lip-reader (in several languages) and, it seems, the degree of hearing loss varied at different stages in her life, the disability took its toll, making her more isolated than she might otherwise have been and making others, who did not know her well, regard her as, somehow, a bit odd.

There would be echoes of his mother's childhood in Prince Philip's own. Her parents loved her dearly, but they left her, frequently for weeks at a time, sometimes for months, in the care of nannies and governesses and assorted family members. When I asked Prince Philip how he felt about his mother's upbringing, he simply shrugged his shoulders and said, 'It was the way it was.' Little Alice spent her peripatetic childhood in Darmstadt, at Sennicotts (the house the Battenbergs rented near Chichester), in Malta (where the Mediterranean fleet was stationed), in London (at different times in Pimlico, Victoria, and Knightsbridge), at Walton-on-Thames, at Sandgate, near Folkestone, and in the various residences of her great-grandmother: at Windsor, at Balmoral, at Osborne House on the Isle of Wight, in the Royal Yacht *Victoria & Albert*, and on the

---

4   At least, not in the 1880s. Some members of the family maintained that Alice's hearing had been impaired because of an accident caused at sea during a rough crossing of the English Channel. The official diagnosis was that she suffered from a thickness of the Eustachian tubes. Today, according to my GP, the condition could be treated relatively simply.

French Riviera, where the Queen-Empress would take her spring holiday.

Despite her deafness, Alice was a bright child, likeable and liked, and mature for her age, in manner and appearance. 'She is eleven,' one of her great-aunts commented in 1896, 'but as big as a girl of fourteen.' By 1900 the Battenberg family was complete. Alice had one younger sister, Louise (1889–1965), who would one day become Queen of Sweden,[5] and two younger brothers, destined to follow their father into the British navy: Georgie (1892–1938) and Louis (1900–79), known as Dick or Dickie almost from birth. He was the last great-grandson born in Queen Victoria's lifetime.

The Queen-Empress died on 22 January 1901. Her funeral took place at Windsor on 2 February. Alice and her parents were there. Sixteen months later, on 26 June 1902, Edward VII was due to be crowned. Alice and her mother were both expected and invited to stay at Buckingham Palace, where the distinguished guest list boasted an array of European royalty,[6] including Crown Prince Constantine of Greece and two of his younger brothers, George and Andrew. Prince Andrew (known in the family as Andrea) was twenty, a young officer in the Greek army, tall, blond, and relatively handsome. 'Interesting', too: he was short-sighted and wore spectacles. Princess Alice was seventeen and a half: beautiful, intelligent, and hard of hearing. The young people fell in love.

There was time for romance. Three days before the day set for his Coronation, Edward VII was suddenly taken ill and operated on for peritonitis. The Coronation was postponed, but the royal house

5   She was sixty-one when, eventually, in October 1950, her husband succeeded his father as Gustaf VI Adolf, King of Sweden. She and her husband were happily married, but she did not find it easy adjusting to her ultimate role. She was ungrand and a little uncertain. In the 1950s, when out in London shopping on her own, in case she was knocked down by a bus and nobody would know who she was, she kept a small card in her handbag which read: 'I am the Queen of Sweden.' More recently, Queen Margrethe II of Denmark told me: 'European royalty like coming to England because no one knows who we are. We can be anonymous. And then when people discover who we are, they are always very helpful, so we get the best of both worlds. Our bread is definitely buttered on both sides. That is an advantage to being a queen. People always behave very nicely towards me.'

6   'You think of us as "European royalty",' the Queen of Denmark said to me. 'We think of ourselves as "family". We are all cousins. That's why we are easy together.'

party went on. The German princess and the Greek prince lingered at Buckingham Palace for a fortnight more. Love blossomed.

Andrea was a Greek prince, serving in the Greek army, living in Greece, the fourth son of King George I of Greece, but he was not really Greek at all. (This is, in part, a comic opera, remember.) He was German, Danish, Dutch, and Russian.

In the late 1820s, when modern Greece managed to shake itself free from Turkish domination, the newly independent kingdom was in want of a monarch. Having nothing home-bred to hand, the Greeks shopped around (literally) for a royal figure of sufficient international standing and authority and shipped in Prince Otto of Bavaria as their first king. He stayed the course for thirty years, but following an unpleasant insurrection in 1862 (not the first), made his excuses and left. The search for a king resumed and, this time round, the lot fell to one Prince William, younger son of King Christian IX of Denmark. He was only seventeen. He changed his name, his nationality, and his destiny. He served as King George I of Greece for fifty years, from 1863 until he was murdered by a lunatic while out for a stroll in the streets of Salonika in the spring of 1913.

George I of Greece had an elder brother (who became King Frederick VIII of Denmark in 1906) and two younger sisters: Alexandra, married to England's Edward VII, and Marie, married to Russia's Tsar Alexander III. George I also married a member of the Russian royal family: the Grand Duchess Olga, a granddaughter of Tsar Nicholas I. Over a period of twenty years the couple had eight children, the youngest-but-one of whom was Andrea: intelligent, humorous, conscientious, committed to Greece (he could speak English, German, Danish, Russian, French, but he spoke Greek with his parents) and committed to a career in the Greek army. In her preface to his volume of military memoirs – the aptly titled *Towards Disaster* – Princess Alice wrote: 'He took his duties very seriously as he loved his profession, and he wished to earn his promotion like any other officer.'

The Coronation of Edward VII was rescheduled for 9 August 1902. The courts of Europe reassembled in London. Alice and Andrea met once more. Indeed, their families seemed happy to encourage the match: Alice and her mother travelled to Westminster Abbey in the same carriage as Andrea and his brother, George.

Fourteen months later (mostly months when they were apart: Andrea's military duties kept him away), in Darmstadt, on 6 and 7 October 1903, they were married. It was a fairy-tale wedding, complete with carriages and kings, three ceremonies (one civil, two religious), feasting, dancing, laughter, and happy tears. She was eighteen, a beautiful princess, with orange blossom in her hair; he was twenty-one, a dashing prince, decked out in the glorious uniform of a Red Dragoon. They did not live happily ever after.

It all began well enough. They had a quietly domestic honeymoon in Darmstadt and, early in the new year, set off for Greece. Having spent several winters in Malta as a child, Alice was at least accustomed to a Mediterranean climate, and her new in-laws evidently did everything they could to give the young bride – still a teenager, partially deaf, in a strange country where she did not yet speak the language – a warm welcome and a sense of security. George I appears to have been a wise man: unstuffy, courteous, considerate, capable, honest, and keenly aware of his position as an 'imported' monarch. He would advise his sons, 'Never forget that you are foreigners among the Greeks, and never let them remember it.'

George I rode the roller-coaster of Greek politics for half a century. He survived censure, insurrections, intrigues, and at least one assassination attempt before the one that killed him. He accepted his destiny, and did what he sensed was his duty, but he made it clear, repeatedly, in public and in private, that he was ever ready to step down from the throne if his services were no longer required.

His grandson, Prince Philip, felt much the same way. It infuriated the Duke of Edinburgh if he was portrayed in the press as someone who revelled in the life of a prince and believed in the survival of the Crown above all else. He didn't. 'If a monarchy serves a purpose, and if, on the whole, most people are mostly comfortable with it, so be it,' he told me. 'If not, fine, let's stop buggering about and have done with it.' The Queen would be saddened no longer to be Queen of Canada or Australia (we know how the Queen feels about the Commonwealth, old and new), but Prince Philip was ready to say, as he did, in Canada in 1969, 'It is a complete misconception to imagine that the monarchy exists in the interests of the monarch. It doesn't. It exists in the interests of the people. If at any time any nation decides that the system is unacceptable, then it is up to them to change it.'

George I of Greece was a family man, by all accounts a good man, decent, God-fearing, and happily married. That said, according to the memoirs of the well-connected Prince von Bülow (gossipy, gripping, but generally considered reasonably reliable), George I did allow himself 'an occasional relaxation' at Aix-les-Bains, on his annual French holiday away from his queen. When his eldest son, Constantine, followed his father's example, the crown prince's dismayed wife, Sophie (another of Queen Victoria's grandchildren), turned to her father-in-law for guidance. 'You must consult your dear mother-in-law,' he is supposed to have told her. 'She will be able to give you the best advice on this point.'

Over ten years, Alice and Andrea had four daughters: Margarita (1905–81), born in the none-too-comfortable Royal Palace in Athens, and Theodora (1906–69), Cécile (1911–37), and Sophie (1914–2000), all born at Tatoï, the royal family's cherished country estate near by. Life at home was fairly placid: Alice rode, sewed, read, played with her children, corresponded with her family. In the streets it was a little livelier. This was a turbulent decade in Greek politics (yet another one), the ups and downs including a *coup d'état* and the resignation of all the royal princes from the Greek army in 1909, followed by their reinstatement at the outset of the first of the Balkan wars in 1912. An incidental side effect of the princes' period outside the army was that they did not venture out socially as much as previously: accustomed to appearing in public in uniform, they felt under-dressed – emasculated, even – in civilian clothes.

During much of this period Alice and her daughters were abroad, visiting her parents and other members of the extended family in Germany, England, Malta, and Russia, joining house parties, attending weddings, christenings, funerals. In May 1910 Alice and Andrea were in London when Edward VII died. They attended his funeral. Alice's father had been a friend of the King's (they had shared Mrs Langtry, after all); Queen Alexandra was Andrea's aunt.

In March 1913 King George I of Greece was murdered outside a café in Salonika, shot in the back by a single bullet from a lone assassin. A motive was never established. The murderer, a Greek, apparently deranged, threw himself to his own death from an upstairs window on the way to his cross-examination. In his will the old King left some words of counsel for his son and successor, now King

Constantine I: 'Be calm and never forget that you are reigning over a southern people who are easily roused and may in a moment do and say many things which they will probably forget a few hours after. For this reason never fall into a passion and never forget that it is preferable that the King should suffer rather than his people.'

He also left Andrea and Alice a useful annuity and gave them his house, Mon Repos, on the pretty island of Corfu. (The British had given Greece the Ionian islands at the time of George I's accession.) Alice mourned the loss of her father-in-law. He had been a good friend to her, had taken her seriously, and admired and encouraged her good works.

The tradition of royal princesses, born to privilege, with time on their hands and status at their disposal, both setting an example and at the same time achieving a degree of self-fulfilment, by giving practical service to the community, is a relatively young one. Prince Albert, Queen Victoria's Prince Consort, very much encouraged it. In Darmstadt, Victoria and Albert's daughter, Alice, had established a sisterhood of young women, known as 'Alice's nurses', committed to giving service to the community as trained district nurses. In Russia, this Alice's daughter (young Alice's aunt), Ella (married to Grand Duke Serge), established a convent of nursing sisters and built a church for her community. In Greece, George I's wife, Queen Olga (another Russian grand duchess by birth), founded four separate hospitals, as well as building a prison for women and a reformatory school for boys.

These women were models for Alice. She was inspired by their example, both by the practical hands-on alleviation of suffering that the nurses could achieve, and, especially in Aunt Ella's case, by the spiritual zeal that fuelled it.

There is certainly a thread of spiritual zeal that runs through the family to this day. Prince Philip was deeply interested in the spiritual – as is his son, Prince Charles. Philip's library contained several hundred volumes on religious and spiritual matters. He told me that he was a 'committed Christian', even if, as he put it, 'I have a few questions to ask.' He also told me that his mother and his great-aunt Ella had used their faith 'to a purpose' and that he had tried, in his way, to do the same. 'I wanted to do something practical.' With Prince Hassan of Jordan and Sir Evelyn Rothschild, for example, he actively encouraged dialogue between Christians, Muslims, and Jews with a series of inter-faith conferences. And in 1986, as president of the World Wide Fund for Nature, he organised a meeting between leaders of the major faiths during WWF's twenty-fifth anniversary conference in Assisi. He proposed the creation of ARC – the Association of Religion and Conservation. To what purpose? 'To encourage the members to feel their responsibility to God's creation and care for the natural environment.'

When I asked the Duke to talk on the record about his interest in religion, he declined: 'If I start talking about religion, the press will say I'm barking. *You'll* say I'm barking.' For many years, some people said his mother, Princess Alice, *was* barking.

Foreshadowing Alice's spiritual crisis, in 1905 her Aunt Ella renounced the grand-ducal life completely and declared with pride to her nursing sisters, 'I am about to leave the brilliant world in which it fell to me to occupy a brilliant position, but together with you all I am about to enter a much greater world – that of the poor and the afflicted.'

When she arrived in Athens in 1904, still a teenager, the first community work young Alice undertook was assisting at the Greek School for Embroidery, where girls were taught a specific skill that would help them support their families. Eight years later, in 1912, at the onset of the Balkan wars, Alice would galvanise the young embroiderers and set them to the task of making and mending warm and durable clothes (jackets, scarves, hoods) both for the troops and for refugees.

The first Balkan war – in which Greece, alongside Bulgaria, Montenegro, and Serbia, sought to reclaim territory from the Turkish European empire and secure Crete for Greece – saw Prince Andrea back in uniform, as a lieutenant colonel with the 3rd Regiment of Cavalry. When he was posted to Larissa, an established garrison town on the old Turkish border, Alice accompanied her husband, but she went with a mission of her own: to establish her own first-aid field hospitals at the front. She sent her mother written reports: 'I went to the Military Hospital and saw the arrival of some 15 to 20 wounded soldiers from a skirmish at Elassona who had taken 14 hours coming here over utterly impossible roads, over a fearful mountain pass – Melouna – at the frontier, where huge boulders and rocks stuck out of the road, and on hearing of their agony and the impossibility of bringing severely wounded at all to Larissa, and news which reached us of the army's tremendously rapid advance, I instantly decided to move my hospital to Elassona.'

Over the next three months – first at Elassona, then at Servia, then elsewhere in Macedonia, and finally at Epirus – Alice displayed the most extraordinary courage, compassion, determination, energy, and organisational skill. She set up hospitals, she marshalled nurses, she bullied doctors, she commandeered vehicles, houses, a school. She attended the sick, she tended the dying, she assisted at an amputation. For days she barely ate or slept and did not change her clothes. She witnessed the full horror of war. 'But, God!' she told her mother, 'What things we saw! Shattered arms, and legs and heads, such awful sights – and then to have to bandage those dreadful things for three days and three nights. The corridor full of blood, and cast-off bandages knee-high.'

Reading her letters to her mother,[7] you can see she was appalled by what she saw, and exhausted by the experience, but she was exhilarated too. There is manic energy here: touches of Joan of Arc as well as Florence Nightingale. Her forcefulness rubbed some people up the wrong way; it left others worrying about the effect on her health when she came down from her 'high'. What no one doubted was her courage and commitment. In November 1913 George V decorated her with the Royal Red Cross, 'in recognition of her services in nursing the sick and wounded among the Greek soldiers during the recent war'.

The Balkan wars, of course, were merely the curtain-raiser for the Big Show, the 1914–18 conflict. Constantine I was resolved that Greece should remain neutral. Britain and the Allies were where Greece's traditional allegiance lay, but Germany under the Kaiser looked formidable and might not prove magnanimous in victory. It was a difficult call. King Constantine hedged his bets. Besides, his family had close kith and kin on both sides of the argument.

In London in October 1914, Alice's father, Louis of Battenberg,

---

7 They are powerful and moving letters, reproduced in Hugo Vickers's authorised biography *Alice: Princess Andrew of Greece*, 2000. Chapter X alone would make an amazing feature film.

First Sea Lord since 1912, resigned. He was married to a grand-daughter of Queen Victoria, he had served with great distinction in the Royal Navy for forty-six years, but he was German. There was no denying it. He had a home in Germany, he spoke German, he kept German staff. The *Daily Mail* did not look kindly on any of that. And Winston Churchill, now First Lord of the Admiralty, wanted him replaced in any event. The Battenberg family was devastated. His younger son, Dickie, a fourteen-year-old naval cadet, vowed to avenge the slight.[8]

Louis of Battenberg's wife, Victoria, railed against the stupidity of those responsible. 'The King is a nobody,' she declared. In fact, the King was somebody of some substance and, though several parts German himself, determined, for reasons of patriotism and self-interest, to assert the Britishness of the British Crown. In 1917 George V disowned the German connection. The House of Saxe-Coburg, also known as Wettin, also known as Wipper, would hence-forward be known as the House of Windsor. (The Kaiser, on hearing the news, was reported to have quipped that he was 'off to the theatre to see *The Merry Wives of Saxe-Coburg-Gotha*'.) The Queen's brothers, from the proud House of Teck, would become the Marquess of Cambridge and the Earl of Athlone, and the Battenbergs would be transliterated into the Mountbattens. Queen Victoria's 'dear Ludwig' was given a peerage and a title with a comforting British ring to every syllable: Marquess of Milford Haven.[9]

Louis was forcibly retired, but his sons, with their new names, continued to serve in the British navy. Alice professed herself resigned to whatever fate might have in store for them. 'I can't be grateful enough that I was given the nature of a fatalist,' she wrote to a

8   He did. Forty-one years later, in 1955, as Winston Churchill stepped down as prime minister for the final time, Admiral of the Fleet Lord Mountbatten of Burma was appointed First Sea Lord.

9   Do I sense this still rankles within the family? Look up the entry for Louis's great-grandson in the 2003 edition of *Debrett's People of Today* and you will see that the 4th Marquess describes the 1st as: 'HSH Prince Louis of Battenberg, who relinquished, at the King's request, the style and title of Serene Highness and Prince of Battenberg, instead assuming the surname of Mountbatten by Royal Licence 1917.' Louis of Battenberg was staying at his elder son's house in Scotland at the time his new title was officially approved. He wrote in his son's visitors' book: 'June 9th arrived Prince Hyde; June 19th departed Lord Jekyll.'

friend. 'All my life I have felt that all of us have our appointed time on earth & that nothing will alter it. Perhaps the way my mother & little sister were swept away by that vile diphtheria has helped me to strengthen the feeling . . . I feel too that if it is Georgie's time to go, he will go & my Dickie too, but not otherwise, & so I hope I shall not worry more than is inevitable when Dickie goes to sea.'

In the event, Georgie died in April 1938, of cancer of the bone marrow, aged forty-five, three days after his mother's seventy-fifth birthday. Dickie died, full of years (and honours), aged seventy-nine, murdered by the IRA in August 1979. At the time, the *Chicago Tribune* calculated that no single family in recorded history, including the Borgias and the Cosa Nostra families of Sicily, Chicago, and New York, was more susceptible to violent death among its members than the family of Queen Victoria and her descendants.

In 1917, in the aftermath of the Bolshevik revolution, George V was unwilling to send a British warship to rescue his first cousin, the overthrown Tsar Nicholas II. In July 1918 the Tsar and Tsarina (Alix, Alice's aunt) and their children were executed and Alix's sister, the Grand Duchess Ella – Alice's aunt and inspiration – and other members of the Russian royal family were thrown alive down a mine shaft, where they were heard singing psalms before Bolshevik soldiers killed them by throwing a grenade into the mine shaft after them. Eighty years on, in July 1998, Ella, now recognised as a saint by the Russian Orthodox Church, was one of ten twentieth-century martyrs whose carved effigies above the Great West Door of Westminster Abbey were dedicated in the presence of Prince Philip and the Queen.

Alice and her four daughters spent much of the First World War in Athens. Andrea was stationed at Salonika until 1916, when his brother sent him on diplomatic missions to London and Paris to assure the Allies of Greece's commitment to neutrality. Constantine I did not play his hand well. He was mistrusted by the Allies, wholly at odds with the Greek Prime Minister, Eleutherios Venizelos, and no longer in step with the Greek people. In June 1917 he was overthrown, driven into exile in Switzerland and replaced, not by the Crown Prince, George (who was thought might be sympathetic to the German cause), but by his second son, Alexander. Andrea,

Alice, and the girls joined the exodus to St Moritz. The hotel accommodation was reasonably priced and the weather quite congenial. The skiing and the skating were both excellent. There are worse spots to endure the humiliation of exile than the shores of a Swiss lake.

Greek politics being what it is, by 1920 they were all back. King Alexander, aged twenty-seven, died of blood poisoning, having been bitten by a monkey. In a plebiscite, King Constantine I was restored to the Greek throne by a vote of 1,010,788 to 10,887, and Prince Andrea, now sporting a monocle, slipped back into uniform, promoted to the rank of major general. He was thirty-eight. Alice was thirty-five. Seven years after the birth of their fourth daughter, they were due to have another child. On 10 June 1921, on the dining-room table at Mon Repos, Prince Philip was born.

Chapter Two

'If one is not caressed . . . one develops thorns.'
Beryl Bainbridge (1934–2010), *According to Queeney*

The sun was high, the day was hot, the scent of orange and lemon, of cypress and magnolia, filled the air. Mon Repos, built by the British in 1824, is a handsome villa by the sea, a family mansion (not a palace), spacious and comfortable, and its setting (at least, in 1921, before Corfu became a major-league holiday destination) near-idyllic. The house, surprisingly cool in summer, was surrounded by olive groves, wisteria, and wild flowers growing in the long grass. Prince Philip was only born on the dining-room table because the doctor felt that it would more convenient than Princess Alice's bed.

'He is a splendid, healthy child, thank God,' his mother reported to one of the family back in Darmstadt. 'I am very well too. It was an uncomplicated delivery & I am enjoying the fresh air on the terrace.' Though the years of wars and revolution – the years of her marriage, in fact – had taken their toll on Alice – on her health, on her spirits, on her looks – her life was not without its consolations. She was a princess and she was treated like one. She had a lady-in-waiting. She had domestic staff. She had a French governess for her daughters and an English nanny, Mrs Nicholas, for her son.

The standing of European royalty might not be what once it was – for a start, the crowned heads of Germany, Austria, and Russia were no more – and the position of the monarchy in Greece had always been precarious, but, nonetheless, Alice and her family – though they faced high drama in their lives, and pain, and personal tragedy – were mostly spared the mundane drudgery that is – and, especially, was – the lot of most working people. Alice and Andrea were not rich – by the standards of the Windsors, say, or the Dukes of Westminster – and there were to be times when their financial worries would be considerable – but they were not truly poor, ever, and all their lives, in one shape or form, there were servants hovering and there was deference in the air.

This is true of royalty, even today, a hundred years on. Prince Charles is – as his father was – generally unstuffy, good-humoured, and easy to talk to, but he is a prince and always treated like one. Cars come, guards salute, breakfast is served, valets press your suits, the fairies clean your shoes. Over the years I watched Prince Philip padding alone along the long, narrow corridors of Buckingham Palace, barely noticing as nodding footmen stepped aside, pages bowed, and private secretaries backed discreetly into doorways. If you were due to meet him in his study, whether for the first time or the thirty-first, his equerry would invite you to stand in the room, at a specific angle in a particular spot, and remind you to bow as His Royal Highness entered and to call him 'Sir'. I didn't and don't have a problem with any of this: I am in favour of due respect, I like old-fashioned courtesy, I even still try to stand up when a lady enters the room: I mention it here only because if this is the way you have lived your life – as Prince Charles does; as Prince Philip and his parents did – it will affect you.

Prince Philip of Greece must have been a beautiful baby: the early photographs show a cherubic child, bonny, smiling, a little chubby. He had the blondest hair and the bluest eyes and was the darling of a household crowded with women. From London, Alice's mother, Victoria, now Marchioness of Milford Haven, wrote to one of her friends: 'I knew you would rejoice with us at Alice having a boy. Poor Andrea had the bad luck of leaving the day before the event & so has not seen his son.' Andrea had just been given command of the Greek army's 12th Division in Asia Minor and, on 9 June 1921, embarked on the campaign that would prove his undoing. It would be several months before he set eyes on his baby boy.

Victoria, in fact, got to see Philip before Andrea did. In September, Louis Milford Haven died, aged sixty-seven, and Alice came to London to console her mother, bringing Philip with her. Alice showed off her son to her assorted English relations, including, of course, her own youngest brother, Dickie Mountbatten, now nearly twenty-two and already smitten with his bride-to-be, the young Edwina Ashley.

Just a month before Louis Milford Haven's death, George V had honoured him – and thrilled him to the core – by appointing him Admiral of the Fleet. Louis might have had a German accent, but he had done the state some service. And the King now offered Louis's widow a home: an apartment in Kensington Palace, where she lived for the rest of her long life.

Prince Philip's grandfather was a naval officer of real distinction. Coming to an exact assessment of the merits of Prince Philip's father as a military commander is not so easy. Andrea enjoyed life as a soldier – his life *was* soldiering. He was committed and conscientious, without question, but, ultimately, his career ended in failure.

The trigger for his downfall was, as I say, the conduct of the campaign launched in the month of Prince Philip's birth. The Greeks and Turks were at war over the possession of Anatolia, once Turkish territory but awarded to Greece after the First World War. There may not have been a great deal to choose between the military capacity of the two sides, but there is little doubt that the Greek forces were seriously over-extended, poorly equipped, inadequately led, and simply unable to sustain a successful campaign in the Anatolian desert, so far away from base.

From the outset, Andrea had been convinced that the Asia Minor campaign was doomed. His own division was manned by new recruits, inexperienced and ill-equipped, and he had no faith in the campaign's overall commander, one General Papoulas, a soldier, according to Andrea, notable for his 'ignorance of the science of war'.

On 9 September 1921, Papoulas sent an order to Andrea in the desert to make an 'immediate violent attack' on the enemy to the north. Andrea considered the proposal absurd – 'a cry of ill-concealed panic', he called it – and replied to his commander-in-chief, 'Attack by 2nd Corps in the direction indicated impossible.' He had an alternative plan, involving different troop movements and no attack. He acted on his plan and sent word to Papoulas that he had done so. Under the circumstances, Papoulas's reaction does not seem surprising: 'Astonished at plan of abandoning positions. I order corps to remain in its position. Only person competent to judge and decide is myself as Commander-in-Chief. Cancel all orders of transfer movements.'

This order Andrea obeyed, but the following day, outraged to discover that overnight the commander-in-chief had relieved him of his chief of staff, he volunteered his own resignation. He sent word to Papoulas: 'It is absolutely impossible for me to continue in command of corps. Please order my immediate relief.'

Papoulas felt unable to oblige: 'I desire, and the situation demands, you should remain in your place.' Andrea did as he was told. The Turks attacked. The Greeks responded. The battle was neither lost nor won, but the drive towards Ankara was halted and then abandoned. Andrea and his men were in retreat.

If, today, you read *Towards Disaster*, Andrea's own account of what took place, you are left feeling (or, at least, I am left feeling) that the Prince protests too much. When ordered to attack, he did not do so. Further, he informed his commander-in-chief of his alternative plan of action as he was undertaking it. In his apologia he concedes that the message he sent Papoulas 'was not in accordance with ordinary practice', but asserts, 'beyond that, it does not constitute an infraction of orders, nor does it show any lack of fighting spirit'. This much – but no more – he is ready to accept: 'There is, however, a breach of formality, and this lies in the fact that in the message the correct phrase "subject to approval" was omitted, but the omission of this phrase cannot possibly form the basis of an accusation for disobedience and abandoning one's position.'

Prince Philip was like his father. As he grew older, he came to look like him – though Andrea had more protuberant ears, a moustache, and a monocle. By several accounts, they shared a joshing sense of humour and a capacity for charming the ladies. And from my reading of Prince Andrea's *Towards Disaster* and my observation of Prince Philip in action, I reckon they also had in common a stubborn streak, a wilful contrariness, a need to have the last word, and a slightly exasperated (occasionally despairing) sense that they were right and the other chap didn't know what he was talking about.

Andrea and Papoulas remained at odds and, at the end of September 1921, the Prince was granted three months' leave and returned to Corfu to meet his baby son for the first time. Within eight weeks, however, he was called back to active service, first as a member of the Supreme Army Council, then as commander of the 5th Army

Corps. General Papoulas was replaced by one General Hadjianestis (for whom Andrea had rather greater regard), but the fighting went no better. Within the year, the Turks had triumphed and the Greeks were in full retreat, forced back, literally, into the sea. Asia Minor was lost, the collapse was complete, the casualties horrendous. There were more than a million Greek refugees.

In the aftermath of the catastrophe, there was a military coup: a colonels' revolt. King Constantine I was overthrown and sent once more into exile. General Hadjianestis and five others were put on trial and swiftly executed. Andrea was arrested, charged with disobeying orders and abandoning his post in the face of the enemy, and tried in Athens, in the Chamber of Deputies, by a jury of junior officers. He was found guilty and expected to be sentenced to death. 'I think you might add,' Prince Philip said to me when he saw the draft of this paragraph, 'that my father was charged by the new republican government as a scapegoat.'

There is a telling photograph that was taken of Andrea during his trial. He is impeccably dressed in an elegant lounge suit, with a white handkerchief in his breast pocket, folded exactly as Prince Philip would fold his all his life. In the picture Prince Andrea sits staring into the middle distance, his attaché case unopened on the table in front of him. He looks gaunt and anxious, but unbowed.

At Mon Repos, Alice, under police surveillance, and denied access to her husband, was sending desperate messages in every direction, pleading for help from all quarters. Internationally, there was little desire to get involved in Greek politics, but, in London, Alice's brother, Dickie, saw the King and lobbied the Prime Minister, and Lord Curzon, the Foreign Secretary, arranged for a British agent – Gerald Talbot, previously naval attaché in Athens, and a man with useful contacts among the high command of the new regime – to slip discreetly into Greece 'to see what might be done'. The upshot was a secret deal, negotiated by Talbot, whereby Andrea was spared his life but condemned to 'perpetual banishment'.

For many years, in the British press and elsewhere, Prince Philip was nicknamed 'Phil the Greek'. Briefly, he had been sixth in line to the throne of Greece, but he has no Greek blood in him and no particular fondness for Greece or the Greeks. As he said to me, more than once, 'A grandfather assassinated and a father condemned to death does not endear me to the perpetrators.' Prince Philip thought of himself as British or Danish, with elements of German and Russian. He never thought of himself as Greek. I remember talking to him once about divided Cyprus: he was evidently more sympathetic to the Turks than to the Greeks. About the traumatic events of 1922 he was less forthcoming: 'I was barely a year old when the family went into exile. What do you expect me to remember?'

His sister Sophie, who was eight at the time, did remember and did talk about the experience before she died. 'It was a terrible business,' she recalled. 'Absolute chaos.' The British had sent a cruiser, HMS *Calypso*, to carry the family into exile. When Andrea was released from gaol, he was driven straight from his prison to the quayside. On Corfu, Alice, her lady-in-waiting, the governess, the nanny, the four girls and baby Philip, were bundled into cars, loaded with all the possessions they could muster in the hours before their escape, and taken in a small boat from the island harbour to the *Calypso* waiting offshore. Sophie's abiding memory of the flight from Mon Repos was of the smell of smoke from the grates in every fireplace: Alice had instructed her daughters to burn everything: letters, papers, documents; to leave nothing behind.

The sea – not having much respect for royalty – was rough. The ship's officers were more gracious, giving up their cabins for the royal refugees and providing an on-board concert to distract and entertain the children and their parents. The exiles were taken across the Adriatic sea to Brindisi, on the heel of Italy, 'a ghastly place', according to Sophie, 'the worst town I've ever been in'. From there, as dawn broke, they took a train to Rome. On the train, Philip made himself filthy, crawling everywhere. 'He was very active,' said Sophie. He even licked the windowpanes. His mother reprimanded him. 'Leave him alone,' said nanny.[10]

---

10 Princess Sophie told her story in 1990 to Tim Heald, Prince Philip's biographer. Heald told me: 'I liked her very much. She could not have been more friendly. I stood with her at Buckingham Palace watching the Guards rehearse for Trooping the Colour. She spoke with a marked German accent and occasionally had to search for the *mot juste*, but if not quite bilingual she was certainly completely fluent. I sensed her relationship with Prince Philip was still very much big sister/ kid brother.'

Their hope and expectation had been to travel on to London, but George V, while ready to help save his cousin's neck, was not so eager to offer him sanctuary. Buckingham Palace took the view, endorsed by the Foreign Office, that it would be politically more comfortable if the exiled Greek prince could settle somewhere quietly on the continent, out of controversy's way. What about Palermo in Sicily, where the overthrown King Constantine had taken refuge?

In the event, the exiles and their entourage (a family of seven, plus six servants) went on from Rome to Paris, then – after several days of awkward diplomatic wrangling – briefly to London and then, finally and permanently, back once more to the French capital. Paris dictated itself as the city in which to settle because Andrea's elder brother, Prince George, now fifty-three, was already living there and had a home to spare that was large enough to accommodate the royal refugees.

In 1907 Prince George (known in the family as 'Big George') had married Marie Bonaparte, great-granddaughter of the Emperor Napoleon's brother, Lucien, and, rather more usefully, granddaughter of the celebrated Monsieur Blanc, founder of the casino at Monte Carlo. She was an interesting woman: an heiress, an antiquarian, a dog-lover, a psychoanalyst of some distinction, and a friend and patroness of Sigmund Freud. George and Marie and their two children (Peter and Eugénie, aged fourteen and twelve in 1922) lived in a substantial mansion at St Cloud, on the outskirts of Paris. In the garden they had a lodge and this became Andrea's and Alice's family home for the rest of the 1920s.

When the exiles had arrived in Rome they were, literally, penniless (the British Ambassador had to lend them money to pay for the train tickets to Paris), but, once they were able to make contact with their bankers, they were not without some means. They were not poor, they did not go hungry, but they were impoverished, and now, to an extent, dependent on the kindness of others. As well as Big George and his wealthy wife, Marie Bonaparte, their principal benefactors were Andrea's younger brother, Christo, and his wealthy wife, Nancy Leeds, and Alice's younger brother, Dickie, and his wealthy wife, Edwina Ashley. Edwina was especially generous, in all sorts of ways. When he was just a toddler, she took out an insurance policy for Philip. When she had her dresses made, she asked the dressmaker to include extra seams so that, in due course, the dresses could be let out and passed on to Alice and her girls.

Prince Philip made it clear to me that what memories he had of life in Paris in the 1920s were good ones. By all accounts, he was a cheerful, active, inquisitive, friendly little boy. He did not lack companionship. He had doting sisters. Big George had children. Another of the brothers, Prince Nicholas, lived in St Cloud, with his young daughters. There were other cousins in the neighbourhood and family lunches in Big George's big house every Sunday. 'It was a normal family life, as far as I was concerned,' said Prince Philip. 'I did not sense anything untoward.'

Nevertheless, for Philip's parents life was now very different from anything they had known before. They dined with family and friends. They travelled quite extensively: to America (without baby Philip) and the south of France, on holiday, to Italy and England and Germany, to visit assorted royal relations. They kept themselves occupied, but they had no occupation. In Paris, Alice gave some of her time to a small Greek shop called Hellas in the Faubourg St Honoré, raising money to help Greek expatriates, and Andrea, who had for so long lived the life of a professional soldier, now spent the best part of most days sitting about in clubs and restaurants, meeting with other Greek exiles, talking politics, regretting the fate that had befallen Greece. He was, by all accounts, enormously charming and, under the circumstances, surprisingly cheerful. He had enthusiasms: he loved animals, he enjoyed painting, he read, he wrote. In his enforced retirement (he was just forty in 1922), *Towards Disaster*, published in London in 1930, was his most significant undertaking, written by him in Greek and translated into English for him by Princess Alice. Alice admired her husband, as a soldier and as a man. She hoped and, sometimes, believed that the family might return to Greece one day. Briefly, energetically, but to little effect, she worked on a plan to install Andrea as president of a reformed Hellenic republic.

But Alice's principal preoccupation was not politics. It was religion. As a young woman she had been inspired by the example of her Russian aunt, Ella. Alice thought a great deal about Ella, and the sisterhood she had founded, and the martyrdom she had suffered. Alice read widely and deeply about comparative religion. She took a particular interest in Christian Science. Encouraged by her young brother-in-law, Christo, she dabbled in the occult. This was a period when interest in spiritualism was widespread. In Britain, Sir Arthur Conan Doyle was attending séances. In America, Harry Houdini was denouncing false mediums. In Paris, Princess Alice was turning over cards and receiving messages from the spirit world. Increasingly, those who met her found her a little strange.

Hugo Vickers, in his biography of Alice, suggests that an unfulfilled love affair may have tipped her over the edge. In 1925, the year she turned forty, when her eldest daughter was twenty and Prince Philip just three, she met a married man, an unidentified Englishman, and fell overwhelmingly in love with him. Nothing 'happened'. According to Vickers, 'Everything in Alice's background was strictly conventional. She herself had high moral principles and nothing in her character was flighty or flippant. She was no Edwina Mountbatten or Nada Milford Haven.[11] The fact of falling in love and resisting temptation almost certainly needed an outlet of some kind. Without even knowing why, Alice turned to religion as a safe outlet for these repressed feelings.'

I am not so sure. My instinct is that the hopeless passion – intense yet impossible, feverishly pursued but ultimately abandoned – and the religious fervour – complete with visions, voices, and the acquisition of the gift of healing – had the same root cause: mania, the kind of mania associated with what we now call bipolar disorder or manic depression. I think the evidence is there.

Alice's behaviour at this time displays the classic symptoms of bipolar disorder: inappropriate elation, impulsiveness, extreme motor activity. When she embarked on her mission to secure for Andrea the presidency of Greece, she did so with manic energy. She pursued politicians and diplomats, she organised a clandestine meeting with representatives of the League of Nations, she dashed to London to

11 In 1916 Dickie's elder brother, Georgie, married Countess Nadejda (Nada) Torby, a daughter of Grand Duke Michael of Russia. Georgie was reputed to have a large and adventurous collection of pornography, and Nada was a noted lesbian, whose lovers included Gloria Vanderbilt Sr. When I put it to Nada's niece, Gina Wernher (later Lady Kennard), that Nada was 'a bit of a goer', she smiled and said, 'Yes, she had many sides to her, and she was a real rebel. There was no stopping her – in all sorts of ways.'

lobby George V face to face at Buckingham Palace. Those she met listened courteously, and then let her down gently. 'Ladies get carried away,' said George V, benignly, to his private secretary, adding, 'I think it would be most unwise for Prince A. to go near Greece.'

When, in 1928, Princess Alice decided to convert to the Greek Orthodox faith (not unreasonably: this was the church into which her husband and her children had been baptised), the English, Anglican, members of her family took her decision comfortably in their stride. When she took to lying on the floor in order to enhance her mystic powers, when she became convinced that her hands contained the gift of healing, when she announced that she was a saint and the bride of Christ, it was a different matter. The medical experts were called in. Alice was clearly not well. Sometimes she seemed quite happy, seraphically so: she would talk incessantly, laugh immoderately, declare herself to be in a state of ecstasy. At other times she would be listless, seemingly exhausted, unable to do anything, unwilling to eat. She lost weight, she had headaches, she recognised that something was amiss.

Her gynaecologist, brought to Paris from Athens, concluded that her condition was not menopausal. Her sister-in-law, Marie Bonaparte, suggested she seek help from a fellow Freudian, Dr Ernst Simmel, at his clinic in Tegel, on the outskirts of Berlin. Simmel diagnosed Alice as 'schizophrenic paranoid'. He concluded that she was suffering from a 'neurotic-pre-psychotic libidinous condition'. Reading between the lines and stripping away the euphemism, it seems the psychoanalyst's view of her situation was that she was a woman who was hungry for sex and no longer getting it. This was disturbing the balance of her mind. Freud himself was consulted and proposed, as a palliative treatment, to help subdue her sexual appetite and so calm her nerves, 'an exposure of the gonads to X-rays, in order to accelerate the menopause'.

Alice was given the prescribed treatment. Whether or not she knew exactly what was being done to her is unclear, but gradually she began to put on weight and, for a while, to feel better in herself. She returned home, but, in truth, she was no better. She was preoccupied with sex and religion. She was obsessed by her relationship with Christ. Andrea could not cope.

In May 1930, with Andrea's agreement, Alice's mother, Victoria, took the decision that Alice should be interned in an asylum. Against her will, and under sedation, Alice was taken to the Bellevue Clinic at Kreuzlingen in Switzerland, the psychiatric sanatorium of Dr Ludwig Binswanger.

To all intents and purposes, Alice's marriage, and her family life, were now over. Things had not been comfortable for some while. There is a formal photograph taken of the family at St Cloud in 1928, at the time of Andrea and Alice's silver wedding anniversary. Everybody in the picture looks miserable. Andrea, seated, arms and legs folded, cigarette holder in hand, is gazing remotely into the middle distance. The two elder daughters look almost haunted, the two younger ones, positively sullen. Oddly, Alice, and young Philip, aged seven, in his sailor suit, holding his mother's hand, both staring solemnly at the camera, appear the most composed, the least ill at ease.

In 1928 Philip was still a pupil at his first school in Paris, The Elms, a pre-preparatory establishment, run by an American couple, Donald and Charlotte MacJannet, and catering largely for the children of wealthy American businessmen and the multi-national offspring of the diplomatic corps.[12]

According to the MacJannets' biographer, Princess Alice told the headmaster that, while her boy had plenty of originality and spontaneity, 'instead of being constantly hushed up he should be working off his boundless energy by practicing games and learning Anglo-Saxon ideas of courage, fair play, and resistance. Philip should develop English characteristics, because his future will be in English speaking lands, perhaps American, and I want him to learn English well.'

Philip, accompanied by his governess, walked to the school every morning and usually arrived half an hour early. According to 'Mr Mac', as the head was known, Philip made himself useful, cleaning blackboards, straightening furniture, and reminding all and sundry of his sisters' *dictum*: 'You shouldn't slam doors or shout loud.' He seems to have been something of a paragon. 'He always got chairs

---

12 When I included this sentence in the account of Prince Philip's life prepared for his eightieth birthday, he wrote to me from Windsor Castle: 'The Elms catered largely for children of the Diplomatic Corps. I am sorry to upset your obsession with wealth!!' (Double exclamation marks are very much a feature of the Prince's writing style. His father wrote letters in the same emphatic vein.)

for visitors, would not let women serve him, carried food from the kitchen but never broke a platter.' Besides loving football, and baseball, he did well enough in his studies to get a silver star and even a gold one, 'making great progress in his three years'. Apparently, he begged to be allowed to be a boarder and live at the school, but 'we can't afford it,' his mother said. As it was, his school fees were paid by his father's younger brother, Christo.

Prince Philip remembered the MacJannets for the rest of his life and always spoke of them with respect and affection. Off and on, over the years, he would write to them. Once or twice he saw them and talked with them happily about the old times. 'Were they the best times?' I asked him. 'They were good times,' he said. 'The MacJannets were good people.' In 1947, when Philip married Princess Elizabeth, they sent an album of school pictures to the couple as a wedding present. Later, when Prince Charles reached school age, they sent him a story entitled 'When Daddy was a Little Boy', in which Charlotte MacJannet told of Philip's school days.

The Elms was an international school. I asked Prince Philip if he thought of himself as an 'international' person. 'I've been a British subject since 1947,' he said, side-stepping the question.

'What language did you speak at home?' I asked.

'English . . . and then we might lapse into French – or German.'

'Greek?'

'Sometimes. We spoke English mainly.'

'So by the time you were ten you spoke English, German, Greek, and French?'

'I could hardly fail to learn French during nearly ten years' residence in Paris,' he replied tartly.

In 1928, though his parents' marriage was under strain and his home circumstances unusual, Philip was happy with his lot. Indeed, every account of him at this time contributes to a picture of a perfectly straightforward little boy: lively, boisterous, adventurous, not especially academic (but by no means a dunce), self-confident, self-reliant, noticeably charming.

In 1929, when he was eight, funds were found to send him to boarding school – in England. He was dispatched to Cheam, in Surrey, England's oldest preparatory school, where his mother's younger brother, Georgie (2nd Marquess of Milford Haven), had once been a pupil, and where Georgie's eldest son, David, was a near-contemporary, and, though two years his senior, would become Philip's closest school friend and, eighteen years later, his best man. Cheam, founded at the turn of the seventeenth century, was a typical, traditional English prep school of the period, complete with cold showers, wet runs, corporal punishment, compulsory chapel, compulsory games, compulsory Latin and compulsory Classical Greek. Philip appears to have thrived in this environment. Years later, in a foreword to an official history of the school, written in 1974 (after Prince Charles had been a pupil at Cheam – and hated it), Prince Philip wrote: 'Children may be indulged at home, but school is expected to be a spartan and disciplined experience in the process of developing them into self-controlled, considerate and independent adults. The system may have its eccentricities, but there can be little doubt that these are far outweighed by its values.'

Philip's arrival at Cheam coincided with a range of dramatic changes in his immediate family's situation. From the age of eight, his mother virtually disappeared from his life for the rest of his childhood. For several years he received no word from her of any kind, not even a birthday card. And within the space of eight months, between December 1930 and August 1931, his four sisters were married to a quartet of eligible German princelings. Margarita, aged twenty-five, married Prince Gottfried of Hohenlohe-Langenburg; Theodora, twenty-four, married Berthold, Margrave of Baden; Cécile, twenty, married George Donatus, Hereditary Grand Duke of Hesse; and Sophie, seventeen, married Prince Christoph of Hesse. It was a parcelling off of daughters that would have done credit to Mrs Bennet in *Pride and Prejudice*.

With Alice in a sanatorium, his daughters in their new family homes, and his son enjoying the spartan, disciplined life at his English boarding school, Prince Andrea gave up the house in St Cloud and moved, on his own, to live in a small flat in Monte Carlo. However much you pressed him on the matter, in my experience Prince Philip would make no complaint about any of this. 'It's simply what happened,' he said to me. 'The family broke up. My mother was ill, my sisters were married, my father was in the south of France. I just had to get on with it. You do. One does.'

Prince Philip's loyalty to the memory of both his parents was impressive. Occasionally, I heard him make withering comments about a member of his own family, but about his parents – who, in effect, left him without a settled home and family from the age of ten – I only heard him speak with sympathy, affection, and even admiration. Fine portraits of them both hung in his study at Buckingham Palace. To the end of his life, arthritis permitting, he liked to wear his father's signet ring.

Princess Alice was incarcerated in the Bellevue Clinic at Kreuzlingen for two and a half years. Her condition did not improve. There were times when she was 'high' – drafting loopy articles and working on a book of spiritual revelations – but, mostly she was depressed and, occasionally, she was suicidal. Philip visited her once, accompanying his grandmother. Andrea visited once, too.

The environment at Kreuzlingen was not uncongenial – I get the impression of a country house hotel set in well-tended parkland – and the clinic's staff appear to have been kindly and intelligent people. There was no electric-shock treatment, no automatic recourse to drugs, and straitjackets would be used rarely and only to restrain the most violent patients. Alice was offered care, kindness, and attention. The hope seems to have been that rest would lead to recuperation. It didn't, and the Princess felt imprisoned. She resented being detained against her will. In July 1932, after jumping through a window, she managed to escape. Her freedom was short-lived. Within hours she was apprehended at the local railway station and forcibly returned to the clinic.

Alice did not want to live with her own family (she was clear about that), but she did want to leave Kreuzlingen, and eventually, later in 1932, she persuaded her mother that the time had come when she should be allowed 'freedom under surveillance'. For the next five years Alice led a nomadic existence, travelling between Italy, Switzerland, and Germany, living quietly in small hotels and in rented rooms. She sent Philip and her daughters the occasional message or birthday card. She did not see any of her children for five years. She lived among strangers. Gradually, she recovered her equilibrium.

Andrea, meanwhile, was making a new life for himself on the French Riviera. The tall, elegant, monocled prince-in-exile, who smoked and drank a little more than was quite good for him, lived variously in a small flat, in hotel rooms, and on board a wealthy friend's smart yacht moored in Cannes harbour. From around 1930 up until the time of his death he had a lady friend, the Comtesse Andrée de La Bigne, granddaughter of a mistress of Napoleon III. Andrea had a reputation as a charmer and enjoyed the company of women, but there is no evidence to suggest that he was a serial philanderer. He died at the Hôtel Métropole in Monte Carlo on 3 December 1944. He was sixty-two.

Young Philip, meanwhile, when not at boarding school, travelled between the homes of assorted relations: his grandmother at Kensington Palace, his English Uncle Georgie (Milford Haven) in Berkshire, his sisters and their new husbands in Germany. He did see his parents together just once more, in late November 1937, when he was sixteen. There was a family reunion as a consequence of a family tragedy. A Hesse-Darmstadt cousin was getting married in London and Alice's and Andrea's middle child, Cécile, and her husband and their two boys (aged six and four), were all killed on their way to the wedding, when the aeroplane taking them from Darmstadt to England crashed in heavy fog outside Ostend.

Alice travelled to Darmstadt from Berlin for the family funeral. Andrea brought Philip from London. At the funeral Alice's brother Dickie (whom she had not seen since 1929) represented George VI and Queen Elizabeth. Both Kaiser Wilhelm (Queen Victoria's grandson, who lived until 1941) and the German Third Reich were represented. Hermann Goering, founder of the Gestapo and commander-in-chief of the Luftwaffe, came in person.

For Alice and Andrea the death of their daughter and two of their grandchildren was a shocking event. They were united in grief, but only briefly. In better health than she had been for several years, Alice was ready to consider the possibility of sharing a life with her husband again. For Andrea, however, it was too late: he had moved on.

From Prince Philip's early childhood, I have three anecdotes to offer, each illustrating a different aspect of his character: his generosity, his get-up-and-go, his pig-headedness. Two of them were recounted by his cousin and exact contemporary, Princess Alexandra of Greece. In 1944 Alexandra married Peter, the last King of Yugoslavia, and, in 1959, in exile in England, she published *Prince Philip: A Family*

Portrait. She was emotionally unstable and her book, according to Prince Philip, is 'largely unreliable'. 'She was a natural journalist,' he said. But, having said this, he did not quibble with the stories.

The first illustrates Philip's instinctive kindness – one of his most attractive and least recognised characteristics. The story dates from the mid-1920s, when Philip was five or six, and on a family holiday, playing on the beach at Berck-Plage, the seaside resort in the Pas de Calais. A well-meaning visitor arrives on the beach one day with toys which he gives out to each of the children in the party – except for one little girl, who is disabled and whose disability, the visitor assumes, will prevent her from playing. Immediately, Philip goes into the house and collects his assorted toys and treasures and presents them to the little girl.

The second story – again set at Berck-Plage – illustrates his initiative. Inspired by the nomadic salesmen – usually from north Africa – who plied their exotic wares along the beach, Philip collected a couple of oriental rugs from the house and set himself up on the beach in direct competition.

The third story demonstrates his stubborn streak. It was told to me by Patricia Mountbatten, his first cousin, Dickie Mountbatten's elder daughter, and dates from a few years later. She remembers: 'I suppose Philip was about twelve and I was about nine. Our mutual grandmother took a great interest in Philip. She played an enormous part in his upbringing. But they were both strong-willed individuals and sometimes they argued – and sometimes Philip was really quite rude. I remember vividly the time when they had an argument about something and our grandmother said, "Philip, go up to your room." And he wouldn't. He just hung about in the hall. He would *not* go up to his room. Eventually, our grandmother came out into the hall and actually had to chase him up the stairs.'

When in England as a boy, and not staying either with his grandmother, Victoria Milford Haven, or her son, Georgie, Philip spent part of his holidays with the Wernher family, either at Thorpe Lubenham, near Market Harborough, or at their splendid Bedfordshire mansion, Luton Hoo. In 1916 Georgie married Countess Nadejda (Nada) Torby, daughter of Grand Duke Michael of Russia and his wife, Countess Torby (an heiress from the Caucasus), and great-granddaughter of Tsar Nicholas I. In 1917 Nada's elder sister Anastasia, known as Zia, married Harold Wernher,[13] for a while considered the richest catch in England. The Wernhers had three children and their daughter Gina, born in 1919, had vivid memories of Prince Philip as a little boy. 'I suppose I was about eight and he was about six when I first met him,' she told me. 'He was a very obstreperous, rough little boy. Very strong, very active. He had a great sense of humour. We had a lot of fun. There were four of us who played together all the time: Philip, Philip's cousin, David Milford Haven (he was my cousin, too, of course), me (I was known as "George") and my younger brother, Alex, who was exactly Philip's age and who was killed in the war, in 1942, aged twenty-one. We called ourselves "The Four Musketeers".'

I asked Gina Wernher – who later became Lady Kennard[14] – whether she thought Prince Philip was happy as a boy. 'As a little boy he was very happy,' she said, 'Very jolly, very lively. As he grew older, he became more thoughtful, more introspective. He never saw his parents, you know. Never. And he minded that. He told me so. He was perfectly happy at boarding school, but he said to me – I remember this clearly – "Everybody has a family to go back to. I don't." He loved his sisters very much and when Cécile was killed in that air crash, in 1937, it affected him deeply. He was very quiet. He didn't talk about it much, but he showed me a little bit of wood from the aeroplane. It was just a small piece, but it meant a lot to him.'

In 1933, aged twelve, Prince Philip first came under the influence of the German educationist Kurt Hahn. Hahn had been secretary and friend to Prince Max of Baden, former Chancellor of the

13 Wernher, who inherited a mining fortune in South Africa (as well as Luton Hoo), was an industrialist of note, chairman of Plessey, chairman of British Telephones, chairman of Associated Theatre Properties (London), and, notably, chairman of Electrolux (1926–63).

14 Georgina Wernher (1919–2011) was married first, in 1944, to Lieutenant Colonel Harold 'Bunnie' Phillips (1909–80), sometime lover, it is said, of Edwina Mountbatten, and, much later, as his fourth wife, to Sir George 'Loopy' Kennard, who commanded the 4th Queen's Own Hussars and whose autobiography, *Loopy*, published 1990, is the most original and entertaining military memoir I know. Lady Kennard's daughters included the present Duchesses of Abercorn (Alexandra, born 1946) and Westminster (Natalia, born 1959). Her only son, Nicolas Phillips, born 1947, committed suicide at Luton Hoo in 1991.

German Empire, whose son Berthold had married Philip's sister, Theodora, in 1931. A decade or so before that, Hahn and Max of Baden had founded a school together, based at the Baden family home, Schloss Salem, on the shores of Lake Constance, and designed as much to build the characters of its students as to educate them. Prince Max said of the school, 'I am proud of the fact that there is nothing original here. We have cribbed from everywhere, from the public schools, from Goethe, from Plato, from the Boy Scouts.'

Philip left Cheam and came to Salem. He explained to me, 'The suggestion came from my sister and brother-in-law, who owned the school: it had the great advantage of saving school fees.' Philip remained at the school for two terms. He might have stayed longer had it not been for Hitler's rise to power (Hitler became Chancellor that year) and the growing and malevolent influence of the Nazi Party. Under the circumstances, Philip's family felt he should return to school in Britain. 'It was certainly a great relief to me,' he said. At Salem, Philip could not take the 'Heil Hitler' salute at all seriously: at Cheam, exactly the same arm gesture was used to indicate to a master that a boy wanted permission to go to the lavatory. (When he saw this paragraph in draft, Prince Philip asked me, 'Do you really want to keep the last sentence?' 'Yes,' I said, 'because it illustrates your contempt for the Nazi Party even at an early age.' When a Jewish fellow pupil had his head shaved by anti-Semites, Philip gave the boy his Cheam school cap to hide the indignity. He had nothing but scorn for the Nazis, yet there are those who persist in portraying him as a racist. I have come across two websites that label him, uncompromisingly, as a crypto-Nazi.)

Kurt Hahn himself – not only Jewish, but also an outspoken critic of Hitler – was arrested by the Nazis in March 1933. He was later released and fled to Britain, ending up in Scotland, in Morayshire, where he founded another school, at Gordonstoun House, in a location close to the sea and mountains, where the wind and weather were appropriate to his challenging educational philosophy. Hahn believed that young people were 'surrounded by a sick civilisation . . . in danger of being affected by a fivefold decay: the decay of fitness, the decay of initiative and enterprise, the decay of care and skill, the decay of self-discipline, the decay of compassion'.

At Gordonstoun – where Prince Philip arrived in the autumn of

1934 – the regime was designed to tackle this decay and, years later, Hahn's radical philosophy and methods would play their part in shaping two of the national and international ventures with which Prince Philip became most closely associated: the Outward Bound Trust and the Duke of Edinburgh's Award Scheme. How would Philip describe Hahn? 'Eccentric perhaps, innovator certainly, great beyond doubt.'

Hahn's chief eccentricity lay in his appearance. As a young man he had had brain surgery which involved a silver plate being implanted in his skull. As a result of the operation he had an aversion to light, wore a huge black cape, a broad-rimmed black hat, and, when travelling by car, covered his face with a dark cloth. 'There was an air about Hahn which commanded instant wariness and respect,' said Philip. 'Apart from that, his famous mannerisms – the stooping gait, the handkerchief screwed up like a ball and held in his mouth, the large-brimmed hat and the flashing quizzical eye – all helped to signal the presence of an exceptional being.'

Hahn was an intellectual. He had read Greats at Oxford. He had studied at the universities of Berlin, Heidelberg, Freiburg, and Göttingen. He believed in books. He also believed in the power of 'the great outdoors'. He said, 'My best schoolmaster is the Moray Firth.' As a teenager Philip learnt to sail in its chilly, challenging waters. 'I was wet, cold, miserable, probably sick, and often scared stiff, but I would not have missed the experience for anything,' he said. 'In any case the discomfort was far outweighed by the moments of intense happiness and excitement. Poets and authors down the centuries have tried to describe those moments but their descriptions, however brilliant, will never compare with one's own experience.'

Prince Philip's experience of Gordonstoun would inform the rest of his life. In 1938, when he left the school – as Guardian, Gordonstoun's equivalent of head boy – Hahn gave him a glowing final report: 'Prince Philip is universally trusted, liked and respected. He has the greatest sense of service of all the boys in the school.' Hahn described the seventeen-year-old as 'a born leader', a boy of 'intelligence and spirit', 'often naughty, never nasty', with 'a natural power of command', a 'sense of humour and a rapid understanding of human nature', but suggested Philip would 'need the exacting demands of great service to do justice to himself'. When he was engaged he had the 'power of meticulous application'; at other times he showed a 'determination not to exert himself more than was necessary to avoid trouble'. Hahn concluded that Philip would 'make his mark in any profession where he will have to prove himself in a free trial of strength'.

Philip was not especially academic and, at Gordonstoun, while he played Donalbain in the school production of *Macbeth*, his enthusiasms were, on the whole, more sporting than artistic. (At this point, reading my text, Prince Philip wrote to me: 'I don't see the connection between not being academic and taking part in a school play. I was just a very bad actor. I did at least pass the Civil Service Exams to enter the Navy!!')

Having passed the necessary exams, on 1 May 1939, six weeks short of his eighteenth birthday, Prince Philip of Greece joined the Royal Naval College at Dartmouth and set himself on course for a career in the Royal Navy. He told me that, left entirely to his own devices, 'I'd have gone into the air force without a doubt.' Flying was one of the great unremarked-on passions of his life. He made his first flight, from White Waltham in Berkshire, in a Chipmunk, on 12 November 1952; his last, in a BAe 146, flying from Carlisle to Islay, on 11 August 1997. Over forty-five years he clocked up a total of 5,986 hours of flying in fifty-nine types of aircraft, including nine helicopters. (An RAF pilot might clock up no more than 8,000 hours in a full career.)

That Philip was persuaded to opt for the navy rather than the air force in 1938 is hardly surprising. As he explained to me, there was something of a family tradition: 'I was following my grandfather [Louis of Battenberg] and two uncles [Georgie Milford Haven and Dickie Mountbatten]. My Danish grandfather had been in the Danish navy and my uncle George (of Greece) served in the Greek navy.'

Who were the key influences on the young Prince Philip?

'Beyond my parents?'

'Yes. You didn't see a great deal of them after you were ten.'

'You can be influenced by people you don't see every day.'

'Who else?'

'Kurt Hahn was one, certainly.'

'And your uncle, Georgie Milford Haven, and the industrialist

Harold Wernher – people with whose families you spent part of your holidays?'

'Yes, inevitably. I also spent time with my sisters and their husbands. I saw more of my third sister's husband (George Donatus of Hesse) as I usually spent most of my holidays with them in Darmstadt or at Wolfsgarten' – their idyllic country house: an old hunting lodge built around a courtyard in a woodland setting, apparently remote, but, in fact, not far from Frankfurt.

'You enjoyed your holidays?' I asked the Prince, trying to coax a few recollections from him.

'Yes,' he said, 'I did. I know you are determined to make a meal out the so-called "deprivations" of my childhood, but I am afraid I can't help you there.'

His Royal Highness did at least concede that working out exactly where he should go for his holidays was sometimes a challenge, not because he was not welcome wherever he went, but because his father, although largely absent, liked to be involved in the plans relating to his son. For example, in late July 1934, Philip's grandmother, Victoria, was with Philip at Wolfsgarten, but, as she explained in a letter to her son, Georgie, in England, she was not quite sure what to do with her grandson next: 'Philip may go there (Hemmelmark) with us & back to England with me via Hamburg & Southampton but we can settle nothing about his movements until having discussed them with Andrea, who after a delay of 4 weeks turns up this evening, we suppose en route for a cure in Marienbad. I hope it is not too inconvenient to leave you without definite news of Philip's movements, but it has been unavoidable.'

Andrea was interested in his son, and proud of his son, but not very hands-on – or reliable – when it came to his care of him.

If Wordsworth is right and the child is father of the man, what effect was Prince Philip's childhood likely to have had on his personality as an adult? As you can imagine, the man himself was not one to indulge in this kind of speculation. The Duke of Edinburgh acknowledged that he had read the writings of Freud and Jung and when I told him that I would be intrigued to know what a practising psychoanalyst like his aunt Marie Bonaparte – his uncle Big George's wife – could tell us about the impact of his upbringing on his later behaviour, he replied, with a raised eyebrow, 'You don't surprise me.'

Marie Bonaparte (1882–1962) is a fascinating figure. Born at St Cloud, a Catholic, and brought up in Paris, she married Prince George of Greece in 1907. Their relationship was not conventional. They had two children, Peter and Marie, born in 1908 and 1910, but when Prince George died in 1957, a few months before their golden wedding anniversary, Marie said, 'I bent over his cold forehead and kissed it. Not his lips, which he had always refused me.'

She was wealthy, glamorous, passionate, intelligent, restless. Her lovers included Aristide Briand, famously depicted by Toulouse-Lautrec and ten times Prime Minister of France. Her enthusiasms included sex, her pet chows, and Dr Sigmund Freud. In 1925 she entered analysis with Freud in Vienna and trained as a psychoanalyst. She went on to become a pivotal figure in the French Psychoanalytical Society and the international psychoanalytical community. She was fascinated by criminal psychopathology and published a gripping account of a woman who had murdered her pregnant daughter-in-law, *Le Cas de Madame Lefebvre*, as well as an acclaimed study of Edgar Allan Poe, whom she described as 'one of the darkest minds there has ever been', and the first full study of female sexuality, *La Sexualité Féminine*. She experimented with early forms of genital surgery and underwent an unusual procedure to alter the position of her clitoris. She was sympathetic to the view of Freud's mentor, Jean-Martin Charcot, that when looking for the root cause of nervous disorders, '*c'est toujours la chose génitale, toujours, toujours*'. It was to her that Freud posed his celebrated question, 'What does a woman want?'

'A good question,' the Duke of Edinburgh said to me, laughing. 'And one to which I think we still don't have the answer.'

Marie Bonaparte became one of Freud's closest friends. She lavished gifts on him. In the aftermath of the Nazi *Anschluss*, she used her connections and her considerable financial resources to help secure his – and his family's – safe passage from Vienna to London in 1938. According to Freud's son, Martin, 'She had most of father's chief characteristics – his courage, his sincerity, his essential goodness and kindliness and his inflexible devotion to scientific truth.' She became a close friend, too, of Freud's daughter, Anna Freud, the pioneer of child psychoanalysis, and maintained a lifelong affectionate interest in her husband's nephew, Prince Philip. What would Marie Bonaparte and the classic Freudians have made of Philip's childhood?

'Do we really need to know?' asked the Duke of Edinburgh.

'It's not essential,' I replied, 'but it might be interesting.'

In search of an authoritative answer to my question I travelled to 20 Maresfield Gardens in Hampstead – the Freud family's London home, now the home of the Freud Museum – to meet Dr Brett Kahr, noted Freudian psychologist, Senior Research Fellow in Psychotherapy at the Winnicott Clinic of Psychotherapy, and a student of the life and work of Marie Bonaparte. He said at once, 'I am not allowed to talk about a person I have never met, but if you want to know what Princess Marie Bonaparte might have made of Prince Philip's childhood history I am happy to speculate.'

Where to begin? 'I think Marie would have begun right at the beginning – with Philip's mother and his birth. Prince Philip was born into a household of women. There was his mother, and his nanny, and probably a wet-nurse, and certainly a lady-in-waiting, and, most significantly, four older sisters. His father was away at the wars. Philip was the only boy, literally a beautiful, blue-eyed boy, born into a household of devoted, doting women. And he is the fifth child, the longed-for son. After four girls, whose ages range from sixteen to seven when Philip is born, here is a boy – and what do boys have that girls do not have? A penis. Into this household of women and girls comes this perfect boy. It is very exciting. There is within the household – in the phrase of Phyllis Greenacre, a Freudian from the 1950s – "penis awe". It is unspoken, but it is there. And the admiration and devotion of these women, especially the four elder sisters, will have given Philip, as he grew up, what might be termed a certain "phallic swagger", a sense of self-assurance and self-confidence, a certain cockiness.'

Will there have been disadvantages to all this feminine attention? 'Possibly,' says Brett Kahr – still, of course in the guise of Marie Bonaparte. 'Children with multiple carers sometimes struggle with depression. And being given lots of different affection from different people – nannies, nurses, sisters, aunts, grandmothers – can leave a child confused as to who is his primary attachment figure. Children with multiple carers, however loving, become sexually promiscuous because they don't have a model of falling in love with just one person.

'In Prince Philip's case there is nothing to suggest that Princess

Alice was not devoted to her son, but she was a princess who would have expected to share the child-rearing with nannies and, from about the time Philip was nine or ten, she virtually disappeared from his life. No child is immune from a mother disappearing. And, in Philip's case, his father virtually disappeared, too. A history of broken parental attachments is one of the keys to depression.

'There is some evidence that Prince Andrea was depressed after his departure from Greece. It would hardly be surprising. He was forced into exile and had to give up a career he loved. Unemployment and enforced idleness can lead to depression. The family moves to Paris. The father is depressed and leaves home. The mother suffers a nervous breakdown and is sent to a sanatorium. How does the child Philip feel about this? Children are self-referential. Children are grandiose and think the world revolves around them. A child can have omnipotent infantile fantasies. Prince Philip was just a year old when his family were forced into exile. The military debacle that triggered Prince Andrea's downfall coincided precisely with Philip's birth. One wonders whether, subconsciously, Philip saw himself as responsible for the fate that befell his parents.'

I point out that Philip himself never complained about any aspect of his childhood. 'It's simply what happened,' is what Prince Philip had said to me. 'The family broke up. My mother was ill, my sisters were married, my father was in the south of France. I just had to get on with it. You do. One does.'

Brett Kahr nods. 'Yes, his mother was ill and in a clinic in Switzerland; his father was depressed and on a boat in the south of France; his sisters were married and living in Germany; and Philip was away at school in England and Scotland. From the age of ten he saw his parents only rarely. He saw his sisters in the school holidays, but seeing them and their husbands became increasingly difficult with the rise of Nazi Germany through the 1930s. And in 1936, his sister Cécile and her husband – who, apparently, is his favourite brother-in-law – they are the sister and brother-in-law he sees most during his holidays – these two key figures in his world, and their children, are all killed in an aeroplane accident. And in 1938, what happens? Georgie Milford Haven, his favourite English uncle and his guardian, dies of cancer. Philip is not yet seventeen. By any standards, Philip has known a lot of loss in his young life and one

66

way people deal with loss is with stoicism. To take on board the full throttle of what has happened to you is too painful, so you use your defence mechanisms well. You rationalise your experience. You don't dwell on it. You don't discuss it. Stoically, you soldier on.'

People who knew Prince Andrea in the 1930s have described him alternately as 'melancholy' and 'as funny as all-get-out'. 'There is a touch of manic depression in most of us,' says Brett Kahr. I think there is little doubt that Princess Alice, in the late 1920s and early 1930s, suffered from quite severe bipolar disorder. Princess Marie Bonaparte took a personal and practical interest in Alice's condition. She kept in touch with Prince Philip through the years as well. As a boy, according to Kurt Hahn, Philip 'felt deeply both joy and sadness, and the way he looked and the way he moved indicated what he felt'. As a man Philip could be urbane and engaging one day and sullen and crabby the next. How does Brett Kahr believe that Marie would have characterised the mature Prince Philip's mood swings? 'She would have believed that everything springs from our childhood experience. Philip was born into a household of adoring women – that's indisputable. Prince Philip suffered from the trauma of parental loss – that's indisputable, too. Marie Bonaparte would not have been surprised, therefore, to find in the adult Philip a man who could, by turns, be charming and swaggering, and then dour, sour-faced, proto-serious.'

Before leaving Brett Kahr and the spirit of Marie Bonaparte (and the actual ashes of Sigmund Freud, now resting at Maresfield Gardens in an ancient urn given to Freud by the Princess), I thought I would risk one final question: 'Is a man with phallic swagger prone to promiscuity?' Brett Kahr's answer surprised me: 'Not necessarily. He will be confident with women because he is confident in himself. Phallic swagger might help if you were planning to woo and wed the next Queen of England – the most sought-after, least attainable girl in the world – but it would not of itself make you a serial philanderer. I know nothing of Prince Philip's private life, but I've heard the stories. He likes the company of attractive, younger women, of his own class and kind. That much we know. I wonder if these women are his attempt to replicate the family of sisters who adored him so? Could he simply be looking for playful friendships? That is possible. Or could he be looking for something more? That is also possible. Prince Andrea spent much of the 1930s in the south of France with his mistress. If Prince Philip had knowledge of his father's marital infidelity during his own teenage psychosexual development, that might have been a model for him and had an effect on his own behaviour later in life. Or not. Who knows? Perhaps you do?'

LILIBET

Chapter Three

'All things bright and beautiful, / All creatures great and small,
All things wise and wonderful, / The Lord God made them all.
. . . The rich man in his castle, / The poor man at his gate,
God made them high or lowly, / And ordered their estate.'

Mrs C.F. Alexander (1818–95)

Queen Victoria's father was Edward, Duke of Kent, fourth of the six sons of George III, 'mad King George'. Edward was the baldest member of the family. The playwright, Richard Sheridan, liked to say this was because grass does not grow upon deserts. Edward responded to the sally rather well. 'If Sheridan means that I haven't genius,' he said, 'I can tell him that such a gift would have been of small value to a Prince, whose business it is to keep quiet. I am luckier in having, like my country, a sound constitution.'

In fact, Edward had a poor constitution and succumbed to a fever in the cruel winter of 1819, and died on 23 January 1820, when his baby daughter, Victoria, his only child, was barely eight months old. Before the madness took hold of him, George III led a calm and continent domestic life, married to Queen Charlotte, one-time Princess Sophia Charlotte of Mecklenburg-Strelitz. George's sons did not follow their father's example. Extravagance, self-indulgence, promiscuity, and adultery characterised their personal lives.

Edward had abandoned his French mistress to marry a German princess in the hope of producing an heir. As a young widow with two small children, Princess Victoria of Saxe-Coburg was, recognisably, a sound breeder. When she married Edward and became Duchess of Kent, she spoke not a word of English, but she produced a vigorous child for him in baby Victoria.

Little Victoria – she never reached five feet in height – was blessed with both a sound constitution and a certain genius. She lived more than eighty-one years, from 24 May 1819 to 22 January 1901. She came to the throne aged eighteen and reigned longer than any other English monarch. She gave her name to a century, and its achievements and constraints, its values and aspirations, and was Britain's first and only Queen-Empress. She was small and round (at nineteen she weighed 125 pounds), but she cast a long shadow. Whenever Queen Elizabeth II appears on the balcony of Buckingham Palace she looks out over the Victoria Memorial. The Queen has much in common with her great-great-grandmother, not least her longevity, sense of duty, acceptance of destiny, and sometimes complicated relationship with her eldest son. Prince Philip, while an admirer of the Prince Consort, did not like to take the comparison very far. 'Queen Victoria was an executive monarch,' he said to me, somewhat brusquely, when I raised the subject. 'Prince Albert was the Queen's secretary. He could do things. It's very different now.'

Victoria adored her husband and it is clear from her journal that, at least when she was young, her approach to the physical aspects of love was anything but 'Victorian': 'I NEVER NEVER spent such an evening!!!¹⁵ My DEAREST DEAREST DEAR Albert sat on a footstool by my side, & his excessive love & affection gave me feelings of heavenly love & happiness, I never could have *hoped* to have felt before! He clasped me in his arms, and we kissed each other again and again! His beauty, his sweetness and gentleness – really how can I ever be thankful enough to have such a *Husband*!'

Despite the discomforts and indignities of childbirth ('I think . . . of our being like a cow or a dog at such moments,' she said), she bore nine children. The first was born on 21 November 1840, nine months and eleven days after her wedding. 'Oh, Madam,' said her physician, Dr Locock,¹⁶ 'it is a Princess.' 'Never mind,' answered the

<hr>

15 A fondness for multiple exclamation marks appears to be a family characteristic!
16 Thirty-five years ago a young woman named Victoria Locock came to my house to give my wife a piano lesson. I said to her, 'It's amazing: you look exactly like Princess Anne.' She said, 'I know.' The piano teacher turned out to be a descendant of Henry Locock, born in December 1867 and brought up as the son of Sir Charles Locock, gynaecologist or 'First Physician Accoucher' to Queen Victoria, but long rumoured within the family to be the illegitimate son of Queen Victoria's sixth child, Princess Louise (1848–1949). In 1870, Louise, said to be something of

Queen feebly, 'the next will be a Prince.' It was. Eleven and a half months after the birth of Princess Victoria, known first as Pussy, then as Vicky, on 9 November 1841, Bertie, the Prince of Wales, the future King Edward VII, was born.

Victoria's reign was long and, overall, hugely successful. When Albert died, on 14 December 1861, the Queen was only forty-two. Utterly bereft, she closeted herself at Windsor Castle, and her sustained seclusion – at Windsor, at Balmoral, at Osborne House on the Isle of Wight – did not endear her to the press or public. She was temperamental, emotional, volatile: there were times when her family, and her ministers, feared for her sanity. She was also able, intelligent, and perceptive, though susceptible to flattery – 'Gladstone treats the Queen like a public department,' said Benjamin Disraeli. 'I treat her like a woman'; of course, the Queen preferred Disraeli – and wilful to the point of obstinacy. She would not give up her devoted, drunken, Highland servant, John Brown, however much her family wanted her to do so. She would not abandon her Indian secretary, Abdul Karim, 'the Munshi', however anxious the Indian Office and others were over his constant presence at her side. Victoria, especially as she grew older, was instinctively conservative, but neither a snob nor, in any way, racially prejudiced.

As Queen, she had dignity, determination, and unique dynastic skills. She came to be known as 'the grandmother of Europe' with good reason. Vicky married a future German emperor. Bertie married the Danish Princess Alexandra, whose brother became King of Greece and whose sister was Empress of Russia. It was her third child Alice who married the Grand Duke of Hesse and launched the line that produced, among others, the last Tsarina and Prince Philip. Her fourth child, Alfred, also married into the Russian royal family and, in time, his daughter became Queen of Romania. After Helena and Louise came two more sons: Arthur, Duke of Connaught, whose

---

a 'goer', married the Marquess of Lorne (heir to the Dukedom of Argyll), often said to be a promiscuous homosexual – although Elizabeth Longford (Princess Louise's biographer) claimed there was 'no evidence whatever' for this 'in Lorne's family archives or traditions'. From 1880, Louise and her husband lived separate lives and Louise was the only one of Queen Victoria's children who apparently had no issue. The Locock family is now hoping to exhume the body of Henry Locock (who died in Canada in 1907, after falling from a train) for DNA testing.

daughter became Queen of Sweden, and Leopold, Duke of Albany. Her youngest child, Beatrice, married Henry of Battenberg, and became the mother of the Queen of Spain.

As a mother, grandmother, and great-grandmother, Victoria was interested and involved, concerned and conscientious. There is a lovely photograph of her, taken in April 1886, with her daughter Princess Beatrice, her granddaughter Princess Louis of Battenberg, and her great-granddaughter Princess Alice (Prince Philip's mother), aged one. They all look contented. The Queen is smiling happily.

When Victoria was not amused[17] it was all too often because of Bertie. Victoria and Albert viewed the young Prince of Wales as a problem child. He was not academic; he was not athletic; he did not inherit his father's appetite for work. Instead, he seemed to have inherited his assorted, dissolute, great-uncles' appetites for good food, fine wines, gaming, and loose women. In 1861, when he was still nineteen and a young officer stationed with his regiment in Ireland, a compliant young actress, Nellie Clifton, was slipped between his sheets. Prince Albert heard all about it and was appalled. What if the liaison were to result in a child? In his anguish, the Prince Consort wrote to the Prince of Wales: 'If you were to try and deny it, she can drag you into a Court of Law to force you to own it & there with you in the witness box, she will be able to give before a greedy Multitude disgusting details of your profligacy for the sake of convincing the Jury, yourself crossexamined by a railing indecent attorney and hooted and yelled at by a Lawless Mob!! Horrible prospect, which this person has in her power, any day to realise! And to break your poor parents' hearts!'

Albert died only a few weeks later, possibly of typhoid, possibly of cancer. In the extremis of her grief, Victoria attributed her husband's death to the distress he had been caused by their son. 'Oh!

17 There is no record of Queen Victoria ever saying, 'We are not amused.' On the contrary, her journals frequently include the phrase, 'I was very much amused.' Elizabeth Longford, one of Victoria's best biographers, told me there are 'many recorded instances' of the Queen laughing out loud, and heartily, often at stories or incidents that other Victorians might have considered quite *risqué*. Like Elizabeth II, Victoria enjoyed the absurd. She regularly repeated the story of the time her mother, the Duchess of Kent, had emerged from the dining room carrying a fork, mistaking it for her fan.

that boy,' she said, despairingly, 'much as I pity him I never can or shall look at him without a shudder . . .'

At five foot seven inches, Bertie was a little taller than his mother, and rounder. At his heaviest he weighed more than sixteen stone – 224 pounds. His nickname was 'Tum-Tum'. He enjoyed five substantial meals a day – breakfast, luncheon, afternoon tea, dinner, supper – and smoked as many as twenty cigarettes and a dozen fat cigars between daybreak and sunset. He coughed and he wheezed, but he safeguarded his own health by requiring others not to smoke while he was doing so. Despite his weight and his wheezing, throughout his adult life he enjoyed a series of mistresses: occasionally actresses, like the young Nellie Clifton and the celebrated Lillie Langtry, more often the willing wives of his complaisant aristocratic and racing friends.

On 10 March 1863 Bertie, aged twenty-one, married Princess Alexandra of Denmark. She was just nineteen, beautiful, tall, sweet-tempered, good-natured, a little vacant, chronically unpunctual, wonderfully tolerant. She endured her husband's selfishness, self-indulgence, and promiscuity for almost half a century. When he was dying in the late spring of 1910, she allowed Alice Keppel, his last and most enduring mistress, to come to his bedside. Queen and mistress shook hands and Alix, with extraordinary generosity, said to Alice, 'I am sure you always had a good influence over him.'

She probably did. In many ways Bertie was a spoilt child and Mrs Keppel ('My little Mrs George'[18] as he called her) could coax and tease him out of his sulks and ill-humour. The present Prince of Wales (Bertie's great-great-grandson) is also reported to have had occasional sulking moments and bouts of ill-humour in the past, and his good-humoured mistress-turned-wife, Mrs Camilla Parker Bowles (the great-granddaughter of Mrs Keppel, as chance

---

18 George Keppel is an intriguing figure, tall, elegant, moustachioed, with more than a touch of the music hall dandy about him. Encouraging his wife to consort with the King enabled him to enjoy a lifestyle he might not otherwise have been able to afford – and pleasuring royalty was, and is, a Keppel family tradition. William III – William of Orange – was bisexual and brought sixteen-year-old Arnold Joost van Keppel with him from Holland to England as his catamite in 1688. In due course he made him Earl of Albermarle.

would have it) is said to have had a similarly useful influence over him.

Prince Charles's first wife, Diana Spencer, was, to an extent, consoled by the affection in which she was held by the public at large and by her strong and loving relationship with her own children. The same was true of Princess Alexandra. She was strikingly beautiful, much admired, and genuinely loved by the people. She did good works. With the Alexandra Rose Day, she introduced a new form of charitable fund-raising to Britain. Despite increasing deafness[19] and a slight limp, triggered by rheumatic fever when she was just twenty-two, she was easy with strangers and especially comfortable with children.

Alix's own children were a special joy to her. She had six, the youngest of whom, a boy, died when only a few hours old. Her daughters called her 'darling Motherdear' and were so devoted that Bertie feared they might never leave the nest. In the event, the eldest, Princess Louise, the Princess Royal, married the Duke of Fife, and the youngest, Princess Maud, married Prince Charles of Denmark, later to become King Haakon VII of Norway. Only the middle girl, another Princess Victoria, remained a spinster all her life.

As seems to be the custom with the British Royal Family, it was the eldest son who proved to be the problem child. Prince Albert Victor, the Duke of Clarence, known in the family as Eddy, was born prematurely at the start of 1864 and died prematurely in the spring of 1892. He was neither bright nor ambitious and devoted most of his short life to the pleasures of the boudoir and the polo field. When the police raided a male brothel in Cleveland Street in central London they discovered a clutch of the Prince of Wales's friends and associates among the regular clientele and learnt that Bertie's eldest boy, the young Duke of Clarence, had not long before visited the establishment in the (forlorn) hope of seeing a display of naked women. Eddy was notorious and his dissolute behaviour fuelled

19 She may have exploited her deafness on occasion. When her sister-in-law Vicky's son, Wilhelm, the German Kaiser, held forth at length, she responded: 'Willy dear . . . I am afraid I have not heard a single word you were saying.' And, a hundred years on, in royal circles, they still tell the story of the equerry who asked her, 'Did you know, Ma'am, that His Majesty has a new car?' to which she replied, 'A new cow?' 'No, Ma'am, a new *car.*' 'Yes, yes, I hear you. I understand the old one has calved.'

the rumours that he was 'Jack the Ripper', the man who murdered and mutilated a number of prostitutes in the Aldgate and Whitechapel districts of east London in 1888.

Just as Albert and Victoria had hoped that marriage would magically transform their eldest son ('marry or burn' was the phrase they used), so Bertie and Alix hoped that matrimony would make a man of the wretched Eddy. Finding a bride for this particular prince was not easy. First, he rejected an anyway reluctant Princess Margaret of Germany; next, he was turned down by Alix of Hesse (the one who went on to become the luckless last Tsarina of Russia); then, he fell passionately in love with Princess Hélène d'Orléans, who was a Catholic as well as French, and consequently (despite her readiness to become a Protestant) wholly *hors de concours.*

In due course he was persuaded to propose to Princess Victoria Mary of Teck, known to all as May, who was three years his junior and not nearly so 'royal', but was willing, able, available, and sound. Queen Victoria invited her to Balmoral and gave a grandmotherly seal of approval, judging May to be 'a superior girl – quiet and reserved *till* you know her well – . . . & so sensible and unfrivolous.'[20]

Princess May agreed to marry Prince Eddy, but she was spared what would certainly have been an ordeal. In the run-up to the wedding, while shooting at Sandringham in the winter of 1891, Eddy was taken ill. He died of pneumonia on 14 January 1892. In his final fever, as May and his mother took turns to keep watch, repeatedly he called out, 'Hélène, Hélène.' His fiancée was understandably disconcerted. His mother was understandably bereft. For years, in her bedroom, Alix kept the hat her hapless son had been wearing on his final shoot, and she preserved his quarters as they been on the day he died: his toothpaste tube as he had left it, a fresh

20 This was not how anybody would have described May's parents. Her mother, Princess Mary Adelaide, who was a granddaughter of George III, was garrulous, extravagant and greedy: she was reckoned to be at least the weight of Bertie, Prince of Wales. Her father, Franz, Duke of Teck, came from a family that had married beneath itself but resolutely refused to recognise the fact. Franz was argumentative, temperamental and sensitive about his status. The parents, as vulgar spendthrifts, embarrassed their daughter, who was a decent, discreet, dignified sort, fair-haired, blue-eyed, clear-skinned, handsome rather than beautiful, with a look we would now recognise in her great-granddaughter, Princess Anne.

cake of soap ready by the washbasin. Her second son, George, wrote to her: 'Gladly would I have given my life for his, as I put no value on mine . . . Such a tragedy has never before occurred in the annals of our family.'

In truth, tragedy (or, at least, melodrama tinged with bathetic comedy) was probably averted by Eddy's death. He was not good-husband or good-monarch material. Prince George turned out to be both. Princess May, having received the old Queen's seal of approval, was too good a catch to let slip, and, within eighteen months, May, having been engaged to one heir apparent, had married the next. It was a fortunate match. George later wrote to his wife: 'People only said I married you out of pity and sympathy; that shows how little the world knows what it is talking about.'

Queen Victoria and Edward VII were the last two monarchs whose names alone would conjure up the flavour of the eras in which they reigned. Since 1952 we have not been living in a new Elizabethan age. Elizabeth II is an impressive woman, with special gifts that have been much to the benefit of Crown and country, but she has not set the tone or temper (or tempo) of the time in which she has lived. Far from it. At moments during her long reign she has struggled to keep pace with the swirling changes taking place around her. In part, this is a reflection of the gradually diminishing power and position of the monarchy, but it also has something to do with the personalities – and the perception of the personalities – involved. A statue of Queen Victoria immediately evokes the Victorian age. A photograph of Edward VII – especially one taken at the races, or at a country house party – at once triggers a wider picture of Edwardian England. There is no image of Elizabeth II that conveys the spirit of Britain in the second half of the twentieth century.

Bertie was in his sixtieth year when Victoria died and he succeeded her as the first king to be called Edward since the middle of the sixteenth century. He had been waiting in the wings a long time. 'I don't mind praying to the eternal Father,' he once said, 'but I must be the only man in the country afflicted with an eternal mother.' Despite the lengthy and chequered apprenticeship, to the surprise of many he managed the transition from playboy Prince of Wales to king-of-some-substance without difficulty. As King, he eased up a touch on the womanising (well, we all get older), but his other appetites remained undiminished and his generous girth was seen as evidence of his humanity and endeared him to his subjects. 'Good old Teddy,' they said, and they meant it. You could argue that the last time Great Britain could be described as 'a nation at ease with itself' was in the Edwardian era, when toffs were toffs, the middle classes were comfortable, and the workers – rather like the King – accepted their lot in life and took their pleasures where they could.

Edward VII took his role seriously. He had the presence of a leader and the skills of a diplomat. His achievement in encouraging a loosening of the national bias towards Germany and the signing of the 1904 Entente Cordiale with France was real. He also took himself seriously. When Bertie was a guest at the Comédie Française and a stranger enquired what His Royal Highness thought of the play, the Prince rebuked him: 'I don't think I spoke to you.' He would tease his friends and indulge in his fondness for practical jokes at their expense,[21] but his intimates were not permitted to respond in kind. If you overstepped the mark, if you answered back, if, in your cups, momentarily, you forgot who you were, and, more to the point, forgot who he was, your bags would be packed and your carriage summoned. The word lese-majesty comes from the French lèse-majesté, which comes from the Latin laesa majestas, meaning 'hurting' or 'injuring' majesty.

In his memoirs, A King's Story, the Duke of Windsor, briefly Edward VIII, grandson of Edward VII, recalled a conversation he had had, when, as Prince of Wales, he had asked a senior courtier, Sir Frederick 'Fritz' Ponsonby, to give him a candid opinion of how he was faring in his role:

21 'According to Mrs Hwfa Williams, sister-in-law of the Prince's friend Colonel Owen Williams, he would place the hand of the blind Duke of Mecklenburg on the arm of the enormously fat Helen Henneker, observing, "Now, don't you think Helen has a lovely little waist?" And he would be delighted by the subsequent roar of laughter – "in which no one joined more heartily than Helen." Similarly, he would pour a glass of brandy over Christopher Sykes's head or down his neck or, while smoking a cigar, he would tell Sykes to gaze into his eyes to see the smoke coming out of them and then stab Sykes's hand with the burning end. Shouts of laughter would also greet this often-repeated trick as the grave and snobbish Sykes responded in his complaisantly lugubrious, inimitably long-suffering way, "As your Royal Highness pleases."' Christopher Hibbert, Edward VII, 1976.

'"If I may say so, Sir, I think there is a risk in making yourself too accessible," he answered unhesitatingly.

'"What do you mean?" I asked.

'"The Monarchy must always retain an element of mystery. A Prince should not show himself too much. The Monarchy must remain on a pedestal."

'I maintained otherwise, arguing that because of the social changes brought about by the [1914–18] war, one of the most important tasks of the Prince of Wales was to help bring the institution nearer the people.

'"If you bring it down to the people," Fritz Ponsonby said coldly, "it will lose its mystery and influence."

'"I do not agree," I said. "Times are changing."

'He replied severely, "I am older than you are, Sir; I have been with your father, your grandfather, and your great-grandmother. They all understood. You are quite mistaken."'

Victoria, Edward VII, and George V understood the requirements of monarchy and, in their different ways, delivered in full measure. Edward VIII did not.

One Saturday morning in May 1910, the future Edward VIII and his younger brother, the future George VI, aged sixteen and fifteen, learnt of the death of their grandfather, Edward VII, when they woke up and looked out of the window of Marlborough House and saw the Royal Standard flying over Buckingham Palace at half-mast. Moments later they were called downstairs. The Duke of Windsor later recalled: 'My father's face was grey with fatigue, and he cried as he told us that Grandpapa was dead. I answered sadly that we had already seen the Royal Standard at half-mast. My father seemed not to hear as he went on to describe in exact detail the scene around the deathbed. Then he asked sharply, "What did you say about the Standard?" "It is flying at half-mast over the Palace," I answered. My father frowned and muttered, "But that's all wrong," and repeating as if to himself the old but pregnant saying, "The King is dead. Long live the King!" he sent for his equerry and in a peremptory naval manner ordered that a mast be rigged at once on the roof of Marlborough House.'

This is an interesting story and makes an important point about the Royal Standard. When Diana, Princess of Wales, died in 1997, there was an outcry in the press about the Royal Standard at Balmoral not being flown at half-mast. The Queen was hurt and angered by the criticism. She felt it showed a lack of understanding of history and tradition. The Royal Standard *never* flies at half-mast. The flagpole at Buckingham Palace was bare because flags are only flown over a royal residence when the sovereign is in residence. The Queen could see no reason to break with precedence. After several days, against her better judgement, she was persuaded to change her mind and allow a compromise: the Union flag – not the Royal Standard – was flown over Buckingham Palace at half-mast.

George V, the Queen's grandfather, was a stickler for the established order of things. As a boy he had been a naval cadet. He spent twenty years in the service and, according to his eldest son, throughout his life 'retained a gruff, blue-water approach to all situations, a loud voice, and also that affliction common to Navy men, a damaged ear-drum'. Apparently, 'Damn fool!' was his favourite expression. He had an explosive temper, a simple sailor's sense of humour, and a horror of change for change's sake. He liked things to be 'ship-shape'; he appreciated order; his chief delight was his stamp collection. He was a creature of habit: carefully, he checked the barometer, every morning and every night. When his wife, Queen Mary (as Princess May was known after the Accession), attempted to shorten her skirts in line with the fashion of the day, the King would have none of it. As their eldest son recalled, 'He disapproved of Soviet Russia, painted finger-nails, women who smoked in public, cocktails, frivolous hats, American jazz and the growing habit of going away for weekends.'

George was in awe of his father and adored his mother. He treated Edward VII with respect, tinged with fear, and Queen Alexandra with an almost puppy-like devotion. Even when he was King, he was Alix's 'darling Georgie boy'. On paper, in correspondence (especially with his 'Motherdear'), he could be sentimental to the point of soppiness. In person, it sometimes seemed that he had an easier, more comfortable, relationship with his beloved pet parrot, Charlotte, than he did with either his wife or children. 'I was frightened of my father,' he once said, 'and I'm damn well going to see that my children are frightened of me.'

Georgie and May had six children.[22] The family was brought up in the main at York Cottage, a comparatively cramped and – by every account – cluttered and uncomfortable house in the grounds of the Sandringham estate. As parents, Georgie and May saw their children twice a day: once, briefly, in the morning, and then, for an hour, at teatime. The eldest, David, the future Edward VIII, had a particular loathing of the family nanny: 'Before carrying me into the drawing room, this dreadful "Nanny" would pinch and twist my arm – why, no one knew, unless it was to demonstrate, according to some perverse reasoning, that her power over me was greater than that of my parents. The sobbing and bawling this treatment invariably evoked understandably puzzled, worried, and finally annoyed them. It would result in my being peremptorily removed from the room before further embarrassment was inflicted upon them and the other witnesses of this pathetic scene. Eventually, my mother realised what was wrong, and the nurse was dismissed.'

Queen Mary was no 'Motherdear'. She was a concerned parent, but not a cosy or a cuddly one. To her children (as to the public as large) she seemed somewhat removed, forbidding, and formidable. She was a devoted and dutiful wife: she accepted her place and her husband's character. She knew that his gruff exterior concealed a kindly nature. He suffered from dyspepsia, smoked excessively, and had a rough tongue. Their son David said his father had 'a most horrible temper': 'He was foully rude to my mother. Why, I've seen her leave the table because he was so rude to her, and we children would all follow her out; not when the staff were present, of course, but when we were alone.'

Nor did Queen Mary have the confidence of being a full-blooded royal. She was naturally diffident, she accepted (as much of the world did in her day) that women were the weaker vessels, and, of course,

22 The future Edward VIII (always known in the family as David), 1894–1972; the future George VI (known as Bertie), 1895–1952; Mary, later the Princess Royal (and mother of the late Earl of Harewood), 1897–1965; Henry, Duke of Gloucester (father of the current Duke), 1900–74; George, Duke of Kent (father of the current crop of Kents: the present Duke of Kent, Princess Alexandra and Prince Michael), 1902–42; and John, 1905–19, who was born brain-damaged, suffered epileptic fits and died young, and whose strange, sad story was brought fully into the open for the first time in Stephen Poliakoff's 2002 television film *The Lost Prince*.

she respected her husband as both master and monarch. She expected her children to do the same. 'I always remember,' she said, solemnly, 'that as well as being their father he is also their King.' She was a serious-minded traditionalist, conversationally limited, emotionally cautious. She and King George brought up their one daughter, Princess Mary, to be the same. Mary's son, George Harewood, remembers a family where emotional inhibition was the order of the day. 'We did not talk of love and affection and what we meant to each other,' he says, 'but rather of duty and behaviour and what we ought to do.'[23]

Mary was the King's favourite and, to a limited extent, indulged. He was much tougher on his sons, especially the elder two. He picked on them, mocked them, made sarcastic remarks about them, and generally found ways of finding fault with them at every turn. According to Bertie, 'It was very difficult for David. My father was so inclined to go for him. I always thought it was a pity that he found fault with him over unimportant things – like what he wore. This only put David's back up.'

Bertie was not spared. He was a left-handed child but, as was the custom of the time, was forced to become right-handed. He was also knock-kneed and, during his pre-adolescence, for several hours every day, and throughout the night, he was made to wear corrective wooden splints. He developed a pitiful stammer, which dogged him all his days and infuriated his father. When Bertie was struggling to speak a word, his impatient papa would bark at him, 'Get it out, boy, get it out!'

David, as he grew older, and especially once he had become Prince of Wales, deliberately defied his father, doing his own thing in his own way, and seemingly taking perverse pleasure in irritating – even

23 Queen Mary wore long Edwardian dresses long after they went out of fashion. She was rarely seen in public without her trademark toque. The diarist 'Chips' Channon said meeting her was 'like talking to St Paul's Cathedral'. At Lord Harewood's wedding, the novelist E.M. Forster, his eyesight failing, bowed to the multi-tiered cake, mistaking it for Her Majesty. (That reminds me: Fritz Ponsonby used to tell the story of how fond George V was of a certain silver statuette of Lady Godiva. The reason? Once upon a time, as she peered at it, the myopic Queen Olga – mother of Prince Andrew of Greece and grandmother of Prince Philip – had been heard to murmur appreciatively, 'Ah, dear Queen Victoria.')

shocking – his unbending parent. Bertie was more compliant. He gave way to occasional outbursts of frustrated rage – known in the family as his 'gnashes' – but, on the whole, he kept out of trouble's way. Bertie was second in line to the throne, so, in any event, his public profile was lower, but his stammer also meant that he had less to say. He was shy, awkward, hesitant, in a way that David was not. Famously, as a little boy, at lunch with his grandfather, Edward VIII, David had dared interrupt the King in full flow. He was immediately reminded that children are to be seen, not heard, and to speak only when they are spoken to. Eventually, he was given permission to say whatever it was he had wanted to say. 'It's too late now, grandpapa,' he chirruped. 'It was a caterpillar on your lettuce, but you've eaten it.'

King George's chaffing of his sons amounted to bullying. Queen Mary chose not to intervene, but others were bolder. Margot Asquith, second wife of Herbert Asquith, Liberal Prime Minister at the start of George's reign, told the King that his treatment of his sons would drive them to drink. During the First World War, to set an example, the King imposed a drinking ban on the entire royal household, but after the war, once they were adults, each of the four surviving royal princes drank much more than was good for him. The third son, Prince George, eight years David's junior, even dabbled with morphine and cocaine.

Henry (created Duke of Gloucester, at twenty-eight, in 1928) was the family dullard, a cavalry officer and a country gentleman, who drank too much whisky, but meant well and did no harm. George (created Duke of Kent, at thirty-two, in 1934) was his mother's favourite and the most socially adept and easy of her boys. He had an artistic temperament, a fondness for high society and low living, and a loathing for the naval career into which he felt he had been forced by his father. He was a notorious ladies' man who was, apparently, equally at home among the homosexual set. He was once arrested, briefly, in a gay nightclub known as the Nut House. In 1934 he married the beautiful Princess Marina of Greece (granddaughter of George I of Greece, niece of Prince Andrea, cousin of Prince Philip), which may have tempered his behaviour but didn't halt the rumour-mongering. It is often said that Noël Coward, playwright, performer, and theatrical darling of the era, was one of his lovers, but when I put the suggestion to Graham Payn, Coward's companion for thirty years, his denial was emphatic: 'Oh, no. That story about Noël and the Duke of Kent, it wasn't true. We can put the record straight on that. I asked Noël about it and he was quite clear. "We did not get over-friendly."'

Graham Payn also told me that Coward 'always preferred the Yorks, long before there was any thought they might be King and Queen. He used to visit them quite often, much to the irritation of Queen Mary, who felt her eldest was being upstaged. Let's face it, the Windsors [as Edward VIII and his wife, Wallis Simpson, became] were not exactly joy unconfined. The Duke, to be honest, was an extremely dull man. Noël said he even danced a boring Charleston, which is no mean feat. One evening Wallis said to Noël, "You know, I don't understand why the British dislike me so much." There was a terrible pause before Noël replied, "Well, because you stole their Prince Charming." She rather liked that. On social occasions, the Duke rarely spoke, not because his mind was preoccupied, but simply because he had nothing to say. Noël used to say, "He had the charm of the world with nothing to back it up."'

Prince George, who became the Duke of Kent, was tall and handsome. David, the Prince of Wales, who became Duke of Windsor after his abdication, and Bertie, who became Duke of York and then King, were shorter, slighter, slimmer, more athletic, more reticent, and wholly heterosexual. They were good-looking (well, they were young, well dressed, well heeled, well mannered) and they were princes (it counts for a lot) and they could pull as they pleased. It seems they did. The Prince of Wales had a series of infatuations and affairs before his obsession with Wallis Simpson cost him the crown and changed the course of royal history. His first heavy-duty love affair was with Freda Dudley Ward, the liberal wife of a Liberal MP, and it is from their correspondence that we learn that, in the pre-marital love stakes, stammering Bertie was not as tongue-tied as earlier biographies have suggested. He lost his virginity, it seems, in Paris towards the end of the First World War. According to David, that's where 'the deed was done'. Back in London Bertie enjoyed the company of several chorus girls and, on at least one occasion, in 1919, entertained Jack Buchanan's leading lady, Phyllis Monkman, star of the happily titled hit *Tails Up*, to a late supper in a private room in Half Moon Street.

David embarked on his affair with Freda Dudley Ward in March 1918 and evidently encouraged his younger brother to find himself a married mistress of his own. Sheila Chisholm was young, lively, Australian, and game. She was married to Lord Loughborough and she had a baby son (Anthony, born in May 1917), but, nevertheless, she was up for some fun. David and Freda, Bertie and Sheila, called themselves 'The Four Do's', and certainly did. 'What marvellous fun we 4 do have, don't we, Angel?' wrote the Prince of Wales to Mrs Dudley-Ward, '& f— the rest of the world.' In 1926 Sheila and Lord Loughborough were divorced, but in 1919 the unfortunate cuckold appears to have been unaware of what his young wife and the two kings-to-be were up to. 'After tea,' David reported gleefully, 'I managed to lure Loughie away on the pretext of wanting to play a few more holes of golf . . . so as to give Sheilie a chance of being alone with Bertie . . . I'm sure Loughie doesn't suspect Bertie at all!'

That was in June 1919. A year later, on 10 June 1920, Bertie, now twenty-five, and created Duke of York by his father, George V, only the week before, accompanied his mother, Queen Mary, to a Derby Night ball in Grosvenor Square. Around eleven o'clock the young Duke saw a smiling girl across a crowded room. She was chatting to his equerry. The Duke asked to be introduced. Lady Elizabeth Angela Marguerite Bowes-Lyon, ninth child and fourth daughter of the 14th Earl of Strathmore and Kinghorne, was nineteen, unattached, and pretty as a picture. Bertie later claimed it was love at first sight.

Chapter Four

'. . . Never take a second mouthful before you have finished the first. Do not finish the last crumb or spoonful, or scrape your plate. When finished do not clutch your knees. *General remarks.* Do not read too much. Do not eat too much butter or jam. Say your prayers. Keep your hair in order.'

Rules drawn up by her sisters for Margaret Gladstone, 1882

'It was always love at first sight. No one could resist her. No one. Everybody who met her fell under her spell. Always.'

This was the verdict of the Hon. Margaret Rhodes, first cousin, childhood playmate, and lifelong friend of Elizabeth II, niece and sometime lady-in-waiting to Queen Elizabeth the Queen Mother. Mrs Rhodes's mother was Lady Mary Bowes-Lyon, one of Lady Elizabeth's three sisters.

Mrs Rhodes was in her late seventies when I first met her, trim and bird-like. She had a smoker's voice and the beady eye of one who had seen the world and, on the whole, been gently amused. Her elegant, slightly faded, drawing room at the Garden House in Windsor Great Park was littered with signed photographs of assorted royals. Her small kitchen table was cluttered with old newspapers, correspondence, invitations, bills. In the downstairs lavatory, beneath the formal picture of the Queen and the Duke of Edinburgh on their wedding day, there was a well-thumbed copy of *The Prince Philip Throneside Book.* Mrs Rhodes was devoted to the memory of her aunt. 'Everybody adored her,' she said. 'Everybody.'

Certainly, I have met few who didn't. Lord David Cecil, who was a childhood friend, told me that 'even as a girl, she had a certain twinkle as well as extraordinary sweetness. She made you feel part of a delightful conspiracy.' Woodrow Wyatt said to me, 'She is the most truly charming person in the world.' Sir John Mills told me, 'No one is more captivating. I have been lucky enough to meet some of the most glamorous women of our time. She outshines them all.' I asked one of her sons-in-law, Lord Snowdon, to sum her up in a single word and, without hesitation, he said, 'Fun.'

In 1920, according to Mabell, Countess of Airlie, who knew her then, Lady Elizabeth's 'radiant vitality', combined with 'a blending of kindness and sincerity', made her 'irresistible to men'. She was pretty, not spectacularly beautiful. She was small (five foot four inches), but not petite. She had flawless skin, bright blue eyes, but shortish, rather dull, dark hair, cut in a noticeably unsexy fringe. She was anything but 'modern'. According to Lady Airlie, 'she was very unlike the cocktail-drinking, chain-smoking girls who came to be regarded as typical of the 1920s'. She came from one of Scotland's oldest, grandest, families. Among her forebears was Robert the Bruce. The family properties included Glamis Castle in Scotland; another, lesser, castle, Streatlam, in County Durham; a fine, eighteenth-century country house, St Paul's Walden Bury, in Hertfordshire; and a handsome town house in London, in St James's Square, between Piccadilly and Pall Mall.

Her father, Lord Strathmore, was a Scottish nobleman of the old school. He was God-fearing, courteous, kindly, conscientious, conservative, and only mildly eccentric. Every day, at breakfast he made his own cocoa and at lunch he ate plum pudding. Mrs Rhodes recalled the huge dining hall at Glamis and her grandfather at the head of the table: 'I can picture the food being sort of thrown on to the plates and him catching it. I remember, too, he had a wonderful droopy moustache and he smoked endless cigarettes. This was before the age of tipped cigarettes and we children kept watch as his cigarette burnt slowly down to see if it would set fire to his moustache. It never did.' Lord Strathmore took his duties seriously (as a land-owner and Lord Lieutenant of Angus) and his recreations were exactly those you would expect: fishing, shooting, and cricket. He was an authority on forestry. According to Mrs Rhodes, 'He really loved his trees. Queen Elizabeth used to tell the story of people telephoning Walden Bury and enquiring, "Is his Lordship down from Glamis yet?" "No," the butler would say, "his lordship only comes when the sap rises."'

Lady Strathmore, born Nina-Cecilia Cavendish-Bentinck, also came from good aristocratic stock. Her father, a clergyman, was heir to the 5th Duke of Portland. She, too, took her religion seriously: the chapel at Glamis was in regular use. She was also outgoing, unpretentious, warm, practical, and creative: she was an enthusiastic gardener and an accomplished pianist. Mrs Rhodes told me, 'She died when I was thirteen, but I can see her clearly – a lovely, voluminous figure, in a long, black dress with a lace collar. She was a heavenly, smiling granny.' She seems to have been pretty perfect as a mother as well. According to Mrs Rhodes, 'Queen Elizabeth always spoke of her mother with enormous warmth and affection.' In a letter to Osbert Sitwell, she once wrote: 'I have nothing but wonderfully happy memories of childhood days at home.' She was ever grateful to her parents for providing 'Fun, kindness, & a marvellous sense of security.'

In July 1920, in the run-up to her twentieth birthday on 4 August, Lady Elizabeth Bowes-Lyon was, arguably, London's most eligible debutante. She had it all: breeding, looks, intelligence, vivacity, charm. She also had a certain maturity. She had seen something of life. During the First World War one of her brothers was killed in action, at the Battle of Loos, and another was severely wounded and captured by the Germans. As part of the war effort, Glamis Castle was turned into a convalescent hospital for wounded soldiers and Elizabeth helped her mother care for the men. If Bertie, newly created Duke of York, fell for her instantly, as he later claimed, he was not alone. Other suitors also made the pilgrimage to Glamis. One of them was Ronald Barnes, 3rd Baron Gorell, who later claimed, 'I was madly in love with her. Everything at Glamis was beautiful, perfect. Being there was like living in a van Dyck picture. Time, and the gossiping, junketing world, stood still. Nothing happened . . . but the magic gripped us all. I fell *madly* in love.'[24] Gorell listed Lady Elizabeth's principal qualities: 'Her charm was indescribable . . . She was also very kind and compassionate. And

24 In 1920 Ronald Gorell became President of the National Council for Combating Venereal Diseases. He was a remarkable character: a poet, a publisher, a pilot, a doer of good works of all kinds. He was sixteen years older than Elizabeth Bowes-Lyon and never a serious suitor for her hand. In 1922, he married Elizabeth Radcliffe, daughter of a lawyer and one of England's most respected collie-fanciers.

she could be very funny – which was rare in those circles. She was a wag.'[25]

The list of eligible young men who took a shine to the waggish, wide-eyed, heart-faced enchantress of Glamis was a long one. It included Prince Paul of Yugoslavia, a good friend of one of her brothers, who did most of his wooing, it seems, by paying court to Lady Strathmore (not a bad stratagem); Henry Gage, the 6th Viscount, who owned Firle Place, in Sussex, plus, he liked to say, 'about 10,000 acres'; the 10th Earl of Airlie's younger son, Brucie, who courted Elizabeth's attention by dancing on the dining-room table while playing the ukulele; Christopher Tennant, the second Baron Glenconner, who was a millionaire and a charmer (and whose first wife, Pamela, would produce Colin Tennant, the future owner of Mustique and friend of Princess Margaret); and James Stuart, the third son of the 17th Earl of Moray, who, at the age of nineteen, had won one Military Cross at the Battle of the Somme and a second at the Battle of Arras. James Stuart was more than a hero: he was reckoned – by many – to be the handsomest man in the kingdom. He was also the new Duke of York's equerry and the man who first introduced Bertie to Lady Elizabeth at the Derby Night ball in Grosvenor Square.

Of her many suitors, none was better connected than HRH The Prince Albert, Duke of York, but most were more obviously attractive: more outgoing, more articulate, less inhibited, less shy. How, then, did Bertie secure his bride? In the old way, it seems: simply, by persistence.[26] James Stuart was delightful: dashing, debonair, dangerous. He was a serial flirt. He was not reliable. Bertie was different. Bertie was dogged. Single-mindedly, he pursued Elizabeth for nearly three years. And he was not unattractive: he was slim, fit, well dressed, well mannered, a good shot, a brilliant dancer (this was an age in which that counted for something), a decent cove – kindly and courteous (in any age that counts for a lot) – with sound instincts and an impeccable pedigree. He was, after all, a royal duke, the second son of the King.

---

25 Famously, as a little girl in want of pocket money, she sent a telegram to her father: 'S.O.S. L.S.D. R.S.V.P. ELIZABETH.'

26 'In time refractory oxen come to plough, in time horses are taught to bear pliant reins, an iron ring is worn by constant use . . . Only persevere, you will overcome Penelope herself.' Ovid, c.1 BC.

Bertie proposed to Elizabeth three times. Twice she refused him. He would not go away. He did not give up. Eventually, he secured his prize. On a Sunday walk in the woods at St Paul's Walden Bury, in January 1923, she said 'yes', and did so wholeheartedly. She belonged to a class and generation where every woman's destiny was to be a wife and a mother – and nothing more. To secure the ideal husband was everything. Elizabeth sensed that in Bertie she had found a good man and that theirs would be a happy match. She was right.

The Strathmores were not besotted with royalty. 'As far as I can see,' Lady Strathmore is said once to have remarked, 'some people have to be fed royalty like sea-lions fish.' She was not one of them, but nonetheless to be the mother of the first 'commoner' to marry legitimately into the Royal Family was undoubtedly 'something'. Bertie's mother, Queen Mary, was equally delighted. 'Elizabeth is charming,' she wrote in her diary, 'so pretty & engaging and natural. Bertie is supremely happy.'

The Duke of York and Lady Elizabeth Bowes-Lyon were married in Westminster Abbey on 26 April 1923. The political situation was uncertain and the economy fragile. The King declared that 'the arrangements should be of as simple a character as possible and that no unnecessary expense shall be incurred'. The wedding – the Abbey's first royal wedding since 1382, when Richard II married Anne of Bohemia – was grand, but not ostentatious. The bride wore a dress of machine-made Nottingham lace, designed in medieval style by Queen Mary's dressmaker, with a veil of Flanders lace lent by the Queen. The groom wore the uniform of a group captain of the recently created Royal Air Force. The ceremony was filmed – in long-shot – for the cinema newsreels, but not broadcast on the fledgling BBC wireless. The Archbishop of Canterbury was concerned that 'disrespectful people might hear the service, perhaps some of them sitting in public houses with their hats on'.

As the wedding drew near, Elizabeth made what seems to have been the only unforced error of her public life. An enterprising reporter from the *Star* newspaper turned up at her parents' Mayfair front door and asked Lady Elizabeth for a brief interview. He was granted one. The King was not amused. 'Those filthy rags of newspapers,' was how His Majesty regarded the press. Elizabeth never spoke on the record to a journalist again – and the coverage she received over the next eight decades was extraordinary and, almost always, adulatory. She had an instinct for doing what was right and doing it in a way that would be well received. On her wedding day, as she entered Westminster Abbey, spontaneously she placed her bouquet of white heather and York roses on the tomb of the Unknown Soldier.

The guests at the wedding included a raft of royals, the cream of the aristocracy, a smattering of the great and the good, and thirty boys chosen by the Industrial Welfare Society to represent the ordinary youth of Britain. The Duke of York was President of the IWS and properly interested in giving sporting, recreational, and training opportunities to young people. He founded – and attended – an annual summer camp where two hundred working-class lads and two hundred young chaps from public schools came together for an integrated adventure holiday. He pioneered 'social inclusion' seventy years before it became government policy. He undertook good works both because he believed in them and because that was what was expected of a king's second son in the aftermath of the Great War. He and his young duchess did their duty as required – he shyly, she gaily – but, once the excitement of the wedding was over, they neither sought, nor received, undue press or public attention. He was not the king and not ever expected to be. The Prince of Wales was not yet thirty. He was the glamorous one who was in the front line and in the spotlight. His younger brother could – and did – lead a relatively private life.

The Yorks honeymooned at Polesden Lacey in Surrey[27] and at Glamis. The weather in Scotland was atrocious and the new duchess

27 The house was put at their disposal by Mrs Ronald Greville, described by Cecil Beaton (Elizabeth's favourite photographer) as 'a galumphing, greedy, snobbish old toad who watered at her chops at the sight of royalty'. Another of my favourite diarists, Harold Nicolson, described her as 'a fat slug filled with venom'. Elizabeth was more charitable. When Maggie Greville died in 1942, the Queen wrote to Osbert Sitwell: 'She was so shrewd, so kind and so amusingly unkind, so sharp, such fun, so naughty.' Mrs Greville, daughter of the brewing magnate William McEwan, left all her jewelry – including Marie Antoinette's diamond necklace – to the Queen, 'with my loving thoughts', and a bequest of £20,000 to Princess Margaret.

contracted whooping cough, 'not', she conceded, 'a very romantic disease'. This dampener behind them, the young couple settled into the life of near-unparalleled privilege – and occasional duty – that was to be their lot. Everybody was utterly enchanted by the Duchess. Most found the Duke a touch awkward. His equerry, James Stuart, who had also been, of course, his rival in love, said of the young Duke, 'He was not an easy man to know or to handle.' The Prince remained capable of sudden, unpleasant, bursts of anger, his notorious 'gnashes'. Margaret Rhodes remembered him 'for his totally schoolboy sense of humour'. She told me, 'He laughed like a drain at ridiculous things, but he had an explosive temper. I saw him once grouse-shooting in a butt. He hadn't shot very well. In fact, he'd shot badly. He threw his guns into the heather in his rage and frustration.'

Elizabeth did her best to tease him out of his ill-humour by taking his pulse and quietly counting: 'Tick, tick, tick, one, two, three.' She also did all she could to help him conquer the speech impediment that was the blight of his life. She went with him on his regular visits to Harley Street to see his speech therapist, Lionel Logue. She lay beside him on the floor as he practised his breathing and relax-ation exercises. She repeated after him the assorted tongue-twisters designed to help him jump the hurdles of especially challenging consonants. ('Let's go gathering heathy heather with the gay brigade of grand dragoons' was a particular favourite, apparently.) She checked the drafts of speeches he was due to deliver to eliminate the worst stumbling blocks – and, when he came to deliver those speeches, she was on hand, with an encouraging smile, willing him to succeed. He never wholly conquered his impediment, but, over time, managed to contain it. Lionel Logue said, 'He was the pluckiest and most determined patient I ever had.'

That Elizabeth was good for Bertie, everyone agreed. She was altogether, as Sellar and Yeatman (two of her favourite historians) would have it, A Good Thing.[28] Naturally, she was not without flaws. Her time-keeping was terrible. More than once, her husband was seen, impatiently pacing the hallway, checking the clock, muttering

28 W.C. Sellar and R.J. Yeatman, a schoolmaster and an advertising copywriter, published *1066 and All That*, their spoof history of England, in 1930. As they explained in the preface, 'History is not what you thought. *It is what you can remember.* All other history defeats itself.'

to himself, 'Where is that damned woman?' But such was her charm, and her lightness of touch, that, it seems, everyone forgave her everything. Even the King – perhaps especially the King – would indulge her. When once, famously, she arrived late for dinner with His Majesty, she, of course, apologised. 'Not at all,' said the King, to everybody else's amazement. 'You are not late, my dear. I think we must have sat down early.'

Elizabeth was not over-awed by her father-in-law. 'Unlike his own children,' she said, after his death, 'I was never afraid of him.' George V and Queen Mary enjoyed Elizabeth's company. She was easy with them in a way that very few others were. Beady-eyed Virginia Woolf – one of the shrewdest and sharpest observers of the period – was at the theatre one evening (at a performance of an Edgar Wallace thriller) and saw the royal party on display: 'There was a cheer, and behold a great golden Queen bowing in a very small bow windowed box. Also, when the lights went up, the King, red, grumpy, fidgeting with his hands; well groomed, bluff; heavy-looking, with one white flower in his buttonhole, resenting the need, perhaps, of sitting to be looked at between one of the acts – his duty to be done. Once the Duchess of York sat with the Queen; a simple, chattering, sweet-hearted little roundfaced young woman in pink; but her wrists twinkling with diamonds, her dress held on the shoulder with diamonds. An odd feeling came to me of the shop window decorated for the public: these our exhibits, our show pieces. Not very impressive – no romance or mystery – the very best goods.'[29]

The young Duchess of York delivered in full measure. In due course, at 2.40 a.m. on Wednesday, 21 April 1926, after a difficult labour, and by Caesarean section, she gave birth to her first child, a

---

29   15 December 1929. The actress Dame Eileen Atkins introduced me to *A Moment's Liberty: The Shorter Diary of Virginia Woolf* when she, Dame Eileen, was playing the part of Queen Mary in a television film about Bertie and Elizabeth. She said to me, 'The joy of the diary is that there's a gem on every page' and proved her point by opening the book at random and putting her finger on the entry for 18 May 1930: 'The thing is now to live with energy and mastery, desperately. To despatch each day high handedly. So not to dawdle and dwindle, contemplating this and that. No more regrets and indecisions. That is the right way to deal with life now that I am forty-eight and to make it more and more important and vivid as one grows old.'

baby girl, 'a little darling', according to Queen Mary's diary, 'with a lovely complexion and pretty fair hair'. The new Princess was named Elizabeth Alexandra Mary, after her mother (at Bertie's insistence: there was no thought of Elizabeth I), her grandmother (Queen Mary) and her great-grandmother (Queen Alexandra, who had died of a heart attack, aged eighty, the previous November). She was born in Mayfair, at 17 Bruton Street, a tall, handsome, eighteenth-century town house that had recently become the Strathmores' London home. She was christened five weeks later, on 29 May, in the chapel at Buckingham Palace. Her godparents included the King and Queen; her other grandmother, Lady Strathmore; her royal aunt, Mary, the Princess Royal; a non-royal aunt, Lady Elphinstone (mother of Margaret Rhodes); and Arthur, Duke of Connaught (1850–1942), Queen Victoria's last surviving son.

Princess Elizabeth was born as the General Strike was reaching its climax. Nineteen twenty-six was a year of political, social, and industrial unrest. It was also the year in which A.A. Milne wrote and published *Winnie-the-Pooh*. The tone of Elizabeth's childhood reflected the latter rather than the former. She was brought up in a golden cocoon: her nursery world, like Christopher Robin's, was cosy, Christian, safe, certain, utterly secure. There were differences, of course. Christopher Robin was a middle-class boy. Elizabeth was a princess and third in line to the throne.

The Yorks never liked the house assigned to them on their marriage. White Lodge in Richmond Park (now the home of the Royal Ballet School) was huge and unappealing, unwieldy and uncomfortable. Soon after Elizabeth's first birthday the family moved to 145 Piccadilly, overlooking Green Park, an impressive town house running to five floors (with electric lift) and featuring assorted reception rooms, a fine dining room, a proper ballroom, a good library, twenty-five bedrooms (including several fit for a king), and an impeccably appointed nursery floor. The indoor staff included a housekeeper, a cook, three kitchen maids, a butler, an under-butler, two footmen, a valet for the Duke, a dresser for the Duchess, an orderly, a handy-man, a night watchman, and a couple of lads: one to wait on the senior servants, one to operate the in-house telephone exchange. Up on the nursery floor, the little Princess had her own retinue. In command was Clara Cooper Knight, known as 'Alah' (to rhyme with Clara), a traditional English nanny, originally from Hertfordshire, who had looked after Lady Elizabeth when she was a baby. Alah, now in her late forties (but looking older in the photographs), was assisted by a young Scots nursery maid, aged twenty-two, the daughter of a railway worker from Inverness, Margaret MacDonald, known as 'Bobo'. Quite soon little Elizabeth would come to be known by her own diminutive: Lilibet – King George's pet name for his favourite grandchild.

The King gave Lilibet the time, attention, and affection he had denied his own children. He played with her – properly, down on all fours. He indulged her, sitting her at his side at breakfast and tea and feeding her titbits from his own plate. He took her with him on holiday, to Sandringham and Balmoral – even to Bognor, in 1929, where he was recuperating from a near-fatal illness.[30] Most significantly, perhaps, he shared with her his love of dogs and horses. He had a passion for racing and racehorses and loved nothing better than to take little Lilibet around the stud at Sandringham. For her fourth birthday, in April 1930, he gave her her first pony, a Shetland called Peggy.

Margaret Rhodes – then Margaret Elphinstone – was ten months older than her cousin, and, when Lilibet was staying in Scotland, at Glamis or Balmoral, a natural playmate. 'What did we play? We endlessly played at horses. That was her idea. We galloped round and round the field. We were horses of every kind. Carthorses, racehorses, circus horses. We spent a lot of time as circus horses.'

Mrs Rhodes laughed and lit another cigarette and gazed into the middle distance. 'We played "Catching happy days". Do you know it? It's a game you play in the autumn. You just run around trying

---

30 When George V died, in 1936, the story quickly circulated that his final words were 'Bugger Bognor!', apparently muttered in response to one of his doctors who had tried to lift his spirits by suggesting that he would soon be well enough to convalesce at his favourite seaside resort. I prefer the version of the story set in 1929. The King is recovering well and about to leave Bognor. A deputation from the town council comes to call on His Majesty, both to pay its respects and to ask that the town might in future be known as Bognor Regis. The request is conveyed to His Majesty by his private secretary, Lord Stamfordham. 'Bugger Bognor!' says the King. The private secretary returns to the delegation: 'His Majesty is touched by your request and graciously pleased to accede to it.'

to catch the leaves as they fall from the trees before they hit the ground. It's a wonderful game.

'I remember, too, we invented a play. We put it on in Scotland and then again at St George's Hall at Windsor Castle. It was the story of one family through the ages. I remember carrying the Queen across the threshold. I was the young man in the play. Anyway, I dropped her. Of course, in those days, there wasn't the faintest idea she might be Queen.'

In fact, by the end of 1930, the possibility that Princess Elizabeth might indeed one day be Queen was being openly discussed. In August the Yorks had produced a second child, but it was a girl. Rumour was rife: as adolescent naval cadets both Bertie and David had contracted mumps, which might have affected their fertility. The Prince of Wales was thirty-six and still unmarried. Even if he found a wife in the foreseeable future, would he be able to father an heir? Producing Lilibet and her sister – Princess Margaret Rose – had taken the Yorks all of seven years. Were they now likely to have a third child, and, if they did, would it be a boy?

The public, the press, even her parents, were speculating as to little Lilibet's destiny. Queen Victoria had succeeded her uncle. Would Princess Elizabeth succeed hers? Did she, even as a toddler, have the makings of a monarch? Osbert Sitwell recalled the Duke of York telling him, 'From the first moment of talking she showed so much character that it was impossible not to wonder that history would not repeat itself.' In September 1928 Winston Churchill – who would, one day, be Elizabeth II's first Prime Minister – stayed at Balmoral as a guest of King George and Queen Mary. He wrote to his wife: 'There is no one here at all, except the family, the household and Princess Elizabeth – aged two. The latter is a character. She has an air of authority and reflectiveness astonishing in an infant.'

Margaret Rhodes remembered her as 'a jolly little girl, but fundamentally sensible and well behaved. Princess Margaret was the naughty one. She was always more larky. She used to tease the servants. There was a wonderful old page and, as he carried the plates around the dining room, Margaret used to stare at him, trying to make him laugh. But she never got herself reprimanded. She got away with everything. She made her father laugh.'

When she was a little girl, Lilibet's closest friend outside the family was Sonia Graham-Hodgson, who became Sonia Berry. Sonia was the daughter of Sir Harold Graham-Hodgson, radiographer to the Royal Family, and a Mayfair neighbour of the Yorks. Sonia and Lilibet met in 1931, playing in Hamilton Gardens, behind Piccadilly. 'I was five and she was four,' Sonia recalled. 'I had no idea who she was, but I can see her now in a pink or red dress. She says I was wearing a blue coat, but we always argue over what we were wearing. I was the bossy one then – I rather rubbed in that I was eight months older. I was tall and she was rather small.'

Sonia and Lilibet played together in the gardens in Mayfair, in the nursery at 145 Piccadilly, in the thatched Wendy House at Royal Lodge, Windsor. Sonia kept evocative photographs of the pair of them (uniformed nannies in attendance) walking hand in hand in the park. Another picture showed them out cycling together: Lilibet, on her tricycle, looking very determined. 'We quarrelled like normal children,' said Sonia, 'but she was a thoughtful and sensitive child, and naturally well behaved. She never seemed aware of her position and paid no attention to the people who stood by the railings to watch her play.' And the Yorks as parents, by the standards of their time and class, were noticeably hands-on. 'The Duchess, having had a very happy childhood herself, was all the more determined that, because the children were royal, they should have an ordinary childhood. The Duke never seemed shy, he didn't stutter, and he played games, like Sardines. I remember my starchy nanny saying that she found it very undignified having to hide in a bush with him.'

When I went to visit Sonia Berry at her home in Bath she showed me some of the letters Lilibet had sent to her when they were little girls. They give a good flavour of the child and the childhood: 'Please excuse blots, messes etc as I am just going to bed because we've just come back from Royal Lodge where there is about four inches of snow. We made an igloo, an armchair and an ice cake. Really I have no other time to write here because we're living in a whirl of excitement. I hope your mother is well. Longing to see you again. With lots of love from Lilibet xxxxxooooo.'

The following spring – in March 1936, when young Princess Elizabeth was not quite ten – in a clear hand (and without any spelling mistakes) she wrote to Sonia from Compton Place in

Eastbourne, one of the homes of the Duke and Duchess of Devonshire: 'I'm so sorry not to write sooner but we have done such a lot that I couldn't find time. We've had such fun here. We went to Beachy Head where the cliffs fall sheer down to the sea. Then we went to Birling Gap and played on the beach. We went to Seaford and saw a waiting steamer coming in to harbour. Then went to Cooden Beach where it was lovely. Papa and all of us, except Mummy who had a cold, went to a place called High and Over where the name suited it very well because you went high and then you went over. The next day we went to Cooden Beach again and we picked up a lot of shells and then we had tea in a hotel – wasn't that lovely? Tarts with cream and jam. It was lovely and I wished you were there. We've got a little chalet on the beach and it's perfectly lovely. Two big lounge chairs and two little basket chairs. I hope you are quite well and Woolly [Sonia's governess] I hope is better. Not having any more colliwobbles! Love from Lilibet.'

It's clear: the Yorks were a happy family. They had reason to be. These were the years of the Great Depression, but – though the King ordered a general tightening of the royal belt – his family was mostly cushioned from the harshness of reality. The Yorks led comfortable, ordered lives. They already had a fine house in Mayfair and, in September 1931, the King had given them, in addition, a handsome weekend retreat in the mock-Gothic shape of the Royal Lodge in Windsor Great Park. They spent Easter at Windsor Castle; Christmas and the New Year at Sandringham; August and September in Scotland. There was nothing rackety about their lives. The Prince of Wales might disport himself on the Continent with one or other of his mistresses, but the Yorks only ever went abroad on duty. They took their duties seriously. They took their role as parents seriously as well.

Yes, they would travel to foreign parts when they had to (in January 1927, when Lilibet was only nine months old, they went without her on an official visit to Australia and New Zealand that kept them away for six months), but when they were at home – and they were mostly at home – they were much more intimately involved in the care and upbringing of their children than many aristocratic parents of their generation. The Yorks gave time and attention to their daughters: they played with them, they bathed them, they read to them, they gathered round the piano after tea and sang songs together. Prince Philip barely saw his parents throughout his adolescence. Lilibet saw hers every day.

'Of course,' said Mrs Rhodes, lighting another cigarette and putting her head gently to one side, 'we were educated at home. The Queen and I were really the last generation of gels who didn't go to school. We thought school would be ghastly. You'd have to play hockey. We didn't want to play hockey. I had a French governess. The Queen and Princess Margaret had Crawfie.' Mrs Rhodes smoothed out her skirt with an anxious hand. 'I knew Crawfie. She was very nice really, but then she wrote the book. I haven't read it.'

A silence fell. 'It's rather good,' I said.

'It probably is,' said Mrs Rhodes, stubbing out her cigarette and laughing. 'I still haven't read it. I don't think I shall.'

'Crawfie' was Marion Crawford, the young Scotswoman who joined the York household as Lilibet's governess in the spring of 1932. 'The book' is *The Little Princesses*, Crawfie's account of the childhoods of Lilibet and Margaret Rose based on her sixteen years of royal service and published – to the dismay and astonishment of the House of Windsor – in 1950. Crawfie was tall, trim, intelligent, ambitious. She had trained as a teacher at Moray House in Edinburgh, working with young children from difficult backgrounds. She had plans to go on to train as a child psychologist. She was introduced to the Yorks by another of the Duchess's elder sisters, not Lady Elphinstone (Margaret Rhodes's mother), but Lady Rose Leveson-Gower, whose daughter, Mary, had been taking lessons with her. Crawfie was an excellent governess and a good friend to Lilibet and Margaret Rose, until, by publishing her book, she betrayed their trust – and became, overnight, a 'non-person'.

There is nothing shocking in *The Little Princesses*. Far from it. The tone is altogether deferential, the literary style overly sweet and sentimental, but the observation is often shrewd and the details revealing. Here is Crawfie's account of her entry into the nursery world of Royal Lodge and her first encounter with Alah Knight, the formidable nanny, 'a tall, noble-looking woman', and little Princess Elizabeth, the heroine of her story, and ours:

'Alah awaited me with that mixture of reserve and apprehension felt by all nannies when the governess is introduced. I like to remember that in all my years at 145 Piccadilly, London, and later at Buckingham Palace, Alah and I remained good friends; and if on her side the neutrality was sometimes armed to the teeth, I was always very careful not to tread on her toes.

'Alah had entire charge in those days of the children's out-of-school lives – their health, their baths, their clothes – while I had them from nine to six. She had to help her an under-nurse and a nursemaid. These two girls are there still – Margaret MacDonald and Ruby MacDonald, two sisters, who have become the personal maids and friends of the two sisters.

'The night nursery was decorated in pink and fawn, the Duchess's favourite colour scheme. A small figure with a mop of curls sat up on the bed. She wore a nightie with a design of small pink roses on it. She had tied the cords of her dressing gown to the knobs of the old-fashioned bed, and was busy driving her team.

'That was my first glimpse of Princess Elizabeth.

'"This is Miss Crawford," said Alah, in her stern way.

'The little girl said, "How do you do." She then gave me a long, comprehensive look I had seen once before, and went on, "Why have you no hair?"

'I pulled off my hat to show her. "I have enough to go on with," I said. "It's an Eton crop."

'She picked up her reins again.

'"Do you usually drive in bed?" I asked.

'"I mostly go once or twice round the park before I go to sleep, you know," she said. "It exercises my horses." She navigated a dangerous and difficult corner, and went on, "Are you going to stay with us?"

'"For a little while, anyway," I replied.

The account has the feel of a novella, but also the ring of truth. We are introduced immediately both to Lilibet's discriminating, observant eye and to her passion for horses. We can picture the child, the nanny and the governess quite clearly. While friends of the Queen who have read the book tell me that much of it is fanciful and not to be relied upon, I reckon that, overall, Crawfie's portrait of the little Princesses is both accurate and telling. Lilibet comes across as an intelligent child, a dutiful daughter, and a responsible elder sister. Her love of dogs and horses – practical as well as passionate – is essential to her happiness. 'Lilibet's first love of all was undoubtedly Owen the groom, who taught her to ride.' She was not yet six. 'What Owen did or said was right in her sight for many years.' In 1933, when Lilibet was seven, her father gave her her first corgi.

Because Crawfie had reservations about some of Alah's methods – Alah was a wholly traditional nanny: she believed in order, discipline, routine, calmness at all times, the virtues of emotional constraint – Crawfie, in her book, may have exaggerated the degree of Lilibet's obsession with orderliness. Alah believed in the regimented life and, from the earliest age, Lilibet was a stickler for domestic order. Crawfie tells us how carefully Lilibet lined up her toy horses, how neatly she folded her clothes, how – night after night – she took care to position her shoes exactly parallel underneath her chair. After a family lunch one day, when their parents allowed the Princesses a spoonful each of sugar crystals, Margaret Rose ate all hers at once: before eating them, Lilibet arranged hers meticulously, one by one, in a straight line according to size.

Crawfie comes back, time and again, to her charges' contrasting personalities:

'Of the two children, Lilibet was the one with the temper, but it was under control. Margaret was often naughty, but she had a gay bouncing way with her which was hard to deal with. She would often defy me with a sidelong look, make a scene and kiss and be friends and all forgiven and forgotten. Lilibet took longer to recover, but she had always the more dignity of the two.

'The Duke was immensely proud of her. He had a way of looking at her that was touching. But Margaret brought delight into his life. She was a plaything. She was warm and demonstrative, made to be cuddled and played with. At one time he would be almost embarrassed, yet at the same time touched and pleased, when she wound her arms round his neck, nestled against him and cuddled and caressed him. He was not a demonstrative man.

'Lilibet took after him. She, too, was reserved and quiet about her feelings. If you once gained her love and affection you had it for ever, but she never gave it easily.'

In January 1936, aged seventy-one, George V died. His favourite grandchild was not quite ten. Crawfie recalls:

'Lilibet in her sensitive fashion felt it all deeply. It was very touching to see how hard she tried to do what she felt was expected of her. I remember her pausing doubtfully as she groomed one of her toy horses and looking up at me for a moment.

'"Oh, Crawfie . . . ought we to play?"'

The old King was much mourned. His face was red, his manner was gruff, his voice was loud, but he had done his duty with dignity and some skill. His reign encompassed the Great War, the Russian Revolution, civil war in Ireland, the Great Depression, the advent of Britain's first Labour government. He had risen to the challenges. He had dropped few catches. He had survived. He would be missed. 'The people of America are mourning, as if for their own King,' Virginia Woolf noted in her diary, 'and the Japanese are in tears.' The BBC suspended normal service and simply broadcast the sound of the ticking of a clock. The Prime Minister, Stanley Baldwin, addressed the nation and Virginia Woolf reckoned Baldwin hit the right note: 'He gave out the impression that he was a tired country gentleman; the King another; both enjoyed Christmas at home; and the Queen is very lonely; one left the other taken, as must happen to married couples; and the King had seemed to him tired lately, but very kind, and quiet as if ready for a long journey; and had woken once or twice on the last day and had said something Kind ("Kind" was the adjective always) and had said to his Secretary "How is the Empire?" – an odd expression. "The Empire, Sir, is well"; whereupon he fell asleep . . . The shops are all black. Mourning is to outlast the London season. A black Ascot.'

'Kind' was not necessarily the word his elder sons would have used to encapsulate the essence of their father. His relationship with each of them – which became very different – was never easy. He was much more comfortable with the women in his family. Perhaps they had the measure of him. The Duchess of York teased him. Playing horse and groom, little Lilibet led him around the drawing room by his beard. Until her death (a few weeks before his own) the old King and his unmarried younger sister Victoria chatted daily on the telephone. Once – Elizabeth Longford told me this story and assured me she had it on good authority – Princess Victoria telephoned the King at Buckingham Palace and said, 'Is that you, you old fool?' The operator interrupted: 'Beg pardon, your Royal Highness, His Majesty is not yet on the line.'[31]

The reign of George V lasted more than a quarter of a century. The reign of Edward VIII came to an abrupt end after eleven months and twenty-one days. As Prince of Wales, David had been popular with public and press alike. He was good-looking, charming, socially adept; he appeared articulate, energetic, and able; he came over as unstuffy and contemporary, both human and humane. Those who saw him at closer quarters got a different picture. Beatrice Webb, socialist pioneer and co-founder of the *New Statesman* magazine, met him at dinner in the summer of 1930 and recorded in her diary: 'He is neurotic and takes too much alcohol for health of body or mind. If I were his mother or grandmother I should be very nervous about his future . . . his expression was unhappy – there was a horrid dissipated look as if he had no settled home either for his intellect or his emotions . . . He must be a problem to the conventional courtiers who surround him.' He was.

In January 1931, at Melton Mowbray in Leicestershire, at the country house of one mistress, Thelma Furness (the second wife of the first Viscount Furness), David met his next mistress, his last, the non-negotiable love of his life: Wallis Simpson. Mrs Simpson was thirty-five, American, chic rather than beautiful, the Baltimore-born second wife of a New York businessman, Ernest Simpson, who had an English-born father and had come to London to run the British end of the family firm. David's interest in Wallis developed gradually. It began as a flirtatious friendship. The affair blossomed in the spring of 1934. By 1935 the Prince was wholly infatuated. Within court circles the affair was an open secret, but it was not a matter that was discussed within the Windsor family. As one of David's nephews, George Harewood, the Princess Royal's son, pointed out: it was a different world, a world in which 'anything awkward' was best avoided. 'People kept much more private and much more quiet about things

31 Possibly less reliable, but equally charming, are the two George V stories recounted by George Lyttelton in his correspondence with Rupert Hart-Davis: 'Much may be forgiven him for (a) when asked what film he would like to see when convalescing, announcing "Anything except that damned Mouse" and (b) when the footman, bringing in the early morning royal tea, tripped and fell with his load and heard from the pillow, "That's right; break up the whole bloody place."'

like that and were much more able to bottle up their feelings. I think the whole of my mother's family tended to bottle up their feelings very much.'

The crisis reached its climax in the autumn of 1936. In August the new King – not yet crowned: his Coronation was set for the following May – holidayed at Balmoral, with his mistress installed in the rooms that, a year before, had been occupied by Queen Mary. In September he asked the Yorks to take his place at the official opening of a hospital in Aberdeen, so that he could meet Mrs Simpson, secretly, at the railway station. In October Mrs Simpson secured her second divorce and became free to marry for a third time. In November the King – Supreme Governor of the Church of England, which did not then recognise divorce – told his mother, his brother, and the Prime Minister that he had decided to marry his American divorcee and, if necessary, to give up his throne in order to be able to do so. 'Oh,' stammered Bertie, 'that's a dreadful thing to hear. None of us wants that, I least of all.'

Of all this, until the beginning of December, the majority of the British public knew nothing. Around the world, especially in the United States, reports of the King's relationship with Mrs Simpson had been widespread. In the United Kingdom, a deferential press had breathed not a word of scandal. Up on the nursery floor at 145 Piccadilly, Crawfie and Alah and the little Princesses sensed something ominous in the air, but no one told them anything. Evidently something was about to happen, but what was it? 'It was impossible not to notice the change in Uncle David,' said Crawfie, in retrospect. 'He had been so youthful and gay. Now he looked distraught, and seemed not to be listening to what was said to him. He made plans with the children, and then forgot them.'

On Thursday, 3 December, Crawfie went out and bought an evening paper. Standing on the doorstep, 'I remember I read the headline while I waited for the front door to open . . . THE KING AND HIS MINISTERS. GREAT CONSTITUTIONAL CRISIS . . . I do not know what we would have done at that time without the swimming lessons. They were a great diversion and took our minds off other matters.'

At Buckingham Palace and in Downing Street, as the drama of the Abdication unfolded, down at the Bath Club, Lilibet and Margaret

Rose, aged ten and six, were learning to swim. ('I remember the Bath Club well,' Gina Kennard told me. 'Princess Elizabeth was always so nicely behaved. I remember she used to have a bag of sweets and, after swimming, would take the bag round, offering everybody a sweet.') The King could not marry Mrs Simpson and make her his Queen. A morganatic marriage, allowing her the position of wife but not the status of Queen, might be possible, but would require legislation. The government advised against it. The King agonised. The press fulminated. The Church pontificated. Mrs Simpson left the country to escape the furore. Queen Mary shook her head in sorrow and in anger. Bertie wept on his mother's shoulder, overwhelmed by the prospect of what was to come. Elizabeth retreated to her bed with a bout of influenza. At the poolside, Crawfie and Alah wrapped Lilibet and Margaret Rose in huge bath towels and, as each was awarded her Life Saving Certificate, rewarded the girls with hugs and a small box of chocolates.

The King was ready to sign the Instrument of Abdication. Edward VIII was about to become Prince Edward, Duke of Windsor. Prince Albert, Duke of York, was about to become King George VI. At 145 Piccadilly, Crawfie was standing in an alcove on the landing outside the Duchess of York's bedroom. The door opened:

'Queen Mary came out of the Duchess's room. She who was always so upright, so alert, looked suddenly old and tired. The Duchess was lying in bed, propped up among pillows. She held out her hand to me. "I'm afraid there are going to be great changes in our lives, Crawfie," she said . . . When I broke the news to Margaret and Lilibet that they were going to live in Buckingham Palace they looked at me in horror. "What!" Lilibet said. "You mean for ever?" . . .

'I had to explain to them that when Papa came home to lunch at one o'clock he would be King of England, and they would have to curtsy to him. The Royal children from their earliest years had always curtsied to their grandparents.

'"And now you mean we must do it to Papa and Mummie?" Lilibet asked. "Margaret too?"

'"Margaret also," I told her, "and try not to topple over."

'When the King returned, both little girls swept him a beautiful curtsy. I think perhaps nothing that had occurred had brought the change in his condition to him as clearly as this did. He stood for a moment touched and taken aback. Then he stooped and kissed both warmly. After this we had a hilarious lunch.'

'Of course, when the Yorks became King and Queen, the family had to move to Buckingham Palace,' Sonia Berry explained to me. 'That was quite a wrench. Lilibet had so many toy horses – dozens of them – she kept them all neatly lined up on the landing outside her bedroom – she groomed them so beautifully – and they had to be packed up. She left her favourite horse, Ben, with me, because she didn't want him to be packed up by the removal people. I didn't hear from her for a week or two, but then she wrote to me.'

The letter was dated Monday, 1 March 1937: 'Thank you very much for keeping Ben whilst we moved into Buckingham Palace. We're quite settled in now and we would like you to come to tea one day next week. We've been very busy and we could not find time for out-teas, but now we'll be able to find some. Crawfie will ring up next week and would you please come to the Privy Purse door – that is the one next to Constitution Hill. I hope you will find it. Please do you think you could bring Ben with you. Could you bear it? I'm sure he enjoyed staying with you.'

PHILIP & LILIBET

Chapter Five

'Behind the complicated details of the world stand the simplicities: God is good, the grown-up man or woman knows the answer to every question, there is such a thing as truth, and justice is as measured and faultless as a clock. Our heroes are simple: they are brave, they tell the truth, they are good swordsmen and they are never in the long run really defeated. That is why no later books satisfy us like those which were read to us in childhood – for those promised a world of great simplicity of which we knew the rules, but the later books are complicated and contradictory with experience; they are formed out of our own disappointing memories.'

Graham Greene (1904–91), *The Ministry of Fear*

'Dickie, this is absolutely terrible.' As Edward VIII prepared to sign the Instrument of Abdication, his younger brother Bertie turned to their cousin Louis Mountbatten –now thirty-six and a rising star in the Admiralty, where, of course, his own father, Louis of Battenberg, had once been First Sea Lord – and shared his sense of desperation, bordering on panic. 'I never wanted this to happen,' he bleated. 'I'm quite unprepared for it. David has been trained for this all his life. I've never even seen a State paper. I'm only a Naval Officer. It's the only thing I know about.'

Mountbatten, a staunch ally of the King's until the moment of Abdication,[32] offered David's reluctant successor an anecdote by way

32 And, in fairness, beyond. David, as Prince of Wales, had been best man at Mountbatten's wedding to Edwina Ashley in 1922. Following the Abdication, Mountbatten offered his services as best man to David. The Duke of Windsor, as he had become, had hoped his brothers, the new King and the Duke of Kent, might be his supporters at his wedding to Mrs Simpson. In the event, there was no royal representation at the wedding at Candé on 4 June 1937. Mountbatten

of consolation and encouragement. 'This is a very curious coincidence,' he said. 'My father once told me that, when the Duke of Clarence died, your father came to him and said almost the same things that you have said to me now, and my father answered: "George, you're wrong. There is no more fitting preparation for a king, than to have been trained in the Navy."'

George V, the second son of Edward VII, was forty-five when he became King in 1910, four years before the outbreak of the First World War. George VI, the second son of George V, was forty-one when he became King in 1936, three years before the outbreak of the Second World War. Wars that are won can do much to enhance the reputation of the reigning monarch. Bertie, as Duke of York, was unexceptional, unexciting, a good family man, a decent chap, not over-stretched, but conscientious when duty called. Bertie, as King, was stretched to the limit and not found wanting. René Massigli, the French Ambassador to London at the time of Bertie's death just over fifteen years later, wrote in a report to the French Foreign Minister: 'If the "greatness" of a king can be measured by the extent to which his qualities corresponded to the needs of a nation at a given moment in history, then George VI was a great king, and perhaps a very great king.'

George VI – decent, dignified, determined – was the right man in the right place at the right time. He might lack his elder brother's obvious glamour and panache, but you could see – and hear – from the way he wrestled with his speech impediment that he had courage. He might not be blessed with great imagination or any very obvious intellectual gifts, but he had palpable integrity. He looked to be what he was: a softly spoken, well-intentioned, quietly uncomplicated, honest English gentleman. And one blessed with a matchless Scottish wife.

Famously, in his Abdication broadcast (which he scripted himself, though he showed the draft to Winston Churchill, who may have

---

had been loyal to David when he was King and would be loyal, too, to Bertie. On 11 December 1936, the day of the Proclamation, he wrote to the new King: 'My dear Bertie, Heartbroken as I am at David's departure and all the terrible trouble he has brought on us all I feel I must tell you how deeply I feel for Elizabeth and you having to shoulder his responsibilities in such trying circumstances. Luckily both you and your children have precisely those qualities needed to pull this country through this ghastly crisis.'

added the odd rhetorical flourish), David had said, 'You must believe me when I tell you that I have found it impossible to carry the heavy burden of responsibility and to discharge my duties as King as I would wish to without the help and support of the woman I love.' Might the same not have been true of Bertie? Could he have coped as King without Elizabeth Bowes-Lyon as Queen? Certainly, he could not have coped as well. And, equally certainly, he found the burden to be a cruelly heavy one. When, later, someone commented on how well the exiled Duke of Windsor was looking, Queen Elizabeth responded, 'Yes. And who has got the lines now?' Sir Alexander Hardinge, who served as assistant and then principal private secretary to George V, Edward VIII and George VI, said of Bertie, 'As a result of the stress he was under the King used to stay up too late and smoked too many cigarettes – he literally died for England.'

There was no love lost between Queen Elizabeth and the Duke and Duchess of Windsor, but her niece, Mary Rhodes, who was also, later, her lady-in-waiting, and spent many hours with her, was anxious to tell me – and you – that 'Not once in all the years I was with her – not once – did I ever hear say anything remotely unpleasant about the Windsors. I know she liked David and, I promise you, I never heard her say anything uncharitable about the Duchess. Becoming Queen was not what Queen Elizabeth wanted or expected, but, when it happened, she accepted it.' And grew into the role and, I suspect, over time, rather relished it.

Sensibly, Queen Elizabeth kept her feelings about Wallis Simpson – and much besides – to herself. The females of the family (Queen Mary, Queen Elizabeth, Queen Elizabeth II, Princess Anne) are good at that. Mrs Simpson was less circumspect. 'Really David,' she wrote to the Duke of Windsor, having seen photographs and newsreel of the new Queen going about her duties, 'the pleased expression on the Duchess of York's face is funny to see. How she is loving it all.'

In March 1937, only three months into the new King's reign, Harold Nicolson, diarist and recently elected Member of Parliament, found himself (in knee breeches and silk stockings – Court Dress – it was a different world) attending the grandest of dinners at Buckingham Palace: 'The dining-table is one mass of gold candelabra and scarlet tulips.' The meal was disappointing, but the wine 'excellent and the port superb'. After dinner, in the drawing room, Nicolson observed the new Queen going the rounds: 'She wears upon her face a faint smile indicative of how much she would have liked her dinner-party were it not for the fact that she was Queen of England. Nothing could exceed the charm or dignity which she displays, and I cannot help feeling what a mess poor Mrs Simpson would have made of such an occasion. It demonstrated to us more than anything else how wholly impossible that marriage would have been.'

The evening over, Nicolson went home with friends and sat, over beer, late into the night, discussing 'the legend of monarchy'. At dinner, George VI had sat with Stanley Baldwin and David Lloyd George discussing affairs of state. In truth, he would have little impact upon them. The King was still head of state, the figurehead, the font of honour, but he was no longer a force to reckon with. Queen Victoria had been (in Prince Philip's phrase) 'an executive monarch' who could 'do things'. As a diplomat, as an operator on the European stage, Edward VII had been able to make a difference. Even George V had had opinions – and taken action – that, to an extent, affected the course of history. But by the time Edward VIII's reign had ended, exactly a century after Queen Victoria's had begun, the *power* of the monarch had all but disappeared. Edward VIII was forced to abdicate because the government and parliament of the day – in the Dominions as much as in Britain – would not let him do as he pleased. George VI was the first of a new kind of monarch: a symbol, not a player.

'Until the King became King,' Margaret Rhodes said to me, 'he was always "Uncle Bertie". Then, overnight, he became "Sir".' The simple fact of being King gave the hesitant Duke of York a new authority. The machinery of the monarchy – well oiled and with its own momentum – swept him, relatively effortlessly, through the first few months of his reign. Privately, he felt the strain, but, so far as the public was concerned, it was a matter of 'business as usual'. Bertie and Elizabeth might, silently, be brooding about David and Wallis across the water,[33] but, at home, the court, the press, and the people were

33 They were not altogether silent. Bertie made it clear there was no prospect of Wallis ever being granted the title Royal Highness, nor of David returning to any kind of public life in the United Kingdom. Encouraged by Queen Mary – who had been quite horrified by her eldest son's behaviour – Bertie and Elizabeth ostracised David's closest and most ardent supporters, notably the celebrated hostess and shipping-line widow Emerald, Lady Cunard.

ready to move on. 'Least said, soonest mended' was the unstated national policy. 'The King is dead! (Well, moved to France, which comes to the same thing . . .) Long live the King!' The Coronation, on 12 May 1937, was not Edward VIII's Coronation *manqué*: it was wholly George VI's, and the day when the new King – according to several observers – seemed, for the first time, wholly to accept his destiny.

Lilibet, now eleven and Heiress Presumptive, seems always to have accepted hers. Her life was to be different from here on in and there was nothing she could do about it. In public, even her closest friend, Sonia, now had to curtsy to her and could no longer call her Lilibet. When the family moved to Buckingham Palace, Sonia told me, 'Princess Elizabeth's parents, who, previously, had simply been "downstairs", were now "miles away" and very much busier. Everything was different.'

'Was the young Princess different?'

'She had always been quite serious, calm and organised. She was still fun to be with, but I think we were all suddenly aware that one day she might be Queen.'

According to Margaret Rhodes, 'I believe, briefly, she hoped that she might have a brother and be let off the hook, but I think she knew that wasn't very likely. She knew she would be Queen one day, but she thought it would be a long way off. She didn't talk about it much. In fact, I don't think she talked about it at all.'

What she did talk about, and take the keenest interest in, according to Crawfie, was her father's Coronation. Crawfie read to her Queen Victoria's account of her own Coronation in 1837. In 1937, as a present for her parents, in a neat hand, written in light pencil on lined paper, the little Princess produced her own record of their great day:

> To Mummy and Papa
> In Memory of Their Coronation
> From Lilibet
> By Herself
> An Account of the Coronation

It's vivid stuff. The day begins with Lilibet, wrapped in an eiderdown by her faithful nursemaid Bobo, gazing out of her nursery window 'onto a cold misty morning'. Once they were breakfasted and dressed, the young Princesses showed off their Coronation outfits 'to the visitors and housemaids':

'I shall try and give you a description of our dresses. They were white silk with old cream lace and had little gold bows all the way down the middle. They had puffed sleeves with one little bow in the centre. Then there were the robes of purple velvet with gold on the edge.

'We went along to Mummy's bedroom and we found her putting on her dress. Papa was dressed in a white shirt, breeches and stockings, and over this he wore a crimson satin coat. Then a page came and said it was time to go down, so we kissed Mummy, and wished her good luck and went down.'

Lilibet and Margaret Rose in their Coronation finery travelled in procession to Westminster Abbey in a glass coach: 'At first it was very jolty but we soon got used to it.' She watched the three-hour-long ceremony sitting alongside her grandmother, Queen Mary, in a specially created royal box:

'I thought it all *very, very* wonderful and I expect the Abbey did, too. The arches and beams at the top were covered with a sort of haze of wonder as Papa was crowned, at least I thought so.

'When Mummy was crowned and all the peeresses put on their coronets it looked wonderful to see arms and coronets hovering in the air and then the arms disappear as if by magic. Also the music was lovely and the band, the orchestra and the new organ all played beautifully.

'What struck me as rather odd was that Grannie did not remember much of her own Coronation. I should have thought that it would have stayed in her mind for ever.

'At the end the service got rather boring as it was all prayers. Grannie and I were looking to see how many more pages to the end, and we turned one more and then I pointed to the word at the bottom of the page and it said "Finis". We both smiled at each other and turned back to the service.'

The service over, the Princesses were escorted to 'our dressing room' and offered 'sandwiches, stuffed rolls, orangeade and lemonade' before taking the 'long drive' home.

'Then we all went on to the Balcony, where *millions* of people were waiting below. After that we all went to be photographed in front of those awful lights.

'When we sat down to tea it was nearly six o'clock! When I got into bed my legs ached terribly!'

The unique souvenir she presented to her parents (carefully tied together with pink ribbon) tells us much about the essential Lilibet. She is observant. She has a nice sense of humour. She lives in a world of nursemaids and housemaids and pages and accepts it completely. She goes out on to the balcony and '*millions* of people' are waiting below. The only thing she doesn't enjoy is being photographed. At the end of a long day her legs ache terribly. It's all a taste of things to come – and there's a telling sentence there, too, that, in many ways, sums up the phlegmatic approach to life that will stay with her – and sustain her – through the years: 'At first it was very jolty but we soon got used to it.'

Lilibet's composition – well structured, with sound punctuation and impeccable spelling – tells us something about Crawfie, too. She was a good teacher. In February 1937 Crawfie, along with Alah and Bobo and their young charges, moved from 145 Piccadilly across Green Park to Buckingham Palace. 145 had been a home, albeit a grand one staffed by eighteen servants. Buckingham Palace was the headquarters of an empire, with a staff in excess of four hundred. 'I still recall with a shudder that first night spent in the Palace,' said Crawfie. 'The wind moaned in the chimneys like a thousand ghosts.' Crawfie was disconcerted by the sheer scale of the place and not impressed by the (in every sense) Victorian quality of much of the accommodation. The rooms were dark and musty. The light switch for Crawfie's bedroom was outside the door, two yards down the corridor. To reach the bathroom and lavatory you had to cross the passageway in your slippers and dressing gown, and risk bumping into the Palace postman on his early morning round. Crawfie did not like it. She was homesick.

Lilibet was less troubled. To her, it was a home – this was where her grandparents had lived – and the corridors, while endless ('People here need bicycles,' she said), were more fun than forbidding. 'There was very little restraint placed on the children,' Crawfie reported. 'The Prime Minister, coming to see the King on affairs of State . . . might easily find himself tangled up with two excited little girls racing down the corridors. Or one stoutish little girl panting, "Wait for me, Lilibet. Wait for me!" Perhaps Dookie, the Queen's devoted Corgi, might take a nip at a passing leg. Dookie adored the taste of strange trousers.'[34]

Gradually, the governess came to terms with her new surroundings. Improvements were made, walls were repapered, facilities were enhanced. The new Queen added her special touch. 'Elizabeth can make a home wherever she is,' said Bertie, proudly. 'Mice continued to be a menace,' said Crawfie, tartly. However, even she had to acknowledge that the gardens at the back of the Palace were a bonus, and there were still the weekends, 'now the best part of all our lives', when 'we escaped from the Palace' and went down to Royal Lodge, Windsor. 'At Royal Lodge, court etiquette was forgotten, and ceremony left behind. We were just a family again.' In fact, nothing was to be quite the same again.

The Yorks were now King and Queen; Lilibet and Margaret Rose were first and second in line to the throne. Queen Mary, who, since her own Coronation, twenty-six years before, had always been the personification of majesty, and had long shown an interest in her granddaughters' upbringing, now insisted that touches of regality be introduced to the children's routine. Meals on the nursery floor were served by liveried footmen. The food was English, but the menus were in French. Crawfie continued to be in charge of the Princesses' education, but her staple fare – Bible, History, Grammar, Arithmetic, Geography, Literature, Poetry, Writing and Composition, with Music, Drawing, or Dancing after lunch – was now supplemented by lessons in constitutional history (for Lilibet) and, later, for both girls, by special classes in French, provided by a Mrs Montaudon-Smith (soon known as Monty), and, later still, French literature and European history, provided by a Belgian aristocrat, the Vicomtesse de Bellaigue (known as 'Toinon': her Christian name was Antoinette).

Lilibet's personal tutor in constitutional history was Henry Marten, co-author of a much-respected standard *History of England* and Vice-Provost of Eton College, the celebrated boys' school conveniently

---

34 And not just of trousers. Crawfie regarded Dookie as generally 'very soured-natured': 'He bit me once quite severely, and on another occasion took a piece out of Lord Lothian's hand. With great fortitude his lordship averred it was nothing! It did not hurt him at all. "All the same, he bled all over the floor," Lilibet pointed out.'

Prince Philip of Greece

Princess Elizabeth of York

Philip's father, Prince Andrea, centre, during the Asia Minor campaign, 1921

Andrea facing trial in Athens, December 1922

Philip's mother with her family in 1917, the year the Battenbergs became Mountbattens. r–l, Alice, her parents, Louis, 1st Marquess of Milford Haven, and Victoria, with their younger son, Dickie, and second daughter, Louise (later Queen of Sweden)

Philip's parents and all
five of their children,
photographed in Paris
for their silver wedding
anniversary in 1928 – the
only known photograph
of the family together

Philip and his mother,
Princess Alice,
October 1928

Philip at St Cloud in 1929

Philip at school: The Elms, 1928; Cheam, 1932; Gordonstoun, 1935

Lilibet at home, in the garden at 145 Piccadilly, protecting Jane and Dookie, July 1936

Elizabeth and Margaret with 'Crawfie', 1939

Philip at Gordonstoun, 1938

The first photographs: Queen Elizabeth and George VI, seated centre, with Elizabeth, far left, and Philip, in uniform, standing next to Dickie Mountbatten

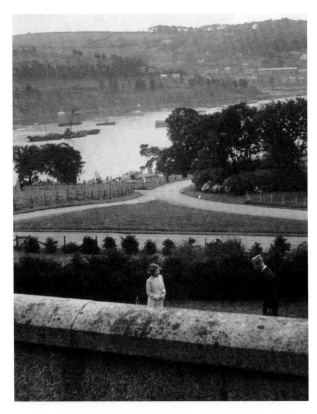

Philip, aged eighteen, and Elizabeth, thirteen, at the Royal Naval College, Dartmouth, July 1939

Elizabeth's favourite wartime photograph of Philip

Elizabeth in her ATS uniform

Elizabeth playing tag on board HMS *Vanguard* on the voyage to South Africa, February 1947

Philip instructing the school for petty officers, HMS *Royal Arthur*, Corsham, Autumn 1947

The first look: the tell-tale photograph of Philip and Elizabeth
arriving at the wedding of Patricia Mountbatten and
John Brabourne, October 1946

The first dance: Lt Philip Mountbatten and his fiancée dance
together publicly for the first time, Edinburgh, July 1947

situated not far from Royal Lodge. Marten described his royal pupil as 'a somewhat shy girl of thirteen who when asked a question would look for confidence and support to her beloved governess, Miss Crawford'. The teacher, a bachelor now in his sixties who had been a master at Eton since 1896, does not seem to have been wholly at ease himself, never managing to look his first-ever female student directly in the eye, frequently addressing her as 'Gentlemen', and alternately biting his handkerchief and nervously crunching lumps of sugar produced at regular intervals from his jacket pocket.

Marten's syllabus covered more than a thousand years of royal heritage, starting with the reign of King Egbert, the king of the West Saxons (802–39), 'the first to unite all Anglo-Saxons', and culminating with the two most significant events of modern times: the advent of broadcasting and the 1931 Statute of Westminster. According to Marten, the Statute, which recognised the independence of the Dominions within the Commonwealth, gave a new significance to the Crown as the one remaining link between the United Kingdom and the Dominions, and the arrival of broadcasting enabled the wearer of the crown to sustain that link, in a personal way, by speaking directly to people around the world.

Gradually, Princess Elizabeth was being groomed for her destiny. Crawfie, meanwhile, was determined to keep the royal feet firmly on the ground: 'I suggested one day that it would be a very good idea for the children to start a Girl Guide Company at the Palace. Besides keeping them in touch with what children of their own ages were doing, I knew it would bring them into contact with others of their own ages and of all kinds and conditions.' So, in 1937, the Buckingham Palace Guide Company was formed, divided into three patrols, with a small Brownie pack tacked on for the benefit of Princess Margaret, who was still only seven. The girls – about three dozen in all – included royal cousins, royal friends, the children of courtiers and, according to Crawfie, 'those of Palace employees'. The Company met on Wednesday afternoons: in summer, in the Palace gardens; in winter, in one of the Palace's many echoing reception rooms. 'Just at first,' noted Crawfie, 'some of the children who joined started coming in party frocks, with white gloves, accompanied by fleets of nannies and governesses. We soon put a stop to all that.'

Princess Elizabeth was in the Kingfisher patrol and second-in-command to Patricia Mountbatten, Louis Mountbatten's elder daughter, who was two years her cousin's senior. 'Princess Elizabeth was a first-class Guide,' Countess Mountbatten told me, 'really efficient and completely level-headed. You could really rely on her. She'd never let you down. She quickly became a leader in her own right.'

The girls enjoyed their Guiding. 'The Company was formed so that Elizabeth and Margaret Rose could meet and mix with ordinary children,' Countess Mountbatten told me, with a charming little chuckle. 'Well, there's ordinary and ordinary, of course. I think the children were quite carefully vetted. I think they had to be "suitable". But we did do ordinary Guiding things. The long corridors at Buckingham Palace were ideal for practising signals and we went on wonderful expeditions in the Windsor forest, trekking and bird-watching and cooking sausages over the camp fire. The King's Piper came and played for us and we did Highland dancing. That was fun.'

What was Lilibet like at thirteen? Henry Marten said she was shy and looked to Crawfie to give her confidence. Crawfie said that, at thirteen, 'when so many are gawky', Lilibet 'was an enchanting child with the loveliest hair and skin and a long, slim figure'. She was growing up. She was no longer biting her nails. She was almost as tall as her mother. Soon her wardrobe of 'very simple afternoon frocks' – 'usually of tussore silk, often hand-smocked, quite short with knickers to match' – would give way to something more sophisticated: a hemline below the knees, silk stockings in place of white cotton ankle socks, a beret instead of a winter bonnet or a summer straw hat. Lilibet and Margaret Rose, who, according to Crawfie, 'were never in the least interested in what they were going to wear and just put on what they were told', no longer appeared, automatically, in matching outfits. The child was giving way to the young adult.

Was she a moody adolescent? 'No,' said Patricia Mountbatten. 'Far from it,' said Margaret Rhodes. 'She was always very controlled – or, should I say, in control?'

Countess Mountbatten said, 'The Queen told me recently that she had been quite nervous of me when we were in the Guides together and she was my second-in-command. That surprised me, but, of course, she has always been guarded about her feelings. Even as a girl, she was careful how she appeared in front of others. For example, if she fell and hurt herself she knew she mustn't be seen to cry.' 'Only once,' according to Crawfie, 'did she walk right into my arms, thinking of nothing but that for the moment she had to have a little comforting . . . "Oh, Crawfie, Grandfather Strathmore is dead," she said, and burst into tears.'

Like her father and, to an even greater extent, her royal grandparents, King George and Queen Mary, Princess Elizabeth was not given to public displays of emotion. She was, from an early age, self-controlled, self-contained, self-sufficient. Was that healthy? We might not think so, living as we do in the let-it-all-hang-out twenty-first century, but things were very different eighty and more years ago. The 'stiff upper lip' wasn't a joke then: it was a much-vaunted national characteristic. Lilibet was a Girl Guide[35] and the daughter of a king – and of a king of England, too.

Besides, as Margaret Rhodes pointed out to me, she had an outlet for her emotions. She might stand, as, by her own account, she did, for hours, gazing out of the window of Buckingham Palace, 'watching the people and the cars there in the Mall', saying little, but wondering 'what they were doing and where they were all going, and what they thought about outside the Palace'. But, then, she could scamper off and play with the corgis and the labradors – with Dookie and Spark, Flash and Mimsey, Scruffy and Stiffy – or go for a ride on Peggy or Comet. Margaret Rhodes stubbed out yet another cigarette and pondered, 'Perhaps she didn't repress her feelings. Perhaps she channelled them through her animals. Dogs are faithful. And they don't tell tales. I don't know. All I do know is that the real love of her life, then, as now, was dogs, followed by horses.'

The real-life Christopher Robin, who had become a character in a story book in the year that Princess Elizabeth was born, blamed his troubled adolescence on his parents and on the global fame attached to his name as a consequence of his father's four best-selling

---

35 The Boy Scouts and Girl Guides movement was founded by Robert Baden-Powell (1857–1941). On 4 July 1911, in a letter to a friend, he wrote: 'I know my weak points and am only thankful that I have managed to get along in spite of them! I think that's the policy for this world: Be glad of what you have got, and not miserable about what you would like to have had, and not over-anxious about what the future will bring.' This is the Queen's philosophy to this day.

children's books. He later accused A.A. Milne of 'building his reputation by standing on a small boy's shoulders'. Princess Elizabeth,
like Christopher Robin, received sackfuls of post from unknown
admirers. Like Christopher Robin, she was photographed, written
about, and featured in newspapers and magazines around the world.
He, in effigy, appeared, with Pooh, in the window of Selfridges
department store in Oxford Street. She appeared, with her pony, as
a waxwork at Madame Tussaud's exhibition in Marylebone Road.
Unlike Christopher Robin, however, Elizabeth did not grumble: she
accepted her lot.

And it was a bizarre lot to have to accept. Aged eleven, when she
was taken to a children's matinée at the Holborn Empire, as she
entered the auditorium, fifteen hundred children got to their feet
and sang a specially written children's verse of the national anthem.
Aged twelve, she was attending the Buckingham Palace Garden
Parties, walking dutifully behind her parents through a throng of
three thousand excited subjects, who bowed and curtsied as she
passed. Aged thirteen, she accepted her first official post: as President
of the Children's League of the Princess Elizabeth of York Hospital,
which had been named after her. From birth, she had been a public
figure: now, she had increasingly to become accustomed to public
life, to exposure to public gaze, to being – literally – the centre of
attention.

Princess Elizabeth was blessed with parents who were loving –
and united. Prince Philip's parents lived apart from each other and
Philip did not live with either of them. In November 1937 Philip,
aged sixteen, saw Andrea and Alice together for the first time in six
years – and for the last time ever. That was when the family gathered
in Darmstadt for the heartbreaking business of the funeral of Philip's
sister Cécile and her husband and two of their three children, all
killed in the aeroplane accident on their way to a cousin's wedding.
Kurt Hahn, Philip's headmaster at Gordonstoun, broke the news of
the tragic accident to the sixteen-year-old boy, who took it on board
with stoical calm. 'His sorrow,' according to Hahn, 'was that of a
man.' Andrea, understandably, was devastated by the deaths: Cécile
had been his favourite daughter. Of the parents, it seems Alice coped
the better. Her sister Louise (now married to the King of Sweden)
said Alice was 'so balanced & so splendid about her sorrow'.

Alice appeared to have regained some of her old equilibrium. She was even ready to consider the possibility of living with her husband once more. That was not a prospect Andrea was willing to entertain. He returned to the south of France and the singular life of a displaced prince. He moved between Monte Carlo and Nice, between hotel rooms and the yachts of friends. He drank, he charmed, he reminisced. At a distance, he followed the complexities of Greek politics. When he could, he visited relations. At the beginning of 1938 he asked Philip to join him on an expedition to Athens to attend the wedding of Crown Prince Paul of Greece and Princess Frederika of Hanover.

Cécile's youngest child, her baby daughter Johanna, had been too small to take on the fatal flight in November 1937. She died, nonetheless, aged barely two, of a fever, in June 1939. Alice, who was at her little granddaughter's deathbed, wrote to Philip: '. . . we had such a sweet picture before our eyes of a lovely sleeping child with golden curls, looking for me so very like Cécile at that age that it was like losing my child a second time and I was thankful that Papa was away travelling and did not see that, for Papa adored Cécile when she was small and could never bear to be parted from her.' This was the month in which Philip turned eighteen. His mother, having disappeared from his life throughout his adolescence, was in touch with her boy once more. A week later she wrote to him again: 'I am quite exhausted by the strain and the sadness of it all.'

The Yorks, undoubtedly, were more conventional parents. Inevitably, as King and Queen, however, they saw less of their daughters than they would have liked. In the summer of 1938, with the clouds of war gathering across Europe, Lilibet and Margaret Rose were left at home as Papa and Mama undertook their first foreign assignment: a state visit to France intended to reinforce the Entente Cordiale. In May 1939, with war now imminent (despite Chamberlain's determination to secure peace), the King and Queen were dispatched on a longer and more ambitious expedition: to Canada and the United States. The American President, Franklin Roosevelt, invited the Princesses along for the ride. 'I shall try to have one or two Roosevelts of approximately the same age to play with them!' he promised.

In the event, the girls were left at home, perhaps wisely. The tour proved arduous and the transatlantic crossing, on board the *Empress of Australia*, potentially perilous. Off the coast of Newfoundland, the fog was treacherous. The Queen reported by letter to her mother-in-law, Queen Mary: 'For three & a half days we only moved a few miles. The fog was so thick, that it was like a white cloud round the ship, and the foghorn blew incessantly . . . We were nearly hit by a berg the day before yesterday, and the poor Captain was nearly demented because some kind cheerful people kept on reminding him that it was about here that the Titanic was struck, & *just* about the same date.'

George VI and Queen Elizabeth were the first reigning British monarchs to visit North America and their tour was a triumph. Even in Quebec, the cry went up: '*Vive le Roi! Vive la Reine!*' The Governor-General of Canada was Lord Tweedsmuir (better remembered as the novelist John Buchan), who chaperoned the King and Queen for much of the Canadian leg of the tour and drafted the text of the King's principal speeches. For Tweedsmuir, the most telling moment came at the unveiling of a war memorial in Ottawa: 'The King spoke admirably and clearly, as he has done each time since he landed. After the ceremony the Queen said to me that she wanted to go down among the veterans, and I thought, knowing what excellent fellows they are, that it would be worth chancing it. A most extraordinary scene followed. The King and Queen, and my wife and myself, were absorbed in a crowd of six or seven thousand ex-soldiers, who kept the most perfect order among themselves, and opened up lanes for Their Majesties to pass through. There was no need of the police, and indeed the police would have had no chance. It was a wonderful example of what a people's king means . . . One old man shouted to me, "Ay, man, if Hitler could see this!" It was extraordinarily moving because some of these old fellows were weeping . . . The capacity of Their Majesties for getting in touch with the people amounts to genius.'

Tweedsmuir was smitten. The King was a 'wonderful mixture' of 'shrewdness, kindliness and humour': 'He is simply one of the best people in the world. I never thought that I should feel the romantic affection for my sovereign that I felt for him.' The Queen 'has a kind of gentle, steady radiance which is very wonderful' and 'a perfect genius for the right kind of publicity, the unrehearsed episodes here were marvellous'. When he had dried his eyes and cleared his throat, the Governor-General reported to the British Prime Minister, 'The Statute of Westminster is now much more than a mere piece of paper, for we have been given a visual revelation of its meaning.' Henry Marten, Lilibet's tutor, would have been gratified.

The King and Queen were as rapturously received in the United States. They took to the President. 'He is so easy to get to know,' wrote the King, '& never makes one feel shy.' Roosevelt was equally charmed, and impressed – and possibly a little surprised – to find his British guests quite knowledgeable 'not only about foreign affairs in general but also about social legislation'. 'The British sovereigns have conquered Washington,' said the *New York Times*. Crowds turned out to cheer and an initially sniffy press was quickly won over. The misty-eyed Lord Tweedsmuir murmured to His Majesty, 'It is a pleasant saying in the United States at the moment that you have taken the "g" out of kingship.' The King himself, whose confidence grew as the tour proceeded, learnt from the experience. 'There must be no more high-hat business,' he reflected during the tour, 'the sort of thing that my father and those of his day regarded as essential as the correct attitude – the feeling that certain things could not be done.'

The royal couple returned to England on 22 June 1939. The imminence of war, combined with glowing coverage of the tour in the British press, ensured a properly patriotic and heart-tuggingly warm welcome home. Lilibet and Margaret Rose had not seen their parents for seven weeks.[36] The girls, accompanied by Alah and Crawfie, travelled by train to Southampton. There they were taken, by destroyer, to meet their parents' ship mid-Channel. While Crawfie and the Princesses ate cherries with the captain on deck, Alah retreated to a cabin ('I think she was not feeling very well,' Crawfie reported, lips pursed). At last, 'The *Empress of India* came in sight and we went

36 The matter of these royal separations bravely borne needs to be kept in perspective. At the time, it was not unusual for middle- and upper-class girls and boys of this age (nine and thirteen) to be away at boarding school for twelve-week terms. There was a half-term 'exeat', but the children of diplomats, serving soldiers and the like often did not see their parents for months at a time – and survived. In my dormitory at my prep school, in the 1960s, I recall that Bowden (aged seven) cried himself to sleep in a quite pitiful manner – but only for the first few nights of term.

below to tidy. The Captain's cabin amused us, with its, to us, almost primitive amenities.' Back on deck, they saw the *Empress* 'heaving to' and the King and Queen amidships. 'The little girls could hardly walk up the ladder quickly enough,' recalled Crawfie, 'but when they reached the top they rushed to Mummie and Papa. They kissed them and hugged them again and again . . . The Queen kissed me and said how much the children had grown and how well they looked, and all the time the King could hardly take his eyes off Lilibet.'

In the ship's dining room happiness reigned. There was much merriment, and balloons and bunting, too. The King pushed some of the balloons through a porthole. Lord Airlie popped some of them with his cigarette. Champagne cocktails were served and Crawfie got a little squiffy. We can imagine what Alah thought. We are told the Queen said, 'Poor Crawfie, I ought to have warned you. They make them rather strong aboard.'

There was rejoicing in the streets as well. From Southampton to Waterloo, all along the railway route, Their Majesties' subjects turned out to cheer. From Waterloo to Buckingham Palace, the King and Queen travelled home in state. According to police estimates, some fifty thousand people crowded into the Mall to salute them, the men raising their caps and bowler hats (and furled umbrellas) in greeting, the women and children waving flags and handkerchiefs. As the royal carriage passed through Parliament Square, MPs of every party came out of the House of Commons to watch the parade. 'Such fun,' Harold Nicolson reported to his wife, Vita Sackville-West. 'The bells of St Margaret's began to swing into welcome and the procession started creeping round the corner. They went very slowly, and there were the King and Queen and the two Princesses. We lost all our dignity and yelled and yelled. The King wore a happy schoolboy grin. The Queen was superb. She really does manage to convey to each individual in the crowd that he or she have had a personal greeting. It is due, I think, to the brilliance of her eyes.[37] But she is in truth one of the most amazing Queens since Cleopatra. We returned to the House with lumps in our throats.'

37 And, I think, to the way she let them rest, however momentarily, upon you. She didn't appear to be scanning the crowd. The way she nodded her head, as well as her wave, added to the effect that she was looking directly at 'you. It was, of course, an illusion, but, as Houdini pointed out, 'That's the nature of magic.'

The King and Queen were riding high. To date, this was their finest hour. Perhaps it needed to be: it was the prelude, after all, to Britain's darkest hour. War was looming. There was a whiff of romance in the air as well. On 22 July, exactly a month after their triumphal return from America, and five weeks and a day before the declaration of war on 3 September, the King and his family and their entourage – Crawfie and Alah and all – set off for a brief excursion on the Royal Yacht *Victoria & Albert*. Their first port of call – part duty, part pleasure – was along the Devon coast, at the mouth of the estuary of the River Dart, at Dartmouth, at the Royal Naval College, where the King – a cadet at the College in the years before the Great War – was to carry out an inspection, and Princess Elizabeth, aged thirteen, was to meet Prince Philip of Greece, aged eighteen. Lilibet later claimed it was love at first sight.

Chapter Six

'He had never kissed me, and I wondered whether he would.'
Vita Sackville-West (1892–1962), *Portrait of a Marriage*

'How do you do?'

He was standing over her, looking gently amused. He was tall and slim, blond and blue-eyed, and his dark blue naval uniform suited him. He was eighteen and achingly handsome.

'I'm quite well,' she said. 'Thank you.' She was sitting on the floor, her knees tucked under her, leaning over the track of a toy railway set, trying to make an engine stand steady on the rolling stock.

'You haven't had mumps then?' he asked. He seemed to be half-laughing as he spoke. She sensed he was teasing her, but she did not mind.

'No,' she said, 'But Papa – the King – he had the mumps when he was a cadet here. He said we should be careful. He says it's really horrid.'

Philip nodded, slowly. 'Yes, beastly. I know one of the chaps who's got it now. He's having a rotten time.' Her brow furrowed. She was trying to look sympathetic. He thought she was anxious. He smiled. It was a kindly smile. 'Don't worry,' he said, 'I'm not contagious.' He crouched down beside her and took the engine out of her hand. 'Let me.'

'Thank you,' she said, again.

'To be honest,' he said, when they had watched the small train rattle around the track four times more, 'I don't see you as a clockwork-railway sort of girl. Do you fancy a game of tennis?'

She looked uncertain. 'I haven't got—'

He interrupted: 'Of course not.' He got to his feet. 'But we could jump the nets or something. Or we could play croquet. Do you play croquet? It's a filthy game. Vicious. Shall we play croquet?'

'Yes,' she said, smiling. 'I'd like that.'

He took her right hand in his and pulled her to her feet. 'Come on,' he said. 'Let's go.'

Well, dear reader, it might have been like that. Who knows? When I asked him he said he couldn't remember much about it, and I don't think you will find her very forthcoming (even if you have the courage to ask her), and all the other witnesses are long since dead.

What we do know is this. Prince Philip of Greece, fresh out of Gordonstoun, just turned eighteen, apparently very engaging (there is evidence), certainly very handsome (there are photographs), was undoubtedly at the Royal Naval College, Dartmouth, on the weekend of 22–23 July 1939. He was coming to the end of his three-month initial officers' training course. He was not a traditional Dartmouth cadet. They came to the College at thirteen and stayed for five years. Philip was a Special Entry recruit. These were public school boys, who joined up at eighteen, and would normally begin their naval careers on a training cruiser. However, in anticipation of war, HMS *Frobisher*, the cruiser in which Philip would have expected to train, was being refitted and rearmed, hence the presence of Philip – and the other 'Specials' – at Dartmouth.

We know, too, that on Saturday, 22 July, the day *Victoria & Albert* arrived at Dartmouth, Philip was invited to join the royal party. It is hardly surprising, since he was a cousin of the King, and his uncle, Louis Mountbatten, was in attendance on board the Royal Yacht. On 22 July, Mountbatten noted in his diary: 'Philip accompanied us and dined on board.' The next day he reported: 'Philip came back aboard V and A for tea and was a great success with the children.'

It seems Philip entertained them ashore as well. According to the ever-present Crawfie, 'On the Sunday morning we were going to the College because there was to be a special service . . . I remember it was a lovely day, though it became a bit cloudy around eleven. Just about the time the service was scheduled to start and the boys had been paraded before the King and Queen, the Dartmouth College doctor said, "I am very, very sorry, but two of the boys have developed mumps." There was a long conversation as to whether the children ought to go into the chapel . . .'

Eventually, it was decided – 'better safe than sorry' – that Crawfie should take the girls across to the Captain's House and that Prince Philip would be detailed to entertain them. Lilibet and Margaret Rose were busy playing with the captain's children's train set when Philip appeared. 'A fair-haired boy, rather like a Viking, with a sharp face and piercing blue eyes,' is how Crawfie remembered him. 'He was good-looking, though rather off-hand in his manner. He said, "How do you do," to Lilibet, and for a while they knelt side by side playing with the trains. He soon got bored with that. We had ginger crackers and lemonade, in which he joined, and then he said, "Let's go to the tennis courts and have some real fun jumping the nets."'

Off they went, chaperoned by Crawfie. 'I thought he showed off a good deal,' she recalled, eleven years after the event, 'but the little girls were much impressed. Lilibet said, "How good he is, Crawfie. How high he can jump." She never took her eyes off him the whole time. He was quite polite to her, but did not pay her any special attention. He spent a lot of time teasing plump little Margaret.'

How much of this happened in fact and how much in Crawfie's imagination, it is impossible to say. There are, however, in existence two photographs taken that weekend, each featuring Philip and Elizabeth, and each telling its own story. The first is a snapshot of the two of them alone playing croquet in the garden of the Captain's House. The focus of the picture seems to be ships moored in the Dart estuary, but in the foreground, glimpsed behind a parapet, are the two teenagers. The eighteen-year-old boy appears to be concentrating on his next stroke. The thirteen-year-old girl, standing by a hoop, in her neat double-breasted summer coat, small hands clasped together in front of her, is gazing at him intently. She does look happy.

The other photograph shows the entire royal party watching the cadets on parade. Sitting in the front row, staring somewhat vacantly into the middle distance, is Lilibet. She is wearing a solemn expression and what looks like a beret to match her coat. She seems very young. Three places along, seated next to a tiny Princess Margaret (who doesn't look plump at all), is the Queen, wearing a fabulous hat and chatting graciously to the captain. Standing immediately behind them, side by side, are Louis Mountbatten and Prince Philip. Mountbatten is looking amused and avuncular. Philip is leaning forward, grinning, gesticulating with his right hand: he is, without doubt, in the middle of telling a funny story. He has the unmistakable look of a charming young man who is often in the middle of telling a funny story.

That weekend the boy certainly made his mark. When the time came for *Victoria & Albert* to set sail, permission was given to the cadets to commandeer what vessels they could – rowing-boats, motor-boats, dinghies – and take to the estuary to give the royal visitors a memorable send-off. As the Royal Yacht made her stately progress out of the harbour she was escorted by a veritable flotilla of small craft manned by enthusiastic young men. 'They followed the *Victoria & Albert* quite a long way,' according to Crawfie, who was on deck with the royal party. 'Then the King got very alarmed and said to Sir Dudley North [the Commander of the Royal Yacht], "It's ridiculous, and most unsafe. You must signal them to go back." Most of the boys did go back immediately, and all the others followed shortly except this one solitary figure whom we saw rowing away as hard as he could, who was, of course, Philip. Lilibet took the glasses and had a long look at him. In the end the King said, "The young fool. He must go back, otherwise we will have to heave to and send him back." At last Philip seemed to realise they did want him to go back – they were shouting at him through the megaphone – and he turned back while we gazed at him until he became just a very small speck in the distance.'

Prince Philip told me that the story, as told by Crawfie, is somewhat exaggerated – the small boats only followed the Royal Yacht for a few hundred yards, then turned round and went home – but he does not deny the essence of it. And nor, I understand, would the Queen deny the essence of it either: that was the weekend when she fell for Philip.

And why not? He was enviably good-looking. He was fit.[38] He was fun. He was funny. At this stage in the story, Louis Mountbatten

---

38 In 2001, at the Royal Variety Performance, I told Prince Philip that a beautiful young pop singer called Myleene Klass (a member of the fleetingly famous band Hear'Say and subsequently a model for Marks & Spencer) had told me that she regarded him as 'right fit' – meaning physically attractive. He was intrigued by the phrase and pleased with the news. He watched his figure: even in old age, he cared about his appearance.

– Uncle Dickie – did not know Philip that well. Through his teens, because he sometimes stayed with him during the school holidays, Philip had been much more under the wing of his other Mountbatten uncle, Dickie's elder brother, Georgie, 2nd Marquess of Milford Haven, the father of David, Philip's best friend at school and later, at his wedding, his best man.

Georgie had died of cancer on 8 April 1938, aged only forty-five, mourned by all who knew him. Dickie wrote in his diary that day: 'The sweetest natured, most charming, most able, most brilliant, entirely lovable brother anyone ever had is lost. Heartbroken.' Gina Kennard, who was nineteen at the time, and whose mother's sister was married to Georgie, told me, 'You couldn't not love Georgie. Everybody adored him. I remember as a girl sitting under the dining-room table, hidden under the table cloth, thinking how lovely he was. Princess Elizabeth told me she loved him, too. His death was another blow for Philip, especially coming, as it did, only a matter of months after his sister Cécile and her family were killed in that awful air crash. It was a difficult time.'

On Georgie's death, Dickie, aged thirty-eight, with only daughters himself, assumed the role of Philip's informal guardian. The month before, in March 1938, Dickie had already had him to stay at Adsdean, the Mountbattens' country house just outside Portsmouth. 'Philip was here all last week doing his entrance exams for the Navy,' Dickie reported to his wife. 'He had his meals with us and he really is killingly funny. I like him very much.'

Prince Philip dismissed the suggestion when I put it to him, but I get the impression of a young man who felt some obligation to sing for his supper. He was handsome, engaging, well mannered. He was also homeless. And, by royal standards, virtually penniless. 'Rubbish,' he said. When he wasn't at boarding school, he stayed with his grandmother (Princess Victoria of Hesse, widow of Louis of Battenberg, 1st Marquess of Milford Haven) in her grace-and-favour apartment at Kensington, or with one of his English uncles, or, until the prospect of war made it impossible, with one of his sisters and their German husbands. He would accept that his parents weren't rich, but 'you could hardly call them poor'. By this time, his father, Prince Andrea, had managed to get some funds out of Greece and Russia and gave Philip a small allowance when he joined the navy. His mother, Princess Alice, now received nothing from Andrea, and depended on an allowance from the ever-generous banking heiress, Edwina Mountbatten.[39] 'We weren't well off,' said Prince Philip, 'but I don't remember wanting for anything.'

While he chose not to complain about any aspect of his upbringing, he did not argue with the fact that from the age of ten or so, until he married Princess Elizabeth when he was twenty-six, he did not have one fixed address. 'Whither the storm carries me, I go,' he wrote in a visitors' book at the beginning of 1946, '– a willing guest.'

And a welcome one. He had the glamour and energy of youth. He was funny. He had an engaging and memorable laugh. He was articulate and he was no fool. When he took the entrance examination to get into Dartmouth he came sixteenth out of thirty-four. At the College, his written work was no more than average, but in the oral exam, he scored 380 out of a potential 400 marks. At Gordonstoun he had become head boy. At Dartmouth he was awarded the King's Dirk as the best all-round cadet of his entry. He had leadership qualities and ambition. He strove to live up to the ideal of manhood set out in Kipling's famous poem. Certainly, he 'walked with kings' without losing 'the common touch'. While studying for the Dartmouth entrance exam, he stayed, as a paying guest, with a Mr and Mrs Mercer in Cheltenham. By day, Mr Mercer prepared young men for their naval examinations. By night, according to Philip's cousin and exact contemporary, Queen Alexandra of Yugoslavia, Mr Mercer's teenage daughter entertained the student prince to 'radio or record sessions' in the family sitting room. Alexandra also recalled Philip enjoying a holiday dalliance in Venice at about the same time. 'He was very amusing, gay, full of life and energy and he was a tease,' she said.

---

39 She was the daughter of Wilfrid Ashley MP (a grandson of the great Earl of Shaftesbury) and Maud Cassel, the only daughter of Sir Ernest Cassel, the banker known as 'Windsor Cassel' because of his role as financial adviser to Edward VII when he was Prince of Wales. Cassel's wife died in 1880. Maud died in 1911. Edwina came to live with her grandfather at Brook House in Mayfair when she was just seventeen. When he died, Edwina inherited some £2.3 million. When Cassel's sister's died, Edwina inherited Brook House and yet more money. When her father died, she also inherited Broadlands, near Romsey in Hampshire, where she and Dickie started their honeymoon in 1922 and Philip and Elizabeth theirs in 1947. Edwina was remarkable: bedazzling, promiscuous, generous, wild.

It is frequently asserted that Saturday, 22 July 1939 was the day on which Philip and Elizabeth first set eyes on each other. 'Not so,' Prince Philip told me. 'It's one of those myths that's just too good to let go. The journalists never like to let the facts get in the way of a good story, do they? But we'd certainly met before. We were cousins, after all.' In Queen Victoria and Prince Albert, Philip and Elizabeth had the same great-great-grandparents. In Queen Alexandra, the wife of Edward VII, they had the same great-aunt. 'We came from different parts of the same family.'

As a small child Philip was taken to tea at Buckingham Palace with Queen Mary, who considered him 'a nice little boy with very blue eyes'. His mother was born at Windsor Castle. His grandmother lived at Kensington Palace. His father, Prince Andrea, had been an aide-de-camp to Queen Victoria, Edward VII, and King George V. At his prep school, Philip had a framed photograph of the King-Emperor, signed 'From Uncle George'. (He did not flaunt it: it was spotted, hidden in his trunk, by a dorm mate.)

Prince Philip told me that he and Princess Elizabeth certainly met – aged thirteen and eight – at Westminster Abbey on 29 November 1934, when his cousin, Princess Marina of Greece and Denmark, married Lilibet's Uncle George, Duke of Kent. 'We might have met before that.' They certainly met again at the Coronation of George VI in 1937. What distinguishes their meeting in July 1939, of course, is not Philip's attitude to Elizabeth – he was interested in girls, girls of his own age, not thirteen-year-olds – but hers to him. In *The Power and the Glory*, Graham Greene says, 'There is always one moment in childhood when the door opens and lets the future in.'

Through her field glasses on the deck of *Victoria & Albert* Lilibet may have gazed at Philip in his rowing boat until he disappeared from view, but romance was some way off. There was a war to contend with first.

At the beginning of August 1939 the Prime Minister, Neville Chamberlain, convinced that war was not, in fact, imminent, set off for a spot of salmon fishing. (Salmon fishing had long been a Chamberlain priority. Declining the office of Chancellor in May 1923, he wrote: 'What a day! Two salmon this morning and the offer of the Exchequer this afternoon.') On 6 August the King, who liked and trusted a good hunting and fishing man, set off for Balmoral for his customary family holiday. The grouse were expected to be particularly good that year.

On 9 August duty called, and the King came down briefly from Scotland to inspect the Reserve Fleet at Weymouth and, after the event, reported to his mother, Queen Mary, 'I feel sure it will be a deterrent factor in Hitler's mind to start a war.'

On 22 August news came that Germany and Russia had signed the Nazi-Soviet Pact. On 24 August Parliament was recalled and the King returned to London. The grouse had been magnificent. On 29 August he told a British ambassador who called at Buckingham Palace that he had never seen so many grouse, that he had bagged 1,600 brace in six days, that it was 'utterly damnable that the villain Hitler had upset everything'. Happily, now that Britain had signed a formal treaty of alliance with Poland, he was convinced there would be peace and that 'this time Hitler's bluff had been called'. Unhappily, His Majesty was mistaken.

On 1 September German troops crossed the Polish border. On 2 September Britain and France issued an ultimatum to Germany: withdraw or face war. A deadline was set of 11 a.m. on Sunday, 3 September. Germany failed to respond with the undertakings demanded. The Second World War was under way.

'Who *is* this Hitler, spoiling everything?' demanded Princess Margaret. 'I remember trying to give the Princess a painstaking and unbiased character sketch,' said Crawfie, 'but it wasn't very easy.' The King and Queen were now based at Buckingham Palace, staying at Windsor Castle overnight and at weekends. Margaret and Lilibet remained in Scotland, at Birkhall on the Balmoral estate, with Alah and Bobo and Crawfie. 'Why had Mummie and Papa to go back, Crawfie?' asked Margaret. 'Do you think the Germans will come and get them?' Crawfie was predictably reassuring and Lilibet, apparently, 'was very calm and helpful, as usual, and at once ranged herself on the side of law and order'. 'I don't think people should talk about battles and things in front of Margaret,' she said. 'We don't want to upset her.'

The Princesses' parents telephoned their daughters every night at six o'clock. 'Stick to the usual programme as far as you can, Crawfie' was the Queen's instruction. 'Up there among the moors and heather it was easy to do this,' said Crawfie. 'The River Muick rippled merrily through the gardens just as usual in those lovely autumn days, while Poland was being over-run and "lights were going out all over Europe".'

Now and then the horrors of war managed to penetrate the peace of the Highlands. The children listened to the wireless. They heard the anti-British propaganda broadcasts made by William Joyce, the notorious 'Lord Haw-Haw', and threw books and cushions at the wireless set in protest. On 14 October they heard the news of the sinking of *Royal Oak* at Scapa Flow with the loss of more than eight hundred lives. 'Lilibet jumped horrified from her chair,' according to Crawfie, 'her eyes blazing with anger . . . "Crawfie, it can't be! All those nice sailors."'

On 18 December, to their surprise and delight, they were summoned to Norfolk to join their parents for the traditional Royal Family Christmas at Sandringham. They did not know what the future would hold. No one did. They listened to their father as he made his Christmas Day broadcast, live, seated in front of two large microphones, dressed in the uniform of an Admiral of the Fleet. The hesitancy with which he spoke – at one point having to start a passage again from the beginning – made what he had to say all the more moving:

'A new year is at hand. We cannot tell what it will bring. If it brings peace, how thankful we shall be. If it brings continued struggle we shall remain undaunted. In the meantime I feel that we may all find a message of encouragement in the lines which, in my closing words, I should like to say to you:

'"I said to the man who stood at the Gate of the Year, 'Give me a light that I may tread safely into the unknown.' And he replied, 'Go out into the darkness, and put your hand into the Hand of God. That shall be better than light, and safer than a known way.'"

'May that Almighty Hand guide and uphold us all.'

The King's children were moved by what they heard. So were the British people. The poem the King had quoted was by a Gloucestershire-born poet and academic, Minnie Louise Haskins, and it first appeared in a collection called *The Desert* in 1908. It was Lilibet who gave the book to her father and it has remained a favourite with her throughout her life. She had the words of the poem engraved on brass plaques and fixed to the gates of the King

George VI Memorial Chapel at Windsor Castle, where her father was interred in 1952 and, fifty years later, the poem was read out at the funeral of her mother, Queen Elizabeth.

George VI had a good war. At first he was frustrated. 'I wish I had a definite job like you,' he wrote to Louis Mountbatten, now captain of HMS *Kelly* and commander of the 5th Destroyer Flotilla. 'Mine is such an awful mixture, trying to keep people cheered up in all ways, and having to find fault as well as praising them.' He was a constitutional monarch: his lot was to advise, counsel, and warn the government of the day. He was Head of State and Commander-in-Chief of the Armed Forces: his role was to look the part, to lead by example, to *be* rather than to *do*. He delivered in full measure. He wore his uniform throughout the war. He paraded, he saluted, he inspected, he handed out medals whenever and wherever was required. When rationing was introduced, he made it clear that he and his family expected – wanted – to share the privations of the people.

And when, in September 1940, Buckingham Palace was bombed, it was akin to a blessing in disguise. 'The King & I saw 2 of the bombs drop quite close to us in the quadrangle,' the Queen wrote to Osbert Sitwell. 'They screamed past the window and exploded with a tremendous boom and crash about fifteen yards away. We both thought we were dead, & nipped quickly into the passage, where we found our two pages crouching on the floor. They rose at once & we then descended to the basement, pretending really that it was nothing.' It was quite something: the King and Queen were in the firing line and seen to be. As the Queen remarked, famously, after the bombing, 'Now I feel I can look the East End in the face.' 'Thank God for a good King,' someone shouted in the street as the sovereign inspected the damage done by yet another enemy air raid. 'Thank God for a good people,' the King replied.

George VI and his family knew, liked, and trusted Neville Chamberlain. When, in May 1940, he resigned as Prime Minister they were much distressed. After his farewell broadcast, the Queen wrote to him: 'My eldest daughter told me, that she and Margaret Rose had listened to it with real emotion – In fact she said "I *cried*, mummy."' Later, the King wrote to Chamberlain, now dying from cancer: 'You were my Prime Minister in the earliest years of my reign, & I shall ever be grateful to you for your help & guidance during what was in many ways a difficult period.' The Queen was unequivocal: 'How deeply I regretted your ceasing to be our Prime Minister.' The King was more circumspect: 'I have sympathised with you very much in seeing your hopes shattered by the lust & violence of a single man.' He was not referring to Winston Churchill – although the King shared Chamberlain's reservations about the arch-opponent of appeasement. Churchill, after all, wasn't just a maverick: he had also been one of Edward VIII's staunchest allies at the time of the Abdication. The King – whose constitutional duty it was to invite the parliamentarian best placed to form an administration to do so – would have liked to see Lord Halifax, the Foreign Secretary, as Chamberlain's successor, but he bowed to the inevitable. 'There was only one person whom I could send for who had the confidence of the country,' he noted in his diary, '& that was Winston.'

At first their relationship was uneasy: at best, joshing; at worst, strained. In time, as they got to know each other better and to recognise each other's strengths, they became close comrades. When, five years later, on VE Day, 8 May 1945, they stood together on the balcony at Buckingham Palace, they did so as firm friends, conscious that each, in his own way, had played his part in the victory. Churchill's task, no doubt, had been infinitely more complex, challenging, and significant, but the King's contribution – as a sounding board, as a figurehead, as a focus for national unity – was also key.

It was George VI who first described the House of Windsor as 'the family firm'. It helped that – while, yes, they lived in castles and palaces and were surrounded by flummery and flunkies – there were only four of them, and they seemed . . . well, almost ordinary. The King's shyness, diffidence, and stammer served to underline his decency. The Queen's charm was simply irresistible. She wasn't slim and chic and brittle (as 'Queen Wallis' would have been): she was soft and round, regal yet real, classy but comfortable and comforting. And the two girls – moving slowly through adolescence but still, mostly, seen dressed in matching outfits – looked to be model daughters: quite unspoilt and thoroughly wholesome.

Lilibet and Margaret Rose lived through the war years at Windsor Castle. They arrived at the beginning of May 1940, as the Germans began their assault on Belgium and the Netherlands, and France prepared to fall, thinking they were to be there for a few days. They remained for five years. Where they were was an official secret. Press and public were simply informed that the royal children had been evacuated to 'a house in the country'. Some in government – fearful that they might be captured by the Nazis and used as hostages – wanted them evacuated to Canada. Churchill was opposed to the idea. So was the King.

Crawfie painted a lurid picture of the Princesses' arrival at the ancient castle 'in the gathering twilight of that May evening': 'We were tired, and it was very gloomy. Pictures had been removed, and all the beautiful glass chandeliers had been taken down. The State Apartments were muffled in dust-sheets, the glass-fronted cupboards turned to the walls. About the stone passages the shadowy figures of servants and foremen loomed, attending to the black-out. I remember one old man remarking to me dryly: "By the time we've blacked out all the windows here, it's morning again, miss." The two little girls clung to me apprehensively. Alah, as always when she was bothered or anxious, was cross.'

The Queen's recollection of her war years at Windsor is rather different from Crawfie's. 'Windsor Castle was a fortress,' said Crawfie, 'not a home.' To the Queen it was a home, and still is, and a favourite home, too. It is frustrating to Her Majesty that, simply because Crawfie wrote a book, every account of her childhood is seen, in part, from her governess's perspective. Emotionally, Lilibet was closer to Alah and to Bobo than to Crawfie. And, perhaps, closer still to Jane and Crackers and Carol and Susan and Ching – some of the dogs – and Jock and Hans, two of the ponies. If, today, you talk to the Queen about the war, she won't mention Crawfie, but she will talk, happily, about her animals.

From 1938 she was taking formal riding lessons from the royal instructor, Horace Smith. She learnt to ride side-saddle. She was introduced to carriage driving. In 1943 and 1944, driving her own pony and cart, she won first prize in the Royal Windsor Horse Show. In 1942 the King took her up on to the Wiltshire Downs, to the Beckhampton Stables, to watch the royal racehorses being trained. She visited the royal stud at Hampton Court. She went to Newmarket to see more royal racehorses in training. In 1943, aged seventeen, she first rode to hounds. She still spent several hours each day closeted with Crawfie, conscientiously learning her lessons – and, twice a week, taking instruction on English history and the British constitution from Sir Henry Marten, who came up to the Castle in his dog-cart – but, undoubtedly, during these years, she was most alive, most at ease, most happy, with her dogs and her horses, the sustaining passions of her life.

These adolescent years were also the ones during which another, quite different, sustaining force took a lifelong hold on the young Princess. On 1 March 1942, when she was not quite sixteen, Lilibet was confirmed and took her first communion. Her father was Supreme Governor of the Church of England, but not just in name. In his most celebrated broadcast, at the beginning of the war, he had said, 'I believe from my heart that the cause which binds together my peoples and our gallant and faithful Allies is the cause of Christian civilisation.' His daughter believed it, too. At his Coronation – and hers – at the heart of the service, the sovereign is given a copy of the Holy Bible, with the words: 'We present you with this Book, the most valuable thing that this world affords. Here is wisdom; this is the royal Law; these are the lively Oracles of God.' The Queen, not as a matter of form, but as a matter of faith, says 'Amen' to that.

So, Lilibet was a teenage girl who played with her dogs, groomed her ponies, said her prayers, and lived in a castle. She had friends: cousins and the children of courtiers. She had dancing lessons on Saturday mornings with Miss Vacani, dancing mistress to the gentry.[40] She continued with the Girl Guides and became leader of her patrol. For four consecutive Christmases she and Margaret Rose appeared in quite elaborate Christmas pantomimes, produced by a master from the local Church of England school and featuring neighbourhood

40 Betty Vacani died on 21 August 2003, aged ninety-five. Princess Elizabeth greatly valued all she learnt from her, and, in due course, invited her to give a weekly class at Buckingham Palace for Prince Charles, Princess Anne and several children of the royal household. Miss Vacani was a passionate teacher and a particular favourite with the Royal Family because, unlike Crawfie, she was wonderfully discreet. She did reveal that Prince Charles was a particular favourite with her because of his seriousness and his commitment to the Highland Fling, but when asked about the abilities of Lady Diana Spencer – who, on leaving school herself, taught briefly at the Vacani School in Brompton Road (a few doors down from Harrods) – she would only say that Lady Di 'had a rather full social life, which distracted her from teaching dancing as a career'.

children and young evacuees as well as the two Princesses. There was a war going on, and a golden childhood, too.

Margaret Rhodes was a year older than her cousin Lilibet. She explained to me, 'I was at Windsor during the war, because I was doing a shorthand and typing course at Queen's College, which had moved out to Egham. I lived at Windsor and went into Egham on the bus. And, later, I worked at MI6 and lived at Buckingham Palace. Queen Elizabeth's great achievement during the war was that she kept family life going, kept it as normal as possible. When we were about sixteen or seventeen, she had little parties with the young Grenadier officers, so we could have a dance. And when the bombs were falling, she was always so calm. I remember there was a wonderful butler who would come in, bow, and say solemnly, "Purple warning, Your Majesty," which meant that the Germans were closer than they ought to be. We had to go to the air-raid shelter, along miles of corridor. Queen Elizabeth would not be hurried. If people tried to hurry her, she simply slowed down.'

At Windsor, Lilibet and Margaret Rose believed they shared the privations of the people. Their food may have been served to them by the nursery footman, but they were told it was subject to the rationing restrictions that applied to the public at large. There were lone lightbulbs hanging from the ceiling in their chilly, draughty bedrooms. Fires were limited and hot water was restricted, with a black line painted around the royal bathtubs as a reminder that the water should not be more than five inches deep. The children were also expected to contribute to the war effort.

In October 1940, when Lilibet was fourteen and a half, she made her first broadcast, introducing a series of 'Children in Wartime' programmes for the BBC. 'She was so good about the endless rehearsals we had to have to get the breathing and phrasing right,' said Crawfie. Her voice was high-pitched, her accent high-falutin', but her performance was flawless. John 'Jock' Colville, then twenty-five and assistant private secretary to the Prime Minister, and, much later, private secretary to Princess Elizabeth herself, listened and was 'embarrassed by the sloppy sentiment' of the broadcast, but, by every other account, the people – in Britain, in the Dominions, in America – loved it. The message was straightforward: 'Thousands of you in this country have had to leave your homes and be separated from your father and mother. My sister Margaret Rose and I feel so much for you, as we know from experience what it means to be away from those we love most of all.' According to Crawfie, 'Lilibet herself put in several phrases that were quite her, and everyone who heard this particular speech will remember the most spontaneous and amusing end. Lilibet, always anxious to bring her small sister forward, said, "Come on, Margaret, say good night," and a small, clear voice piped in rather pompously, "Good night, children."'

In fact, the end was not spontaneous. It was fully scripted and Margaret's farewell line actually read: 'Good night and good luck to you all.' Nor did Lilibet need to do much to bring her small sister forward. Margaret was naturally precocious. She was always the livelier and naughtier of the pair. She appears to have been encouraged in this by Crawfie, who claimed, 'Margaret and I were very given to practical jokes and we each egged the other on.' The Heiress Presumptive did not approve. 'Lilibet was always too serious-minded,' said Crawfie. On one occasion Margaret and Crawfie wanted to ring the alarm bell on the Castle terrace to see if it would bring out the guard from all over the Castle. On another, they took one of the elderly gardener's brooms from his wheelbarrow and hid it in the bushes. 'Lilibet was always ashamed of us on these occasions,' reported Crawfie, without any apparent sense of remorse, 'and walked away from us rather pink in the face.'

Sarah Bradford, in her biography of George VI, quotes an unnamed courtier as saying of Margaret Rose, 'She was a wicked little girl, there were moments when I'd have given anything to have given her the hell of a slap.' These were moments that the general public were not privy to. 'They spoiled her,' said the courtier of Margaret's parents. 'They adored her; the King used to look at her as if he couldn't believe anybody could be so much fun. But I think he fully realized that much as he admired Princess Margaret – he said something once that made it quite clear – he realized the Queen was the best of the two.'

Their cousin, Margaret Rhodes, said to me, 'The Queen and Princess Margaret were such different people. Occasionally, she was driven mad by her, but they were sisters.' From an early age, Margaret was spoilt, outspoken, playful, and flirtatious. Lilibet was not. During the war years at Windsor, young Grenadier Guards officers would sometimes join the girls and their governesses for lunch or tea. Margaret would chatter away gaily. Lilibet was more restrained, more formal, more dignified. Cosmo Lang, the Archbishop of Canterbury, who conducted her confirmation, spent some time alone with her and concluded that 'though naturally not very communicative, she showed real intelligence and understanding'. Eleanor Roosevelt, wife of the American President, came to tea and reported that the Princess was 'quite serious and with a great deal of character and personality. She asked me a number of questions about life in the United States and they were serious questions.'

Lilibet was a serious young woman. She listened to the BBC news bulletins with care. She charted the progress of the war with her own large wall map with little flags that were moved from place to place. Under the instruction of Sir Henry Marten, she was taken through the niceties of *The English Constitution* by Walter Bagehot (1826–77), required reading for monarchs in the making. She was being prepared – and preparing herself – to fulfil her destiny.

To mark her sixteenth birthday, in 1942, she was made Colonel of the Grenadier Guards, in place of her great-great-uncle and godfather, the Duke of Connaught, who had died recently, aged ninety-one. 'It was a bit frightening inspecting a regiment for the first time,' she reported to a friend, 'but it was not as bad as I expected it to be.' She had her father at her side, and, in truth, all that was required of her was to stand stock still while the troops marched to and fro. More of an ordeal for her would have been the small talk she had to make afterwards, mingling with the officers and men, and the photographers she had to face. Ten press cameramen were admitted to the event and the unofficial court photographer, Cecil Beaton, was invited to take a special birthday portrait. It is a fabulous shot, both sexy and innocent: the sixteen-year-old Princess, looking straight into the camera, is not quite smiling. She is in uniform, but her jacket is unbuttoned and her hat is at an angle that is almost provocative. The picture was reproduced around the world. A life of being photographed had begun.

Today the Queen is not comfortable with the idea of 'image making'. She is wary of being involved in what we now call 'spin'. In fact, whether consciously or not, seventy years ago George VI and his private secretary, Alexander Hardinge, allowed carefully wrought images of the young Princess to be used as visual propaganda for both the war effort and the House of Windsor. Different kinds of image were required to tell different aspects of the story. Cecil Beaton – whose brilliantly lit and composed pictures (often with painted backdrops) had helped transform the bosomy, somewhat cosy and domestic Duchess of York into a fully-fledged Queen – was used to give the world a romantic Princess Elizabeth. (His eighteenth-birthday portrait has her set against an idealised skating scene, eyes wistfully cast down.) Another photographer, Lisa Sheridan, was brought on board to produce more of a home-and-hearth series of pictures of Lilibet and Margaret Rose: nice girls, in sensible clothes, with perfect manners and adorable pets, the princesses-in-the-castle-next-door. When, in February 1945, Lilibet joined the Auxiliary Territorial Service as No. 230973 Second Subaltern Elizabeth Alexandra Mary Windsor, 'aged 18, eyes blue, hair brown, height 5ft 3in', she was photographed, on her knees, spanner in hand, on the ATS car mechanics' course at Aldershot, learning how to change a wheel.

Nearly sixty years later, in October 2003, at the opening of an exhibition at the Imperial War Museum, the Queen was reunited with six of her wartime ATS colleagues. Betty Royle, aged eighty-two, said, 'I think she has never quite forgotten us, because those were the days when she had a kind of freedom.' Pat Blake, eighty-two, who had been an ATS sergeant, said, 'You've got to remember that in those days people knew little about royalty. There was no telly. Once in a while you saw them on a newsreel in a local cinema. She really did seem a remote person to us all . . . She and her sister seemed like fairy-tale people. The fact that we were going to work alongside her doing night driving, learning first aid, military law and theory and practice of mechanics was quite spellbinding . . . She seemed very, very young – but she was very easy and just very unaffected and pleasant.'

In theory, on the course young Princess Elizabeth was 'to be treated in exactly the same way as any other officer learning at the driving training centre'. Well, she was – and she wasn't. She was taught alongside the others (who were instructed to call her 'Your Royal Highness' and then 'Ma'am to rhyme with jam') and barked at when they were barked at, but, in class, she sat in the centre of the front row, and at night, when the rest of the girls kipped down in the dormitory, she was driven back to Windsor Castle. Her 'normal' life was anything but normal. For her wardrobe she was dependent on clothing coupons like everybody else, but, somehow, the royal household was issued with more coupons than everybody else. The world was told she received just five shillings a week in pocket money and more than half of that the kind Princess donated to good causes. It was true, and it was good of her, but, of course, to her, money had no real meaning. She wanted for nothing. Her life was never – would never be, could never be – 'real'.

But the war was real enough. In August 1942 it claimed the life of her uncle, the Duke of Kent, killed on board an RAF Sunderland flying boat bound for Iceland, where he was due to inspect RAF installations. In atrocious weather the craft flew into the side of a Scottish hill. The King was devastated. It was a family tragedy: the Duchess of Kent was a widow at thirty-five, with three small children, the youngest of whom, Prince Michael of Kent, was only seven weeks old. The Duke's nieces shared in the family sadness. 'It was the second uncle they had lost completely,' Crawfie observed, 'for though the first, Uncle David, was not dead, they did not see him any more. The Royal conspiracy of silence had closed about him, as it did about so many other uncomfortable things. In the Palace and the Castle his name was never mentioned.'

Lilibet's adolescence coincided with the Second World War. She was a child of thirteen at the outset in September 1939, a woman of nineteen when victory came in the summer of 1945. In the intervening six years, she grew up: she was confirmed; she made her first broadcast; she shot her first stag; she inspected her first regiment; she launched her first ship; she learnt to drive; in her ATS training she tested herself, for the first time (perhaps for the only time), against contemporaries from ordinary backgrounds; indeed she mixed, after a fashion, with ordinary people for the first time; she rode her horses; she loved her dogs; she learnt to dance; she became a Counsellor of State and, in her father's absence, visiting the Eighth Army in Italy in 1944, she performed her first constitutional functions, signifying the Royal Assent to Acts of Parliament. 'There was always a strong sense of duty mixed with *joie de vivre* in her character,' according to her tutor in French, the Vicomtesse de Bellaigue. Princess

Elizabeth had a good war, and she remembers it as, essentially, a happy time in her life.

She is not alone, of course. A number of her contemporaries, and those just a little older than her, still speak of the war as the happiest time of their life. In a conversation about what brings happiness to people's lives – of which more later – I asked the late eminent Irish psychiatrist Professor Anthony Clare why that might be. 'Among those who fought in the Second World War there was a comradeship,' he told me. 'People who might otherwise have found it difficult to socialise were thrown in together. They had no choice. And there was a shared philosophy, a common purpose. The basic fighting man felt he was doing something worthwhile. That was why the 1939–45 war was so different from Vietnam, or even the Gulf wars. And those engaged in the war were testing themselves. That seems to be rather important. Happy people are rarely sitting around. They are usually involved in some ongoing interchange with life. Of course, we're talking about people who survived the war, not those who were wounded or killed. And I'm not sure how many back home felt that way, other than those in the blitzed cities where, again, there was this comradeship.'

Prince Philip of Greece had a good war, too. His mother, Princess Alice, who had returned to live in Athens in November 1938, had hopes that her son might choose to serve in the Greek navy. From Philip's point of view, it was not an inviting prospect. The Greek navy was tiny. Philip's knowledge of the Greek language and people was sketchy. He was a prince of Greece, but he had spent most of his life in England, France, and Germany. Where did his loyalty lie? He could see there was a dilemma and he was torn – but not for long. King George II of Greece (the son of King Constantine I, Prince Andrea's eldest brother) let him off the hook. Philip had started his naval training in Britain. The King decided it was only sensible he should continue it there.

Philip had no regrets about the decision. He was not greatly given to 'regrets', as we know. Nor was he given (despite the presence of C.S. Forrester's *Hornblower* novels on his bookshelves) to recounting tales of his wartime adventures on the high seas. He was 'mentioned in dispatches', but he would not want to exaggerate his contribution or achievement. In 1948, when, as the Duke of Edinburgh, he was presented with the Freedom of the City of London, he looked back on his war service and said, 'In every kind of human activity there are those who lead and those who follow . . . I would like to accept the Freedom of this City, not only for myself, but for all those millions who followed during the Second World War. Our only distinction is that we did what we were told to do, to the very best of our ability, and kept on doing it.'

His first appointment, as an eighteen-year-old midshipman, in January 1940, was to an old battleship, HMS *Ramillies*, then in Colombo, Ceylon, and working as an escort to convoys that were part of the Australian Expeditionary Force moving from Australia to the Middle East. The ship, a veteran of the Great War, was uncomfortable; the appointment – at least in the eyes of a young man eager for action – somewhat unexciting. He was, of course, Prince Philip of Greece, and Greece was not yet at war. That was an issue. For the time being, the powers that be felt it necessary to keep him out of the main line of fire. Did he find that frustrating? He shrugged his shoulders. 'Inevitable,' he said. 'And it was useful experience. I was quite young.'

It turns out that Louis Mountbatten had proposed to George VI that Philip be sent to a ship on the China station. When I raised this with him, Prince Philip bridled at the suggestion that Mountbatten was the orchestrator of his career. Uncle Dickie took an avuncular interest, certainly – 'He put in a good word where he could, I've no doubt' – but Prince Philip made it pretty clear to me that he hoped whatever he achieved in the navy he achieved through his own best endeavours. In fact, he was not entirely sure that being a prince, and nephew to a noted 'operator' like Mountbatten, may not have been positively to his disadvantage.

In September 1943, when Mountbatten, aged only forty-three, was appointed Supreme Allied Commander, South-East Asia Command, and promoted to the rank of Acting Admiral, Philip, still only twenty-two, wrote teasingly to him: 'What are they going to make you? Acting Admiral of the Fleet or something? You had better be careful . . . before you know what you will have the prospect of 40 years without promotion in front of you. What a thought! As a string-puller, of course, you've practically lost all value, you're so big now that it might smell of nepotism (just to make sure I had the right word, I looked it up in the dictionary, and this is what it says: undue favour from holder of patronage to relatives, originally from Pope to illegitimate sons called nephews).'

In 1940, after four months in *Ramillies*, Prince Philip served briefly in HMS *Kent*, in a shore station in Ceylon, and in HMS *Shropshire*. 'Action' continued to prove elusive. 'We have something to look forward to,' he noted, optimistically, in his logbook at one point in his time in *Kent*: 'there is an enemy raider in the Indian Ocean and there is just a chance our tracks will cross'. They didn't. The only 'fun' to be had was thanks to the swirl of the ocean: 'On one occasion a particularly heavy sea completely smothered the bridge and platform, and even the crow's nest felt the spray from it. Steaming with the sea on the beam and at twenty-one knots the rolling was greatly emphasised, and a lot of innocent fun was had in the mess, watching the Goanese stewards diligently laying the table, and then the plates, knives, forks, spoons, butter dishes, toast racks and marmalade landing in a heap on the deck.'

The catering arrangements were clearly taken seriously on board HMS *Kent*. When the ship was off Bombay, the first lieutenant noted in his log: 'It rained most of the Morning Watch. Luckily had Prince Philip as the snotty[41] and he makes the best cup of cocoa of the lot.'

In 1999, in a tribute to his friend and fellow snotty Terry Lewin – who became First Sea Lord in 1977 and was Chief of the Defence Staff at the time of the Falklands conflict in 1982 – Prince Philip recalled what happened next: 'I remained in the East Indies Station until June 1940, when the Italians invaded Greece and I became a combatant. I was appointed to HMS *Valiant* in the Mediterranean Fleet, where I found Terry as Senior Midshipman of the Gunroom. I remember it as a very happy Gunroom, which was a reflection of his good humour and powers of leadership. The fact that he had a typical rugby player's build and an all-round athletic ability helped to establish his authority. *Valiant* saw quite a lot of action during the latter part of 1940, including Malta convoys, the bombardment of Bardia, and the night action off Cape Matapan in March 1941, and the evacuation of Crete in May.'

---

41 Slang for 'midshipman'; etymology unknown; first recorded use, 1903; used by Kipling, 1904.

It was for his contribution to the success of the Battle of Matapan, manning the searchlight on board his battleship, that Prince Philip, not yet twenty, received his 'mention in dispatches' – and the Greek War Cross. (According to his cousin, Alexandra, when she congratulated him on the honour, 'he simply shrugged'.)

On the night of 28 March 1941, as darkness fell off the coast of Cape Matapan, at the southernmost point of the Peloponnese, Admiral Sir Andrew Cunningham, Commander of the British Mediterranean Fleet, in his flagship, HMS *Warspite*, was leading his battleships – including HMS *Valiant* and HMS *Barham* – towards three Italian cruisers. 'My orders,' Prince Philip noted in his log, 'were that if any ship illuminated a target I was to switch on and illuminate it for the rest of the fleet, so when this ship was lit up by a rather dim light from what I thought was the flagship I switched on our midship light which picked out the enemy cruiser and lit her up as if it were broad daylight.' Then the fun started: 'She was only seen complete in the light for a few seconds as the flagship had already opened fire, and as her first broadside landed and hit she was blotted out from just abaft the bridge to right astern. We fired our first broadside about seven seconds after the flagship with very much the same effect . . . By now all the secondary armament of both ships had opened fire and the noise was considerable. The Captain and the Gunnery Officer now began shouting from the bridge for the searchlights to train left. The idea that there might have been another ship, with the one we were firing at, never entered my head, so it was some few moments before I was persuaded to relinquish the blazing target and search for another one I had no reason to believe was there. However, training to the left, the light picked up another cruiser, ahead of the first one by some 3 or 4 cables. As the enemy was so close the light did not illuminate the whole ship but only about ¾ of it, so I trained left over the whole ship until the bridge structure was in the centre of the beam . . . she was illuminated in an undamaged condition for the period of about 5 seconds when our second broadside left the ship, and almost at once she was completely blotted out from stern to stern.'

It was at this point that 'all hell broke loose, as all our eight 15-inch guns, plus those of the flagship and *Barham*'s started firing at the stationary cruiser'. Through the noise and the pounding – 'the glasses were rammed into my eyes . . . flash almost blinding me' – Philip kept his searchlight on target. 'More than 70% of the shells must have hit,' he recorded, with justifiable satisfaction. 'When the enemy had completely vanished in clouds of smoke and steam we ceased firing and switched the light off.'

The Battle of Matapan was, for the time being, the last British victory in the Eastern Mediterranean. It was made possible, not only by Prince Philip's steady hand on the searchlight – the action which brought his 'mention in dispatches' – but also by British supremacy in the air. The Italians had no aircraft at Matapan. British aircraft – from Cunningham's aircraft carrier, *Formidable* – had been deployed during the afternoon of 28 March and had done serious damage to a number of the Italian ships. When it came to the Battle of Crete seven weeks later, it was a different story. Here the Germans had command of the air. On 22 May, within fifteen miles of Crete, Philip recorded in his log: 'We were bombed from a high level by a large number of small bombs dropped in sticks of 12 or more. One Dornier came straight for us from the port beam and dropped 12 bombs when he was almost overhead. We turned to port and ceased firing, when suddenly the bombs came whistling down, landing very close all down the port side.'

Within forty-eight hours three cruisers and six destroyers were lost, among them HMS *Kelly*, under the command of Louis Mountbatten. At 0800 hours on the morning of 23 May, twenty-four Junkers dive bombers appeared in the sky above his ship. 'Christ, look at that lot,' Mountbatten is said to have said, quite calmly. Within thirty seconds of being hit, with guns firing and the captain standing firm on the bridge, *Kelly* was capsizing. 'I felt I ought to be last to leave the ship,' Mountbatten wrote to his daughter, Patricia, soon after, 'and I left it a bit late because the bridge turned over on top of me and I was trapped in the boiling, seething cauldron underneath. I luckily had my tin hat on, which helped to make me heavy enough to push my way down past the bridge screen, but it was unpleasant having to force oneself deeper under water to get clear.' He managed it. He 'suddenly shot out of the water like a cork released' and, with his first lieutenant, set about swimming desperately through the oily water around the wreckage, rescuing wounded men and dragging them to the safety of a raft. As *Kelly* finally went down, he called for three cheers for the ship, and, bobbing up and down in the treacherous water, led his surviving crew in an extraordinary chorus of 'Roll out the Barrel!' It was the heroic stuff of which movies are made.[42]

Mountbatten and his surviving crew were picked up by HMS *Kipling* and taken to Alexandria, where Uncle Dickie, to his surprise, was met by 'the cheery grinning face' of his nephew, Philip. 'He roared with laughter on seeing me,' Mountbatten reported to his wife, 'and when I asked him what was up he said, "You have no idea how funny you look. You look like a nigger minstrel!" I had forgotten how completely we all were smothered in oil fuel.'

Separately, Uncle Dickie and his nephew now returned to England: Mountbatten, to brief Churchill (unbidden) on the need for greater air support in the Mediterranean and to take command of the aircraft carrier *Illustrious*; Philip, to take his sub-lieutenant's courses and exams at Portsmouth. He worked hard and he played hard. In the exams – covering seamanship, signals, navigation, gunnery, and torpedoes – he secured the top grade in four sections out of five. In March 1942, staying in London with the Mountbattens, he went out on the razzle with his cousin, Dickie's other nephew, David Milford Haven, who was also in the navy. The young men borrowed the Mountbatten Vauxhall to help transport themselves around the more fashionable West End and Mayfair nightspots and, at 4.30 a.m., collided with a traffic island, wrote off the car, and returned to their uncle's residence, bloodied if unbowed. 'So,' reflected Mountbatten, 'after facing death many times over at sea, they got their first wounds in a London blackout.'

In June 1942 Philip was appointed to the destroyer HMS *Wallace* and, that October, when *Wallace*'s first lieutenant was appointed

---

42 In July 1941, back in England, Mountbatten went to the pictures with Noël Coward. 'Dickie told whole story of the sinking of *Kelly*,' Coward noted in his diary. 'Absolutely heart-breaking and so magnificent.' In 1942, Coward turned the story into a fine propaganda film, *In Which We Serve*, and Mountbatten – who was involved at every stage, although officially the film was based 'on no Royal Navy destroyer in particular' – took the King and Queen and their daughters to Elstree Studios to watch some of the filming. Coward admired Mountbatten inordinately ('I would do anything in the world for him') and Mountbatten was suitably appreciative of Coward's cinematic skills. He saw the film at least fifteen times.

elsewhere, the Commanding Officer asked that Prince Philip take his place. At just twenty-one, Philip became one of the youngest first lieutenants in the Royal Navy. More than forty years later, his friend Lord Lewin said to me that if Prince Philip had stayed in the navy, 'he'd have gone right to the top'. When I put the possibility to Prince Philip, he shook his head. 'No,' he said, emphatically. 'Given the way of the British press, I wouldn't have got very far. Every promotion would have been seen as me being treated as a special case.'

HMS *Wallace* was one of the destroyers on convoy duty on the British east coast, constantly moving up and down 'E-Boat Alley', as it was known, from Sheerness to Rosyth and back. It wasn't glamorous, but it was necessary, arduous, and, given the effectiveness of the German E-boats' torpedoes, not without its hairy moments.

At the beginning of July 1943 *Wallace* joined the armada of ships (and 150,000 men) amassed off the coast of Sicily ready to invade the island. According to Harry Hargreaves, a yeoman aboard the ship, 8 July was the night when Prince Philip of Greece saved the day. 'The stars were bright and the sea was black,' recalled Hargreaves. 'There was only one problem: the water shone and sparkled, and our progress created a long, glowing trail which made it extremely easy for enemy aircraft to spot us.' At midnight the first plane struck. 'We were sitting ducks. It was inevitable that one of the bombs would hit us. We had little chance of survival and all 163 of us on board thought we were facing death.'

After the first attack – which hit the side of *Wallace* – the enemy aircraft disappeared. 'We knew it would return in minutes – with other aircraft.' At this point, according to Hargreaves, Philip came up with 'a brilliant plan that was destined to save our lives'. He got a group of men to lash together large planks of wood to make a raft, attaching smoke floats at each end. They launched the raft into the sea and activated the smoke floats. 'Billowing clouds of smoke and small bursts of flame made it look like the flaming debris of our ship floating in the water.' *Wallace* then steamed away from the raft for 'a good five minutes' before the captain ordered the engines stopped. When, shortly afterwards, the enemy aircraft returned, 'I heard the scream of bombs falling,' Hargreaves recalled, 'but they were aimed at the raft, not at us. The first lieutenant's ruse had worked.'

Hargreaves had only good memories of Philip, who, on the day they first met, when *Wallace* was docked at Tilbury, rustled up a meal of sausages and powdered egg for them both, despite the fact that Philip was an officer and Hargreaves 'merely a yeoman': 'He was a down-to-earth, ordinary man. He had no airs or graces, and when the captain told me he was a prince, I said, "He doesn't look like that to me."'

In 1944, as the war in Europe moved decisively the Allies' way, Philip was appointed to a brand-new destroyer, HMS *Whelp*, still building in Newcastle when he joined her, and, subsequently, set off with her for more exotic climes: the Far East and the climax of the war against Japan in the Pacific. En route, *Whelp* called at Colombo and Philip spent a memorable Christmas Eve with Uncle Dickie, now Supreme Commander, South-East Asia Command, and Mountbatten's new Chief of Staff, Lieutenant General Frederick 'Boy' Browning. According to Philip Ziegler, Mountbatten's official biographer, the night went gloriously awry because 'the Singhalese cook, overawed by the occasion, took refuge in drink and served dinner cold, late, and back to front: Christmas pudding at midnight, turkey at 1 a.m. Nobody minded – least of all Mountbatten.'

Dickie was increasingly a father figure for Philip. Earlier in December he had had to break the news to his nephew that his actual father, Prince Andrea, was dead. Andrea, aged sixty-two, unreachable in Vichy France, had died of a heart attack in his bedroom at the Hôtel Métropole in Monte Carlo in the early hours of 3 December. His lady friend, the Comtesse Andrée de La Bigne, was with him. His widow, Princess Alice, living reclusively in Athens, received the news two days later. Somehow she got word to Dickie, who sent a naval message to Philip on board *Whelp*. The message was deciphered precisely as follows: 'So shocked and grieved to hear of the death of your (?) father and send you all my heartfelt sympathy. Following has been received from your mother: "Embrace you tenderly in our joint sorrow. Your loving mama."'[43]

43 The family seems rarely not to have been in mourning. In February 1938, Andrea's brother, Prince Nicholas, had died. Nicholas's daughter, Marina, was married to the British Prince George, Duke of Kent, who was killed in a flying boat accident over Scotland in August 1942. In April 1938, Alice's brother, Georgie, 2nd Marquess of Milford Haven, had died. In January 1940, another of Andrea's brothers, the

In November 1938 Princess Alice had returned to live in Greece. From Athens, on 5 December that year, she had written to Philip: 'I have taken a small flat just for you and me. Two bedrooms, *each* with a bathroom and two sitting rooms, a little kitchen & pantry. I found some furniture stored away in various places from our rooms in the Old Palace, which I had not seen again since 1917, a most agreeable surprise & the family here are giving me things to complete it.' Philip was happy to visit his mother in Greece, but he had been educated in Britain and he was joining the Royal Navy: Athens was to him a port of call, not his home. Just before the outbreak of war, in August 1939, he stayed with his mother in her small flat in Athens. In January 1941, on leave from HMS *Valiant* in Alexandria, he visited her again. George II, still King of Greece (if only just), wrote to Alice's mother, Victoria, at Kensington Palace: 'With Alice we talk and think of you often. She is very busy looking after the needy families of soldiers and we only get to see her on Sundays. A few days ago Philip arrived here on leave, which naturally is a great source of joy for her. He is looking very well and happy.'

Philip had returned to his ship in the middle of February 1941. By the end of March that year he had become one of the heroes of the Battle of Matapan. On 6 April 1941, the Germans had come to the rescue of the defeated Italians and invaded Yugoslavia. By 17 April the German forces were advancing through Greece. On 23 April King George II and his immediate family were on their way into exile: first to Crete, then to Egypt, then to London. On 26 April German troops marched into Athens and the Nazi flag was raised above the Acropolis. Alice stayed put. Her mother wrote to Dickie: 'I rely on her pluck & common sense to carry her through these times, which must be very painful to her.'

Alice lived in Athens throughout the German occupation, and beyond. As her biographer, Hugo Vickers, says, 'Alice was no threat to the Germans, politically or personally, and she moved about

---

youngest, Prince Christo, died, aged sixty-one, followed, later in the same year, by his closest sister, Princess Marie, aged sixty-four. At least some of those who died in these years had lived long lives: Queen Victoria's last surviving daughters (Alice's great-aunts), Princess Louise and Princess Beatrice, died in 1939 and 1944, aged ninety-one and eighty-seven respectively. Prince Arthur, Duke of Connaught, died in 1942, aged ninety-one.

relatively unnoticed. She did her best to alleviate the suffering of the Greeks, but more as a nurse than as a princess.' She shared in the privations of the Greek people. Food was in scant supply. During the first bitter winter of the occupation she lost fifty-seven pounds in weight. She was sometimes lonely, often hungry, frequently cold, but she had spirit – and hope. She imagined herself and her son – a Prince of Greece – living together in Athens after the war. In December 1941 she had written to Philip: 'Even in these anxious times I am full of hope and when I go for walks I look at all the houses to see if there is not a suitable one for us later on, as I am tired of flats and prefer a whole house . . . I am still busy with my charities . . . Don't worry about me. I am really and truly in good heart.'

She was of good heart, too. She worked in one of the largest soup kitchens in Athens; she worked in a refuge for orphans; she organised a group of district nurses to provide care in the poorest areas of the city. She was in no way ostentatious about her good works. She was quietly determined, dogged, devoted, and ready to take risks. When the Nazi threat to the Jews of Athens was at its height, Alice offered refuge to a family of Cohens. When neighbours enquired, she said that Mrs Cohen was a former Swiss governess to her children. When the Gestapo questioned her, she simply exaggerated her deafness and looked uncomprehending.

She never talked about hiding the Cohens. When I tried to talk to Prince Philip about his mother, he was reluctant to be drawn. When I told him how moving I had found Hugo Vickers's account of her life, Philip said, in a very matter-of-fact way, 'Yes, he did a lot of research.' When I said Princess Alice seemed to me to be an extraordinary woman, he said, 'Mm' and changed the subject, asking me if I had yet read a new book that told the story of the Royal Yacht *Britannia*.

It is clear to me that from his father Prince Philip inherited his appearance, his charm, his humour, his flirtatious way with the ladies. But with his mother he shared a wider, and perhaps more significant, range of characteristics. He guarded his privacy. He kept his own counsel. He did not wear his heart on his sleeve. He hid his light under a bushel. He found it uncomfortable to talk about himself – and had a feeling that it would have been both unmannerly and unmanly to do so. His manner was deceptive. He was a kindly person, and a caring one. He was more sensitive than he wanted us to think or know. He could be prickly and perverse, stubborn and wilful. He could also be visionary. His spiritual life was important to him. He was his mother's son.

In the late 1980s, some years after her death in 1969, surviving members of the Cohen family sought to honour the memory of Princess Alice. They secured for her a 'Certificate of Honour' as one 'Righteous among the Nations': she 'risked her life to save persecuted Jews'. In October 1994 Prince Philip and his surviving sister, Sophie, went to Jerusalem, to the Holocaust Memorial at Yad Vashem, to accept the posthumous award on their mother's behalf. In his speech on the day, Philip said of her, 'As far as we know she had never mentioned to anyone that she had given refuge to the Cohen family at the time when Jews throughout Greece were in danger of being arrested and transported to the death camps. I suspect that she never thought of it as something special. She was a person with deep religious faith and she would have considered it to be a totally natural human action to help fellow human beings in distress.'

I would have been intrigued to know the range of thoughts passing through Sophie's mind as, with her brother, in her mother's memory, she laid the wreath in the Holocaust Museum in 1994. Sixty years earlier, her beloved husband, Prince Christoph of Hesse, had joined the Nazi Party and become a member of the SS – the *Schutzstaffel*, 'Hitler's bodyguard'. In 1945 Sophie told her grandmother: 'Since 2 years my eyes have been open & you can imagine what feelings one has now about those criminals.' As time went by, Prince Christoph grew less enamoured of the Führer, but in 1935 he was thirty-four, patriotic and ready to serve the greater German cause. He joined the Luftwaffe. In October 1943 he was killed in a flying accident in the hills outside Rome. Alice, in German-occupied Athens, was given permission to travel to Germany to visit her widowed daughter.

Alice's daughters suffered from the dilemma that faced several of Queen Victoria's grandchildren and great-grandchildren during the two world wars of the twentieth century: divided loyalties. Their grandmother lived in Kensington Palace, under the protection of the British king. Their grandfather had become a British marquess. Their brother, Philip, and their uncle, Dickie, were officers in the British navy. They were married to Germans. Whose side were they on?

Hermann Goering had attended the funeral of Cécile and her husband in 1937. Sophie's husband had been a member of the Nazi Party. Theodora's husband, Berthold, was a German, but not a Nazi. He was severely wounded in the leg in France at the outset of the war and was invalided out of active service. The eldest sister, Margarita, had the oldest husband, Gottfried (known as Friedel), who was already in his forties when war was declared. Relatively speaking, through the hostilities, they managed to keep a low profile and out of harm's way.

While Athens was occupied by the Germans, Alice was able to get permission to visit her sister in Sweden and her daughters in Germany and Switzerland. In October 1944, when, three and a half years after being driven out, British troops returned to Greece, Alice's daughters were, once again, behind enemy lines. Throughout the war years Philip was unable to make contact with his sisters. While Greece was in German hands, he was unable to see his mother. He was twenty-three, and in a ship bound for Colombo, when his father – whom he hadn't seen for five years – died in his hotel bedroom in the south of France.

'You're a poor bloody orphan just like me,' thought Mike Parker when he met Philip at the time. 'A poor bloody orphan.'

ELIZABETH & PHILIP

Chapter Seven

'Don't praise my charm too much . . .
Don't take my arm too much,
Don't keep your hand in mine . . .
People will say we're in love!'
Oscar Hammerstein II (1895–1960), *Oklahoma!*

Mike Parker was an Australian, from Melbourne. Born in June 1920, he was a year older than Prince Philip. They met in 1942, as fellow first lieutenants – Philip in HMS *Wallace*, Parker in HMS *Lauderdale* – on convoy duty on 'E-boat Alley'. They became lifelong friends. Parker's father was a captain in the Royal Australian Navy. Parker came to Britain to join the Royal Navy to prove his independence. 'I was an orphan,' he liked to say, 'because I came from Australia. Philip was an orphan because he came from nowhere. His parents weren't anywhere to be seen.'

The two men had much in common. They were young. They were ambitious. 'We were highly competitive,' said Parker. 'We both wanted to show that we had *the* most efficient, cleanest, and best ship and ship's company in the Navy'. And they shared a sense of humour. For a prince, Philip was remarkably unstuffy. As an Australian, Parker did not stand on ceremony. In an unlikely way, each felt he was the other's equal. The traditional middle-class British naval officer was relatively well heeled. Not so Philip of Greece and Parker of Melbourne. 'He was better off than I was,' said Parker, 'but compared with many people he didn't have a brass razoo!'

Prince Philip dates the beginning of their close friendship to 1944, when, by coincidence, they found themselves in sister ships – Philip in HMS *Whelp*, Parker in HMS *Wessex* – on their way to the Pacific as part of the 27th Destroyer Flotilla under Admiral Sir James

Somerville. They were looking forward to some action against the Japanese; they arrived just in time for the Japanese surrender in September 1945. In Tokyo Bay, *Whelp*'s final wartime assignment was to ferry newly released prisoners of war to light fleet carriers which then brought them back to Britain.

En route for the Far East and after the Japanese surrender, Philip and Parker took shore leave together, in both north Africa and Australia. In 1990, interviewed by Tim Heald for his biography of Prince Philip, Parker recalled: 'Of course we had fun in north Africa, but never anything outrageous. We'd drink together and then we'd go and have a bloody good meal. People are always asking, "Did you go to the local estaminets and screw everything in sight?" And the answer is, "No! It never came into the picture. There was so much else to do." ' He did admit, however, 'There were always armfuls of girls.'

What exactly did he mean by that? When I asked him, Mike Parker simply exploded: 'Nothing, for Christ's sake.' Commander Parker (as he became, and MVO, CVO, and Order of Australia, too) died at the very end of 2001, aged eighty-one, a plain-speaking Australian to the last.[44] 'Jesus, I wish I'd never used that phrase,' he said to me. 'Yeah, there were always "armfuls of girls", showers of them, but nothing happened – nothing serious. What I meant was this: we were young, we had fun, we had a few drinks, we might have gone dancing, but that was it. In Australia, Philip came to meet my family, my sisters, and their friends. There were girls galore, but there was no one special. Believe me. I guarantee it.'

In 1945 Philip was twenty-four, a bearded Adonis. According to his cousin, Alexandra of Yugoslavia, who wasn't there, 'Philip, with a golden beard, hit feminine hearts, first in Melbourne and then in Sydney, with terrific impact.' According to Mike Parker, who was, 'Philip was actually quite reserved, quite restrained really. He was always good company, but he was self-disciplined, too. And self-contained. And careful. He didn't encourage gossip. He certainly didn't wear his heart on his sleeve. He didn't give away a lot. There

---

44 He was, among other things, chairman of Australian Dredging and General Services, a director of Spacelift Australia, and chairman of the Australian Plain English Foundation.

have been books and articles galore saying he played the field. I don't believe it. People say we were screwing around like nobody's business. Well, we weren't. You didn't. We didn't. That's the truth of it.' Besides, in 1943, Parker got married. 'In those days, if you slept with a girl, you married her.'

Robin Dalton – in time a London-based film producer; in 1945 a twenty-three-year-old Australian girl working as secretary to the commanding officer of the ordnance department of the Southwest Pacific Area – remembered it a little differently. In her *Incidental Memoir*, she wrote: 'What would seem like shocking promiscuity – not only physical but emotional – in peacetime, was felt as a beneficence of the heart. The fact that it was also rarely that one was caught out in one's perfidious spread of affection blinded one to the dangers. The pleasures were freshly minted each week, as the turnover in admirers was brisk. If possible, our affections were limited to one per squadron, or PT boat, or Marine battalion, and the chief dread was that their leaves would overlap. They seldom did. We did not consider ourselves promiscuous. We were in love.'

Robin was in love with Philip's cousin, David Milford Haven. 'We met in 1944, in Sydney, at a cocktail party on one of the warships. He was a signals officer working for Admiral Vian. He was adorable. It was love at first sight.' Their affair lasted five years. 'I met Philip through David,' she told me. 'They were like brothers, you know.' She told me that Philip had two special girlfriends in Australia at the end of the war: 'A society girl called Sue Other-Gee, and then Sandra Jacques – that was a terrific love affair.'

Perhaps there was a licence to be more uninhibited in Australia?

Sixty years on, in London, sitting with Gina Kennard in the elegant drawing room of her third-floor flat off Sloane Square, Prince Philip's childhood friend said to me, emphatically, 'It was a different world. Unmarried girls didn't sleep with their boyfriends. It really wasn't done. You went for dinner, you went dancing, you went shooting, you had fun, but you knew where to draw the line. Of course, some girls stepped over the boundary, but that was the exception, not the rule.' Gina and her sister and their friends were brought up in an age when the Church of England's traditional teaching on sexual morality went virtually unquestioned and mostly unchallenged. Married women (like Dickie's wife, Edwina) might have affairs, and, because there was a war on, some unmarried sweethearts might indulge their boys on the way to the front, but, on the whole, most nice girls expected to be married as virgin brides. And there were practical considerations as well as moral ones: contraception was uncertain, illegitimacy a stigma, abortion illegal.

I asked Gina Kennard if Prince Philip had been her boyfriend. She laughed. 'Everybody said he was in love with me. My mother used to say that his mother – who was a saintly person, deaf but lovely – would have been very happy for Philip to marry me, but it never came up. I said to him recently, "Are you still in love with me?" and he said, "Yes, of course, I am." The truth is, he was wonderfully attractive – he still is – and we were friends, best friends, and we went out together and had just the best time, but nothing really serious happened. It wasn't like that. He was young and handsome and, of course, I loved him. At that age, you fall in love all the time, don't you? Philip knew lots of girls. There was Osla Benning, wasn't there? We were just young people having fun.'

According to Alexandra of Yugoslavia, Philip started 'having fun' when he went on holiday to Venice in the year before the war and, aged seventeen, stayed with Alexandra and her mother, Aspasia (widow of Prince Alexander of Greece, nephew to Philip's father, Andrea). Andrea cautioned Aspasia that his boy had exams to pass and urged her to 'keep him out of girl trouble'. In the event, in Alexandra's account, Philip discovered 'blondes, brunettes and redhead charmers' and 'gallantly and I think quite impartially squired them all'.

That said, one charmer, it seems, did stand out from the crowd: a seventeen-year-old American model and aspiring actress named Cobina Wright Junior, daughter of Cobina Wright Senior, established actress and ambitious hostess. Cobina Jr was a considerable beauty: tall and blonde, with large blue eyes and a contract from Twentieth Century Fox. Philip met her in Venice, in Harry's Bar, and was seriously smitten. He met her again in London and, according to her friends, wrote her 'impassioned love letters', but the passion, apparently, was not entirely reciprocated. Cobina returned to the United States and, in November 1941, not long after featuring on the cover of *Life* magazine, she married Corporal Palmer T. Beaudette, the son of a wealthy automobile family from Pontiac, Michigan.

(In the 1980s, by odd coincidence, Cobina Jr's daughter, Cobina

Caroline, known as CC III, was linked, fleetingly, to Prince Philip's second son, Prince Andrew.)

Osla Benning was another of Philip's youthful flames. She was a Canadian-born, London-based debutante, with 'dark hair, alabaster white skin, an exquisite figure and a gentle loving nature', according to Sarah Norton, who shared a flat with her in 1939 – when Osla was just sixteen. Sarah, daughter of Richard Norton (soon to become the 6th Lord Grantley) and god-daughter of Louis Mountbatten, introduced Osla to the eighteen-year-old Philip and, from the start, 'they got on like a house on fire'. When I asked Prince Philip how he remembered times with Osla, he simply said, 'Fun.' By all accounts – including her own – she was larky, high-spirited, and innocent. For the first two to three years of the war, when Philip wasn't at sea he'd see Osla in London when he could – and then he saw her less. And less. And in 1944 she became engaged to someone else. 'But you remained friends?' I asked Prince Philip.

'Yes.'

'And you kept in touch?'

'Yes.' Osla did not marry her first fiancé. In 1946 she married a thirty-year-old diplomat, John Henniker-Major, later the 8th Baron Henniker, and in 1947 Philip became godfather to their first-born son, who was given 'Philip' as one of his Christian names.

As an old man Prince Philip would sigh at what he described as my 'obsession with personalities and gossip'. But even as a young man, according to Mike Parker, 'Philip wasn't one for tittle-tattle. He was much more reserved than you'd think. Circumspect.'

Richard Norton, 6th Lord Grantley, Sarah Norton's father, was a banker turned film producer. Norton got to meet Prince Philip when the young naval officer came to call on his daughter and her friend Osla. What struck Norton about the youthful Prince was his 'forceful intellect'. 'When asking me questions about films, for instance,' he said, Philip 'did not want to know about the stars but about the technicalities of how films were made'.

In his despair at my 'obsession with personalities and gossip' Prince Philip quoted Eleanor Roosevelt: 'Great minds discuss ideas; average minds discuss events; small minds discuss people.'

Prince Philip was fascinated by 'ideas'. He gave all sorts of ideas his time and careful attention. As just one example of his questing, challenging, intellectual nature I refer you to *A Windsor Correspondence between The Duke of Edinburgh and The Right Reverend Michael Mann, Dean of Windsor*. The correspondence, an exchange of letters triggered by Prince Philip, concerns evolution, science, religious conservatism, and morality. It is worthwhile, if not easy, reading. It was published in 1984 by St George's House, at Windsor Castle, an institution that came into being in the mid-1960s, on the Duke's initiative, 'to provide a place where men and women in positions of influence and responsibility, drawn from every area of society, might consider and evaluate current questions in which important value judgements are involved'.

Considering and evaluating ideas was central to Prince Philip's life. At St George's House, at the Royal Society for the Encouragement of the Arts, Manufactures and Commerce from 1952 to 2011, through the British Association for the Advancement of Science, of which he became President in 1951, through the Commonwealth Study Conferences he established in 1956, and in any number of other settings, public and private, Prince Philip probed and tested 'ideas' in every area of endeavour and experience. Over sixty years he delivered more than five thousand properly considered speeches and lectures and was proud of the fact that his collected 'works' took up more than a yard of shelf space.[45]

I was not surprised that Prince Philip approved of Eleanor Roosevelt's dictum. To him, ideas were paramount. Events he accepted: he took them in his stride. 'You take what life gives you,' he said, 'and make the best of it you can.' People he kept at bay. When once I asked him who was the most impressive individual he had ever met, he began to answer – mentioning Vincent Massey, the Governor-General of Canada in the 1950s, and Sir Robert Menzies, twice Australian Prime Minister, 1939–41 and 1949–66 – and then stopped himself, saying, 'No, that's invidious. I don't want to talk

---

45 His published books included: *Selected Speeches 1948–1955* (1957); *Prince Philip Speaks* (1960); *Birds from Britannia* (1962); *Wildlife Crisis* (with James Fisher, 1970); *The Environmental Revolution* (1978); *A Question of Balance* (1982); *Men, Machines and Sacred Cows* (1984); *A Windsor Correspondence* (1984); *Down to Earth* (1988); *Survival or Extinction: A Christian Attitude to the Environment* (1989); plus *Competition Carriage Driving* (1982, revised 1994); *Driving and Judging Dressage* (1996); *30 Years On and Off The Box Seat* (2004).

about individuals. Why do you have to bring everything back to people and personalities?'

Because mine's a small mind, perhaps, and because I am fascinated by people – I confess it. How people behave, in private as well as in public, provides clues to who they are – and who they are as people, as *personalities*, affects the way they behave and what they achieve. I said to His Royal Highness, 'People are intrigued by people. That's allowable, surely?' He made no reply.

I was certainly intrigued to read in the diaries of James Lees-Milne the story told by June Hutchinson (daughter of Diana, Countess of Westmoreland, and near-contemporary of Prince Philip) of a friend of hers who 'swore that when in her teens she used to lie in the same bed with Prince Philip, a bolster between them. They would talk for hours. She was much in love with him. He would not transgress the bolster.'

Lees-Milne was not sure he could believe the story. I think I do.

Through the war years, while he was seeing Osla Benning, Prince Philip kept in touch with his young cousin, Princess Elizabeth. He wrote to her 'from here and there'. He saw her 'now and again'. That's about as much as I got out of him. Around the time of his golden wedding anniversary he said to me, 'I don't remember much about it. It *was* a long time ago.' In 1970, talking to his official biographer, Basil Boothroyd (whom he liked and trusted), he said, with the diffidence and touch of defensiveness that were the hallmarks of any conversation about his personal life: 'During the war, if I was here [in Britain] I'd call in and have a meal. I once or twice spent Christmas at Windsor, because I'd nowhere particular to go. I thought not all that much about it, I think. We used to correspond occasion-ally. You see it's difficult to visualise. I suppose if I'd just been a casual acquaintance it would all have been frightfully significant. But if you're related – I mean I knew half the people here, they were all relations – it isn't so extraordinary to be on kind of family rela-tionship terms. You don't necessarily have to think about marriage.'

However sketchy he claimed his recollections to be, Prince Philip was adamant on one point. He did not think about marriage in any serious sense until more than a year after the war, when he went to stay at Balmoral in 1946. 'I suppose one thing led to another,' he conceded. 'It was sort of fixed up. That's really what happened.'

By 'fixed up', he did not mean arranged by others. He meant that was the time when he and Princess Elizabeth came to a mutual understanding that met with the approval of their families. If he did have thoughts of marriage much before 1946, he kept them to himself. He certainly did not share them with Mike Parker, his contemporary and closest wartime friend. 'He was the same, then as now,' Parker told me in 2000, 'good at keeping his feelings to himself. He didn't tell me anything and I didn't ask. I might have had my suspicions, but until around 1946, when an engagement was in the air, I didn't know a thing.'

Others, however, had their suspicions as far back as 1941. Henry 'Chips' Channon was one such. A wealthy American from Chicago, Channon came to Britain aged twenty-one in 1918, married Lady Honor Guinness, and became an English MP. He liked to feel he knew everybody and everything. He was a waspish chronicler of the social scene and took a special interest in royalty. In January 1941 he found himself staying at the British Legation in Athens and noted in his journal: 'The Royal set-up at Athens is complicated: there is the isolated King who sees no-one; there are the Crown Prince and Princess (Frederika) who, madly in love, remain aloof from the world with their babies and their passion. She is a touch unpopular, being German (I met her first dining with General Goering in 1936); there is Princess Andrew who is eccentric to say the least and lives in semi-retirement: there is Prince Andrew, who philanders on the Riviera whilst his son, Prince Philip, is serving in our Navy . . .' This was the January when Philip, on leave from HMS *Valiant*, was staying in Athens with his mother. On the 21st, Channon was taken to 'an enjoyable Greek cocktail party': 'Philip of Greece was there. He is extraordinarily handsome, and I recalled my afternoon's conversation with Princess Nicholas [Ellen, Philip's aunt, widow of Andrea's brother Nicholas]. He is to be our Prince Consort, and that is why he is serving in our Navy. He is charming, but I deplore such a marriage; he and Princess Elizabeth are too inter-related.'

Prince Philip deplored the kind of tittle-tattle in which 'Chips' Channon revelled. In January 1941 Philip was nineteen, Elizabeth was fourteen, and, whatever his match-making aunt or her gossip-mongering teatime companions might care to invent, as far as Philip was concerned, marriage was not on the agenda. Channon, nevertheless, retained his watching brief. On 16 February 1944 he noted in his diary: 'My parents-in-law, the Iveaghs, called to see me, after having had tea with the King and Queen at Buckingham Palace . . . I do believe that a marriage may well be arranged one day between Princess Elizabeth and Prince Philip of Greece.' In October the same year, Channon's nose went into an overdrive of twitching when he found himself a guest of Princess Marina, Duchess of Kent, at Coppins, her country house in Buckinghamshire. 'As I signed the visitors' book,' he reported to his journal, with a note of triumph worthy of Sherlock Holmes, 'I noticed "Philip" written constantly. It is at Coppins that he sees Princess Elizabeth. I think she will marry him.'

Prince Philip had no time for *The Diaries of Sir Henry Channon*. He and Princess Elizabeth were cousins; they became friends; they got to know each other better; they became closer; in due course, they became engaged. 'That's about it, really,' he said to me, with a shrug. What Philip felt exactly, and when he felt it, is, as far as he was concerned, (a) frankly, none of our business, and (b) honestly, quite difficult to recollect at this distance in time.

Getting an insight into Philip's feelings about his relationship with Elizabeth was never going to be easy. Getting an insight into her feelings about him is more straightforward – if you are content to go along with the well-worn legend. As almost every one of the obituaries of the Duke of Edinburgh put it, Princess Elizabeth's heart belonged to Prince Philip from the moment she saw him on that momentous day at Dartmouth when she was just thirteen. Once she had set her course, she did not waver from it.

Horace Smith, her riding instructor, when she was both a child and a young woman, had the measure of her. He saw that she was single-minded, not one to take up interests 'lightly, only to drop them just as easily a short time later. If and when her interest is aroused, she goes into whatever subject it is with thoroughness and application, nor does her interest wane with the passing of time or the claim of other new matters upon her attention.'

As it was with her horses – and her dogs, and her faith, and her duty – so it was with Philip. Her first cousin, near contemporary, and friend, Margaret Rhodes, said to me, 'Princess Elizabeth was enamoured from an early age. I've got letters from her saying, "It's so exciting. Mummy says that Philip can come and stay". She never looked at anyone else. She was smitten from the start.' 'Yes,' agreed Lilibet's grandmother, Queen Mary, 'it does happen sometimes and Elizabeth seems to be that kind of girl. She would always know her own mind. There's something very steadfast and determined in her – like her father.'

'Once she had set her course she did not waver from it.' Is that really so? 'She never looked at anyone else.' Without doubt, that is the line that everyone takes and always has done. I took it, too, when I published the original edition of this book. Since then, however, I happened one day to find myself filming a television documentary at a country auction house when I was shown a letter that was up for sale, vendor unnamed. The letter was from Princess Elizabeth to her first cousin, Diana Bowes-Lyon.[46] It was dated Tuesday, 30 November 1943 – so the young Princess would have been a little more than halfway between her seventeenth and eighteenth birthdays. It begins as a thank-you letter to 'Darling Diana': 'I hope you will forgive me for not having written sooner to thank you for the handkerchief which you sent me. You know, it really was wicked of you to give me another one as I only wanted the other one as it belonged to a set, which I've had for years. It was angelic of you to give me a hanky but an unforgivable thing to do nowadays.'

---

46 Diana Cinderella Mildred Bowes-Lyon was born on 14 December 1923 – hence her second Christian name. She was the daughter of Queen Elizabeth the Queen Mother's elder brother, 'Jock' Bowes-Lyon, who married Fenella Hepburn-Stuart-Forbes-Trefusis, daughter of the 21st Lord Clinton, in 1914. Diana had four sisters, including Patricia, who died in infancy, and Nerissa and Katherine, who inherited a mental disability from their mother's side of the family and lived out their adult lives in institutions for the mentally frail. In 2011, a television documentary claimed that, at one of the hospitals where they were patients, 'there is no known record that the sisters were ever visited by any member of the Bowes-Lyon or royal families, despite their aunt, the Queen Mother, being a Patron of Mencap, the charity for people with learning difficulties'. According to the family, while their mother had told *Burke's Peerage* that the girls were dead when they were still alive, that was a matter of 'vagueness' on her part and she had, in fact, continued to visit them regularly until her own death in 1966, when family visits were then 'discouraged by their carers'. William Shawcross quotes another of the Queen Mother's nieces describing the girls as 'lovely children . . . like easily frightened does'. Their father, Jock, died of pneumonia in 1930, aged forty-three.

So far not so surprising. Anyone familiar with William Shawcross's splendid collection of the letters of Queen Elizabeth the Queen Mother will be familiar with the effervescent family style. Anyone familiar with Princess Elizabeth's ordered mind and thoughtful character will understand her delight at having her incomplete set of hankies made whole once more and her horror at the extravagance entailed at a time of war, privation, and clothes rationing. The opening of the letter is interesting – and charming in its way – but it is with what follows that there comes the revelation: 'I saw Andrew for a moment last week. And the more I see of him, the more I wish he wasn't my first cousin, as he's just the sort of husband any girl would love to have. I don't think one could find anyone nicer.'

Well, there you have it. 'He is just the sort of husband any girl would love to have.'

And who was Andrew? He was Andrew Charles Victor Elphinstone, born 10 November 1918, the younger son of Queen Elizabeth's eldest surviving sister, Mary (May), and Sidney, 16th Lord Elphinstone. The Elphinstones had five children in all: Elizabeth, John, Jean, Andrew, and Margaret – our Margaret Rhodes. Mrs Rhodes told me that she 'hero-worshipped' her brother Andrew, who had Victor added to his Christian names because his birth coincided with Armistice Day marking the Allied victory at the end of the First World War. When Andrew was staying with the Windsors during the Second World War, in May 1944, Queen Elizabeth wrote to Elizabeth Elphinstone to say: 'It is delicious having Andrew. He is such fun, & so intelligent & so good-looking.' He was bright – educated at Eton and New College, Oxford – and musical, too. 'He has just bought me a piano, or rather he found it & I paid for it and he plays on it, & I listen.'

And Lilibet listened, also. And she liked what she heard. She enjoyed her tall and handsome first cousin's company very much. As a boy he had suffered from a stammer. It had not been as debilitating as her father's, but it was a point of sympathy. And Lilibet was taken with her cousin, too, because, while he was fun to be with, he was so palpably decent. And he was fundamentally serious. He was destined to become a clergyman.

He was not destined to marry Lilibet. In the summer of 1946 he married a young war widow, Jean Gibbs (née Hambro), then twenty-three, a friend and lady-in-waiting to Princess Elizabeth. Andrew and Jean had two children and Lilibet became godmother to the first, Rosemary Elizabeth, in September 1947. It was one of her last engagements before her own wedding seven weeks later.

The Reverend Andrew Elphinstone died in March 1975, aged only fifty-six. From photographs he looks to have been a kindly as well as a handsome man. He became one of Princess Anne's god-parents and remained one of the Queen's close friends for the rest of his life. 'I don't think one could find anyone nicer.' That was Lilibet's verdict in 1943. From what I have read and heard, that seems to be the general verdict.

It was not a line that everyone would have used about Prince Philip of Greece. He was fun, too, and intelligent, and quite as hand-some as Andrew (if not more so), but much less easy to read. By 1943 Philip had made his mark, for sure, but I do not believe that Lilibet had yet quite made up her mind. Philip is there, alongside Andrew, in that same letter to Diana Bowes-Lyon: 'I still think he is charming and he is great fun. Hardly ever serious. But when he is, I think he talks good sense. We had a terrific time on Sunday night. We danced to the gramophone, which was great fun.' The war notwithstanding, it seems they danced to Austrian tunes. 'You go waltzing madly round the room, but it's not like an ordinary waltz as your partner holds you round the waist and you hold his neck. Sounds odd, but it holds you together much better and you feel safer on a slippery floor.'

At that Christmas of 1943, when the Windsor Castle pantomime was *Aladdin*, and Lilibet, aged seventeen and three-quarters, in fetching tights and tunic, was 'principal boy', and Margaret Rose, thirteen, played the heroine, Princess Roxana, Philip, now twenty-two, attended the third and final performance and sat in the very front row. Crawfie was impressed: 'He looked more than ever, I thought, like a Viking, weather-beaten and strained, and his manners left nothing to be desired.' Lilibet was positively pink with excitement. 'I have never known Lilibet more animated,' said her governess. 'There was a sparkle about her none of us had ever seen before.' According to Crawfie, 'From then on, the two young people began to correspond.'

But what did Crawfie know? The two young people had, in fact, been corresponding for some time. Writing to a friend in January

1944, Queen Mary insisted that they had actually 'been in love for the past eighteen months. In fact longer, I think . . . But the King and Queen feel that she is too young to be engaged yet. They want her to see more of the world before committing herself, and to meet more men.'

'Poor darlings,' the King wrote of his daughters in his diary as the war rumbled to a close, 'they have never had any fun yet.' His Majesty need not really have worried. Princess Margaret was to have plenty of 'fun' in the years to come and Princess Elizabeth never complained that her life lacked excitement or romance. She was not a natural gaiety girl: she never felt she was missing out on what her mother's friend Noël Coward called 'cocktails and laughter – and what comes after . . .' As Margaret Rhodes puts it, 'She was not a flibberty-gibbet, by any stretch of the imagination.'

And she did have fun, in her own way. At Windsor, as the war was ending, she was allowed her own space, beyond the nursery and the schoolroom. Crawfie described it: 'There was a little boudoir done in pink tapestry between the schoolroom and her bedroom . . . This she could use as her private apartment. Lilibet was enchanted . . .' At Buckingham Palace, as the war ended, she was given her own suite: a bedroom (in pink and beige, her mother's favourite colours), a bathroom, a sitting room, all of her own, along the corridor from Margaret's rooms, and Crawfie's and Bobo MacDonald's. Alah, the nanny, was no longer part of the nursery family: she died of meningitis, at Sandringham, at Christmas 1945. Lilibet was growing up – and having fun, albeit pretty innocent fun by today's standards. When Philip came to call, reported Crawfie, 'The three of them [Philip, Elizabeth and Margaret Rose] had dinner together in Lilibet's sitting-room, and later romped in the corridor.' Elizabeth was nineteen, Philip was twenty-four. According to Crawfie (who appears to have been as taken with the golden prince as her young charge), 'There was nothing of the polished courtier about him. He came into the Palace like a refreshing sea breeze . . . Presently he began to come up as a matter of course, and have dinner informally, in the old comfortable nursery fashion, in the old nursery, which Margaret now used as her sitting-room. The food was of the simplest. Fish, some sort of sweet, and orangeade. Philip does not smoke and drinks very little.'

After dinner, apparently, along the corridors of the Palace, there would be what Crawfie liked to describe as 'high jinks': 'Philip removed from the door the old card with "Nursery" on it, and substituted another marked "Maggie's Playroom". They would play ball (a good many electric-light bulbs suffered) and race about like a bunch of high-spirited children. It was always a threesome, unless I took a hand and did something about it by removing Margaret on some pretext or other. I felt the constant presence of the little sister, who was far from undemanding, and liked to have a good bit of attention herself, was not helping on the romance much.'

The playful presence of little Margaret notwithstanding, the romance was blossoming. In February 1945 Lilibet, approaching her nineteenth birthday, reported to her cousin, Diana: 'I am now the proud possessor of a very large photograph of Philip, which stands on the mantelpiece and glowers at me. I had to go through a lot of ragging when it arrived − though I admit Mummy said, "He is a good-looking boy", at which I agreed! I am sure all the housemaids at Sandringham looked at the photograph and said, "Ooh! I wonder who that is?"'

Princess Elizabeth did meet other men, of course. Her parents encouraged her to do so. Her mother organised small dances, to which young courtiers, Guards officers, and aristocrats were invited. Crawfie, apparently, tried to encourage Lilibet to give 'little cocktail parties of her own, in her own sitting room, to return the hospitality of her many friends', but could never persuade her. 'She was too accustomed to leaving it all to Mummie. Mummie always had done all the entertaining, and the habit was hard to break.'

Princess Elizabeth's paternal grandfather, great-grandfather, and great-great-grandmother had been royalty who had married royalty. Her father, however, only second in line to the throne, had married aristocracy ('a different gether altothing', as Princess Margaret liked to quip), but his marriage was universally accepted as a success, and, consequently, it was generally accepted that it would be equally acceptable for Elizabeth, although Heiress Presumptive, to settle for an aristocrat (top-of-the-range, of course), as Papa did when he married Mummie.

Heading the list of potential candidates were two young Grenadier Guardsmen, both born in 1919, who were the heirs to the dukedoms of Rutland and Grafton. Each became a good friend of the Princess, but neither caught her fancy and both married other girls during the course of 1946. The Duke of Rutland's marriage lasted just ten years. The Duke of Grafton[47] (a direct descendant of one of Charles II's illegitimate children) was more fortunate. His marriage survived (and thrived), and his wife, Fortune Smith (daughter of Captain Eric Smith MC), became one of Elizabeth's closest companions: Lady of the Bedchamber to the Queen from 1953 to 1966, Mistress of the Robes from 1967. When I was travelling with the Queen's party on one of her regional tours in 2001, we overheard someone in the crowd asking if the Duchess of Grafton, seated next to the Queen in the royal limousine, was the Queen's sister. This really delighted the Duchess. 'I do feel like her sister,' she said to me, proudly.

The Duke of Grafton died, aged ninety-two, in April 2011. The Queen attended his memorial service at St George's Chapel, Windsor, and mourned a friend she had known for seventy years. In February 1945, when Lilibet was confined to bed at Windsor Castle, she wrote to her cousin, Diana: 'On the second day of mumps and a long letter from Hugh which made me feel much better. He gave a very amusing description of tiger shooting with Nepalese generals. It is awful to think he has been out in India for over a year, nearly eighteen months.' The separations of war made building relationships difficult in a way that is not so easy for us to understand today – and the war took its toll, too. In October 1944 Lilibet wrote to Diana from Balmoral Castle in Scotland: 'It's awful how all the particularly charming people seem to get killed. People who had a wonderful

47 He was the Earl of Euston at the time. He succeeded as 11th Duke of Grafton on his father's death in 1970. The best aristocratic families will have acquired a series of titles over time – the Duke of Grafton, for example, is also Viscount Ipswich as well as Earl of Euston – and the custom is to give the eldest son, as a courtesy title, the second most senior title in the series. It is known as a courtesy title because it is there merely for courtesy's sake, conferring no privileges – specifically, no seat in the House of Lords. In descending order the ranks of the British aristocracy are as follows: Royal Duke, Duke, Marquess (also spelt Marquis), Earl, Viscount, Baron. A few years ago, when I presented a weekly radio show in London, I set myself the task of having a different titled guest over successive weeks, presenting them in the correct order of precedence. My guests were: the Duke of Edinburgh, the Duke of Devonshire, the Marquess of Bath, the Earl of Snowdon, Viscount Norwich, and Lord Montagu of Beaulieu.

future before them. One sometimes gets rather despairing about one's friends as one hears about more casualties, but I do hope the war will be over very shortly. We are coming south next week, which we are not looking forward to wildly. It is so peaceful up here and the thought of coming down back to bombs and sirens, and complete blackout, is not a very pleasant one. However, I expect we shall get accustomed to it again.'

Another young Guards officer of the same generation who did survive the war, and became one of Elizabeth's closest friends, was Henry, Lord Porchester. Known simply as 'Porchey', he was born in 1924, the grandson of the 5th Earl of Carnarvon, who had been a distinguished racehorse breeder (and co-discoverer of the tomb of Tutenkhamun in 1922), and the son of the 6th Earl, who, following the family tradition, bred the 1930 Derby winner, Blenheim. Shortly before he died – on 11 September 2001, the day of the al-Qaeda attacks on the United States – I asked Lord Carnarvon (who became the 7th Earl on his father's death in 1987) how he first came to meet Princess Elizabeth. 'My father knew the King and I think the King thought I might be the right kind of chap to accompany the Princess to the races. I'm glad he did. We hit it off at once.' And ever after. From October 1945 – when he accompanied her to Newmarket – until the end of his life, Elizabeth and Porchey were regular racing companions, and special friends.

Horse breeding has long been an interest of the British Royal Family. A royal stud was established at Hampton Court back in the sixteenth century. In the late nineteenth century Elizabeth's great-grandfather, Edward VII, as Prince of Wales, established a royal stud at Sandringham. In 1962 Elizabeth II, encouraged by Porchey, took on the Polhampton Lodge Stud in Hampshire to breed royal race-horses. In 1969 Porchey was officially appointed Her Majesty's racing manager. Porchey and Elizabeth shared a passion for horses, for racing, for breeding. 'We've learnt a lot together,' he told me, 'and from one another. And we've had a great deal of fun.'

I asked Porchey's son, Geordie, now the 8th Earl of Carnarvon (who was born in 1956 and is also one of the Queen's godchildren), what he felt the Queen gained from her relationship with his father. 'The Queen is completely at ease in the world of horses,' he said. 'It's a world she knows and loves. It's quite separate from the rest of the universe she inhabits. When she's in it, she is wholly absorbed by it. And I suppose my father was the centre of that part of her life. The Queen has a long and successful history as an owner and breeder. She knows the background of the stallions, she knows all the good bloodlines. My father had a photographic memory – he could remember the names of all the descendants of the great horses with no difficulty at all. The Queen and he could talk about horses for hours. They had a shared interest that was all-consuming – and a shared sense of humour. When my father and the Queen were together, there were always a lot of laughs. The Queen is more comfortable around men, anyway. She is easy with them, more chatty. And I think their relationship was special because they knew each other so well. They were happy together. You could tell. When he died, quite unexpectedly, the Queen came to his funeral. She very rarely goes to funerals, as you know.'

Princess Anne once said that Porchey was the one person in the world who could telephone the Queen and always be put through at once. In seven months, between 11 September 2001 and 30 March 2002, the Queen lost three key figures in her life: Porchey, her sister, and her mother.[48] With Porchey and Queen Elizabeth, she shared a

48   The Queen's telephone conversations with her mother and her racing manager were
     a regular, and very happy, feature of her adult life. They would discuss every aspect
     of the horsey world, including the form of the day's runners – but not with a view
     to placing bets. In the week of Queen Elizabeth's death, when I interviewed her
     niece and lady-in-waiting, Margaret Rhodes, she was anxious to dispel the myth
     that Her Majesty was a betting woman. 'What was the other thing I read in the
     paper this week?' she said to me. 'Queen Elizabeth had rung up her turf accountant
     from Concorde? Well, I don't think she knew what a turf accountant was, apart from
     anything else. And I should think she never had a bet in her entire life. In fact, I'm
     perfectly sure she'd never had a bet in her entire life.' Mrs Rhodes was eager to
     scotch quite a few myths that day. With a laugh, and while offering me a glass of
     sherry, she said, 'Her drinking. I read in one of the papers somebody saying Queen
     Elizabeth had hollow legs and that she'd start drinking gin and Dubonnet after
     breakfast. That is total fallacy. She would have a glass of gin and Dubonnet before
     lunch and a Martini before dinner and that was it. She enjoyed it. She'd have red
     wine with dinner. She drank normally, like we would – but absolutely not to excess.'
     'And what about her famous high teas?' I asked. Mrs Rhodes exploded: 'High tea?
     She never had high tea. She had ordinary tea at a quarter to five. If she was at Birkhall
     and people had been out shooting or stalking or fishing, then there'd be scones and
     jam and cake and biscuits – but high tea? Never.'

passion — and, according to the psychiatrist Anthony Clare, having a passion is one of the secrets of achieving happiness. Prince Philip is a serious equestrian with a passion for carriage driving, but he has never shared his wife's commitment to the turf or her passion for horse breeding. He left that to Porchey.

On 8 May 1945, VE Day, Prince Philip was on board HMS *Whelp* in the Far East and Princess Elizabeth was at Buckingham Palace with her parents. Dressed in her ATS uniform, she joined the King, the Queen, Princess Margaret, and the Prime Minister, Winston Churchill, on the Palace balcony, and waved to the cheering multitude below.

Later in the day, the King and Queen, a little reluctantly, allowed their daughters to go down into the streets and join the throng. According to the Vicomtesse de Bellaigue, who, with Crawfie and a Guards major, were the Princesses' chaperones for the expedition, 'The King drew the line about Piccadilly Circus, which was to be avoided.' Porchey, who was also among the party, recalled, 'We went down Birdcage Walk, up Whitehall, up Piccadilly, into the Ritz Hotel and back to Hyde Park Corner down to the Palace. Everyone was very jolly, linking arms in the streets, and singing "Run, Rabbit Run", "Hang Out the Washing on the Siegfried Line", "Roll out the Barrel", that sort of thing . . .' The Comtesse de Bellaigue said, 'I shall never forget running wildly down St James's Street, with a puffing Major of the Grenadiers, to keep pace with the Princesses. When we reached the Palace they shouted like the other people, "We want the King", "We want the Queen". On the whole we were not recognised. However, a Dutch serviceman, who attached himself to the end of our file of arm-in-arm people (the Princesses being in the centre of the file) realised who the Princesses were. He withdrew discreetly and just said, "It was a great honour. I shall never forget this evening." All our group got back to the Palace through a garden gate. The Queen was anxiously waiting for us. Her Majesty provided us with sandwiches she made herself.'

By the time the Princesses took to the streets again, thirteen weeks later, for a similar expedition on VJ Day, 15 August 1945, Churchill was no longer Prime Minister. With victory in Europe achieved, the Labour Party, under Clement Attlee, reckoned the time had come to end the wartime coalition. Churchill had no choice but to dissolve

Parliament and call a general election. Polling began on 5 July, with the voting and counting period specially extended to allow the troops overseas to vote. When the result was announced on 26 July, it was a landslide victory for Labour. Churchill's Conservatives lost 160 seats. Attlee's Labour Party gained 230. The age of nationalisation was upon us: the Welfare State was about to be born: King George VI was a monarch with misgivings.

The King was instinctively conservative, wary of change, and apprehensive about the pace and degree of his new government's socialist agenda. He appears to have done rather well at keeping his personal feelings under wraps. Herbert Morrison, chief architect of Labour's election victory, and second-in-command in the new administration, said the King 'accepted calmly and willingly the changes of political outlook and of personality in the kind of minister he had known throughout his reign'. Morrison found the monarch 'fair in his observations' and 'meticulously observant in his constitutional position'. Princess Elizabeth learnt much from her father's example.

Privately, the King said (to his brother, the Duke of Gloucester) that he found the new government 'difficult to talk to' and his new Prime Minister 'positively mute'.[49] Churchill, of course, was positively verbose (and elaborately solicitous when it came to his dealings with any monarch), but the King had been wary of him, too, back in 1940. In due course – in fact, quite quickly – George VI and Clement Attlee came to understand, respect, and even value each other. Michael Foot, who became an MP in 1945 and, later, leader of the Labour Party, knew Attlee well. 'Clem was not an emotional man,' he told me. 'He was not given to public shows of feeling. The only time – ever – that I saw tears in his eyes and sensed a crack in his voice was when he spoke of the death of George VI.'

The King made it his business to work harmoniously with his Prime Minister. The relationship prospered. In November 1951 he honoured Attlee with the Order of Merit. In July 1945, however,

49 His colleague Aneurin Bevan said of Attlee: 'He brings to the fierce struggle of politics the tepid enthusiasm of a lazy summer afternoon at a cricket match.' Attlee was aware of how others viewed him, and, in retirement, composed a wry limerick about himself: 'Few thought he was even a starter / There were many who thought themselves smarter / But he ended PM / CH and OM / An earl and a knight of the garter.'

he was simply appalled by Attlee's triumph and Churchill's defeat. 'I was shocked at the result,' he told Churchill, '& thought it most ungrateful to you personally after all your hard work for the people.' With a heart 'too full', he wrote at length (and by hand) to say 'how very sad I am that you are no longer my Prime Minister', concluding:

> For myself personally, I regret what has happened more than perhaps anyone else. I shall miss your counsel to me more than I can say. But please remember that as a friend I hope we shall be able to meet at intervals.
> Believe me,
> I am,
> Your very sincerely and gratefully,
> GRI[50]

The King's world was changing.

With the war in Japan at an end, Philip and HMS *Whelp* came home. In January 1946, in Portsmouth, as the destroyer's first lieutenant, Philip's immediate post-war duty was to preside over her decommissioning. His next postings – to Pwllheli in north Wales and Corsham, near Bath, in Wiltshire – were land-based and less romantic, but, he would insist, no less rewarding. He used to speak with particular pride of his time at the Corsham naval training establishment, HMS *Royal Arthur*. It was a school for petty officers and, by all accounts, Philip was an innovative, imaginative, and effective instructor. 'We had some new ideas,' he said. 'It was satisfying work.'

Away from his naval base, he still had no home to call his own. When I first went to meet Countess Mountbatten and Lord Brabourne, they showed me their first visitors' book – from 1946, the year they were married – and there, marking his visit over the weekend of 20–22 December, was Philip's signature and, next to it, in the address column, he had written: 'No fixed abode!'

He had a base with his grandmother at Kensington Palace; he stayed with his cousin, Princess Marina, and her family, at Coppins; regularly, at weekends, when the Mountbattens were away at

<hr />

50 *Georgius Rex Imperator* – George King Emperor.

Broadlands, he cadged a bed for the night at 16 Chester Street, their London house. According to the Mountbattens' butler, John Dean, the Mountbatten household servants all adored him: 'He was so considerate, so anxious to avoid giving trouble to people who, after all, were paid to look after the family, that we all thought the world of him and looked forward to his visits.'

Dean later went to work for Prince Philip as his valet and, eventually, 'did a Crawfie', publishing a memoir of his happy years as the Prince's trouser-presser. From start to finish, the Prince remained a hero to his valet. Dean noticed how, immediately after the war, Philip seemed to have very few clothes and what he had wasn't in the best nick. Philip would come up to town, in his black MG, with just his razor in his pocket. Overnight, Dean would wash and iron the young Prince's only shirt and darn his threadbare socks for him. 'He was very easy to look after, and never asked for things like that to be done for him, but I liked him so much that I did it anyway.'

Philip worked hard. He played hard. He drove hard. In April 1946 he managed to borrow an army vehicle, to drive across war-torn Europe, to Salem, to attend his youngest sister Sophie's second wedding. 'Tiny', as she was known, left with five young children when her husband, Prince Christoph of Hesse, was killed in Italy in 1943, was marrying Prince George Wilhelm of Hanover, now headmaster of Salem, the school founded by Prince Max of Baden and Kurt Hahn, where Philip had briefly been a pupil before moving to Hahn's Scottish outpost, Gordonstoun, in 1934. After years of separation, Philip was reunited with his sisters. He was reunited with his mother, too. Alice travelled to London to stay with her own mother at Kensington Palace and to see her son again: it was the first time they had been together for five years. 'She is full of energy & good sense,' Alice's mother reported of her daughter, '& she and Philip get on well together.'

Philip also made a post-war pilgrimage, in 1946, to Monte Carlo – accompanied by Mike Parker – to meet up with his late father's lady friend, the Comtesse de La Bigne, and collect a few of Prince Andrea's personal effects: some books, some pictures, some clothes, a pair of hairbrushes, his ivory-handled shaving brush, his signet ring. Andrea left his son very little because he had very little to leave – other than debts. (The debts were not finally cleared until 1947, and then only thanks to help from Dickie and Edwina Mountbatten, and Nada Milford Haven's brother-in-law, Sir Harold Wernher.)

Philip arranged to meet the Comtesse at the Café de Paris – founded in 1868 and, to this day, described on its website as 'the mother of all meeting places'. Mike Parker told me, 'We got there first, ordered cocktails and waited. Then she arrived. It was like a scene from a film. We realised it must be her at once. She made a proper entrance. She was elegant. She wore blue glasses, I remember. Very striking. She seemed totally at home. She and Philip hit it off at once.'

Andrea had been laid to rest in the Russian Orthodox church in Nice. In 1946 his body was taken by Greek cruiser to Athens and buried in the gardens of the royal palace at Tatoï. He had been the son of King George I of Greece. In September 1946, following a plebiscite, George I's grandson, Andrea's nephew, George II, was restored to the Greek throne. His renewed reign was short-lived. In April 1947 he suffered a sudden stroke and died, unexpectedly, aged fifty-six. His younger brother, Paul (husband of the formidable Princess Frederika of Hanover), succeeded him.

King Paul was Prince Philip's first cousin. Prince Philip was a great-great-grandson of Queen Victoria. If Princess Elizabeth was to follow the custom, long established, of British monarchs-in-waiting marrying into European royalty, there was a certain inevitability about her match with Prince Philip. That is certainly how his immediate family all felt – in Greece, in Germany, in England. He acknowledged the fact himself. 'After all,' he said, 'if you spend ten minutes thinking about it – and a lot of these people spent a great deal more thinking about it – how many obviously eligible young men, other than people living in this country, were available?'

One of 'these people' thinking about it, long and hard, over several years, was undoubtedly Lord Louis Mountbatten. Thus far, I have tried to tell the story of the royal romance without too much reference to Uncle Dickie, simply because that is the way the Duke of Edinburgh would have preferred it. In every other published account of the lead-up to the royal engagement of July 1947, Mountbatten stands centre stage. I think the principals saw it differently. To them the off-stage murmurings and machinations of others were neither here nor there. This affair was their affair and nobody else's – right from the start. They were cousins – though, happily, not first cousins. Their families knew one another. They met. They fell in love – she, quite quickly; he, over time. They thought about it; they talked about it; eventually they decided to make their lives together, for better or worse. It is as simple as that.

That Dickie Mountbatten was anxious to encourage the union is not in question, but his eagerness to be involved may have been more of a hindrance than a help. On more than one occasion Philip had to urge his uncle to moderate his enthusiasm. In September 1945 he wrote to him: 'Please, I beg you, not too much advice in an affair of the heart, or I shall be forced to do the wooing by proxy.' In January 1947, as the prospect of the engagement grew closer, Philip wrote to Dickie about the impact his uncle's attitude might have on Lilibet: 'I am not being rude, but it is apparent that you like the idea of being the General Manager of this little show and I am rather afraid that she might not take to the idea as docilely as I do. It is true that I know what is good for me, but don't forget that she has not had you as Uncle *loco parentis*, counsellor and friend as long as I have . . .'

Mountbatten was a well-intentioned control freak. He was also a loving uncle, rightly proud of his impressive young nephew, and understandably excited by the possibility of being *in loco parentis* to the next Prince Consort. Indeed, as the engagement appeared ever more likely, he began looking into the precedent and encouraged his sister Alice to help him with his research. Mountbatten revelled in royalty; he was ambitious for his kith and kin; he was fascinated by genealogy; he was an instinctive match-maker. According to his biographer, Philip Ziegler, some time in the early 1930s he prepared for his cousin David, then Prince of Wales, a list of eighteen unmarried European princesses, ranging from the thirty-three-year-old Alexandra of Hohenlohe-Langenburg to Princess Thyra of Mecklenburg-Schwerin, who was a mere fifteen. He knew his *Almanack de Gotha*. He knew there was no more glittering match for the son he never had than the Heiress Presumptive to the British throne.

Other members of the family were almost as excited by the prospect of the union as Dickie. But Philip gave them no encouragement. In February 1944 Philip's grandmother, Victoria, having had Philip to stay on leave, reported to Mountbatten, 'As he has not touched on the subject you spoke about to me with reference to his future, I also refrain from doing so.' In March, having seen more of Philip, she wrote again to Dickie: 'I touched on the subject on which you gave him advice, but he was not inclined to confide in me, so I did not press him.' In June, Alice wrote to her son from Athens, hoping to tickle some titbits from him: 'I heard you stayed with Marina [at Coppins] at Easter and paid an interesting visit, as well as lunching with a certain young lady & her parents before you left . . .' Philip did not rise to the bait.

Philip was his own man, resistant to all outside interference. Yes, his cousin Marina was helpful in providing a discreet venue for the young couple to meet. Where else could they meet, after all? He had no home of his own and they could hardly have romantic trysts in public places – but she was not party to any intriguing. In January 1945 she wrote to Dickie: 'Of course the less said about the question we have sometimes discussed the better – & as you say it must take its course.'

Lilibet did not hide her feelings from her mother or her sister or her closest friends. Margaret Rhodes told me, 'She'd say, "Philip's written again" or "Philip's coming to stay – isn't that exciting?" She was happy to be in love.' On the mantelpiece in her sitting room she kept her framed photograph of Philip. 'Is that altogether wise?' asked Crawfie. 'A number of people come and go. You know what that will lead to. People will begin all sorts of gossip.' The teenage Princess removed the offending portrait – and replaced it with another one, featuring her adored first lieutenant hidden behind a full naval beard. 'There you are, Crawfie,' she said. 'I defy anyone to recognise who that is.'

Philip had a picture of Lilibet, too, a small one, kept – according to John Dean, who discovered it in the Prince's overnight travelling bag – in a scuffed leather frame. Philip did not discuss his love life with his uncle's butler, nor even, if he could help it, with his uncle. He did not discuss it, either, with the women in his family or – until the engagement was imminent – with his two closest contemporary male friends: his first cousin, David Milford Haven, and his fellow first lieutenant, Mike Parker. I think he was a man (like many) who did have difficulty in openly expressing his feelings. He would deny it, of course. He would simply say that he was not a man who liked to wear his heart upon his sleeve – for daws to peck at, and hacks to feed upon.

Where young Philip did cooperate with his uncle was in the matter of achieving British nationality. Philip was a Prince of Greece, but he did not feel Greek and, as I say, had never professed any particular sympathy for the Greek people.

In terms of blood, Prince Philip of Greece was not Greek at all. He was Danish, German, Russian, and English. He was born in Greece, but spent his early childhood in France and Germany. From his adolescence onwards he was based in England. Once he had joined the Royal Navy, therefore, and started to make headway as a young officer, becoming a naturalised British subject seemed to be a wholly sensible move. Mountbatten took the initiative, and did so with the family's general approval. In September 1944 Victoria wrote to Dickie: 'I think it is the best thing for him & it will give a firm basis for his life, which without a fixed career or home country it was wanting in, poor boy.' Princess Marina concurred: 'I think it is a very good idea & apart from it being a help in his naval career it might also be an asset for other "matters".'

Turning Philip from Greek prince to British subject proved a more challenging undertaking than Mountbatten had envisaged. For a start, the blessing of both George II of Greece and George VI of Britain was an essential requirement, and, initially at least, neither monarch seemed in a hurry to give it. In George II's case, it may have been a matter of national pride, a reluctance to have Greece lose any prince to another country. In George VI's case, it may have been because the King suspected that Mountbatten's concern over Philip's nationality was as much to assist his nephew with the 'other matters' as with his naval career. In August 1944, when the King's private secretary, Sir Alan Lascelles, called on the Permanent Secretary of the Home Office to discuss the matter, he noted in his diary: 'I suspect there may be a matrimonial nigger in the woodpile.'

This hesitation of the two kings, combined with sustained doubts in government circles about the wisdom of getting embroiled in any aspect of Balkan politics except when absolutely necessary, and simple bureaucratic delay (there was a war on and this was not a priority), meant that it took three years – and much toing and froing and huffing and puffing, lobbying, and letter-writing by Mountbatten

– to arrive at a satisfactory outcome. Eventually, on 18 March 1947, the deed was done.[51] The news of Philip's naturalisation was officially posted in the *London Gazette*, alongside that of several hundred others, many of them Poles who had fought with the British through the war, many of them German Jewish refugees. Once, when I asked Prince Philip how he thought he was seen by most people in Britain, he said, after a moment's consideration, 'Refugee husband, I suppose.'

Along with a new nationality he needed a new name. The surnames on offer on his father's side of the family had little to commend them. Prince Andrea was the grandson of the King of Denmark and the family name of the Danish royal house was Schleswig-Holstein-Sonderburg-Glücksburg. Another, more manageable, paternal family name was Oldenburg and a bright spark at the College of Arms suggested that 'Oldcastle', as its English equivalent, might find favour. It didn't.[52] Instead (apparently at the suggestion of James Chuter Ede, Clement Attlee's Home Secretary), Philip agreed to take the already established anglicised version of his mother's surname, Battenberg. On 18 March 1947 Prince Philip of Greece became Lieutenant Philip Mountbatten, RN.

In time (in the mid-1980s), his mother-in-law, Queen Elizabeth, would describe Prince Philip as 'an English gentleman – completely'. In the mid-1940s she was less certain. Her younger brother, David Bowes-Lyon, to whom she was very close (Elizabeth and David were the Benjamins of the family, seventeen and nineteen years younger

---

51   It transpired, subsequently, that it need not have been done at all. As the result of a case brought, in 1955, by Prince Ernst August of Hanover to establish his own British nationality, it became clear that, as a consequence of the Act of Settlement of 1701 – designed to assure the succession of Queen Anne should she die without issue – all direct descendants of the Electress Sophia of Hanover (granddaughter of James I and mother of George I) would, by Act of Parliament, be deemed British. As a direct descendant of the Electress Sophia, Prince Philip, like Prince Ernst August (and some four hundred others, mostly Germans), was, it appears, from birth, automatically a British subject.

52   Fortunately perhaps. While Oldcastle is a good old English surname with an interesting pedigree, Sir John Oldcastle (c.1375–1417) served in the Welsh campaigns of King Henry IV and was a friend of Prince Hal, before converting to the doctrines of John Wycliffe and leading a Lollard conspiracy to capture Henry V. Oldcastle ended his days hanged and burned at St Giles's Fields. In Shakespeare's *Henry IV* the character of Falstaff was originally named Oldcastle.

than their eldest sister), did not believe that Philip was an appropriate husband for the future Elizabeth II.

According to Gina Kennard, 'David Bowes-Lyon was a vicious little fellow. He had it in for Philip right from the start. He was completely against him.' He was not alone. Lord Salisbury (whose ancestor had been on hand to advise Elizabeth I, after all) had profound reservations. As did Lord Stanley and the Earl of Eldon. As did most of the senior men at court. Philip might now be eligible for a British passport, but he wasn't really British. He was German and you couldn't trust a Hun. Yes, he was royal (of sorts), but Greek royalty was a standing joke. The Greek throne was notoriously unstable and the Greek royals undeniably the bottom of the pack. All right, he was serving in the Royal Navy – and that 'mention in dispatches' was to his credit – but where had he been to school? Gordonstoun? What was that all about? And where were his parents, for God's sake? And wasn't he a *protégé* of Dickie Mountbatten's? Need more be said?

Many at court, and much of the Establishment, were wary of Mountbatten. As his daughter, Patricia, put it to me, with a smile, 'My father was a progressive and the one thing the courtiers were not was progressive.' Never mind 'progressive': the courtiers considered Mountbatten dangerously Left-wing. And not quite as royal as he liked to think he was. Hadn't his grandfather, Prince Alexander of Hesse (whose own parentage was doubtful), run off with a lady-in-waiting – a Polish girl called Julie Hauke? She might have been elevated to the rank of Serene Highness eventually, but she was certainly a blot on the Battenberg escutcheon. ('I believe that the Battenbergs have always behaved somewhat peculiarly,' commented Heinrich Himmler after studying the Gestapo file on Mountbatten and his family.)

Mountbatten had a questionable pedigree and a rum set of *louche* and Left-leaning friends – such as Tom Driberg.[53] He was also, in the eyes of those who did not take to him, inordinately full of himself, impossibly pushy, and incurably inclined to interfere where he wasn't wanted.

53 Tom Driberg (1905–76) was a journalist, Labour MP, and notoriously promiscuous homosexual. It was Mountbatten's easy way with people like Driberg – and Noël Coward – that fuelled the rumours of his possible bisexuality. In his official biography Philip Ziegler explores these exhaustively and dismisses them.

'Yes,' chuckled Patricia Mountbatten, 'My father had colossal energy and drive. He was a dynamo. He made things happen. He got things done. And he didn't go through "the usual channels". He by-passed the officials. That really infuriated them. If he wanted to speak to the King, he just picked up the telephone. I'm sure they thought he'd be a very bad influence on Philip and that Philip might prove to be a chip off the old block.'

Sir Alan 'Tommy' Lascelles (*Educ*: Marlborough; Oxford; *Address*: Sutton Waldron House, Blandford; *Clubs*: Travellers', Pratt's, MCC; *TA*: Fontmell-Magna), assistant private secretary to the Prince of Wales throughout the 1920s, assistant private secretary and private secretary to successive kings from 1935,[54] encapsulated some of the family's and most of the courtiers' initial estimation of Lieutenant Philip Mountbatten: 'They felt he was rough, uneducated, and would probably not be faithful.'

In time the King's private secretary warmed to Philip, describing him (to Harold Nicolson in June 1948) as 'such a nice young man', and 'not a fool in any way', saluting his 'sense of duty', and acknowledging him to be 'so much in love poor boy'. The King himself warmed to the young Prince from the start. In the spring of 1944 he told Queen Mary, 'I like Philip. He is intelligent, has a good sense of humour & thinks about things in the right way.' The King's only real reservation in the early days of the romance was his daughter's youth, but by the summer of 1946 Lilibet was twenty, so when Philip, now twenty-five, came to stay with the Royal Family at Balmoral – and proposed to her, and was accepted – there was little the doting father could do but bow to the inevitable – and play for a bit more time. The King agreed, in principle, to the union, but made two conditions: there could be no formal engagement until

---

54 In *Friends, Enemies and Sovereigns*, Sir John Wheeler-Bennett described Lascelles: 'Tall and aristocratic of bearing, with a long face and long thin hands and feet, his manner was at the outset austere.' He typified the courtier of his time: a 'jealous guardian of the royal prerogative; a man who had the reputation not only of not suffering fools gladly, but of rarely enduring their presence in the same room.' Apparently, those who knew him well appreciated his 'caustic wit' and 'the delightful and unusual workings of his mind'. Of course, appearances can be deceptive. You would have thought he was a Balliol man with a First. In fact, he was a Trinity man with a Second.

after the Princess's twenty-first birthday in April 1947 and, before that, there would be a period of reflection while the King and Queen took their two daughters with them on a twelve-week tour of southern Africa.

The tour was memorable on several counts. Princess Elizabeth was unhappy to be going away – Crawfie reports 'tears in her eyes' at the moment of departure – but ready, as ever, to do her duty, and excited by the prospect of her first trip outside the British Isles. The timing, however, was unfortunate. As the Royal Family set off from Portsmouth – 'us four', as the King called them – on 1 February 1947, on board HMS *Vanguard*, the Royal Navy's newest battleship, the weather in the English Channel was appalling. The weather on the mainland was even worse. Britain was suffering its cruellest winter of the century.

By 12 February, when the royal travellers were basking in sub-equatorial sunshine, the news from home was dire: 'Heavy snowstorms and sub-zero temperatures are combining with a serious fuel shortage to bring Britain to its economic knees. More than four million workers have been made idle by power cuts, and with hundreds of coal trains unable to battle their way through 20-feet high snow-drifts, thousands of homes are without heat or light for long periods of the day.' The Thames at Windsor had frozen over. Buckingham Palace was candle-lit. The King volunteered to return home. The Prime Minister, Clement Attlee, said, 'Thank you, but no thank you': a dramatic return would simply exacerbate the crisis, advertising it worldwide. Besides, the African trip was also designed, in part, to give the King – exhausted by the war and in failing health – a well-deserved opportunity for rest, recuperation, and sunshine.

On board ship, when the calmer seas were reached, there was certainly some of that. The King and Queen relaxed. The Princesses had fun. There are delightful photographs of Lilibet and Margaret Rose playing deck games with the younger officers. They look really happy. (There is a key to these people in those pictures: as a rule, the Windsors are most comfortable and carefree, not in conversation or contemplation, reading books or listening to music, but when they are playing games, playing sport, riding, shooting, having larks, enjoying practical jokes, taking part in Scottish country dancing.) Off-duty in *Vanguard*, picnicking in Southern Rhodesia, visiting the

Orange Free State, Basutoland, and Bechuanaland in a special 'White Train', almost as tourists: the trip had many highlights. The girls sent regular reports to Crawfie:

'The letters I got back were a great pleasure to me. They were also a wonderful picture of the different make-up of the two sisters. Margaret [now sixteen] wrote with her usual gaiety, all about the fun they were having, how beautiful the White Train was, how warm the sun, how wonderful the food.

'Lilibet wrote, immensely distressed by all that was going on in England in the bitter weather. It bothered her to feel she was far away having a good time, in a land so full of everything. She felt she ought to be at home.'

The South African leg of the tour was the longest and most trying. The King was in sympathy with the ageing South African Prime Minister, Field Marshal Jan Christian Smuts,[55] who was striving valiantly against the odds to achieve Anglo-Afrikaner unity. The Boers – whose Nationalist Party would defeat Smuts and his United Party government in the election of 1948 and usher in the era of apartheid – were not in sympathy with the King, nor with the 'mingling' of Europeans and non-Europeans in the crowds that came to greet him. The atmosphere was tense. The King was tired and tetchy. At Benoni, a gold-mining town in the south of the Transvaal, there was an unfortunate incident when a man broke from the jostling crowd and rushed towards the open royal car. The King, unnerved, began shouting angrily at the driver to get a move on. The Queen, fearing an attack, hit at the man with her parasol. The man was immediately felled by one of the attendant policemen, and half beaten up, before it became apparent that he was not a would-be assailant at all, but an ardent royalist who was trying to present Their Majesties with a ten-shilling note as a twenty-first birthday present for Princess Elizabeth. The King, distressed by the misunderstanding, sent to

55 Smuts (1870–1950) was twice prime minister: 1919–24 and 1939–48. He had enlisted South Africa on the side of the Allies during the Second World War, while the Nationalist Party refused to support Britain and expressed sympathy for Nazi Germany. Smuts described apartheid as 'a crazy concept, born of prejudice and fear'. Nelson Mandela saw Smuts's defeat as a defining moment in South African history: 'From the moment of the Nationalists' election, we knew that our land would henceforth be a place of tension and strife.'

enquire after the unfortunate man, and, later, apologised for his own behaviour to his equerry, Group Captain Peter Townsend. 'I'm very sorry about today,' he said, 'I was very tired.'

The South African tour had a profound impact on Princess Elizabeth. It was her first first-hand experience of the reality of the British Commonwealth and Empire, of a divided country, of native people, of the tensions of African politics, and the nastiness of white supremacists. The Nationalists – who sneered at the King's halting attempt to say a few words in Afrikaans at the opening of parliament – trumpeted the '*swart gevaar*' ('black danger') and campaigned to keep '*Die kaffer op sy plek*' ('the nigger in his place') and '*Die koelies uit die land*' ('the coolies – i.e. the Indians – out of the country'). Lilibet was not impressed.

The Princess was taken with Africa and the African people – and the feeling was reciprocated. According to Peter Townsend, the Africans really loved her. As she drove past, they shouted, 'Leave the Princess behind!', 'Stay with us!' A popular song was composed in her honour:

> Princess, in our opinion,
> You'll find in our Dominion
> Greetings that surely take your breath,
> For you have a corner in every heart,
> Princess Elizabeth.

The climax of the tour coincided with her twenty-first birthday. Field Marshal Smuts declared 21 April a national holiday. There was a birthday parade, a birthday ball, and a civic reception at City Hall in Cape Town; Smuts presented the Princess with a gemstone necklace and a gold key to the city; the Princess reviewed hundreds of troops, shook scores of hands, and delivered a short speech at a celebratory 'youth rally of all races'. She also made one of the key broadcasts of her life.

Her old tutor in constitutional history, Sir Henry Marten, had impressed on her the special significance to the modern monarchy of both the advent of broadcasting and the development of the Commonwealth. He must have been mighty proud of his diligent pupil's birthday broadcast to the Empire and Commonwealth.

'Although there is not one of my father's subjects, from the oldest to the youngest, whom I do not wish to greet,' the Princess began, 'I am thinking especially today of all the young men and women who were born about the same time as myself and have grown up like me in the terrible and glorious years of the Second World War. Will you, the youth of the British family of nations, let me speak on my birthday as your representative?'

The essence of the message was unsurprising and comfortably generalised: in the dark days of the war, the British Empire had saved the world and 'has now to save itself'. With determination – faith, hope, and endeavour – the future of the Commonwealth might be yet more glorious, prosperous, and happy than its past. Then came the peroration – much less predictable and much more personal – spoken in a steady, high-pitched voice and heard by many millions around the world:

'There is a motto which has been borne by many of my ancestors – a noble motto, "I serve". Those words were an inspiration to many bygone heirs to the throne when they made their knightly dedication as they came to manhood. I cannot do quite as they did, but through the inventions of science I can do what was not possible for any of them. I can make my solemn act of dedication with a whole Empire listening. I should like to make that dedication now. It is very simple.

'I declare before you all that my whole life, whether it be long or short, shall be devoted to your service and the service of our great Imperial family to which we all belong, but I shall not have the strength to carry out this resolution alone unless you join in with me, as I now invite you to do. I know your support will be unfailingly given. God help me to make good my vow and God bless all of you who are willing to share in it.'

She meant it, and you could tell. She did not write it. The author was Dermot Morrah (1896–1974), historian and leader-writer and correspondent for *The Times*. Morrah sent his draft of the speech to the King's private secretary, Sir Alan Lascelles, who was travelling with the royal party on board the White Train. At first the draft went missing. According to Lascelles, who wrote to Morrah from the train on 10 March, 'The steward in the Protea diner had put it in the bar, among his bottles, little knowing that it was itself of premier cru.' Lascelles saluted Morrah's achievement: 'I have been reading drafts for many years now, but I cannot recall one that has so completely satisfied me and left me feeling that no single word should be altered. Moreover, dusty cynic though I am, it moved me greatly. It has the trumpet-ring of the other Elizabeth's Tilbury speech, combined with the immortal simplicity of Victoria's "I will be good."' Lascelles told Morrah how it had pleased Princess Elizabeth and her mother: 'The ladies concerned, you will be glad to hear, feel just as I do. The speaker herself told me that it had made her cry. Good, said I, for if it makes you cry now, it will make 200 million other people cry when they hear you deliver it, and that is what we want.' And so it proved. When the speech was broadcast, there was barely a dry eye on the planet.

On 24 April, as the royal party set off once more for home, Lascelles reported to his wife, 'From the inside, the most satisfactory feature of the whole business is the remarkable development of P'cess E.' He summed up her essential characteristics: 'A perfectly natural power of enjoying herself . . . Not a great sense of humour, but a healthy sense of fun. Moreover, when necessary, she can take on the old bores with much of her mother's skill, and never spares herself in that exhausting part of royal duty. For a child of her years, she has got an astonishing solicitude for other people's comfort; such unselfishness is not a normal characteristic of that family.'

Elizabeth was – and is – a conspicuously unselfish individual. But uniquely so? In 1936 Elizabeth's Uncle David selfishly abandoned his duty to pursue the love of his life – no question – yet, nineteen years later, in 1955, Elizabeth's sister Margaret – certainly spoilt and undoubtedly self-indulgent in many ways – sacrificed the love of her life when she agreed not to marry a divorcee in the becoming shape of her father's former equerry, Peter Townsend. Elizabeth's grandfather, George V, was not an easy parent, but he was a conscientious king, wilful but not notably selfish. His wife, Elizabeth's grandmother, Queen Mary, shared her husband's stern sense of duty, but liked to get her own way. Famously, when she came to call, if there was a *bibelot* in your drawing room that took her fancy, she expected you to present it to her. Elizabeth's mother was justly celebrated for her courtesy, charm, and commitment, and while, on the whole, she did as she pleased, and led a wonderfully pampered – and nonchalantly extravagant – life, enhanced by an enviable capacity for ignoring the unpleasant, she, like her daughter, was always solicitous for other people's comfort.

That said, when Crawfie – while her charges were in South Africa – came to see Queen Mary to tell her of her own plans to marry, the old Queen, then in her eightieth year, 'spearing for me a muffin on a small silver fork: Her Majesty never touches any food with her fingers', said at once, "My dear child. You can't leave them!"' Crawfie, then in her thirty-eighth year, pointed out that Margaret Rose, at seventeen, was nearly done with her schooling and that Princess Elizabeth was likely to get married before too long. The Queen was unmoved. 'I don't see how they could manage without you,' she said. 'I don't think they could spare you just now.' Queen Elizabeth, on her return from South Africa, was equally unbending. 'Does this mean you are going to leave us?' she asked the governess. 'You must see, Crawfie, that it would not be at all convenient just now. A change for Margaret is not at all desirable.' Crawfie hoped Her Majesty might say something about the family's plans for Lilibet's future, but, according to Crawfie, the Queen 'said nothing further, and I curtsied and withdrew'.

From my observation of them, the members of this family are masters of the art of saying nothing. Sometimes they do it to protect themselves. Sometimes they do it to indicate that a conversation is at an end. Often they do it to indicate disapproval.[56] In Queen Elizabeth the Queen Mother's very first letter to Prince Philip at the time of his engagement to her daughter, Her Majesty warned her future son-in-law of the challenges that lay ahead and that chief among them would be 'remaining silent when one is *bursting* to reply'.

56 In October 2003 the press carried reports of an employment tribunal that turned down a claim for unfair dismissal brought against Princess Anne, the Princess Royal, by one Caroline Brown, who for thirteen years was housekeeper at Gatcombe Park, the Princess's home in Gloucestershire. Ms Brown told the tribunal what happened when she took an unexpected day off: 'That evening when HRH returned from London she was plainly not speaking to me. This is the royal way of showing disapproval.'

Crawfie reflected on Queen Mary's silence and settled on a compromise. On 16 September 1947 she married her man (Major George Buthlay, a divorcee from Aberdeen, fifteen years her senior), but, after the honeymoon, the royal governess returned to her duties at Buckingham Palace.

She was not there much longer. By the end of 1948 Princess Margaret had turned nineteen and Princess Elizabeth had given birth to her first son. After sixteen years of loyal and effective service, Crawfie retired. She had been a good teacher: intelligent, imaginative, and quite adventurous by the standards of her time. Queen Elizabeth wrote thanking her for the 'devotion and love' and she was awarded one of the honours in the sovereign's personal gift, becoming a Commander of the Royal Victorian Order. (She had been hoping to become a Dame, but she was a little too junior for that, both in years and in station. She had a good opinion of herself – and why not? – but, possibly, *des idées au dessus de sa gare.* She was just the governess, dammit.) Her happiest reward – besides, of course, her fond memories of her years with the little Princesses – was the lifetime tenure of Nottingham Cottage at Kensington Palace, a dream home of 'seasoned red brick . . . with roses round the door . . . in the little square garden' – or £100 per annum in lieu. She did not enjoy the charms of Nottingham Cottage for very long.

In 1949 she wrote *The Little Princesses*, her account of her years in royal service. The book was originally published in the United States and serialised in the *Ladies' Home Journal.* Queen Elizabeth's friend Nancy, Lady Astor, happened to know the magazine's editors and was able to send Her Majesty a copy of the manuscript. The Queen was appalled. The invasion of her family's privacy and the betrayal of their trust left Her Majesty 'shocked and distressed'. Her private secretary wrote to Lady Astor: 'Such a thing is utterly alien to the spirit and custom of Their Majesties' households and staff and great regret is felt by all those who care for the sanctity of their family life at this unhappy breach of decency and good taste.'

Crawfie was not to be silenced. She received $6,500 for the US serialisation and £30,000 when the book appeared in the UK, serialised in *Woman's Own.* The money was good, and she was pleased with her own writing, but, in her heart, she knew she had done wrong. John Gordon, editor of the *Sunday Express*, tried to persuade her to write for him. He reported to the *Express*'s proprietor, Lord Beaverbrook, 'Persuasion is difficult at the moment because she has been brought to the edge of a nervous breakdown by all the trouble, but she will bend in good time.' She didn't – at least, not for the *Express* – but for *Woman's Own* she continued to exploit her erstwhile royal connections with a weekly column that ultimately proved her undoing. In the summer of 1955 she gave her readers vivid and personal accounts of both the Sovereign's Birthday Parade and Royal Ascot – annual events that, unfortunately for Crawfie, were unexpectedly cancelled that year due to a national rail strike.

Crawfie abandoned Nottingham Cottage (which Queen Mary had helped furnish for her) in the autumn of 1950. (It later became the home of Brigadier Sir Miles Hunt-Davies, GCVO, secretary to the Duke of Edinburgh, and subsequently the first London home of Prince Harry and Meghan Markle.) The court's low opinion of the errant former governess was made plain. Her neighbours, according to John Gordon, 'were afraid even to be seen speaking to her. So she decided to pack up and go.' Five years later, when her reputation as a reliable royal correspondent was finally exploded, she retired to Aberdeen, childless, largely friendless, and living in a marriage that turned out to be a disappointment. She died on 11 February 1988. There were no flowers from Lilibet or Margaret Rose at her funeral. It had been very different forty years before. At her wedding in 1947, Crawfie had been showered with royal gifts, including a complete dinner service from Queen Mary, a coffee set from Lilibet, and three bedside lamps from Margaret Rose.

Crawfie had been determined to marry her man and Their Majesties had had no choice but to accept her decision, however inconvenient. Lilibet, in her way, was just as determined. She had accompanied her parents to South Africa; she had done her duty: she had passed her twenty-first birthday and broadcast her solemn commitment to the world; now she was coming home to claim her prize. One of the ladies-in-waiting accompanying the royal party reported that, as the *Vanguard* steamed into harbour, Lilibet 'danced a little jig of sheer delight at being home again'.

Philip was determined, too – and clearly had been for a while. In June 1946 he had invited himself to Buckingham Palace and, after the visit, had written to Queen Elizabeth to apologise for his 'monumental cheek' in so doing – adding, as if to compound his cheek while claiming to be 'contrite', 'there is a small voice that keeps saying "nothing ventured, nothing gained" – well I did venture and I gained a wonderful time.'

Later that summer, after he had spent three weeks holidaying with the Windsors at Balmoral and the young couple had shared their feelings with each other and with the King and Queen, Philip wrote another thank-you letter to his future mother-in-law. 'I am sure I do not deserve all the good things which have happened to me,' he said to the Queen. 'To have been spared the war and seen victory, to have been given the chance to rest and readjust myself, to have fallen in love completely and unreservedly, makes all one's personal and even the world's troubles seem small and petty.'

In an age of comparative deference and discretion, long before the advent of the internet and the tweet, it took a while for rumours of the royal romance to spread. On 29 May 1946 Philip was photographed next to Princess Elizabeth at the wedding of her new lady-in-waiting, Mrs Jean Gibbs, to her favoured first cousin, Andrew Elphinstone, but Philip was described in the press as 'a figure still largely unknown to the British public'. They were photographed together again five months later, on 26 October 1946, at the wedding of Philip's first cousin, Patricia Mountbatten, to John Knatchbull, 7th Baron Brabourne. This time the picture appeared to tell a story: the young couple were caught on camera gazing into each other's eyes. Then they were sighted walking in the park at Windsor – holding hands. The moment they realised that they had been spotted, they sprang apart, but their secret was gradually seeping out. When Princess Elizabeth went to visit a factory, on one of the solo official outings that she was now beginning to undertake, someone in the crowd called out, 'Where's Philip?'

On 30 April 1947 the Rodgers and Hammerstein musical *Oklahoma!* opened at the Theatre Royal, Drury Lane. Philip and Elizabeth went to the show and, as a consequence, for ever after, 'People Will Say We're in Love' was said to be 'their song'. I happen to know that the Queen has a good recall of popular songs of the 1940s,[57] but I know, too, that the Duke of Edinburgh regarded the notion of 'our song' as 'sentimental codswallop' and was 'utterly infuriated' whenever it was played. In 2012, at the time of the Queen's Diamond Jubilee and the Duke's ninety-first birthday, I took part in a special edition of BBC television's *The One Show* broadcast live from Buckingham Palace. The producers were keen to feature 'People Will Say We're in Love' in the programme. I said, 'Why?' They said, 'Because it's their tune – it's their *favourite* tune.' I said, 'It isn't. I know it isn't.' They said, 'It is. It really is.' When I reported this to the Duke of Edinburgh he laughed somewhat despairingly: 'Once these myths take root there's nothing you can do to dislodge them.'

Did Prince Philip marry for love? It is not a question that I dared to ask him – nor one that he would have deigned to answer. But every one of those to whom I did put the question who knew him at the time – and knew him well – answered with an unequivocal 'yes'. His first cousin, Patricia Mountbatten, said to me, 'He may have had his doubts about what he was getting himself into – the whole business of marrying the King of England's daughter, I think that did concern him. But he had no doubts at all about Lilibet as a person – as a future wife. He adored her. He loved her deeply – you could tell. It was definitely a love match.' Mike Parker, Philip's closest male friend at the time, said to me, 'He loved her – absolutely.' Parker was an Australian and added, for good measure, 'And he fancied her, too. No question about that.'

Prince Philip married Princess Elizabeth for love. I think that he married her for family as well. As he never ceased to remind me, he had 'a perfectly good family' of his own. 'I had parents, I had sisters,' he insisted. But from his adolescence onwards he saw very little of them. Through the years of the Second World War he

---

57 Deborah Bean, for many years senior correspondence secretary at Buckingham Palace, told me that when the George Formby Society wrote asking if the Queen remembered their hero, Her Majesty told her, 'I still remember all his songs and sing them!' When the next movie of her life comes to be made and there is a sequence of Her Majesty walking steadily down a red-carpeted Palace corridor quietly trilling, 'When I'm cleaning winders', you'd better believe it. Well, stranger things have happened. We have seen the Queen on screen with Daniel Craig as James Bond, after all.

could not see his sisters: they were in Germany, literally sleeping with the enemy. His father was in Vichy France until his death in 1944. His mother was in Athens, occupied by the Germans until October 1944. In the summer of 1944, after he had spent part of his leave staying with the Windsors, Philip wrote to the Queen and told her how much he had valued his time at Balmoral: 'It is the simple enjoyment of family pleasures and amusements and the feeling that I am welcome to share them. I am afraid I am not capable of putting all this into the right words and I am certainly incapable of showing you the gratitude that I feel.'

'Showing' his feelings was not something that came easily to Prince Philip. Gina Kennard told me, 'Philip used to speak to me about Princess Elizabeth before they were engaged. He was extremely fond of her, always. He said, "I think we could do a lot together."' Robin Dalton told me, 'Philip's a cold fish. Always charming and fun, but I couldn't tell you what he really felt. All I know is that in 1945 David [Milford Haven] told me Philip was definitely planning to marry Elizabeth one day. He saw it as his destiny.'

And so it proved. On 7 July 1947, from Buckingham Palace, Queen Elizabeth wrote to her sister May: 'This is one line to tell you *very secretly* that Lilibet has made up her mind to get engaged to Philip Mountbatten. As you know, she has known him since she was 12, & I think that she is *really* fond of him, & I do pray that she will be very happy . . . We are keeping it a deadly secret, purely because of the Press, if they know beforehand that something is up, they are liable to ruin everything!'

'At last things were moving,' wrote Crawfie. 'Suddenly that look of strain we had all been conscious of disappeared from Lilibet's eyes. One day she poked her head into my room looking absolutely radiant . . . "He's coming tonight," she said, and then she kissed me and danced away. Next morning was Wednesday, July the ninth. Lilibet came to my room much earlier than usual. I have never seen her look lovelier than she did on that day, not even on her wedding morning. She wore a deep yellow frock, a shade that has always suited her very well. She closed the door behind her and held out her left hand. Her engagement ring sparkled there. It was a large square diamond with smaller diamonds either side. At the same time it was too large for her, and it had to go back to be made smaller.

It was a ring they had chosen secretly, but of course she had been unable to go and try it on.'

In fact, neither Lilibet nor Philip had been able to choose the ring personally. Phillip's mother, on one of her visits to London, undertook the task. Princess Alice had managed to reclaim her own jewelry – deposited for safety's sake at an English bank in Paris in 1930 – and took a selection of her diamonds to a jewellers in Old Bond Street, 'as Philip dared not show his face at jewellers,' she explained to her brother, Dickie, 'for fear of being recognised. I think the ring is a great success.'

On 9 July 1947 the engagement was formally announced from Buckingham Palace: 'It is with the greatest pleasure that the King and Queen announce the betrothal of their dearly beloved daughter The Princess Elizabeth to Lieutenant Philip Mountbatten, RN, son of the late Prince Andrew of Greece and Princess Andrew (Princess Alice of Battenberg), to which union the King has gladly given his consent.'

Chapter Eight

'To have and to hold from this day forward, for better for worse, for richer for poorer, in sickness and in health, to love and to cherish, till death us do part, according to God's holy ordinance.'

The Book of Common Prayer

How great was their pleasure? How glad was the King's consent? Was George VI truly happy with the engagement? Yes, overall, I think he was. Naturally, he was loath to lose a daughter – he was a fond father and they were good companions to each other – but he saw Philip's merits. He liked the fact that Philip was royal – and therefore 'one of us'. He liked the fact that Philip was making a career in the Royal Navy, as he had done. He appreciated his future son-in-law's intelligence, energy, and sense of humour. Above all, he saw that Lilibet was wholly in love and, now she was of age, could find no reason to deny her her heart's desire.

Queen Elizabeth, too, welcomed the engagement – although not in person on the day of the announcement. On 9 July she wrote to Philip from Buckingham Palace: 'I am *so* disappointed to be laid aside with this laryngitis, because I particularly wanted to see [you] & tell you how happy we feel about the engagement, and to say how glad we are to have you as a son-in-law. It is so *lovely* to know you so well and I know that we can trust our darling Lilibet to your love and care.' She signed the letter, 'Ever your affect aunt'. Whoever you are, it is never easy knowing what to call your mother-in-law.

To friends, acquaintances, and well-wishers offering congratulations on the news of the engagement the Queen gave a uniform response: 'We feel very happy about it, as [Philip] is a very nice person, & they have known each other for some years which is a great comfort.' But, privately, Her Majesty had reservations. Her doubts fuelled by her younger brother, David Bowes-Lyon, and some of her closest aristocratic friends, and by the senior courtiers led by Sir Alan Lascelles, she was not entirely sure about her future son-in-law. Was Philip really right for Lilibet? Was he good enough? Was he, in truth, a suitable consort for a future Queen?

To the senior courtiers, to the aristocrats in Queen Elizabeth's immediate circle, Philip did not feel like 'one of us'. He spoke perfect English, he had impeccable manners, but he was by no stretch of the imagination a classic English gentleman. He was neither an Etonian, nor a Guards officer, nor a huntsman.[58] And what little was known of his parents was not encouraging. The royal establishment did not welcome Philip with open arms. Far from it. According to John Brabourne, 'They were bloody to him. We were at Balmoral that summer' – the summer of the engagement – 'and they were absolutely bloody to him. They didn't like him, they didn't trust him, and it showed. Not at all nice.'

What was Philip's reaction to the hostility? I asked.

'I think it hurt,' Lord Brabourne said to me. 'But he didn't let it show. He just got on with it.' It certainly rankled with Philip – and continued to do so, even into old age. He was snubbed by snobs. He was treated as an outsider, when he knew he was anything but. His father, after all, had been an ADC to Queen Victoria, Edward VII, and George V. Prince Philip told me the story of the first time he visited Windsor Castle after his engagement, when a courtier, patronisingly, began to tell him about the history of the place. Philip interrupted and silenced the man, saying, 'Yes, I know. My mother was born here.'

Princess Alice was in England at the time of her son's engagement. She was staying with her own mother at Kensington Palace. She was happy to see Philip and, together, they spent hours sorting through cases of Andrea's old possessions – his papers and books,

---

58 Even today, fox-hunting is at the heart of country life for many in the Queen's immediate circle. Despite the controversy it attracts, Prince Charles continues to hunt. Prince Philip never did. He said, 'I don't think I've even seen a fox hunt.' He was opposed to a ban on fox-hunting – 'I don't understand the prejudice against it,' he said – but, even after sixty years of rubbing shoulders with them, there was almost nothing of the huntin'-shootin'-fishing' English aristo in his manner or his attitudes.

clothes, and bric-a-brac – sent up from the south of France following Philip's visit to the Comtesse de La Bigne. Alice now spoke of Andrea almost as if they had never parted. She had high hopes for her son's future happiness.

The betrothal was announced on 9 July, because a Buckingham Palace garden party was scheduled for the 10th and the young couple could make their first public appearance there. Alice sent a happy report to Dickie, now in India in his new role as Britain's last Viceroy: 'It amused me very much to be waiting with the rest of the family, for Philip to come down grandly with Bertie, Elizabeth & Lilibet. The young couple made their rounds of the garden alone, accompanied by the court people & received ovations from the guests. This morning the two came alone to visit Mama, who was delighted as she is very fond of Lilibet & likes her character very much.' Alice told Dickie that Philip was at his most exuberant: 'He was so excited he hardly knew what he was doing.'

The engagement announced, preparations for the wedding began at once. By royal standards, it was not to be an extravagant affair. Times were hard: the winter had been cruel, the economy was fragile, rationing was the order of the day. Tom Driberg, the Labour MP, wrote to his friend Dickie Mountbatten to warn him that the government's backbenchers would not look kindly on public funds being lavished either on his nephew's wedding or on his subsequent lifestyle. From India (where he had been transformed from Viceroy to Governor-General following India's independence) Mountbatten sent a swift response to Driberg: 'You can rest assured that he [Philip] thoroughly understands this problem and indeed he spoke to me about it when I was home in May. I am sure he is entirely on the side of cutting down the display of the wedding, and his own personal feelings are against receiving any civil list for the very reasons you give. I have, however, persuaded him that he should take something.' Mountbatten explained that Philip had virtually no money beyond his navy pay and that his 'little two-seater' (his beloved MG) made 'a big hole in his private fortune'. 'As a future Prince Consort, however,' he went on, 'I think you will agree that Third-class travel would be regarded as a stunt and a sixpenny tip to a porter as stingey . . . It really amounts to this: you have either got to give up the Monarchy or give the wretched people who have to carry out the functions of the Crown enough money to be able to do it with the same dignity at least as the Prime Minister or the Lord Mayor of London is afforded.'

As it turned out, Philip was not destined to be Prince Consort. It would be ten years, in fact, before he would become a prince of the United Kingdom. At the outset of his marriage he did not go entirely without honours, however. The wedding was set for 20 November 1947. At the beginning of the month the King reported to Queen Mary, 'I am giving the Garter to Lilibet next Tuesday, November 11th so that she will be senior to Philip, to whom I am giving it on November 19th. I have arranged that he shall be created a Royal Highness & that the titles of his peerage will be: Baron Greenwich, Earl of Merioneth & Duke of Edinburgh . . . It is a great deal to give a man all at once, but I know Philip understands his new responsibilities on his marriage to Lilibet.'

Mountbatten (who had become a Knight of the Garter himself at the end of 1946) returned from India for the wedding. For the eve of the great day, Mike Parker organised a stag night for Philip at the Dorchester Hotel. He told me about it: 'It was a great night. Everyone was in naval evening dress. Mountbatten was the senior guest, alongside David Milford Haven and captains and first lieutenants of the 27th Destroyer Flotilla, the flotilla that wound up in Japan at the end of the war. It was a very happy occasion. It was an evening of comrades. Philip was an orphan of sorts and we were family.[59] Philip was happy and we were happy for him.' At the beginning of the evening, the gentlemen of the press were invited to take photographs of the guests. When they had done so, Mountbatten suggested that the guests might now borrow the press cameras to take a group photograph of the gentlemen of the press. Having done so, the guests, at Parker's bidding, removed the flash bulbs from the

59 The concept of fellow officers forming one's 'family' was best expressed for me by a soldier called John Kenneally, another orphan, the illegitimate son of a prostitute, who won the Victoria Cross in the final assault on Tunis in 1943. His regiment, the Irish Guards, were his 'family': 'It was a hard school to learn in. Without being over-sentimental, men can love each other. It is born of mutual suffering, hardships shared, dangers encountered. It's a spiritual love and there is nothing sexual about it. It's entirely masculine, even more than brotherly love, and it's called comradeship.'

cameras and smashed them against the wall, so preventing any further photography. 'We were just having fun,' Parker told me. 'It was a good-humoured evening all round.'

At the time, that's how the newspapermen saw it, too. Over the years, however, the incident has been cited, time and again, as an illustration of Philip's fundamental hostility towards the press. He denied it absolutely. He said to me more than once, 'I go out of my way to line people up for the photographers, to make sure everyone in the group is in the picture, to make sure the photographers have got what they need. I always have.' He added, with a sigh, 'Of course, they always want one more. They're never satisfied. But I do my best. I do try to help.' On the morning of his wedding, seeing the photographers huddled in the cold outside Kensington Palace, he ordered cups of hot coffee and tea to be sent out to them.

There is additional confusion about the eve-of-wedding stag night, confusion inadvertently caused by Larry Adler,[60] who, in interviews reproduced in several books and used in a Channel Four documentary about Prince Philip, said, 'I was at his bachelor party the night before his wedding to Princess Elizabeth.' He wasn't. Adler was at a different dinner, an earlier event, organised by the photographer Baron Nahum (always known simply as 'Baron'), who had met Philip at Broadlands when he had been taking photographs of the Mountbattens, had become a friend of Philip's, and was to take the official photographs of the royal wedding. When, not long before his death in 2001, I asked Adler about the stag night he remembered, he said, 'I may have got the date wrong, but I've not forgotten the occasion – or the atmosphere. There were about twenty to thirty guys there, all cracking jokes at Philip's expense – you know, dirty jokes, wardroom stuff. I couldn't join in because it wasn't comfortable. Philip wasn't comfortable. He was getting married and he was

60 Larry Adler (1914–2001) was an American-born, London-based virtuoso mouth organ player. He was both gifted and preposterous, a name-dropper on an epic scale (Gershwin, Churchill, Einstein, he had known them all) and a raconteur who rarely stopped. Once, when he was very old, he was a guest on a radio show I was presenting, and inadvertently slipped off his chair and fell to the floor. Flat on his back, feet in the air, he carried on talking. Many regarded him as a bore. I liked him, even if – like Prince Philip – I would not rate him as an altogether reliable witness.

scared. His face was white. He was beginning to realise what he'd let himself in for.'

Philip and his best man, David Milford Haven, spent the night before the wedding at Kensington Palace. John Dean, the Mountbattens' butler who became Philip's valet, said, 'Their rooms were astonishingly poor and humble – floors scrubbed boards with worn rugs.' (Robin Dalton recalled her boyfriend David's room being 'in the servants' attic'. 'We had a flat together in Chelsea,' she told me, 'but in the run-up to the wedding it was thought advisable that David, as Philip's best man, move in with his grandmother. I remember David and me, on our nights together, creeping up the back stairs of her apartment at Kensington Palace as silently as possible.') John Dean recalled bringing Philip his early-morning tea promptly at 7 a.m. and finding his young master in happy form and not the least bit nervous.

Patricia Mountbatten's recollection was a little different. 'I saw him just after breakfast that morning,' she told me. 'We were alone together – we were cousins and we knew each other very well – and I said something about what an exciting day it was and, suddenly, he said to me, "Am I being very brave or very foolish?"' I asked Lady Mountbatten what she thought he meant by that. 'He was apprehensive,' she said. 'He was uncertain – not about marrying Princess Elizabeth, but about what the marriage would mean for him. He was giving up a great deal. In many ways, nothing was going to change for her. Everything was going to change for him.'

For a start, that very morning he stopped smoking cigarettes. The King was a heavy smoker. (It was a family habit: Queen Mary was a smoker, too.) Princess Elizabeth saw the effect cigarettes had on her father and did not want her husband to smoke. Philip was happy enough to oblige his bride-to-be – and disciplined enough to be able to do so overnight. At 11 a.m., fortified by a gin and tonic, and dressed in naval uniform, sporting the insignia of a Knight Companion of the Order of the Garter, and wearing the ceremonial sword that had belonged to his grandfather, Prince Louis of Battenberg, Philip, accompanied by his best man, set off for Westminster Abbey.

Over at Buckingham Palace, Elizabeth, too, had an early start. It was still dark when Bobo brought her little princess a cup of tea. 'I don't think any of us had very much sleep,' reported Crawfie. 'I went along to Lilibet's room very early, and found her in her dressing-gown, peeping excitedly out of the windows at the crowds.' Despite the bitter cold, people had slept out overnight to secure their view. Along the Mall and down Whitehall, the pavements were packed, fifty people deep. 'I can't believe it's really happening,' Lilibet told Crawfie. 'I have to keep pinching myself.'

Norman Hartnell, who had designed the Princess's wedding dress, delivered it personally to the Palace the night before. At 9 a.m. he and his entourage were on parade again for the final fitting. It took an hour and a quarter. 'She looked so beautiful,' recalled Margaret Rhodes, who was one of the eight bridesmaids. 'We were all dressed by Mr Hartnell, too. It was very exciting. There was rationing, of course, and we used up all our clothes coupons.' The bride's dress alone absorbed three hundred coupons and cost £1,200. Given the prevailing austerity, the extravagance was considered controversial by some. Most, however, went along with the Leader of the Opposition, Winston Churchill, who welcomed the wedding and all that it involved as 'A flash of colour on the hard road we have to travel.' Norman Hartnell used to enjoy telling the story of how his manager – who had travelled far and wide gathering materials for the dress – was stopped at customs on his return from a buying trip to the United States and asked if he had anything to declare. 'Yes,' the man replied, 'ten thousand pearls for the wedding dress of Princess Elizabeth.' The dress was made of ivory silk, decorated with pearls arranged as white roses of York, entwined with ears of corn embroidered in crystal. The effect was ravishing.

Inevitably, there were last-minute dramas, 'the tensions common to any home on a wedding morning', according to Crawfie. The bride's bouquet was lost. A footman remembered receiving it and bringing it upstairs, but what happened to it after that, he couldn't recall. Panic ensued and then, suddenly, happily, the footman remembered he had placed it in a cool cupboard near by for safekeeping. Next, the precious tiara given to the Princess by Queen Mary snapped as it was being put on her head. More panic, until nervous hands managed to repair the damage. Finally – and most dramatically – the Princess went to put on the double string of pearls that her parents had given her as a wedding present – and realised that they were half a mile away at St James's Palace, where all the wedding presents were to go on public display.

The Princess's recently appointed private secretary, Jock Colville, was summoned to her sitting room. 'She stood there, radiant and entrancing in her wedding dress,' he recalled. Could he, somehow, make his way to St James's Palace and retrieve the necklace? she asked. 'I looked at my watch,' he said. 'I rushed along the corridor. I galloped down the Grand Staircase and into the main quadrangle of Buckingham Palace. Take any car, the Princess had called after me. So I ran towards a large Royal Daimler. "To St James's Palace," I cried to the chauffeur, and I flung open the door of the car. Before I could leap in, a tall, elderly man, ablaze with Orders and Decorations, began to emerge. It was King Haakon VII of Norway. "You seem in a hurry, young man," he said. "By all means have my car, but do let me get out first."'

When Colville reached St James's Palace, the detectives guarding the royal wedding gifts were not inclined to believe his story. He pleaded with them. He asked them to telephone Buckingham Palace. The line was dead. With his heart beating and the minutes ticking by, he told them his name and, when they discovered it printed in the official Wedding Programme, they reluctantly allowed him to escape with the necklace. Pushing his way through the crowd, apologising as he went, 'with one hand firmly pressed against the pocket of my tunic where the pearls lay', Colville made his way back to the car and reached Buckingham Palace with only moments to spare.

At 11.15 a.m. the Princess, carrying her bouquet, wearing her parents' pearls, her grandmother's tiara, and Mr Hartnell's fairy-tale dress, clambered into the Irish state coach. Her father, slight and pale, but smiling, dressed in his uniform as an Admiral of the Fleet, sat next to her. Together, escorted by the Household Cavalry in full ceremonial dress uniform for the first time in six years, father and daughter travelled along the Mall and down Whitehall towards Westminster Abbey, crowds up to fifty people deep cheering them all the way. 'The King looked unbelievably beautiful,' Sir Michael Duff wrote to his friend, the photographer Cecil Beaton, 'like an early French King and HRH the Bride a dream.' It was a poignant journey for them both, but more so for the King than his daughter. For Lilibet a new life was about to begin; for George VI an era was coming to an end. 'It is a far more moving thing to give your daughter away than to be married yourself,' the King told the Archbishop of York later that day.

The Archbishop, Cyril Garbett, officiating alongside the Archbishop of Canterbury, Geoffrey Fisher, described the wedding – to the congregation of two thousand in the Abbey, to the few thousand more watching a film of the occasion on fledgling television in the evening, and to the millions tuned in to the live broadcast on the wireless around the world – as 'in all essentials exactly the same as it would have been for any cottager who might be married this afternoon in some small country church in a remote village in the Dales'. Well, up to a point, Lord Archbishop. The Princess had chosen traditional hymns ('The Lord Is My Shepherd', sung to the tune of Crimond, was Crawfie's favourite moment) and vowed, until death, to 'love, honour and obey' her husband, 'for richer or poorer, for better or worse', so the essentials were certainly familiar, but everything else was truly beyond the ken of the average British cottager of the period. For a start, there were eight bridesmaids (led by Princess Margaret, walking alone, three paces ahead of the other bridesmaids, in recognition of her rank), two kilted page boys (Prince William of Gloucester and Prince Michael of Kent, who inadvertently stepped on the Tomb of the Unknown Warrior), and the guests – the men in uniform and morning suits, the women in full-length dresses with long white gloves and glittering tiaras – included a remarkable array of royalty, some still reigning, others retired, hurt. According to one of the bridesmaids, Pamela Mountbatten, 'Crown Princess Juliana of the Netherlands caused a stir, remarking that "Everyone's jewelry is *so* dirty," which may or may not have been the case; to me it was just remarkable that all those royal jewels had survived the war.'

On Lilibet's side of the family, her Uncle David and his American wife, the Duke and Duchess of Windsor, were conspicuous by their absence. On Philip's side, the principal non-invitees were his three sisters and their German husbands. It was only two years since the end of the war, too soon for the British Royal Family to be seen extending the hand of friendship to the enemy. Philip's youngest sister, Sophie, had three brothers-in-law still awaiting denazification, one of them still interned.

Alice wrote a twenty-two-page description of the wedding for her daughters, to 'console them for their absence'. She was there, seated with her mother, the Marchioness of Milford Haven, and her sister, Louise, and her husband, Crown Prince Gustaf of Sweden, and her brother, Dickie, who, with Edwina and their younger daughter, Pamela, had come home briefly from India for the occasion.

From Philip's father side of the family the contingent was smaller: of Andrea's seven brothers and sisters, all but one was dead. Philip's uncle, 'Big George', was there from Paris, with his wife, Marie Bonaparte, and their daughter, Eugénie, alongside assorted first cousins, second cousins, and cousins by marriage, including Queen Helen of Romania, Queen Alexandra of Yugoslavia, and Queen Frederika of Greece.

There were so many foreign royals in the best seats for the wedding that members of the British Parliament had to draw lots to secure access to the 'parliamentary enclosure'. Chips Channon was one MP who managed get in. 'I thought Princess Elizabeth looked well,' he noted in his diary, 'shy and attractive, and Prince Philip as if he was thoroughly enjoying himself.' A few days later Channon gave a spectacular post-wedding party – 'a great, great success' by his own account: 'I "laced" the cocktails with Benzedrine, which I find always makes a party go' – and entertained some of the royalty who were in town, including the Queens of Spain and Romania. 'I am sorry that Queen Freddie [of Greece] and the Duchess of Kent [Princess Marina, Philip's first cousin] could not come,' he told his diary. 'They are on a secret visit to the affronted German relations to tell them about the Wedding.' They took Alice's twenty-two-page account with them.

Noël Coward was at both Channon's party and Westminster Abbey, where he found, to his surprise and pleasure, that he was placed in the fourth row, next to Beatrice Lillie. Coward recorded in his diary: 'A gala day . . . The wedding was most moving and beautifully done. English tradition at its best.' The Coward verdict was the general one. As the young couple left the Abbey, Philip bowing smartly to the King and Queen, Elizabeth dropping a low, slow curtsy to her parents, they looked like figures from a story-book: a princess with her prince from a foreign land, destined to live happily ever after. Jock Colville was one of those who, in the lead-up to the marriage, had been sceptical about its prospects. 'As the day drew nearer,' he confessed, 'I began to think, as I now sincerely do, that the Princess and Philip really are in love.' That's what the cheering crowds thought, too, as the Abbey's bells pealed, and the bride and groom, beaming and waving, were taken back to Buckingham Palace in the Glass Coach.

At the Palace, Baron took the official photographs and luncheon was served. It was billed as an 'austerity' wedding breakfast, a modest affair for just 150 guests: family, close friends, and courtiers. Crawfie was excited to be included:

'It was a gay and merry lunch party. The tables were decorated with smilax and white carnations, and at each of our places there was a little bunch of white heather, sent down from Balmoral. The famous gold-plate and the scarlet-coated footmen gave a fairy-tale atmosphere to it all, and I was in a veritable dream. The skirl of the bagpipes warmed the hearts of those of us who came from north of the Tweed. The French gentleman seated next to me, however, winced from time to time, but he bore it with fortitude.

'There were no long speeches. The King hates them and has always dreaded having to make one. He was brevity itself. The bridegroom, another sailor, had just as little to say. It was a very large room and there were no microphones, so few people even heard the little that *was* said. The French gentleman kept hissing in my ear, "*Qu'est ce qu'il dit?*" I was unable to help him.'

The younger members of the family, and their nannies, had a quiet lunch and 'a nice lie down' in another part of the Palace. According to Crawfie, the page boys, Prince William and Prince Michael (the six- and five-year-old sons of Lilibet's uncles, the Dukes of Gloucester and Kent), were 'thoroughly overtired', 'grew peevish', and almost came to blows: 'Shocked nannies enveloped them in those vast white shawls royal nannies always seem to have handy. Like sheltering wings! They were borne off, but not before they had made ceremonious bows to the King and Queen. In royal circles manners are taught young.'

The little ones reappeared to see the bride and groom set off on their honeymoon. Mr Hartnell was especially proud of his going-away outfit for the young Princess: a love-in-the-mist crêpe dress with blue velvet cloth travelling coat, and a blue felt bonnet trimmed with ostrich pompom and curved quills in two tones of blue. It needed to be warm because the November weather was bitter and, for the benefit of the crowds, the newly-weds were to travel from Buckingham Palace to Waterloo Station (en route for Winchester and their first stop at Broadlands, the Mountbattens' country house in Hampshire) in an unheated open landau. (It was foggy, but at least it wasn't raining and, under their lap rugs, discreet comfort was provided by hot-water bottles and Lilibet's favourite corgi, Susan.) As, hand in hand, the newly-weds came down the Palace staircase, the family, cheering, gathered round and threw rose petals. As the couple's carriage trundled through the Palace gates, the King and Queen stood watching, holding hands. Princess Alice kept waving until the carriage disappeared from view. In some ways, perhaps it was like any cottager's wedding. All three proud parents had tears in their eyes.

A few days later, back in Athens, Alice wrote to Philip: 'How wonderfully everything went off & I was so comforted to see the truly happy expression on your face and to feel your decision was right from every point of view.' And, from London, the King wrote, touchingly, to Lilibet, as she embarked on married life and he contemplated a future without his elder daughter at his side:

I was so proud of you & thrilled at having you so close to me on our long walk in Westminster Abbey, but when I handed your hand to the Archbishop I felt that I had lost something very precious. You were so calm and composed during the Service & said your words with such conviction, that I knew everything was all right.

I am so glad you wrote & told Mummy that you think the long wait before your engagement & the long time before the wedding was for the best. I was rather afraid that you thought I was being hard-hearted about it. I was so anxious for you to come to South Africa as you knew. Our family, us four, the 'Royal Family' must remain together with additions of course at suitable moments!! I have watched you grow up all these years with pride under the skilful direction of Mummy, who as you know is the most marvellous person in the World in my eyes, & I can, I know, always count on you, & now Philip, to help us in our work. Your leaving us has left a great blank in our lives but do remember that your old home is still yours & do come back to it as much & as often as possible. I can see that you are sublimely happy with Philip which is right but don't forget us is the wish of

Your ever loving & devoted

Papa

The newly-weds began their honeymoon at Broadlands, by the River Test and not far from Winchester. They were not alone. As well as Lilibet's corgi, the young lovers' entourage included a personal detective, a personal footman, Bobo MacDonald (the Princess's nursery maid turned dresser and confidante), and John Dean (the Mountbattens' former London butler, now Prince Philip's valet). John Dean and Cyril Dickman, the footman, looked after the luggage: the bride had fifteen cases, the groom just two. The detective did his best to keep the public at bay. At Winchester Station there were crowds waiting to cheer the young couple. At Broadlands there were more sightseers, gawping at the gates. Despite the cold, eager rubber-neckers (loyal subjects as well as representatives of the press) hovered, day and night, at the edge of the estate hoping for glimpses of the happy pair. On Sunday morning, when the couple went together to a service at nearby Romsey Abbey, frantic royal-watchers scrambled across tombstones to get a better view. Several came equipped with chairs and stepladders to enable them to peer through the windows into the Abbey itself. For the royal newly-weds, life in the goldfish bowl had begun.

A few years ago, when visiting Broadlands as a tourist,[61] I recollect there was some sniggering among our party when we were shown the bedroom in which Elizabeth and Philip spent their wedding night. A fellow visitor reached over the security cordon to touch the nuptial bed and announced happily, 'The Queen is very keen on sex, you know.' I didn't know, but I was happy to hear it. And I have heard it said by others, quite often, since. I recall Lord Longford telling me, 'The Queen enjoys sex, as I do. People who

---

61 A visit is highly recommended. The house – a grey-brick Palladian villa – was once the country home of Lord Palmerston, features a fascinating exhibition on the life of Earl Mountbatten of Burma, and is usually open to the public on weekdays from 1 p.m. to 5.30 p.m. between June and September. See www. broadlandsestates.co.uk for details.

ride tend to. It's very healthy.' Lord Longford was a Knight of the Garter, a God-fearing man, wholly honest and utterly devoted to Her Majesty, but I do wonder: how did he know? Sarah Bradford, in her comprehensive and compelling biography of the Queen, states boldly, but without giving us any authority for the assertion: 'Elizabeth was physically passionate.' I don't doubt it, but I do ask myself: who told Miss Bradford? I have not raised the matter with Her Majesty, and I would be very surprised if anyone else has either.

Thanks to servants' tittle-tattle (reliable in this instance) we do know that Prince Philip, in the early days of his marriage, did not wear pyjamas. We are told, too, by Patricia Mountbatten, that, once, when she remarked on Lilibet's flawless complexion, Philip laughed and said to his cousin, beaming, 'Yes, and she's like that all over.' One of David Milford Haven's friends told me that David had told her that Philip had told him that Lilibet was 'very keen on sex, quite a goer'. Well, for both their sakes, let us hope so – but let us not pretend that we know. I can just about visualise Prince Philip giving a nod and a grin to David Milford Haven in response to a jocular enquiry on the subject, but I do not think he was the sort of man who would – for a moment – discuss the most intimate aspects of his married life with his men friends.

What happened between the sheets on the night of the royal wedding I cannot tell you. I was not there. However, I can report, because there were witnesses, that the evening at Broadlands was not especially peaceful. The telephone rang incessantly; the staff at Broadlands (in the absence of the Mountbattens in India) were not as well organised as they might have been; Bobo and Cyril and John were exhausted. The day had been a long one. The bridal couple retired as soon as supper was over: they looked weary but very happy, Lilibet especially so.

By several accounts, the bride and groom certainly had a jollier evening in Hampshire than the groomsman and bridesmaids had in London. Elizabeth's cousin, Margaret Rhodes, was one of the brides-maids and she told me, 'We didn't have a girls' party before the wedding, but, on the day itself, we did have the traditional evening where the best man entertains the bridesmaids. It was not a success. The best man was Milford Haven, not my favourite man. Let's not talk about him.'

The engagement picture: Elizabeth, photographed with her engagement ring and on Philip's arm for the first time, Buckingham Palace, 10 July 1947

The best man: David Milford Haven with his girlfriend, Robin Dalton, on holiday in France, 1946

Philip, with Mike Parker and Dickie Mountbatten, at Philip's Stag Night at the Dorchester Hotel, 19 November 1947

Wedding Day: Thursday 20 November 1947

The Wedding group photographed by Baron in the Throne Room at Buckingham Palace. David, 3rd Marquess of Milford Haven is standing on Elizabeth's right; Princess Margaret is on Philip's left; the page boys are Prince William of Gloucester and Prince Michael of Kent. In the front row, left to right, are: Elizabeth's grandmother, Queen Mary; Philip's mother, Alice, Princess Andrew of Greece; Elizabeth's parents, King George VI and Queen Elizabeth; and Philip's (and David Milford Haven's) grandmother, Victoria, Dowager Marchioness of Milford Haven. Among the bridesmaids, on the far left of the picture, is The Hon Margaret Elphinstone, now Margaret Rhodes.

Into the woods: Philip and Elizabeth on their honeymoon
at Broadlands, 23 November 1947

Elizabeth and Philip at the Royal Windsor Horse Show, May 1949

The Thursday Club cricket match, 1948, with Baron and Philip, seated centre, in top hats, and James Robertson Justice, in back row, far left

The best of times: surveying the harbour at Malta, 1949

Letting go: Philip water-skiing in the Mediterranean, August 1951

Baron's photograph of the sponsors at Prince Charles's christening in
the Music Room at Buckingham Palace, 15 December 1948.
Seated, l-r, The Dowager Marchioness of Milford Haven, Elizabeth
and Charles, Queen Mary; standing, l-r, Patricia Brabourne, Philip,
George VI, David Bowes-Lyon (Queen Elizabeth's brother),
the Earl of Athlone (Queen Mary's brother), Princess Margaret

Elizabeth and Anne with Queen Elizabeth, Prince Charles and
Queen Mary at Princess Anne's christening, 21 October 1950

14 November 1951: George VI, 'recovered' from his operation, pictured eleven weeks before his death, with Prince Charles on his third birthday, Princess Anne and Queen Elizabeth. (The Edinburghs were returning from their American tour.)

6 February 1952, the day George VI died: Princess Alice, Philip's mother, arriving in Chicago and telling reporters, 'The King looked exceptionally well when I last saw him on January 16th.'

7 February 1952, the new Queen Elizabeth, dressed in mourning for her father, arriving at Heathrow Airport on her return from Kenya

Summer holiday:
Philip and Elizabeth
with Charles and Anne,
August 1951

Off duty:
Charles and Anne
with Elizabeth II
at Balmoral castle,
September 1952

'Why not?' I asked.

Mrs Rhodes assumed a very pinched look and said, rapidly, stubbing out her cigarette, 'We went to somewhere like Quaglino's and he was much keener on some dolly bird at the other table than he was on us. He was not my idea of a gentleman.'

Milford Haven's girlfriend at the time, Robin Dalton, fears that she was probably the 'dolly bird at the other table'. (In her memoir of the wedding day, another of the bridesmaids, Pamela Hicks, describes her as 'a dazzling girl at the next table'.) Looking anything but pinched, Robin Dalton told me, smiling into her Bloody Mary, 'I think the party was at Ciro's in Orange Street, not Quaglino's. I do remember Princess Margaret getting cross because David was spending too much time with me. I wasn't a bridesmaid, of course. I was only at the wedding because David got me a ticket. I sat at the back with the servants. I had been married, albeit briefly. I was a divorcee, so not a suitable bride for a descendant of Queen Victoria. I couldn't accompany him into the Royal Enclosure at Ascot, even had I wished to. I loved David. He was so sweet and we had five happy years together. Then, understandably, and very suddenly, David got married to someone else, through the mistaken idea that she was very rich, leaving me with his dog, his car, and both of us in tears.[62] As a wedding present, I think Philip gave David a pair of cufflinks Philip had been given by the Duke of Gloucester.'

As best man, David gave Philip and Lilibet a present that was both practical and sought after: the most up-to-date (and expensive) record player on the market, the new Deccola. According to Robin Dalton, 'David and Philip had very little money. They survived on their naval pay, and £5 a week each from Lord Mountbatten. One

62 Milford Haven's first marriage – to Romaine Simpson – ended disastrously. (It did not begin too well, either: his mother, Nada, decided the prospects were so poor, she could not bear to attend.) He then became infatuated with the Hungarian film starlet Eva Bartok, before marrying Janet Bryce, the mother of the 4th and current Marquess. Lord Brabourne told me, his wife nodding assent: 'David was awfully nice. We liked him. Girls adored him. But he was hopeless. He was gullible. He died young.' He left the Navy, he drank too much, he got involved in unfortunate financial ventures, he died in 1970, aged fifty, running to catch a train. When Prince Philip and David Milford Haven stayed at Windsor over Christmas 1943, the King's private secretary, Sir Alan Lascelles, sized them both up and came to a definite conclusion: 'I prefer the latter.'

night at a dinner party, I sat next to a businessman who proudly told me he was manufacturing the Deccola. By the end of dinner, I had procured free for David the very first one off the production line and the manufacturer had procured valuable publicity because all the wedding presents went on prominent display.'

Philip and Elizabeth received around fifteen hundred wedding gifts, ranging from five hundred cases of tinned pineapple from the Government of Queensland to a turkey from a woman in Brooklyn who had heard that 'they have nothing to eat in England'. 'The people of Kenya' generously gave the royal couple a hunting lodge; the people of Britain generously sent Lilibet dozens of pairs of nylon stockings. The Aga Khan pleased Elizabeth with his present of a thoroughbred filly; Mahatma Gandhi impressed Philip with his gift of a personally woven piece of cloth, intended as a cover for a tea tray. As she toured the exhibition of the presents displayed at St James's Palace, Queen Mary, not an admirer of Gandhi, decided the material was intended as a loincloth and was not amused. Philip protested, but the old Queen did not want to be enlightened. She muttered, 'What a horrible thing' and, lips pursed, moved quickly on.

One gift that seems not to have been put on display was that of a tiny gold bicycle, apparently given to Prince Philip by a French friend of his and David's, a hotelier from the south of France called Félix. During the summer before the wedding Philip joined David at Nada's holiday home above Cannes. Every day during the holiday (so the story goes), Philip would borrow a bicycle from Félix to ride over to the home of a certain married lady . . . Félix thought the little gold bicycle would be an amusing souvenir of the bachelor prince's last summer holiday as a 'free man'.

After five nights at Broadlands, the honeymooners returned briefly to London for lunch at Buckingham Palace with the King and Queen before setting off by train for Scotland and a further two weeks of honeymoon at Birkhall on the Balmoral Estate.[63] Here the

---

63 You too could honeymoon on the Balmoral Estate. The Estate – which was purchased by Prince Albert for Queen Victoria in 1851 – is owned and funded by the Queen personally (rather than as Sovereign) and Her Majesty lets out a number of holiday cottages: for details see www.balmoralcastle.com. Overall, the estate comprises 18,659 hectares owned between Balmoral, Birkhall, and Glen Doll, 2,940 hectares of grouse moor at Corgarff, and 4,688 hectares of sporting

young couple had a quieter, cosier, more secluded time. They went for walks in the snow. They warmed themselves by roaring log fires. They got to know each other. They had time alone – or, as much time alone as you get when there are servants always hovering. It is the privilege of princes to be waited on, but the price they pay for that privilege is a heavy one: someone is always close at hand, waiting, watching, listening, standing in silent judgement; sometimes reporting this and that to others in the servants' hall; occasionally reporting that and this to the world at large. Marion Crawford (governess), John Dean (valet), Paul Burrell (footman turned butler), in their way, in their day, showed real dedication as royal servants. They served their mistresses and masters with devotion, and then repaid the royal trust placed in them by spilling the beans in best-selling books, protesting their continuing loyalty all the way to the bank.

Philip had had an odd childhood, but, at boarding school and in the Royal Navy, he had, to some extent, lived in 'the real world', fending for himself. Lilibet, on the other hand, was a girl, born before the era of female emancipation, brought up as a princess, living in palaces and castles, surrounded by servants. She, more than Philip, was wholly accustomed to being fed, and bathed, and dressed, and watched over, by others. At Broadlands, at Birkhall, at Buckingham Palace, the entourage was always there: the detective, the driver, the footman, the valet, and Bobo. Especially Bobo.

Margaret MacDonald was the daughter of an Inverness railway worker. As a child she lived by a railway line in a small railway company cottage. At twenty-two – in 1926, when Princess Elizabeth was born – she joined the Yorks' household as nursery maid and assistant to Alah Knight, the royal nanny. When Princess Margaret Rose was born in 1930, Alah, naturally, concentrated on the new baby, and Bobo (as Miss MacDonald was soon nicknamed) began what would become a lifetime of single-minded devotion to Princess Elizabeth. When Lilibet was a little girl, Bobo shared her bedroom.

---

rights rented from a neighbour. The land is poor (mainly granitic) and most lies over 1,000 feet above sea level. There are seven Munros (mountains over 3,000 feet), 3,000 hectares are afforested, and 190 hectares are arable or pasture, of which ninety are farmed by a tenant and a hundred by the Estate with twenty-nine Highland Cows, their progeny, and the Queen's Highland, Fell, and Haflinger ponies.

When the Princess grew up, Bobo became her dresser, confidante, and friend. John Dean described her as 'a small, smart, rather peremptory Scotswoman' whose years with the royal household 'seemed to be imprinted on her face and stature'. She was formal – 'We have to keep a certain standing in the house' was her line – and seemed formidable to some, but, according to Dean, she was 'quite friendly when thawed'. She was a redhead when young. Dean reported, 'She was a lovely dancer and very good fun, with a nice sense of humour, but even when we were staying in some village, and were out socially in the local pub, she always addressed me as "Mr Dean". She always referred to Princess Elizabeth as "My Little Lady".' In private, with the Princess, Bobo would call her mistress "Lilibet", one of the very few outside the royal family to feel comfortable doing so. (Playfully, Princess Margaret occasionally called her sister "Lil".)'

Officially, Bobo was simply Elizabeth's dresser. She looked after the royal wardrobe. She dealt with the royal dressmakers: Mr Hartnell, Hardy Amies, and, later, Ian Thomas. She kept them in their place, both by the manner with which she handled them and by not allowing any one of them complete control over Elizabeth's appearance. 'You're here for the clothes not the accessories,' she would tell the designers, firmly. Bobo was a personally disciplined, conservatively inclined, frugally minded Scotswoman: she saw no virtue in Lilibet being kitted out with expensive handbags. Officially, Bobo looked after Elizabeth's wardrobe. Unofficially, Bobo looked after Elizabeth. Her devotion was absolute, her commitment total, her access almost unlimited. By the time she died, in 1993, aged eighty-nine, she had become a legendary figure in royal circles: the one person to whom the Queen always listened.

For sixty-seven years, Bobo lived for Elizabeth. She loved her, protected her, respected her. She was wholly loyal and ever-present. I imagine that at times she must have got on Prince Philip's nerves. Mike Parker said to me, 'Let's face it, he had a hell of a time with her. Miss MacDonald was *always* there. And in charge. Princess Elizabeth was Bobo's baby and that was that. But I don't think he ever complained. Anyway, he didn't to me. He didn't say a word. Not a word. He just put up with it.' Patricia Mountbatten told me that Bobo would prepare Lilibet's bath and then potter in and out of the bathroom while she was having it, effectively keeping Philip at bay: 'He couldn't share the bathroom with his wife, because Bobo saw it as her territory and I don't think Princess Elizabeth had the heart to say, "Bobo, please go away." I think Philip must have found it quite irritating.'

After two weeks at Birkhall, the honeymoon was over and Elizabeth and Philip (and the detective and the dresser, the footman and the valet, the seventeen cases, and the corgi) returned to London in time for the King's fifty-second birthday on 14 December. 'The Edinburghs are back from Scotland,' Jock Colville noted in his diary. 'She was looking very happy, and, as a result of three weeks of matrimony, suddenly a woman instead of a girl. He also seemed happy, but a shade querulous, which is, I think, in his character.'

I go along with Colville's judgement. In many ways, Prince Philip was remarkably good-humoured and long-suffering. He put up with Bobo; he shrugged off his press coverage; he endured more than six decades of footling royal flummery and thousands of hours of mind-numbing small talk with strangers and civic dignitaries. But he was 'a shade querulous'. He would grumble. He could be difficult. His impatience sometimes showed. And, though he denied it, he was always contradictory. He liked to be his own man.

On 1 December 1947 Queen Elizabeth wrote to him from Buckingham Palace – 'the first time I have written to you as my son in law'. This letter, running to several pages, she signed 'with much love, dearest Philip, ever your devoted Mama'. It is full of warmth and encouragement: 'I *do* hope that you won't find public life too trying; for the people *are* demanding when they like you, but you will have the comfort of knowing that you are giving so much towards the happiness and stability of the country.' The letter also contains a telling observation: 'I remember at Balmoral last year, you told me that you had always played a lone hand, and had had to fight your own battles . . .' To an extent, for the rest of his life Prince Philip continued to play 'a lone hand' – notwithstanding his public advocacy of team games. Within a fortnight of his wedding, his new mother-in-law told him, 'You will now have a great chance for individual leadership, as well as "married couple" leadership which is so important as well. As a family we do try to work as a team, but each going their own way, and I am sure you will make very valuable contributions towards the common pool.'

In 1947 Princess Elizabeth was twenty-one and, though self-possessed, still quite shy. I asked her cousin, Margaret Rhodes, what she made of Philip when she first got to know him in the 1940s. 'I used to dread sitting next to him,' she told me, pulling a rather anxious face. 'He'd be so contradictory. You'd say something just to say something, and he'd jump down your throat. "Why do you say that? What do you mean?" Quite frightening, until you got used to it. I think he's always had that debunking element in him. It was just his way.'

'Was he like that with Elizabeth?' I asked.

'Yes,' said Mrs Rhodes, 'he was like that with the Queen. He'd say, "Why the bloody hell? What the bloody hell?" I think she did sometimes find it very disconcerting.'

Patricia Mountbatten – whose manner was more robust than that of Mrs Rhodes: she was her father's daughter – told me that while, in her experience, the Queen did not respond to her husband's intemperate outbursts in kind, she enjoyed it when others did. 'I remember a big party at Balmoral,' said Countess Mountbatten, 'a shooting party, when, at dinner, Philip and I had a right old ding-dong about South Africa. It was a terrific argument and the Queen kept encouraging me. "That's right, Patricia," she said. "You go at him, nobody ever goes at him."'

When the Duke was critical of his wife, berating her for paying attention to the dogs when she should be listening to him, or wondering out loud why she was spending so much time on the telephone, or telling her she was wearing the wrong clothes for a shooting expedition, the Queen was quite capable of answering back, saying to him, 'Oh, do shut up.' According to family and friends, over the years she became bolder with him, and he gentler with her.

Why was Prince Philip contradictory and querulous? His cousin, Patricia Mountbatten, said, 'He has a very similar character to my father. He's a dynamo. He wants action. He wants to get things done. He likes getting his own way and it's frustrating for him when he doesn't.'

'And life at court was very, very frustrating for him at first,' according to Patricia's husband, Lord Brabourne. 'It was very stuffy. Lascelles was impossible. They were absolutely bloody to him. They patronised him. They treated him as an outsider. It wasn't much fun. He laughed it off, of course, but it must have hurt. I'm not sure that Princess Elizabeth noticed it. She probably didn't see it. In a way, marriage hardly changed her life at all. She was able to carry on much as before. In getting married, she didn't sacrifice anything. His life changed completely. He gave up everything.'

According to Lord Brabourne and the Mountbatten girls (Philip's first cousins), and according to Mike Parker and other male friends of Philip's at the time, as a young man Philip was funny, charming, wilful, dynamic, and occasionally impatient. As a bridegroom, Pamela Mountbatten said, he was 'so dashing that it made you realise why every girl in England seemed to think she was in love with him'. Of course, not every girl in England was. His best man's girlfriend, Robin Dalton, described him to me as 'a cold fish'. When I asked Princess Elizabeth's childhood friend Sonia Berry what she made of the young Prince Philip, her back stiffened and she answered crisply, 'No comment.'

Margaret Rhodes said that Philip 'mellowed a lot' in his later years. He must have done. When I first became involved in the work of the National Playing Fields Association in the 1970s, I was warned that Prince Philip was a 'hands-on' president, but not always easy. He could be abrupt, I was told. In my experience he was sometimes demanding and occasionally testy, but he was never rude.

Yes, he was challenging: he automatically questioned everything. Whatever you said, he countered it immediately. And he could certainly be wilful as well as contrary. I recall an event at Buckingham Palace at which an equerry was introducing children who had won a poetry-writing competition into the presence of the Prince and the Queen. The equerry made a point of asking the assembled guests not to applaud each child individually. As each child's name was read out, the Duke of Edinburgh made a point of leading the applause.

Yes, he could be impatient. 'Why hasn't this happened?' he would ask, eyebrow raised. 'What are we waiting for? Let's get on with it, for heaven's sake.' With those he knew like me, he would indicate his disapproval with a grimace or a sigh and a weary shake of the head, but, on the whole, with the general public, and with those he met undertaking his array of public duties, he was surprisingly equable: easy-going, unaffected, and good-humoured. I would see him looking grouchy now and again (and keep my distance), but I only once saw him positively bad-tempered. He expected to find a folder of papers in their usual place on the desk in his study at Buckingham Palace. A footman had moved the papers. Philip gave him short shrift. I blanched. The footman retreated, chastened and abashed. Lord Brabourne said to me of Philip in his seventies, 'He's naughty now. He shouts at people sometimes.' Gina Kennard said to me, 'Let's face it, he can be really quite bad-tempered.'

Jock Colville's assessment of the mood and manner of the royal couple in 1947 is borne out by other witnesses: the bride was very happy; the groom, happy but a touch querulous. Philip still did not have a home to call his own. The plan had been for the newly-weds to have a country home at Sunninghill Park in Windsor Great Park and a London home at Clarence House, next to St James's Palace, overlooking the Mall – where Prince Charles and the Duchess of Cornwall live today.

Unfortunately, the substantial house at Sunninghill Park burnt to the ground before the Edinburghs could move in, and Clarence House was in need of substantial refurbishment and repair.[64] Eventually, they rented a comparatively small country house, Windlesham Moor, in Berkshire (just two floors: four reception rooms, five bedrooms, plus staff quarters) and, in May 1949, eighteen months after their wedding, moved into their London home, a handsomely restored Clarence House. (The restoration cost £78,000, rather more than the £50,000 voted for the work, somewhat grudgingly, by Parliament.) Meanwhile, for their London base, they perched briefly at Clock House in Kensington Palace (the home of the Earl and Countess of Athlone, who were on a three-month trip to South Africa) and then spent a year living with the King and Queen at Buckingham Palace. For Lilibet, the Palace was 'home

64 Clarence House was built in the late 1820s for Queen Victoria's uncle, who was Duke of Clarence until he became William IV in 1830. Queen Victoria's son, the Duke of Connaught, lived there until his death in 1942, aged ninety-one. During and after the Second World War, it was used by the Red Cross and the Ministry of Works. Sunninghill Park eventually became the site of a new house, mocked in the media as a ranch-style house in the tradition of the TV series *Dallas* and *Dynasty*, the home of the Queen and Prince Philip's second son and his wife, the Duke and Duchess of York.

from home'. For Philip, given a bedroom and sitting room of his own alongside his wife's established apartments, the arrangement was less satisfactory. Queen Elizabeth told him to think of it as 'Hotel Buckingham'. He did.

There was one area in which Philip, however, was able to do exactly as he pleased: the appointment of his first equerry-in-waiting. He chose his friend, contemporary, and fellow naval officer Mike Parker. 'I was honoured,' Parker told me, 'and I felt I could do the job. Philip and I were mates and I felt I could be a useful ally to him at court. The King was fine, very friendly, very helpful, but the traditional courtiers weren't always so easy. I had been planning to return to Australia, but my wife, Eileen, who was Scottish, didn't want to leave the UK, so it worked out all round.' Parker was Philip's right-hand man – equerry, ADC, secretary, friend – for ten years, until 1957, when the 'scandal' of his divorce from Eileen obliged him to resign.

Princess Elizabeth's private secretary, Jock Colville, was chosen for her by the King's, Tommy Lascelles. Born in 1915, educated at Harrow and Trinity College, Cambridge, Colville was a career diplomat who started out (as personable and bright young men from the Foreign Office sometimes do) as an assistant private secretary in Downing Street. He worked for Chamberlain, Churchill, and Attlee in turn, so he knew his way around the corridors of power. He was also wholly at home with the Palace culture. His mother, Lady Cynthia Colville, was a lady-in-waiting to Queen Mary. As a boy he was a Page of Honour to George V. In 1948 he married Lady Margaret Egerton, known as 'Meg', daughter of the 4th Earl of Ellesmere, who had been recruited by Princess Elizabeth as one of her first ladies-in-waiting. He was a class act, as smooth and British as Parker was rough and Australian, but they rubbed along well and came to see each other's strengths.

Completing the team, as Comptroller and Treasurer to the Edinburgh household, was an older man, Lieutenant General Sir Frederick 'Boy' Browning, born 1896, a dashing war hero, considered by Baron to be the handsomest man he ever photographed, married to the novelist Daphne du Maurier, and Chief of Staff to Philip's uncle, Louis Mountbatten, in his South-East Asia Command. Mountbatten recommended Browning to his nephew unreservedly:

'Boy has drive, energy, enthusiasm, efficiency and invokes the highest sense of loyalty and affection in his subordinates. His judgement is absolutely sound, and he would sooner die than let his boss down . . . he is not a "yes man" or even a courtier and never will be. He will fearlessly say what he thinks is right . . . Frankly, Philip, I do not think you can do better.'

It was a strong team. It had to be. The Princess and the Duke, aged twenty-one and twenty-six, were about to embark on a curious and exhausting adventure: a relentless, endlessly repetitive roller-coaster ride of royal duties and good works, from which only death or revolution could release them. When I asked Prince Philip if he felt frustrated that his marriage had ultimately curtailed his naval career, he said, 'In 1947 I thought I was going to have a career in the navy, but it became obvious there was no hope. The Royal Family then was just the King and the Queen and the two Princesses. The only other male member was the Duke of Gloucester. There was no choice. It just happened.' Philip had joined the family firm: he had to play his part in the family business. 'You have to make compromises,' he said to me. 'That's life. I accepted it. I tried to make the best of it.'

For the first four and a quarter years of his marriage, the Duke combined his royal duties with his naval ones. He had plenty of energy, a well-run office, and an enviable ability to successfully juggle the competing demands of the Admiralty and Buckingham Palace. He worked hard; he played hard. In May 1948 Chips Channon observed the Edinburghs dancing the night away at a fancy-dress party at Coppins. They were still going at 5 a.m. – two hours after everyone danced the Hokey Cokey 'hilariously'. According to Channon, Philip 'looked worn out', but he was the success of the ball, 'wildly gay with his policeman's hat and handcuffs. He leapt about and jumped into the air as he greeted everybody . . . His charm is colossal, like all the Mountbattens, and he and Princess Elizabeth seemed supremely happy.'

Quickly, and seemingly effortlessly, Philip slipped into the role of supportive consort and interested royal visitor. He had the ability to live in the moment, to concentrate intently on the job in hand. He was good at compartmentalising his life, switching from one interest/duty/activity to another in an instant, as required. In a day, he might wear several hats (metaphorically) and several uniforms (literally): he seemed at home in each of them. In the space of sixteen hours he would move from parade ground to business meeting to memorial service to charity lunch to factory tour to award ceremony to state banquet, changing kit four times, appearing up-to-speed throughout, but not letting the agenda or mood of one engagement affect the next. It is a useful skill to acquire – if you aspire to the royal life. (It also, I think, explains something that those who become friendly with royalty sometimes find puzzling. I have a number of 'show-business friends' who have enjoyed the company of Prince Philip – or Prince Charles or Prince William or Prince Harry – at charitable events, felt they were getting on famously, even been invited to Windsor Castle or Highgrove House for a meal, and then been disconcerted because the camaraderie of the moment isn't sustained. The royal is being thoroughly jolly – really friendly, intimate, and confidential – and then, suddenly, he's gone. It's 2.45 p.m., the car is waiting, he gets up, he goes: he may not even say goodbye. That's it – until next time. And, on the whole, *you* cannot organise next time: the ball is in their court. The royal life provides opportunities for countless brief encounters, many of them happy, some of them intense: it is not conducive to forming and sustaining a wide range of everyday friendships.)

In 1948, with the Edinburghs living at Buckingham Palace, Philip could walk to work, and did. He started the year with a desk job at the Admiralty, as an operations officer 'pushing ships around'. Later in the year he went on a Staff Course at the Royal Naval College, Greenwich, and chose to spend the week in Greenwich, coming home to Lilibet at weekends. Spending nights, and weeks, and sometimes months, apart from your spouse is the lot of married servicemen and women. It may be unsatisfactory, it may cause tensions and difficulties in a relationship, but it is not unusual: in the navy especially, it is the way things are. In the years to come, the time Elizabeth and Philip would spend apart would give rise to comment. To them it was simply an inevitable fact of life.

Understanding the lives of other people is not easy if their way of life is very different from your own. I have spent my married life sharing a bedroom – and a bed – with my wife. If we started to sleep in separate rooms, I would be dismayed: I would see it as the beginning of the end. The truth is it might be more comfortable and convenient sometimes to sleep apart, but we don't – we never have. Why? Because we are middle-class, and comfortably married middle-class couples of our generation always share the same bedroom. That's the way it is. Among the upper classes, especially three or four generations ago, it was different. Men and women led much more separate lives, they lived in larger houses, they had separate (if adjacent or adjoining) bedrooms. That's just the way it was. When Elizabeth and Philip moved into Clarence House they had separate but communicating bedrooms. It was what they – and their staff – would have expected. In his memoir the Duke's valet, John Dean, described the arrangement as though it was the most natural thing in the world. Of an evening, John would be assisting Philip in his bedroom, while Bobo would be tending to Elizabeth in hers, and the royal couple 'would joke happily through the left-open door'.

In July 1982 an intruder – a thirty-one-year-old schizophrenic named Michael Fagan – found his way into Buckingham Palace and disturbed the Queen, alone, asleep in bed. This alarming incident prompted a double dose of outrage from the tabloid press: why was the Palace's security so lamentable and where was Prince Philip? Why was he not on hand to come to his wife's rescue? Indeed, the 'revelation' that the Queen and her husband did not appear to share a bedroom caused more comment in certain quarters than the fact that a lunatic could wander off the street into the sovereign's bedroom without let or hindrance. The Queen, who, at the time, handled the intrusion with commendable calm, was nevertheless shaken. The popular press had the answer: 'Give her a cuddle, Philip,' instructed one newspaper headline. In fact, when sleeping under the same roof, the Queen and Prince Philip usually did share the same bed. It just happened that on the morning of Fagan's intrusion Philip had a crack-of-dawn start for an out-of-town official engagement and so spent the night in his own quarters.

Their long-standing friend Gina Kennard told me, 'At Balmoral that year – after that man got into her bedroom – the Queen began snapping at Philip. She was really quite snappy with him. Which was unusual for her. Not for him, of course. He's always been a bit snappy. But the man getting into her room was horrid.' It was. The man had a broken glass ashtray in his hand and was bleeding. The intrusion occurred at around 7.15 a.m. on 9 July. The Queen pressed the alarm button by her bed, but her overnight police guard had gone off duty at 6 a.m. and her footman was out walking the corgis. The intruder simply wandered in, wholly unhindered, drew the curtains and sat on the bed. He wanted to share his troubles with Her Majesty. (Later he told police he had planned to cut his wrists in front of the Queen.) Eventually, when he asked for a cigarette, the Queen managed to manoeuvre him out of the bedroom and the alarm was raised. The incident prompted a review of Palace security, which was, in the words of the intruder himself, 'diabolical'. This was not Fagan's first dawn raid on the Palace: on the previous occasion he had stolen a bottle of wine. The Home Secretary at the time was Willie Whitelaw. Ultimately, he was responsible for the Metropolitan Police and the Queen's security. He offered his resignation. It was declined. Some years later, he told me, his eyes brimming with tears, 'I felt utterly ashamed, utterly miserable. It was the worst moment of my public life.'

Back in May 1948, Princess Elizabeth and the Duke of Edinburgh undertook their first official foreign assignment: a four-day visit to Paris, a trip designed – as had been the King and Queen's French tour in 1939 – to burnish the Entente Cordiale. It did the trick. The programme was packed and predictable: Versailles, Fontainebleau, a night at the Opéra, a trip down the Seine. There were lunches, dinners, receptions, and a banquet – the stuff of every royal tour. The French press was charmed: the Princess was beautiful, the Duke was handsome, and both spoke surprisingly good French – he, thanks to his decade in Paris as a child; she, thanks to the tutoring of Antoinette de Bellaigue. 'In four hectic days,' Jock Colville noted with satisfaction, 'Princess Elizabeth had conquered Paris.' Forty years before the phrase 'the Diana effect' became common currency, Colville watched Elizabeth going about her business and described what amounted to the same phenomenon: 'Quite mysteriously, a visit by a young princess with beautiful blue eyes and a superb natural complexion brought gleams of radiant sunshine into the dingiest streets of the dreariest cities. Princes who do their duty are respected, beautiful Princesses have an in-built advantage over their male counterparts.'

One of the things that saddened – and worried – the Queen and

Prince Philip about Diana, Princess of Wales, was not that she was popular, but that she allowed her popularity to go to her head. Elizabeth was once adored, too – as much as Diana was, perhaps even more so. In the late 1940s and early 1950s, in Britain, in France, in countries around the world, thousands – tens of thousands, sometimes *hundreds* of thousands – turned out to cheer her. Once upon a time Philip and Elizabeth were seen – and talked about – and written up – as characters from a fairy tale. The difference between them and Princess Diana, I think, is that they did not take it personally. When I discussed this with the Duke of Edinburgh in his library at Buckingham Palace, he said to me, 'You won't remember this, but in the first years of the Queen's reign, the level of adulation – you wouldn't believe it. You really wouldn't. It could have been corroding. It would have been very easy to play to the gallery, but I took a conscious decision not to do that. Safer not to be too popular. You can't fall too far.'

Years later, when Catherine Middleton came along as a potential bride for his grandson, Prince William, the Duke of Edinburgh was, he told me, 'relieved to find her such a level-headed girl'. 'If you believe the attention is for you personally,' he warned, 'you're going to end up in trouble. The attention is for your role, what you do, what you're supporting. It isn't for you as an individual. You are not a celebrity. You are representing the Royal Family. That's all. Don't look at the camera. The Queen never looks at the camera. Never. Look at who you're talking to. Look at what you've come to see. Diana looked at the camera.' I have been on walkabout with the Duchess of Cambridge. She never looks at the camera.

The four-day trip to Paris was the Edinburghs' first overseas triumph. As a diplomatic and public relations exercise it was an unqualified success. At a personal level it was hell. The weather was unbearable: it was the hottest Whitsun weekend of the century. The schedule was alarmingly crowded: the couple were allowed one night off – 'a private evening' – and it was not a success. According to Jock Colville, 'We went to a most select three-star restaurant; the French had been turned out, so we found a table, just a party of us all alone in this vast restaurant. Prince Philip spotted a round hole in a table just opposite us, through which the lens of a camera was poking. He was naturally in a frightful rage. We went on to a nightclub, again the French [were] all turned out. One of the most appalling evenings I have ever spent. Everybody dressed up to the nines – nobody in either place – except the lens.'

Philip was in a rage and he had an upset stomach. Rumour had it that the kitchens at the British Embassy were to blame. Elizabeth stayed calm, of course. 'She is always calm,' according to her childhood friend Sonia Berry. 'She might get annoyed about something, but as a rule she stays on an even keel. I have never seen her lose her temper.' Elizabeth stayed calm, but she, too, felt a little queasy. She was three months pregnant. Back in London, in June, she wrote to her cousin, Diana Bowes-Lyon: 'Life is very busy at the moment, but after this month I'm taking a rest for the baby's sake. I am so excited about it and I really can't believe it's true.'

THE QUEEN & THE DUKE

Chapter Nine

'Love does not consist in gazing at each other,
but in looking in the same direction.'
      Antoine de Saint-Exupéry (1900–44), *Wind, Sand and Stars*

'Her Royal Highness the Princess Elizabeth, Duchess of Edinburgh, was safely delivered of a Prince at 9.14 o'clock this evening. Her Royal Highness and the infant Prince are both doing well.'

On Sunday, 14 November 1948, at a little after 11 p.m., Commander Richard Colville RN – a cousin of Jock Colville's, but an older man and less subtle, who had joined the Palace as press secretary to the King the year before – took the formal announcement, written out in his own neat hand, and, accompanied by Jock, scrunched his way across the courtyard of Buckingham Palace and fixed it to the railings. The waiting crowd – some three thousand strong – greeted the news with sustained cheers and an impromptu chorus of 'For He's a Jolly Good Fellow'.

By daybreak word had spread across the nation – and the world. In the United States, radio programmes were interrupted with the news. In South Africa and India, in Kenya and Canada, in Australia and New Zealand, guns were fired, bells were rung, bonfires were lit. In the streets of London, news vendors cried, 'It's a boy!' and across the mountain ranges of Wales a chain of beacons was lit. On the high seas, the ships of the Royal Navy – every one of them – put out more flags, and on the River Thames the humblest boats were festooned with celebratory bunting. In homes, and pubs and clubs and churches, there was – in a way that seems incredible to us now – genuine rejoicing. At Westminster Abbey the bells rung out with a peal of five thousand changes. In the chamber of the House of Commons, the Prime Minister, Clement Attlee, on behalf of a grateful nation, saluted the virtues of the constitutional monarchy, 'which have won the hearts of the people', and spoke of the 'great responsibilities' that would one day settle on the shoulders of the infant Prince. The Leader of the Opposition, Winston Churchill, now seventy-four, rose to the occasion with a typical rhetorical flourish: 'Our ancient monarchy renders inestimable services to our country and to all the British Empire and Commonwealth of Nations. Above the ebb and flow of party strife, the rise and fall of ministries and individuals, the changes of public opinion and fortune, the British monarchy presides ancient, calm and supreme within its functions, over all the treasures that have been saved from the past and all the glories that we write in the annals of our country. Our thoughts go out to the mother and father and, in a special way, to the little prince, now born into this world of strife and storm.'

At the very moment of the little Prince's birth, his father was on the squash court at Buckingham Palace, having a game with his friend and equerry, Mike Parker. The Prince and Parker had had more than one game that evening – and a swim in the Palace pool. Princess Elizabeth's confinement – in the Palace's Buhl Room, specially converted into a well-equipped surgery – had been a painfully long one. The King's private secretary, Tommy Lascelles, brought the good news hotfoot from the Buhl Room to the squash court. Philip raced back, with Lascelles and Parker trailing, on the way picking up the carnations and champagne he had at the ready, and went in to congratulate his young wife and admire his new son. 'It takes a man to have a son!' was the signal Philip sent to Parker when Parker's first child was born. Parker told me, 'Philip was thrilled to have a son. He was over the moon. Absolutely delighted.' That same night Philip sent a telegram bearing the glad tidings to his mother in Greece.

Princess Alice, now aged sixty-three, had recently moved to the Greek island of Tinos. She planned, she told her family, to 'withdraw from the world' and found 'a religious sisterhood of Martha & Mary', training girls to become nursing sisters. She was not a nun herself, but she dressed as one, and rose early every morning to attend to her devotions. Prince Philip said, in a typically matter-of-fact way, 'Wearing the habit meant that she did not have to worry about clothes or getting her hair done.' She led a life of comparative simplicity, in a modest house, where the electricity supply was erratic and there was no telephone. She was thrilled to receive her son's telegram. She wrote to him at once: 'I think of you so much with a sweet baby of our own, of your joy & the interest you will take in all his little doings. How fascinating nature is, but how one has to pay for it in the anxious trying hours of the confinement.'

Princess Elizabeth recovered quickly from her confinement. She spent ten days in bed recuperating (as new mothers were encouraged to do) and breast-fed her son from the start. The Princess wrote to her former music teacher: 'The baby is very sweet and we are enormously proud of him. He has an interesting pair of hands for a baby. They are rather large, but with fine long fingers quite unlike mine and certainly unlike his father's. It will be interesting to see what they become. I still find it hard to believe I have a baby of my own!'

The first cot-side report to reach the public came from one of Elizabeth's aunts, her mother's younger sister, Rose, by now Countess Granville, who told a gathering of Girl Guides in Northern Ireland that the new mother was 'wonderfully well and radiantly happy' and the new Prince 'could not be more angelic looking': 'He is golden-haired and has the most beautiful complexion, as well as amazingly delicate features for so young a baby . . . The Queen says that she thinks the baby is like his mother, but the Duke is quite certain that the baby is very like himself.' After a few days, in small clusters, Palace servants were allowed to gather round the royal crib ('done up in buttercup yellow silk, with lace trimmings', according to Crawfie: 'The Royal Family do not observe the old tradition of pink and blue') and coo and ooh and ah at the bonny little Prince, who had weighed in at a satisfactory seven pounds six ounces. John Dean described the infant as 'a tiny red-faced bundle, either hairless or so fair as to appear so'. Crawfie thought that, like all royal babies in her experience, he bore a strong resemblance to George V, with 'an absurdly mature look, and ridges under his eyes'.

After the initial excitement of the royal birth – four thousand congratulatory telegrams were received at Buckingham Palace within twenty-four hours of the news breaking, closely followed by an avalanche of cards, letters, flowers, and assorted gifts, from teddy bears to hand-knitted bootees – a macabre rumour started. Around the land the whisper went: something is wrong with the child: he is disfigured, he might not live. Crawfie later wrote: 'The stories that went around at that time about him were entirely without foundation of any kind.' She believed the root cause of the stories was the Royal Family's own obsession with privacy, what she called a 'strange campaign of secrecy': 'For a long time no pictures were issued, and even the household did not know what the baby's names were to be.'

There was a news vacuum and on the streets it was filled with wild speculation. The baby might be 'healthy and strong, and beautifully made', as Crawfie insisted, 'with a flawless, silky skin', but, if so, why not show him off to the world? And why not name him? The answer to both questions, it seems, was a simple desire on the part of the Princess for privacy. Just as fifty years later, on the death of Diana, Princess of Wales, the Queen's first instinct was to shield her grandsons, protect their privacy, and keep her own counsel, so, in November 1948, on the birth of Prince Charles, Princess Elizabeth instinctively wanted to guard her baby son's privacy. There would be photographs – of course[65] – and the baby's names would be made known – naturally – but all in good time . . . Why should the Heiress Presumptive and her little boy have to dance at once to the public's tune?

Throughout her life the Queen has fulfilled her public duty conscientiously and with complete commitment, and has hoped, as a consequence, to be allowed some private space for her private life. Do we really need to know how the infant Prince took to the breast (quite well, apparently), or whether and when he was circumcised (yes, on 20 December 1948, it seems: Dr Jacob Snowman performed the operation)? Of course, we don't need to know. It is none of our business. And yet, we are curious.

From the birth of her son to the present day, Elizabeth II has struggled to maintain a degree of privacy for herself and her children. It has not been easy. Hugh Dalton, the Labour MP and sometime Chancellor of the Exchequer, wrote in his diary in the week that Prince Charles was born: 'If this boy ever comes to the throne . . . it will be a very different Commonwealth and country he will rule

65 And the first were taken by Cecil Beaton, who reported to his diary: 'Prince Charles, as he is to be named, is an obedient sitter. He interrupted a long, contented sleep to do my bidding and open his blue eyes to stare long and wonderingly into the camera lens, the beginning of a lifetime in the glare of public duty.'

over.' Dalton was prescient. Elizabeth had been born in the reign of George V, King-Emperor. She grew up in an age of deference and discretion, when bowing and curtsying to royalty was automatic, when you did not speak to a royal unless first spoken to, when her Uncle David could conduct an open affair with a married divorcee and know that it would go unreported by a self-denying press. The world has changed. The Empire has gone, deference has disappeared, and newspapers will print what they like – and the more intimate and salacious it is, the more they like it. When Edward VIII and his girlfriend, on holiday together, swam naked off the coast of Albania, there were no paparazzi hiding on the hillside. When, half a century later, the Duchess of York, on holiday with her boyfriend in the south of France, appeared topless by their swimming pool, the revealing photographs, taken with telephoto lenses from the adjacent hillside, appeared on front pages in Britain and around the world. In the summer of 2012, when the Duke and Duchess of Cambridge were holidaying at the Château d'Autet, near Viens in Provence, another photographer with a telephoto lens managed to take a series of pictures of Prince William's wife, Catherine, topless. The French edition of the magazine *Closer* splashed three of the photographs on its cover and, on the inside pages, published more pictures – with captions to match: 'On the terrace of Château d'Autet, Kate has decided to release the pressure, to get rid of convention, to free herself from the protocol, but also to get rid of her bikini top! At the time of feminist struggles, militants were burning their bras. Kate doesn't wear hers, and that's her absolute right. Exulted by the fragrance of lavender from the neighbouring fields, Kate takes advantage of those delicious moments of doing nothing and offers her breasts to the soft caress of the Provence sun.'

For Princess Elizabeth in 1948, the desire for privacy was more than a matter of personal preference and natural reticence. It was a matter of policy. In 1867 Walter Bagehot, writing about the role of the monarchy in *The English Constitution*, declared: 'We must not let daylight in on magic.' Bagehot believed that sustaining the mystique of the monarchy was essential to its authority – and survival. Elizabeth had studied Bagehot, and Commander Richard Colville, who was the Palace's press secretary from 1947 until 1968, believed in Bagehot's maxim completely. When Colville got the job he had no experience of press relations: he had been in the navy for twenty-two years. For the next twenty-one years he dealt with the press in a manner that suggested that relations with them were the very last thing that either he or the Royal Family desired.

According to Kenneth Rose, a journalist and biographer who dealt with him on a regular basis, Commander Colville did not discriminate between hacks: 'All were made to feel that their questions were impertinent if not downright vulgar.' Colville would supply information about the sovereign's public engagements, and that was all. In his view, as he explained to the Press Council, the Queen was 'entitled to expect that her family will attain the privacy at home which all other families are entitled to enjoy'. Somewhat impertinently, the Press Council begged to differ, maintaining that 'the private lives of public men and women, especially royal persons, have always been the subject of natural curiosity. That is one of the consequences of fame or eminence or sincere national affection. Everything therefore that touches the Crown is of public interest or concern.'

All their adult lives Elizabeth and Philip remained wary of the press. Take it from those who know her, the Queen is a delightful person – amusing, engaging, and intelligent – but she is not comfortable with journalists. She has never given an interview and has no desire to do so. When she comes face to face with a journalist or broadcaster, at a public event or a private reception, she watches her words. She is determined to give nothing away. Jennie Bond was the BBC's royal correspondent for fourteen years. When she gave up the job in 2003, she told me, 'I never got to know the Queen. I barely got to meet her. As a royal reporter you don't. You are kept at arm's length. And on the rare occasions when you are admitted to the royal presence, the small talk is very desultory. When the Queen went to South Korea, I covered the visit for the BBC and met Her Majesty briefly at a reception. She said, "Oh, have you come here specially?" I felt like saying, "No, I just happened be in South Korea and thought I'd drop by." I think it's sad that, after fourteen years, I still had the most distant relationship with the Queen and Prince Philip. I think, from their point of view, it's bad public relations. From my point of view, I didn't dislike them. I just didn't get to know them. There were endless opportunities when they could have made their mark with the media, and they simply didn't take them. They avoid journalists. They walk away from them. They dismiss them. The Duke's even worse than the Queen. He's really perfected the art of saying hello and goodbye in the same handshake.'

Prince Philip, in fact, was almost invariably good company and, in my experience, usually went out of his way to be agreeable to strangers. He did not trust the press, however. 'If I'm doing something I care about,' he once said to me, 'I really hope the press won't come along too, because I know they'll only ruin it.' When I reminded him that he was the member of the Royal Family who, in the 1950s, first talked to the press, giving a series of newspaper, radio, and television interviews, he said, 'Yes, I made a conscious decision to talk to the media – but not about me, only about what I'm doing, what I'm supporting.' When I told him that, fifty years on, that was no longer enough, that the modern media need something more sexy, they need 'personalities', he nodded. 'Yes,' he said, with a sigh, 'the press have turned us into a soap opera.'

In 1948 the soap opera had something of the fairy tale about it. A month and a day after the royal birth came the royal christening. On the morning of Wednesday, 15 December, in the White and Gold Music Room at Buckingham Palace, wearing the flowing silk and lace christening robe his mother had worn for her christening twenty-two years before, the infant Prince was baptised into the Church of England and named Charles Philip Arthur George. His godparents included the King, Queen Mary, the King of Norway, Prince George of Greece, the Dowager Marchioness of Milford Haven, Elizabeth's uncle, David Bowes-Lyon, and Dickie's daughter, Patricia Brabourne. Patricia told me that she thought Philip and Elizabeth chose 'Charles' as a name simply because they liked it. Boy Browning was one of those who felt the name was 'bad news', given the precedents of Charles I and II, to say nothing of the unhappy fate that befell Charles Stuart, 'Bonnie Prince Charlie'. Princess Margaret, however, was delighted with the choice of name, explaining that henceforward she would be known as 'Charley's Aunt', 'probably my finest title'.

After lunch, and the taking of the formal photographs (including a fine study of the sleeping Prince in the crisply starched arms of his nurse), Queen Mary invited the assembled company to gather round Queen Victoria's photo albums to decide who among his forebears the new Prince most closely resembled. She decided, without doubt, it was Prince Albert. Queen Mary took the keenest interest in family history. Her christening gift was a silver cup and cover given by George III to a godson in 1780, 'so that', she noted in her diary, with allowable satisfaction, 'I gave a present from my great-grandfather to my great grandson 168 years later.' Queen Mary entertained few doubts about her family's place in history. Baby Charles's other great-grandmother, Victoria Milford Haven, was more circumspect. She wrote to Dickie of her 'latest & important great-grandson': 'Let us hope he may live in a more peaceable & prosperous time than we & live to be some sort of reigning king.'

Alice did not attend the christening, but she received news of her new grandson's progress from other members of the family. She got a full report from her younger sister, Louise, the Queen of Sweden, which she shared with Dickie: 'She says that Lilibet was looking so well & fresh, a good recovery after a hard time she had, 30 hours in all. The baby is sweet with a well-shaped head, an oval face & a little bit of fair fluff of hair. She says he is like Philip, but Marina says he is like Lilibet, so you can choose. I am so happy for Philip for he adores children & also small babies. He carries it about himself quite professionally to the nurse's amusement.'

By every account, Prince Philip was especially good with babies and small children. 'They like him and he likes them,' is what Countess Mountbatten told me. 'No question about it, Philip was a very good father to his children when they were young.' According to Lady Kennard, 'He was a wonderful parent. He played with his children, he read them stories, he took them fishing, he was very involved. I remember we stayed with them in Scotland when Charles must have been about one. The three of them were so happy together, easy and relaxed. Philip has been marvellous with his grandchildren, too. He's just good with the little ones.' In the summer of 2002, when the Prime Minister, Tony Blair, and his wife, Cherie Booth, went to stay at Balmoral, Philip took a special shine to the Blairs' two-year-old son, Leo. Proudly, Leo sang the whole first verse of the national anthem to Philip and Philip responded happily by singing Leo the second verse. Cherie Blair told me, 'I have to say that both the

Queen and Prince Philip are really, really good with little children. You couldn't fault them.' (Whether you could fault Mrs Blair is another matter. I was told, on good authority, that when the Queen came to see Leo in the nursery at Balmoral, Mrs Blair had instructed her nanny not to curtsy to Her Majesty.)

Philip and Lilibet were very happy with their new baby. Parenthood suited them. According to all of their friends to whom I have spoken – friends who have known them across all their adult lives – the first few years of their marriage were, in many ways, the happiest. 'Perhaps inevitably,' Gina Kennard said to me, 'Princess Elizabeth was not yet Queen, Philip was still in the navy. They were young, they were relatively carefree.' And they were cosseted. They were devoted to little Prince Charles, but they did not have to tend to him unaided. He had two Scottish nurses in constant attendance: Helen Lightbody, who arrived on the recommendation of the Duchess of Gloucester, whose sons she had looked after, and Mabel Anderson, who placed an advertisement in a nursing journal and was amazed to find herself invited to Buckingham Palace for an interview with the Princess.

Before Charles was born, Elizabeth had declared, 'I'm going to be the child's mother, not the nurses.' Well, she was – but, inevitably, because she was a princess as well as a mother, because 'royal duty' called and all her life Elizabeth has made answering the call of royal duty her first priority, and because it was the way of her class and her time, much of the nitty-gritty of childcare was left to Mrs Lightbody and Miss Anderson. (Both nurses were maiden ladies. Because Helen Lightbody was the more senior, she was given the courtesy title of 'Mrs', as Alah Knight had been in her day.) Until Clarence House was ready for the family to move into in July 1949, the baby lived and was looked after in the country, at Windlesham Moor, only seeing his parents when they came down from London at weekends. The breast-feeding had stopped in January, when Charles was not quite two months old. Elizabeth had contracted measles and the doctors advised that, until she was better, mother and child should stay apart.

The Edinburghs rented Windlesham Moor from a Mrs Warwick Bryant. It had useful grounds – fifty acres and a fine garden noted for its azaleas – but the house itself – two storeys, five bedrooms, four reception rooms, plus staff quarters – was by no means a mansion. According to John Dean, Philip was particularly happy there: 'I believe that in those early days the Duke was uneasy in the atmosphere of the Palace with its formalities, and that this heightened his pleasure in having a country home that was so different.' Clarence House, of course, was much grander, but, again according to Dean, Philip made it 'his own'. The Duke, reported the valet, loved 'home-making' and was particularly keen on every kind of new-fangled labour-saving device. The facilities for the staff were 'wonderful', said Dean, 'as near ideal as could possibly be imagined.' Even so, the turnover in the ranks of the junior members of the household was quite high. The hours were long – when the royals were in residence, staff got just one half-day a week free and alternate Sundays off – and the wages were modest. The Edinburghs were not extravagant. The Princess was a 'considerate employer', according to Dean, concerned about the health and welfare of her servants,[66] but, overall, the Duke was in charge, the undoubted captain of the domestic ship, 'pleasant and courteous to servants', but quite demanding, and liable to speak his mind 'in naval fashion'. When the Duke called Dean 'a stupid clot', master and servant did not speak to each other for several days.[67] Dean did not find Philip altogether easy to work for. 'He is difficult to dress,' he complained, 'because he's not interested in clothes and is set on his own ideas – he wears suede shoes with evening dress and he simply cannot tie a tie.' The Princess, in her dressing room, would hear her husband and his valet arguing next

---

66 Paul Burrell, who first went to work at Buckingham Palace as an under-butler in the 1970s and later became one of the personal footmen to the Queen, told me that when once he asked Her Majesty how many servants she had, she replied, 'I have many members of staff, but no servants.'

67 Who would be a servant? Burrell also tells of the time when, while he was butler to the Princess of Wales, servant and mistress fell out and were not on speaking terms for a matter of *weeks*. 'Silence,' someone said, 'is the unbearable repartee.' But it may be preferable to verbal abuse. More than one royal servant has reported being barked at by the Duke of Edinburgh, and Burrell, in his book *A Royal Duty*, gives a hair-raising account of a book being thrown in his direction by a ranting, screaming, and foot-stamping Prince of Wales, who, minutes later, apologised shame-facedly, only to be told by Burrell, as he picked up the missile from the floor, 'If you can't vent your feelings on me, Your Royal Highness, who can you vent them on?'

door. 'Listen to them, Bobo,' she would say to her own, ever-present dresser, 'they're just like Papa and Jerram [the King's valet]. Only sometimes I think they're worse.'

In fact, the Edinburgh household was a contented one. At Windlesham Moor, Mr Huggett, the head gardener, and an ex-Guardsman, playfully encouraged the Princess to take an interest in his team's handiwork, saying, 'Ma'am, from one Grenadier to another, I think you ought to come round the garden after church,' while Philip encouraged general team spirit by getting the staff of all ranks to come together to play cricket on summer Sunday afternoons. At Clarence House, when films were shown in the Edinburghs' home cinema, the members of staff were invited to join the guests for the show. In the staff sitting room at Clarence House there was even a television set.

In 1949 there were very few households in Britain that could boast of having a television set, fewer still that could boast of having two. In an age of austerity the Edinburghs wanted for nothing. Their country house was thoroughly comfortable; their town house was unostentatiously palatial. The high-ceilinged reception rooms were filled with elegant eighteenth-century furniture. The Princess's bedroom was freshly decorated in pink and blue (with a crowned canopy over the royal bed); the Duke's bedroom and bathroom featured light wood panelling, red furnishings, and framed photographs of the ships in which he had served; Prince Charles's nursery was all in white, with blue trimmings. The young couple took an active interest in the detail of the refurbishment of Clarence House. The Duke chose and arranged all the pictures, and personally supervised the installation of the kitchen and laundry-room equipment. The Princess helped mix the light lime-green paint for the dining room's walls with her own hand and offered her own practical solution to the problem of the lingering smell of paint: 'Put a bucket of hay in there and that'll take it away.'

One of the witnesses to Philip and Elizabeth's early married life that I most enjoyed meeting during my researches for this book was John Gibson. He began his working life as a kitchen porter at Buckingham Palace in 1946. He went on to train as a footman and observed the romance between Philip and Elizabeth as it blossomed. Before the wedding, when Philip came to Sandringham to stay, John noticed that Philip's socks needed darning and that he had to borrow a tie from one of the valets. When Prince Charles was born, in November 1948, John found himself working temporarily in Winston Churchill's household. He told me, 'When I heard the news on the radio I went in to tell Mr Churchill and he jumped up in the air and gave three cheers. He was over the moon for the Princess. He ran round the room waving his hands above his head and shouting, "Hooray! It's marvellous news!" Tell everybody to come in, John. And bring the champagne. We must toast the heir to the throne.'

Two months after Charles was born, John Gibson returned to royal service as 'nursery footman' at Windlesham Moor. 'I had sole responsibility for the royal pram,' he told me proudly. He assured me that Princess Elizabeth was 'very hands-on' with Charles, 'like a real mother – not a princess'. He could not fault the young royal couple: 'When they were on their own it was a very simple life. They were quite normal people really. They were waited on hand and foot, obviously, but they sat at the table and they had a natter about what was going on in the day.' Princess Elizabeth loved lemon and sugar pancakes and chocolate cake. Much of the domestic conversation overheard by John related to home-making. 'They couldn't wait to get into their new home at Clarence House. They talked about it all the time. "I think Grandma is giving me a nice sideboard. I'm sure she is." Grandma was Queen Mary, of course.'

When John Dean, Philip's valet, had a day off, John Gibson would take the young Duke of Edinburgh his early morning tea. Philip would look in on Elizabeth in her intercommunicating room and tease her for not being out of bed yet. When they were up at Birkhall in Scotland, Philip and Elizabeth would drive over to Balmoral with the staff piled into the back of the shooting brake. 'He'd drive like mad over the country roads,' according to John Gibson. '"Philip, Philip, slow down for God's sake, slow down, you're killing all the rabbits," she said. "What's the matter with you?"'

These were the golden years. Elizabeth conceived her second child towards the end of 1949. Princess Anne Elizabeth Alice Louise was born at Clarence House at 11.50 a.m. on Tuesday, 15 August 1950. Elizabeth reported to a friend, 'Both Philip and I are very thrilled about the new baby and we only hope that Charles will take kindly to it. He has only seen Fortune Euston's baby at close quarters and he then tried to pull her toes off and poke her eyes out, all of which she took very kindly, having a brother of 2 who presumably did the same.'

Elizabeth and Philip were proud parents and happy ones. They were good parents, too. That is certainly the impression I got, speaking to, say, the Duchess of Grafton (Fortune Euston, as was) or Countess Mountbatten (one of Prince Charles's godmothers), but it is not the impression you will have gained if you have read any of the many books that have touched on the matter. Every one of them – without exception, I think – portrays Elizabeth as a well-intentioned but somewhat distant mother and Philip as a forbidding, formidable, and usually absent father. Sarah Bradford, for example, in her widely acclaimed portrait of the Queen, says of the young mother's relationship with baby Charles: 'Elizabeth, although fond of him, was not particularly maternal.' Anthony Holden, in his acclaimed biography of Charles, describes the young children's routine at Clarence House like this: 'The royal nursery settled into a rigid daily routine in the care of the two nannies, "Mrs" Lightbody and Miss Anderson. Charles and Anne were got up each day at 7 a.m. sharp, dressed, fed, and played with in the nursery until nine, when they enjoyed a statutory half-hour with their mother. They rarely saw her again until tea-time, when Elizabeth would try to clear two hours in her day. She liked to bath the children herself when her schedule permitted, after which they were dressed up again to be introduced to distinguished visitors. Even before his third birthday, Charles had learned to bow before offering his cheek for a kiss from "Gan-Gan", Queen Mary, and not to sit down in the presence of his grandfather. It was a formidable introduction to the complexities of any child's life – basking but sporadically, and unpredictably, in the attentions of his mother, with his father all but a stranger. Already a pattern was being set that would come to haunt Charles's life even in adulthood, even at times of his greatest need.'

The tone and content of this account of nursery life at Clarence House is accepted as a reflection of the truth by nearly one and all – including Prince Charles, who, in 1994, allowed his authorised biographer, Jonathan Dimbleby, to reveal that the Prince felt 'emotionally estranged' from his parents and, all his life, had yearned for the kind of affection that, in his view, they were 'unable or unwilling to offer'. Charles's strictures hurt his parents. (That he chose to make them in public angered them as well.) All that Prince Philip would say to me on the record about his and his wife's parenting skills was, 'We did our best.'

In fact, Elizabeth saw her young children as much as any aristocratic mother of her generation and more, perhaps, than many busy working mothers today. And Philip, on the evidence of those who witnessed him in action as a young father in the late 1940s and early 1950s, far from being distant and forbidding, was hands-on and loving – more so than many of his stiff-upper-lip, Eton-educated, Guards officer contemporaries. The royal couple did not spend as much time with their children as they might have liked, for the simple reason that, as well as being parents, Elizabeth was Heiress Presumptive to an ailing King and Philip was a serving officer in the Royal Navy.

George VI was fifty-three when Prince Charles was born in November 1948. He looked much older. In the preceding eighteen months he had lost seventeen pounds in weight. He was, he said, 'in discomfort most of the time', suffering from numbness and cramp in his feet and legs. He carried on with his duties – standing, in considerable pain, at the Remembrance Day service at the Cenotaph in Whitehall and reviewing the Territorial Army in Hyde Park – but summoned his doctors. Two days before Charles's birth, he was diagnosed as suffering from arteriosclerosis, a condition brought on by his chronic smoking. Two days after the birth, he agreed, reluctantly, to postpone a planned tour of Australia and New Zealand. In March 1949 he underwent an operation to help regulate the blood supply to his legs, and felt much better. Because of the continuing danger of a sudden thrombosis, he was advised to reduce his commitments, to rest more and worry less. He did his best. He promised his mother that he was trying to 'worry less about political matters' – he was an inveterate worrier – and avoid the bursts of bad temper – his notorious 'gnashes' – that were brought on by frustration and irritation. 'Since he has become a recognised invalid,' a courtier told Harold Nicolson, 'he is as sweet and patient as can be.'

As the King curtailed his workload, so the pressures on the young Princess increased. 'It was inevitable,' Prince Philip said to me. 'You've got to remember that the Royal Family then was just the four of them: the King and the Queen and the two Princesses. It's very different now. Now we have to avoid tripping over one another, so Charles goes off and does the arts, Anne does the prisons, and so on. Then, there was just the four of them – and the Duke of Gloucester – for everything. Because of the King's health, it was inevitable that we did more. There was no choice.'

But there were compensations. As well as dutiful days, there were glamorous nights. To mark Elizabeth's twenty-third birthday in April 1949, they went to see Laurence Olivier and Vivien Leigh in *The School for Scandal* at the New Theatre and then went on for supper and dancing with the Oliviers at the Café de Paris, off Leicester Square. The American entertainer Danny Kaye, then the toast of the town, danced attendance on them – literally. (John Dean reported watching the star of *The Court Jester* 'capering round Princess Elizabeth' at Windlesham Moor.)

They consorted with stars of stage and screen (as royalty has often done) and they had a lot of fun, too, in their own way with their own set. Gina Kennard told me, 'I remember lots of laughter, lots of old-fashioned gaiety. Country weekends. Shooting – not hunting in Philip's case. We used to pot at rabbits. Serious shooting, too, of course. Shoot suppers. Hunt balls. Proper house parties. With tennis. And croquet. And dancing. They are both wonderful dancers. You should have seen Philip's samba! And games. Sardines. Hunt the Thimble. So much fun.' And some dressing up, too. At the American Ambassador's fancy-dress ball, Philip came as a waiter and Elizabeth as a maid.

In the summer of 1949 the world was an uncertain place. The Cold War was upon us. The Soviet Union was testing the atomic bomb. In China, Shanghai had just fallen to Mao Zedong's People's Liberation Army. The British Empire was no longer what it once had been. India and Ireland had become republics. There were race riots in Durban. In Britain, the economy was enfeebled. The Chancellor of the Exchequer spoke of 'the crushing difficulties' faced by the British people as he prepared to devalue the pound sterling by a staggering 30.5 per cent. But at Windsor Castle the champagne still flowed. At the end of Royal Ascot, a royal ball. They danced till dawn. There was magic in the air. In his diary Chips Channon described the scene: 'The rooms were banked with flowers . . . Windows were open on to the terrace . . . The doors were flung open, and we saw the King and Queen waiting to receive us, side by side: he seemed brown and she, though unfortunately very, very plump, looked magnificent in a white satin semi-crinoline number with the Garter and splendid rubies . . . We walked along a long passage with magnificent Canalettos and Zoffanys, by the dozen, many of which have been rehung and cleaned since the war . . . The King had his foot up on a foot stool to rest, though he seemed quite well and often danced . . . The Edinburghs made a somewhat late appearance (he had been to the Channel Islands or somewhere) and they looked divine. She wore a very high tiara and the Garter – he was in the dark blue Windsor uniform, also with the Garter. They looked characters out of a fairy tale . . . At a quarter to five, [the Queen] told the band to stop; everyone bowed and curtseyed to the remaining Royalties and we left, and drove back in the dawn – looking back, the Castle rose romantic in the pink morning light. I was enchanted with the evening.'

Philip had boundless energy. He could indeed make a flying visit to the Channel Islands ('or somewhere') and then dance till dawn. Patricia Mountbatten said to me, 'He was a dynamo.' Mike Parker told me, 'He crackled with energy. He made things happen. He made things jump.' As well as fulfilling his naval and his royal duties, he was beginning to take on a range of 'good works' – starting with the presidencies of the London Federation of Boys' Clubs and the National Playing Fields Association. He was not inclined to be a docile figurehead: he wanted to be proactive and hands-on. Mike Parker said to me, 'He wanted to make a difference and, if necessary, he was ready to make a noise.'

Elizabeth was altogether quieter. She was still quite shy. She didn't have her husband's ability to swing into a room of strangers and talk easily to anybody. She sometimes felt, as they went out on official visits together, that the crowd would rather see the Duke than the Princess. She was wrong, of course. She was beautiful and she was the Heiress Presumptive. She knew her duty, and did it conscientiously. Encouraged by Jock Colville, she was now regularly reading Foreign Office telegrams because – as Colville put it to the King's private secretary, Tommy Lascelles – they 'would give HRH an idea of world affairs which she cannot possibly get from the newspapers'. She was also making speeches – speeches drafted by Colville and

Lascelles – whose content, when not simply anodyne, reflected the essentially conservative views and values of the Establishment of the day. In October 1949, for example, the young princess and mother, aged twenty-three, addressed a massed meeting of the members of the Mothers' Union in Central Hall, Westminster, and, in her thin, high-pitched voice, deplored the 'current age of growing self-indulgence, of hardening materialism, of falling moral standards' and nailed her colours firmly to the unshakeable, unbreakable matrimonial mast: 'We can have no doubt that divorce and separation are responsible for some of the darkest evils in our society today.'

In the same October, Philip, now twenty-eight, was appointed first lieutenant and second-in-command of HMS *Chequers*, the Leader of the 1st Destroyer Flotilla of the Mediterranean Fleet at Malta. The appointment was a good one – Philip was the youngest of the first lieutenants in the Flotilla – and reunited him with his old friend from HMS *Valiant*, the future First Sea Lord and Chief of the Defence Staff, Terry Lewin. 'I found him doing the job of Flotilla Gunnery Officer,' Philip recalled. 'We served together until August 1950 in what was a very happy wardroom, four of whose members were destined to become flag officers.'

The posting also brought Philip back into daily contact with his uncle, Dickie Mountbatten, recently translated from Viceroy to Vice Admiral. Mountbatten, having overseen the end of empire in India, was reconnecting with the Royal Navy in Malta in a relatively humble role as Commander of the 1st Cruiser Squadron. Philip arrived on his own in Malta and went to stay with Dickie and Edwina at the house they were renting, the Villa Guardamangia. The two men took a little while to get used to each other again. Philip, according to Dickie, was 'very busy showing his independence'. Within three weeks, however, everything was much jollier. 'Philip is right back on 1946 terms with us,' Mountbatten reported in a letter to his daughter, Patricia, 'and we've had a heart-to-heart in which he admitted he was fighting shy of coming under my dominating influence and patronage!' Mountbatten's joy was wholly unconfined when, towards the end of November, Princess Elizabeth came out to Malta to join her husband. 'Lilibet is quite enchanting,' declared Mountbatten, 'and I've lost whatever of my heart is left to spare entirely to her. She dances quite divinely and always wants a Samba when we dance together and has said some very nice remarks about my dancing.'

This is the period in Elizabeth's adult life that can perhaps be described as the most 'normal' – or, at least, 'the least unreal', the most like that of other young couples of Philip and Elizabeth's generation. He was a serving officer; she was a naval wife. Buckingham Palace was a thousand miles away and the British press left them largely unmolested. 'It was a good time,' according to Philip. 'It was a fabulous time,' according to Mike Parker. 'I think it was their happiest time,' said John Dean. 'They were so relaxed and free, coming and going as they pleased.' Of course, the very fact that Parker, as equerry, and Dean, as valet, were in Malta as well, is a reminder that, when it comes to royalty, nothing is ever entirely 'normal'. The Princess arrived in Malta comfortably attended: as well as Parker and Dean and the inevitable police officer, there was the ever-faithful Bobo MacDonald and a new lady-in-waiting, Lady Alice Egerton, sixth and youngest daughter of the 4th Earl of Ellesmere and sister of Meg Egerton, who had recently married Jock Colville.[68]

The Edinburghs, plus retinue, stayed with the Mountbattens at the Villa Guardamangia where the indoor help included a butler, a

68 Alice Egerton was born on 7 August 1923 and died on 7 October 1977. She committed suicide. She was a lady-in-waiting to Princess Elizabeth until 1952 and a Woman of the Bedchamber to the Queen from 1953. In 1957 she was appointed a Commander of the Royal Victorian Order. In 1996, Sarah Bradford, in the first edition of *Elizabeth: A Biography of Her Majesty The Queen*, suggested that Lady Alice, who was unmarried, committed suicide after being dismissed as a lady-in-waiting for telling the Queen of the Duke of Edinburgh's infidelities. When the book was published, Lady Alice's brother, the 6th Duke of Sutherland, issued a denial. In November 2003, as an admirer of her meticulously researched biographies, I went to see Sarah Bradford at her home in Fulham – in Britannia Road, appropriately. Over a glass of wine, in flickering candlelight, she said to me: 'I believed my information had come from a reliable source, but Lady Alice's family told me that, in fact, Lady Alice had suffered from depression over a number of years and it was her depression that led to her suicide. I accepted that, apologised to Lady Meg, and took the suggestion out of the paperback edition of the book.' As I understand it, Lady Alice suffered from manic depression and her behaviour was consequently erratic. Interestingly, in the 1950s, she became a particular friend of Prince Philip's mother, Princess Alice, who, of course, had her own experience of manic depression in the 1930s. Meg Egerton, Lady Colville, died, aged eighty-five, in May 2004 and the Queen, unusually, attended her memorial service.

housekeeper, three cooks, six stewards, two housemaids, two cleaning ladies, and a valet. 'We are not too grossly overstaffed,' protested Dickie, who was accustomed to living on a fairly grand scale. Clearly, however, he felt a little sheepish about the valet, writing to Edwina: 'I fear you think I'm very spoilt wanting a valet and I do admit I am, but if one is working hard it does help if there is a second man in the house who can look after my clothes.'

John Dean, who was there looking after Philip's clothes, paints a very sunny portrait of the Edinburghs in Malta. There were parties and picnics, swimming expeditions and boat trips. Elizabeth went out for coffee and shopping and visits to the hairdresser with the other young officers' wives. Philip – encouraged by his uncle – took to the polo field and discovered one of the great sporting pleasures of his life.

Princess Anne was conceived in Malta. Prince Charles was just one year old and back in England, being looked after by his nurses and devoted grandparents. The King sent a progress report to Lilibet: 'He is too sweet for words stumping around the room.' Elizabeth had been in London for Charles's first birthday on 14 November. Six days later she flew to Malta to join Philip and, after a few duty nights as a guest at the Governor's residence, settled in happily to life at the Villa Guardamangia, 'although,' according to John Dean, 'she was probably a little sad at leaving Prince Charles behind.' She was away from her boy for five weeks. She stayed in Malta until 28 December, when Philip and HMS *Chequers* (along with six other warships) were sent on manoeuvres to patrol the Red Sea. Neither Philip nor Elizabeth was with Charles for his second Christmas, and, when Elizabeth did get back to England, she did not rush immediately to Sandringham to be reunited with her little boy. She spent four days at Clarence House, attending to 'a backlog of correspondence', and fulfilling a number of engagements, including a visit to Hurst Park races, where she had the satisfaction of seeing Monaveen, a horse she owned jointly with her mother, win at 10–1.

Today it is evident that Prince Charles has mixed feelings about his upbringing. Overall his memories of his childhood are not happy ones and they go back a long way. He told his biographer, Anthony Holden, that he could still recall his first pram, 'lying in its vastness, overshadowed by its high sides'. Charles believes he was neglected by his parents when he was small. His parents, understandably, saw it differently. When I raised it with him, Prince Philip shrugged and pointed out that, at the time, he was serving in the Royal Navy and that servicemen and their families are often apart. 'It's the way it was. It's the way it is.' He also made it clear to me that Elizabeth believes that, all her life, she has done her best to balance the range of her responsibilities – as a princess and monarch, as a mother and wife – but, of course, 'it has not always been easy'. The Princess was with Charles for his birthday. That was important. She was with Philip in Malta. That was important, too. And, as his father reminded me, Charles was far from being either neglected or unloved: when he was not with his parents, he was with doting nurses and grand-parents who adored him.

At the beginning of 1950 Princess Elizabeth spent three months in England before returning to Malta – again without Charles – on 28 March. On her twenty-fourth birthday, 21 April 1950, at 8.45 a.m., the telephone rang in her bedroom at the Villa Guardamangia. When she picked up the receiver she was greeted with a rousing chorus of 'Happy Birthday to You' performed by a group of young naval officers accompanied by some of the band of HMS *Liverpool*. According to Bobo, who was there (of course), 'Lilibet was wildly excited and kept saying, "Oh! Thank you, thank you! That was sweet but who are you?"' She was answered by a second chorus of the song, harmonised by the officers' Glee Club, then a burst of bagpipes. Bobo reported to Dickie Mountbatten – whose flag officer had been responsible for organising the surprise birthday greeting – that 'Lilibet first went white, then quite red, and ended up with tears in her eyes'. Mountbatten was enchanted with the birthday girl: 'I think she's so sweet and attractive. At times I think she likes me too, though she is far too reserved to give any indication.' Elizabeth's birthday treat was to watch her husband and her uncle playing polo.

The young wife spent six weeks with her husband in Malta and then returned to England on 9 May and did not see him again for three months until he, too, came home, for five weeks' leave, at the end of July. Princess Anne was born on 15 August at Clarence House. The birth was a cause for general rejoicing. Among the first callers was Philip's mother, Princess Alice, who had come over specially from Greece, determined not to miss the birth of her latest

252

grandchild. She was dressed in her nun's habit and was spotted by a sharp-eyed reporter from the *Daily Mail* who decided to describe her, intriguingly, as 'one of the few remaining mystics in the Greek church'.[69] It was a happy time for the whole family – with the possible exception of Prince Charles. This is how Sarah Bradford puts it in her biography of the Queen: 'For Prince Charles, the return of his father closely followed by the appearance of a new baby must have been something of a shock. A photograph of the time shows him peering into the cradle with a slightly puzzled air. He was two years old and had not seen his father for nearly a year, his mother only at intervals. Now the appearance of a new sister as the focus of everyone's attention must have been very confusing; only his loving grandparents and his unchanging nursery retinue provided stability. His father left again for Malta on 1 September and in December his mother went out to join him. At Christmas Prince Charles and his new sister went as usual with their grandparents to Sandringham.'

Philip did not and Elizabeth does not dispute the facts. What they found frustrating is the gloss. There is another photograph of Charles, taken at the time, looking quite content. Princess Elizabeth was devoted to her son and knew that when she went away – always after several months at home and usually for no more than four or five weeks at a time – her boy was in good hands – the best. And her mother, Queen Elizabeth, sent regular and enthusiastic reports from the home front: 'What a joy Charles and Anne are to me . . . I shall miss them quite terribly when you return.'

In July 1950, a few weeks before Princess Anne was born, Philip was promoted to the rank of lieutenant commander and given his first command: the frigate HMS *Magpie*. Queen Elizabeth wrote, sending him 'a thousand congratulations'. The promotion was not automatic: it involved an exam, part of which the Duke failed first time around. Apparently, the Commander-in-Chief was all for over-ruling the examiner. Philip was having none of it. 'If they try to

---

69 Earlier, in January 1949, when the *Daily Mail* first learnt about her and the home and religious school for district nurses that she planned to found on the island of Tinos, they sent a reporter to interview her. He did not get very far. 'I don't like talking about my work,' she said. 'Duty is its own reward. I am not a politician or a film star. Taking pictures of me at work would be posing.'

fix it,' he said, 'I quit the navy for good.' He took the exam again and, according to Mike Parker, 'went through like a breeze'. Parker told me, 'Philip was first-class at his job and popular with his men.' Terry Lewin agreed: 'They admired him because he was good.' Some did not admire him. According to Sarah Bradford, 'One said he'd rather die than serve in that ship again, while another described him as "stamping about like a —— tiger".' The Duke's biographer, Tim Heald, probably has the balance about right: 'His command of *Magpie* was a success. He was tough, hard, mucked in with everybody, and if he had a fault it was a tendency to intolerance. It is not just his enemies who have commented on this last trait.'

As a young naval officer Philip was ambitious and fiercely competitive. He was determined that *Magpie* would be the smartest, sharpest frigate afloat, and that her eight officers and 150 men pull their weight at all times. He led from the front. He demanded the best and gave his all. In the annual Mediterranean Fleet regatta, the officers and men of *Magpie* rowed to victory in six out of the ten races, with 'Dukey', as he was known to his men, rowing at stroke in the Destroyer Command Officers' race – which they won (of course) by half a length from a field of fifteen. As well as taking part in routine naval manoeuvres, *Magpie* – or 'Edinburgh's Private Yacht' as some called her – was sent on sundry ceremonial exercises. In December 1950, when Princess Elizabeth came to Malta, there was an expedition to Athens to call on Philip's cousins, King Paul and Queen Frederika. Elizabeth travelled on board the Commander-in-Chief's dispatch vessel, HMS *Surprise*. One morning there was a jovial exchange of signals between the ships:

Surprise to *Magpie*: Princess full of beans.

Magpie to *Surprise*: Can't you give her something better for breakfast?[70]

Happy days. But the fun – and Philip's career – did not last. The King's health was gradually deteriorating. On 4 May 1951, when

70 The exchange fairly reflects the family sense of humour, which tends to be broad rather than subtle. There also appears to be a family weakness for practical jokes. When Queen Frederika came to dinner on board Mountbatten's ship in the summer of 1949, she made him an apple-pie bed. Six months later, when Mountbatten was staying with Queen Frederika and King Paul, he had his revenge. 'Put packet of brown sugar in Freddy's bed,' he noted, gleefully, in his diary.

George VI and Queen Elizabeth went to the official opening of the Festival of Britain on the south bank of the Thames,[71] the King looked grey and weak. Three weeks later, on 24 May, at Westminster Abbey, during the installation of the Duke of Gloucester as Great Master of the Order of the Bath, the King appeared seriously ill. His doctors diagnosed 'catarrhal inflammation' on the left lung and prescribed a course of penicillin injections. The King felt relieved, confident, he told his mother, that the condition would resolve itself with treatment.

In the event, his condition worsened. In July he started to undergo a series of tests that would eventually establish the presence of a malignant tumour in his lung. That same month the Edinburghs returned from Malta. The Princess and her husband were required for public duty. Elizabeth had revelled in the relative freedom she had enjoyed as a naval officer's wife. 'They're putting the bird back in its cage,' said Edwina Mountbatten. Philip had relished his year in command of his own ship. 'That's that,' he said to Mike Parker. 'It was bloody for him,' Parker told me. 'Absolutely bloody.' 'No,' Prince Philip said to me. 'It's what happened. That's all. It happened sooner than might have been expected, but it was inevitable. I accepted it. That's life.'

That autumn the King and Queen had planned to make a state visit to Canada and the United States. The Princess and the Duke were sent in their place. They were due to leave on 25 September, sailing on the liner *Empress of Britain*, but their departure was postponed as the King's condition deteriorated further. On Sunday, 23 September, in a two-hour operation at Buckingham Palace, the King had his left lung removed. A crowd of 5,000 waited outside the Palace for news and, when it came at 5 p.m., the bulletin, written in black crayon, encased in a picture frame, and hung on the Palace gates, told the truth, but not the whole truth: 'The King underwent

71 The King and Queen arrived at the Festival's centrepiece: 'The Dome of Discovery', described at the time as 'Morrison's Folly', in honour of the Labour government minister Herbert Morrison, who was responsible for promoting the Festival. Forty-eight years later, Morrison's grandson, Peter Mandelson, was a member of the Labour government that presided over the Millennium Dome, also sited south of the Thames, and officially inaugurated by George VI's daughter, Elizabeth II, on 31 December 1999.

an operation for lung resection this morning. Whilst anxiety must remain for some days, His Majesty's immediate post-operative condition is satisfactory.' In 1951 cancer was a word rarely spoken above a whisper.[72] On 24 September Harold Nicolson wrote in his diary: 'The King pretty bad. Nobody can talk about anything else – and the Election is forgotten. What a strange thing is Monarchy!'

Clement Attlee, the Prime Minister, had already told the King that he proposed dissolving Parliament at the beginning of October to hold a general election on the last Thursday in the month. Despite the King's frailty, on 25 October the election went ahead. Attlee's Labour Party lost. The Liberals were routed. Winston Churchill and the Conservatives were returned to office with a majority of seventeen. Churchill was coming up to his seventy-seventh birthday and had suffered a stroke. He was hard of hearing, not altogether mobile, and not always wholly alert. He had no doubt, however, that he was ready for office.

The King was approaching his fifty-sixth birthday and far from well. Lord Moran (Winston Churchill's doctor) reckoned 'he can scarcely live more than a year', but since the King himself was not told he had cancer, he was ready to believe the operation had cured him. He did all he could – mentally and physically – to rally his strength and determined on a policy of business as usual. On 8 October, with his blessing and encouragement, Princess Elizabeth became the first member of the Royal Family to fly the Atlantic when she and Philip went ahead with their postponed North American tour. It was essentially a visit to Canada – George VI was King of Canada, after all – with a brief foray into the United States

72 In fact, it was a word rarely spoken at all. Because cancer, in those days, almost invariably spelt death, the word was taboo. Some talked euphemistically of 'the big C'; most avoided the subject – like the plague. And even when relatives of a patient were told 'the worst', the patient himself was usually kept in the dark. This approach – 'fearing' the disease, 'protecting' the patient – continued at least until the 1960s. (When, in the 1970s, my aunt was dying of cancer, my parents travelled to Lourdes to collect some holy water. They wanted to give it to her in the hope of a miracle cure, but because her doctor had not told her of her condition, my parents were unable to administer the water openly. Instead, they used it to make my aunt a cup of instant coffee. She died soon afterwards. The local priest explained that the expected miracle had not occurred because my parents, by boiling the Lourdes water, had steamed the efficacy out of it.)

thrown in for good measure. When the royal couple reached Washington, DC, the thirty-second President of the United States, Harry S. Truman, introduced the young Princess to his elderly and nearly deaf mother-in-law. 'Mother!' boomed the President, 'I've brought Princess Elizabeth to see you!' The old lady beamed at the young Princess. 'I'm so glad your father has been re-elected,' she said.

Travelling with the Edinburghs on the thirty-five-day, twelve-thousand-mile, cross-continental tour was the Princess's new private secretary, Martin Charteris. Jock Colville, having completed his two-year secondment to Clarence House (and happily married one of Elizabeth's ladies-in-waiting) had returned to the Foreign Office in 1949.[73] Charteris had come on board because he knew Jock Colville and because his wife was friendly with the King's private secretary, Sir Alan Lascelles. 'It was as simple as that,' he told me forty years later, still chuckling. 'No vetting, no board interviews, no security clearance, no qualifications required, no training given. That's the way it was.' Certainly, Charteris had no technical qualifications for the job – he was neither a courtier nor a diplomat – but he was evidently the right kind of chap. His background was thoroughly sound: born 1913, second son of Lord Elcho (killed in action, 1916), grandson of the 11th Earl of Wemyss; educated at Eton and Sandhurst, he was a career soldier who had a decent war, much of it spent in the Middle East, where he eventually wound up running Military Intelligence in Palestine. He went to work for Princess Elizabeth in January 1950 and stayed at her side for twenty-seven years. He loved her – in the best sense – and loved to talk about her – in the best way. He was wholly loyal (he was devoted to her), but his anecdotes about her, while always affectionate, were both well observed and

73 He did a two-year stint as Head of Chancery at the British Embassy in Lisbon before being summoned back to 10 Downing Street to serve as joint principal private secretary to Churchill from 1951 to 1955. When I met him in the 1970s, he was in his sixties and a director of Hill Samuel, the merchant bank. Urbane, discreet, with matchless connections, he padded contentedly about the corridors of power. He was also a very elegant writer and kindly gave me a copy of what he called his 'memories', *Footprints in Time*, a volume of 'vignettes' of some of the many extraordinary figures he encountered during his enviable career. (The book, published by Collins in 1976, is long out of print, but well worth chasing up.)

usually revealing.[74] He liked to tell the story of the day he went for his first interview with his prospective employer and how impressed he was by her style before they even met. Charteris arrived early at Clarence House for his 11.30 a.m. appointment. At 11.25 a.m. Boy Browning rang through to the Princess. 'Major Charteris is here to see you, Ma'am. Shall I bring him in?' 'Yes,' said the Princess, coolly, 'at half-past eleven.' Charteris told me – and anyone else who cared to listen – that the moment he set eyes on her he was smitten. 'She was wearing a blue dress and a brooch with huge sapphires. I was immediately struck by her bright blue eyes and her wonderful complexion. She was young, beautiful, and dutiful. I knew at once that I would be proud to serve her.'

She was dutiful, and prepared for the worst. On the flight to Montreal on 8 October 1951, Charteris took with him the documents of accession in case they should be required. The Princess was already privy to a range of state papers. Throughout her time in Canada she carefully monitored the news from home, conscientiously reading the air-mail edition of the London *Times*.[75] The tour was not an unmitigated triumph. The programme was exhausting – it took in every province in the dominion – and the Princess was anxious about her father. The Canadian press, who had been bowled over by the effortless charm of Queen Elizabeth when she and the

74 The older he got the less discreet he became. He died just before Christmas 1999, aged eighty-six. I met him properly at the beginning of the 1990s with Sir Peter Morrison, the MP for Chester, whose sister, Mary, has been one of the Queen's ladies-in-waiting since 1960. Lord Charteris of Amisfield, as he then was (and Provost of Eton, President of the Prayer Book Society, a director of Claridge's and the Connaught hotels, and an amateur sculptor, among other things) travelled to Chester to give a talk to the local Conservative Association about his life with the Queen.

75 These were the days when *The Times* was still owned by the Astor family and regarded as 'the newspaper of record'. Later, the Queen and Prince Philip read the *Daily Telegraph* and, whenever possible, the Queen completes both the *Telegraph's* daily crossword puzzles. Given the Duke of Edinburgh's open contempt for the newspapers owned by Rupert Murdoch, I am always surprised that, when you go to Buckingham Palace, the two papers provided in the waiting room at the Privy Purse entrance are *The Times* and the *Telegraph*. The Queen has six national daily newspapers laid out for her to scan at breakfast time each day: *The Times*, *Telegraph*, *Mail*, *Express*, *Mirror*, and *Racing Post*. By all accounts, she reaches for the last first, rarely sees the *Sun*, and never sees the *Daily Star*.

King had toured the country twelve years before, complained that the twenty-five-year-old Princess was shy and unsmiling. 'Please smile more, Ma'am,' pleaded Charteris. 'But my jaws are aching,' sighed the Princess. (Exactly fifty years later, accompanying the Queen on a tour of the West Country, the Duchess of Grafton told me, 'She does find this constant smiling very exhausting, you know. After a day like today, her jaw really aches.') The royal couple did their best, of course. They scored well when – kitted out like characters from *Oklahoma!* by the ever-present Bobo and John Dean – they gave their all dancing a Canadian square dance. Philip did less well when – hoping to be humorous – he nonchalantly referred to Canada as 'a good investment'. Forty-nine years later, in October 2002, when the royal couple were back in Canada for an eleven-day Golden Jubilee tour, Canadian newspapers were still quoting the remark.

Martin Charteris said to me, 'It was a long trip and it wasn't plain sailing. It wasn't easy for either of them.' Is it true, I asked him, that, at breakfast one morning on the Governor-General's train, the Duke called the Princess 'a bloody fool'? 'He might have done,' said Charteris, smiling. 'He had a naval turn of phrase.' Was he often ratty with the Princess? I asked. 'Not so much ratty,' said Charteris, 'as restless. He was impatient. He was frustrated. You must remember he had just turned thirty and he was obliged to give up a promising career in the navy to do – what? He hadn't yet defined his role, found his feet as consort. He was certainly very impatient with the old-style courtiers and sometimes, I think, felt that the Princess paid more attention to them than to him. He didn't like that. If he called her "a bloody fool" now and again, it was just his way. I think others would have found it more shocking than she did. Although she was very young, she had a wise head on her shoulders. She has always understood him – and his ways. And valued his contribution – which has been immense and is underestimated. I believe history will come to judge him well.' When, in 2003, to discuss this book, I had lunch with the Queen's then private secretary, Sir Robin Janvrin, in referring to Prince Philip, he used almost the same phrase: 'Whatever the papers say about him now, I have no doubt at all that history will come to judge him well.'

Fifty-two years after Elizabeth and Philip's visit to President Truman in Washington, DC, in November 2003, George W. Bush, the forty-second US President, made a state visit to the United Kingdom. The Queen and the Duke of Edinburgh, of course, hosted a state banquet in honour of the President at Buckingham Palace. During the reception, before dinner, there was a telling moment. On one side of the room stood the Queen and President Bush, alone, chatting quietly – amiably but with little animation – while two yards away, on the other side of the room, stood Prince Philip at the centre of a small group that included the First Lady, Laura Bush, and the American Secretary of State, Colin Powell. They were all laughing. Prince Philip was leaning forward, gesticulating with his hands, entertaining his guests, telling a funny story. This – exactly this – was what Prince Philip succeeded in doing for more than sixty years. While the Queen made intelligent, interested small talk, always amiably, but sometimes a little awkwardly, the Duke kept the party going. 'He has done the state some service,' Martin Charteris said to me. 'I think the Queen appreciates his sense of humour, and values it.'

On the long train ride across Canada in the autumn of 1951, Philip did his best to entertain his wife with a range of practical jokes. According to John Dean, these included surprising her with a booby-trapped can of nuts and chasing her down the corridor wearing a set of joke false teeth. When they flew to Washington, DC, on 31 October, the smiles were rather more forced when, at the British Embassy's reception in their honour, they were expected to shake hands with each of the 1,500 guests. In terms of public relations, however, the brief visit to the American capital was an unqualified success. 'We have many distinguished visitors here in this city,' declared President Truman, welcoming his British visitors to the White House Rose Garden, 'but never before have we had such a wonderful couple, that so completely captured the hearts of all of us.' Sir Oliver Franks, the British Ambassador, reported to the King that when the sixty-seven-year-old President appeared with the twenty-five-year-old Princess in public he gave 'the impression of a very proud uncle presenting his favourite niece to his friends'. According to Martin Charteris, 'Truman fell in love with her.' The President was captivated, certainly. Memorably, he said, 'When I was a little boy I read about a fairy princess, and there she is.' When the royal couple had returned to Canada to complete their tour, he wrote himself to the King in England, 'We've just had a visit from a lovely young lady and her personable husband . . . As one father to another we can be very proud of our daughters. You have the better of me – because you have two!'

The Princess and the Duke returned to England by sea in the middle of the month, missing Prince Charles's third birthday on 14 November. In a birthday photograph, taken at Buckingham Palace, the toddler Prince and his grandfather, sitting on a sofa side by side, look very much at ease. The photograph when it was published, combined with the King's determination to think positively and the Queen's ability to avoid the unpleasant by ignoring it (what Martin Charteris later called her capacity for being 'a bit of an ostrich'), encouraged the public to believe that the King's health was on the mend. On 2 December a day of national thanksgiving for the sovereign's recovery was celebrated in churches throughout the kingdom. When, early in November, Princess Elizabeth, in a transatlantic call from Canada, had spoken to her father on the telephone, she reported that he sounded 'much better'. When she saw him on her return home, later in the month, he 'looked awful', according to Charteris, 'quite dreadful'.

The King had hoped to travel to Australia and New Zealand in the spring of 1952, to undertake the antipodean tour his health had forced him to postpone in 1948. Now he knew that would be impossible. Again, Elizabeth and Philip would go in his place. On their return from Canada, by way of tribute to what they had already achieved, he made them both Privy Councillors. His own hope for the New Year was to enjoy a recuperative holiday in South Africa in March. First, there was Christmas and the ordeal of the 3 p.m. Christmas Day broadcast. Customarily, the King gave the broadcast live so that he could speak 'directly' to his people. Because of its significance, and because of his stammer, it was a ritual he dreaded. One Christmas morning he barked at his family, 'I can't concentrate on anything because I've got that damned broadcast coming up this afternoon.' This year, his difficulty with breathing precluded a live broadcast. A BBC engineer, Robert Wood, came to Buckingham Palace on 21 December and, over two hours, painstakingly pieced together the ten-minute recording. Wood said afterwards, 'It was very, very distressing for him, and the Queen, and for me, because I admired him so much and wished I could do more to help.'

Christmas at Sandringham was a family affair and, by all accounts, the King – particularly because he did not have the cloud of 'that damned broadcast' hanging over him – was in mellow mood throughout. He was well enough to go shooting. He showed a revived interest in the business of the estate. He caught up with official correspondence, writing to, among others, President Truman and his successor, General Eisenhower. He began the New Year in a positive and determined frame of mind. On 29 January he travelled to London and saw his doctors, who, remarkably, pronounced themselves 'very well satisfied' with their patient's progress. The next day, by way of celebration, there was a family outing to the theatre. The King and Queen took their daughters and their son-in-law (and the King's equerry, Peter Townsend) to the Theatre Royal, Drury Lane, to see a performance of *South Pacific*. Next day, Thursday, 31 January, the King and Queen, with the Prime Minister in attendance, went to Heathrow Airport to see Elizabeth and Philip off to Kenya, on the first leg of their journey to Australia and New Zealand. They were due to be away for almost six months. In photographs of the farewell, the King, standing on the tarmac, windswept, hat in hand, looks gaunt and bleak and lonely. But Churchill, who was there, said he was 'gay, and even jaunty, and drank a glass of champagne'. 'I think,' Churchill added, 'he knew he had not long to live.'

On 1 February the King returned to Sandringham. It was the end of the shooting season. On 5 February he was out on the estate shooting hares and rabbits. In the evening there was a jolly dinner with the Queen and Princess Margaret, and members of the royal household, and one or two shooting friends. At 10.30 p.m. the King retired to bed. At midnight he was seen by a watchman in the garden standing at his bedroom window. At some time in the early hours of Wednesday, 6 February, he died, in his sleep, of a coronary thrombosis. 'He died as he was getting better,' said Princess Margaret.

When George VI died, the Heiress Presumptive was in east Africa, in Kenya, about one hundred miles north of Nairobi, at Treetops, a three-bedroomed 'hotel' set, amazingly, in the branches of a giant fig tree, overlooking a salt lick, a unique vantage point for observing the wild animals ranging below. 'She became Queen,' Harold Nicolson wrote in his diary, 'while perched in a tree in Africa watching the rhinoceros come down to the pool to drink.' In fact, at the very moment of her father's death, Elizabeth was either asleep, or taking a photograph of the sunrise, or having breakfast, watching, not watering rhino, but a troop of playful baboons who had captured paper rolls from the Treetops lavatory and were throwing them over the branches. The news from England did not reach her for several hours.

At Sandringham, the King's death was discovered by his valet at 7.30 a.m. when he took in his early morning tea. The Queen, a widow at only fifty-one, was heartbroken. 'He was so young to die,' she wrote to her friend Osbert Sitwell, 'and was becoming so wise in kingship. He was so kind too, and had a sort of natural nobility of thought & life which sometimes made me ashamed of my narrower & more feminine point of view. Such sorrow is a very strange experience . . .'

The King's private secretary, Sir Alan Lascelles, telephoned the assistant private secretary, Edward Ford, in London and instructed him to break the news to the King's mother and to the Prime Minister. At 10 Downing Street, Ford found Churchill, propped up in bed, cigar in hand, surrounded by paperwork. 'I've got bad news,' Ford said. 'The King died this morning. I know nothing more.' 'Bad news?' said Churchill. 'The worst.' He threw aside the papers he had been working on. 'How unimportant these matters seem,' he said. Later, when Jock Colville arrived, he found the Prime Minister in tears. Colville said that he tried to console Churchill with the thought of how well he would get on with the new Queen, but 'all he could say was that he did not know her and that she was only a child'.

The child, meanwhile, still unaware that she was now Queen, had finished breakfast at Treetops, clambered to the ground down the rickety ladders (she was wearing jeans), and, with Philip and the rest of her party, had driven the ten or so miles back to Sagana Lodge – the royal couple's wedding present from the people of Kenya – to spend the rest of the morning fishing for trout in the River Sagana before preparing for the onward journey to Mombasa and the boat that was due to take them on to New Zealand and Australia via Ceylon. The party included Bobo and John Dean, Pamela Mountbatten as lady-in-waiting, Mike Parker as equerry, and a celebrated local 'white hunter', Jim Corbett, armed with a high-velocity rifle, to guard the Princess both from rampaging elephants and the possibility of an attack by local Mau-Mau terrorists. Martin Charteris was staying near by, at the Outspan Hotel in Nyeri, once the home of Robert Baden-Powell. It was at the Outspan, at lunchtime, that Charteris got the news – given to him, in a garbled version, by a local newspaper reporter. The King's secretary at Sandringham had sent a telegram to Charteris in Nyeri, but it never reached him.[76] From the Outspan, Charteris telephoned Parker at Sagana Lodge. Parker found a wireless, fiddled with the dial, and eventually tuned in to the BBC. Philip was having a siesta. Parker woke him and gave him the news.

'I never felt so sorry for anyone in all my life,' said Parker. 'He looked as if you'd dropped half the world on him.' The Duke said nothing, according to Parker, 'nothing at all. He just breathed heavily, in and out, as though he were in shock.' Philip found Elizabeth and took her into the garden. He told her what had happened. Did he hold her? I asked Parker. 'I can't remember,' he said. 'We were all in a state of shock. But she was quite calm, I do remember that. She said very little. They were out on the lawn together, alone, away from the rest of us. They walked slowly up and down the lawn, up and down, up and down, while he talked and talked and talked.'

When Martin Charteris arrived back at Sagana, he found them in the sitting room. 'I can still picture the scene,' he told me. 'The Queen, sitting at her desk, pencil in hand, making notes. She was sitting upright, erect, utterly resolved. Her cheeks were a little flushed, but there were no tears. Philip was lying back on a sofa, silent, holding a copy of a newspaper wide open over his face.' Parker was busy making the arrangements for their immediate return to London. The new Queen was anxious to send messages back home and to Ceylon and New Zealand and Australia. She apologised for all the inconvenience she was causing. 'I'm so sorry we've got to go back,' she said to Pamela Mountbatten. 'I've ruined everybody's trip.' Charteris asked her what name she wanted to use as Queen. 'My own name, of course,' she told him. 'Elizabeth.' Charteris said later, 'I never imagined that anyone could grasp their destiny with such safe hands.'

76 Edward Ford told me he thought this was because the telegram was in the form of a pre-arranged coded message: 'Hyde Park Corner', three words that would signify the King's death to those in the know. Ford reckoned the telegraphist mistook the message for the address.

They changed, they packed, they got into their cars and drove to Nanyuki Airport. By now, reporters and photographers had arrived at Sagana. 'I asked them not to take any pictures,' Charteris told me, 'and, as our cars left the Lodge, though the world's press lined the road, not a photograph was taken.' They flew first to Entebbe. There they were reunited with the rest of their luggage, flown up from Mombasa – including the black mourning clothes which Bobo and John Dean had carefully packed against this very eventuality. For two hours they waited in the airport lounge while a storm abated and then, at last, climbed aboard the BOAC Argonaut for the long flight home. Little was said on the journey. John Dean recalled that he saw the Queen get up once or twice and return to her seat looking as if she had been crying. Martin Charteris told me, 'We slept for much of the first part of the journey. I discussed some of the details of the Accession with Her Majesty. She was completely calm, utterly composed. For a long time she simply gazed out of the window.'

It was mid-afternoon on Thursday, 7 February when the plane touched down at Heathrow. Waiting to greet his new sovereign was her Prime Minister, Winston Churchill, who had first become a Member of Parliament more than fifty years before, when Victoria was Queen. Elizabeth II, Victoria's great-great-granddaughter, a tiny figure in black, solemn and self-possessed, descended the aircraft's steps alone. Philip lingered inside the door, hidden, watching and waiting until the new Queen had touched British soil. Only then did he emerge and come down the steps to join her. 'Oh yes,' he said to me, 'when the late King died, everything changed.'

Chapter Ten

'A King is a thing men have made for their own sakes, for quiet-
ness' sake. Just as if in a family one man is appointed to buy the
meat.'

John Selden (1584–1654), *Table-Talk*

'When King George died,' I asked Prince Philip, 'did you know
what to expect?'

'No,' he said, laughing a little bleakly. 'There were plenty of people
telling me what *not* to do. "You mustn't interfere with this." "Keep
out." I had to try to support the Queen as best I could without
getting in the way. The difficulty was to find things that might be
useful.'

'But there was the example of Prince Albert, the Prince Consort,'
I suggested. 'You'd read biographies . . .'

'Oh, yes.' An exasperated sigh. 'The Prince Consort . . .' A pause.
'The Prince Consort's position was quite different. Queen Victoria
was an executive sovereign, following in a long line of executive
sovereigns. The Prince Consort was effectively Victoria's private secretary. But after Victoria the monarchy changed. It became an institution. I had to fit in with the institution. I had to avoid getting at
cross purposes, usurping others' authority.'

The institution had its own momentum and Philip had very little
authority of his own. As darkness descended on that cold, dank
February afternoon, the new Queen and her husband were driven
from Heathrow to Clarence House, where they found the old King's
private secretary already waiting for them. Only, of course, Sir Alan
Lascelles was not waiting for Philip. He was waiting for the Queen.
He had a sheaf of state papers that he needed Her Majesty to sign.
Within the hour, Queen Mary also came to call. She was eighty-four

and frail, full of dignity and grief. The day before, her son, the King, had died. Today she had come, not to hug her granddaughter, but to curtsy to her new Queen. 'Her old Grannie and subject must be the first to kiss her hand,' she said. Elizabeth's eyes pricked with tears as she accepted her grandmother's obeisance. Martin Charteris told me, 'For the young Queen, it was a moment that must have sorely tested her reserve and her resolve, but she loved her father and wanted to carry herself courageously as he would have done.'

Elizabeth said as much the following day, at St James's Palace, where her Privy Councillors gathered for the formal meeting of the Accession Council – many of them, according to Hugh Dalton, a former Chancellor of the Exchequer, who was there, 'people one didn't remember were still alive, and some looking quite perky and self-important'.[77] The Queen, looking 'very small', according to Dalton, entered alone and read the Declaration of Sovereignty in a 'high-pitched, rather reedy voice'. 'She does her part well,' said Dalton, 'facing hundreds of old men in black clothes with long faces.' Harold Wilson, another of the Privy Councillors and one of her future prime ministers, said it was 'the most moving ceremonial I can recall'. When the Queen had read the formal Declaration, she added, 'My heart is too full for me to say more to you today than that I shall always work as my father did.'

Outside, on the ramparts of the Palace, the Garter King of Arms, in Tudor tabard, proclaimed the Accession: 'Queen Elizabeth the Second, by the grace of God Queen of this Realm and of all Her other Realms and Territories, Head of the Commonwealth, Defender of the Faith.' Inside, Philip, only eight weeks a Privy Councillor himself, stepped forward to take his sovereign by the hand and escort

77 The Privy Council was originally an active advisory council to the sovereign. As a body, the Privy Council is no longer asked to give advice, but members of the Cabinet must be Privy Councillors (and some other senior ministers are as well) and Orders in Council and Proclamations are still approved by the sovereign in the presence of three Privy Councillors (enough to form a quorum). On leaving the Cabinet, individuals remain Privy Councillors for life, entitled to style themselves 'The Right Honourable' – unless (like Jonathan Aitken on his imprisonment for perjury) they resign from the Council in disgrace. Other 'eminent persons' – archbishops, senior members of the judiciary, the Queen's private secretary, etc – are also appointed to the Privy Council, which is only summoned in full 'upon the demise of the Crown'.

her out of the chamber and down to her waiting car. 'In the back of the car,' according to Sarah Bradford's biography of the Queen, 'she finally broke down and sobbed.' Someone who was there at the time said to me, 'The Queen may have cried – that would only be natural, the experience was overwhelming – but I assure you that she did not "break down and sob". That is not her way. Why does everything have to be exaggerated?'

There is no need to exaggerate the national sense of grief at the passing of George VI or the degree of admiration bordering on adulation expressed for the new Queen. When news of the King's death was broadcast, drivers stopped their cars, got out, and stood to attention as a mark of respect. When his body lay in state in Westminster Hall, more than 300,000 people filed slowly past in tribute. 'The world showed a large and genuine measure of grief,' said Jock Colville. 'The King was universally loved and respected,' said Martin Charteris. 'He gave his life for his country.' 'The King's outstanding quality,' said Dean Acheson, the US Secretary of State, was 'his selfless dedication to duty.' 'He was a grand man,' President Truman noted in his diary. 'Worth a pair of his brother Ed.' George VI had been King through the six long years of the Second World War and had not flinched. At his funeral at St George's Chapel, Windsor, the card accompanying Winston Churchill's wreath bore just two words, the inscription to be found on the Victoria Cross: 'For Valour.'

In his broadcast on the night of the King's death, Churchill, as Prime Minister, paid tribute to the courage and fortitude of the late King and then, with typical Churchillian bravura, heralded a new Elizabethan age: 'Famous have been the reigns of our Queens,' he rumbled prophetically. 'Some of the greatest periods in our history have unfolded under their sceptre.' Churchill might not yet know Elizabeth well, might consider her no more than a child, but, very quickly, he became utterly enchanted by her. 'You've got to remember,' Charteris said to me, 'Churchill was nearly eighty and the Queen was no more than twenty-five, but it was not simply her youth and beauty that entranced him. He was impressed by her. She was conscientious, she was well informed, she was serious-minded. Within days of her Accession she was receiving prime ministers and presidents, ambassadors and High Commissioners – all those who had come to London for the King's funeral – and doing so faultlessly. She had authority and dignity as well as grace.' Within a year, Churchill was confiding to his doctor, Lord Moran: 'All the film people in the world, if they had scoured the globe, could not have found anyone so suited for the part.'

Meanwhile, the Duke of Edinburgh, when he was being noticed at all, was not being so rapturously received. Within three weeks of the Accession, Churchill had received a formal letter of complaint about the Duke from a Conservative MP, Enoch Powell. Philip had visited the House of Commons to listen to a debate – something, according to Powell, a royal consort had not done since 1846 – and, while sitting observing the proceedings from the peers' gallery, the Duke was deemed to have expressed his own opinions about the matters under discussion below, in a manner neither seemly nor constitutional. The government chief whip endorsed Powell's complaint: Philip's demeanour had not been 'exactly poker-faced'. Philip was quietly reprimanded. 'It kept happening,' according to Patricia Mountbatten's husband, Lord Brabourne. He said to me, 'Philip was constantly being squashed, snubbed, ticked off, rapped over the knuckles. It was intolerable.' Mike Parker told me, 'The problem was simply that Philip had energy, ideas, get–up–and–go, and that didn't suit the Establishment, not one bit.' In his diary another, more senior, Conservative MP, Harold Macmillan (another of Elizabeth's future prime ministers), summed up the 'Establishment's' reservations succinctly: 'I fear this young man is going to be as big a bore as Prince Albert. It was really much better when royalty were just pleasant and polite.'

Among the many who came to London for the lying-in-state and funeral of the late King was his elder brother, David (or 'Ed' as President Truman called him), whose abdication as Edward VIII, of course, had led to George VI's reign. The Duke of Windsor, as he had become, was now fifty-seven and destined to live a further twenty years. Queen Elizabeth, privately, may have blamed her brother-in-law's selfishness for her own husband's premature death, but now she entertained him to tea and spent some time alone with him. He reported to his Duchess – who, diplomatically, had stayed behind in New York – that the widowed Queen had 'listened without comment' (they are very practised at that) '& closed on the note that it was nice to be able to talk about Bertie with somebody who had known him so well'. 'Officially and on the surface,' David told Wallis, 'my treatment within the family has been entirely correct and dignified.' Superficially, he acknowledged, he was handled impeccably by courtiers and relations alike. 'But gee,' he added, 'the crust is hard & only granite below.' Unsurprisingly perhaps – given that he had lived away from the court for sixteen years, and that most of those at court had little affection and still less respect for him – he found the mood and way of life at Buckingham Palace stiff and uncompromising. 'Gosh, they move slowly within these Palace confines,' he said. He found the tone and atmosphere at Clarence House, the Edinburghs' base camp, much more congenial. 'Clarence House was informal and friendly,' he reported to Wallis. 'Brave New World, full of self-confidence & seem to take the job in their stride.'

According to Martin Charteris, 'the operation at Clarence House was a good one.' 'We were a good team,' said Mike Parker. 'Philip ran a tight ship.' As well as being the Edinburghs' office, Clarence House was also their home – and Philip's first and only family home since he had last lived with his parents in Paris when he was ten. Philip wanted to go on living there. He put his thoughts on paper in a note to Boy Browning. He proposed that Queen Elizabeth the Queen Mother – as she decided she wished to be known – should remain at Buckingham Palace and that the new Queen and her family should remain at Clarence House. One day, he suggested, Clarence House might also be an appropriate London home for Prince Charles. (It now is.) The business of the monarchy could be conducted from Buckingham Palace, while the family of the monarch could continue living where they were. Sir Alan Lascelles was having none of it. 'God, he was bloody,' Lord Brabourne told me fifty years later. Lascelles was adamant: the traditional home of the British monarch was Buckingham Palace; it always had been; it should remain so. In fact, the Palace – built by the Duke of Buckingham in 1703 and rebuilt between 1825 and 1837 – had only been the official London residence of the sovereign since Queen Victoria's reign, but Lascelles, as the Queen's private secretary, had authority that Philip, as the Queen's husband, lacked, and – significantly – he also had the backing of the Prime Minister. Churchill said, 'To the Palace they must go.' So, to the Palace they went.

At the same time, in another, even more sensitive matter, the young Queen did as her private secretary and Prime Minister advised, rather than as her husband wished. She decided that her children – and her children's children – should bear her family name rather than his. Philip was incandescent. 'I am nothing but a bloody amoeba,' he protested. 'I am the only man in the country not allowed to give his name to his own children.'

'It hurt him, it really hurt him,' Patricia Mountbatten said to me when I went to see her. Sitting facing her and her husband, John Brabourne, in their drawing room at Mersham half a century after the event, from the pained expressions on their faces you would think the wound had been inflicted yesterday. 'Can you imagine doing such a thing?' asked Lord Brabourne. 'It so hurt him,' repeated Countess Mountbatten. 'He had given up everything – and now this, the final insult. It was a terrible blow. It upset him very deeply and left him feeling unsettled and unhappy for a long while.' 'A long while,' echoed Lord Brabourne. A silence fell in the room. The fire crackled. Suddenly, jointly, the Brabournes seemed to sense that they had gone too far. 'Of course, I don't blame the Queen,' said Lady Mountbatten. 'It was Churchill,' said Lord Brabourne, emphatically, 'encouraged by Lascelles. They forced the Queen's hand.' Lady Mountbatten said, 'I remember hearing the Queen say herself that she was in favour of the name Mountbatten-Windsor.'

The issue arose when it did, as it did, because, at a house party at Broadlands, within days of the old King's death and the new Queen's Accession, Dickie Mountbatten was heard to declare that 'the House of Mountbatten now reigns'. Prince Ernst August of Hanover, who was there, swiftly reported this boast to Queen Mary – whose own husband, George V, had created the House of Windsor in 1917. Queen Mary, outraged, summoned the Prime Minister's secretary, Jock Colville. Colville duly reported the dowager Queen's concerns to Churchill, who had his own reservations about Mountbatten – and was by no means alone. The Duke of Windsor, after the King's funeral, wrote to Wallis: 'Mountbatten – one can't pin much on him but he's very bossy & never stops talking. All are suspicious & watching his influence on Philip.'

Churchill decided on 'action this day' and immediately raised the issue with his senior ministers. According to the Cabinet minutes of

18 February 1952, 'The Cabinet's attention was drawn to reports that some change might be made in the Family name of the Queen's Children and their descendants. The Cabinet was strongly of the opinion that the Family name of Windsor should be retained; and they invited the Prime Minister to take a suitable opportunity of making their views known to Her Majesty.' The Prime Minister did exactly that and, within six weeks, despite her husband's furious protestations, the Queen made her position plain before the Privy Council: 'I hereby declare My Will and Pleasure that I and My children shall be styled and known as the House and Family of Windsor, and that My descendants who marry and their descendants shall bear the name of Windsor.'

'Philip was not happy,' said Martin Charteris. 'Philip was spitting,' said Mike Parker. 'Personally,' reflected Dickie Mountbatten, 'I think it was Beaverbrook's hatred of me coupled with Winston's disenchantment with what I did in India that brought all this about.' Certainly, Lord Beaverbrook had Churchill's ear and, not long before George VI's death, John Gordon, the editor of the *Sunday Express*, had reported to his newspaper's proprietor that a member of the Greek royal family had told him that those 'dangerous people', the Mountbattens, were 'determined to be the power behind the throne when Elizabeth succeeds', though he sensed they would not succeed, as 'Elizabeth was developing into a strong-minded woman who would not be controlled by him'. Gordon told Beaverbrook that the Mountbattens were plotting to get Philip pronounced King or King Consort. But Arthur Christiansen, the editor of the *Daily Express*, who knew Philip through their shared membership of the photographer Baron's Thursday Club (of which more anon), assured Beaverbrook that Philip 'sees through his uncle and fully realizes how great are the Mountbatten ambitions'.

There is no evidence that Philip ever wanted to be called Prince Consort – let alone King Consort or King – and I do not believe he was particularly concerned about the actual name 'Mountbatten'. It was not his father's name. It was not his mother's name. It was the anglicised version of his maternal grandfather's name. What concerned Philip was the principle that a father be allowed to pass on his surname to his children. He believed he had precedent on his side. Victoria of Hanover had married Albert of Saxe-Coburg-Gotha: their son,

Edward VII, had reigned as a member of the House of Saxe-Coburg-Gotha.

He also, unfortunately, had precedent against him. During the First World War, George V showed that a sovereign could change the name of the Royal House at will.

'What the devil does that young fool Edinburgh think that the family name has got to do with him?' asked Queen Mary in the spring of 1952. In the spring of 1953, ten weeks before the Coronation, Queen Mary died. In the summer of 1953, shortly after the Coronation, Tommy Lascelles retired. In April 1955 Winston Churchill, aged eighty, resigned as Prime Minister. On 8 February 1960, eight years to the day after her Accession Council, and shortly before the birth of Prince Andrew, the Queen issued a new declaration of her 'Will and Pleasure': 'While I and my children will continue to be styled and known as the House and Family of Windsor my descendants, other than descendants enjoying the style, title or attributes of Royal Highness and the titular dignity of Prince or Princess, and female descendants who marry and their descendants, shall bear the name Mountbatten-Windsor.'

It was a compromise. 'The Queen has always wanted,' announced the Buckingham Palace press office, 'without changing the name of the Royal House established by her grandfather, to associate the name of her husband with her own and his descendants. The Queen has had this in mind for a long time and it is close to her heart.' She had certainly been brooding about it. Harold Macmillan, her Prime Minister between 1957 and 1963, liked to tell the story of calling on the Queen at Sandringham and encountering the old Duke of Gloucester in the hall. 'Thank heavens you've come, Prime Minister,' says the Duke. 'The Queen's in a terrible state. There's a fellow called Jones in the billiards room says he wants to marry her sister, and Prince Philip's in the library wanting to change the family name to Mountbatten.'

It was a compromise – and kindly meant – but it did not amount to much. Essentially, the Queen's descendants, if non-royal, could be called Mountbatten-Windsor. Dickie, delighted to find the door even slightly ajar, did his best to push it further open. In 1973 Princess Anne married Captain Mark Phillips. In June that year Mountbatten wrote to Prince Charles: 'When Anne marries in November, her marriage certificate will be the first opportunity to settle the Mountbatten-Windsor name for good . . . if you can make quite sure . . . that her surname is entered as Mountbatten-Windsor it will end all arguments. I hope you can fix this.' It seems he did, for – though clearly contrary to the stipulations of the Queen's declaration of 1960 – it was as a Mountbatten-Windsor that Princess Anne was married.

In fact, the first properly named Mountbatten-Windsor did not appear on the scene until more than fifty years after the Queen's Coronation. Lady Louise Alice Elizabeth Mary Mountbatten-Windsor, the daughter of the Earl and Countess of Wessex, was born on 10 November 2003 – and her Christian names nicely reflect both the Windsor and the Mountbatten heritage. Princess Louise (1848–1939) was the sixth child of Victoria and Albert; Princess Louise of Hesse-Cassel (1817–98) married Christian IX of Denmark and was grandmother to Prince Andrea, Prince Philip's father. Prince Philip's mother was Alice; the Queen's mother was Elizabeth; the Earl of Wessex's great-grandmother was Queen Mary; the Countess of Wessex's mother is Mary Rhys-Jones. The Mountbatten family's delight at the arrival of the first unquestioned 'Mountbatten-Windsor' may have been a little dampened by the Buckingham Palace spokesman who, having announced the new royal baby's full name, added, 'She will, however, be generally known by the more easily remembered title of Lady Louise Windsor.'

Dickie Mountbatten himself was obsessed with the issue of the Mountbatten name. 'His vanity, though child-like, was monstrous,' wrote his biographer, Philip Ziegler, 'his ambition unbridled.'[78] I think Philip always had the measure of his uncle. He loved him, liked him, respected him, admired him – and was grateful to him. But (in my experience at least) Prince Philip spoke with equal affection – and gratitude – and almost as frequently – of his other maternal uncle, George Milford Haven. Dickie was a great achiever (and a

78 Ziegler's official biography of Mountbatten, first published in 1985, is a wonderful book, sympathetic, scrupulous, and gripping. When writing it, there was a point when Ziegler became so frustrated by aspects of his subject that he found it necessary to place on his desk a notice that read: 'REMEMBER, IN SPITE OF EVERYTHING, HE WAS A GREAT MAN.' If you read *Mountbatten*, you will be in no doubt of that.

great operator), but at times he had to be taken with a pinch of salt. Philip always understood that. Elizabeth understood it, too. They knew Mountbatten's strengths and his weaknesses and his foibles – and were enormously fond of him. In 1974, five years before he was murdered by the IRA, they took him on a cruise aboard the Royal Yacht. He was seventy-four, and delighted to be in *Britannia* once more, 'but what moved me most of all,' he wrote in his diary, 'is the increasing kindness of Lilibet and Philip who treat me more and more as a really intimate member of their immediate family.' They understood him and he, perhaps, understood them, too. When the cruise was over, Mountbatten wrote to Philip: 'You sometimes seemed rather disappointed, perhaps frustrated would be a better word, but I feel you underestimate your effect on the UK, and especially the Commonwealth. I hear more and more praise and appreciation from people in all walks of life.'

For Philip, in 1952, frustration and disappointment were already the order of the day. His children were not to inherit his name. He was not happy about that. He was obliged to move house. He was not happy about that. He was treated as something of an extraneous nuisance by both the court and the Prime Minister – and there was very little he could do about that. Mike Parker said to me, 'There were a lot more of them than there were of us.' At Clarence House, Philip and Elizabeth had essentially shared a secretariat, and Philip was head of the household. It was his domain. At Buckingham Palace, it was very different. Elizabeth was Queen. The Palace was the sovereign's domain. Naturally, she inherited her father's Household (huge and hidebound), to which she added Martin Charteris (more flexible and fun, but still relatively inexperienced), leaving Philip pretty isolated, with just Parker and Boy Browning. 'You can imagine,' Countess Mountbatten said to me, 'Bobo MacDonald sitting by the bathtub' – and 'Tommy Lascelles sitting in judgement,' chipped in Lord Brabourne – 'it can't have been easy.'

It was not easy. In most households in Britain in the early 1950s, the husband and father was the dominant figure. He was the head of the household, the breadwinner, the law-maker; he ruled the roost, he was the cock of the walk. For Philip, it was not like that. 'It was bloody difficult for him,' said Mike Parker. 'In the navy, he was in command of his own ship – literally. At Clarence House, it was very much his show. When we got to Buckingham Palace, all that changed.' 'It was an unsettling time for him,' said Martin Charteris. 'He had no defined role, while the Queen's role was clearly defined and she assumed it with an extraordinary and immediate confidence and ease. For the rest of us, it was wonderful to behold, but I can see that he might have found it somewhat disconcerting.'

According to Elizabeth Longford, soon after her Accession the Queen told a friend, 'I no longer feel anxious or worried. I don't know what it is – but I have lost all my timidity somehow becoming the Sovereign and having to receive the Prime Minister.' She was now leading a life from which her husband was necessarily – constitutionally – excluded. When the Prime Minister went to the Palace for his weekly audience with the sovereign, the old man and the young Queen would sit together, alone, sometimes for up to an hour. 'What do you talk about?' Jock Colville asked Churchill. 'Oh, mostly racing,' answered Churchill, with a twinkle. And polo, apparently. And the state of the world, of course.

The Queen was – and is – supplied daily with a mass of 'state papers': Cabinet minutes, Foreign Office telegrams, documents, briefs, drafts – boxes of 'secret' documents relating to all manner of United Kingdom, Commonwealth, and international affairs. Philip never had access to any of these. When I told him that, as a Lord Commissioner of the Treasury, I used to sign mandates that were then sent to Her Majesty for counter-signature, he was bemused. 'I had no idea she did that,' he said. 'I've no idea what goes on.'

In 2012, at the conclusion of her Diamond Jubilee year, the Queen went to 10 Downing Street to attend a meeting of the British Cabinet. Her father, George VI, had attended gatherings of the War Cabinet during the Second World War, but on 18 December 2012 Elizabeth II became the first monarch to attend a normal Cabinet meeting since George III in 1781. (George I chaired the Cabinet personally until 1717.) The Duke of Edinburgh did not accompany her. His absence caused some press speculation. Was the ninety-one-year-old Duke unwell? No, not at all. He was undertaking his own official engagements elsewhere. He was not privy to attend the Cabinet meeting because constitutional matters are entirely the sovereign's preserve.

The Duke of Edinburgh did not complain about this. He accepted it as a matter of fact. 'When the Queen became Queen, I was told "Keep out" and that was that.'

'So, what did you do?' I asked him.

'I tried to find useful things to do,' he said. 'I did my best. I introduced a Footman Training Programme. The old boys here [at Buckingham Palace] hadn't had anything quite like it before. They expected the footmen just to keep on coming. We had an Organisation and Methods Review. I tried to make improvements – without unhinging things.'

The Organisation and Methods Review involved the Duke and Mike Parker treading on a number of toes. 'Some of the old guard weren't too happy,' Parker told me. 'We met with a fair bit of resistance. But I think we made a few improvements, dragged some of them into the twentieth century. We explored the whole Palace. We didn't find a wicked fairy in a turret with a spinning wheel, but we did discover the wine cellar. It's deep underground and goes on for miles and miles. There were some great old vintages and menus dating back to the early days of Queen Victoria.'

When I suggested to Prince Philip that he was an instinctive moderniser, and always had been, he interrupted me: 'No, no, not for the sake of modernising, not for the sake of buggering about with things in some sort of Blairite way. Not at all.'

Back in December 1949 his mother-in-law had written him a very friendly and loving letter in which she had said, among other things, 'I sometimes wonder if you think Papa & I are rather olde worlde about some things – I expect you do.' He wrote to Queen Elizabeth by reply, denying it. 'I don't really think that my own ideas are sufficiently clear to be able to stigmatize anybody least of all yourself,' he said. 'Perhaps my education and life so far have caused me to think differently and therefore hold different views but I hope that they are sufficiently open-minded not to be "modern" for modernity's sake. If and when we disagree I assure you that I listen to and digest your views as those of an exceptionally intelligent and enlightened person and try to reconcile them with my own. It seems to me that the best way to form an opinion is to rub views with other people.'

When I talked to him sixty years later he took exactly the same line. 'I'm not interested in change for change's sake. Far from it. And

I think I do listen to people with opinions that are different from my own. In fact, I make a point of it.'

'But you do get impatient,' I suggested.

'With other people?'

'Yes.'

'There's usually a reason,' he insisted.

This conversation took place on the morning after His Royal Highness had attended the Royal Variety Performance. During the interval he had been introduced to some of the team involved in putting the show together. 'But I've already met these people,' he protested irritably. 'We were introduced when we arrived. Shouldn't we meet some new people? Let's use the time we've got usefully.'

On another occasion he said to me, 'I'm anxious to get things done. That's all. I'm interested in the efficient use of resources.'

'Weren't you the first member of the Royal Family to use a helicopter?' I asked.

'Yes,' he said, 'in the run-up to the Coronation.'

In 1952 he was appointed Chairman of the Coronation Commission. He believed it was 'a real job' and he took it seriously. Large numbers of Commonwealth and Colonial troops arrived in the country to take part in the event and were stationed in barracks across the land. The Duke decided to visit them all. He and Mike Parker looked at the logistics and reckoned they should go by helicopter. They borrowed one from the Royal Navy. 'It was just more practical,' the Duke explained to me, 'but it caused a ruckus. I didn't go through the proper channels. There was a lot of pettifogging bureaucracy.' Parker was hauled before the Prime Minister and given a severe dressing-down.

The Coronation when it came – on 2 June 1953 – was more than a logistical triumph. 'Never has there been such excitement,' wrote Jock Colville, 'never has a Monarch received such adulation.' The country felt on top of the world – literally. The 29,028-foot summit of the world's tallest mountain had been reached at 11.30 a.m. on 29 May. The news reached London on the morning of the Coronation. The triumphant mountaineers were a New Zealander, Edmund Hillary, and a Nepalese Sherpa, Norgay Tenzing, but the leader of the expedition, John Hunt, was British and the feat was hailed as a British achievement. Everest had been conquered and Elizabeth was to be crowned!

In London the day itself was dank and overcast, but the mood was universally sunny. Hundreds of thousands of people – happy and curious – braved the drizzle and filled the streets. Millions more – in Britain and around the world – followed the day's events on television. Never before in human history had so many people witnessed the same events at the same time.

Inevitably, there were a few republicans with reservations, but, sensibly, they kept their heads down. And the Duke of Windsor stayed away because he was not wanted. Elizabeth felt his presence would be inappropriate. He came to England to attend the funeral of his mother, Queen Mary, on 31 March, but reckoned he had not received a warm welcome. Elizabeth would not pay him the £10,000 annual allowance he had been given by her father. A family dinner was held at Windsor Castle following Queen Mary's funeral. He was not invited. He wrote to his wife: 'What a smug, stinking lot my relations are and you've never seen such a seedy worn-out bunch of old hags most of them have become.'

The Duke of Edinburgh was Chairman of the Coronation Commission, but most of the detail was out of his hands. The pageantry was largely in the gift of his Vice Chairman, Bernard Fitzalan-Howard, 16th Duke of Norfolk, hereditary Earl Marshal and Chief Butler of England, a seasoned campaigner whose family titles dated back to 1139 (when Stephen was King) and whose past personal triumphs included the management of the funeral of George V and the Coronation of George VI. Norfolk was a 'character'. When asked by a peer if his invitation to the Coronation might be prejudiced because of his divorce, he replied, 'Good God, man, this is a Coronation, not Royal Ascot.' And when asked if it was true that the peers were hiding sandwiches inside their coronets during the service, he answered, 'Probably. They're capable of anything.' When one of the Coronation rehearsals was running behind schedule, his voice echoed round Westminster Abbey: 'If the bishops don't learn to walk in step, we'll be here all night.'

The Queen herself attended several of the rehearsals at the Abbey and learnt her moves from the Duchess of Norfolk, who also acted as her stand-in. At Buckingham Palace – where the ballroom was marked out with ropes and posts replicating the Abbey's floor plan – she put in hours of extra practice on her own. She listened to recordings of her father's Coronation. She walked the course with sheets pinned to her shoulders representing the robes she would wear. To become accustomed to its weight, she sat at her desk wearing the actual St Edward's Crown first used at the Coronation of Charles II in 1661. It was heavy – five pounds – and its weight was of significance, symbolising, according to the Archbishop of Canterbury, the burden of the demands that would be made upon her 'to her life's end'. (It was because of the weight of the crown that Queen Victoria and Edward VII chose not to wear it at their Coronations.)

The Archbishop, Dr Geoffrey Fisher, a muscular Christian (at Oxford he was a noted footballer, rugby player, and oarsman), went to great lengths to ensure that the spiritual significance of the Coronation was not obscured by the pomp and pageantry. In the lead-up to the great day, he gave a series of sermons exploring and explaining the Coronation liturgy. He was an experienced teacher (he had been headmaster of Repton) and in Elizabeth, of course, he had a willing pupil. Martin Charteris said to me, 'People will have their own memories of the Coronation – of the pageantry, the processions, the Queen of Tonga in her open carriage,[79] the street parties and what have you – but for the Queen herself, the Coronation was not about celebration, it was about dedication. It was a religious event.' A few days after the event, the Archbishop looked back on it in awe: 'The wonder of it, the unforgettable bearing of the Queen, the overwhelming sense of dedication to God, of worship of God, consecration by God and communion with God, embracing everyone in the Abbey.' And beyond. In the United Kingdom in 1953, the Anglican faith was alive and well – and popular. In London in the early 1950s, more than forty per cent of all adults regularly attended church. Today fewer than three per cent do.

Westminster Abbey, the setting for Elizabeth's Coronation, was where William the Conqueror was crowned on Christmas Day in 1066. The essential elements of the ceremony were much as they had been for a thousand years. For the Queen, the most significant part of the service was the Act of Anointing, the moment that

---

79 Queen Salote of Tonga was a huge lady and she travelled to the Abbey in an open carriage sitting opposite the comparatively diminutive Sultan of Kelantan. Someone asked, 'Who is that with Queen Salote?' 'That,' said Noël Coward famously, 'is her lunch.'

brought her, in the Archbishop's phrase, 'into the presence of the living God'. It was a moment, both intimate and sacred, that, at her own request, was neither filmed nor televised. As she sat on the Coronation Chair, under a canopy held by four Knights of the Garter, the Archbishop made a sign of the cross on both of her hands, on her breast, and on her head. 'Be thy head anointed with holy oil,' he said, 'as kings, priests and prophets were anointed. And as Solomon was anointed King by Zadok the priest and Nathan the prophet, so be thou anointed, blessed and consecrated Queen over the Peoples, whom the Lord thy God hath given thee to rule and govern.'

For Philip, the most significant part of the service came a little later. This was, in every sense, the Queen's day — and, in truth, hers alone. He was there as her attendant lord. Dressed in the uniform of an Admiral of the Fleet,[80] he accompanied her to and from the Abbey in the great Gold State Coach. He shared in the waving, not the crowning. This was her Coronation, not theirs. In the Abbey, she processed alone. She took the Coronation oath alone. She alone was anointed with holy oil. She alone was crowned. When the Coronation was done — when St Edward's Crown had been placed upon her head — the nobility paid homage to their Queen. The first to do so was the Lord Archbishop of Canterbury. Next was the Duke of Edinburgh. He stepped forward and knelt before her. He placed his hands between hers and said, 'I, Philip, Duke of Edinburgh, do become your liege man of life and limb, and of earthly worship; and faith and truth will I bear unto you, to live and die, against all manner of folks. So help me God.'

He said it and he meant it. When, once, I asked Prince Philip what his life had been about, he narrowed his eyes and flinched away from the question. I decided to persist. 'Supporting the Queen,' I suggested, 'isn't that what it's all been about?' He looked away — which was unusual for him: normally, he looked directly at you — and said, very slowly and almost inaudibly, 'Absolutely. Absolutely.' He may have been disappointed that his naval career was cut short. He

80   On giving up his active naval career, Philip had been appointed Admiral of the Fleet – and Field Marshal and Air Chief Marshal. When Mountbatten was promoted to Admiral, in February 1953, Philip sent him a telegram: 'Congratulations on your promotion. Keep it up – you may catch up one day!'

may have been angered that he could not give his own name to his own children. He may have been infuriated by the way he was patronised by some of those he met at court. But never – not once – in more than sixty years – did he flinch in the performance of what he saw as his one, essential duty: to support the Queen.

Margrethe, the Queen of Denmark – who is another direct descendant of Queen Victoria – said to me, 'I think people in your country undervalue Prince Philip because he makes what is a very difficult job look so easy. He does it so well people don't realise what a complicated and difficult job it is. It has not been easy for my husband being Prince Consort and it has not been easy for Prince Philip. Philip does have one advantage. He comes from a royal family. He has always understood what monarchy is about.' Margrethe's husband was a Frenchman, an aristocrat, and former diplomat. Philip was the grandson and nephew of kings. All his life he had had royalty all around him. He never questioned his place at the Queen's side, one step behind her. He never complained about that. From start to finish, he took it 'as read'. At her Coronation the Queen stood at the altar, laid her hand on the Holy Bible, and swore, 'The things which I have here before promised, I will perform and keep. So help me God.' And Philip knelt before his sovereign, and with his hands in hers, vowed to become her 'liege man of life and limb, and of earthly worship . . . So help me God.' Today, in a largely Godless country where the hereditary principle – for more than a thousand years, central to our governance – survives only in the case of the Royal Family, the ritual of the Coronation will seem to many archaic and absurd, the words used an almost meaningless mumbo-jumbo from a bygone age. In June 1953 Elizabeth and Philip understood what they were saying and meant every word. Uncle David would not have done, which is why Elizabeth did not want him there. She kissed the Bible and signed the Coronation oath. Philip promised her 'faith and truth'. For neither of them was any of this a hollow ritual.

When Philip had completed his homage, he stood up, touched the Queen's crown, and kissed her left cheek. Next to pay homage were the Dukes of Gloucester and Kent, followed by England's premier baron, Mowbray, Segrave and Stourton, whose titles dated back to 1283 (when Edward I was King) and whose appearance provided some unexpected light relief. The Archbishop recalled: 'He came down from his homage all over the place, bunching up his robe and, as the Queen said, with moth balls and pieces of ermine all over the place.' When the homage was over, the trumpets sounded and the congregation – 7,500 strong – called out, 'God Save Queen Elizabeth, Long Live Queen Elizabeth, May the Queen Live for ever.'

As the choir sang a valedictory *Te Deum*, the Queen stepped down from her throne. In St Edward's Chapel she changed her velvet robes once more – the ceremony had involved a lot of dressing and undressing – and swapped the historic St Edward's Crown for the slightly lighter, but undeniably fancier, Imperial State Crown, studded with many of the most precious stones on earth – including the Black Prince's ruby, Elizabeth I's pearl earrings, and Charles II's sapphire. Bearing the crown jewels, carrying the sceptre in her right hand and the orb in her left, while the congregation sang the national anthem, Elizabeth II processed through the Abbey to the West Door, where the Gold State Coach again awaited her. She clambered aboard, accompanied by Philip, and, drawn by eight grey horses, the coach – a proper fairy-tale affair, over-the-top, baroque, and bedazzling, with door panels painted by Cipriani in the 1760s – took them, slowly and steadily, on a circuitous seven-mile route back to Buckingham Palace. They were cheered, long and loud, by hundreds of thousands of the Queen's subjects, many of whom had camped out for several nights, in the cold and wet, to secure a good view of the passing parade. They were escorted by twenty-seven further carriages, twenty-nine military bands, and thirteen thousand troops. The Chairman of the Coronation Commission reckoned it 'not a bad show'.

Back at the Palace, in the Green Drawing Room, Cecil Beaton was waiting to take the official photographs. 'In came the Queen,' he recorded in his diary, 'cool, smiling, sovereign of the situation.' (She looked so perfect thanks, in part, to Oscar Wilde's daughter-in-law. Thelma Holland, married to Wilde's younger son, Vyvyan, was, for several years, the young Queen's beautician. She was responsible for the Queen's make-up on Coronation Day.) Beaton is a useful witness because he has a photographer's eye and an artist's sensibility. 'The Queen looked extremely minute under her robes and Crown, her nose and hands chilled and her eyes tired. "Yes," in reply to my question, "the Crown does get rather heavy." She had been wearing it now for nearly three hours.' Beaton's description of Philip rings especially true: 'The Duke of Edinburgh stood by making wry jokes, his lips pursed in a smile that put the fear of God into me. I believe he doesn't like or approve of me. This is a pity because, although I'm not one for "Navy-type" jokes, and obviously have nothing in common with him, I admire him enormously, and think he is absolutely first-rate at this job of making things comparatively lively and putting people at their ease. Perhaps he was disappointed that his friend, Baron, was not doing this job today; whatever the reason he was definitely adopting a rather ragging attitude towards the proceedings.'

Beaton was homosexual, and camp in manner, and his favourite royal sitter on Coronation Day – on any day, come to that – was Queen Elizabeth the Queen Mother, always the queens' favourite Queen. He found her in 'rollicking spirits' and so immediately warm and helpful towards him that, at once, all his 'anxieties and fears' were dispelled: 'The Queen Mother, by being so basically human and understanding, gives out to us a feeling of reassurance. The great mother figure and nannie to us all, through the warmth of her sympathy bathes us and wraps us in a counterpane by the fireside. Suddenly I had this wonderful accomplice – someone who would help me through everything. All at once, and because of her, I was enjoying my work. Prince Charles and Princess Anne were buzzing about in the wildest excitement and would not keep still for a moment. The Queen Mother anchored them in her arms, put her head down to kiss Prince Charles's hair, and made a terrific picture.'

Prince Charles would endorse every word of Beaton's description of his grandmother. In the Abbey, Charles, not yet five years old, in white silk shirt and shorts, had watched the Coronation from the Royal Box, perched between his aunt and his grandmother. His other grandmother, Princess Alice, was near by, 'a contrast to the grandeur', Beaton noted, 'in the ash-grey draperies of a nun'.

For Alice, it was a wonderful experience, moving and exciting. She ordered a special, brand-new nun's habit for the occasion. (She was an interesting mix: she craved the simple life, but travelled widely; mostly she lived modestly, but sometimes she was immoderately extravagant; she advocated self-discipline, but she smoked like a chimney.) For the Queen Widow (as Beaton called the Queen Mother) it was a more poignant occasion. At the Palace she was 'dimpled and chuckling, with eyes as bright as any of her jewels': at the Abbey, in her expression 'we read sadness combined with pride'. Martin Charteris told me that he believed that the Queen Mother was jealous of her daughter. 'Queen Elizabeth was not yet fifty-two when the King died,' he reminded me. 'She was accustomed to being centre-stage, the focus of attention, universally loved. She was still loved, of course, and admired, but she was no longer the star of the show and I don't think she found that easy. In the early days of the new Queen's reign, there was an awkwardness about precedence, with the Queen not wanting to go in front of her mother and Queen Elizabeth, of course, accustomed to going first.'

I want to quote one last time from Beaton's diary, for two reasons: to illustrate Elizabeth's sense of humour (which is rarely seen in public) and to suggest something about the Queen Mother's attitude to her son-in-law. Beaton had not expected to be asked to take the Coronation pictures. Because Baron, 'a most unexpected friend of Prince Philip's', had been taking all the recent royal photographs, Beaton assumed that Baron would get this special assignment, too. He didn't, and when, in early May 1953, Beaton learnt that the job was going to be his, after all, the news came 'as an enormous relief':

'The same night that this message was relayed to me, at a ball at the American Embassy, I saw the Queen for a brief moment and thanked her. "No, I'm very glad you're going to take them," she said, "but, by the time we get through to the photographs, we'll have circles down to here" (she pointed halfway down her cheeks), "then the Crown comes down to here" (to the eye), "then the court train comes bundling up here, and I'm out to here" (sticks stomach out). "There are layers upon layers: skirt and mantle and trains." She spoke like a young high-spirited girl.

'I also had a short opportunity to thank the Queen Mother for what I am sure must have been her help in bringing about this "coup" for me. She laughed knowingly with one finger high in the air.'

I can picture her. She could be very naughty. And worse, perhaps. Famously, Sir John Wheeler-Bennett, the official biographer of

George VI, remarked of her that there was 'a small drop of arsenic in the centre of that marshmallow'. Philip was the Chairman of the Coronation Commission. He might have preferred to have the official Coronation photographs taken by his friend Baron, but, if so, he was thwarted. Beaton secured the assignment, not only because he was an exceptional photographer who wooed Queen Elizabeth with flattery and flowers,[81] but also because Baron was Philip's man and Philip was someone Queen Elizabeth did not entirely trust. When first he had appeared on the scene, she had had her misgivings about him – encouraged by her brother David and his set – but, according to several of Philip's friends, her doubts and reservations about her son-in-law persisted until the end of her very long life.

Her published letters betray none of this – unsurprisingly. According to her editor, William Shawcross, she 'made it a rule never to talk (let alone write) about her new relations, even to her Strathmore family.' Shawcross commends her 'wise discretion' and tells us that she maintained it for the rest of her life. Certainly, her letters to Philip are consistently affectionate – though she suffered the dilemma faced by many mothers-in-law. She was not quite sure what to call herself. In the 1940s she was signing her letters to Philip 'Ever your devoted Mama Elizabeth' and 'Much love, Mummy or Mama' and 'Ever your loving Mum, Elizabeth'. In the 1950s she tried 'Your loving Mama, Elizabeth', 'Your loving m-in-l, E', and 'Your loving Mama in law, Elizabeth'. Eventually she settled for 'Your affec Elizabeth M' or, most often, a simple 'Much love, Mama E'.

When Philip and Elizabeth were married, Queen Elizabeth told her son-in-law, 'We are so fond of you, and *so so* glad that you and darling Lilibet are so happy.' Margaret Rhodes told me that was the essence of it: 'Queen Elizabeth was happy that her daughter was happy. That's all she asked. That's what every mother wants, isn't it?' And Prince Philip was a conscientious son-in-law. When George VI died, Philip sent the Queen Mother a 'comforting & wonderful' letter full of 'understanding and sweetness'. When Princess Margaret was married, Prince Philip walked his sister-in-law down the aisle

81 'I took enormous care to choose a bouquet of all the first spring flowers to be sent to that adorable human being living in that cold, bleak Palace.' You couldn't make it up!

287

and his mother-in-law thanked him 'with all my heart', not only for providing 'the arm of a strong and loving person', but also for 'being so sweet to her during the last years. It must have helped her a lot, for I think she felt terribly lost when her father died.' Philip was a committed family man, on the whole better at expressing his feelings in action or by letter than in conversation. He wrote thoughtful letters to his mother-in-law; he gave her presents (including two landscapes he had painted himself); he lent her books that he thought would be of interest to her. He always behaved towards her with dutiful affection and punctilious courtesy.

At around the time of Queen Elizabeth's one hundredth birthday, I happened to interview Prince Philip (seventy-nine himself at the time) for ITN Radio and tried to nudge him into saying something about his mother-in-law. Apart from insisting that he had no desire to live so long himself, he would not be drawn. I have had no reports of his having ever made any disparaging remarks about her, but several people have told me how, within their hearing, Queen Elizabeth made slighting comments about Philip and referred to him – not entirely humorously – as 'the Hun'. One of Philip's close female friends told me that the coolness between Prince Philip and Prince Charles was, in part, a by-product of the unspoken tension between Philip and his mother-in-law. Charles adored his grandmother and Queen Elizabeth was extravagantly, effusively, fond of Charles. There was an intimacy and mutual sympathy between them that Philip did not share. 'She laughed knowingly with one finger in the air.' Yes, there was a small drop of arsenic in the centre of that marshmallow.

On Coronation Day, Cecil Beaton described Princess Margaret at Buckingham Palace, sailing towards him, 'her purple train being held aloft by four pages', 'with pink and white make-up and a sex twinkle of understanding in her regard'. Perhaps Beaton knew her secret. Margaret was twenty-two and in love with a married man sixteen years her senior.

Group Captain Peter Townsend was born in 1914, at the outset of the First World War, and, in 1940, in the Battle of Britain, became one of the heroes of the Second World War. He was a fighter pilot who led the B Flight of Hurricanes in the celebrated No. 43 Squadron. He was mentioned in dispatches. He won the DFC and Bar. But the war took its toll: he had a nervous breakdown. 'I knew in my bones that I should never again be the pilot I once had been,' he confessed in his memoirs. 'I had gone too far down the hill ever to get to the top again . . . The more I flew, and there could be no relenting, the more fear, stark, degrading fear, possessed me. Each time I took off, I felt sure it would be the last.'

By 1944 Townsend was no longer flying, but he was still a hero, and when the King expressed the desire to have an RAF officer as an equerry for the first time, he seemed a first-rate choice. He was handsome, agreeable, distinguished, and came from a solid, if middle-class, background. (His brother, Michael, a naval captain, served with Philip in HMS *Chequers*.) He was also complex, troubled, and deeply religious. The King took to him at once and Townsend was, in turn, immediately sympathetic: 'The King did not try, or even need, to put me at my ease . . . the humanity of the man and his striking simplicity came across warmly, unmistakably . . . sometimes he hesitated in his speech, and then I felt drawn towards him . . .' Townsend was said to be the only member of the Household who could successfully soothe the King when he was overwhelmed by one of his 'gnashes'. He arrived at Buckingham Palace anticipating a three-month attachment. He remained in the King and Queen's service for nearly ten years. On the day he came for his initial interview, in February 1944, Lilibet and Margaret, then aged seventeen and thirteen, saw the beautiful, brown-haired, blue-eyed hero, who was just twenty-nine, arrive at the Palace, and, as he came into view, so the story goes, Lilibet whispered to her younger sister, 'Bad luck. He's married.'

Townsend married young and unluckily. Rosemary Townsend was attractive, vivacious, and flirtatious. She was also socially aspirational. She liked to flirt with the King. According to Townsend, when he secured the job as equerry, his wife's immediate reaction was: 'We're made.' In fact, they were undone. Townsend gave his all to the Royal Family: he was devoted to the King, charmed by the Queen, and, before very long, innocently enamoured of the teenage Princess: 'One day after a picnic lunch with the guns, I stretched out in the heather to doze. Then, vaguely, I was aware that someone was covering me with a coat. I opened one eye to see Princess Margaret's lovely face, very close, looking into mine. Then I opened the other eye, and saw behind her, the King leaning on his stick, with a certain look, typical of him: kind, half-amused.'

In 1947, when the Royal Family took their three-month trip to southern Africa, Townsend was in attendance, of necessity leaving Rosemary behind. Rosemary had an affair with a young Guards officer, and then another, with John de László, son of the painter Philip de László, whose portraits of Prince Philip's parents used to hang in his study at Buckingham Palace. Townsend's marriage was breaking down and he was falling in love with the second in line to the throne. He was sixteen years older than Margaret and a married man. He should have known better. He should have resisted temptation. But he didn't. He was besotted: 'What ultimately made Princess Margaret so attractive and lovable was that behind the dazzling façade, the apparent self-assurance, you could find, if you looked for it, a rare softness and sincerity. She could make you bend double with laughing; she could also touch you deeply. There were dozens of others; their names were in the papers, which vied with each other, frantically and futilely, in their forecasts of the one whom she would marry. Yet I dare say that there was not one among them more touched by the Princess's *joie de vivre* than I, for in my present marital predicament, it gave me what I most lacked – joy. More, it created a sympathy between us and I began to sense that, in her life too, there was something lacking.'

When the King died, Margaret was twenty-one years old and bereft. 'He was so kind and brave all his life,' she said, 'the very heart and centre of our family and no one could have had a more loving and thoughtful father.' His death left a void and Townsend filled it. Having served as the King's equerry, he was now appointed Comptroller of the Queen Mother's Household. At the end of 1952 he secured a divorce from Rosemary on the grounds of her adultery. He was the innocent party; he was the wronged husband; he was now a free man and he wanted to marry the new Queen's sister. With a sense of timing that, according to their detractors, serves to illustrate Townsend's naivety and Margaret's selfishness, in the spring of 1953, with the Coronation not far off, the young Princess told her sister and her mother that she and Townsend were in love and wished to marry. Townsend later recalled: 'If they were disconcerted as they had every reason to be, they did not flinch, but faced it with perfect calm and, it must be said, considerable charity.'

Sir Alan Lascelles, the new Queen's private secretary, who was set to retire after the Coronation, was less understanding. 'You must be either mad or bad or both,' he told Townsend when he heard the news. Martin Charteris, then the Queen's assistant private secretary, said to me, 'I don't think he was mad or bad, but he was naive. Incredibly so. He was a commoner and a divorcee. Rightly or wrongly, divorcees were not presented at court, were not invited to garden parties, were not formally introduced to royalty. I don't think there was ever a serious prospect of a marriage. If the King had still been alive I don't believe the matter would have arisen. I don't think Townsend would have dared.'

Queen Elizabeth the Queen Mother seemingly put the matter out of her mind – 'the old ostrich approach', as Charteris had it. The young Queen, not yet crowned, put the matter on hold. 'Under the circumstances,' she said, 'it isn't unreasonable for me to ask you to wait a year.' In the event, Margaret and Townsend waited more than two years before bowing to the inevitable.

Elizabeth wanted Margaret to be happy. As their cousin, Margaret Rhodes, put it to me, 'Margaret drove the Queen mad frequently, but she was her sister and she loved her.' Prince Philip was not unsympathetic, either. He was infuriated by the amount of publicity the romance generated, and annoyed, especially, that it was a photograph taken at Westminster Abbey on Coronation Day – of Margaret brushing Townsend's lapel 'with a tender hand' – that triggered the worldwide media interest in the story, but there is no evidence to support repeated press suggestions that he was positively hostile towards Townsend. When stories of his alleged plotting against his would-be brother-in-law appeared in the papers, Philip bleated, despairingly, 'What have I done? I haven't done anything.' In truth, he tried to keep out of the way. As he said to me once, with reference to his own children's marital difficulties, 'I try to keep out of these things as much as possible.' Charteris said to me, 'Prince Philip had a sort of ragging, joshing way with Princess Margaret, treated her as the wayward younger sister, but I don't believe he interfered in any way. The Queen was naturally sympathetic towards the Princess, but I think she thought – she hoped – given time, the affair would peter out. Townsend really was unsuitable. He was older, he had two sons already. It just wasn't going to happen. Churchill wouldn't wear it. Salisbury wouldn't wear it. The Commonwealth wouldn't wear it. It wasn't going to happen.'

It didn't. Under the Royal Marriages Act of 1772 the Queen's sister required the Queen's blessing before she could marry. If the Queen decided not to sanction marriage, Princess Margaret could wait until her twenty-fifth birthday and then marry without the sovereign's consent provided she could secure the approval of Parliament. In 1953, when Margaret was still twenty-three, Churchill, whose momentary first instinct had been that 'the path of true love must be allowed to run smooth', quickly advised against the marriage. Lord Salisbury, a senior figure in the government, was adamantly opposed. The Commonwealth prime ministers, when consulted, expressed their misgivings. The Queen was Supreme Governor of the Church of England: her sister's union with a divorced man was not to be condoned.

For two years the issue simmered on, with the publicity surrounding it coming to the boil at regular intervals. In the hope that distance might lessen enchantment, under pressure from Lascelles and Churchill, the Queen agreed that Townsend be 'let go' from court. He was dispatched to the British Embassy in Brussels as air attaché. Margaret took up her public duties. She accompanied her mother on a tour of Rhodesia. Alone, she undertook a tour of the West Indies. For nearly two years the lovers remained apart, but in touch. They were lovesick and the malady lingered on. It all came to a head in the summer and autumn of 1955, as Margaret approached and passed her twenty-fifth birthday. At twenty-five she would be free to marry without the sovereign's consent. The new Prime Minister, Anthony Eden (himself, incidentally, divorced), advised the Queen that the Government still could not sanction the union – Lord Salisbury, for one, would resign if it attempted to do so – and, while the legislation required to enable the marriage to take place might be passed by Parliament, it would necessitate the Princess sacrificing her right of succession. Margaret was third in line to the throne. Eden advised the Queen that 'neither the proposed marriage nor her renunciation of her right to the Succession need in themselves affect her style and title as Her Royal Highness Princess Margaret or the provision made for her under the Civil List', but, inevitably, if she married Townsend, her status would be changed, irrevocably.

In the end Margaret decided against the sacrifice. She met with Townsend on 22 October 1955. 'We were both exhausted,' he recalled, 'mentally, emotionally, physically.' He knew his Princess loved her life as a princess. He knew he could not expect her to abandon it for a life in Brussels as the not-quite-as-royal-as-once-she-was second wife of a middle-aged air attaché. They met again. 'We looked at each other,' he said, 'there was a wonderful tenderness in her eyes which reflected, I suppose, the look in mine. We had reached the end of the road.'

On 31 October they met at Clarence House and had a last drink together, toasting the happiness they had shared and the future they would not. At seven o'clock that same evening the young Princess issued a public statement that, within hours, became the lead story on front pages around the world:

'I would like it to be known that I have decided not to marry Group Captain Peter Townsend. I have been aware that, subject to renouncing my rights of succession, it might have been possible for me to contract a civil marriage. But, mindful of the Church's teaching that Christian marriage is indissoluble, and conscious of my duty to the Commonwealth, I have resolved to put these considerations before any others.

'I have reached this decision entirely alone, and in doing so I have been strengthened by the unfailing support of Group Captain Townsend. I am deeply grateful for the concern of all those who have constantly prayed for my happiness.'

Sarah Bradford, in her biography of the Queen, says, when she reaches this point in the story: 'Amazingly, the royal family did not rally round Margaret on the night of her formal renunciation. She dined alone while her mother kept an official engagement at London University. The Queen Mother did not say goodnight to her daughter on her return. For some time they had barely been on speaking terms; for the Queen Mother, the Townsend affair had been as traumatic as the Abdication had for Queen Mary. Elizabeth telephoned for a brief conversation, after which Margaret returned to watching boxing on television. The King's death and his widow's subsequent withdrawal, Elizabeth's marriage and Margaret's romance had weakened the family bonds that had linked "us four" so closely together.'

Certainly, the 'family dynamic' had changed, but I believe that, today, the Queen – who, I understand, admires Sarah Bradford's biography of George VI – would quarrel with the implications of the Bradford account of 'the night of the formal renunciation'. Of course, the Queen Mother fulfilled a long-standing official engagement. Duty always comes first. Of course, the Queen telephoned her sister, but the conversation was neither cursory nor unsympathetic. As Queen Elizabeth the Queen Mother pointed out to Princess Margaret in a letter that October: 'It is so difficult talking of anything personal on the telephone, because one feels that so many people are listening most eagerly.' And if the telephone is not secure, a meeting is not always easy either. The Queen's position – and her lack of any kind of anonymity – mean that she cannot simply jump into the car and go round to see people on a whim.

Townsend did not entirely disappear from Margaret's life. He went around the world, slowly, to help himself forget her, but found himself unable to do so. He contacted her once more in the spring of 1958. They met again at Clarence House, apparently with the Queen Mother's somewhat uncertain blessing. This was in March 1958, when the Queen and the Duke of Edinburgh were on a state visit to the Netherlands. Unfortunately, news of the reunion reached the press, and salacious, sensationalised coverage of the Princess's tryst at Clarence House quite eclipsed more responsible reporting of the state visit. Elizabeth and Philip were not amused. Margaret and Townsend knew there was no hope, and parted for a final time. Within a year, Peter Townsend, aged forty-five, was engaged to a Belgian girl, aged nineteen. Marie-Luce Jamagne looked uncannily like the teenage Margaret.

In May 1960 Princess Margaret, approaching thirty, married a man her own age ('and almost her own height,' quipped friends: in fact he was several inches taller): Tony Armstrong-Jones, a gifted theatre and society photographer, and one of the most alarmingly charming people a girl (or boy) could hope to meet. They did not live happily ever after. Far from it. Their marriage was a roller-coaster ride: at times exciting, at times quite frightening: ultimately disastrous. As personalities they had much in common: both were charismatic, creative, charming, manipulative, selfish, and self-absorbed. Their marriage was turbulent almost from the start, characterised by

Happy and glorious: Coronation day, 2 June 1953

In the swing: Anne and Charles with their parents
at Balmoral in 1955

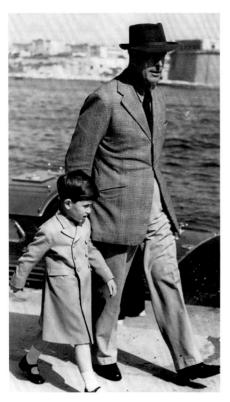

Guiding spirits: Charles coming ashore at Malta with his great-uncle Dickie Mountbatten, April 1954

Charles with his grandmother, Queen Elizabeth going to watch his father play polo in Windsor Great Park on 10 June 1957, Philip's thirty-sixth birthday

Together: Fortune Euston, Elizabeth II, Mike Parker and the Duke of Edinburgh, Nigeria, February 1956

Hats on: Mexico, 1954

Action man: Preparing for take-off in a Westland helicopter

Apart: Philip in Antarctica, on the Grahamland Peninsula, January 1957

Behind the camera: Elizabeth II with her sister and her mother, and her subjects looking on, at the Badminton Horse Trials, April 1957

Sailing at Cowes in *Bluebottle* with Prince Charles and Uffa Fox, 1958

Playing polo in Jamaica with Prince Charles, 1966

A second family: The Queen playing with Prince Edward, aged fifteen months, and Prince Andrew, aged five at Windsor Castle, June 1965

Look at the time: The Queen with Prince Edward, aged five and Prince Charles, aged twenty, April 1969

Princess Alice with her grandchildren, Charles and Anne, on their arrival in Athens for the wedding of King Constantine of Greece, September 1964

Guiding hands: Charles and his grandmother, Queen Elizabeth, 1969

Charles and his great-uncle Dickie Mountbatten, 1977

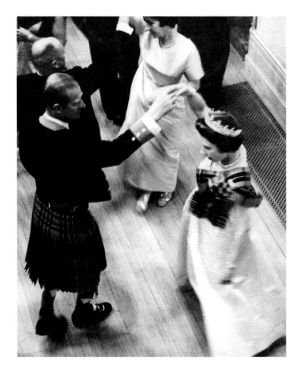

Philip and Elizabeth dance the Gay Gordons at the annual Ghillies' Ball at Balmoral, in the run-up to their silver wedding anniversary, 1972

'We are a family': The Queen with Princess Diana and her bridesmaids, July 1981

self-indulgence, recrimination and mutual infidelity. And yet, as parents, they seem to have been enormously successful. As adults the Snowdon children have been happy and fortunate in their relationships in a way that the children of Philip and Elizabeth, on the whole, have not. The Snowdon children – children of a broken home – made good marriages and got on well and easily with both their parents. Three of the children of the Queen and the Duke of Edinburgh have had failed marriages, and their relationship with their eldest son was, for many years, uncomfortable. It is interesting to ponder why.

I talked about this with Margaret Rhodes. She was quite shy, a little nervy, but with a sensible head on her shoulders and a countrywoman's values. She also had a beady eye. She had seen all conditions and types of relationship in her long life. She could sense what worked and did not work. Of the Queen and Prince Philip's marriage, she said to me at once, and emphatically and convincingly, 'On the whole, it ranks as one of the most successful marriages. One of the most successful.'

'And as parents?' I asked.

'I've seen Philip being absolutely sweet with his children's babies,' said Mrs Rhodes, 'absolutely sweet.' She paused and poured out more coffee. She sighed. 'But with their own children it hasn't been easy. There's no use denying it. Things have gone slightly awry with Prince Charles. I've been at Birkhall when he's been there. He's very conscientious, very committed. He'll have dinner, and go back to work. He works so hard, but then he's so extravagant.' Another pause. 'The Queen finds Prince Charles very difficult. He is extravagant and she doesn't like that.'

Mrs Rhodes looked directly at me. 'It's incredibly sad,' she said. 'It's a fractured family. Terribly sad.'

'Why do you think that is?' I asked. 'What's at the root of it?'

'Philip can't bring himself to be close with Charles,' said Mrs Rhodes. 'Perhaps you don't learn to give love if you haven't had love.'

We talked for a while about Prince Philip's childhood and the years when he barely saw – nor heard from – either of his parents.

'But what about the Queen?' I asked. 'Her childhood was very loving, wasn't it?'

Mrs Rhodes pondered for a moment. 'The Queen was always reserved, even as a child. And when she became Queen that did add to her reserve, very definitely. But you're right. The King adored both his daughters. And Queen Elizabeth was brimming with love.' At this point, Margaret Rhodes, who was by nature a woman of restraint, flung her arms wide open to illustrate the warmth and breadth of the Queen Mother's embrace. She smiled and looked at me again. 'Perhaps,' she said, 'having married someone who is like Philip, it is difficult to go on expressing emotion to an unemotional person. You find, in time, you can't express love any more. Princess Margaret could. Completely. And her children have been so successful.'

MA & PA

Chapter Eleven

'To marry is to domesticate the Recording Angel. Once you are married, there is nothing left for you, not even suicide, but to be good.'

Robert Louis Stevenson (1850–94), *Virginibus Puerisque*

Gina Kennard, a childhood friend of each of them, who knew them both almost all her life (and was godmother to Prince Andrew), said to me, 'The Queen and Prince Philip were good parents, *really* good parents, *always* interested in their children and *always* actively involved. Whatever Charles says about it now, Philip was a wonderful father. He used to read them stories, play with them, go fishing – the lot. So much nonsense is talked about the Queen and her family. We saw quite a lot of them in the 1950s. They were a young family, full of energy and life, and a very happy one. I remember lots of fun and games, lots of laughter.'

Martin Charteris, a trusted courtier, who was close to Elizabeth from 1949 onwards, told me, 'There's this myth that the Queen cares more about her dogs and her horses than she does about her children. I believe it was fuelled when someone who had written to Her Majesty commiserating on the death of one of her corgis received a six-page handwritten response. Certainly, the Queen is devoted to her animals – absolutely devoted: they're what help keep her sane – but she loves her children deeply, as any mother would. Both she and the Duke of Edinburgh did their level best to give their children a normal family life. Not always easy, under the circumstances.'

Elizabeth II was Queen, after all. In November 1953 Elizabeth and Philip, without their children, embarked on a post-Coronation Commonwealth tour lasting five and a half months. They took in

Bermuda, Jamaica, Fiji, Tonga, the Cocos Islands, Aden, Uganda, Malta, and Gibraltar. They spent three months in Australia and New Zealand, and ten days in Ceylon. As Ben Pimlott put it in his biography of the Queen: 'Such a marathon of travel, speeches, national anthems, handshakes, troop inspections, Parliament openings, performances, banquets, bouquets and gifts, had never been before undertaken by a British Head of State – or perhaps by anybody.' 'I can't remember much about it,' Prince Philip said to me, laughing, 'but I can tell you the crowds were incredible, the adulation was extraordinary. You wouldn't believe it, you really wouldn't.' It was reckoned that three-quarters of the entire population of Australia turned out to see the Queen in person.

While their parents were away, Charles and Anne, aged five and three, were looked after by their grandmother, the Queen Mother. At the end of the grand tour the children were to be reunited with their parents in Malta, where their great-uncle, Dickie Mountbatten, was now Commander-in-Chief of the Mediterranean Fleet. The children, sent from England in the newly commissioned Royal Yacht *Britannia*, arrived in Malta ten days ahead of their parents. Mountbatten was not amused to receive a message from Boy Browning – his one-time Chief of Staff who had become Comptroller of the Edinburghs' Household in 1948 – to the effect that Mountbatten should submit a programme of proposed 'excursions for the children' to be laid before Her Majesty for her approval. Understandably indignant, Mountbatten reported the request to his wife, Edwina, telling her he had told Browning that Lady Mountbatten, the children's great-aunt (and, incidentally, mother of Pamela Mountbatten, who was accompanying the Queen on the royal tour as lady-in-waiting) 'would organise the trips, etc, as desirable each day. Really!'

When you become sovereign, nobody treats you quite as they did before. According to Sonia Berry, perhaps Lilibet's closest childhood friend, 'She would never have chosen to be Queen. She would much rather have lived in the country with horses and dogs and been a normal housewife.' Lilibet and Sonia's friendship did not end with the Queen's Accession, but its nature changed. Suddenly there was a new formality – a sense of strain and distance – in the air. Overnight, the old, easy intimacy disappeared. Letters and invitations were no longer sent to 'you', but to 'Your Majesty'. When Philip was away, the Queen might come to Sonia's for tea or dinner – 'She used to say how nice it was to get out of Buckingham Palace' – but informality and spontaneity were no longer possible. Security was required. Guest lists had to be checked. Curtains had to be drawn so that the sovereign might not be observed. 'Once she arrived, she was completely at ease,' said Sonia Berry. But for everybody else, inevitably, having the Queen in your midst is an honour, may be exciting, can be exhilarating, but, as experiences go, is rarely wholly comfortable. Sonia Berry reflected, 'Looking back, perhaps the formality was a mistake, but it takes time to change.'

On her Accession, Elizabeth II was in no mood for change. Naturally shy, instinctively conservative, she was content to follow in her father's footsteps, to do her duty as he had done his. Her court had much of the character – and personnel – of his. Soon after her Coronation, her private secretary, Sir Alan Lascelles, who had been the late King's private secretary also, was succeeded by Sir Michael Adeane, who had joined the royal household in 1937, aged twenty-seven, as an assistant private secretary to George VI. Adeane, on his mother's side, was a grandson of Lord Stamfordham, assistant private secretary to Queen Victoria and influential private secretary to George V as Prince of Wales and King. Adeane had the traditional courtier's manner: he was effortlessly courteous, he had a nice sense of humour, he understood the ways of the world. Like his father (who was killed in action in 1914), he was an officer in the Coldstream Guards, and, while he was no radical, he was no fool either: he got a First in History at Cambridge.[82] For nineteen years, until 1972, he

---

82 In *Who's Who* he listed his recreations as shooting and fishing (naturally) and his clubs as Brook's and the Beefsteak (of course). I was still a teenager when I first met him and was much impressed. He seemed to me the epitome of courtliness: formal yet easy, and wholly unpatronising. (Perhaps he was accustomed to dealing with children. He once said, 'Because you happen to be in Whitehall terms the equivalent of a Permanent Under-Secretary, it is no use thinking you are a mandarin. One moment you may be writing to the Prime Minister. The next you are carrying a small boy's mac.') The humorist Basil Boothroyd (who was writing an authorised biography of Prince Philip at the time) liked to tell the story of the morning he encountered Adeane crossing the forecourt at Buckingham Palace. Boothroyd was arriving, Adeane was departing. Boothroyd paused to greet the Queen's private secretary. Pleasantries were exchanged. Courtesies were extended. The weather was discussed, the Queen's blooming health was touched on, the vigour and charm of

served the Queen with intelligence, quiet efficiency, and complete devotion. He was cautious, he was careful, he was kindly: Her Majesty liked his style. It suited her own.

As monarch the Queen had role models: her father and grandfather. According to Martin Charteris, 'She took on the mantle of monarchy as to the manner born – which, of course, she was. Right from the start, she performed all her duties, not only conscientiously – never chafing against her lot – but with a quiet confidence that was moving to behold. Remember, she was not quite twenty-six at the start of her reign.' Dutifully, and thoroughly, she read through her 'boxes', absorbed Cabinet minutes, digested Foreign Office telegrams, signed state papers, met her Prime Minister, gave audiences to ambassadors, judges, generals, held meetings of the Privy Council, conducted investitures. Her husband was involved in none of this. As consort the Duke of Edinburgh had no role models (Prince Albert died sixty years before Prince Philip was born) and – in a way – no role. As he put it to me, 'I had to find a way of supporting the Queen, without getting in the way.'

According to Patricia Mountbatten, Philip in the 1950s was 'a dynamo, an absolute dynamo – he was very like my father at the same age'. In her autobiography Wallis Simpson described Dickie Mountbatten as she found him when they first met and Dickie was in his early thirties: '[He] bubbled with ideas on every conceivable subject – housing, relieving unemployment, new strategies of attack in polo, or how to cure the chronic maladies of the British Exchequer. The more baffling these problems, the more convinced Dickie was that he had a fundamental contribution to make and was determined to make it.' According to Mrs Simpson, the hyperactive Dickie 'bombarded' her lover, then Prince of Wales, 'with pamphlets, books, and clippings, all carefully annotated or underlined and all urgently commended to the Prince's attention'. Philip – equally bubbling with ideas and initiative – might have liked to 'bombard' the Queen, as his uncle had once 'bombarded' hers, but he chose not to. He knew there was no point. It did not occur to the Queen to involve

---

the Queen Mother marvelled at, progress on Boothroyd's book reported – then Adeane threw in gently: 'If you'll forgive me, I must be on my way now. I've just heard that my house is on fire. I wouldn't mind, but as it's part of St James's Palace . . .'

her husband in affairs of state: it would not have been constitutionally appropriate, and Her Majesty, a firm believer in the value of precedent, tradition, and continuity, has always been one for observing the proprieties.

Besides, as Prince Philip put it to me, her advisers made his position crystal clear. 'Keep out,' they said. 'You mustn't interfere with this.' Lord Brabourne, Patricia Mountbatten's husband, told me that, at the time, Philip found the traditional courtiers' hostility towards him 'intolerable and deeply frustrating'. Fifty years on, the Duke of Edinburgh simply shrugged and said to me, 'I had to fit into the institution. I had to avoid getting at cross purposes, usurping others' authority. In most cases that was no problem. I did my own thing.'

To get a flavour of Philip's 'own thing' turn to page 464 and scan the official list of his 'offices and involvements'. It is a long list – and extraordinarily varied – and each line represents many hours, weeks, and months of activity: meetings, minutes, briefings, speeches, arm-twisting, fund-raising, travelling hither and yon. As you will see from the list, 1956 was an especially fruitful year. Philip was just thirty-five. As well as publishing a collection of speeches (his thoughts on competitive sport, science, technology, and the environment), he initiated the Commonwealth Study Conferences that year. They were his own idea: three-week-long, high-powered international gatherings, to be held every six years or so, and designed to take a big issue, examine it, worry it, look at it in depth and from different perspectives. The delegates were to be ambitious, questing people from across the Commonwealth who wanted to ask challenging questions and seek out practical answers. The first conference, held in Oxford in 1956, focused on work and the changing demands of industrial society. In 1998 the conference was held in Canada and the theme was the impact of technology in a global 'infodustrial' society. The ninth conference was held in October 2003 in Australia and New Zealand. The theme was 'People First in the Global Century'. In October 2011 Prince Philip, aged ninety, hosted a reception in Australia for some of the 2,500 Conference 'alumni'. Fifty-five years after he started the 'experiment' (as he called it), the objective of the Conference remained the same: he said it was for 'its members to look, listen, and learn in the hope that the process will help them to improve the quality of their decision-making when they reach the peaks of their occupations'. It was an 'experiment' little noticed by those not directly involved, but one that mattered to him and in which he stayed involved until the end of his life.

Nineteen fifty-six was also the year when, with the Australian stockbroker and grazier Sam Hordern, Prince Philip founded the Royal Agricultural Society of the Commonwealth, and, with his old headmaster, Kurt Hahn, he founded the Duke of Edinburgh's Award Scheme. The Award Scheme is arguably Philip's 'great achievement'. Prince Edward, the next Duke of Edinburgh, who has been actively involved in promoting the scheme since he achieved the Gold Award in 1986, said to me, 'It's my father great legacy. The scheme has spread to more than a hundred countries around the world. Since it started at least six million young people have taken part and some three million have achieved awards. As we speak, today, there are around six hundred thousand young people actively participating in it – and since community service is one of the components of the award that means that right now, this year, there is something like thirty million hours of community service taking place around the world as a direct result of my father's initiative. That's amazing when you stop to think about it.'

The Award Scheme is indeed amazing. And the qualities the Award encourages – self-reliance, compassion, fitness, skill, enterprise, endeavour – were among those Prince Philip considered the most important. I asked Prince Edward if his father had ever discussed with him the best way to 'run' the Award Scheme – or if they had talked about the values that underpinned it. He said, 'Not really. He just got on with it and I watched how he did it and I've done my best to follow his example.'

More than once I tried to talk to Prince Philip about his 'philosophy of life'. I did not get very far. I suspect that the best way to get the measure of the man is to look at the organisations he gave his time to – and to consider the books he chose to read and keep on his shelves. He owned more than 11,000 volumes, all carefully arranged and catalogued. The collection was both predictable and surprising: plenty of military history, science, and engineering; more than a thousand books on wildlife and conservation; six hundred books on matters equestrian; 494 on sport; a complete run of cartoon annuals by Giles; more than two hundred volumes of poetry; 990

books on art. Not many novelists were represented on the Duke of Edinburgh's library shelves, but C.S. Forester was one of them. The heroes of the *Hornblower* stories exemplify the virtues Philip valued: decency, daring, courtesy, comradeship, kindliness, loyalty, courage. These were the very virtues that the youth organisations he headed, such as the Duke of Edinburgh's Award Scheme and the Outward Bound Trust, were, in large part, designed to foster.

Some years ago, while I was making the smallest of small talk with the Queen at a drinks reception (where she wasn't drinking, or eating the nibbles, so nor was I), the subject of the National Playing Fields Association came up. The Queen is the charity's patron; the Duke of Edinburgh was its president. 'I don't know very much about the Playing Fields, I'm afraid,' Her Majesty said to me, with a slightly apologetic laugh. 'That's Prince Philip's department. He doesn't tell me much about it. He has his departments, I have mine.'

Inevitably, since the Queen's Accession, she and her husband, to an extent, led separate, parallel lives. As Head of State she does what heads of state must. (She is also Head of the Commonwealth, of course, and Supreme Governor of the Church of England.) Philip was her consort and, as consort, dutifully, and with some style, did whatever was required. And, when not required, he did his own thing. She has her role, her duties, her enthusiasms, her friends. He had his obligations, his interests, his enthusiasms, his friends. Frequently, they overlapped: often, they did not.

At the start of her reign, the courtiers surrounding the young Queen were of a type, and it was not Philip's type. Mike Parker, Philip's private secretary until 1957, said to me, 'They were old school – Eton, Oxbridge, the Brigade of Guards – which Philip was not, and which I most definitely was not. I think he had the measure of them, but I'm not sure they had the measure of him.' Parker told me that Philip 'understood, sort of' that Elizabeth was required to exclude her husband from affairs of state; in return, said Parker, Philip was left 'in charge of the home front'. Elizabeth wore the crown, but Philip wore the trousers. The Queen, it seems, was ready – anxious, even – to allow her husband the man's traditional authority in their domestic and private life. Readily, Elizabeth bowed to Philip's wishes in the matter of their children's upbringing and education. (Prince Charles followed in his father's footsteps by attending Cheam

School and Gordonstoun – and was not at all happy, as we shall see.) She positively encouraged her husband to take on her late father's role and responsibilities in the active management of the royal estates. 'She was head of state,' said Parker, 'but he was head honcho.'

In public he walked one step behind her. In private he treated his wife much as any strong-willed, independent-minded, intelligent, able, and energetic naval husband of his temperament and generation might. He questioned her judgement, he called her 'a bloody fool', he swore at her and them when he tripped over a clutch of her corgis. Martin Charteris said to me, 'It sounds worse in the telling than it actually was. He can be grumpy. He is outspoken. He can be argumentative. But it's just his way. If she hadn't been Queen, you wouldn't have noticed.' But she was Queen and people did notice. Lord Mountbatten liked to tell the story of driving with the Queen and Prince Philip through Cowdray Park. Philip was at the wheel and driving far too fast. The Queen started drawing in her breath and flinching at the way her husband was driving. Philip turned to her and said, 'If you do that once more I shall put you out of the car.' When the hair-raising journey came to an end, Mountbatten asked the Queen why she hadn't protested. 'But you heard what he said,' replied the Queen. 'And he meant it.' Charteris recalled an unhappy half-hour once on *Britannia*. 'I'm not going to come out of my cabin until he's in a better temper,' said Her Majesty. 'I'm going to sit here on my bed until he's better.'

Philip could be irascible – even with his wife. 'It means nothing,' Mike Parker insisted when I raised the subject with him. 'Philip is an outspoken kind of a guy. Everyone knows that. He might use colourful language talking privately with the Queen – for all I know, they might have the odd barney, as couples do – but he is devoted to Her Majesty, absolutely devoted, don't be in any doubt about that.' And, according to several reliable witnesses, as the years went by, the Queen got better at holding her own with Prince Philip and, on occasion, giving as good as she got. Martin Charteris smiled impishly when I tackled him on the matter. 'Have I heard Her Majesty say, "Oh, do shut up, Philip, you don't know what you're talking about"?' he said, tapping his chin with his forefinger. 'Possibly.' 'More than once?' I persisted. 'Perhaps.'

In public and on parade – and the Duke of Edinburgh was

relentlessly on parade with Her Majesty: at the State Opening of Parliament, at the Cenotaph on Remembrance Sunday, at the distribution of the Royal Maundy, at the Queen's Birthday Parade, at Royal Ascot, at the Garter Ceremony, at the Thistle Service, at the Braemar Royal Highland Gathering, at garden parties and state banquets: the royal year is nothing if not predictable – towards his sovereign, Prince Philip's manner and his manners were impeccable. Mike Parker said to me, 'From day one, he was clear that his duty was to support the Queen, first, second, third and last. That's what he's there for. That's what he does. And I don't believe he has failed in his duty. Ever.'

Together the Queen and the Duke undertook thousands of engagements within the United Kingdom, and overseas completed more than 260 visits to 128 countries. Their travels ranged from the Cocos Islands (5.4 square miles with a population of 655) to the People's Republic of China (3.7 million square miles with a population of 1.25 billion).

At the beginning of 1956 the royal couple spent three weeks in Nigeria, where, shaded from the African sun by an elegant canopy designed in London by Norman Hartnell, their programme included a spectacular Durbar at Kadona and countless cheerful encounters with colourfully clad and broadly beaming tribal chiefs. In Lagos, ten thousand masked 'tribal warriors' danced for them, and a crowd, conservatively estimated at a million strong, chanted, 'Our Queen! Our Queen!' with apparently heartfelt enthusiasm. (Within a decade Nigeria was a republic and soon after embroiled in a devastating civil war: the 'tribal warriors' turned tribal warriors.) In April of the same year Nikita Khrushchev and Nikolai Bulganin, the new leaders of the Soviet Union, visited Britain, took tea with the Queen and Philip at Windsor Castle, and presented Her Majesty with a thoroughbred horse as a thirtieth birthday present. Khrushchev, General Secretary of the Soviet Communist Party, and once a farmhand, plumber, and locksmith, had expected 'haughtiness' from a queen, but, to his surprise, found her 'completely unpretentious', 'the sort of woman you would be likely to meet walking along Gorky Street on a balmy summer afternoon'. In June, Queen and Duke paid a state visit to King Gustaf VI Adolf and Queen Louise of Sweden and, in July, received a state visit from King Faisal of Iraq.

The Queen rarely travelled abroad without the Duke. Her solo foreign forays were usually related to her interest in horse breeding, visiting stud farms in Normandy in France and flying to Kentucky in the United States, where her host was William Farish, Texan racehorse owner and breeder and US Ambassador to London from 2001 to 2005. But the Duke undertook frequent overseas assignments without Her Majesty. Between the beginning of 1952 and the end of his life, on behalf of the United Kingdom, the Commonwealth, and the range of causes he supported, he took part in more than 620 overseas visits to over 140 countries.

He set off on his single longest tour in October 1956. He was away for four months – 124 days to be precise. His travels took him to Australia, New Zealand, Ceylon, the Gambia, Antarctica, and the Falkland Islands. The tour was controversial. To an extent, it still is. In 1999 Channel Four screened a two-part television documentary, produced by an independent company, Seven Sisters Productions, entitled *The Real Prince Philip* and designed to reveal just that. The Prince and his office cooperated with the film-makers, giving the programmes' researchers a long list of names (including mine) to contact in the hope that – in the words of Prince Philip's then private secretary, Miles Hunt-Davis – 'they would be able to produce a fair and honest portrayal of His Royal Highness'. In the event, the Prince and his team were disappointed – 'extremely disappointed' – by the result. Miles Hunt-Davis took particular exception to the second programme and wrote to the film's producers to say so: 'Your portrayal of the 1956/57 World Tour in *Britannia* in Programme 2 was marred, firstly by implying that the journey was undertaken in order to get away from The Queen and the Court and secondly that it was a spree. This is totally wrong. The journey was planned to allow His Royal Highness to open the Olympic Games in Melbourne and the use of *Britannia* was specifically planned to enable Prince Philip to visit as many of the remote British Dependent Islands as possible. Most of these were only accessible by sea and had never before been visited by a Member of the Royal Family. The result of this trip was that Prince Philip had visited more of the then British Empire than any other member of the Royal Family.'

The timing of the tour was unfortunate. In July 1956, on the fourth anniversary of his overthrow of King Farouk, President Gamal

308

Abdel Nasser of Egypt announced that he was nationalising the Anglo-French-controlled Suez Canal Company, declaring that if the imperialist powers did not like it they could 'choke to death on their fury'. In August, while she was attending a race meeting at Goodwood, the Queen was required to approve a proclamation, to be read out in the House of Commons that very afternoon, ordering 20,000 army reservists to be called up for service in the Canal zone. In October, as the Duke of Edinburgh, Mike Parker, and their party, in *Britannia*, were sailing east of Trincomalee, on the north-east coast of Ceylon, one of the world's outstanding natural harbours, in the Middle East British and French bombs – and paratroops – were dropping on Egypt. In the event of war *Britannia* was designated a hospital ship. There was momentary uncertainty about whether or not the tour could proceed. It did. Within days, international uproar and the United States' opposition to the Anglo-French action in Egypt brought about a ceasefire. The crisis was resolved. Anti-British riots in Singapore meant abandoning a proposed stop-over at the south end of the Malay peninsula, but, other than that, the royal itinerary was unaffected. On 22 November, in Melbourne, as planned, the Duke of Edinburgh formally opened the sixteenth Olympic Games, the first to be held south of the equator.

The length of the tour was unusual, but, as Prince Philip pointed out, its scope was ambitious. 'We were reaching parts of the Commonwealth that, in some cases, had never before been visited by a member of the Royal Family. And they seemed quite pleased to see us.' To some in those days (and, perhaps, to many more today), for a young husband and father to be separated from his wife and family for four months may have seemed out of the ordinary, but to a naval officer – especially one with experience of war – a sixteen-week tour of duty is not so remarkable. Philip regarded the tour of 1956–7 as a duty to be done and a job worth doing. The Queen agreed and encouraged him to go. As she said in her Christmas message that year, 'If my husband cannot be at home on Christmas Day, I could not wish for a better reason than he should be travelling in other parts of the Commonwealth.'

To the end of his days, it infuriated the Duke of Edinburgh that this arduous tour was portrayed perennially as something of a princely 'jolly' and was used as the platform from which to launch a raft of what Miles Hunt-Davis called 'innuendoes about Prince Philip's private life which [are], in my view, overstated and unbalanced'.

Back at the beginning of 1957, what first set the rumour-mill a-grinding – and allowed 'innuendo' to be translated from a whisper behind the hand to a headline on the front page – was really nothing to do with Prince Philip at all. It was a classic case of 'guilt by association'. Mike Parker, Philip's wartime naval friend, his Australian boon companion, and, since 1947, his private secretary, was being sued for divorce by Eileen, his wife of fourteen years. 'We should never have got married in the first place,' Parker said to me. 'It was a wartime romance, exciting at the time, but we weren't suited long-term. And Eileen wasn't suited to royal life either.' She called her memoirs *Step Aside for Royalty*. 'I didn't behave that well,' admitted Parker. 'It was a helluva mess.' And a mess made public when news of Mrs Parker's petition for divorce was published in February 1957, just as *Britannia* – with Parker and his boss on board – was cruising calmly towards Gibraltar on the final leg of the world tour. 'When we reached the Rock,' said Parker, 'the world's press was waiting. It was not a pretty sight.'[83]

Parker told me, 'I decided to get back to London as soon as possible. We had been on this remarkable voyage, testing the newly commissioned *Britannia*, visiting Ascension Island, Tristan da Cunha, and goodness knows where, but all that was instantly forgotten. I'd become the story – and a liability to Philip.' Surrounded by rapacious hacks ('Literally – I think they bought every other seat on the plane'), Parker, unusually tight-lipped, and accompanied by his solicitor, flew from Gibraltar to London. At Heathrow Airport he found yet more of the world's press awaiting him – together, surprisingly, with the habitually reticent Commander Richard Colville, the Queen's press secretary, who had motored down from London, not

83 At a later date, Prince Philip, visiting Gibraltar, gazed up at the Rock, covered with the limestone promontory's celebrated monkeys, and saw a posse of newsmen and photographers awaiting his arrival. 'Which are the monkeys?' he asked. Philip and Parker shared a sense of humour. One year, Commander Parker listed his 'recreations' in *Who's Who* as follows: 'enjoying young people, including himself, de-pomping, promoting style in anything, sailing in the Pacific and through red tape and tennis anyone?' He told me his address in Queensland was 'Banana Creek – great address, isn't it?'

to give the Duke of Edinburgh's friend and secretary a helping hand, but to say to him this, and nothing more: 'Hello, Parker, I've just come to let you know that from now on, you're on your own.'

Colville made this excursion to Heathrow on his own initiative. Parker was not 'on his own' as far as the Queen and the Duke were concerned. 'The Duke saw me off at the airport in Gibraltar and the Queen was wonderful throughout,' Parker told me. 'She regarded a divorce as a sadness, not a hanging offence. Her Prime Minister at the time was a divorcee, after all.[84] The Queen telephoned me and could not have been more sympathetic.' Initially, Parker – and his employer – hoped he might be able to weather the storm. 'But pretty damn quickly I could see it wasn't going to be possible. It was going to take a year for my divorce to come through. I had to resign. I had no choice.' The Queen was sorry to see him go and appointed him a Commander of the Royal Victorian Order in recognition of his years of loyal service to her husband.

Parker flew to London, but Philip remained on board *Britannia*. Since it was now the beginning of February and he had been away from hearth and home since mid-October, the *Sunday Pictorial*, for one, wanted to know why. The Royal Family, the newspaper reminded its readers, 'is loved and envied throughout the world because it *is* a family'. Why wasn't Philip at home with the kiddies? Anne was six and Charles was eight. 'How can you expect youngsters to understand that Daddy is so near yet cannot come home?'

The reason that Philip remained where he was was simple. It was convenient. And he was not about to dance to the *Sunday Pictorial*'s tune. As planned many months before, the Queen was scheduled to pay a state visit to President Craveiro Lopes of Portugal between 18 and 21 February and Philip was due to join her. He did. 'But,' as they sigh wearily at Buckingham Palace to this day, 'why let the boring facts get in the way of the salacious innuendoes?' Fairly or unfairly, the collapse of the Parker marriage, combined with Philip's prolonged separation from his wife and children, created a flood of

---

84 In fact, Sir Anthony Eden, Prime Minister since April 1955, had resigned on grounds of ill health on 9 January 1957. He was married first to Beatrice Beckett in 1923, divorced in 1950, and, in 1952, married Clarissa Spencer Churchill, who said, famously, of the autumn of 1956: 'For the past few weeks I have really felt as if the Suez Canal was flowing through my drawing room.'

speculation – and eventually the dam burst. The *Baltimore Sun* – the premier newspaper of Wallis Simpson's home town – broke 'the story', with the paper's London correspondent reporting that the British capital was awash with rumour that the Duke of Edinburgh was romantically involved with an unnamed woman whom he met on a regular basis in the West End apartment of a society photographer. 'Report Queen, Duke in Rift Over Party Girl,' ran the headline.

According to Mike Parker, 'The Duke was incandescent. He was very, very angry. And deeply hurt. There was no truth in the story whatsoever.' The Queen was equally dismayed, and, surprisingly (given her instinct to follow precedent and the unwritten rule that royalty never answers back), authorised the normally uncommunicative Commander Colville to issue an official and complete denial: 'It is quite untrue that there is any rift between the Queen and the Duke.' Having received the Palace's reassurance, *The Times*, *Daily Telegraph*, *Mail*, and *Sketch* did the decent thing and ignored the story altogether: if it wasn't true it wasn't to be reported. (Those were the days!) The *Daily Express*, *Mirror*, and *Herald* were less circumspect, however, and splashed the Palace's denial on their front pages. On 11 February, from New York, for the *Manchester Guardian*, Alistair Cooke reported to his readers, no doubt accurately: 'Not since the first rumours of a romance between the former King Edward VIII and the then Mrs Simpson have Americans gobbled up the London dispatches so avidly.' Tongues were wagging, all over the world.[85]

The Queen and the Duke did their best to rise above it. They were reunited at Lisbon's military airport. The scene was a memorable one, and not at all as depicted in the Netflix TV series, *The Crown*. During part of the tour Philip had grown a full set of naval whiskers. Photographs of the bearded Adonis had found their way back to London. When Philip, now clean-shaven in anticipation of the state

---

85 This was the week, incidentally, when Bill Haley and his Comets (with record sales of 22 million) landed in London for the first time. Haley, twenty-nine, told the British press, 'Everyone wants to get into the act.' He was referring to rock and roll rather than royal rumour-mongering, but the media, anxious to find a royal angle to any story wherever possible, declared that 'See you later, alligator / In a while, crocodile', catchphrases from one of Haley's hit songs, had now become 'popular greetings within Princess Margaret's set'.

visit to Portugal, bounded up the steps of the Queen's plane in Lisbon, he was greeted by an extraordinary sight: his wife and her entire entourage, sitting in their seats, all sporting false ginger beards! (This is a family that is fond of practical jokes.) Minutes later, when the royal couple emerged from the plane, both were beaming, and an eagle-eyed reporter, with a sentimental streak, was sure he spotted a telltale smudge of lipstick on the Duke's cheek.

Her Majesty decided to deal with the rumour-mongers' cheek as well. In 1947, when Philip became a naturalised British subject, he ceased to be a Prince of Greece and, technically at least, a 'prince' of any kind at all. On his wedding day, 20 November 1947, George VI created him Baron Greenwich of Greenwich, Earl of Merioneth, and Duke of Edinburgh. The late King had made his son-in-law a Royal Highness, but not a prince. In March 1955 Sir Winston Churchill, a month before his retirement as Prime Minister, proposed to the Queen, 'in informal conversation', that she might like to consider making her husband 'a prince of the United Kingdom'. She agreed, but, at the time, did nothing about it. Two years later, in February 1957, Harold Macmillan, a month after his appointment as Prime Minister, put forward the same proposal. Her Majesty warmly welcomed the suggestion and, this time, took action. On 22 February, the day following their return from the state visit to Portugal, Queen Elizabeth II announced that, henceforward, His Royal Highness the Duke of Edinburgh would carry 'the style and dignity of a prince of the United Kingdom'. This was not merely 'in recognition of the great services which His Royal Highness has provided to the country', but also – and pointedly – 'of his unique contribution to the life of the Commonwealth, culminating in the tour which he has just concluded'.

In 2011, when Prince William married Catherine Middleton, the press talked up the possibility that the Queen might make her grandson's bride a princess on her wedding day. It did not happen – and, so long as the Queen is Queen, I do not believe it will until William and Catherine have been married for ten years. The Queen always uses the honours at her disposal carefully and to a purpose. On Prince Philip's ninetieth birthday, for example, she found for her husband a unique honour that was singularly appropriate. It was a title she held herself until she transferred it to the Duke of Edinburgh: Lord High Admiral of the United Kingdom.

In 2013 Prince Philip spent his ninety-second birthday at the London Clinic, recuperating from an exploratory operation on his abdomen. A few days before, on 6 June, on the morning of his admission to hospital, the Queen presented him with yet another honour to add to his collection: the Order of New Zealand. (Well, what else do you give to a man who has everything?)

The Queen gives honours to recognise achievement and service – and to silence critics. In February 2011 Her Majesty gave her second son, Prince Andrew, Duke of York, one of the highest honours at her personal disposal. She made him a Knight Grand Cross of the Royal Victorian Order. The honour was a fifty-first birthday present for the Prince, a 'thank you' from his mother for the support he had given her and an acknowledgement of his work as un unpaid United Kingdom trade ambassador. The announcement of the honour coincided with both the Prince's birthday and a barrage of bad press for 'Airmiles Andy' as the British media chose to dub him. At the time, Andrew was getting an especially rough ride in the British press because of his association with an American billionaire financier sent to jail and placed on the US sex offenders' register after admitting soliciting teenage girls into prostitution. At the end of March 2011, when Prince Andrew called on his mother at Windsor Castle to be invested with his new honour, the *Daily Mail* reported that 'the revelations' about Andrew's 'associations' had led to questions in Parliament about his suitability as a representative of British industry abroad: 'Critics argue that the Prince's public profile has been fatally damaged. Matters have been made worse in recent weeks by further accusations that he has deliberately befriended rich and powerful foreign figureheads – particularly in Eastern Europe and the Middle East – for personal gain. This has always been vehemently denied by Buckingham Palace.'

When the Queen honoured Prince Andrew in February 2011, she was showing her support for her son in as forthright and public a way as she could. It was the same – but only more so – when, in February 1957, she honoured her husband with 'the style and dignity of a prince of the United Kingdom'. But the critics and the rumour-mongers were not silenced then, either.

Prince Philip told me that he was aware that 'from the earliest days' of his marriage there were those who were convinced that he was what used to be termed 'a ladies' man', one of those husbands who, publicly, support their wives, while at the same time, albeit discreetly, managing to play the field.

Prince Philip was sensitive to this. I know because he raised the issue with me. I did not bring it up: I would neither have dared nor presumed to do so. He raised it himself and did so repeatedly. You might think that, after all those years in the public eye, and knowing how people love to gossip, and seeing the way the press behaves, he would have simply shrugged his shoulders and laughed it off. To an extent he did. In 1995, for example, when a German newspaper reported that His Royal Highness had twenty-four illegitimate children and that this had been confirmed by Buckingham Palace, he did laugh. It transpired that the newspaper had misinterpreted 'godchildren' as 'love children'. But, as a rule, he did not consider the widespread speculation about his alleged love life – in print and private – to be any kind of laughing matter. These stories 'damage your reputation', he said, 'chip away at it insidiously'. I came to realise that the Duke was both more sensitive and more vulnerable than he seemed.

What really surprised me was that he kept copies of some of the most offensive material. Once, he sent me a photocopy he had made of ten pages from an Australian magazine, *Woman's Day*, which on its front page promised readers a full exposé of 'Prince Philip's torrid sex life' with 'famous lovers named'. Inside – under the banner headline 'Philip's Outrageous Affairs' – Australian readers were offered a 'sizzling extract' from a book 'they daren't publish in Britain'. The book's author, Nicholas Davies, purported to reveal 'a shocking world of royal adultery, passion and betrayal' and stated – as fact, not surmise – that the Duke of Edinburgh's liaisons with his cousin, Princess Alexandra, with the film star Merle Oberon, and with the Duchess of York's mother, Susan Barrantes (among others!) were the reason 'why the Queen banned her husband from her bed'.

'It's the most terrible tosh,' I said to Prince Philip.

'I know,' he said, 'but it's out there, in print, between hard covers, and available to one and all. And some of those who read it, may believe it. And those who don't believe it all, may think, "Well, there's no smoke without fire . . ."'

The book itself is not published in the United Kingdom, but, via the internet, of course, it is available worldwide, and, internationally, it has enjoyed wide circulation. In the United States, according to *Publishers Weekly*, the initial print run was 50,000 copies.

What could Philip do about it? He wanted to do something. He wrote to me from Windsor Castle: 'I am sure you will appreciate my dilemma. My only defence would be to sue for libel, but that is a ponderous and expensive business and might well involve me in giving evidence. Either way, it would be valuable publicity for the book! Furthermore, the problem for any individual suing for libel in such a case is that they have to specify which are the statements claimed to be libellous. This means that if any statement is not complained about, it could be taken as being true!!'

Typically, Prince Philip offered me his own practical solution to the dilemma: 'It would be so much easier, and fairer, to be able to draw the attention of some sort of complaints tribunal to the publication of unsubstantiated statements about the behaviour of individuals of this, or of any other, nature. It would then be up to the author to satisfy the tribunal that there was sufficient acceptable evidence to prove the truth of the statements. Needless to say, quoting unsubstantiated reports in the media ought not to be considered acceptable evidence.'

In 1995, when I was an MP and parliamentary private secretary to Stephen Dorrell, then Secretary of State for National Heritage, I took the minister to see Prince Philip at Buckingham Palace to hear the Duke's views on privacy and the press, among other things. The minister listened sympathetically and said, frankly, there was not much he could do. Given the beleaguered state of John Major's government at the time, and the number of stories of 'sleaze' sloshing round its ankles, action of any kind that could be interpreted as restricting the freedom of the press was not likely to find favour. Sixteen years later, when Lord Justice Leveson was appointed to head a judicial public inquiry into the culture, practice, and ethics of the British press, the Duke of Edinburgh followed its proceedings with interest, but was not optimistic that the new, independent body that Leveson proposed to replace the existing Press Complaints Commission would either 'have teeth or make much difference'.

Lies were told about Prince Philip's private life and he did not like it.

'I want my book to tell the truth,' I said to him.

'Good luck,' he said.

What was the truth?

Was the Duke of Edinburgh a philanderer?

And, if he was, why do we need to know? Is it any of our business? As the great Cervantes puts it in *Don Quixote*: 'Suppose they were lovers, what's that to me? Plenty of people expect to find bacon where there's not so much as a hook to hang it on.' Surely, as Dr Johnson insists, even in death (perhaps especially in death) 'a man is to have part of his life to himself'?

Well, yes. And no. Prince Philip was in a special position. He was the Queen's consort, and Her Majesty is Supreme Governor of the Church of England. At her Coronation, he knelt before her, placed his hands between hers, and vowed, 'I, Philip, Duke of Edinburgh, do become your liege man of life and limb, and of earthly worship; and faith and truth will I bear unto you . . .' I do not believe that he took that vow – or, indeed, his marriage vows – lightly. It was at his insistence that, in 2011, his biography on the official Buckingham Palace Royal Family website included the sentence: 'The Duke is a committed Christian.' And although he instructed me not to 'bang on' about his interest in religion, when in a draft of my book I said that his shelves contained 634 volumes on religion, he corrected the figure in his own hand to 670.

Prince Philip was a committed Christian who disapproved of his eldest son's adultery. He said it was 'wrong'. Prince Philip was also a role model – especially to the young and those in the armed services. He was founder of the Duke of Edinburgh's Award Scheme and patron of the Outward Bound Trust. He was a Colonel or Colonel-in-Chief, Field Marshal, Admiral, and Air Commodore forty-two times over. He took these appointments seriously. Honour, duty and example counted with him. But was he a hypocrite? Did he criticise his son for doing what he had done himself? Did he betray the Queen?

I believe we can take it as read that the Queen remained faithful throughout her married life. There are those who persist in believing that Prince Andrew's natural father was the Queen's racing manager, Henry Porchester, 'Porchey', 7th Earl of Carnarvon, suggesting the conception occurred at some point between 20 January and 30 April

1959 when Philip was away on another of his long sea voyages in *Britannia*. Never mind that the dates don't stack up (Andrew was born on 19 February 1960, a happy by-product of the Queen and Philip's post-*Britannia* reunion): the idea of the Queen committing adultery is simply preposterous.

I asked Geordie, 8th Earl of Carnarvon (and one of the Queen's godchildren), if his father and Her Majesty knew of the rumour and what they made of it. Were they amused? 'They knew all about it,' Geordie told me, 'and were not in the least amused. They were angry. My father was very annoyed by it, and embarrassed. It was dreadful.' The Queen and Porchey were best friends. They had known each other all their adult lives: they shared a passion for racehorses and a sense of humour. They may even have been a little in love – in the nicest possible way – but the idea of a romance between them is risible. 'Both my parents were friends of the Queen and Prince Philip,' Geordie told me. 'Obviously my father saw a lot of the Queen throughout the year, but in October he used to invite them to Highclere [Castle, near Newbury in Berkshire, the Carnarvon family home, now familiar to television viewers around the world as the setting for *Downton Abbey*] for a shooting weekend – partridge shooting. Prince Philip sometimes came, not always. He's an extremely good shot. And the Queen, of course, has always been good at working dogs. On Saturday night, my mother would do dinner, the best of English country house cooking, using old recipes of my great-grandmother's. And on Sunday my father and the Queen might walk round the stables or visit Highclere stud. The Queen adored going on the gallops early in the evening. It was just a perfect, relaxing weekend.' Porchey died in 2001, but two years later the family reinstated the weekend. 'The Queen came again,' said Geordie, 'and Prince Philip, too. Without my father it couldn't be quite the same, but it was very jolly.' In 2012, when I visited Highclere at the height of its *Downton Abbey* celebrity, I was pleased to see from the visitors' book that the Queen and Prince Philip were maintaining the tradition.

In the United Kingdom, as I write, there are two 'republican movements' (self-styled) who have taken to the worldwide web to demand DNA testing to establish the true paternity of, not one, but two of the Queen's children. Not content with suggesting that

Porchey fathered Prince Andrew, they also allege that the Queen's youngest child, Prince Edward, born in 1964, was the product of the union between Her Majesty and the Deputy Master of her Household, Patrick, 7th Baron Plunket.

Patrick Plunket was a delightful individual, good-looking and good-humoured, born in 1923, so only three years older than the Queen, and more like a brother than a lover. His parents were 'characters'[86] and great friends of Elizabeth's parents, dating back to the days when they were still the Yorks. In 1938, when Patrick was not yet fifteen, they were both killed in a plane crash on their way to a party William Randolph Hearst was giving in their honour in California.

Educated at Eton and Cambridge, Patrick joined the Irish Guards, rose to the rank of lieutenant colonel and became an equerry to George VI in 1948. He had charm and taste (he was a trustee of the Wallace Collection and the National Art Collections Fund), and, as the Queen's Deputy Master of the Household from 1954 until his early death from cancer in 1975, masterminded the Queen's official entertaining with style and devotion. Martin Charteris told me, 'Patrick Plunket's death was a real loss to the Queen, a personal loss. He was a lifelong courtier, but he wasn't a stuffed shirt. He was great fun. He had a wonderful flair for entertaining, of course, but he was also very good at human relations. He was very easy with the Queen and she was very relaxed with him. He treated her almost as an equal, certainly as a friend. If you wanted to say something awkward or difficult to Her Majesty, you could do it through Patrick. When he died a bright light went out in her life.' The Queen

---

86 Terence 'Teddy' Plunket, 6th Baron, was an Anglo-Irish charmer (of Wilton Crescent, SW1, and Old Connaught House, Bray, County Wicklow) who, in 1922, married Dorothé, a petite beauty and noted dancer. Dorothé's mother was Fannie Ward, actress and protégée of Cecil B. de Mille. Officially, her father was Joseph 'Diamond Joe' Lewis (who had made a fortune in South Africa in the diamond rush of the 1870s), but, biologically, it seems she was fathered by Lord Londonderry. When Dorothé married Teddy Plunket, she was the widow of Captain Jack Barnato, a First World War air ace (and son of 'Babe' Barnato, another South African diamond king) who died in the great influenza epidemic of 1918. They had three sons. When the Plunkets were killed in 1938, Queen Elizabeth wrote to a mutual friend: 'They both gave so much happiness to so many people . . . Those dear little boys make one's heart *ache*.'

mourned the loss of Patrick Plunket: he was a true friend, but he was not the father of Prince Edward. Lord Plunket was a confirmed bachelor: in many ways, that was part of his attraction.

Given her nature and her upbringing, you would expect the Queen to be wholly faithful to her marriage vows. Her role models, after all, were her mother and father and her grandparents, George V and Queen Mary. Yes, there were stories about George V when he was a young Duke of York, but what did they amount to? 'I say, May,' the Duke told his fiancée, Mary of Teck, in the spring of 1893, 'we can't get married after all. I hear I have a got a wife and three children . . .' The alleged 'wife' was an American living in Plymouth. 'Why there, I wonder?' pondered the Prince. At first he found the rumour 'really very amusing', but it rumbled on and gathered momentum. When, eventually, it appeared in print, the year was 1910, the Duke of York was King, and the charge was specific. E.F. Mylius, in an article headed 'Sanctified Bigamy', published in a republican paper in Paris and sent to every British MP, alleged that in 1890, in Malta, the future king had married an admiral's daughter who bore him several children: 'Our very Christian King and Defender of the Faith has a plurality of wives just like any Mohammedan Sultan.' His Majesty found this less amusing and decided to nail the lie. The Crown instigated libel proceedings and Mylius was sentenced to twelve months' imprisonment. George V's second son, the eventual George VI, as a young Duke of York, was briefly led astray by his elder brother, the Prince of Wales, but, as husbands, George V and George VI were continent and loyal, and, as wives, Queen Mary and Queen Elizabeth were, without doubt, above reproach. Lilibet, as a child and adolescent, had a stable and happy home life and the example of parents who were as devoted and loving to their children as they were to each other.

The black sheep of the family, of course, was the Duke of Windsor: his love life as Prince of Wales had been chequered; his married life, living in exile with a double divorcee, was not a bed of roses. Elizabeth II is not judgemental – Prince Philip told me that his wife's most notable virtue is her tolerance – but she is observant. Her younger sister's love life may have been more colourful than her own – it was certainly more varied and adventurous – but the Queen will have noticed that Princess Margaret's romantic relationships, and her marriage to Tony Snowdon, while they brought her undoubted 'highs', did not provide her with lasting happiness.

Who were Prince Philip's role models? What is the pattern – the template – within his immediate family? His royal grandfather, King George I of Greece, had a good marriage, but apparently allowed himself some light romantic relaxation during his annual holiday (without the Queen) in the French spa town of Aix-les-Bains. Philip's uncle, King Constantine I of Greece (King George's eldest son), had a less happy marriage, holiday dalliances similar to those his father enjoyed, and, at the climax of the Balkan war in 1912–13, caused consternation at home and a scandal at court by conducting an almost open affair during his wife Sophie's sixth and final pregnancy. Philip's father, Constantine's younger brother, Andrea, was not a philanderer, but he was attractive to women, and, as we have seen, following his separation from Princess Alice in the 1930s, eventually settled with a lady friend in the south of France. As a young man Prince Philip's maternal grandfather, Louis of Battenberg, was a self-confessed Lothario. His memoirs of his bachelor days included a page marked '*NOT* FOR MY DAUGHTERS'. So lively was his love life, and so notorious, that Queen Victoria, fearing that he might have been contemplating marriage with her youngest daughter, Princess Beatrice, instructed the Admiralty to send him abroad – and keep him there. In due course, of course, he made a good marriage to Queen Victoria's granddaughter, Princess Victoria, and had four children: Princess Alice, Prince Philip's mother, Princess Louise, Prince Philip's aunt, and George and Louis, Prince Philip's uncles.

Georgie, 2nd Marquess of Milford Haven, and his wife, Nada de Torby, were a charismatic couple. In the 1930s Georgie acted as Philip's guardian. Philip stayed with Georgie and Nada during the school holidays. They were two people of considerable personal charm, but their marriage was not conventional. Nada had a reputation as a bisexual and Georgie as a collector of pornography. Louis Mountbatten, 'Dickie', and his wife, Edwina Ashley, were a charismatic couple, too – and charming also. And glamorous, rich, restless, and achieving as well. In its imperfect way, their marriage was a good one, though, again, not unduly constrained by the letter of their wedding vows.

'Edwina and I spent all our married lives getting into other people's beds,' Mountbatten once confessed to a friend. Philip Ziegler, Mountbatten's official biographer, while accepting that Edwina was, in every sense, 'a goer', doubts that Mountbatten was promiscuous. He conducted two protracted love affairs outside his marriage, but, according to Ziegler, 'though he liked to imagine himself a sexual athlete, he seems in fact only to have had slight enthusiasm for the sport'. Mountbatten's daughter, Patricia, told me she concurred with Ziegler's conclusion that her father 'loved the company of women, sought their affection and had an almost irresistible urge to use them as confidantes', but that his real energy – his colossal life force – was channelled into his working life: 'If asked to choose between seduction by the most desirable of houris and a conversation about service matters with a person of influence, he would unfailingly have chosen the latter. Never would he have sacrificed his career for lust.'[87]

In May 1945, as the Second World War reached its climax in Europe, Mountbatten was Allied Supreme Commander, South-East Asia. The professional challenges he faced were formidable. On 8 May he confided to his daughter, Patricia, 'I do feel the need of opening my heart to a woman and not another man when I'm worried.' Now and again, though not very seriously, he had contemplated a divorce, simply to give Edwina her freedom (he was extraordinarily understanding and tolerant of his wife's passionate commitment to other men), but, that spring, when Edwina's current lover suddenly announced his engagement to another woman, it seems the Mountbattens decided to make a concerted effort to clear the air and come to a mutual understanding. On 7 May, Dickie wrote to Edwina: 'I am so glad that you felt as happy as I did about our new-found relationship. I have always wanted to have you as

---

87 Ziegler also concludes that there is no evidence whatsoever to suggest that Mountbatten was homosexual. He had a number of homosexual friends, like Noël Coward, but, despite a raft of rumours, no homosexual life himself. A gay friend of mine introduced me to him, at the Garrick Club in London one night in the 1970s. Because Mountbatten happened to be with Sir Richard Attenborough that evening, my friend exclaimed, 'Ah, the two Dickies together at last!' Mountbatten appeared amused. He put his hand on my shoulder and kept it there, but only, I think, because he was old and I was young and he liked the company of young people. My friend took me on for a nightcap to a nearby gay club called Heaven. Lord Mountbatten did not join us.

my principal confidante and friend, but as long as A. was yours – it made it literally impossible for me. I hope you don't mind about my mentioning about my girl-friends – it was only to show you that they have never meant to me what A. meant to you, and so can never come between us, provided you no longer make difficulties about my seeing them, within reason, as you were apt to do in the old days!!'

Was Prince Philip like his uncle? Or his father? Or his grandfather? 'Men,' says my wife, 'they're all the same', but, in truth, they are different, aren't they? Some men find fidelity impossible; others find it hugely rewarding. Margaret Thatcher told me that President Reagan once told her that his single-minded devotion to his wife, Nancy, had given him 'strength and freedom'.[88] President Clinton's marriage, by contrast, seems to have enjoyed strength and freedom of a different sort. Some men of distinction, leading public lives, seem to me to take extraordinary risks with their own reputations – and with their marriages. Clinton is a spectacular example: he risked impeachment for lust. John Major is another. When Major's illicit affair with a fellow MP was revealed, he said he had 'long feared' it would be made public and it was 'the one event in my life of which I am most ashamed'. Lord Jenkins of Hillhead, another high-achieving politician, another happily married man, told me that he had enjoyed a number of affairs while holding office, adding, emphatically, and with the broadest of grins, 'I've done nothing of which I'm ashamed.'

Otherwise-decent men do have affairs and sustain successful marriages. Some years ago, for a national newspaper, I was sent to

---

88 In 1971, Reagan wrote a letter of advice to his son, Michael, who was twenty-six and about to be married: 'You have entered into the most meaningful relationship there is in all human life. It can be whatever you decide to make it. Some men feel their masculinity can only be proven if they play out in their own life all the locker-room stories, smugly confident that what a wife doesn't know won't hurt her. The truth is, somehow, way down inside, without her ever finding lipstick on the collar or catching a man in the flimsy excuse of where he was till 3 a.m., a wife does know, and with that knowing, some of the magic of this relationship disappears . . . Any man can find a twerp here and there who will go along with cheating, and it doesn't take all that much manhood. It does take quite a man to remain attractive and to be loved by a woman who has heard him snore, seen him unshaven, tended him while he was sick and washed his dirty underwear. Do that and keep her still feeling a warm glow and you will know some very beautiful music.'

interview the 11th Duke of Devonshire, born in 1920, so belonging to exactly the same generation as the Duke of Edinburgh. Andrew Cavendish was a quintessential English gentleman: effortlessly courteous, urbane, tolerant, good-humoured, self-deprecating, gently eccentric. For sixty-three years, until his death in 2004, he was married to Debo, the youngest of the celebrated Mitford sisters. 'She is on the bossy side,' he told me, 'but I like that in a girl.' He acknowledged a weakness for 'fast women and slow horses'. The degree of his soft spot for the ladies was exposed in 1985 when three blank cheques were stolen from his house in Mayfair. At the trial following the theft, his former butler gave evidence about the Duke's habit of handing out cheques to ladies who came to call. When the judge asked him if the ladies were young, middle-aged, or elderly, the Duke was forced to admit that they tended to be young, and that he was on holiday with one of them at the time that the robbery occurred. The Duchess was apparently unperturbed by this revelation. The Duke confessed to me that he feared it might cost him the Garter. It didn't. He was appointed a Knight of the Garter in 1996, aged seventy-six. He told me the honour gave him 'real joy every hour of every day': 'I know I don't deserve it, but it is our oldest order of chivalry and I take the idea of English chivalry seriously. It's important.' He also told me, 'English girls are the loveliest in the world and an Englishman should marry an Englishwoman, without a doubt. As to a dalliance? Well, the French have their strengths and the Italians are very agreeable, but if you want my advice stick to Englishwomen. They know the rules.' It seems that John Major (a Knight of the Garter since 2005) had the misfortune to have a dalliance with an Englishwoman who did not know the rules and the 6th Duke of Westminster (a Knight of the Garter since 2003) had his extramarital liaisons with Lithuanian and Russian prostitutes.

As Andrew Devonshire reminded me, the Order of the Garter is the most senior and the oldest British Order of Chivalry, founded by Edward III in 1348. The origin of the emblem of the Order, a blue and gold garter worn just below the Knight's left knee, is obscure. Tradition says it was inspired by an incident which occurred while the young King, fresh from his triumph against the French at Crécy and celebrating the capture of Calais, danced at court with Joan, Countess of Salisbury. As King and Countess danced, the lady's garter fell to the floor: the King retrieved the garter and tied it to his own leg. The courtiers watching the scene were apparently amused, but the King admonished them with the words, 'Honi soit qui mal y pense' – 'Shame on him who thinks evil of this.' The phrase has been the motto of the Order ever since.[89] The Duke of Edinburgh had been a Knight of the Garter since 1947. Was he yet another member of the Order whose girlfriends knew the rules? Or should we be ashamed of thinking evil and giving time and attention to the innuendoes about his private life?

Prince Philip was careful never to dignify tittle-tattle with comment of any kind. When the journalist from the Sunday broadsheet suggested to him that he might have a raft of illegitimate children and have enjoyed a liaison with the President of France, he sat impassively, gazing steadfastly into the middle distance, incensed but silent. Privately, he would say, 'How could I? I've had a detective in my company, night and day, since 1947.' He liked to point out that he was accompanied everywhere he went, that his face was not entirely unknown, and that, over six decades and on three continents, reporters had been trying to dig up some dirt on him that would stick but, thus far, had managed to come up with 'bugger all'!

Mike Parker told me, 'Philip has been one hundred per cent faithful to the Queen. No ifs, no buts. Take it from me, I know.' Lord Charteris said, 'I am aware what people say, and have said for years, but I know of no evidence of any kind, no evidence at all, and, if there were any, I rather think I would.' Geoff Williams, Prince Philip's former pilot, who accompanied his boss to fairly faraway places, put it even more succinctly: 'I have no information that would make two lines in the *Sun*.' And yet the murmuring went on. 'When

89 Less romantic historians reckon it is more likely that the Order was inspired by the strap used to attach pieces of armour, and that the motto referred to critics of Edward's claim to the throne of France. For those who want to learn more on the subject, I recommend *Royal Orders: The Honours and the Honoured* by Hugo Vickers, 1994. Hugo gave me my copy of his book on a memorable morning in 2000 when, for a TV documentary I was making on the honours system, we visited Spink, suppliers of medals and orders since 1666, and tried on a variety of decorations. The one I would have liked to take home was the Ugandan VC. Spink, as I recall, had created just six of these, at the behest of Idi Amin, when he was President of Uganda. Only one was ever awarded – by Amin to Amin.

I see the tabloids,' Prince Philip once sighed to Patricia Mountbatten, 'I think I might as well have done it.'

Well, did he or didn't he?

Countess Mountbatten was in no doubt. 'He has been completely faithful to the Queen,' she said to me, 'I'm sure of it, completely and utterly sure.' Just as her father, Lord Mountbatten, would never – in his biographer's phrase – 'sacrifice his career for lust', so her cousin, Prince Philip, would never betray the Queen for a mere roll in the hay. 'Supporting the Queen has been his life,' Countess Mountbatten reminded me emphatically. 'He wouldn't endanger his reputation or betray her trust. How could she retaliate? He simply would not allow himself to humiliate her in that way. He wouldn't risk it. He wouldn't want to. He is bound to the Queen by duty – and by love.' But when I raised the issue with Margaret Rhodes, the Queen's cousin and childhood friend, she was less certain. 'I don't know,' she said to me, brow furrowed, staring into her coffee cup, 'I just don't know.' Now that the Duke of Edinburgh is dead, will there be posthumous 'revelations'? Possibly, but I doubt if anything of substance will be proven.

Buckingham Palace first put the matter of the royal marriage into the public domain in February 1957, with Commander Colville's question-begging official statement flatly denying 'any rift between the Queen and the Duke'. As we have seen, what prompted the unfortunate statement was the torrent of speculation unleashed by the *Baltimore Sun*'s story that London was awash with 'whispers' that 'the Duke of Edinburgh had more than a passing interest in an unnamed woman and was meeting her regularly in the apartment of a court photographer'. The 'court photographer', of course, was Baron, Philip's friend, who would, in fact, have been with the Duke, and Mike Parker and company, in *Britannia* on the 1956–7 world tour, as 'official photographer', had he not gone into hospital for a hip operation at the beginning of September 1956 and died unexpectedly on the operating table, aged only forty-nine.[90] Almost all

90 Needing a replacement photographer for the tour, Mike Parker went round to Baron's studio to see if one of his assistants might be suitable. He met Tony Armstrong-Jones, then twenty-six, but decided 'the young man was far too bohemian' to join the royal party. Within four years, Armstrong-Jones had joined the Royal Family, marrying Princess Margaret and becoming the Earl of Snowdon. He said to me once, 'I always feel so sorry for those people from Bohemia.'

the lurid 'stories' about Philip, from the late 1940s through the 1950s, revolve in some way around Baron and his 'set'.

Baron Henry Stirling Nahum − known to all as 'Baron': 'Lordly by name and lordly by nature,' said one obituary − was born in 1907. His family were Italian Jews from Tripoli who settled in Manchester and made a success in the Lancashire cotton trade. Baron, and his twin brother, Jack, came to London at the turn of the 1930s and cut a dash: Baron as a society photographer, Jack as a barrister. According to Robin Dalton, the film producer, who knew Baron well ('he was one of my dearest friends; he gave me away at my wedding; was godfather to my daughter; we spoke every day on the telephone until his death'), his success was due to 'his talent, his unique and lovable personality, and his connections': 'In the late 1920s he and Dickie Mountbatten had both been madly in love with a fascinating Frenchwoman, Yola Letellier,[91] and had met at her fete in Paris. They remained friends. In time Uncle Dickie introduced Baron to his nephew Philip − I think it was when Baron was taking pictures of the Mountbattens at Broadlands − and then Philip introduced Baron to David [Milford Haven] and me. David and I were living together in a flat in the Kings Road. It cost £8 per week. We paid half each.'

Robin Dalton, in her *Incidental Memoir*, remembers clearly that Baron 'was reputed to be at the centre of a very disreputable world indeed'. 'With me,' she says, 'he was a loving and gentle friend,' but, she admits, 'one heard lurid tales of orgies.' Robin and Baron became proper friends when 'David had gone skiing for two weeks and asked Baron to look after me'. Meeting 'Baron's set' (or 'Baron's Court' as it was sometimes known) opened up what Robin Dalton calls 'avenues of enjoyment: painters, writers, photographers − skimming the surface, I now realise, of a murkier world underneath of which I remained largely innocent'.

Baron's gifted artist friends included Stephen Ward, who drew a

91   She does sound intriguing. She was married to a hotelier, Henri Letellier, who was also the Mayor of Deauville, when Mountbatten first met her in 1926. According to Philip Ziegler, she was Mountbatten's closest female friend until his death: 'Edwina was wise enough to make her into a friend; she once told her husband that she liked Yola very much but that he was not to marry her if ever he found himself a widower.'

portrait of the Duke of Edinburgh, among others, and, more famously, in his capacity as an osteopath and social intermediary, introduced the call girl Christine Keeler to the Conservative government minister John Profumo. In June 1963 Profumo, who had lied to Parliament about his association with Keeler, resigned – and the press, remarkably, found a way to link Prince Philip to 'the Profumo affair'. Ward, Philip's Thursday Club acquaintance and Christine Keeler's landlord, was charged with living 'wholly or in part on the earnings of prostitution'. He took an overdose on the final night of his trial and never recovered. He was found guilty on two charges, but died without sentence being passed. Ward's drawings of Prince Philip and other members of the Royal Family were put up for sale to help defray his legal costs: Sir Anthony Blunt, Surveyor of the Queen's Pictures since 1945 (and a Soviet spy since 1936 – you couldn't make it up!) bought them, privately, to save the Royal Family public embarrassment.

There was embarrassment nevertheless. Ward had hosted parties at which a feature was that 'the man who serves dinner' – in the words of Lord Denning's official report into the affair – 'is nearly naked except for a small square lace apron round his waist such as a waitress might wear. He wears a black mask over his head with slits for eye-holes. He cannot therefore be recognised by any of the guests. Some reports stop there and say that nothing evil takes place. It is done as a comic turn and no more. This may well be so at some of the parties. But at others I am satisfied that it is followed by perverted sex orgies: that the man in the mask is a "slave" who is whipped.'

Was the Duke of Edinburgh 'the man in the mask'? On 24 June 1963 the *Daily Mirror* filled its front page with a huge headline, 'PRINCE PHILIP AND THE PROFUMO SCANDAL', and managed to get the best of both worlds, opening the story with the words, 'The foulest rumour which is being circulated about the Profumo Scandal has involved the Royal Family,' adding, immediately, a much smaller headline: 'Rumour is utterly unfounded.'

From 1963 until his death in 2006, aged ninety-one, John Profumo kept his own counsel and devoted himself to good works. He became a CBE in 1975 and, in 1995, at a dinner held at Claridge's Hotel to mark Margaret Thatcher's seventieth birthday, the disgraced former minister found himself seated at the Queen's right hand. At the reception after the dinner, he saw Prince Philip and thanked him for the honour of being allowed to sit next to Her Majesty. 'Nothing to do with me,' said Prince Philip dismissively. His Royal Highness was not impressed by Profumo. Jack Profumo was one of the most effortlessly charming men I ever met: Prince Philip was instinctively wary of that kind of charm. And, more to the point, the Duke of Edinburgh was not amused to have been associated, however briefly, tangentially, and irrelevantly, with 'the Profumo affair'.

Another colourful member of 'Baron's Court' was the painter Vasco Lazzolo. He also sketched a portrait of Prince Philip. 'Lazzolo,' Robin Dalton remembers, 'discovered a magic pill which was supposed to make us all madly sexy. You put it underneath your pillow and at the crucial moment of intercourse you were supposed to pop it and inhale. David [Milford Haven] and I tried it once, but as we were madly sexy anyway it didn't appear to do more than slow up proceedings. We were always losing the pills under the pillow. I think they were yellow and I expect they were the first primitive precursors of amyl nitrite.' Talk to Tony Snowdon, Baron's some-time assistant, and later Prince Philip's brother-in-law, and he gossiped happily about the 'madly sexy' goings-on in the London of the 1950s and 1960s. Talking to Prince Philip on the same subject the most I got out of him was: 'All that passed me by.'

In 2008, when the author James Hogg published a biography of another of the Baron set, the actor James Robertson Justice, he asked Prince Philip if he would consider contributing a foreword. James Hogg told me, 'The book originally featured a story given to me by Molly Parkin [James Robertson Justice's mistress], which involved her, JRJ, and a fluorescent light tube. It was extremely graphic! Anyway, I received a very polite letter from Prince Philip's private secretary, saying he'd be delighted to write a foreword, but would I please consider removing said story, as he couldn't really put his name to something so pornographic.'

Philip remembered James Robertson Justice with affection as an 'adventurer, man of many actions, naturalist, intellectual and incidental film actor'. He said, 'He lived every bit of his life more than to the full and gave his friends endless pleasure and entertainment.'

I asked Prince Philip, 'Have you lived your life more than to the full?'

'No,' he answered, firmly. 'Certainly not.' He added, 'James Justice was an eccentric and I'm not.' The Duke of Edinburgh recalled that the actor best remembered by the rest of us as Sir Lancelot Spratt in the *Doctor* films was a wonderful anecdotalist who did indeed tell 'some racy stories', but the Duke remembered him best from the times during the summer in Scotland in the 1950s and 1960s when, staying at Balmoral, he would take his children to visit Justice and his wife Irina at their house at Spinningdale. 'His passion for hawking – and spearing flounders in the nearby Fleet estuary – was infectious; activities that were thoroughly enjoyed by my two older children.'

Through Baron, Prince Philip was introduced to some intriguing characters. Having met at Broadlands in 1947, the photographer and the Duke became friends. Philip asked Baron to take his wedding photographs, and Baron invited Philip to join his informal luncheon club. The Thursday Club, as it was known, met originally in an upstairs room at Wheeler's Restaurant in Old Compton Street, Soho. The purpose of the club was purely convivial: an excuse to start the weekend early, eat Wheeler's finest fish (Bernard Walsh, the restaurant's proprietor, was a founder member), and drink Wheeler's cheap-and-cheerful house white wine – and plenty of it. According to Robin Dalton, 'Thursday night was a lost cause if you happened to be the wife or girlfriend of any of the members.' Her boyfriend, David Milford Haven, joined the club, as did Philip and Mike Parker. The members (all male) included Baron's brother, Jack, artists like Vasco Lazzolo, newspaper editors (Arthur Christiansen of the *Daily Express*, Frank Owen of the *Daily Mail*), actors (James Robertson Justice, David Niven), scriptwriters (Don Stewart, Monja Danischewsky), amusing men about town: Compton Mackenzie, Peter Ustinov, Lord Glenavy (better known as the stammering raconteur and columnist Patrick Campbell), Larry Adler. The gatherings were high-spirited, occasionally raucous, but never debauched. There was gossip and banter, but no birds – other than the cuckoo . . .

The cuckoo became notorious. It lived inside a cuckoo clock in the room where the lunch was held. Predictably, it emerged on the hour and the half-hour, but its appearances on the half-hour were inevitably brief. One day, by way of an amusing wager, the club members bet Baron that he and his camera would not be quick enough to take a snapshot of the cuckoo when it popped out at half past one. Baron rose to the challenge – and failed. Next week, he tried again – setting his camera on a tripod this time. He failed again: Mike Parker, apparently, nudged him as the cuckoo appeared. At the third attempt, Baron insisted that none of the club members be allowed within reaching distance of him or his camera. He was foiled once more: Parker had come equipped with three thunder-flashes – small, safe, lightly explosive smoke bombs, used in military training, and useful for japes like this. Just as the hands of the cuckoo clock reached half past one, Parker, Philip and either James Robertson Justice or Arthur Christiansen deployed the thunder-flashes: one burst immediately under Baron's camera, one landed on a table, and the third ended up in the fireplace, where its explosion prompted a downfall of soot from the chimney. There was laughter – and black-ened faces: the Duke was right by the fireplace – but when the smoke cleared, and the police arrived, general agreement that perhaps it was time to call off the wager.

'We had fun at those lunches,' Parker recalled, 'plenty of laughter, but nothing *louche* or lewd, I assure you.' He also claimed that, even then, at the beginning of his public life, Philip had 'an instinct for self-preservation'. 'He was always correct,' Parker told me, 'always kept just that little bit of distance, never went too far. Most of the chaps were absolutely above board, but we had a nose for those that weren't.' They were always wary of Larry Adler,[92] and Parker said

---

92 I liked Larry Adler. Others found him tiresome: he talked too much (largely about himself), he had a weakness for exaggeration, and his capacity for name-dropping rivalled my own. (This may be why I was in sympathy with him.) I met a number of other Thursday Club regulars in the 1960s. James Robertson Justice (1905–75), actor, was the first grown man I ever saw stark naked. I knocked on his door at the Randolph Hotel, Oxford, and disturbed his pre-prandial snooze. He answered, 'Come!' I entered the room and found him spread-eagled on the bed, unadorned except for a hip flask which was nestling in the thicket of silver hair on his chest. Monja Danischewsky (1911–94), film producer and scriptwriter, wrote an hilarious autobiography (*White Russian, Red Face*, 1966), kept pigs (explaining, since he was Jewish, that he was sure, as a matter of honour, they would never attack him), and introduced me to the Famous Last Words of the Fatted Calf: 'I hear the young master has returned . . .' I shared a literary agent with Patrick Campbell (3rd Baron Glenavy, 1913–80) and appeared on *Call My Bluff* as a member of his team. When the other team captain, Frank Muir, was telling us (at length) about how he had recently been made captain of his local rifle club, Campbell muttered to me, under

that, from the outset, he thought there was 'something unsavoury' about Stephen Ward. When Kim Philby turned up as a guest one Thursday (some time before his exposure as a Soviet spy), Parker's nose twitched, but only because Philby was 'the dullest man in the place'.

Courtiers of the old school (the likes of Tommy Lascelles) always had their doubts about Mike Parker. He was Australian, after all, brash and breezy, and inclined to sail too close to the wind. They had their reservations about Baron, too. 'Baron was a gambler,' said Peter Ustinov, shortly after his death, 'and it sometimes seemed to me as I watched him at work and at play that for him the whole of existence was a pastime with a score.' Baron took risks, and he knew all types and conditions of men – and women.

It was Baron who introduced the Duke of Edinburgh to the first of the 'leading ladies' with whom he is supposed to have had an affair. Pat Kirkwood was an actress, singer, and celebrated pantomime principal boy. The critic Kenneth Tynan (who knew about these things) once described her legs as 'the eighth wonder of the world'. In 1948 she was twenty-seven and starring in a musical revue called *Starlight Roof* at the London Hippodrome. According to Miss Kirkwood, one night, after the show, Baron (who, by his own admission, was besotted with her) turned up with Philip and an equerry, and the four of them went off to dine. They had a late supper at Les Ambassadeurs in Mayfair and then went dancing at the nearby Milroy nightclub. Philip asked Pat to dance. And she did. 'But nothing happened,' she assured me. 'Nothing happened at all. Then, or later. It was innocent fun. He was out on a night with the boys and I just happened to be there.' At the nightclub, she recalled, 'people stopped and stared, and there was some tut-tutting and disapproving looks, and Philip responded by pulling a face – but that is as shocking and outrageous as his behaviour got.' When the dancing stopped, they went back to Baron's place for scrambled eggs. And then it was time for bed. Philip went off with his equerry, and Baron drove Pat home to her mother in St John's Wood.

---

his breath, 'Small bore, I suppose.' These were funny men, and, in the best sense, men of the world. It must have been fun to have dined at the Thursday Club when they were there and on song.

Pat Kirkwood did meet Prince Philip half a dozen times more – at show-business charity events, in the official line-up after a televised command performance, in another line-up, after a charity concert at the Theatre Royal, Drury Lane. On each occasion friendly handshakes and brief pleasantries were exchanged. And that's it. There is nothing more to tell. Yet on the fragile foundation of one night of dancing and a handful of handshakes rests a massive mountain of myth that has managed to sustain itself across sixty years and is usually summed up in the headline, 'The Prince and the Showgirl'. In 2012 the episode even became the basis of a one-woman musical, *Pat Kirkwood is Angry*, in which the star was portrayed by the operatic mezzo-soprano Jessica Walker.

According to Miss Walker, 'The inescapable fact is that Kirkwood's first encounter with the Duke of Edinburgh, and six other meetings with him that followed, ruined her life and robbed her of official recognition in the Honours list, so they are crucial to any proper understanding of her character.' Pat Kirkwood was twice recommended for an OBE, but never received the honour. She certainly felt that the whispers about her and the Prince damaged her career as well as her reputation. She felt hounded by the press. She wrote to Buckingham Palace in sorrow and in anger: '. . . if there had been some support from your direction, the matter could have been squashed years ago, instead of (my) having to battle a sea of sharks single-handed'. Prince Philip's response was sympathetic, but to the point: 'Short of starting libel proceedings, there is absolutely nothing to be done. Invasion of privacy, invention and false quotations are the bane of our existence.'

'Actually, it's quite hateful,' Katie Boyle said to me. She was another celebrated beauty from the 1950s who was regularly mentioned in dispatches as one of Philip's flings. According to the book the Duke of Edinburgh brought to my attention, 'Philip's affair with Katie was very steamy. They had the most extraordinary times together.' On one occasion, claims author Nicholas Davies, when Katie Boyle – a blonde, glamorous, television personality, seven years the Duke's junior – 'entertained Philip at her London home, she received an urgent message that her husband had returned unexpectedly and was on his way home. Philip rapidly exited through the back entrance just as Katie's husband put his key in the front door.'

'Yes, I've met Prince Philip several times,' Katie Boyle told me, when I raised the story with her. 'I think he's the most fantastic man. I love his dryness. But an affair? It's ludicrous, pure fabrication. When it appears in print, people believe it. You can't take legal action because it fans the flames, so you just have to accept people telling complete lies about you.'

I knew Katie Boyle from childhood. I knew her quite well. I believed her completely. I believe Hélène Cordet, too.

In the 1950s in Britain, Hélène Cordet was celebrated, in a moderate way, as a cabaret artiste, television performer, and the hostess of a chic Mayfair nightclub, the Saddle Room in Hamilton Place. In the 1920s, in France, Hélène Foufounis, as she then was, and Prince Philip of Greece were childhood friends. The Foufounis family were Greeks in exile, royalist to the core, comfortably off, with a country house and farm near Marseilles and a seaside holiday home at Berck-Plage, near Le Touquet. Philip's mother and Madame Foufounis were friends; Philip's English nanny, Emily Roose, and the Foufounis's English nanny were allies. On holiday, in the country and at the seaside, Philip and the younger two of his elder sisters, Cécile and Sophie, played with Hélène and her brother, Iaini, and her sister, Ria. Apparently, Ria, an invalid, bedridden with a diseased hip, was especially fond of Philip. (I can believe it: I have seen a photograph taken of them together at Berck-Plage: she looks adoring, he looks adorable: he must have been about four at the time.) Hélène was four years older than Philip and, more than sixty years later, recalled, 'I was very jealous of him when he was a small boy. I don't think he disliked me as much as I disliked him, but my feelings were more jealousy than anything. Everyone adored him so much, particularly my mother, because he was so good-looking. My father had died when I was very small and I felt as if I wasn't loved by my stepfather, and was the least loved of all my family. So when this blond, blue-eyed, German-looking little boy came along, and my mother paid so much attention to him, I was livid. And he and my brother Iaini used to gang up on me.'

Philip and Hélène were childhood friends. They met again a few years later, in London, when Philip was fourteen or fifteen. Hélène's stepfather had died and the family fortune had taken a tumble, and she and her mother were living in a flat in Bayswater: 'I thought,

"Oh God!" He had been so beautiful as a child and now he was growing up. It gave me a bit of a shock.'

Hélène was growing up, too. Aged just twenty, she married her first husband, an Oxford undergraduate, William Kirby. The civil ceremony took place in Oxford, followed by a blessing at the Greek Orthodox Church in Bayswater, with Philip, aged sixteen, in attendance. According to Hélène, 'He was the best man *and* gave me away at my first wedding.' He also, apparently, trod on her veil. The marriage to William Kirby failed and the young Hélène sought consolation in the arms of a French airman, Marcel Boisot. Hélène and Marcel had two children: a son, Max, born in December 1943, and a daughter, Louise, born in February 1945, shortly after their marriage at Paddington Register Office the previous month. It is these two children that many of the rumour-mongers would have you believe were fathered by Prince Philip. (The rumour-mongers have even gone to the trouble of dating Philip's wartime shore leave to prove it might be possible.) Philip was godfather to both Max and Louise and, over the years, took an interest in them. He encouraged Hélène to send Max to Gordonstoun (rather than Winchester) and Hélène's grandson, named Philip, went to Gordonstoun, too.

Philip and Hélène were friends, not lovers. He was not the father of her children. The rumours started because, when Max was born, Hélène was still married to William Kirby, though they had lived apart for two years. At the time, no one knew about Marcel Boisot. Hélène allowed the paternity of her children to remain a mystery. Even in her memoir, *Born Bewildered*, published in 1961, years later, she does not name him. I got the impression (though she denied it) that Hélène Cordet (sometime Foufounis, Kirby, and Boisot) rather relished the *frisson* created by the rumours surrounding her friendship with Prince Philip. I also got the impression that Prince Philip thought so, too, and it irritated him. Hélène said that, when the rumours were at their height, she sought his advice about how best to handle the situation: 'It used to make me really mad, not so much for me, as for the Royal Family. It wasn't right, that chit-chat. So I said to Philip, "What do I do?" He said, "Look, if you like you can sue them, but I don't think it's worth it. On the contrary, it will just stir up more trouble."'

Is that, in fact, what I am doing now, stirring up more trouble, reheating old stories under the pretext of dismissing them, creating a whole new sensation while claiming to be throwing a wet blanket over old ones? I hope not, but I am aware of the risk. I am taking that risk, nonetheless, partly because I am interested in the phenomenon of how a raft of rumours without foundation can become immovably embedded in the public imagination; and partly, too, because I recognise that a general policy of *never* commenting, explaining or denying stories (which has much to commend it) can sometimes encourage even good people to think, perhaps, there is some truth in a lie. And now the man is dead, is there any harm in the whole truth being told? And what is 'the whole truth'? It is not easy to uncover.

For example, a few years ago, the writer Graham Lord published an entertaining and carefully researched biography of the actor David Niven. In the book he wrote that Niven, an occasional attendee at the Thursday Club gatherings, was 'very proud of his friendship with the Duke of Edinburgh'. Lord went on, 'According to actress Lauren Bacall, Niven and his Hollywood pal, Douglas Fairbanks Jr, lent themselves as "beards" to cover up the Duke's alleged dalliances in the early years of his marriage to the Queen. "Philip always had women," Bacall told me, "and they covered for him and pretended that his women were their women."' It simply is not true, though it may well be what Niven told Bacall at the time and the impression she gained on the few occasions in the late 1940s and early 1950s when there was a London show-business party and Philip was there.

In his book Graham Lord made something of the fact that he approached Buckingham Palace hoping to talk to Prince Philip about Niven and was rebuffed. Niven and the Duke were friends, insisted Lord. Prince Philip's secretary responded coolly that the Duke recalled meeting David Niven a couple of times. Lord then sought to establish the depth of the friendship by quoting a letter – brief but thoughtful – sent by the Duke of Edinburgh to Niven in the aftermath of the murder of Lord Mountbatten. The Duke's letter begins 'Dear David' and is signed 'Philip'. It is a courteous and friendly response to Niven's letter of condolence. It does not make the Duke of Edinburgh and David Niven bosom friends.

Lord may have thought that the Duke did not want to talk about his friendship with Niven because he had something to hide, because there was possibly some truth in Lauren Bacall's suggestion that Niven and Fairbanks Jr were the young Duke's 'beards'. If so, Lord misunderstood the situation and misread the Duke. Many did.

Prince Philip had the widest range of acquaintances imaginable: Nelson Mandela, the Pope, Frank Sinatra – he met them all. People in the armed services, in the Church, in the voluntary sector, in the entertainment business – industrialists, environmentalists, athletes, academics, politicians – year in year out, the Duke of Edinburgh was meeting, greeting, saluting, chatting to, talking with, encouraging, challenging, teasing, annoying, pleasing, all manner of men, women, and children. They *always* recollected meeting him, and remarkably, more often than might seem possible, he recalled meeting them – especially on second or third encounter; particularly if he had read about them or seen them on TV; notably, of course, if their particular occupation or achievement was in an area that already engaged him. He was affable and chatty, unselfconscious and at ease with himself. He was good (much better than the Queen) at picking up a conversation or a relationship at exactly the point where it was left off – whenever that was: a month, a year, even a decade ago. He was good at living in the moment, appearing (and being) interested in who you were and what you had to say. If he was concentrating, and giving you his full attention, he could establish a sense of intimacy that was deceptive.

Prince Philip was a great letter-writer. He told me he would never write an autobiography. 'Good God, no!' he said when I suggested it. I told him that he should publish a collection of his letters. 'That's a possibility, I suppose,' he said, without much conviction. 'I could edit it,' I volunteered. 'No doubt,' he said. I have quite a number of letters from him. They are addressed 'Dear Gyles' and signed 'Philip' and so – like his letter to David Niven – give an exaggerated impression of familiarity. As he had no surname, he had no choice but to sign his letters 'Philip'. As he was unstuffy, he addressed people he knew by their first name. He did have close friends – his first secretary, Mike Parker, was one; Sir Brian McGrath, his secretary from 1982 until the mid-nineties, was another; Lord Buxton of Alsa (television executive, conservationist, wildfowl enthusiast) a third – but David Niven was not one of them.

Like the Queen, the Duke of Edinburgh was remarkably self-contained. Unlike the Queen, he might have grumbled and growled, and occasionally snapped, but, like her, as a rule, he kept his true feelings under wraps. And, even with those with whom he was intimate, he was still guarded. Mike Parker told me, 'Philip did not discuss his feelings – at least, not with me. I certainly did not know about him and Princess Elizabeth until virtually the day of the engagement. He's not one to let it all hang out. That's not his style.'

In the public arena, the Prince Philip you would see – the outer man – was accessible (if a little forbidding), confident, bantering, outspoken. The private Prince Philip – the inner man – was infinitely more difficult to reach. He was, from all I saw myself and from what I heard from those who knew him well, more sensitive, more thoughtful, kinder, and more tolerant than the well-known caricature would suggest, but he kept these things hidden. His manner appeared open, but his instinct was watchful. Whoever you were, he did not let you get too close. I said as much to him once. He replied briefly, smiling a wintry smile, 'It's safer that way.'

The Duke of Edinburgh was careful of his reputation and conscious of his position, and of the responsibility that came with it. And he had been, from the day he married Princess Elizabeth. As I write, I am looking at a photograph, taken in 1948, at a Thursday Club cricket lunch: it is a picture of a dozen of the regular club members, some with wives or girlfriends, seated at a long table, out of doors, in the sunshine, waiting for lunch. It is an informal shot – we are among friends: there is laughter, joshing, David Milford Haven's dog, Simon, has his paws on the table – but one figure stands out from the crowd: in the centre of the picture sits the Duke of Edinburgh, just a tad more formal than the rest, looking straight at the camera, smiling, spruce, present and correct, knowing, in truth, that though this is just a snapshot, he is still the focus of attention.

In his diaries Kenneth Tynan gives an account of a memorable evening, in the mid-1960s, when, at his house, after dinner, by way of entertainment, he rigged up two screens 'to show some American experimental films simultaneously with outtakes from British nudipix (cf. scenes when the model accidentally dropped towel, bra or knickers) and Jean Genet's erotic film *Chant d'Amour*'. Tynan's guests that night included Peter Cook, the comedian, Harold Pinter, the playwright, and the Queen's sister, Princess Margaret, and her husband, Tony Snowdon. 'I had warned Tony that there would be some pretty blue material,' recalled Tynan, 'and he said, "It would be good for M."' At first, apparently, the nudie picture show went well – 'the English bits were amateurish and charming', according to Tynan, 'with odd flashes of nipple and pubic bush' – but when Genet's homo-erotic fantasy crackled into life 'the atmosphere began to freeze'. The 'unmistakable shots' of male members, many and various, in assorted states of arousal, rapidly brought a 'gelid silence' to the room: 'no one was laughing now'. Happily for Tynan, Peter Cook came to the rescue, by suddenly improvising a spurious commentary for the film, 'treating the movie as if it were a long commercial for Cadbury's Milk Flake Chocolate . . . Within five minutes we were all rocking with laughter, Princess M included.'[93] My point in relating this story is this: the Duke of Edinburgh would never have allowed himself (let alone his wife!) to have been put into a position like this. He was careful about where he went and what he did. Baron, and some of Baron's friends, might have had a darker side to them – a side that wasn't quite cricket – but, if they did, Philip never joined them there.

The Duke was no prude, but neither, in my experience, was he given to off-colour humour or lewd behaviour. More than once, I saw him, with a look or a raised eyebrow, silence someone, a little in their cups, who might have been on the edge of telling a story that went 'too far'. In several accounts of the Duke, I have read reports of him appreciatively eyeing up shapely women and simultaneously making suggestive remarks. In my experience, while he evidently enjoyed the company of good-looking women, his manners were impeccable. In the 1980s, when I was Appeals Chairman of the National Playing Fields Association, as fund-raisers we organised a number of royal charity evenings at the pantomime. After the show, backstage, I would escort Prince Philip along the line-up of charmingly shapely and scantily clad chorus girls. The Prince shook them

93 How times change. Kenneth Rose tells the story of Princess Margaret's grand-parents, George V and Queen Mary, staying with Lord Derby in 1921 and also being offered post-prandial cinematic entertainment. However, according to Rose, 'The royal party were spared the impropriety of watching a nature film in which a duck laid an egg. The egg episode was cut out.'

firmly by the hand and looked them only in the eye. More recently, at a Royal Variety Performance, while the Queen's equerry and I nudged each other knowingly and agreed that Jennifer Lopez was indeed a fine figure of a woman (petite but perfectly formed), the Duke of Edinburgh directed his small talk entirely at J-Lo's forehead. He was careful. He was no fool. And he was not interested in show-girls, actresses,[94] and starlets. On that, at least, Sarah Bradford and I were agreed.

I bring Sarah Bradford – Viscountess Bangor[95] – into the narrative at this point because, of all the more distinguished and reliable royal biographers, she is the only one who used to speak openly and without equivocation of 'the fact that Philip has not remained faithful' throughout his marriage. In the revised edition of her acclaimed biography of the Queen, published in 2002, she wrote of the royal couple: 'Theirs is a very royal marriage; Elizabeth's generation was not brought up to expect fidelity but loyalty. Affairs are one thing, passion another. Philip is not the man to fall hopelessly in love; his affairs make no difference to a marriage as firm and indeed fond as theirs.' Other royal biographers would hedge their bets and write of Philip's 'friendships with women' (Ben Pimlott) and 'supposed romances' (Robert Lacey); Sarah Bradford, alone, wrote boldly, baldly, of his 'affairs'.

Because Sarah Bradford's work is widely respected and carefully researched, when I was researching the first edition of this book, back in 2002, I went to see her, to discover why she was so uncom-promising in her assertion of Prince Philip's infidelity. We met on a winter's evening at her house in Fulham. She was open, friendly, and hospitable. By candlelight, over a glass of wine, she told me, 'There is no doubt in my mind at all. The Duke of Edinburgh has had affairs – yes, full-blown affairs and more than one. Not with Pat Kirkwood or Merle Oberon or any of those people. You're quite

94 One actress often mentioned in association with him (notably by *Private Eye*) is Anna Massey. It turns out that she met Philip just once, in the 1950s, when her uncle, Vincent Massey, was Governor-General of Canada.

95 Sarah Bradford, born 1938, married to the 8th Viscount Bangor, is an Oxford-educated historian who has written biographies of Cesare Borgia, Benjamin Disraeli, Sacheverell Sitwell, Princess Grace of Monaco, and Jaqueline Kennedy Onassis, as well as of the Queen and King George VI.

right, all that was nonsense, complete nonsense. I don't think there was ever anything in any of that. But he has affairs. And the Queen accepts it. I think she thinks that's how men are. He's never been one for chasing actresses. His interest is quite different. The women he goes for are always younger than him, usually beautiful, and highly aristocratic.' In her book Sarah Bradford put it like this: 'Philip has learned to carry on his flirtations and relationships in circles rich and grand enough to provide protection from the paparazzi and the tabloids.'

In her drawing room, as the candles spluttered, and her husband sat in the kitchen watching the early evening television news, Sarah Bradford recounted what clearly she believed was a telling story of a private party given in Scotland and attended by the Queen and Prince Philip. The Queen, apparently, was seated at a table by the dance floor, talking to friends about racing, but, as she talked, her watchful eyes were elsewhere, gazing across the dance floor, observing her husband as he danced very close – too close – to their hostess's daughter. 'Well,' I said (fully understanding for the first time why Philip pulled that face on his one night of dancing with Pat Kirkwood back in 1948), 'by all accounts he's a great dancer and the Queen is the Queen – she can't really get up and dance as he might. I think we can excuse – even understand – a little light flirtation with the hostess's daughter on the dance floor.' Sarah Bradford did not agree. 'I wouldn't like it if William [Viscount Bangor] behaved like that,' she said.

I told Sarah Bradford that one of the reasons I admired her books was because of the amount of authenticated detail she provides. I asked her, if she was so certain about these 'affairs', why she had not named any names in her book. 'I wanted to give an accurate picture without hurting people,' she said, reasonably enough. The problem, of course, is this: if you make a highly charged assertion, but do not back it up with evidence, or give your sources, or name the names of any of those who might be involved, it is very difficult to make your assertion stand up. I told Sarah Bradford I was trying to get to the bottom of the raft of rumours about Prince Philip and his love life – to either establish them as fact or scotch them once and for all. 'How do you know you are right about this?' I asked her. 'I do know,' she said, smiling. 'Believe me.' 'Who are these women?' I persisted. 'You know you they are,' she said. 'They're the ones people talk about.' 'You mean, women like Sacha Abercorn,' I suggested. 'Yes,' said Sarah Bradford, putting down her wine glass. 'She is certainly one of them. Philip and Sacha Abercorn certainly had an affair. Without a doubt.'

My reporting this conversation in the first edition of my book infuriated Sarah Bradford. There was evidently a misunderstanding. I had gone to her house, notebook in hand, to interview her. She, it transpired, thought I had gone for an off-the-record briefing. She considered my behaviour underhand and unprofessional – the behaviour, as she put it, of 'a creep'.

I was sorry to have caused her distress, but I did not feel too guilty about it. She, after all, was the author who had told the world in her best-selling biography of the Queen that the Duke of Edinburgh was unfaithful. It was quite an accusation to make – and, coming from Sarah Bradford, an author with authority, it was an accusation that was taken seriously and consequently caused distress to both the Queen and Prince Philip. Sarah Bradford made the charge in public, in print, and without equivocation. As an admirer, ally, and biographer of Prince Philip, I felt justified in challenging her face to face and in publishing the account of our encounter.

Happily, Sarah Bradford and I met again more recently, in 2019, at the home of mutual friends. We shook hands and agreed to let bygones be bygones. I was pleased to do so because in the intervening years Sarah Bradford had changed her mind about Prince Philip. He was no longer a philanderer. It appears her original accusation was misplaced. She got it wrong. She was misinformed.

In June 2011, at the time of Prince Philip's ninetieth birthday, Sarah Bradford explained to the journalist John McEntee, 'I was told a lot of things by people who should have known better. I now don't believe he was unfaithful. He hasn't got that sort of temperament. He does like women and you can see his reaction to someone like Carla Sarkozy [the Italian-born wife of the then French president]. I was told about these affairs by people who should know better.'

Whatever Sarah Bradford's view of me, I am grateful to her. As a direct consequence of our candle-lit conversation on that winter's night all those years ago I went to meet one of those alleged mistresses

Sarah Bradford and I had discussed. In doing so, I believe, I came as close as we will ever be to the truth of Prince Philip's special relationship with the women who were not his wife.

Sacha Abercorn, who died in 2018, was tall, slim, and striking. She was quietly spoken: intelligent, articulate, and thoughtful. She was born in 1946, the daughter of Lieutenant Colonel Harold Pedro Joseph Phillips (known as 'Bunnie', a friend of Dickie Mountbatten, and sometime lover of Edwina) and Georgina Wernher (later, of course, Lady Kennard, known to friends as 'Gina' and to Prince Philip, when they were children, as 'George'). Sacha was christened Alexandra Anastasia – her Russian heritage was important to her. Her mother's mother was Zia Wernher, married to Sir Harold Wernher, but born Countess Anastasia Mikhailovna, elder daughter of His Imperial Highness Grand Duke Mikhail Mikhailovich, the grandson of Tsar Nicholas I.

When I went to see Sacha Abercorn she gave me a copy of *Feather from the Firebird*, a collection of her 'prose poems', published by the Summer Palace Press in County Donegal in 2003. The poems are short, powerfully felt, highly evocative, and beautifully observed. Many of them feel autobiographical, coded tributes to people she had known and loved and lost: her younger brother, Nicholas, who committed suicide in 1991, her father, who died in 1980, her father's friend, Lord Mountbatten, murdered in Ireland by the IRA in 1979. The 'biographical note' in the book reads in full: 'Sacha Abercorn is the founder of the Pushkin Prizes Trust. She received an Honorary Doctorate from the University of Ulster in 2003. She is a descendant of the Romanovs and of Alexander Pushkin, the great Russian poet.' Her husband was James, 5th Duke of Abercorn, twelve years her senior, an officer in the Grenadier Guards, briefly an Ulster Unionist MP, and for fifty years a force for good and a power to reckon with in the social and economic life of Northern Ireland. The Abercorns' family home (since 1612) in Omagh, County Tyrone, is called Baronscourt[96] – a very different milieu from the Baron's Court that surrounded Prince Philip's photographer friend Baron, the founder of the Thursday Club.

---

96 'Through hills at the foot of Bessy Bell . . . we come to Baronscourt, Lord Abercorn's magnificent seat . . . the great number of fine oaks and three long lakes which ornament this place give it an air of great grandeur.' Daniel Beaufort (1739–1821).

When I arrived to talk to Sacha Abercorn at her London mews house, near Victoria Station, a stone's throw from Buckingham Palace, she was just back from a trip to Russia. She was in happy form, fielding telephone calls from her mother and her daughter while making me tea. We moved from the kitchen to the drawing room and, sat, facing each other, perched on the edge of sofas. Notebook and pen in hand, I asked her when she first remembered meeting the Queen and Prince Philip.

'When I was a child,' she said. 'I must have been eight or nine. It was in the 1950s. We lived in Leicestershire, at Thorpe Lubenham, and they came to stay. They came with Charles and Anne, who were a bit younger than us. What do I remember best? I think the fun we all had – so much fun. The adults and the children all playing together. I remember dressing up as monsters. I remember huge bonfires and cooking potatoes in the ashes.

'In the evening, indoors, in the dark, after tea, we played a wonderful game called Stone. Do you know it? All the lights are turned out – you are in total darkness. Someone is chosen to be "He" and, in the darkness, when you are touched by "He" you have to stand absolutely still – like stone. There was fear and fun. It was fantastic. The Queen and Prince Philip loved it. They used to play it at Balmoral – all the grown-ups.' Sacha laughed, and covered her mouth with her hand, then said, 'I shouldn't tell you this, but once, my father was "He" and, in the dark, he felt this figure hidden behind the curtains – and then the Queen giggled and he realised who it was. Can you imagine? The Queen hiding behind the curtains and my father feeling her up and down?' I asked Sacha how the Queen and Prince Philip seemed to relate to their own children. 'Then?' she asked. 'Yes,' I said. 'Really well. Really, really well. Philip was wonderful. I remember how he used to help Charles with his Go-Kart. And he used to tell them stories that he'd invented. I can't recall any gruff words – ever. Or any tension. I would go with my parents to Balmoral and their children would be there, too. It was always fun and jolly. I loved the picnics. They were good times. I remember, once, in the stables, there was a dog fight and the Queen arrived and calmed it immediately. She's intrepid. She doesn't get thrown by things. They were good times for us and, I think, good times for them – human times, filled with good humour. They don't get that much time off, you know. The heavy duty is relentless.'

I asked Sacha how she had got to know Prince Philip, not as a family friend of her parents but as a personal friend of her own. She smiled and sat back and thought for a moment. 'I remember going to Cowes one year,' she said. 'My parents were going to go, but my father had cancer and couldn't come, so I went on my own.'

Cowes, on the north coast of the Isle of Wight, is the headquarters of the Royal Yacht Squadron (founded 1812) and home of the annual Cowes Week yachting regatta, held every August. In 1947 the Island Sailing Club of Cowes gave Philip and Princess Elizabeth a Dragon-class yacht as a wedding present. It was painted dark blue and Philip named it *Bluebottle*. For several years he sailed her competitively in Cowes Week, with a regular crew that included the larger-than-life local character, yachtsman, and boat-builder Uffa Fox. Fox and Philip became firm friends. Fox persuaded the people of Cowes to give Philip one of the first of the small Flying Fifteen yachts, which Fox designed and Philip christened *Coweslip*. Probably the best known of Philip's yachts was *Bloodhound*, a pre-war, twelve-metre yacht designed for ocean racing. He raced her at Cowes and, for several years, cruised the west coast of Scotland in her with Prince Charles and Princess Anne. He ended his years of competitive sailing in a series of yachts called *Yeoman*, all owned by another friend and fellow sailing enthusiast, Sir Owen Aisher, founder of Marley Tiles and 'Yachtsman of the Year, 1958'. While Queen Victoria's favourite home was Osborne House in East Cowes, as a rule Queen Elizabeth did not accompany Prince Philip to Cowes Week.

'It was the chaps who did the sailing,' Sacha Abercorn explained. 'I think the girls were there to have fun. It was great fun. All the secretaries from his office were there. And I remember Princess Anne and myself, dressed up as serving wenches. It was hilarious. I remember Uffa Fox telling stories – telling, endless, endless stories. I suppose I was seventeen or eighteen, in that funny in-between world.

'And then I got married – at twenty – in 1966. The Queen and Prince Philip came to the wedding. Oh, yes, everyone was there. They all rolled up. It was extraordinary. It was in Westminster Abbey. It really was amazing. And then we would see them, now and again, at weekends, particularly in November, when they came to Luton

Hoo.[97] My grandparents were there, and uncles and aunts. And the Brabournes. There were ten or twelve in the house party. There was shooting as usual and then, in the evening, some great entertainment. I remember Victor Borge particularly. And I remember the dinners – my grandmother being bossy, my grandfather bringing his heart and soul with him. The talk was always interesting. I remember my grandfather talking, and Prince Philip. I remember when they spoke, they took it in turns, they gave each other time, and we gave them full-blast attention. It was good.

'But it was later that we became close. I think it was at The Gables – when Nicky was running the shoots – that we particularly got interested in each other. What brought us together? Jung. Yes, Jung. I've always been interested in Jung, his work, his ideas. And Philip is interested in Jung. Prince Philip is always questing, exploring, searching for meaning, testing ideas. We had riveting conversations about Jung. That's where our friendship began.'

The Duke of Edinburgh was not the caricature to which all became accustomed. He was fascinated by Carl Gustav Jung (1875–1961), the great Swiss psychoanalyst, who eschewed Freud's obsession with sex and the power of the sexual impulse, and focused instead on what he termed the inherited 'collective unconscious' with its universal ideas or images: the 'archetypes'. Jung wrote on subjects as diverse as nature, mythology, and religion – subjects of deep interest to the Duke of Edinburgh. Philip read Jung, T.S. Eliot, Shakespeare, the Bible. From the 1950s his interest in psychology, philosophy, and religion developed and deepened, and became increasingly intermeshed with his concern for the natural world and the environment.

---

97   One mile south of Luton in Bedfordshire. Set in a thousand acres of parkland (laid out by Capability Brown), the original house, built by Robert Adam in 1767, was destroyed by fire in 1843, rebuilt, and bought by Sacha's great-grandfather, Julius Wernher, in 1903. Wernher was a railway engineer's son who made his fortune as a young man in the South African diamond rush of the 1870s and used it to acquire Luton Hoo, decorate it in lavish French style, and fill it (to bursting) with jewelry, porcelain, paintings, and *objets d'art*. Julius's son, Harold (1893–1973), added to the collection, the best of which is now on public display (loaned to the British people for 125 years) at the Ranger's House in Greenwich Park. Luton Hoo itself is now a luxury hotel: you can sleep where the Queen slept. For further details see www.lutonhoo.co.uk.

Philip's interest in life's spiritual dimension was given additional focus in 1962, with the appointment of Robin Woods as 'Dean of Windsor, Domestic Chaplain to the Queen and Register of the Most Noble Order of the Garter'. Woods (son of a bishop; chaplain to the forces, mentioned in dispatches, 1944; 'interests: sailing, shooting, painting') and Philip became friends. With the Duke's active support and involvement, Woods developed St George's House at Windsor as a training college for clergy and a conference centre where clergy and laity could meet to explore issues and ideas. St George's held its first weekend 'consultation' in October 1966. The theme: 'The Role of the Church in Society Today'. In 1970 Woods moved on from Windsor to become Bishop of Worcester. Philip wrote to him: 'It has been simply marvellous having you at Windsor and your help and guidance for us and for our children has been invaluable.' Woods paid tribute to Philip as a 'man I had come to respect very deeply, not only for the integrity of his religion but for his ability to judge men and situations'.

As Dean of Windsor, Woods was succeeded, briefly, by Launcelot Fleming, sometime Antarctic explorer and Bishop of Norwich, and then, in 1976, by Michael Mann, whose background, in several respects, echoed that of Woods (he, too, had been mentioned in dispatches) and whose education – at Harrow, Sandhurst, Wells Theological College, and Harvard Business School – and range of experience – as an officer in the King's Dragoon Guards during the war, as a colonial administrator in Nigeria for nine years before his ordination in 1957 – made him a figure Philip could reckon with and relate to.

Together the Duke of Edinburgh and Michael Mann embarked on a series of intellectual and philosophical adventures, and their collaboration and friendship led to the publication of three books. The first, *A Windsor Correspondence*, is simply an exchange of letters, between Duke and Dean, sparked by a lecture given by the astronomer Fred Hoyle entitled 'Evolution from Space'. The themes they touch on are science and Christianity, fundamentalism, evolution, and morality. The second is *A Question of Balance*, which explores 'the crucial part that human nature plays in every aspect of communal life'. The Duke evidently had reservations about some of what the Church of England gets up to, but his conclusion was clear: 'religious conviction is the strongest and probably the only factor in sustaining the dignity and integrity of the individual.' The third book is *Survival or Extinction: A Christian Attitude to the Environment*.[98] In 1986 the twenty-fifth anniversary of the World Wide Fund for Nature was celebrated with a conference held, at the Duke's suggestion, at Assisi, in Umbria, home of St Francis, patron saint of birds and animals. The aim was to forge 'a permanent alliance between conservation and religion'. By all accounts, the Buddhists stole the show, but, at the end of the conference, Hindus, Muslims, Jews, and Christians each issued 'Declarations on Nature'. The World Wide Fund was later appointed 'consultant to the Roman Catholic Church in programmes related to nature conservation' and the Duke went to Rome for a private audience with His Holiness Pope John Paul II. In *Survival or Extinction* the Duke and Michael Mann explore some of the themes touched on at the Assisi conference. The book also distils thoughts and ideas contributed at seven separate 'consultations' held at St George's House and includes a list of the various participants, beginning with 'Her Grace the Duchess of Abercorn, Counsellor in Transpersonal Psychology'.

Sacha Abercorn poured me another cup of tea and continued with her story. 'It began with Jung,' she said. 'Philip was having these consultations at Windsor, and he said, "Could you get some of your Jung people to come along?" And I did. These consultations went on for three years. Michael Mann was very involved and, between them, they brought together a really interesting pool of thought.' Sacha sat forward on her sofa and said, with feeling, 'Prince Philip cares about the environment. He has a feeling for nature – in a practical way. He is totally a sentient human being – in a practical way. I saw that at first hand when we travelled with him several times on *Britannia* – James and myself, Aubrey Buxton and Kay [his second wife]. We went to Borneo, Sarawak, the Galápagos. Philip's feeling for the environment is not sentimental – not sentimental at all. It's emotional and practical.

'He's always asking questions, searching for answers. I think it was

98 These three books, published by Michael Russell in the 1980s, give a useful insight into the Duke's way of thinking. The other books of which he is author reflect the range of his enthusiasms, from *Birds from Britannia* (Longman, 1962) to *Competition Carriage Driving* (Horse Drawn Carriages Ltd, 1982).

at Lubenham, and my mother and he were walking back to the house from church, and she said something like, "I don't believe in anything." That made him stop, suddenly, and ask out loud, "What is it? What's behind it all?" He asks the difficult questions and that's what drew me to him. I remember, in the 1980s sometime, we were staying at Windsor for Royal Ascot, and I had just discovered Anthony Stevens's book *Archetypes*[99] and I told Prince Philip about it and he was riveted. Riveted. We both were. One of the things that Stevens writes about is left-brain/right-brain theory. [In a nutshell, the left hemisphere of the brain controls logic and language: the right controls creativity and intuition.] People think of Philip as being "left-brain", but he is so full of "right-brain". Yes, he is practical, unsentimental and logical, but he is also emotional and intuitive. He is deeply sensitive. Deeply sensitive. His senses are so super-charged.'

Sacha was sitting forward now, smiling, her eyes shining. 'Our friendship was very close. The heart came into it in a big way. There's a hugely potent chemical reaction in him. It's a highly charged chemistry. We were close because we understood one another. He felt he could trust me and I felt I could trust him.'

Silence fell in the little drawing room and the tea had gone cold. 'In Eluthera,' I said – the Abercorns have a beautiful holiday home on the island of Eluthera in the Bahamas – 'In Eluthera, someone told me they had seen you and Prince Philip on the beach holding hands.'

Sacha smiled and said, without any awkwardness, 'It was a passionate friendship, but the passion was in the ideas. It was certainly not a full relationship. I did not go to bed with him. It probably looked like that to the world. I can understand why people might have thought it, but it didn't happen. It wasn't like that. He isn't like that. It's complicated and, at the same time, it's quite simple. He needs a playmate and someone to share his intellectual pursuits.'

99 *Archetypes: A Natural History of the Self*, 1982. Stevens, a British Jungian with thirty years' experience as a practising psychiatrist, used the book to explore ways in which 'the archaic' influences our lives in fundamental areas – e.g. the development of attachment bonds, the maintenance of group solidarity, the contribution of myth, ritual, and religion to the development of personality. He also began to link basic Jungian concepts with the structural elements of the brain. In 2003 he published *Archetype Revisited: An Updated Natural History of the Self*, described by one admiring reviewer as 'the overdue marriage of Darwin and Jung'.

'Do you think he sleeps with his other playmates?' I asked.

'I doubt it, I doubt it very much.' Sacha paused and thought a moment and said, 'No, I'm sure not. But he's a human being. Who knows? I don't. Unless you are in the room with a lighted candle, who knows?'

'And what about the Queen?' I asked.

Sacha smiled and said, 'She gives him a lot of leeway. Her father told her, "Remember, he's a sailor. They come in on the tide."'

'Do you see much of him nowadays?' I asked, as Sacha began to stack up the tea things and I put my pen and notebook away.

'Not really. He used to come to Eluthera. And he'd come carriage driving at Baronscourt with Penny [Romsey], but we've stopped having the carriage driving. It was too expensive. I am sorry I don't see him properly any more. Really sorry. He is a very special man.'

As I walked away from Sacha's house, along Buckingham Palace Road, over Grosvenor Place, past the Royal Mews, I thought back on what she had told me – and the way she had told it to me: easily, fluently, without any sense of defensiveness or artifice – and I said to myself, 'Yes, that's it. That is all we need to know. It makes sense.'

It makes sense of the story told, nearly fifty years after the event, by Norman Barson, a royal footman, a former Grenadier guardsman, who worked for Philip and Princess Elizabeth at Windlesham Moor, the house, near Ascot, that was their weekend home at the beginning of their marriage. According to Barson, Philip would visit Windlesham Moor midweek, usually on a Tuesday or a Wednesday, early in the evening, and he would come, driving himself in his beloved MG convertible, accompanied by a young lady who was not the Princess. She was young, slim, pretty, well spoken. Philip made no secret of the visits. He telephoned in advance to say he was coming. Barson prepared them beef sandwiches and gin and orange. 'He always poured the lady's drink,' said the footman. 'He hardly drank at all. I could later hear them laughing and joking, but I never once heard him refer to her by name ... I never saw them kiss or canoodle. I remember thinking he acted exactly the same with her as with the Queen. He was charming to both of them. He stared into their eyes with his head on one side and made them laugh.'

It makes sense of Sir Angus Ogilvy – the delightful husband of Princess Alexandra, granddaughter of George V, fifteen years Philip's junior and long reported as one of the Prince's 'romantic interests' – coming up to me at a party (at the London home of the newspaper publisher Conrad Black – not long before his imprisonment) and congratulating me on an article I had written about the Duke of Edinburgh. Ogilvy, who died in 2004, aged seventy-six, must have known what people used to whisper about his wife and the Duke, but it did not trouble him because he understood the Duke and the nature of the Duke's relationship with his women friends. Sir Angus said to me, 'Prince Philip's a good man, a really good man, hopelessly misreported, misrepresented, and misunderstood.' The Queen appointed Princess Alexandra as one of only a tiny handful of Lady Companions of the Order of the Garter in 2003.

It makes sense of Penny Romsey. Dr Johnson once said, 'If I had no duties, and no reference to futurity, I would spend my life in driving briskly in a post-chaise with a pretty woman.' The Duke of Edinburgh had duties, and an eye to the future, but nevertheless he was wholly at ease carriage driving with Penny Romsey, thirty years his junior, because he knew that the Queen knew that Penny was his playmate, not his mistress.

I think the Queen wanted us to know it, too. Her Majesty used to make a point of being on parade to cheer her husband and his carriage-driving companion as they took part in competitions. And memorably, one Saturday evening, on a day when the *Daily Mail* had carried photographs of her husband and his friend at a carriage-driving event – photographs with captions dripping with innuendo – the Queen said to Penny Romsey, who was staying for the weekend, 'Penny, are you planning to go to church in the morning? If you are, would you like to come to church with me?' The Queen was ready to send out a signal to the world that she was happy to be pictured on her way to church with her husband's much younger friend. She was, and is, the Queen's friend, too, of course.

Penny Romsey, the daughter of a butcher who made his fortune as founder of the Angus Steak House chain, married Dickie Mountbatten's grandson, Norton, in 1979. The Romseys have two children, Nicholas and Alexandra. Nicholas, who is one of Prince Charles's godsons, has struggled with drug addiction. The Romseys had another daughter, a little girl called Leonora, who died of cancer in 1991, aged five. I recall having lunch with Prince Philip one day in 2003 (it was a fund-raiser for the Playing Fields Association, held in the Cabinet War Rooms) and he told me that in the evening he was going to the theatre, to Drury Lane, to see *Anything Goes*, with the Queen and Lord and Lady Romsey. These people were kith and kin, cousins as well as friends.

At the start of 1996 there was a brief outburst of media frenzy when a hospital worker surfaced with a tape of a seventeen-minute late-night telephone conversation between Prince Philip and an unnamed woman. Using a simple £200 scanner the hospital worker had inadvertently intercepted a mobile call from Sandringham House and, somehow, a transcript of the 2,200-word exchange between the Queen's husband and an unknown confidante fell into a newspaper's hands. Who was Philip calling? *Cherchez la femme!* Given the clues in the conversation, she was both posh and horsey, and someone who could make His Royal Highness laugh. She was comfortable calling Charles and Diana – and Camilla – by their Christian names and chatting about the operation on the Queen Mother's hip. The lucky lady was also due to be the recipient of a present from Prince Philip that he wanted her to be sure to unwrap in her bedroom . . . Speculation was rife. Was the lady Sacha Abercorn? Or was she another aristocratic lovely in her forties, Grania, wife of Hugh, Baron Cavendish of Furness, Conservative politician, owner of Holker Hall, and third in line to the Dukedom of Devonshire? It transpired that the lady on the line was none other than Penny Romsey, that the Prince was suggesting she open her Christmas present out of sight of the servants, and that as well as talking to his carriage-driving companion, during the call His Royal Highness also chatted with her husband. The tape was duly handed over to Farrer & Co, the Queen's solicitors, and destroyed, but not before the press had enjoyed a few happy days fanning the flames of gossip and innuendo.

Penny Romsey's mother-in-law, Countess Mountbatten, said to me at the time, 'Philip is a man who enjoys the company of attractive, intelligent younger women. Nothing wrong in that. He's always had somebody there, sharing one or other of his particular pursuits. He has special friends, like Penny. But I am quite sure – quite sure – absolutely certain – he has never been unfaithful to the Queen.'

Eventually Penny Romsey's marriage foundered – but no one

suggested that the Duke of Edinburgh was to blame. In September 2005 Penny's father-in-law, John Brabourne died, aged eighty, and her husband succeeded to the family title as 8th Baron Brabourne. In August 2010 Penny Brabourne gathered together the staff at Broadlands to tell them her husband had flown the nest – and moved to the Bahamas to start a new life with a new companion. Lady Brabourne promised to stay put and manage the family estate. She was not going to leave Broadlands; apart from anything else, her daughter was buried in the grounds. Her husband, it seems, had one of those crises that afflict some men as they turn sixty, not long after a parent dies. In due course he came back from the Bahamas, without his mistress. Then he and his mistress appeared together in London, apparently reconciled. 'It was all rather confusing,' said his mother, 'and sad.' Penny Brabourne, however, showed her mettle and stuck to her last. In 2011, in the absence of her husband, she took over the four-hundred-year-old office of High Steward of Romsey. In 2014 Norton Brabourne returned to live in a converted barn on the family estate. In June 2017, when Patricia Mountbatten died, he succeeded as the new Earl Mountbatten of Burma and attended his mother's funeral with his stoical wife, now the new Countess Mountbatten at his side.

The Queen and Prince Philip were saddened by the failure of Norton and Penny's marriage. Philip was Norton's godfather, as well as Penny's carriage-driving companion. But as the Duke of Edinburgh put it to me once, 'All families have their ups and downs. That's life.'

The Queen is not much interested in gossip, nor swayed by it. She remained on good terms with her brother-in-law, Tony Snowdon, despite the collapse of his marriage to Princess Margaret and lurid reports of the vagaries of his private life – including the suicide of one of his mistresses and the birth of at least one illegitimate child. 'The Queen and Prince Philip have always been marvellous,' Lord Snowdon told me, 'understanding in every way and not in the least judgemental.' To prove his point, he showed me notes and Christmas cards sent to him from them and always signed 'with love'. When he died in 2017, almost forty years after his divorce from Princess Margaret, both the Queen and Prince Philip attended his memorial service at St. Margaret's, Westminster.

And the Queen maintains her friendship with the Abercorns, too, regardless of the stories about Philip and Sacha. In 1999 James Abercorn became a Knight of the Garter. In June 2011, as Prince Philip turned ninety, the Duke of Abercorn accompanied the Duke of Edinburgh and the Queen in their carriage to Royal Ascot. In October 2012 the Queen appointed James Abercorn Chancellor of the Order of the Garter.[100] (Sacha Abercorn's younger sister, Natalia Ayesha, known as Tally, was married to Gerald, 6th Duke of Westminster, who, as we have seen, became a Knight of the Garter in 2003, notwithstanding the stories about *him*.)

In 2004, when the earlier version of this book was serialised, my account of the friendship between the Duke of Edinburgh and the Duchess of Abercorn became front-page news. Sacha later wrote to me from Baronscourt: 'In their usual manner, the media proceeded to quote things out of context, misconstrue meanings and traffic in innuendo.' On the day of the serialisation, she telephoned me from Northern Ireland to say, 'It's fine.' The call was a kindness on her part because I felt uncomfortable that what I had written had prompted headlines around the world. I said I hoped that it was not going to cause her terrible problems vis-à-vis the Queen and Prince Philip. 'No,' she said. 'We have had a call from Balmoral. They are due to come over here next week. They're still coming.'

The Queen's press secretary at the time, Penny Russell-Smith, wrote to me from Buckingham Palace: 'The tabloids have predictably focussed on the Duchess of Abercorn's comments on her friendship with Prince Philip. These days, few columnists seem to believe in platonic friendship!'

Now that Prince Philip is dead, it is possible that some secret scandal will be revealed, but I doubt it. I believe in the story told

---

100 As well as being 5th Duke of Abercorn, he is also 6th Marquess of Abercorn, 5th Marquess of Hamilton, 14th Earl of Abercorn, 9th Viscount Strabane, 7th Viscount Hamilton, 14th Lord Paisley, 14th Lord Abercorn, 14th Lord Paisley, Hamilton, Mountcashell and Kirkpatrick, 13th Lord Hamilton of Strabane, 9th Baron Mountcastle. His father, the 4th Duke of Abercorn, was the brother of Cynthia, who became Countess Spencer and the grandmother of Diana Spencer, later Princess of Wales, so he is also a cousin of Prince William, Duke of Cambridge, who became a Knight of the Garter in June 2008, becoming the thousandth knight in the register.

by the Countess of Westmoreland's daughter of the girl who 'swore that when in her teens she used to lie in the same bed with Prince Philip, a bolster between them. They would talk for hours. She was much in love with him. He would not transgress the bolster.' I believe the testimony of the Duchess of Abercorn.

That said, the question remains: what lay at the root of these passionate platonic friendships of Prince Philip's, these unconsummated *amitiés amoureuses*? Countess Mountbatten – Philip's first cousin and Penny Brabourne's mother-in-law – would say it was the old 'Mountbatten energy', that Philip was like his Uncle Dickie: a dynamo who needed the occasional confidential companionship of a sparky, larky girl who was flattering, intelligent, and fun. A respected Freudian analyst (like his Uncle George's wife, Princess Marie Bonaparte, or my friend Brett Kahr) would say that he was recreating what he had – and loved and lost – in early childhood: the company of adoring girls, devoted playmates like his four elder sisters or the Foufounis girls. A wise young woman, born in 1981, would say that these friendships are what kept him young. Jessica Hay used to go out with Nicholas Knatchbull, the Romseys' only son, and, when she was still a teenager, she stayed at Broadlands for a weekend shoot. 'The Queen's a fantastic shot,' she recalled. 'She shot more partridge than anyone else that day. At one point my trousers got caught as I climbed over a stile and I got stuck. Everyone had gone but Philip. He came back and helped me. Then he said, "What am I going to get in return?" He's got a twinkle in his eye. He knows he won't get the younger women, but I think the flirting keeps him young.' At dinner Jessica sat next to Philip. 'I wouldn't call the royals affectionate,' she said, 'but they are very thoughtful towards one another. At dinner Prince Philip would always check that the Queen was all right, although you still got the sense that she is the one in control of their relationship.'

The Duke of Edinburgh spent a lifetime being talked about and being misunderstood. He knew it. 'I've just go to live with it,' he said to me, 'It happens to a lot of people.' It happened to Charles Dodgson – the Victorian writer Lewis Carroll, creator of Alice in Wonderland. Dodgson had many girlfriends: children and young women who were his playmates, his special friends. In 1893 his sister, Mary, wrote to him about the gossip that was attached to these relationships. On 21 September that year he replied to her, 'You need not be shocked at my being spoken against. *Any*body who is spoken about at all, is *sure* to be spoken against by *somebody*: and any action, however innocent in itself, is liable, and not at all unlikely, to be blamed by *somebody*. If you limit your actions in life to things that *nobody* can possibly find fault with, you will not do much!' (I am surprised he did not run to a double exclamation mark.) Lewis Carroll told his sister that as a result of his experience he was convinced 'that the opinion of "people" in general is absolutely worthless as a test of right and wrong'. He said that, for him, there were only two tests when 'having some particular girl-friend as a guest': did he have her family's '*full* approval for what I do'? And did he 'feel it to be entirely innocent and right in the sight of God'? Lewis Carroll told his sister his conscience was clear. The Duke of Edinburgh's conscience was clear, also.

And how about the Queen? How did she feel about all this in the dark watches of the night? She could not say, fully, freely, as Robert Browning said in his poem 'By the Fireside': 'We stood there with never a third.' But Robert Browning was a sentimentalist, which the Queen is not. She knew her husband. She loved, admired him, and accepted him as he was. She is also Sovereign of the Order of the Garter. *Honi soit qui mal y pense.*

Chapter Twelve

'Children begin by loving their parents. After a time, they judge them. Rarely, if ever, do they forgive them.'

Oscar Wilde (1856–1900), *A Woman of No Importance*

Dr Johnson was characteristically clear-cut in his advice to those about to embark on matrimony. 'Now that you are going to marry,' he said, 'do not expect more from life than life can afford.' His definition of the family was to the point, as well: 'A family is a little kingdom, torn into factions and exposed to revolutions.'

Princess Elizabeth, in fact, was brought up within a family unit that was small, close-knit, loving, and giving – 'us four' as George VI put it. Elizabeth was an adorable child: she was adored by both her grandfathers, and adored them in return. George V died, aged seventy, in 1936, when Elizabeth was ten; 'Grandfather Strathmore', the 14th Earl, died eight years later, in 1944, aged eighty-nine. 'Grandma Strathmore' died suddenly, in the summer of 1938, aged sixty-five. Her daughter, Queen Elizabeth, wrote to the Prime Minister, Neville Chamberlain:

'I have been dreading this moment ever since I was a little girl and now that it has come, one can hardly believe it. She was a true "Rock of Defence" for us, her children, & Thank God, her influence and wonderful example will remain with us all our lives.

'She had a good perspective of life – everything was given its *true* importance. She had a young spirit, great courage and unending sympathy whenever and wherever it was needed, & such a heavenly sense of humour. We all used to laugh together and have such fun.'

George VI died in February 1952, aged only fifty-six, followed to the family mausoleum within fourteen months by his mother, Queen Mary, aged eighty-five, formidable and forbidding in appearance, frail and in pain at the end, heartbroken by her second son's early death. In the year of her Coronation, the new young Queen, at the age of twenty-six, was left with just two of her immediate family: her mother, then aged only fifty-two, and her sister, aged twenty-two. Happily, both lived on for almost half a century more.

Elizabeth II had a good relationship with her mother – 'loving and normal' is how Margaret Rhodes described it to me. Queen Elizabeth the Queen Mother was blessed with many of the virtues she recognised in her own mother: a good perspective of life, a young spirit, a heavenly sense of humour. Elizabeth II loved her mother, respected her, liked her. Yes, the Queen did occasionally shake her head when contemplating her mother's insouciant extravagance. At the time of her death, Queen Elizabeth's overdraft at Coutts was reported to be in the region of £4 million. She was supposed to have said at a dinner party once, 'Golly, I could do with £100,000, couldn't you? Had such an awful afternoon today with my bank manager scolding me about my overdraft.' Yes, the Queen might, now and again, express an envy of her mother's extraordinary capacity for avoiding all unpleasantness, but, fundamentally, mother and daughter were good friends, on the same wavelength, with mutual interests (especially horses), comfortable in each other's company, each looking forward to their regular, easy, uncomplicated chats on the telephone. Prince Philip said to me once, eyebrows raised in amazement, 'They're always on the phone!'

The Queen recognised her mother's special star quality and had no desire to compete with her. Queen Elizabeth recognised her daughter as an exemplary sovereign and was always careful to show due deference. On the occasions when she momentarily forgot herself – stepping through a doorway ahead of the Queen, for example – she was always quick to apologise. Margaret Rhodes's description of the Queen coming by to have a drink with Queen Elizabeth on a Sunday morning after church would be the envy of many a mother and daughter. 'There was mutual respect and deep affection,' said Mrs Rhodes, 'but, most of all, they just got on really, really well.'

Mrs Rhodes's description of the Queen's relationship with Princess Margaret is less dewy-eyed. 'The Queen was sometimes infuriated by Margaret, inevitably,' she told me. 'She found her behaviour exasperating at times, of course she did. But Margaret was her sister and she loved her.'

From all the people I have spoken with who are close to the Queen – courtiers, friends, and family members – I get the impression of someone who, though conservative by upbringing and conventional in her own life, is not judgemental when it comes to others. She looks for the best in people and hopes for the best from them and for them. When things go wrong, she prays (on her knees, with her hands folded together) that they will go better. She is sure of the values, principles, and beliefs that have guided her life, but she is neither prescriptive nor dogmatic with regard to the lives of others. She may be Queen, but she does not lay down the law. She is reluctant to interfere in the private lives of members of her family, although she has done, now and again, in the case of her children, as we shall see. She was sorry to be depicted, as she felt she was, in a series of articles published in the *Daily Telegraph* before her Golden Jubilee,[101] as someone who is emotionally inhibited, buttoned-up, psychologically repressed, awkward when it comes to being loving and giving. She may not express her emotions in the manner of the Prince William and Prince Harry generation, but that does not means she is unfeeling.

The Queen was profoundly fond of her younger sister, for all Princess Margaret's waywardness. The Queen really loves Margaret's two children, David and Sarah, and sometimes seems more at ease in their company than she does in the company of one or two of her own offspring. In the 1950s, when Margaret Rose wanted to marry her father's equerry, Peter Townsend, the Queen was not unsympathetic. It was just a very difficult situation. When, in 1960, Princess Margaret married the photographer Tony Armstrong-Jones, the Queen hoped they would live happily ever after. That they didn't was, from the Queen's point of view, a matter for sadness, not recrimination. Again, it was not easy. Divorce is commonplace nowadays (almost routine in the case of the Queen's children), but a generation ago, things were different. The Duke of Windsor had married a divorcee in 1937, but it was not until thirty years later

101 Articles, based on a wide-ranging series of interviews by Graham Turner, published in book form as *Elizabeth: The Woman and The Queen*, 2002.

that someone in line to the throne (albeit eighteenth in line) was divorced themselves. In 1967 George, 7th Earl of Harewood, aged forty-four, became the first of George V's direct descendants to be divorced. His wife sued him on the grounds of his adultery with an Australian violinist, which he acknowledged. He wanted to marry his mistress (also a divorcee, and the mother of his son – oh yes: what a mess!) and to do so, under the terms of the Royal Marriages Act, required the sovereign's consent. The Queen sighed a sad sigh and, having taken advice from the Privy Council, granted it. Lord Harewood sighed a different sort of sigh and slipped discreetly out of the country (to the United States) to marry for the second time.[102]

The Queen loved her sister. And she liked Tony Snowdon. And Lord Snowdon – talented and engaging and an almost pathological 'charmer' – went out of his way to be solicitous to both the Queen and his mother-in-law, Queen Elizabeth. When the Snowdon marriage began to deteriorate, as early as the mid-1960s, the Queen was dismayed, and concerned, especially for the Snowdon children, but there was little or nothing she could do, except hope and pray – which, we can be sure, she did. The Snowdons had relationships beyond their marriage and rows within it. By 1976 the position was untenable and separation unavoidable. The Queen was saddened by what had happened, but when her press secretary declared, 'There has been no pressure from the Queen on either Princess Margaret or Lord Snowdon to take any particular course', he was speaking nothing but the truth. The Queen would have liked her sister to have had a happier, more fulfilled, less complicated life. In the 1970s and early 1980s she read in the news-papers – you couldn't not – about her sister's relationship with young Roddy Llewellyn – a sandy-haired charmer (a gentleman gardener and garden designer) eighteen years Princess Margaret's junior – and, no doubt, felt that the publicity was not very good for the Royal Family and that the romance would, all too probably, end in tears.

It did, after seven years. Roddy moved on and married someone else, very happily; Margaret lived on, but ended her life without a partner – though not without friends. I did not know her, but I know and knew both Roddy Llewellyn and Tony Snowdon, both

102 Lord Harewood's first wife, Marion, subsequently married the Liberal politician Jeremy Thorpe, later tried and acquitted on a charge of conspiracy to murder.

of them delightful: gifted, engaging, playful, funny. (Kenneth Williams heard Roddy tell a story over dinner at my house and recorded in his diary that he had never heard a story better told.) Princess Margaret did not treat her body as a temple: she smoked and drank and paid the price. She was spoilt; she could be self-indulgent; the stories of her rudeness and bad behaviour are too many not to have had some truth to them. However, from all I have heard of her, from her husband, from her lover, from her friend Angela Huth, among others, it is clear that, at her best, she was great fun: witty, giving, thoughtful, musical, and gay. She was loyal to the Queen, proud of her country, and did her duty, as and when required. Several said to me that she never quite recovered from the death of her father in 1952.

From the 1940s onwards Lilibet was concerned for Margaret, but her attitude was sympathetic. She was sometimes despairing, but never 'holier than thou'. Sarah Bradford, in her biography, quotes the Queen as referring to 'my sister's guttersnipe life'. Those who know the Queen well tell me this does not sound like the Queen they know. It simply is not her kind of turn of phrase.

While the drama of the disintegrating Snowdon marriage unfolded, the Duke of Edinburgh stayed out of the way – figuratively speaking, and, often, literally, too. 'I don't go looking for trouble,' is how he put it to me. In terms of education, upbringing, experience, attitude, temperament, and physique, Prince Philip and Lord Snowdon could not be more different, but each seems to have made it his business to be on relatively good terms with the other. (Up until his death, Lord Snowdon had a small, framed, solo portrait of the Duke standing on his desk.) Doubtless, like the Queen, Philip had reservations about the somewhat rackety nature of the extramarital adventures of his in-laws (and the attendant publicity), but was there anything very helpful he could do in the matter? Not really. Besides, he had his own sisters and mother to think about.

Throughout their lives Prince Philip maintained a fond and active interest in his sisters and their families. Cécile, the third of his four sisters, her husband, and their three children, all died in or after the tragic air crash of 1937. Sophie, known as 'Tiny', the youngest of the four, lived on into the twenty-first century, dying at the age of eighty-seven, in November 2001. She was widowed in 1943, and left with the title of Princess but no very princely income, and the challenge of bringing up five small children on her own. In 1946, aged thirty-two, 'pretty little widow Tiny' (as Queen Mary called her) married Prince George Wilhelm of Hanover,[103] aged thirty-three, headmaster of Salem School (reckoned a sound appointment by Kurt Hahn), and went on to have three more children. Theodora, known as 'Dolla', Philip's second sister, had married Berthold, Margrave of Baden,[104] in 1931, and had three children. Berthold died, aged fifty-seven, in 1963. Dolla died six years later, in 1969, aged sixty-three. (Philip was on an official tour of Canada and the United States at the time and, as duty comes first, decided he could not return for her funeral. Prince Charles, recently invested as Prince of Wales, was dispatched to Salem to represent him.) Dolla's health had been poor for several years. Even before her husband's death, when she was still in her fifties, Alice described Dolla (in letters to Philip) looking 'old & haggard', with a bad heart, 'arteries narrowing', walking with a stick. Philip's eldest sister, Margarita, born in 1905, married Prince Gottfried of Hohenlohe-Langenburg, known as 'Friedel' Hohenlohe, another German princeling and descendant of Queen Victoria, in 1931. They had four sons and two daughters and a handsome home at Langenburg, one of seven Hohenlohe castles that now feature on the 'Castle Trail' promoted by the Rhine Valley Tourist Board. Friedel died in 1960, aged sixty-three, and not long after, Margarita suffered a further loss, when, in January 1963, an extensive fire at Langenburg destroyed much of the castle and all of her personal possessions. She died in 1981, aged seventy-six.

103 For his biography of Princess Alice, Hugo Vickers interviewed Prince George of Hanover, who told him of his mother-in-law's habit of having a ready answer for everything: 'She would say: "That is because . . ." and then she would pause until she came up with the answer!' Prince Philip was certainly his mother's son.

104 'Margrave, a German nobleman of rank equivalent to an English marquis' – *Chambers Dictionary*. 'Baden, bounded S and W by the Rhine, contains the Black Forest and part of the Swabian Jura. Formed (1771) from the Margraviates of Baden-Baden and Baden-Durlach. Became a Grand Duchy 1806. In 1952 in the new arrangement of *Länder* ('States') it became part of Baden-Württemberg' – *Penguin Encyclopedia of Places*. Berthold was the son of Max of Baden, former Chancellor of the German Empire, and co-founder, with Kurt Hahn, of Salem School. Berthold and Theodora (and Philip) were related in sundry ways, including being descendants of George III.

Before the war Philip visited his sisters and their husbands in Germany. After the war he was again in regular touch. The fear of anti-German sentiment meant that they were not invited to Philip and Elizabeth's wedding in 1947 – about which they were unhappy and not wholly understanding – but they were very much on parade at Elizabeth II's Coronation. Within weeks of the Accession, Margarita reported to Uncle Dickie that the sisters had firmly 'fixed that in Philip's mind!!' Philip saw them when he could and corresponded with them regularly. He paid private visits to them in Germany and regularly invited them to visit Britain, to stay with him and the Queen in Scotland. In 1965, twenty years after the end of the war, the Queen and Prince Philip paid their first official state visit to Germany and the ten-day programme allowed time for a number of unofficial excursions: Philip took Elizabeth to Wolfsgarten, the Hesse-Darmstadt family heartland; to Salem for a weekend with Dolla; to Langenburg to visit Margarita. They kept in touch. They were his family. To the end of his days, he kept in touch with nephews and nieces and a multitude of German cousins. 'You have a life outside the United Kingdom that nobody really knows about,' I once said to him. 'I have a family,' he said, 'like anybody else.'

Well, not quite like anybody else. To begin with, Philip's mother was an unusual lady. She died in 1969, aged eighty-four. More than once, in response to letters of condolence, Philip described her life as one 'of wars, revolutions, separations and tragedies'. She was a survivor. She had many strengths: she was intelligent, thoughtful, kind-hearted, honest, honourable, determined. She could also be infuriatingly wilful and contrary. She had visionary qualities and a spiritual dimension that was always sincere, if occasionally difficult to pin down. There was evidently much of her in her only son. In the 1930s her mental breakdown and her separation from her husband destroyed her family life, but she recovered and soldiered on. During and after the war she lived in Greece, relatively modestly, travelling, when it became possible, and travelling widely – to Britain, to Germany, to Sweden, around Europe, even to India and the Middle East. Philip saw as much of his mother as their unusual lives allowed. For example, in the summer of 1966, visiting Sophie in Germany, Alice was taken ill, with liver and heart problems, and admitted to a hospital in Munich. Philip paid the hospital bills and, then, eight weeks later, returning to Balmoral from the Commonwealth Games in Jamaica and hearing that his mother was not well enough to travel and anxious to get home, immediately flew from Scotland to Germany, collected his mother, and flew her on to Athens, where he spent the night to settle her in, and then flew immediately back to Scotland. Again, early in 1967, travelling to and from Australia on official business, he visited her in Athens, this time bringing some new carpet with him for her flat.

Later that year the fall-out from the 'Colonels' Coup' of 21 April – which led, effectively, to the end of the Greek monarchy – and Alice's own failing health forced her to accept her son and daughter-in-law's invitation to come to live at Buckingham Palace. She had been reluctant to leave the country she regarded as home for the land of her birth, but when she was told the invitation had come from 'Lilibet personally', she said, 'We go this afternoon.'

According to Stephen Barry, another royal servant who disobliged his former employers by publishing a volume of reminiscences,[105] the Palace staff found the Duke's mother, in her grey nun's habit, 'strange but likeable'. She was, said Barry, 'eccentric and deaf, and smoked like a chimney. If we could tell when the Queen was coming by the pattering of the corgis' feet, we always knew when Princess Andrew was about from the clouds of smoke that followed her. And the coughing. The poor lady coughed incessantly as she lit another cigarette. Not surprisingly, she was often in hospital with bronchitis.'

Alice died at Buckingham Palace, in her sleep, on 5 December 1969, aged eighty-four. Her granddaughter, Princess Anne, who had just turned nineteen, asked to see her and later told Princess Alice's biographer, Hugo Vickers, 'I am glad I did that. She looked very peaceful. All the lines in her face had gone and for the first time I could see the resemblance to the de László portrait.' Philip de László's handsome portraits of Prince Philip's parents, painted when Edward VII was King and they were still in their twenties, used to hang in Philip's study at Buckingham Palace. Philip almost never spoke of

105 *Royal Secrets*, 1985. The book does not quite live up to its enticing title, but I enjoyed it. Then again, I enjoyed the telltale books by Marion Crawford, John Dean, and Paul Burrell (the governess, the valet, and the butler), while understanding how infuriating and intrusive the Royal Family will have found them.

his parents in public, but he guarded their memory and, in my experience, brooked no criticism of them, of any kind. He was fiercely loyal. They were his family.

'We are a family,' the Duke repeated to me, somewhat exasperated when I was quizzing him about his relationships with his children and their partners. 'We are a family,' he said. 'What do you expect?' You expect ups and downs, good times and bad – that's the truth. And we all know it. The Queen and Prince Philip had a family life that was complex and sometimes complicated. That is true of most of us. Need more be said?' The Queen is weary, as Prince Philip was – 'thoroughly fed up' was his phrase – of the media's apparently insatiable appetite for the meanest morsel of tittle-tattle about their own and their children's and their grandchildren's private lives, not only because much of what gets published is simply inaccurate, but also because, as individuals, the Queen and the Duke belonged to a more discreet generation. There are some things you just don't talk about.

The Emperor Napoleon – whose younger brother Lucien was the forebear of Princess Marie Bonaparte, who married Prince Philip's father's elder brother, 'Big' Prince George of Greece – used to say that if you truly want to know a person you should think of the world as it was when that person was twenty. When Philip and Elizabeth were twenty the world was not as it is now. Couples had their problems, families had their feuds, but, on the whole, and as a rule, they were not much discussed at home, and never broadcast abroad. You simply did not wash your domestic dirty linen in public. Now we let it all hang out. The Duke of Edinburgh complained to me more than once that 'the media have turned us into a soap opera'. Well, like it or not, this is the age of the soap opera. Flick through the popular magazines and newspapers of the 1940s – the decade in which Philip and Elizabeth each turned twenty – and you will read about war, history, travel, fashion, home-making, hobbies. Flick through the most popular publications of today and you will read, almost exclusively, about celebrity, sex, and 'relationships'. We are gripped by 'relationships'.

Within the Queen and Prince Philip's immediate family there was only one relationship that presented them with real difficulty: their relationship with their eldest son, Prince Charles. As I mentioned in the introduction, once, when talking with the Duke of Edinburgh about him being somehow at odds with Prince Charles, I began to say that I found it strange because the two of them seemed to me to be remarkably similar – similar in mannerisms, similar in interests. The Duke interrupted me. 'Yes,' he said, 'but with one great difference. He's a Romantic – and I'm a pragmatist. That means we do see things differently.' He paused and shrugged, and said, with a slightly despairing laugh, 'And because I don't see things as a Romantic would, I'm *unfeeling.*'

Prince Philip was pragmatic and unsentimental, but, in my experience, far from unfeeling. At times in his life, Prince Charles has begged to differ. He still recalls – still talks about – the mortifying day when his father came to Gordonstoun, to see his son, just turned seventeen, play the title role in the school production of *Macbeth* – and laughed. 'It was the "Scottish play",' remembers Charles. 'I had to lie on a huge, fur rug and have a nightmare. My parents came and watched, along with other parents. I lay there and thrashed about and all I could hear was my father and "ha, ha, ha." I went up to him afterwards and said, "Why did you laugh?" and he said, "It sounds like *The Goons*."'

You could fill a book with tales from the Prince of Wales of hurtful moments from his childhood – and, to an extent, he already has. In the early 1990s Charles cooperated with the broadcaster Jonathan Dimbleby to produce a television film and biography that made plain that Charles was profoundly unhappy about his childhood. Then in his forties, going grey and with a pained expression, he let the world know that, as he was growing up, he felt that he was 'emotionally estranged' from both his parents, craving 'the affection and appreciation' from them that they were either 'unable or unwilling' to offer. His stories of small slights that left their scars are many and similar. When, as a little boy, he forgot to call his detective 'Mr' and simply used his surname, as he heard his parents do all the time, he was made to apologise. When he left a door open and a footman went to close it, Philip stopped the footman, barking, 'Leave it alone, man. The boy's got hands.' When, one winter on the Sandringham estate, young Charles was throwing snowballs at a police officer, Philip called to the policeman, 'Don't just stand there, throw some back!' When, again at Sandringham, Charles came back from playing in the grounds one afternoon, having lost a dog lead, his mother sent him straight out again, instructing him not to return until he had found what he had lost, reminding him, 'Dog leads cost money.' When, this time in London, young Charles was seen sticking his tongue out at the crowd watching him drive down the Mall, his father gave him a spanking.

Talking to Jonathan Dimbleby (and, before him, to those of his friends and family who cared to listen), Charles gave the impression that he regarded his father as a bully and a tyrant and his mother as distant and ungiving. As a little boy at Buckingham Palace he passed his mother's study one day and asked her to come and play with him. Gently closing the door against him, she said, 'If only I could.' When his parents returned from their post-Coronation tour and Charles, aged five, was taken in *Britannia* to the port of Tobruk to greet them, the little boy attempted to join the line of dignitaries waiting to shake Her Majesty by the hand. 'No, not you, dear,' were the mother's first words to her son after five months of separation.

Charles felt neglected at home and abandoned at school. The Queen, educated at home, and, though Head of State herself, brought up traditionally to accept the father as the natural head of the family, was content to be led by her husband in the matter of her own children's education. 'The Queen and I,' said Philip in 1956, when Charles was seven, rising eight, 'want Charles to go to school with other boys of his generation and learn to live with other children, and to absorb from childhood the discipline imposed by education with others.' In September 1957, two months before his ninth birthday, Charles was sent to his first boarding school, Cheam, in Hampshire. The school had changed its location since Philip had been a pupil a quarter of a century earlier, but its spirit remained the same. Charles later reflected that his first weeks at Cheam had been the loneliest of his life. Five years later, in 1962, again following in his father's footsteps, Charles moved on to Gordonstoun, on the Moray Firth in Scotland. His new school's spartan regime was not to his taste. 'It's absolute hell,' Charles wrote home. 'It's near Balmoral,' his father told him. 'There's always the Factor there. You can go and stay with him.[106] And your grandmother goes up there to fish. You can go and see her.'

---

106 'Factor, *n*, an agent managing heritable estates for another (*Scottish*)' – *Chambers Dictionary.*

Charles did indeed seek comfort and companionship from family retainers. He was close to the nannies of his early childhood, Helen Lightbody and Mabel Anderson, and to his governess, Catherine Peebles, known as 'Mipsy'. She recalled how sensitive and tentative Charles was as a small boy: 'If you raised your voice to him, he would draw back into his shell, and for a time you would be able to do nothing with him.' But, as his father knew, his chief comforter was Queen Elizabeth. She was a doting grandmother who always gave her favourite grandson an understanding shoulder to cry on and a warm bosom to embrace.

Queen Elizabeth was explicitly against Charles being sent to Gordonstoun. 'It is miles & miles away,' she wrote to her daughter in May 1961, '& he might as well be at school abroad . . . He would be terribly cut off and lonely up in the far North.' Prince Charles agreed with Grannie. She wanted her grandson to go to Eton. 'All your friends' sons are at Eton,' she told her daughter, '& it is so important to be able to grow up with people you will be with later in life. And so nice, & so important when boys are growing up, that you & Philip can see him during school days, & keep him in touch with what is happening.' She apologised for interfering, 'but I have been thinking & worrying about it all'.

In due course Prince Charles sent his own sons to Eton. He did not consider Gordonstoun for a moment. Prince Philip sent his sons to Gordonstoun. He did not consider Eton for a moment. Charles resented his father because of this and he adored his grandmother because of the way she championed and cosseted him. In 2002 his distress at her death was pitiful to behold. He was bereft and felt no need to disguise the fact. 'She was quite simply the most magical grandmother you could possibly have and I was utterly devoted to her,' he said. 'For me, she meant everything, and I have dreaded, dreaded this moment.'

Back in 1962, when asked how Prince Charles was getting on at Gordonstoun, Prince Philip replied, 'Well, at least he hasn't run away yet.' In fact, Charles stayed the course and did rather well. He may have regarded it as 'a prison sentence – like Colditz with kilts', but he ended up as Guardian, or head boy, as his father had done before him (and Prince Edward would later do) and secured two A levels (Grade B in History, Grade C in French), becoming the first heir to the throne in British history to secure a university place on the strength of academic credentials alone. Later, while recalling the bullying to which he was subjected at Gordonstoun and the rigours of its spartan regime, he would come to acknowledge that the school had developed his 'will power' and helped his self-discipline, 'not in the sense of making you bath in cold water, but in the Latin sense, of giving shape and form to your life'. The philosophy of Kurt Hahn that helped form Prince Philip, helped form Prince Charles, too. The values that inspired the Duke of Edinburgh's Award Scheme and the Outward Bound Trust are not dissimilar to those that underpin the work of the Prince's Trust.

Prince Philip acknowledged many of his son's achievements, but not uncritically. He left it to the Queen to sing the Prince of Wales's praises and, over the years, Her Majesty has gone out of her way to praise her eldest son in public and to thank him – sincerely, and from the heart – both for the support he has given her and for the range of good works he undertakes, with imagination and dedication, on behalf of the wider community. Privately, she has been more critical. She used to grumble about Charles's extravagance. The Queen keeps her breakfast cereals fresher longer by storing them in Tupperware containers. The Prince of Wales does not. He has a style and taste and panache – and way with money – that reflect his maternal grandmother rather than his parents. He entertains, and entertains royally. The Queen is reported to have said, 'The amount of kit and staff he takes about – it's obscene.' I think he thinks that's part of the point of being Prince of Wales. At a party at Highgrove, I thanked him for his superb hospitality and congratulated him on the wonderful way it was all done: the silver, the crystal, the lighting, the flowers – especially the flowers. 'They came from the garden,' he said. 'It's a joy to behold,' I murmured. 'Isn't it?' he said, beaming. 'I'm so glad you like it. I want you to like it. I'm so lucky to have all these lovely things around me. I simply want to share them. I want everyone to love my garden. It is a joy, isn't it? Such a joy.' That simply is not the way his parents ever talked.

The Queen, of course, does not talk to the press. The Duke of Edinburgh did. Indeed, I made the point to him once that he started it all, that he was the first senior member of the Royal Family to give any kind of extended interview. 'Yes,' he said. 'I made a conscious decision to talk to the media – but not about me, only about what I'm doing, what I'm supporting.' That Prince Charles should voluntarily talk to a broadcaster and journalist about family matters, about his private life, and let the journalist have access to his diaries and private correspondence, seemed to his parents sheer foolishness. The Queen and the Duke were appalled by the Dimbleby book. They could not see how their son's indiscretions – or special pleading on his own behalf – could serve his cause, or that of the Royal Family, in any way. They were also hurt by their son's public complaints about the quality of their parenting. They had meant well, they had done their best, and their recollection of Charles's childhood was rather different from his own. They recalled fun and games, bath times, story-telling, picnics and bonfires, laughter not tears. Prince Philip remembers taking Charles and Anne, regularly during the summer holidays, cruising in his twelve-metre yacht *Bloodhound* and believes that these were 'good times, happy days'.

I am on the Duke's side, but he was not above reproach. Charles may have whinged about his childhood now and then, but Philip could rarely resist firing cheap shots at his son's expense. Indeed, he did it all the time. It was a habit. Gina Kennard, who knew him and his family all her life, said to me, 'He just can't resist coming out with these personal remarks. He can't stop himself. He's at his worst with Charles, but he could be quite sarcastic with Anne, too, you know.'

That something went wrong in his relationship with Prince Charles is undeniable. Charles could be a sensitive flower. He was shy. He was uncertain. As an adolescent he bruised easily. The poet Kathleen Raine (1908–2003), only a little younger than Charles's grandmother, met him when he was in his early twenties and thought, 'That poor young man – anything I can do for him, I will do, because he is very lonely.' The Queen Mother, not deliberately (though she was capable of mischief), but, effectively, made him feel that she understood him in a way that his parents did not. 'He is a very gentle boy,' she said, 'with a very kind heart, which I think is the essence of everything.' Queen Elizabeth offered Charles a safe haven and warm waters, away from the cool breeze of his mother and the harsh wind of his father. Gina Kennard told me, 'When he was a little boy, there didn't seem to be a problem at all, but, as he was growing up,

I think probably the Queen was too tolerant, and Prince Philip too tough.'

Countess Mountbatten, Philip's first cousin and one of Charles's godparents, said to me, 'You can see it from both sides, can't you? A resilient character such as Prince Philip, toughened by the slings and arrows of life, who sees being tough as a necessity for survival, wants to toughen up his son – and his son is very sensitive. It hasn't been easy for either of them.' Patricia Mountbatten paused and then added, with a dry laugh, 'Anne, of course, as a natural tomboy, presented no problems.'

Mabel Anderson, who was nanny to both Prince Charles and Princess Anne, said, 'He was never as boisterous and noisy as Princess Anne. She had a much stronger, more extrovert personality. She didn't exactly push him aside, but she was certainly a more forceful child.' Anne is like her father. She will make no complaint of any kind about her upbringing. Father and daughter always got on well. They were alike in many ways: undertaking their public duties in the same brisk, no-nonsense fashion, competing with each other as to who could fulfil the more engagements in the year, vying with each other as to who had the more efficient private office. They had an easy, good-humoured, comfortable relationship. They didn't brood about it: they just got on with it.

Philip was separated from his mother throughout his adolescence, but refused – absolutely – to use that as an excuse for anything. He would not find fault with his mother, however hard you pressed him. Anne will not find fault with hers, either – whatever Charles may say. The idea that, as a mother, the Queen was remote and uncaring – an idea spread by Prince Charles via Jonathan Dimbleby in 1994, and more recently fostered by anonymous courtiers quoted by Graham Turner in his Golden Jubilee portrait of the Queen – is flatly rejected by the Princess Royal. 'I'm not going to speak for anyone else,' she says, 'but I simply don't believe that there is any evidence whatsoever to suggest that she wasn't caring. It just beggars belief. We as children may have not been too demanding, in the sense that we understood what the limitations were in time and the responsibilities placed on her as monarch in the things she had to do and the travels she had to make, but I don't believe that any of us, for a second, thought she didn't care for us in exactly the same way as any other mother did. I just think it's extraordinary that anybody could construe that that might not be true.'

Anne found her father demanding in a way that was encouraging and her mother tolerant in a way that allowed her children to find their own feet. 'If she'd been a disciplinarian,' says Anne, with a wry smile, 'and said "no" to everybody, we'd have all been psychoanalysed out of existence on the basis that we had too controlling a mother. We've all been allowed to find our own way and we were always encouraged to discuss problems, to talk them through. People have to make their own mistakes and I think she's always accepted that.'

'We are a family,' Prince Philip said to me. In much the same way, Princess Anne adds, 'Judging by some families, I think we are all on pretty good speaking terms after all this time, and that's no mean achievement for quite a lot of families. I think we all enjoy each other's company.'

The family grew in the early 1960s. Prince Andrew, now Duke of York, was born on 19 February 1960. Prince Edward, Earl of Wessex, was born on 10 March 1964. (There is a lovely, informal photograph, taken in June 1964, of the Queen carrying baby Edward in her arms on their way by train to Balmoral. She looks anything but unmotherly.) Martin Charteris told me that, when Andrew was conceived, 'the Queen and Prince Philip had been trying for another baby for quite a while.' 'How on earth do you know?' I asked him. 'Because Her Majesty told me so,' he chuckled. 'She wanted me to pass it on to President Nkrumah, you see.' I didn't see, so Lord Charteris, beaming broadly, obligingly explained, 'In late 1959, the Queen was due to visit Ghana. It was going to be a big thing. In May she discovered she was pregnant and realised that the Ghana trip would have to be put off. She knew that Dr Nkrumah was a sensitive chap[107] and might take offence unless he knew the whole

107 Kwame Nkrumah (1909–72) studied theology in the United States in the 1930s, attended the London School of Economics in 1945, returning in 1947 to his native Gold Coast, where he founded the Convention People's Party and spent two years in prison charged with 'political agitation'. In 1951 he was appointed first prime minister of the Gold Coast (known as Ghana from 1957) and became first president of the republic in 1960. His vanity was boundless. He created a one-party state and proclaimed himself 'Redeemer'. He was deposed in a military coup in 1966.

story, so I was dispatched to Accra to put him in the picture – which I did. At first he was appalled, then he decided that if the Queen couldn't come to him, he'd go to her – at Balmoral – which he did. I have to say, she has a way with these Commonwealth leaders. They trust her. Absolutely.'

In due course, without any interference from Queen Elizabeth the Queen Mother, Andrew and Edward followed Charles to Gordonstoun – and survived. In 1979, aged nineteen, exactly forty years after his parents' celebrated encounter there, Andrew enrolled at Dartmouth Royal Naval College. At twenty-one he qualified as a helicopter pilot and joined 829 Naval Air Squadron, flying Sea Kings from the carrier HMS *Invincible*. In April 1982 *Invincible* sailed for the South Atlantic with the British naval task force to recapture the Falkland Islands from the invading Argentines. He put his life on the line.[108] 'Prince Andrew is a serving officer,' said Buckingham Palace in answer to suggestions that the Queen might want to keep her son out of harm's way, 'and there is no question in her mind that he should go.' When Port Stanley was liberated and the conflict over, Andrew telephoned home. 'My mother was in,' he said, 'it was about the right time of evening.' She told him that she was relieved he was safe and how proud his parents were of him, and then, immediately, she asked him 'to pass on how proud she was of everyone and to say how marvellously the troops had done'.

In June 1986 Prince Edward, having graduated from Cambridge (with a degree in history), joined the Royal Marines, notoriously the toughest billet in the armed services. Given his slight build and his reported ambition at the time to be an actor, it seemed an odd choice for the twenty-two-year-old to make, but he had signed up before going to university and was determined to make a go of it. He tried, and he failed. It was the psychological as much as the

---

108 Two hundred and fifty-five British officers and men died in the conflict – and 652 Argentines, lest we forget. The senior members of the British Royal Family are impressively sanguine about putting their lives on the line. They live with the ever-present threat of assassination. Twenty months after the murder of Lord Mountbatten, in June 1981, six shots were fired at the Queen as she rode on horseback down the Mall to attend Trooping the Colour. Her horse, Burmese, reared up, but Her Majesty brought the animal under control at once and rode on regardless.

physical demands of the training that overwhelmed him. And, apparently, the attitude of his commanding officer was unsympathetic. In January 1987, with the acquiescence of his parents, Edward resigned his commission. His father (Captain-General of the Royal Marines) was disappointed, but coped. Martin Palmer, a friend of the Duke's, told me how he happened to be having dinner with Prince Philip 'the week after all this'. Prince Edward came into the room and 'Prince Philip got up and gave him the most enormous hug and brought him to the table. Yes, they'd had a humdinger of a row, but it was over.'

Philip, in my experience, spoke of Edward with an ease and warmth that was not in evidence when he talked of the Prince of Wales – who, of course, having secured his own, adequate, degree from Cambridge (BA Hons, Class II, Division II), went on to serve in Her Majesty's armed services for six not unchallenging years. At the Royal Air Force College at Cranwell, in Lincolnshire, Charles showed immediately that he shared his father's aptitude for flying. He then followed his father to the Royal Naval College at Dartmouth, and served in a series of warships: *Norfolk*, *Minerva*, *Jupiter*, and *Hermes*. At the time of the Falklands conflict, Charles expressed regret that he had not been 'tested' in action as Andrew had been, but, throughout his years of service (1970–76) – culminating with a stint as a helicopter pilot in the Fleet Air Arm – he was as gung-ho and courageous as any father could wish. There was, however, something perverse about Prince Philip. He was not always easy. He liked to be contrary and, perhaps, just because nobody would expect it, he seemed to prefer Edward, who flunked the Royal Marines, to Charles, who served in the services with distinction and pushed himself to the limit. Gradually, Edward took on more and more of his father's commitments, notably as the front man for the Duke of Edinburgh's Award, and then the Queen let it be known that, when Prince Philip died, Prince Edward would succeed his father as the new Duke of Edinburgh. Edward's first-born, Louise, became the first royal child to bear the surname Mountbatten-Windsor.

Perhaps inevitably, the youngest of the royal children was the most indulged. In June 1987, a year after he joined the Royal Marines, Edward, aged twenty-three and settled on a new career in entertainment, joined forces with the BBC and John Broome, then owner of the Midlands-based visitor attraction Alton Towers, to present a spectacular royal version of the slapstick-and-games TV show *It's A Knockout!* According to Edward, 'Both the BBC and John Broome positively drooled at the idea.' Of course they did! Edward persuaded his sister Anne, his brother Andrew, and Andrew's new wife, Sarah Ferguson (who needed little persuading), to dress up in mock-Tudor costumes and lead teams of celebrities – Rowan Atkinson, Les Dawson, and Barbara Windsor among them – as they competed in a series of silly fun and games loosely disguised as a medieval joust-about. It was well meant, and useful sums were raised for charity, but *It's A Royal Knockout* did nothing for the dignity of the House of Windsor or the standing of the new generation of young royals. Everyone at Buckingham Palace at the time (from the private secretary to the press office) claims to have been against it, but Edward was determined (utterly determined) and the Queen did not have it in her to say 'no'. The embarrassment of the spectacle itself was compounded by Prince Edward's post-show press conference. The attendant hacks, hot and weary after a long day, not satisfied with the access they had been given to the 'royal celebrities', failed to show any enthusiasm for what Edward hoped the world would regard as his finest hour. Faced with the media's indifference, he made a couple of sarcastic remarks and stalked out of the press tent. 'Edward Storms Out After Game Show,' ran one headline; 'It's a Walkout,' ran another.

The press for the young Prince did not improve much as the years went by. Journalists were relatively gentle with him when he worked as a backroom boy and production assistant for Andrew Lloyd Webber's Really Useful Group, but when he turned his attention to television film-making, and founded his own production company, Ardent, the gloves were off again. The films were rubbished; he was accused of exploiting his family name to get them made; Ardent was repeatedly reported to be making losses – losses of almost £2 million over seven years, according to the *Guardian*. The knock-out blow came in April 2001 and was delivered by the *News of the World*. (No wonder Philip was close to Edward: they shared a loathing for Rupert Murdoch's brand of tabloid journalism. Philip, you will recall, dated the decline in the tone and standards of Britain's popular press to Murdoch's arrival in the United Kingdom.)

In June 1999 Edward, aged thirty-five, had married Sophie Rhys-Jones, aged thirty-four, a pretty, wholesome, blonde public relations executive who appeared to have a sensible head on resolute shoulders. Appearances can be deceptive – as Sophie, now Countess of Wessex, found to her cost when, in the spring of 2001, on behalf of her PR company, she took a meeting with a potential 'client', an Arab 'sheikh', who turned out to be an under-cover reporter for the *News of the World*. Sophie's small talk, as recorded by the 'sheikh', was hardly treasonable, but it was unfortunate. She referred to the Queen as 'the old dear' and the Queen Mother as 'the old lady' and described the Prince of Wales and Camilla Parker Bowles as 'number one on the unpopular people list', only likely to be married after the death of 'the old lady'. She was not discreet. She mocked the Prime Minister, calling him 'President Blair'; she poured scorn on the Prime Minister's wife, calling her 'horrid, absolutely horrid'; and she described the Leader of the Opposition (William Hague) as 'deformed'. Most damagingly, she let slip that, while her company's prestige and royal connections were not officially for hire, 'that is an unspoken benefit'.

When Sophie discovered the truth about the sting, on advice from Buckingham Palace she sought to bury her indiscretions and buy off the *News of the World* by giving them 'a personal interview' – and promptly fell between two stools. Rival newspapers tumbled over themselves to publish edited highlights of her secretly recorded conversation with the 'sheikh' (leaked to them – goodness knows how!) and the *News of the World* carried a sensational interview that was as personal as anyone could hope for. 'My Edward Is Not Gay,' ran the headline, above a story in which the Countess denounced the rumours of her husband's homosexuality and revealed that they were determined to have a baby and were even contemplating in-vitro fertilisation in order to be able to do so.

And the consequence of all this was . . . well, you can see for yourself by checking out the official Buckingham Palace website at www.royal.gov.uk: 'The Earl of Wessex announced in 2002 that he and The Countess of Wessex had decided to concentrate on supporting The Queen during the Golden Jubilee and beyond, and helping the Royal Family shoulder some of the increasing workload into the future. They therefore withdrew from their respective companies, Ardent Productions and R-JH, in order to focus their energies more into supporting those organisations, charities, individuals and companies who deserve to be recognised for their effort, initiative and entrepreneurship.'

Prince Edward features in a number of other, less dignified websites, where he is listed, variously, as a 'celebrity gay', 'a royal gay icon', and 'the Queen's queen'. He is not homosexual and never has been, though the rumour was rife in London throughout the 1980s. At the time, I was working at the breakfast television station TV-am, where, despite the assurances of Edward's best friend at the station (James Baker, son of the newsreader Richard Baker) and the close (and charming) attention paid by Edward to our beautiful young weather girl, Ulrika Jonsson, we would not accept that the seventh in line to the throne was anything but a closet screamer. There was something about his mouth, his manner, his handshake, his hairline, his record – leaving the Marines, that petulant performance after the royal *It's A Knockout!* – that convinced us he was homosexual. Had he been, I believe his parents, born and brought up long before the decriminalisation of homosexual acts between consenting adults in private (which only happened in 1967), would nevertheless have coped – and coped quite well. The Queen is a devout and traditional Christian, the Duke of Edinburgh was very much a man's man, but neither ever betrayed the least hint of homophobia. She is and he was instinctively tolerant, accepting others as they found them, as a rule. In the case of their children, and their children's choice in partners, the Queen and Prince Philip did their level best not to interfere. It was not always easy.

Princess Anne was the first of the royal children to be married. As far as her parents were concerned, she was free to marry anybody she chose. She chose to marry Lieutenant Mark Phillips, born 1948, educated at Marlborough and Sandhurst, a guardsman (The Queen's Dragoon Guards), the soldier son of a soldier, and, more to the point, an achieving equestrian: a key member of the British three-day-eventing team that had triumphed in the World Championships in 1970, the European Championships in 1971, and the Olympic Games in Munich in 1972. Anne, too, was an achieving equestrian: in 1971 she won the individual European Three-Day-Event at Burghley; in 1976 she would be a member of the British Olympic Team in Montreal. On 14 November 1973 (Prince Charles's twenty-fifth birthday), at Westminster Abbey, before a congregation of a thousand and a television audience of many millions, Anne and Mark were married. 'I shouldn't wonder if their children are four-legged,' the Queen is supposed to have remarked.

Once upon a time, not so long ago, the only daughter of the Queen of England would have been expected to marry a prince of some kind – or, at least, a high-ranking aristocrat. There were sound reasons for this: he would know the rules, he would know his way around the court, he might even have land and money enough to keep the royal daughter in the style to which she was accustomed. The twentieth century changed all that. Gradually, over several decades, the rigid British class structure – so clear, so certain, in its own way, so helpful, when Queen Victoria's granddaughter, Princess Victoria, had married Prince Philip's grandfather, Prince Louis of Battenberg, in 1884 – began to collapse. The Great War changed much, the Second World War changed more. The invention of the refrigerator, the washing machine, and the dishwasher, the 1944 Education Act, the arrival of television, the advent of the Pill, the Angry Young Men of the 1950s, the Beatles, the Rolling Stones, Harold Wilson – they all played a part. At the beginning of the Queen's reign, at royal investitures, as Her Majesty passed, everybody bowed or curtsied to the ground. Now, nobody does. The age of deference is dead. Old money has given way to new money. Meritocrats outrank aristocrats, and celebrities outclass them both.

The Queen and the Duke of Edinburgh helped their children adjust to this changing world quite effectively by sending them away to boarding school. Philip was as royal as they come, but he was nothing like an English aristocrat. He was an outsider; a European; in many ways, an iconoclast. Philip chose Gordonstoun – Kurt Hahn's Gordonstoun – for his sons – not Eton or Harrow. Anne went to Benenden, a girls' school in Kent, because Gordonstoun was not yet coeducational. (Both Anne's children, Peter and Zara, born in 1977 and 1981, went to Gordonstoun and then to Exeter University.) As a child, educated at home, Princess Elizabeth did not mix and mingle – let alone live and play – with the middle classes. At Benenden, Princess Anne did. At Gordonstoun and Benenden the royal children met middle-class children, with middle-class values, and shared the middle-class experience.

Mark Phillips was from solidly middle-class stock, thoroughly respectable, if a little unexciting. When I met him I liked him. He seemed on the shy side and sparing with the small talk – but what do I know about dressage? In royal circles he was reckoned dull and a bit dim, and Prince Charles is credited with giving him the nickname 'Fog'. Four months after their marriage, however, Anne's new husband came into his own. One night in March 1974, as they were being driven along the Mall on their way back to Buckingham Palace after a charity film show, an armed man yanked open their car door and attempted to abduct the Princess. Shots were fired. The assailant pulled Anne frantically by one arm while she held tight to Mark with the other. Eventually, police arrived in sufficient numbers to subdue the attacker, who turned out to have a history of mental illness. The world was rightly impressed by the Princess's cool under fire. 'Her bravery and superb obstinacy were unbelievable,' Prince Charles recorded in his diary when he heard about the incident. 'My admiration for such a sister knows no bounds!' Anne was unhurt, but her personal protection officer was shot and wounded during the assault, and later awarded the George Cross for his bravery. Mark Phillips was appointed a Commander of the Royal Victorian Order and Anne was given the Grand Cross.[109]

Mark Phillips was a handsome husband, an outstanding horseman

---

109 The Royal Victorian Order was founded on 21 April 1896 by Queen Victoria as a way of rewarding outstanding personal service to the Sovereign. The lowlier long-serving royal staff get the MVO; the Queen's private secretaries get the KCVO; ladies of the Royal House get the GCVO. Princess Alexandra, the Duchess of Kent, and the Duchess of Gloucester all have the Order, as do the Countess of Wessex (Sophie received it in 2010) and the Duchess of Cornwall (2012), but Sarah, Duchess of York, does not, nor did Diana, Princess of Wales. The Queen has another personal order at her disposal: the Royal Family Order, created at the beginning of her reign. She has given it to almost every royal lady you can think of: her mother, her sister, assorted cousins and aunts; in 1969 she gave it to the Duchess of Kent and Princess Anne; in 1981 she gave it to the Duchess of Gloucester and the Princess of Wales. Conspicuously, she did not give it to the Duchess of York and has not given it to Princess Michael of Kent, but has given it to Edward's wife, Sophie, Countess of Wessex. Yes, the Queen (perhaps alone in the world) can give those who have everything something they do not have. In 1987, Her Majesty accorded her daughter the title 'The Princess Royal'; in 1994, Anne became a Lady of the Garter; in 2000, in recognition of her fiftieth birthday and her years of public service, she became a Lady of the Thistle.

and a good father. He sired two fine bipeds and moved on. The marriage failed, as marriages do, and, since the passing of the Divorce Reform Act in 1969, nobody needed to take the blame. The couple separated in 1989, the marriage was dissolved in April 1992, and, on 12 December the same year, the Princess Royal married Commander Timothy Laurence, RN, at a private ceremony at Crathie Church, near Balmoral Castle in Scotland.

Tim Laurence, the naval son of a naval father, is also from solidly middle-class stock, thoroughly respectable, if a little unexciting. When I met him I liked him. He seemed on the shy side and sparing with the small talk – but what do I know about nautical manoeuvres? He is five years younger than Princess Anne. The couple met when he was the assistant navigating officer in the Royal Yacht *Britannia*. He was an equerry to the Queen from 1986 to 1989 and in consequence became an MVO. Soft-eyed, rosy cheeked, and chinless, he is brighter and more determined than he looks. In July 2004, promoted to Rear Admiral, he was appointed Assistant Chief of the Defence Staff, making him the armed services' highest-ranking member of the Royal Family since Lord Mountbatten was appointed Chief of the Defence Staff in 1959. He went on to even higher things and ended his naval career as a Vice Admiral in charge of the Defence Estates. The Queen made him a Knight Commander of the Royal Victorian Order in June 2011. I got the impression from Prince Philip that his daughter's marriage has not been a bed of roses, but what marriage is? There have been ups and downs, and reported rifts and separations, but Tim Laurence keeps himself busy and the Princess Royal keeps herself busy (her commitment to duty is almost obsessive), and the marriage has survived and, with the advent of grandchildren, some say has once again begun to thrive. Anne's parents were saddened by her divorce, but, as Prince Philip put it to me, 'What could we do?' They were hopeful that her second marriage would bring lasting happiness. Prince Philip worried openly and in a caring way about his daughter.

Now and then Philip sent Anne letters, offering his daughter support, encouragement, and good advice. The Duke of Edinburgh was an assiduous correspondent. He typed his letters himself. He wrote with head and heart, and always to a purpose. It was his most effective means of personal communication. In conversation he could be hectoring and difficult to read. On paper he seemed calmer, more considered, more considerate. He used letters to show he cared. He used them, too, to think out loud, to explore, to question, to offer ideas and advice, and to say those things that, within a family, are sometimes more comfortably written down than spoken out loud.

At the beginning of 1981, when his eldest son was thirty-two and flirting with the idea of marrying Lady Diana Spencer, then nineteen, Philip wrote to Charles, as perhaps a father should write to a son, encouraging him to make up his mind. The girl was young and vulnerable, and the press speculation about a possible match was at fever pitch. The child was in the spotlight and Charles was dithering. He was, he admitted to himself, in 'a confused and anxious state of mind'. Seven years earlier, on Valentine's Day 1974, his great-uncle, Dickie Mountbatten, had written to Charles with his own brand of matrimonial advice: 'I believe, in a case like yours, the man should sow his wild oats and have as many affairs as he can before settling down but for a wife he should choose a suitable, attractive and sweet-charactered girl before she met anyone she might fall for. After all Mummy never seriously thought of anyone else after the Dartmouth encounter when she was 13! I think it is disturbing for women to have experiences if they have to remain on a pedestal after marriage.'

By 1981 Mountbatten, whom Charles regarded as 'infinitely special', the one man in his life who combined the roles of 'grandfather, great uncle, father, brother and friend', was no longer around to offer advice. From the Duke of Edinburgh I got the distinct impression that he regarded the 'infinitely special' relationship between his uncle and his son as somewhat self-indulgent on both their parts. The Duke was his own man, unsentimental and dispassionate. He was a cool and shrewd judge of character. He would never speak of anyone as Prince Charles speaks of Lord Mountbatten or Queen Elizabeth the Queen Mother. The Duke admired his uncle greatly, but he had the measure of him. And it irritated him that some people seemed to think that he was virtually brought up by Mountbatten. He complained once, 'I don't think anybody thinks I had a father. Most people think that Dickie's my father . . .' He told me that his grandmother, Victoria Milford Haven, probably had a greater influence on him than either of his uncles, Dickie or Georgie.

Dickie Mountbatten was murdered by the IRA in August 1979, leaving Charles bereft, overwhelmed by 'a kind of wretched numbness', convinced that 'something' should be done about the IRA, but admitting to his diary that he felt himself to be 'supremely useless and powerless'. In January 1981, 'confused and anxious', he told his diary he was 'terrified' of making a promise 'and then perhaps living to regret it'.

Throughout his twenties Charles appeared to have been following his great-uncle's advice. He had fallen in love ('whatever that means') a number of times. In the summer of 1971, at Smith's Lawn, the Guards' polo ground at Windsor, he had met Camilla Shand, a year older than him, already the girlfriend of Andrew Parker Bowles, but a game girl, with a reputation as something of a goer and proud to be the great-granddaughter of Alice Keppel, celebrated mistress to Charles's great-great-grandfather, Edward VII. Charles and Camilla had an affair – Uncle Dickie allowed them to use Broadlands for illicit weekends – but, in March 1973, Camilla announced her engagement to Major Parker Bowles. Charles heard the news while serving in HMS *Fox* somewhere in the Caribbean. He wrote to Uncle Dickie, mourning the end of an idyllic relationship, bleating that now he had 'no one' to return to in England, but, concluding, stoically, that 'the feeling of emptiness would eventually pass'. It did and it didn't. Other girls came and went – Mountbatten's granddaughter, Amanda Knatchbull, among them – but the yearning for Camilla never wholly disappeared and, in the aftermath of Uncle Dickie's murder, Charles turned to Mrs Parker Bowles for consolation. She was ready to give it, and her husband, an older man and not inexperienced in the ways of women, was ready to look the other way.

Uncle Dickie had indulged Charles at Broadlands, but, before he died, he had also cautioned his great-nephew against selfishness and self-indulgence. In April 1979, five years after sending Charles his Valentine's Day advice, Lord Mountbatten wrote to his great-nephew again, holding out before him this time, not the prospect of wild oats, but the fearful ghost of the black sheep of the family, Charles's other great-uncle, the Duke of Windsor. Uncle Dickie confessed to his great-nephew that his behaviour was the cause of sleepless nights: 'I thought you were beginning on the downward slope which wrecked your Uncle David's life and led to his disgraceful Abdication and his futile life ever after.'

Deep down, Mountbatten knew that Charles would not continue on what he called 'your Uncle David's sad course'. Charles knew it, too. In his diary entry of 29 January 1981 he recognised the absurdity of his own confusion: 'It all seems so ridiculous because I do very much want to do the right thing for this Country and for my family.'

That is all the Duke of Edinburgh wanted, too. What Mountbatten would have termed 'a suitable, attractive and sweet-charactered girl' was now on the scene. She was innocent and eligible, ready and willing. It was time for Charles to put up or shut up. He should either propose to Diana, counselled his father, so 'pleasing his family and the country', or release her. He really should not let her go on dangling in the wind like this.

Mountbatten's daughter, Patricia, Charles's godmother, said to me when I went to see her, 'I take it you've seen the letter? It wasn't a bullying letter at all. It was very reasonable. It was fair. It was sensible.' That is not how it seemed to Charles at the time. He said that his father's letter made him feel 'ill-used and impotent'. Faced with what he regarded as a parental 'ultimatum', Charles felt emasculated, cornered, compelled almost, to do what he did next. He telephoned Diana and suggested they meet. On Friday, 6 February, at Windsor Castle, the Prince of Wales, aged thirty-two, asked Lady Diana Spencer, aged nineteen, to marry him. Apparently, she giggled nervously, and said, 'Yes, yes, of course, yes.'

Charles and Diana were married at St Paul's Cathedral on 29 July 1981. Fifteen years later they were divorced. The decree nisi was granted on 15 July 1996, the decree absolute on 28 August – the feast day of St Augustine of Hippo, the fourth-century divine, famous for his maxim 'Audi partem alteram': 'Hear the other side.'

There are certainly two sides to the sorry story of the marriage of Charles and Diana, and, having friends who were good friends of each of them, I have heard both sides, *in extenso*. Charles, according to Diana's camp, was selfish, self-indulgent, thoughtless, unsympathetic, uncaring, and cruel. He made no effort to share her interests and took no trouble to like her friends. He was older than her and more experienced: he had a duty of care which he neglected, almost from the start. Faced with her frailty – her post-natal depression, her mood swings – he was unable to cope. Faced with her cries for help – her bulimia, her attempts at self-injury – he turned away and sought solace in the arms of the one woman he had loved all along, Camilla Parker Bowles. He was weak yet wilful, pathetic yet petulant. He behaved like a spoilt child. He lacked emotional intelligence and generosity of spirit. Above all, he was jealous of his young wife's popularity with the public.

Diana, according to Charles's friends, was a sad case, almost from the start. She was in love with the position, not the Prince. She never came close to understanding her man – or trying to.[110] She was self-regarding, self-absorbed, self-obsessed. She resented her husband's range of interests: she demanded a cull of some of his closest friends. She came from a difficult background – a dysfunctional family with a history of marital and mental instability – and it showed. Diana was difficult, deceitful, and manipulative. She made up stories, she told lies, she had affairs. She really was beyond the pale.

Interestingly, both camps – so pitilessly vituperative in their attacks on the integrity and character of their villain of choice – offer a guarded truce in the matter of the Wales's children. When it comes to William (born 21 June 1982) and Harry (born 15 September 1984), it seems to be agreed by both sides that both parents, in their different but equally loving ways, meant well and did their best. And it is clear now, though it was not at the time, that, throughout the whole unhappy saga, Charles's parents meant well and did their best, too. They did not take sides and, at first at least, they tried not to interfere.

The tradition of the Prince of Wales having a difficult relationship with his parents is as old as Prince Hal. Edward VII, as Prince of Wales, fell foul of Queen Victoria and Prince Albert. Victoria blamed her son for her husband's premature demise. Edward VIII, as Prince of Wales, disappointed George V and Queen Mary. Her son's

110 In March 1996, at the House of Commons, I happened to have dinner with Dame Barbara Cartland, the romantic novelist, long-standing friend of Lord Mountbatten, and mother of Raine, who married Diana's father, the 8th Earl Spencer, in 1976. Dame Barbara was full of concern for the plight of the Prince and Princess of Wales. 'It's so sad for them both,' she said. 'It's heartbreaking. Of course, you know where it all went wrong? She wouldn't do oral sex, she just wouldn't. It's as simple as that. Of *course* it all went wrong.'

Abdication in 1937 blighted the rest of Queen Mary's life. The Queen and Prince Philip had their reservations about their eldest son – about his self-indulgence and tendency to self-pity, in particular – but they recognised and admired his many gifts and achievements, and they loved him dearly and wished him well. They were delighted with his engagement to Diana and full of hope for the success of the marriage. When it began to go wrong and others said, 'I told you so' – Charles's friend Nicholas Soames, Philip's friend Penny Romsey, the Queen Mother's friend Lady Fermoy (Diana's maternal grandmother), among them – Elizabeth and Philip said nothing. They kept their own counsel. They looked on, silent and dismayed. Unlike almost everybody else involved in the drama, Philip and Elizabeth could see both sides of the story, and had some sympathy with both sides, too. They cared about Charles and they cared about Diana. They cared about their grandchildren, especially. And they cared about the Crown and the country, also.

Initially, as the marriage began to disintegrate, the Queen did not intervene, because, in fairness, what could she do? Unlike Queen Elizabeth the Queen Mother, the Queen does not avoid unpleasantness by putting her head in the sand, but nor is she an interfering busybody. She is naturally reticent. Time heals so much and 'Least said soonest mended' is a policy that often pays dividends. She believes in prayer and patience and hoping for the best. Philip believed in steering clear of trouble – 'I try to keep out of these things as much as possible,' was his line – unless he thought he had something useful to contribute. By the summer of 1992, however, both Philip and Elizabeth reckoned 'something must be done'.

In June the *Sunday Times* began to serialise Andrew Morton's book *Diana: Her True Story*. Essentially, the book laid bare the devastation at the heart of her marriage. It portrayed Diana as a wronged woman, locked in a loveless union, psychologically battered by an unfeeling husband who refused to hear or respond to her cries of anguish. It was a gripping read – and everybody read it, or at least got the gist of it from the never-ending reports of what it both said and implied. Morton's sources were acknowledged to be Diana's friends. At Buckingham Palace they suspected Diana herself. They were right, of course. Diana had not met Morton, but, through an intermediary – James Colthurst, an Old Etonian doctor with an excellent bedside manner and sympathetic ear – she poured her heart out to him, recording tapes in which she told her story her way and answering any supplementary questions that Morton (via Colthurst) fed back to her. Challenged by the Queen's private secretary, her own brother-in-law, Robert Fellowes[111] (who had married her level-headed elder sister, Jane, in 1978), Diana flatly denied any involvement in Morton's book. When Prince Philip told her directly that many feared that she had in some way cooperated with the book's author, she told her father-in-law, equally directly, that she had not. She lied.

That same June, during the week of Royal Ascot, the Queen and Prince Philip sat down with Charles and Diana at Windsor, to listen to their woes and talk about the way ahead. According to Diana, the meeting was frank and, under the circumstances, almost friendly. Charles said very little, but Diana laid her cards on the table. Her husband's behaviour was unreasonable, unjust, and unfair. She believed the time had come for a trial separation. The Queen and Prince Philip (again, according to Diana) listened sympathetically, but firmly resisted any suggestion of a formal separation. They counselled the unhappy couple to search for a compromise, to think less of themselves and more of others, to try to work together to make their marriage work, for their own sakes, for the sake of the boys, for the sake of Crown and country. The Queen and the Duke were totally as one. The Prince and the Princess were hopelessly at odds. The Queen hoped that the meeting had done something to clear the air and proposed a second meeting on the following day. Diana apparently agreed, but failed to turn up. The Queen, the Duke, and Prince Charles remained at Windsor. Diana returned to Kensington Palace.

As his son's marriage teetered on the brink of total collapse, Philip

111 Lord Fellowes of Shotesham since 1999. Born 1941, the son of Sir William Fellowes KCVO, land agent to the Royal Family at Sandringham, 1936–64. Robert (Eton, Scots Guards) was assistant private secretary to the Queen from 1977, deputy private secretary from 1986, private secretary 1990–99, and, consequently, LVO 1982, CB 1987, KCVO 1989, PC 1990, KCB 1991, GCVO 1996, GCB 1998, QSO 1999. He once said to me that he thought his lasting legacy would be that he was the man who persuaded the Queen to allow herself to be painted by Lucian Freud. I don't think he was joking. Andrew Parker Bowles may hope that he will be remembered by posterity, not as the man who gave his surname to Camilla, but as the subject of one of Lucian Freud's last great portraits.

initiated a correspondence with his daughter-in-law that he hoped might prove helpful. This correspondence has been the subject of much misunderstanding. A garbled version later appeared in the tabloid press, suggesting that Philip had written to Diana to scold and upbraid her. He was accused of calling her 'a trollop' and 'a harlot'. He was not amused. Nothing could have been further from the truth.

Not long after Diana's death I said to the Duke of Edinburgh, 'The public view of you, for what it's worth, is of a grouchy old man, unsympathetic to his daughter-in-law, but I happen to know – not from you, but I know it – that when things were difficult you wrote to Diana – kind letters, concerned, fatherly, loving, caring letters from Pa, explaining how you knew, first hand, the difficulties involved in marrying into the Royal Family.' He smiled at me. 'The impression the public have got is unfair,' I said. He shrugged. 'I've just got to live with it,' he said. 'It happens to a lot of people.'

Philip's letters to Diana were typical of his correspondence overall. They were sympathetic, but unsentimental, direct, but to a purpose. Here is a problem: let's worry it, let's unravel it, separate the strands, see if we can't make sense of them, come closer to a proper under-standing of what's wrong in the hope of being able to do something towards putting it right. He did upbraid her for failing to come to the second meeting with himself and the Queen when they had set aside time for the purpose; he did ask her to look at her own behaviour and acknowledge that there had been faults on both sides; he did remind her that, while Charles was sometimes difficult, she was not always easy. He talked about the canker of jealousy, and the problem of Camilla. He did not condone his son's ongoing relation-ship with Camilla – not for a moment – but he did want Diana to at least try to see the situation from Charles's point of view. Her post-natal depression and her irrational behaviour after Prince William's birth had not made her easy to live with. Her constant 'suspicion' of her husband was wearing. In his letters Philip confronted his daughter-in-law with home truths: he invited her to face the facts. Essentially, he wanted to make Diana think about her marriage, long and hard. And he did. He also made her cry.

When Diana received the letters she was at her most vulnerable and volatile. As soon as one arrived, she opened it, scanned it, usually burst immediately into tears and then shared it, as soon as possible, with her closest friends. Rosa Monckton, then managing director of Tiffany's in London, and Lucia Flecha da Lima, wife of the Brazilian Ambassador, were probably Diana's two closest girlfriends at the time of her death.[112] In the aftermath of Diana's death I had lunch with them and they described to me the ritual of receiving, reading, and replying to the Duke of Edinburgh's correspondence. 'When the letters came,' explained Rosa, 'they caused excitement and alarm at the same time. Diana was very up and down. Something he said might make her cry, something might make her laugh. She very often got the wrong end of the stick, misinterpreting what he meant.' 'We went through each letter, so carefully, thinking about what he said, talking about it, explaining it to her,' Lucia recalled. 'We would get into the car and all go to the [Brazilian] Embassy and sit together and read the letters, line by line.' 'Then,' said Rosa, 'we helped her draft her replies. She took the correspondence very seriously.' The correspondence continued for more than a year. For a while Philip's letters, carefully tied together with ribbon, were stored for safe keeping in a box in the Brazilian Ambassador's safe. 'They were good letters,' said Lucia, emphatically. 'He is a good man.' Rosa Monckton agreed. 'Actually, he was pretty wonderful,' she said to me. 'All he was trying to do was help. And Diana knew that.'

According to Paul Burrell, Diana found many of Philip's letters

112 They were both older than Diana (by eight years and more) and, as well as being her girlfriends, had a sisterly/motherly relationship with her, pastoral as well as playful. (Diana's father, Earl Spencer, died in 1992. Diana's relationship with her own mother, Frances, was fraught, from the time her mother 'bolted' from home to run off with Peter Shand Kydd when Diana was only six; at the time of Diana's death mother and daughter were not on speaking terms.) In the weeks leading up to her death, Diana had spent time with both Lucia (staying with her in Washington, DC) and Rosa (cruising together around the Greek Islands). For a while after her death, Lucia and Rosa were regarded as Diana's representatives on earth. It was not their fault. Diana was arguably the most celebrated woman of the twentieth century: her death eclipsed that of Mother Teresa. After Diana's death I recall having supper with James Hewitt, one of her lovers in the darker days of her marriage. He is very easy to be with: you can see why Diana fell for him. 'I hope I made her a little happier,' he said to me. 'That's all.' The point of the story is this: as we left the restaurant, people reached out to shake Hewitt's hand – they wanted to be close to him because he had been close to Diana.

hard to take, describing them as 'brutal'. In his book, *A Royal Duty*, Diana's butler and much-advertised 'rock', maintained that 'the inherent problem of using Prince Philip as a mediator was that he rarely pulled any punches, and as someone who didn't understand the princess, he could hardly be expected to know how to handle her personality and temperament'. I think Burrell is wrong. I think Philip did understand his daughter-in-law and, acting *in loco parentis*, was offering her what she needed: tough love. He accepted that her bulimia was an illness and that consequently she could not always be answerable for her behaviour. He acknowledged that Charles was wrong to have returned to Camilla, but told her that she, too, was wrong to have taken other lovers, and asked her to reflect on why her husband had sought out his old flame. He praised her achievements, but invited her, also, to consider where and when she might have got it wrong. Some of his remarks were undeniably negative, but his underlying message was always positive, and his purpose was practical: to guide her towards the possibility of a reconciliation with her husband. In one letter he even drew up a numbered list of things – activities, interests, people – that the pair of them had in common. I doubt that the trained counsellors from Relate could have done very much more.

Ultimately, Philip's mission failed. 'To be fair,' says Paul Burrell, 'Prince Philip did more to save the marriage than Prince Charles.' Burrell was once a personal footman to the Queen and his then wife, Maria, was the Duke of Edinburgh's maid. He professes to admire them both, but they certainly remained not at all happy with him. Members of staff who write books about their years in royal service are betraying the trust their former employers once placed in them. Burrell (though not his wife) was disinvited to the Windsor party marking the Duke of Edinburgh's eightieth birthday in 2001. Diana's friends Lucia Flecha da Lima and Rosa Monckton, once quite cosy with the Princess's butler, and ready to stand up for him at his trial, now have no time for him. 'He was just a servant,' the ambassador's wife reminded me, skewering a lettuce leaf over our light lunch at Le Caprice. 'He opens doors, he closes door, then he goes. He is the butler, he is the servant. We were her friends.' 'It's very sad,' said Rosa. 'He shouldn't have written that book. He shouldn't have sold his story. He is exploiting Diana now – for money. It's bad.'

It got worse. When I first recorded a conversation with Paul Burrell, not long after Diana's death, he was quite circumspect. He talked of her with enormous affection, but with a certain reserve. He told me how she loved to watch her favourite weepie, *Brief Encounter*, on the television, feet curled under her on the sofa, box of tissues to hand. She invited him to sit with him to watch, but he wouldn't. He was the butler, after all. He described her at breakfast time, pressing him to join her at the table to help open the post, but he was reluctant. When I saw him a few years later, the reserve had gone. He now talked of Diana with a frankness and familiarity that felt uncomfortable. He said, 'I knew she wasn't pregnant when she died, because of all sorts of things – her menstrual cycle, the pills she was taking . . .' He described 'the privilege of attending to her personally' in the French hospital, after she was dead, in mawkish detail. He remains devoted to Diana's memory, but he no longer guards it with the tenderness and discretion that once he did.

In 2004 Burrell published the paperback of his book about Diana, with an 'extra chapter' of hotly touted revelations. The new material prompted the headline in the *Daily Mail*: 'Charles "had a deal with Philip to dump Diana in five years".' According to Burrell, Diana suspected that Prince Philip had been 'a collaborating architect in the marriage's downfall', that he had given Charles 'his blessing, with a nudge and a wink, to renew his liaison with Camilla'. Burrell claimed that Diana was told by Charles himself – in the heat of a row – that 'he had always had his father's blessing – from the outset of the marriage – to return to Camilla if the Princess did not make him happy'. Diana was capable of saying many things – and different things on different days – but her friends, Rosa Monckton and Lucia Flecha da Lima, are quite clear on this: Diana had great respect and affection for her father-in-law, she trusted him and knew that he wanted only to help. The idea that Prince Philip would have arranged 'a five year get-out clause' on his son's marriage is simply not credible. Philip told Diana, in terms, what he thought of his son's mistress. 'I cannot imagine anyone in their right mind leaving you for Camilla,' he wrote to her, and she believed him.

Paul Burrell still speaks of the Queen with respect and acknowledges that the Duke of Edinburgh's intentions towards Diana were

Philip with Princess Beatrice, aged three, the daughter of Prince Andrew and Sarah Ferguson, May 1991

Philip with Zara Phillips, aged nine, the daughter of Princess Anne and Captain Mark Phillips, February 1991

50 years on: Philip and Elizabeth together at 'Omaha' beach in France, marking the fiftieth anniversary of the D-Day Landings of June 1944

THE Sun 25p

Wednesday, November 25, 1992 25p Audited daily sale for October 3,572,450 Today's TV: Pages 20 and 21

ONE'S BUM YEAR

Or as Queen admits: I've had an *Annus Horribilis*

I know how you feel Ma'am Troubled John Major leans over the Lord Mayor to speak to the Queen

By RUKI SAYID

THE Queen opened her heart to the nation yesterday — and admitted 1992 has been one of her worst years ever.

In the most revealing speech of her 40-year reign, she said: "It has turned out to be an 'annus horribilis'" — Latin for a horrible year.

Her remarks came after a year in which she has seen

Charles' and Andrew's marriages hit the rocks, Anne's end in divorce and the blaze at her beloved Windsor Castle.

The Queen also signalled she is ready to start paying income tax on her estimated £6billion fortune.

Following the barrage of public criticism, she said: "This sort of questioning can act — and it should do so — as an effective engine for change."

Looking weary and fighting a heavy cold, the Queen made her astonishing speech at a banquet in London's Guildhall to mark her 40th year on the throne.

Guests including Premier John Major heard her say: "1992 is not a year on which I shall look back with undiluted pleasure. In the words of one of my more sympathetic correspondents it has turned out to be an annus horribilis." In a

Continued on Page Four

'Annus horribilis'
Inspecting the fire damage at
Windsor, 21 November 1992

Mourning Diana: outside Buckingham Palace in September 1997,
the week Princess Diana died

Mourning Britannia: at Portsmouth in December 1997, witnessing the
decommissioning of the Royal Yacht, Britannia

The memorial service for those killed in the terrorist attacks of 11 September 2001, the day 'Porchey' also died

The funeral of Queen Elizabeth, the Queen Mother, 9 April 2002

Prince William and Prince Harry with their grandfather on the steps of Old College, Royal Military Academy Sandhurst, after the Sovereign's Parade, April 2006

The Queen and Prince Philip visiting Prince William at RAF Anglesey, April 2011

Royal weddings: at the wedding of Prince William and Catherine Middleton at Westminster Abbey, 29 April 2011; walking down the same aisle after their wedding, 20 November 1947

The Queen and Prince Philip on the Royal Barge during the Thames Diamond Jubilee River Pageant, 3 June 2012

The author listens to Prince William pay tribute to Prince Philip at an event for the National Playing Fields Association, June 2012

Four sovereigns in one photograph. In the morning room at Clarence House on 23 October 2013, Prince Philip (grandson of the King of Greece) with his wife, Elizabeth II, his son, the Prince of Wales, who will be Charles III, his grandson, the Duke of Cambridge, a future William V, at the christening of Prince Philip's great-grandson, Prince George, a future George VII.

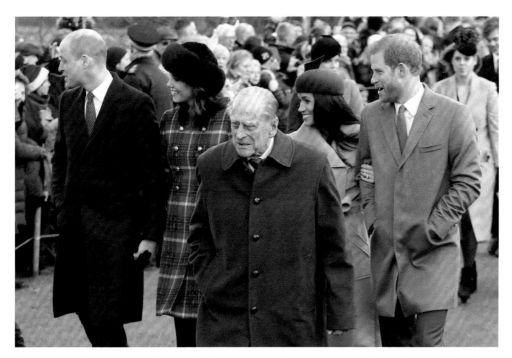

Christmas Day, 2017. Prince Philip leading the way, with the Duke and Duchess of Cambridge and Prince Harry and his American wife Meghan Markle

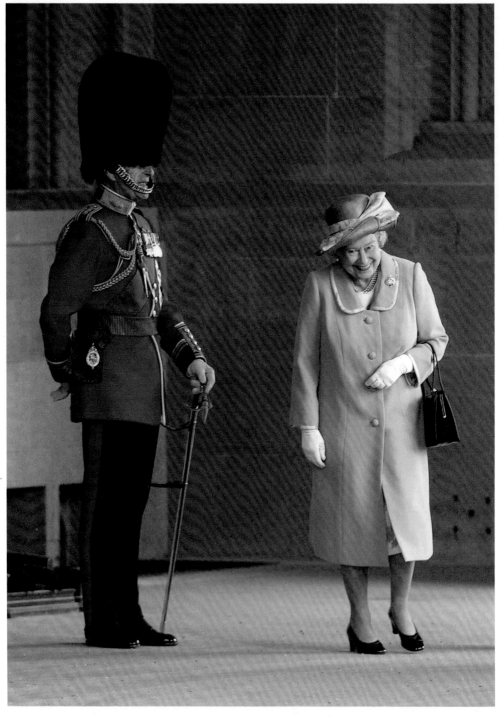

In 2005, HRH The Duke of Edinburgh, Colonel of the Grenadier Guards, doing what he did for HM The Queen for more than seventy years: making her laugh.

essentially well meant, even if Philip 'wore steelworker's gloves for a situation that required kid mittens'. He no longer much cares what the rest of the royal establishment thinks of him. He has some cause, of course. In the aftermath of Diana's death he was arrested, charged, and eventually put on trial at the Old Bailey, accused of stealing three hundred and ten personal items belonging to Diana, Prince Charles, and their children. The case came to trial because, as Burrell put it to me, 'Charles and the boys had been told by the police that I'd dressed up in Diana's clothes and already sold some of her stuff in America.' The case collapsed because, as the trial was reaching its climax, on 25 October 2002, the Queen and Prince Charles and Prince Philip – travelling by car to St Paul's Cathedral to attend a memorial service for the victims of the Bali bombings – had a brief conversation in which the Queen, prompted by her husband, told her son that she recalled having had a meeting with Paul Burrell, shortly after Diana's death, at which Burrell confided to her that he had taken some of Diana's possessions from Kensington Palace to his home, where he was storing them for safe keeping.

This revelation – relayed by the Prince to his private secretary, who confirmed it with the Queen and then transmitted it to the proper authorities – established that Burrell had had no intention to deceive. The prosecution case crumbled, no further evidence was offered, and he was found not guilty and released from the dock with words from the judge that must have sounded sweet indeed: 'Mr Burrell, you are free to go.'

It was a good day for the butler, but an uncomfortable one for the Queen. For a start, the case that collapsed was 'Regina v Burrell' and what brought it to its knees was an intervention from Regina herself. Had Her Majesty really only just recalled her meeting with her former footman? Or had she chosen this moment to mention the matter because she was fearful of what damage might be done if the trial continued and the defence offered evidence about her son and his marriage that might be better left unheard? If her intent was not Machiavellian (and I am happy to accept that it was not), then, at best, the eleventh-hour timing of the Queen's contribution illustrated all too clearly how little and how poorly mother and son communicated.

In his book Paul Burrell recalled, in vivid detail, his celebrated meeting with the Queen. It took place in the Queen's private apartments at Buckingham Palace on Thursday, 19 December 1997, not quite four months after Diana's death. According to Burrell's book, the encounter lasted almost three hours and culminated with Her Majesty looking at her former footman over her half-rimmed spectacles and uttering an eerie warning. 'Be careful, Paul,' she said, fixing him with a penetrating stare. 'There are powers at work in this country about which we have no knowledge.'

When, later, I challenged Burrell to tell me what he thought Her Majesty meant by this, he wouldn't or couldn't tell me. I told him that it didn't, to me, sound very much like the Queen's way of speaking. I told him, too, that the idea of the Queen granting anyone a three-hour audience seemed a bit improbable. He conceded that, perhaps, three hours had been a bit of an exaggeration. 'It was about 2.30 when the meeting began. She had just finished coffee – her dining room is next to her sitting room. Her personal page said, "Paul, Her Majesty will see you now." We stood throughout, of course. I can see Her Majesty lifting her feet as we chatted. She does that. She's used to standing, but she lifts her feet. We talked about much more than Diana. We talked about family problems. Then she said, "I must take the corgis for a walk." They normally go at 3.30 and she has her tea at five, so it was after 3.30. We must have been talking for at least an hour. She's a lovely Christian lady. You know, she gets up at six in the morning to go into her private chapel to pray at Christmas and Easter.'

Paul Burrell's respect for the Queen and devotion to Diana are not in doubt. He fell completely in love with Diana and, after her death, hoarded her possessions because he could not bear to be parted from her. He said as much in a letter to the Prince of Wales: 'All I ever wanted to do was "take care" of what I considered to be "my world".' I said to Paul, 'Your trouble was that you fell in love with Diana because Judy Garland was dead.' He laughed, but I think he understood what I meant. Diana was a star and she was dazzling.

Diana was a star and that was her strength. From the perspective of the Royal Family, that was her weakness, too. The Queen and Prince Philip were not, for a moment, envious of Diana's phenomenal popularity with the public (as Charles may well have been), but they were troubled by it. For them, royalty is not about 'celebrity' or 'star quality', hysterical crowds, or newspaper column inches. It is about duty and service, and providing a thread of continuity that links the past with the future and helps binds communities together, whether it is a local community or the country or the Commonwealth. In one of his letters to Diana, Philip praised her for her good works, but reminded her that being consort to the Prince of Wales 'involves much more than being a hero with the British people'. More than once, in conversation, the Duke of Edinburgh reminded me that, in the 1950s, he and the Queen were objects of 'adulation – such adulation – you wouldn't believe it, you really wouldn't'. The Queen was 'the world's sweetheart'[113]: hundreds of thousands – no, millions – filled the streets to cheer her. But the Queen did not take it personally. Diana believed in her own publicity. The press used her and she used the press. As the Duke of Edinburgh put it to me, 'Diana played to the gallery. It is a dangerous game.'

Prince Philip also reminded me that while Diana did much that was worthwhile, what she did was not unique. For example, early in 1956, in Nigeria, the Queen and Prince Philip, aged twenty-nine and thirty-four, young and oh-so-glamorous, visited a leper colony. They did so, not simply to visit Commonwealth citizens suffering from leprosy, but, more significantly, to allay the widespread, irrational fear that was attached then to any physical contact with the disease. This was a lifetime before Diana – with the same good intentions – got stuck into AIDS. Diana did much that was wonderful, but the way in which she did it was not necessarily the only way in which it might be done. Princess Anne, a loving mother and proactive President of the Save the Children Fund since 1970, says pointedly, 'The very idea that all children want to be cuddled by a complete stranger I find utterly amazing.'

The Queen and Prince Philip did not find Diana easy, because

---

113 At time of the Coronation the phrase was used on radio and television, in newspapers and magazines, all over the world. In January 1953, Jock Colville recorded the American financier Bernard Baruch saying to him that 'England now had three assets: her Queen, "the world's sweetheart", Winston Churchill, and her glorious historical past'.

she was not easy. They found some of her behaviour frustrating, bewildering, and troublesome, because that is what it was. In his book about the Queen, Graham Turner quoted an unnamed courtier who recalled hearing Her Majesty refer to Diana as 'that impossible girl' and 'quite mad'. Those are phrases the Queen could well have used, and with some justification. The 'war of the Waleses' was an unhappy time for all concerned.

On 9 December 1992 Buckingham Palace announced the formal separation of the Prince and Princess of Wales. If the sovereign and her consort hoped for a cessation of hostilities, they were soon disappointed. In the autumn of 1994 Jonathan Dimbleby published his authorised biography of the Prince of Wales. In print, and on television, Charles confessed to his own adultery. In the autumn of 1995 Diana sought her right of reply and gave an interview to Martin Bashir for *Panorama*. Even today, it remains one of the most watched television programmes in the history of broadcasting. Millions tuned in to see Diana, dewy-eyed, pouring scorn on her husband, confessing to her own adultery, but blaming Charles – and Camilla. She expressed her opinion that Charles would never become King and defined the role she sought for herself. 'I would like to be queen of people's hearts,' she said. Nicholas Soames, a close friend of Prince Charles (and a government minister at the time), said Diana 'seemed on the edge of paranoia'. The Queen said, 'Enough is enough.'

The Queen and the Duke talked it through. Her Majesty consulted the Prime Minister (John Major), the Archbishop of Canterbury (George Carey), her private secretary (Robert Fellowes). She then wrote concisely, but unequivocally, to both the Prince and the Princess, giving it as her decided opinion, supported by her husband, that an early divorce was now desirable. In the event, the Wales's divorce settlement took many months to negotiate. The Duke of Edinburgh was not amused by reports that his daughter-in-law's demands included the suggestion that any future children she might have by another husband should bear hereditary titles. The Duke's view was that, as well as losing her rank as a Royal Highness, Diana should be downgraded from Princess of Wales to Duchess of Cornwall – on the basis, as he put it, that 'when it's over it's over'. 'I am not vindictive,' he said to me, emphatically, 'I am not vindictive.' In the

394

end, Diana surrendered her royal status,[114] and agreed to be known as 'Diana, Princess of Wales', in return for a lump-sum sweetener of £17 million and an annual staff and office allowance of £400,000. And that was that.

Except, of course, it wasn't. The worst was yet to be. In the early hours of Sunday, 31 August 1997, the chauffeur-driven Mercedes in which Diana and her current lover, Dodi Fayed, were travelling across Paris at speed, pursued by paparazzi on motorbikes, entered the tunnel at the Place de l'Alma and crashed into a concrete pillar. Diana and Dodi and the driver were all killed. The Queen was at Balmoral, on holiday with her family. At 2 a.m. she was woken with news of the accident. At 3.30 a.m. the British Embassy in Paris confirmed that Diana, Princess of Wales, was dead.

That day the Queen and Prince Phillip did exactly what anyone who knew them would have expected them to do. They comforted their grandsons in private and, in public, went about their business as usual. They took William and Harry to church with them on that fateful Sunday morning because William and Harry wanted to go, and because the Queen believes that, at times of tribulation, there is no better place to be. Her faith is her rock and doing things much as they have always been done is a practice that, on the whole, has served her well. There is comfort to be had from familiar hymns and prayers. There is solace to be found in form and custom long established, and in doing what you have to do in the way that you normally do it.

While Prince Charles flew to Paris to accompany Diana's body on its journey home, the Queen and Prince Philip kept William and

114 As well as losing the letters HRH before her name (the letters Uncle David had so wanted for his wife all his life), Diana's departure from the Royal Family also meant that her name was no longer included in the prayers said for the Royal Family in churches throughout the Church of England. I was an MP at the time and, at the House of Commons, at the start of every day's business, led by the Speaker's Chaplain, we would pray for the Queen and her family, including, by name, the Princess of Wales. One day she was there, the next she was not. Anthony Holden, in his most recent biography of Prince Charles, says the 'letters patent' detailing all this 'were rather brutally published, on the Queen's personal instructions, in "the noticeboard of the Establishment", the *London Gazette*'. This is unfair. The Queen had no desire to be vindictive. This is how such royal announcements are always published.

Harry at Balmoral, out of harm's way, out of the public eye. The Queen viewed Diana's death as a private tragedy for William and Harry. The public displays of grief – worldwide and extraordinary – caught her by surprise. Her instinct and upbringing had taught her – and her generation – that you kept your tears for the pillow. Crying in public was not something the Queen would allow herself, or expect of her children and grandchildren. It is not the royal way. It is neither dignified nor necessary – nor helpful. But, on television, in the first week of September 1997, it seemed the whole world was openly weeping and wailing – and baying for Her Majesty to shed some tears, too.

'Show Us You Care' chorused the headline writers. The Queen was at Balmoral, invisible, unhappy, and confused. Above Buckingham Palace, the flagpole, traditionally empty except when the sovereign is in residence, remained bare. The people – or, at least, the tabloids on their behalf – demanded a sign from the sovereign: a flag above her principal residence flying at half-mast. By tradition, the only flag to fly above the Palace was the Royal Standard and, famously, even at the death of his own father, Edward VII, his son, George V, would not countenance the Royal Standard flying at half-mast. But that was then and this was now. 'Your Majesty, Please Look and Learn,' read a handwritten notice left, amid the field of flowers, outside Buckingham Palace. Her Majesty – pressed from all sides: by family, friends, and Tony Blair – took notice and, biting the inside of her bottom lip, did as she was counselled. She broke with all precedent and commanded that the Union flag be flown above the Palace at half-mast. She returned to London. With Philip at her side, she got out of her car and inspected the tributes – the single flowers, the bouquets, the poems, the teddy bears – left, in their thousands, in remembrance of her late daughter-in-law. On Friday night, 5 September, on the eve of the funeral, the Queen gave a live broadcast that changed the national mood. She said no more than she meant, that Diana was 'an exceptional and gifted human being' whom she admired 'for her energy and commitment to others, and especially for her commitment to her two boys'. She spoke of the 'extraordinary and moving reaction to her death' and the 'lessons to be learnt' from it. She spoke as a Queen and 'as a grandmother' – and what she said and how she said it, simply and directly, with sincerity but without false sentiment, reminded the people who watched that she wasn't such a bad old stick after all. With dignity, and retaining her integrity, she showed us she cared. (Is it any wonder the Queen and Prince Philip despised the tabloid press?[115])

On Saturday morning, before the funeral, the Queen, with her family, stood at the gates of Buckingham Palace, and Her Majesty led by example, bowing her head slowly as Diana's coffin was driven past. In the funeral procession, Diana's former husband and younger brother, Prince Charles and Charles Spencer, were due to walk behind the gun carriage bearing her coffin along the route to Westminster Abbey. Prince Harry and, in particular, Prince William were uncertain as to whether or not they wanted to walk behind the coffin, too. Prince Philip, who had not planned to walk, said to William, 'If I walk, will you walk with me?' As grandparents Philip and Elizabeth did their best by their grandsons that week.

The funeral itself was not a comfortable experience. Elton John was never one of Prince Philip's favourite performers. Tony Blair's over-emotional reading of the Lesson was embarrassing. And Charles Spencer's address, while perhaps forgivable under the circumstances, was, from the point of view of the Queen and the Duke, both illogical and insulting. In the course of it, Earl Spencer spoke directly to Diana's sons and, on behalf of his mother and his sisters, with a catch in his throat, solemnly vowed that 'we, your blood family, will do all we can to continue the imaginative way in which you were steering these two exceptional young men so that their souls are not simply immersed by duty and tradition, but can sing openly as you planned'. Outside the Abbey, the listening crowd applauded the Earl's oration. The noise of applause spilt into the Abbey. The congregation began to clap. The applause rumbled down the nave. William and Harry, a little uncertainly, clapped, too. The Queen and the Duke of Edinburgh did not join in. Later, privately, Her Majesty said that what disappointed her about Charles Spencer's address was that it

115 The Queen understands and accepts that a modern monarchy requires sensitive and effective press and public relations, but having to dance to the tabloid tune sticks in the royal craw. Her Majesty did not like having to break all precedent in the matter of the flagpole. She was initially uncertain about the broadcast, but, once she had agreed to it, did it with a will and in a way that rang true. Her script was drafted by Robert Fellowes, with input from 10 Downing Street.

failed to do justice to his sister's memory. He devoted so much of his address to castigating the media and disparaging the Royal Family that he left himself no time to pay proper tribute to Diana's many gifts and achievements. The Queen was especially saddened by the fact that her godson Earl Spencer failed to acknowledge the importance to Diana of her personal faith.

When I talked to Charles Spencer about his sister's funeral, he told me he had had no intention of upsetting the Royal Family with his remarks. He had simply spoken as he had felt at the time, from the heart. I asked him how much hands-on involvement the 'blood family' now had with the boys and their upbringing, and he admitted, 'Not a lot', because it was not necessary. He said, 'Prince Charles is obviously a good father and the boys are doing really well. I think Diana would be very happy about the way they have grown up. She'd be very proud of them.' I asked him how he felt about Camilla. He said, 'It's none of my business. I wish Charles every happiness. He should do whatever he wants to do.'

Diana despised Camilla. She had good cause. She thought about her rival a great deal, but tended to avoid mentioning her by name, referring to her simply as 'you-know-who' or 'her' or 'that woman' or 'the third party'. What Diana would have felt about Charles and Camilla marrying is anybody's guess. She changed her opinion with her mood – and with the company she kept. On one occasion, she said, 'Marry her? Over my dead body.' On another, 'Oh, what the hell, let him marry her. Why not? I'm past caring.'

She was never past caring what those in the Royal Family whom she respected thought about her – though, in the view of the Queen and Prince Philip, especially after the *Panorama* interview, she had a funny way of showing it. She spoke well of Princess Anne and of Princess Margaret, each of whom, of course, had had matrimonial difficulties of their own. She said that Anne 'could be surprisingly supportive at times' and that Margaret 'even defended me against the occasional tirades of my father-in-law'. Often, she said, she wanted 'to give my mother-in-law a great big hug', but she knew that was not exactly her mother-in-law's style. She conceded that the Queen, who felt sorely tested at times, 'behaved pretty impeccably throughout'. She reckoned that the Queen would never approve of Charles marrying Camilla, 'And he wouldn't without her blessing.'

On 9 April 2005 Charles did marry Camilla, of course – and with his mother's blessing. A few days earlier I had lunch at St James's Palace with the Duke of Edinburgh and found him in a mellow mood. He spoke of Prince Charles without the usual asperity and seemed content at the prospect of his son's second wedding. 'At least it's settled,' he said, 'and that's good.' When Lord Howard of Rising (a Norfolk neighbour) reminded him of the saying that 'when a man marries his mistress it creates a vacancy', His Royal Highness chuckled obligingly and muttered, 'Don't, please.' I reminded him of one of his best jokes – 'If you see a man opening the car door for his wife, it's either a new car or a new wife' – and asked him if he was planning to use it in his father-of-the-groom's speech. 'I shan't be saying a word,' he replied, firmly.

When the wedding day arrived, all went well. The Queen and Prince Philip did not attend the civil marriage at the Guildhall in Windsor, but they were there for the blessing in St George's Chapel at Windsor Castle. The order of service included the General Confession taken from the Book of Common Prayer, so that Charles and Camilla (along with the rest of the congregation) acknowledged their 'manifold sins and wickedness' and sought God's forgiveness 'with hearty repentance and true faith'. The Confession gave the press the excuse for a churlish final fling. The *Daily Express* described the couple's public act of repentance as 'too little, too late'. The *Daily Mirror* filled its front page with a picture of Charles and Camilla both sporting a cuckold's horns and devil's tail, under the stark headline: 'We have SINNED.'

In the streets of Windsor the crowds were not vast, but they were sympathetic and good-humoured. As the couple arrived at the Guildhall for the civil ceremony, I heard one half-hearted 'boo'. It came from a middle-aged man who was quickly hushed by those around him. Inside St George's Chapel, as the guests arrived for the service of blessing and dedication, there was a sense of nervous excitement. 'So far, so good,' said Camilla's father, Major Bruce Shand. 'I'm terribly relieved it's finally happened,' said the actor Timothy West, who was to read Wordsworth's 'Ode: Intimations of Immortality' during the service.

For Camilla, the day was not easy. She was nervous (understandably) and she was suffering from sinusitis (which nobody knew). Her head was throbbing. But she looked wonderful – exactly right – and there was something endearing about her moments of awkwardness. Outside the Guildhall, she knocked her hat with her hand. Outside St George's Chapel, she held on to her hat for fear the wind was going to whisk it away. It was touching, too, to see Charles helping her find her place in the order of service, holding her hand to display the ring, whispering to her, 'You're doing so well.'

The reception was a triumph. Everyone was happy – including, it seemed, the Duke of Edinburgh. He was his genial, joshing self, but he did not give much away. Congratulated on the way it was all going, he said, 'Nothing to do with me.' There was a sense of both relief and good humour in the air. When Charles ended his speech with the words, 'Down with the press!', everybody cheered. When William gave Camilla a congratulatory kiss, it was not cursory: it was done with real affection. When Charles thanked 'my darling Camilla who has stood with me through thick and thin, and whose precious optimism and humour have seen me through', there were tears in many eyes. Charles also paid tribute to 'my sons' ('they would be annoyed if I called them my children') and 'my dear mama' for meeting the bill for the occasion. The Duchy champagne flowed freely and the much-mocked 'finger food' went down a treat.[116]

True to his word, Prince Philip did not say a word. The Queen spoke and her speech stole the show. She gave the marriage her unqualified seal of approval. She did not speak for long, but what she said was funny, apt, and profoundly touching. The wedding coincided with the Grand National and the Queen began by saying she had two important announcements to make. The first was that Hedgehunter had won the race at Aintree; the second was that, at Windsor, she was delighted to be welcoming her son and his bride to 'the winners' enclosure'. She said, 'They have overcome Becher's Brook and The Chair and all kinds of other terrible obstacles. They have come through and I'm very proud and wish them well. My son is home and dry with the woman he loves.'

116 The sandwiches included smoked salmon on brown bread, roast venison with Balmoral redcurrant and port jelly on white bread, and egg and cress on granary. There were potted shrimp bridge rolls and mini Cornish pasties; scones with Cornish clotted cream and Duchy strawberry jam; lemon tarts, caramel banana slices, and miniature ice cream cornets.

After years of anxiety and reservation, the Queen accepted Camilla and did so wholeheartedly. And her reward was to discover quite quickly that Camilla is very much her sort of woman – much more so than Diana could ever have been. Camilla can talk easily (and amusingly) about dogs and horses. She is comfortable with the Queen's view of life (for the most part, she shares it); she is politically incorrect (in a good way), funny, self-deprecating, realistic; and, like the Queen, she is a mother and a grandmother who has been a bit tempest-tossed but has managed to weather the storms. In 2012, to mark Charles and Camilla's seventh wedding anniversary, the Queen honoured her daughter-in-law as she had not honoured Diana: she made her a Dame Grand Cross of the Royal Victorian Order.

Prince Philip accepted Camilla into the family because, as he put it to me, 'You can't argue with the inevitable.' There is no doubt that Prince Charles has not handled his life as his father would have done. And there is no denying that Philip was often critical of his son. At times he regarded him as self-indulgent, self-regarding, and naive. He did not approve of Charles's affair with Camilla, nor with his handling of it, but once Diana was dead he could see no objection to Charles marrying Camilla. Being a pragmatist and a man with an orderly mind, he was pleased to see Charles's situation 'regularised'. When I asked him what he made of Camilla, he was circumspect. 'She's a good sort,' I said. 'Yes,' he agreed. 'I've seen her at Highgrove with the boys,' I said. 'They get on well.' 'Yes,' he said, 'she's good with the boys.'

Prince Philip was content that for the last decade of his life he did not have to lose any sleep over the matter of his assorted daughters-in-law. Diana was dead. Camilla he accepted. Sophie he could rely on. And Sarah Ferguson he did not think about at all.

'I think Sarah still obsesses about you,' I said.

He snorted derisively.

'You clearly love her daughters,' I persisted. 'You obviously get on well with them. Is their mother completely beyond the pale?'

'Her behaviour was a bit odd,' he said.

When Sarah Ferguson joined the Royal Family, in the summer of 1986, hopes were high. She was twenty-six and full of fun. I recall being told at the time by Philip's cousin, King Constantine,

'Everybody agrees that Sarah is the best thing to have happened to the Royal Family in years. She's a breath of fresh air.' She was certainly as lively as they come. She had a past (a live-in relationship with the racing driver Paddy McNally, twenty-two years her senior), but she also had a pedigree (her maternal grandmother was a first cousin of Princess Alice, Duchess of Gloucester, and, on her father's side, she was a second cousin to Robert Fellowes, the Queen's private secretary from 1990 to 1999), and Prince Andrew was head over heels in love with her. On their wedding day he was created Duke of York (the Queen's father's old title), and the wedding itself, at Westminster Abbey on 23 July 1986, was as glamorous and optimistic an occasion as anyone could wish for. Sadly, the Yorks' honeymoon with the press and public was not prolonged.

As the United Kingdom moved into one of its most punishing economic recessions since the war, Andrew and Sarah were building for themselves a £3.5-million mansion on the Sunninghill Estate. Sarah, initially acclaimed by the press as fun and feisty, was soon depicted as freeloading, grasping, and ridiculous. She was mocked for her fashion sense, berated for charging *Hello!* magazine £200,000 for a family photo shoot, and accused of bringing out the worst in her sister-in-law and fellow Sloane, Diana. 'Vulgar! Vulgar! Vulgar!' is how the senior courtier Lord Charteris described her.

At first the Queen and Prince Philip thought she was rather jolly. Philip had known her father, Ronald Ferguson, 'Major Ron', when he had played in Prince Philip's polo team in the 1960s. Philip had been friendly, too, with the major's first wife, Susie, Sarah's mother, who ran off to Argentina with her lover, Hector Barrantes, when Sarah was twelve – much as Diana's mother had run off with Peter Shand Kydd when Diana was a little girl. The Queen liked Sarah because she was 'outgoing and outdoorsy' and because her son evidently adored her and their two daughters (Beatrice and Eugenie, born 1988 and 1990) were very sweet indeed. When the marriage went wrong, Andrew's parents were disappointed and saddened, but understanding. Throughout their divorce Andrew and Sarah remained friends, continuing even to live under the same roof, and Sarah hoped that she would be able to remain on intimate terms with the rest of the Royal Family, too. She might have managed it, had it not been for press reports of her extramarital behaviour.

On 20 August 1992, while Sarah and Andrew, with their children, were holidaying at Balmoral with the Queen and her family, the *Daily Mirror* published photographs, taken earlier in the month, of the Duchess of York enjoying a rather different kind of summer break. At the beginning of August, Sarah had rented a villa in the south of France and gone there, with her daughters, to soak up some Mediterranean sun. John Bryan, her American 'financial adviser', had come along for the holiday, too. Unhappily for Sarah, across the valley from the villa, lurking up on the hillside, was an eagle-eyed jumbo-lensed freelance photographer who managed to take a series of gobsmackingly lurid holiday snaps of Sarah, topless, cavorting with her financial adviser beside the pool, clearly tickling his fancy as — wait for it — he sucked her toes.

The Queen and Prince Philip were, understandably, unamused. Andrew stood by his errant wife, completely and without hesitation, and Sarah, for the sake of form and the children, stayed on at Balmoral for a further three days. The atmosphere was distinctly frosty. At mealtimes Sarah, as usual, sat next to her husband, but she spent most of the time staring at her plate. She told me later that the Queen had been 'furious, really cross'. She had 'a session with her' after breakfast on the morning that the photographs appeared and the Queen kept repeating to her 'how dreadfully let down she felt'. Prince Philip's actions spoke louder than words. He decided to steer clear of Sarah altogether. 'It was ridiculous,' she told me. 'As soon as I came in through one door he'd be falling over the corgis to get out of the other. It was very funny. Except, of course, it wasn't.'

After their separations from her sons, the Queen continued to see Sarah and Diana from time to time, to have tea with them and find out how they were. Prince Philip had no desire to see Sarah again. This she knew and it pained her. 'Of course I want to see him,' she said to me after her divorce. 'I am the mother of his granddaughters, after all.' When I raised this with Prince Philip, he shrugged and said, 'But the children come and stay.' When I asked him why he would not see Sarah any longer, he said simply, 'I don't see her because I don't see much point.'

Sarah was determined to keep on trying. For Philip's eightieth birthday, she sent him a handsome dinner service. (It was supposed to have twelve settings, but it arrived with thirteen: the 'sample' had been included with the set. With Sarah, somehow, something always goes wrong.) He sent her a nice thank-you note and signed it, 'With love' from 'Pa'.

Sarah cannot speak too highly of the Queen. 'She's my icon,' she told me, her eyes glistening. 'I look up to her. I think she's the finest woman I know. HM has got a wonderful sense of humour. She loves to sing. She is the widest-read woman in the world and yet she has this wonderful compassion and total and utter understanding. She is very forgiving. She doesn't poke her nose in. She lets you have free rein, but she doesn't miss a trick.'

When they were small, Sarah made sure that her daughters were on their best behaviour when they went to see the Queen. 'We have three sets of table manners,' she explained to me. 'This is very important. Table Manners C is for at home, when it's just Andrew and me. Anything goes. Table Manners B is for in a restaurant. You can have fun, but always remember people are looking at you. I tell the girls always to smile – because it costs so little and it means so much. Table Manners A is for Granny – their granny – the Boss.'

'And what does that involve?' I asked.

'If we go to tea at Windsor or Balmoral, we do it properly,' Sarah explained to me, acting it out as she described the correct royal teatime etiquette. 'We have our little napkin. We offer Granny the sandwiches first, before we take the whole lot on to our plate. We don't take the raisins out of the scones halfway through a conversation – or flick them across the table. We don't ask for ketchup when the Duke of Edinburgh is sitting there. We don't say, "Oh, the Ribena tastes old", which it probably is. We don't say, "We don't eat pâté sandwiches." We just shut up and eat what we're given. We can have fish fingers when we get home.'

Sarah Ferguson is a huge admirer of the Queen – 'If we're voting for the best granny in the world,' she says, 'I have to tell you the Boss is the best granny' – but she no longer has any time for the 'repressed emotions' that she found were part and parcel of life at the heart of the House of Windsor. She sees it as a generational thing. 'They believe in the virtues of the stiff upper lip. I don't any more.' Sarah reckons that bottling up your feelings is positively harmful. 'My mother's generation said, "Don't speak. Don't say you're unhappy. Don't say you're angry." I think that's all wrong. I say to my girls, "Go on, tell me. Are you angry with me? Have I annoyed you?" We sit down and talk. "Was that a grubby day? Why was it a grubby day?" Or I'll make them stand in the middle of Sunninghill Park and scream – which is what I do.' Sarah suddenly goes, 'Aargh!' for me. 'I make them scream. They say, "Mummy, we can't." I say, "Why not? Who's going to hear? Scream."'

The prospect of encountering his former daughter-in-law screaming in the middle of Sunninghill Park could have been one of the reasons the Duke of Edinburgh decided to give her a wide berth after her separation from his son. Prince Philip was not a screamer. He regarded reticence as a virtue and self-control as a quality to be admired. In 2011, in the week of his ninetieth birthday, the Oprah Winfrey Network in the US aired *Finding Sarah*, a six-part TV series in which the former Duchess of York shared her tears and her heartache with a TV psychiatrist and the viewing millions. The Duke of Edinburgh did not tune in.

Prince Philip's aunt, Princess Marie Bonaparte, was a noted Freudian; Prince Philip himself was fascinated by Jung; but he told me, 'I've not spent much time psychoanalysing myself. I'm not sure how useful it would be.' He told me he was in favour of 'self-awareness', but against 'the endless introspection that seems to be so prevalent these days'. I came across a sentence by the writer and philosopher Iris Murdoch and showed it to him because I thought he would like it: 'Happiness is a matter of one's most ordinary everyday mode of consciousness being busy and lively and unconcerned with self.' 'That's it exactly,' he said. 'You can put that in your book.'

Iris Murdoch's observation sums up much of Prince Philip's philosophy and describes an attitude to life that, by precept and example, he fostered in his grandchildren. He admired Princess Anne's children, Peter and Zara, because they had both taken Gordonstoun in their stride and 'got on with it'. Peter played a good game of rugby and followed his grandfather in becoming head boy at Gordonstoun. After taking a degree in sports science at Exeter University, he embarked on a career in sports management, largely eschewing royal life. In 2008 he married Autumn Kelly, a Canadian management consultant he had met at the Canadian Grand Prix in Montreal. The couple caused some consternation within the family by selling a pre-wedding story with pictures to *Hello!* magazine, but otherwise they have kept a low profile and earnt Prince Philip's admiration. 'It can be done,' he said. Their daughters – Savannah Anne Kathleen (born in 2010 and named after Peter's and Autumn's mothers), and Isla Elizabeth (born in 2012, the year of the Golden Jubilee, and named after the Queen) – are currently thirteenth and fourteenth in line to the throne, but they have no titles and their parents fondly hope they will lead normal, private lives. Peter Phillips's younger sister, Zara, leads a public life, but as an achieving equestrian rather than as a royal. As a member of the Great Britain Eventing Team she won a silver medal at the London Olympics in 2012. The previous year she married former England rugby union player Mike Tindall. She is at the heart of the next generation of the Royal Family – as is her brother, who is particularly close to Prince William – but she does not play the 'royal card'.

Prince Andrew's daughters do have titles. Their Royal Highnesses the Princesses Beatrice and Eugenie of York may be the daughters of Sarah Ferguson but that does not seem to have diminished their paternal grandparents' affection for them. Prince Philip (who could be deliberately perverse) appeared especially fond of them and was happy to see them set out on the road to becoming 'working royals'.

I asked Prince Philip what advice he had given his grandchildren. 'I'm not in the business of giving anyone advice,' he protested. 'They are getting on very well without any interference from me.'

However, he did acknowledge to me that he was particularly happy with the career paths chosen by Prince Charles's two sons. Prince Harry, born in 1984, may have been sent to Eton rather than to Gordonstoun, but, as Prince Philip put it, 'he was lucky – he knew what he wanted to do with his life'. Harry was not interested in going to university: after a gap year spent in Australia and Lesotho, he joined the army. He was commissioned as a second lieutenant into the Blues and Royals of the Household Cavalry and completed his training as a tank commander. He served two tours of duty on the front line in Afghanistan. While his son was there, Prince Charles confessed that he 'worried about him every night' and the enemy let it be known that – because of who he was – they had Harry 'specially in their sights'.

Harry was a target of a different sort in August 2012. On leave and holidaying with high-rolling friends at a hotel in Las Vegas, he found himself being photographed naked in his £5,000-a-night suite during a game of 'strip pool'. The pictures of the royal lieutenant 'covering his privates' while 'romping with naked girls he'd only just met' were taken on a mobile phone by one of the party-goers and swept around the world. 'I was in a private area,' protested the Prince, while ruefully accepting the reality of his position: 'I don't believe there is any such thing as a private life any more. I'm not going to sit here and whinge. Everybody knows about Twitter and the internet and stuff like that. Every single mobile phone has got a camera on it now. You can't move an inch without someone judging you, and I suppose that's just the way life goes.'

It is. And, on the whole, the public judge Harry well. In Las Vegas, he conceded, 'I probably let myself down. I let my family down. I let other people down. It was probably a classic example of me probably being too much army and not enough prince.' By contrast, in Belize, the Bahamas, and Jamaica, earlier in the same year, representing the Queen during her Diamond Jubilee, the Prince did himself – and his family and his country – proud. I was in Jamaica and I can report that he delivered the goods right royally. Even the avowedly republican Prime Minister of Jamaica, Portia Simpson-Miller, was charmed.

In Jamaica, Harry was outgoing, easy, interested – concerned when it mattered and playful when appropriate. The Queen and Prince Charles do what they do very well, but Harry as a public performer has inherited the apparently effortless ease with the public that was the hallmark of his mother and his paternal grandfather at their best.

The only royal I have seen outclass both Diana and Prince Philip is Prince William. I have watched him at close range – at Highgrove, on the polo field, on the streets, and in the crowd. I have seen him with the aristocracy and everyday folk: he is comfortable with both and they are comfortable with him. He shows concern and empathy, in the way that Diana did but without those touches of self-consciousness and self-absorption that her manner sometimes suggested. William is natural, friendly, and completely easy with the people he meets – as Prince Philip was. But William's sense of humour is gentler and his banter never borders on the hectoring, as the Duke of Edinburgh's sometimes would.

Prince William has the charm and good manners of the Old Etonian, but he has had 'real life' experiences, too. He went to the University of St Andrews, where he met his wife-to-be, Catherine Middleton, an indisputably middle-class English girl. He spent parts of his gap year in Chile, Belize, Tanzania, and Kenya. He took Kiswahili studies at universities in Kenya and Tanzania. He was commissioned as a lieutenant in the Blues and Royals (serving briefly with Prince Harry) and, two years later, earnt his wings by completing pilot training at RAF Cranwell. In 2009 he was promoted to flight lieutenant and underwent helicopter training in order to become a full-time pilot with the Search and Rescue force based in Anglesey in north Wales, where he and Catherine managed to live a relatively normal young officer's life – in its way not dissimilar to the experience enjoyed by Philip and Elizabeth when the Duke of Edinburgh was a young officer serving in the Royal Navy in Malta sixty years before.

William is set to be a sovereign and father to a sovereign. Hours before his wedding he was created Duke of Cambridge, Earl of Strathearn, and Baron Carrickfergus. One day he will be Prince of Wales. In time he will be William III. Between now and then, he will continue to fulfil an increasing number of royal duties while doing what he can to keep the press both on side and at bay – providing interviews and photo opportunities *and* taking robust legal action against the media (usually French or Italian) who attempt to invade his wife's privacy by taking long-lens photographs of her on holiday, either naked or nearly so.

Prince Philip told me he was not party to William's legal action against intrusive media, but he thoroughly approved. He conceded that he might have helped Catherine with her shooting, but would take no credit for the successful way in which Catherine has merged into the Royal Family – becoming a star, but somehow managing not to behave like a celebrity.

When Prince Philip was ill in the summer of 2012, as vice-president of the National Playing Fields Association I spent a day in attendance on William and Catherine. I watched them 'doing their thing' on a playing field in Nottingham – meeting and greeting, walking and talking, making a speech, playing with some children, managing a crowd – and they did not put a foot wrong. At all times their focus was entirely on the people immediately in front of them. Not once did either of them play to the cameras – or even acknowledge them. Occasionally, Prince William put out a hand to touch his wife's fingers or elbow or shoulder and she reciprocated with a smile. You would only have noticed these fleeting signals of mutual support if you had been on the lookout for them – which I was. And I noticed, too, that just as the Duke of Edinburgh, in more than seventy years of royal duty, never once put himself above, before, or ahead of his wife and sovereign – in the best sense, he knew his place – so Catherine, it seemed to me, was careful, in the best sense, to know hers. The crowds were not there for Catherine Middleton: they were there because Catherine had married the prince who is heir to the heir to the throne. She did not take the adulation for herself. She did not play to the gallery. She appeared to have learnt all the lessons that Prince Philip could have taught her.

I reported all this back to the Duke of Edinburgh. He nodded.

'It was a wonderful day,' I said.

'I was sad to miss it,' he said, simply.

'And I think Prince William and Prince Harry have given us a million pounds from their charitable foundation.'

The Duke raised his eyebrows appreciatively. (In my experience, the senior royals give substantial sums to a range of good causes, but usually anonymously or without the amount being advertised.) 'And William made a lovely speech – mostly in your praise.'

'Was anyone listening?'

'I was. It was out of doors and a bit windy. But it was on the one o'clock news. And it was a good speech – a tribute to you and your sixty-five years with the Playing Fields Association. A tribute to the Queen, too – for all you've done, for the example you've set.'

His Royal Highness took a deep breath. He was never good at taking compliments. 'I am sorry I missed it.'

PHILIP & ELIZABETH

Chapter Thirteen

'A happy marriage perhaps represents the ideal of human relationships – a setting in which each partner, while acknowledging the
need of the other, feels free to be what he or she by nature is: a
relationship in which instinct as well as intellect can find expression, in which giving and taking are equal; in which each accepts
the other, and I confronts Thou.'

Anthony Storr (1920–2001), *The Integrity of the Personality*

In March 2004, on the day, as it happened, of the funeral of the late
Queen Juliana of the Netherlands, Queen Elizabeth II hosted a
private party in London to celebrate the fiftieth anniversary of her
Coronation. The party took place a year later than originally planned.
It had to be postponed from 2003 because of the war on Iraq. The
Duke of Edinburgh attended the party, of course, but he arrived a
little later than scheduled – not on account of his age (he was then
eighty-two), but because he had spent the day in The Hague, on
duty, representing the United Kingdom at Queen Juliana's funeral.

Queen Juliana was an interesting woman. She reigned from 1948
until 1980, when she abdicated in favour of her eldest daughter,
Crown Princess Beatrix, who, in due course, in April 2013, abdicated
in favour of her son, Crown Prince Willem-Alexander. In her day
Juliana was Europe's richest reigning monarch, but she eschewed
pomp and ceremony, and abolished the curtsy, among other court
formalities. She was kindly, deeply religious, devoted to her four
daughters and her people (in that order), and married, for sixty-seven
years, to Prince Bernhard, a German princeling whose way with
women and money did him little credit and, on more than one
occasion, came close to toppling the Orange throne.

Bernhard and Juliana each had their foibles. In 1956, for example, it came to light that, for the previous eight years, the Dutch Queen had been relying heavily on the spiritual services of a faith healer named Greet Hofmans. Hofmans, apparently, used her position to obtain posts at the palace for her friends and tried to influence government policy. She also persuaded the Queen to move from her quarters 'because the earth waves were not right'. In 1959 the Queen and the Prince invited a self-styled American 'professor' (and former hamburger vendor) named George Adamski to visit them privately to report on what he described as his flight around the moon in a spaceship from Venus. More seriously, in 1976, Prince Bernhard was accused of soliciting money from the Lockheed Corporation of America and found – by the official inquiry into the case – to be a man 'open to dishonourable requests and offers'.

We have had none of these embarrassments with Queen Elizabeth II and the Duke of Edinburgh. I wonder if we appreciate how fortunate we have been. Elizabeth II is neither eccentric nor quixotic, and her husband was as honest and straightforward as the day is long.

If there is one word that sums up Elizabeth II, it is 'dutiful'. Her life has been driven by duty. She was a dutiful daughter. She has been a dutiful Queen. Because I have met her – because, at close quarters, I have observed her as she carried out a range of her official duties – people sometimes ask me, leaning forward, narrowing their eyes, 'What's the Queen really like?' My answer disappoints them. 'She's seems very nice,' I say. 'Rather normal, actually; quite straightforward; much as you'd expect, in fact.'

The truth is, the Queen is wholly predictable. On 30 April 2002, in Westminster Hall, I watched her as she addressed the joint Houses of Parliament on the occasion of her Golden Jubilee. In the outfit you would expect (peacock blue, matching hat, smashing pearls, lovely brooch, black gloves, spectacles firmly in place), in the voice you recognise (Gainsborough Studios, circa 1947), she said all the things you knew that she would say. The speech – brief, balanced, well phrased – reflected both the moderate and modest nature of the monarch, and the decent, enduring values she holds dear. As she concluded with her pledge to continue to serve her country in the years to come, the journalists sitting around me twitched with excitement. 'She's staying,' hissed one. 'That's our story,' whispered another. In the following morning's newspapers it was, indeed, everybody's lead story, but it was hardly news.

Anyone who has had five minutes – let alone fifty or sixty and more years – to consider the Queen knows that when, as Princess Elizabeth, aged twenty-one, she said, 'I declare before you all that my whole life, whether it be long or short, shall be devoted to your service', she meant it. At her Coronation she made a commitment to God as well as to her people, and her faith sustains her in all she does. She is God's anointed monarch. 'Be thou anointed, blessed and consecrated Queen over the Peoples, whom the Lord thy God hath given thee to rule and govern . . .' were the words addressed to her by the Archbishop of Canterbury at the most solemn moment of her Coronation – and she has not forgotten them. Queen Juliana of the Netherlands abdicated in favour of her daughter, Queen Beatrix, just as her mother, Queen Wilhelmina, had abdicated in her favour, but the Dutch way is not the British way. Pope Benedict XVI might resign the papacy on grounds of frailty, but Elizabeth II is made of sterner stuff. Her Majesty will never abdicate, not – as some commentators suggest – because she does not want to see her son become King, but because her faith, her sense of duty, and her heritage mean that abdication is simply not a possibility. Her Uncle David abdicated and his is not an example she would want to follow. And a commitment made before God is an absolute commitment so far as the Queen is concerned. 'It's a job for life,' she says. 'It's a question of maturing into something that one's got used to doing and accepting the fact that it's your fate, because I think continuity is very important.'

The Queen's has been a life of duty, but also one of privilege. She has met everyone and been everywhere. She has never wanted for anything. Wherever she goes she is cosseted. And the corgis come, too – flown, if need be, in an Andover of the Queen's Flight. Her days are sometimes long, and often arduous, but she has staff ever in attendance and the comfort of a routine that rarely varies. At 8 a.m. Her Majesty's dresser enters the royal bedroom with the 'calling tray' and a pot of Earl Grey tea. The curtains are drawn, the bath is run (to a depth of seven inches and a temperature of 72 degrees Fahrenheit – tested by thermometer), the Palace begins to stir. (No vacuuming is permitted before 8 a.m.) Her clothes are laid out for her, her hairdresser is at hand. At 9 a.m., as her personal piper plays beneath her windows, the Queen walks from her bedroom, through her sitting room to her dining room, holding her Roberts radio, listening to the news of the day. Breakfast is modest: cereal (from those Tupperware containers), a slice of granary toast, a layer of Oxford marmalade. At ten o'clock the business of the day begins: her private secretary appears; correspondence is considered, state papers scanned; if it is a morning for receiving ambassadors or the day of an investiture, Her Majesty studies her briefing material. At one o'clock, before a light lunch (she is not fussy about her food), she might treat herself to a gin and Dubonnet: equal measures, two lumps of ice and a slice of lemon. (The lemon is sliced for her.) At 2.30 p.m. she walks the corgis. At five she takes tea. At six the drinks tray reappears and Her Majesty might allow herself a moderate gin and tonic. At 8.15 p.m. it is dinner time.

On some days the Queen and Prince Philip would share breakfast, lunch, and dinner – but not every day. For example, a few years ago, on the day I happened to visit Buckingham Palace to begin the picture research for this book, I noted that Philip and Elizabeth had breakfast alone together. At one o'clock that day, together, they hosted one of their regular, informal Buckingham Palace luncheons for the great, the interesting, and the good – an idea instituted by the Duke in 1956. (The party of eight included representatives of the worlds of business, music, and sport, the director of the National Maritime Museum and the chairman of the Shah Jahan Mosque at Woking.) In the evening, the Duke of Edinburgh, without the Queen, attended a dinner at Drapers' Hall in the City of London on behalf of the Royal Academy of Engineering. The Queen has long been accustomed to evenings on her own. She watches television, she completes the *Daily Telegraph* crosswords, she gives the corgis their late supper. She telephones her racing manager. She chats with her personal page.

I can tell you exactly what the Queen is like. She has the interests, attributes, and tastes of an English (or Scottish) countrywoman of her class and generation. Dogs and horses, courtesy, kindliness, and community service count with her. Essentially conservative (with radical flourishes), intelligent (not intellectual), pragmatic (not introspective), 'immensely tolerant' (Prince Philip's phrase), even-tempered, and utterly reliable, she is what she is and makes no pretence of being what she is not. She may be formally apolitical, but she is definitely not politically correct. If she chooses, she will wear fur, she won't wear a seat belt, she will go out riding without a hard hat, and, in her assorted residences, cigarettes are freely available to her guests. (I am told she even smokes one herself from time to time. Can that be true? If it is, it will make her more understanding of her daughter-in-law Camilla's weakness for the weed.)

Occasionally I heard Prince Philip use four-letter words, though rarely in the presence of ladies. The Queen is averse to bad language, but she is by no means a prude – or an innocent. When Lech Walesa was President of Poland and came to stay, she told an aide, 'He only knows two English words.' She paused, before adding, 'They are quite interesting words.' More recently, at an art gallery, she was confronted by a series of Lucian Freud nudes: heavy, spreading bosoms, weighty, blue-veined thighs. Sensing that the photographers present were eager to get a shot of her gazing up at one of them, Her Majesty moved herself adroitly out of range. When her host enquired, 'Haven't you been painted by Lucian Freud, Ma'am?', she smiled and said, *sotto voce*, 'Yes, but not like that.'

Famously, the Queen is a skilful mimic – not so much of individuals, but of accents, be it cockney or Norfolk – and she has a lively, even impish, sense of humour. We all know that: we all gasped in amazement when she appeared on film with James Bond as part of the opening ceremony of the London Olympics in 2012. She was amused to be asked; she was happy to do it; she played her part without fuss and in just one take; she enjoyed the surprise on the night – she had not confided to her family that she was making this unique contribution to the Olympic celebrations.

Given the weirdness of her life (imprisoned by her fate: destined to be Queen from the age of ten), the Queen seems to me to be quite remarkably well balanced, rounded, grounded, and at ease with herself, the world, and her place in it. Friends who knew her when she was younger tell stories of her sitting on the sofa after dinner, her feet tucked up under her, chatting late into the night. People (even those who know her well) still find it difficult to treat her normally, but she behaves normally nonetheless. She arrived a little late for a supper at a private house in Belgravia. 'Cooee,' she called up the stairwell as she was taking off her coat, 'it's us. Sorry we're late. Terrible traffic.' This essential normality – combined with fundamental decency – presents a problem for the media. Where's the story? It is something of a dilemma for her biographers, too. At the heart of the biographies (and autobiographies) that become best-sellers nowadays is trauma – true 'trauma' from the Greek for 'wound'. The Queen's story has known moments of high drama, but her own life, her personal life – in my view, at least – has not been traumatised.

Others disagree. At the time of her Golden Jubilee, my psychologist friend Brett Kahr (the disciple of Lucian Freud's grandfather, Sigmund), told me he was quite concerned for the Queen. 'She has lost her only sister and her mother at the anniversary of her father's death,' he said solemnly. 'She is vulnerable.' (He also told me that, in psychiatric circles, a rumour has circulated for years that the Queen once had ECT treatment for depression.) As a psychologist I am unqualified, of course, but I told Brett, 'For what it's worth, my hunch is that Her Majesty has not had and will not be having a breakdown in this or any other year.'

There was a streak of hysteria in Diana, Princess of Wales: you sensed it even with a brief acquaintance. There is none in the Queen. The Queen is sane. The Queen is sensible. She has her feet on the ground. She is not self-conscious: she will apply her lipstick whoever is watching. She is not easily flustered: however hectic the schedule, however many stops on the tour, her own steady pace never varies. She has a good team around her: senior courtiers who know what they are doing (unstuffy, for the most part; unfussy, with a couple of exceptions), and loyal ladies-in-waiting who are real friends. Yes, she lost her sister and her mother and, before them, her dresser and confidante Bobo MacDonald, who died at Buckingham Palace having given sixty-seven years of devoted service. (The Queen came down from Balmoral to the Chapel Royal at St James's Palace for her funeral.) But Bobo was succeeded by another dresser, Angela Kelly (a Liverpool dock worker's daughter, twenty-five years younger than the Queen), who has become an ally and friend. The Queen has a good team around her and a large family only a telephone call away.

418

Inevitably, given the length of her reign, she has had her ups and downs. In 1957 a thirty-three-year-old peer, writer, and historian, the 2nd Lord Altrincham,[117] became internationally notorious overnight for publishing what many regarded as an unforgivable personal attack on the Queen. Altrincham accused the thirty-one-year-old Queen of being out of touch, living entirely within the confines of her own class, surrounded by courtiers of 'the "tweedy sort"', making speeches that amounted to 'prim little sermons' in the manner of 'a priggish schoolgirl' and speaking with a voice that was 'a pain in the neck'. 'Like her mother,' wrote Altrincham, the young Queen 'appears to be unable to string even a few sentences together without a written text.' He went on, 'When she has lost the bloom of youth, the Queen's reputation will depend, far more than it does now, upon her personality. It will not then be enough for her to go through the motions; she will have to say things which people can remember and do things on her own initiative which will make people sit up and take notice. As yet there is little sign that such a personality is emerging.'

Sixty years on, the Queen's reputation does indeed rest upon her personality. With a handful of exceptions, she has not said things which people can remember, or done things which have made people sit up and take notice, but her personality has emerged nonetheless. We know what the Queen stands for and cares about. Take, for example, her dogged commitment to the Commonwealth. When her reign began, the British Empire was already set on its inevitable decline and the Commonwealth, as we know it, still in its infancy. In 1952 there were eight members of the Commonwealth. Today there are fifty-four, of which sixteen are still constitutional monarchies with the Queen as head of state. Whitehall and Westminster may be more preoccupied with the United Kingdom's relations with

117 John Grigg, as he became when he was able to renounce his title in 1963. In the 1950s, others attacked the monarchy – John Osborne spoke of it as 'a gold filling in a mouth full of decay', Malcolm Muggeridge called it 'soap opera . . . ersatz religion' – but Altrincham's strictures caused the real scandal because they were so personal. Grigg (1924–2001) was denounced as a republican and attacked in the street by outraged royalists. By the time I met him, the young firebrand had become a cosy old buffer. He told me he thought the Queen was 'charming' and chuckled at the recollection of the furore he caused all those years ago.

Europe and the United States, but the Queen's interest in Commonwealth has never wavered. Indeed, her knowledgeable enthusiasm for what she describes as a 'free and voluntary association of equal partners' that 'in all history has no precedent' is a wonder to behold.

The novelist Daphne du Maurier, when her husband Boy Browning was still Comptroller of the Duke of Edinburgh's household,[118] stayed at Balmoral and was struck by the way Prince Philip could talk about anything – literature, art, murder, military manoeuvres – while the Queen's range of interests – and conversation – was much more limited. Her Majesty's face only really 'lit up' when the talk was of horses – and world affairs.

The Queen is exceptionally well informed. This is because she is conscientious. She does her 'boxes' week in, week out, throughout the year. She says she is a quick reader, 'though I do rather begrudge some of the hours that I have to do instead of being outdoors'. She knows the presidents and prime ministers of the Commonwealth personally. The way they speak of her – invariably with respect, often with affection, occasionally with awe – suggests their admiration is genuine, not simply a matter of form. In the United Kingdom she has had thirteen prime ministers. She has maintained a cordial relationship with them all. Margaret Thatcher told me that the talk of her having a strained relationship with the Queen was 'a lot of nonsense'. 'The Queen,' said Lady Thatcher, 'is simply marvellous. And her commitment to the Commonwealth and to our armed services has been especially important.' When Parliament is sitting, Queen and Prime Minister meet once a week, and, in September, Prime Minister and consort are briefly guests of Her Majesty at Balmoral. (It is reckoned that the Blairs' baby Leo, born a tad prematurely on 20 May 2000, was conceived under the royal roof.) The Queen sees herself as a 'sounding board' for her prime ministers. She says, 'They unburden themselves, or tell me what's going on. If they've got any problems, sometimes one can help in that way, too. I think it's rather nice to feel that one's a sort of sponge. Some things stay there and

118 Browning left the Duke's service in 1959. In 1957 he had suffered a nervous breakdown. His marriage was under pressure and he drank too much. He died in 1965, aged sixty-nine.

some things go out the other ear and some things never come out at all. Occasionally you can put one's point of view when perhaps they hadn't seen it from that angle.'

On the whole, the Queen has accepted what the politicians have thrown at her across the years. In 1964 Sir Anthony Blunt, Surveyor of the Royal Pictures, confessed to an MI5 interrogator that he had been a Soviet spy since before the Second World War. In return for his confession he was offered legal immunity, and, to avoid alerting the KGB, Her Majesty was asked to keep him in royal service until the due date of his retirement. She acquiesced. She does. She has little choice, in the end. That is why the Civil List has gradually been curtailed and, from 1993, the Queen and the Prince of Wales paid tax on their private income. There was nego-tiation – a bit of give and take on either side – but, ultimately, the government of the day calls the shots. The Queen successfully resisted an attempt by Tony Benn (when Postmaster-General in the mid-1960s) to have the sovereign's profile removed from British postage stamps, but, in the 1990s, failed to secure a successor to the Royal Yacht *Britannia*.

Once I asked Lord Charteris, Her Majesty's longest-serving private secretary, if the Queen herself ever felt she had put a foot wrong. He said, at once, 'Aberfan. She got that wrong and she knows it.' In October 1966, in the south Wales mining village of Aberfan, a slag heap collapsed, engulfing the village school and killing one hundred and forty-six people. The Queen expressed her anguish in a press release and dispatched Prince Philip and Lord Snowdon to the scene. She did not immediately go herself. 'It was a mistake,' Charteris told me, 'and one she regrets. The scale of the tragedy called for an immediate response, but she is not a spontaneous person and she is not given to emotional gestures. Custom, form, and precedent count with her. She tends to do what she has done before.' She made up for her error in the years that followed. She has visited Aberfan four times, most recently during her Diamond Jubilee tour in 2012, when she unveiled a plaque at Ynysowen Community Primary School and made a speech. (She is ever-present and always highly visible, but she does not make that many speeches.) 'I have travelled the length and breadth of this country during my sixty years as your Queen,' she said. 'Prince Philip and I have shared many of the joys and sadnesses of the Welsh people in that time and have always been struck by your sense of pride and your undimmed optimism.'

The Queen is still charged by some with being out of touch and slow to react (for example, in the case of Paul Burrell's trial and at the outset of the week of Diana's death) and even her keenest admirers, who regard her as a force for good, would not describe her as a force for change. But while that might have mattered when she was a younger woman, now she is old it does not matter at all. The world changes: the Queen, thank God, does not. Amid life's uncertainties, she is reassuringly familiar. She keeps the show on the road. She keeps her profile on the postage stamps, not for reasons of vanity, but because that is where it belongs, that is where you expect it to be.

On 24 November 1992 I attended the lunch at the Guildhall in London at which the Queen gave probably the most memorable speech of her reign. She had a cold and a sore throat, but she had some things she wanted to say and she hoped to be heard and was not sure how long her voice would last, so she decided to speak before we all tucked into the turbot, partridge, and Ruby soufflé, rather than after. The speech – wry, reflective, personal – was made all the more moving by being spoken in a husky voice. The Queen talked of her *annus horribilis*, 'not a year I shall look back on with undiluted pleasure'. (The phrase was suggested by her former assistant private secretary, Sir Edward Ford, and the next day brilliantly translated by the *Sun*'s headline writer as 'One's Bum Year'.) She did not mention Princess Anne's divorce, Prince Andrew's separation, or Prince Charles's marriage on the rocks, but they were in her mind – and ours. She talked, poignantly, about the fire that had done so much damage to Windsor Castle the weekend before and – because the lunch was to mark the fortieth anniversary of her Accession – reflected on lessons learnt over four decades. She said, rather wistfully, that, of course, any institution – monarchy included – must accept scrutiny and criticism, but asked, 'Couldn't it be done with a touch of humour, gentleness, and understanding?' She commended loyalty and 'moderation in all things'.

'*Annus horribilis*' is one of just a few of the Queen's turns of phrase that will not be forgotten. 'My husband and I . . .' is another. It was a phrase that the Queen used in almost every public utterance in the early years of her reign. She used it to such an extent that it became a joke and she was forced to drop it. She used it because, it seemed, wherever she went, he came, too. They were a double act. At every key moment in the Queen's reign – at every significant event – every one – until he was over ninety and illness began to take its toll, the Duke of Edinburgh was there.

I once asked him what he considered to be his lifetime's chief achievements. We were sitting in his library at Buckingham Palace. It is a large room, with a workmanlike feel, airy, ordered, user-friendly, serviceable rather than cosy. I put my question and a silence fell. He snorted. He spread his hands across the sofa and sighed. The Duke of Edinburgh's Award Scheme was clearly a considerable 'achievement', though, as we talked of it, his one anxiety seemed to be to give credit to John Hunt as its first director. The creation of the Commonwealth Study Conferences was clearly another 'achievement'. His impact on the World Wide Fund for Nature was certainly a third. But all these fine endeavours – and there is a list including many more on page 464 – are almost incidental. The essence of his role in life was to support the Queen. He never talked openly about his feelings for the Queen, because that was not his style,[119] but it was clear from his every action that he was fiercely protective of her. On walkabout, if a photographer or cameraman was encroaching on Her Majesty, he would bark at them to get out of the way. When, once, a journalist asked him about the overseas tour on which he was reported to have fallen asleep during the Queen's speech, he retorted sharply, 'Not at all, it wasn't during the Queen's speech, it was during the president's!' In almost forty years, beyond occasional complaints about her

119 Perhaps we should be grateful. Here is Crown Prince Haakon of Norway addressing his bride, Crown Princess Mette-Marit, at their wedding banquet in August 2001: 'Your soul sparkles with light. Everything we do with love comes alight. Mette-Marit, you are sensitive, easy to please, obsessed with detail, sometimes a bit apathetic, intensely committed, highly strung, courageous, inscrutable. You can be defensive or resolute. You have a good sense of humour and a big warm heart. In other words you are an absolutely fantastic, complex person. I don't think I have ever been so angry, adrenalin angry, with anyone as with you. I don't think I have ever been so weak or so strong as when I've been together with you . . . Thank you for your love and for everything you've done. Mette-Marit, I am proud to call myself your husband. For now we are here. Now we are together. Mette-Marit, I love you!'

devotion to her corgis and the amount of time she seemed capable of spending on the telephone, I did not hear him speak one critical word of her.

To friends, the Queen did occasionally complain about her husband's 'pig-headedness' and about the speed at which he sometimes drove through Windsor Great Park, but on the whole it is evident that she accepted him as he was – she never tried to 'change' him – and admired and loved him deeply for what and who he was. 'He is someone who doesn't take easily to compliments,' she said in a speech at the Guildhall at the time of their golden wedding anniversary in 1997, but she continued, 'He has, quite simply, been my strength and stay all these years, and I, and his whole family, and this and many other countries, owe him a debt greater than he would ever claim or we shall ever know.' In 2012, addressing the joint Houses of Parliament in Westminster Hall for the sixth time in her reign, she said it again: 'Prince Philip is, I believe, well known for declining compliments of any kind. But throughout he has been a constant strength and guide.'

By the time he died Prince Philip was getting a good press. It was not always so. In the 1990s one of the Duke's alleged gaffes prompted the *Daily Mirror* to address him thus: 'You are an arrogant, over-bearing, insensitive, tactless, patronising, boorish and now sickening fool.'

Less surprisingly, the Murdoch *Sun* took much the same line, describing the Prince as a '75-year-old aristocrat who is totally detached from reality', and in the *Independent* Anne McElvoy opined: 'Prince Philip, whose mind remains steeped in the casually ignorant racialism of his youth, is beyond redemption and can only be regarded as an asset on the days he is kept indoors.'

The Duke of Edinburgh endured this kind of press coverage because he had no choice. He told me, 'I have become "the gaffe man" and there is nothing I can do about it. I say something in passing and it's blown up out of all proportion, or taken out of context, or totally rephrased so it suddenly means something it was never intended to mean.' He wrote to me from Buckingham Palace on 4 June 1999: 'That is the trouble when the media give you a reputation. When we were in South Africa some years ago, I flew to Kimberley and was persuaded to take some people with me. On the way back, one of them said to my policeman that it had been a waste of time as I had not put my foot in it!!!'

In February 2002 the *Guardian* published an extended profile of the Prince by the journalist Sally Vincent. She portrayed the Duke as 'a subscriber to the forlorn hope that the male of the species is, in some profoundly genetic and spiritual sense, superior to the female'. He was 'a homophobe and a misogynist', who was 'not cut out to be a consort, since the concept of playing second fiddle to a female would have dismayed him to the point of self-disgust'. To anyone who knew the Prince at all this was so totally wrong (and so at odds with all the evidence) as to be almost comical, but Ms Vincent did not know her man. She saw him as a disappointed individual who had 'covered his helplessness and anger with the rough-hewn mask of arrogance and began to self-destruct'. Her conclusion:

'As the years rolled on, Philip grew increasingly disenchanted with his private and public role in life. In 1983, the Queen and Prince Philip were in California as the guests of President Reagan and his wife. According to American reports of the tour, Philip experienced the darkest night of his soul on the streets of San Francisco while sitting in the back of a limousine accompanied by Her Majesty, his wife. Already exasperated by what he took to be the excessive attention to detail of the US secret service agents assigned the task of protecting their royal persons, he lost his rag while waiting for Reagan's car to lead the ceremonial motorcade. Reagan was a few minutes behind schedule. Philip demanded the chauffeur move the bloody car. The driver demurred. "Move this fucking car," he screamed and, taking a magazine from the seat pocket, rolled it up and beat the driver across the back of his head. The Queen, meanwhile, sat impassively next to her husband, staring silently ahead.

'And there, writ large in one unseemly episode, is the dynamic of the Windsor-Mountbatten alliance. If the health of a marriage can be defined by the flexibility of the balance of power between partners, this liaison has been set in stone, the scales immutably weighted as to who has the last word, the casting vote, the moral high ground. Her dignified silence outweighs his impotent wrath. Every time.'

That was the *Guardian*'s 'take' on Prince Philip on the fiftieth anniversary of the Queen's Accession. To those who knew the Queen and Prince Philip it seemed as preposterous as it was inaccurate and insulting, but there it was in print, the perception of one observer, possibly shared by many others.

Of course, even the Prince's admirers must concede that he did not always help himself. Some of his unguarded remarks were unduly provocative for a sensitive age and his frustration and irritation in the presence of journalists worked against him. For example, in May 2011, his ninetieth birthday interview with Fiona Bruce for the BBC was scratchy, uncomfortable, and unrevealing – and the fault was his, not hers. His Royal Highness was not in a giving vein that day. Martin Palmer, who co-founded the Alliance of Religions and Conservation with the Duke, warned the BBC's programme makers what they might expect. 'Get him on a bad day and it's quite hard work. Get him on a good day and you don't want to be with anyone else. I hope you have a good day.' They didn't.

Mostly when I met him, I got him on a good day. I confess that when I sensed it was a bad day, I kept my distance. I recall a number of occasions – two receptions at Buckingham Palace, an evening at the Royal Academy, once after a service at Westminster Abbey – when I steered clear of him because I could see from his gimlet eye that he wasn't in the mood for the likes of me. At the lunch I organised for his seventieth birthday I introduced him to Joanna Lumley and he took to her at once. 'I love her,' he told me later, at a dinner at the RSA (Royal Society for the encouragement of Arts, Manufactures and Commerce), where I was speaking and she was sitting next to him. It was her energy and intelligence and 'spiritual awareness' that he liked (a touch of the Sacha Abercorns), as well as her beauty, of course. Joanna summed up the experience of meeting Prince Philip rather well: 'It's extraordinary. You get the impression of meeting a bird of prey, a hawk or an eagle. There's something absolutely penetrating about the eyes . . . You feel like you're being scanned . . . You raise your game. You rather hope he'll like you.'

Most of the things I learnt about Prince Philip I learnt incidentally – and many of them surprised me. For example, he was more knowledgeably interested in music and drama than I would have expected. He had met and rather liked Benjamin Britten. In 1958 he asked Britten to compose settings for the *Jubilate* and *Te Deum* for the choir of St George's Chapel at Windsor. Dogs. He told me that he had dogs he had named after assorted British conductors. ('Boult, come here! Sargent – down, boy!') And while he might not have acclaimed his eldest son's appearance in the title role of *Macbeth*, he was hugely supportive of the American actor Sam Wanamaker's project to recreate Shakespeare's Globe Theatre on the south bank of the Thames at Southwark. He put potential donors Wanamaker's way and, in the words of the project's administrator, 'telephoned personally from time to time to hear of (the slow) progress and (frequent) problems'. Philip admired Wanamaker both because he was someone who was making something happen against the odds and because Wanamaker was an outsider – an American in London.

In my experience, the Duke of Edinburgh was a shrewd judge of character, though once in a while he would follow his inclination and favour the maverick rough diamond over the smooth Establishment figure and get it wrong. For example, he was for many years the active president of the national alliance of sports bodies known as the Central Council for Physical Recreation. He championed the cause of the independent CCPR over the government-subsidised activities of the Sports Council and he particularly admired the no-nonsense, cut-a-few-corners style of the CCPR's general secretary, Peter Lawson. The more others voiced their reservations about Lawson, the more Prince Philip appeared to favour him. In 1998, when Peter Lawson, and his son (who also worked for the CCPR), were jailed for embezzling funds from the sports body, it was a sad day all round.

In great things and small, Prince Philip's contrary spirit burned bright to the end of his days. I recall an event at Buckingham Palace where the equerry introducing proceedings suggested that applause would be out of place, prompting Prince Philip to start the clapping. Even in his ninety-second year, the Duke was making mischief. In March 2009 the Prince of Wales warned the world that there were 'less than 100 months to act' to save the planet from irreversible damage due to climate change. Begging to differ, forty-eight months later, in March 2013, in his capacity as an honorary fellow of the Chartered Institute of Water and Environmental Management, the Duke of Edinburgh invited the noted global-warming sceptic David Bellamy to give a lecture at Buckingham Palace.

The Duke of Edinburgh's mind remained engaged and he stayed active almost to the last. 'I'm falling to bits,' he said, 'but what can you do?' At Sandringham at Christmas 2011, when he was ninety, he was airlifted to Papworth Hospital in Cambridge with chest pains. He had emergency surgery to clear a blocked artery and spent nine days in hospital. One of the doctors from the hospital told me that a patient of the Duke's age with a heart in the condition of the Duke's could expect to live for 'about a year'. Nine weeks after his heart surgery, His Royal Highness was back on the box seat, holding the reins, doing a spot of carriage driving around Windsor Great Park.

At the beginning of June 2012, after four hours spent standing in the rain on the royal barge for the jubilee pageant on the Thames, he was admitted to hospital in London with a bladder infection. Five days later, on the eve of his ninety-first birthday, he was discharged. On 15 June, with the Queen he was hosting a reception for the Sultan of Oman at Buckingham Palace. The next day he was on parade for Trooping the Colour. The next week he turned up every day for Royal Ascot. At the end of June he joined the Queen for an historic two-day tour of Northern Ireland, followed by the unveiling of the Bomber Command Memorial in London. Then came jubilee visits to Scotland, to the West Midlands, to the North-East, to Hampshire and the Isle of Wight, as well as a lunch in Downing Street and half a dozen official events connected with the London Olympics. In August, with the Queen he hosted a garden party for 3,000 guests at Balmoral and then, on his own, flew down to the Isle of Wight, as Admiral of the Royal Yacht Squadron, to attend Cowes Week. On 15 August he was flown back to Balmoral by helicopter and, taken ill again, admitted once more to hospital – this time the Aberdeen Royal Infirmary.

In 2011 he undertook 330 official engagements; in 2012 he upped it to 347. On the day in 2013 when he saw members of the Alliance of Religions and Conservation and representatives of Chinese cultural traditions *and* met a team from the Naval Review *and* turned out as Colonel-in-Chief of the Corps of Royal Electrical and Mechanical Engineers, I said to him, 'Why are you still doing all this?' He replied, 'What else am I going to do?'

He did what he did for more than sixty-five years, and beyond saying to me, 'I hope some of it was useful', claimed no special credit.

He read both the first and the second drafts of this book, but the only corrections he offered were to 'facts', not 'opinions' – and he always focused on detail. For example, of one of the ships on which he had served during the war, I had written: 'HMS *Wallace* was one of the destroyers on convoy duty on the British east coast, constantly moving up and down "E-Boat Alley", as it was known, from Sheerness to Rosyth and back.' He corrected me: '*Wallace* was a member of the Rosyth Escort Force based at Rosyth, so it would be more accurate to say "from Rosyth to Sheerness and back".'

He was right, of course. He almost always was. I recall having a heated exchange with him about the address of the London head-quarters of the old British Railways Board. I insisted it had been at Marylebone. I was sure of it. He was certain it had been at Euston. The ding-dong between us lasted several minutes. His equerry looked on in amazement. Prince Philip won the argument with the killer line: 'I should know. I opened the place, dammit.'

I asked him if there were aspects of his life and character that he thought I should write about more extensively. He shrugged unhelp-fully. I asked him if I should have written something about his many improvements to the royal estate. Following the fire at Windsor Castle, from 1992 to 1997 he chaired the Restoration Committee. 'Yes, well, people can see what we've done.' I reminded him that the conversion of the chapel to the picture gallery at Buckingham Palace was his doing. I mentioned how he had built log cabins at Sandringham and demolished the dry-rotten Victorian addition to Abergeldie Castle at Balmoral. I said that perhaps people did not know of his interest in gardening. He planted avenues of trees, created water gardens, laid out borders and beds.

'Do you want a list?' he asked.

The question was not sarcastic. The Duke of Edinburgh was a man who believed in lists – in detail, in facts, in order. Indeed, a psychiatrist might say that his need for order and control in his everyday life was a direct consequence of the insecurity, confusion, and lack of order that were the defining characteristics of his adoles-cence. Whether he accepted it or not, he had a chaotic childhood, with neither a settled home nor proper parenting. As an adult he imposed order on everything he did.

George Carey, the Archbishop of Canterbury between 1991 and

2002, told me about a service that Prince Philip had attended marking the sixtieth anniversary of the liberation of the Channel Islands. 'I preached the sermon and afterwards the Duke came up to me and remarked that during the service the word "reconciliation" had been used 109 times. He said the word was overused and repeating it 109 times did not make it any more likely. I said, "Were you counting?" He said, "Yes." His approach to everything was scientific and quite meticulous.'

Prince Philip was a man who kept control by keeping count. He ordered his thoughts. He ran his office and his life with precision. His books and papers were carefully catalogued. His clothes were correct in all respects: check out the line of the breast-pocket hand-kerchief in each and every photograph of him. It never varied. His wardrobe was catalogued, too, but 'not for the sake of it,' he insisted, '– to a purpose'. For example, in 2012 he went to the Isle of Wight for Cowes Week and sported a double-breasted yachting jacket with distinctive gold buttons. The buttons bore royal crests dating back to the reign of William IV. The jacket itself appeared to be a little on the small side for the Prince – and it was. It had belonged to Sir Eric Penn, sometime Comptroller of the Lord Chamberlain's Office. When Sir Eric died in 1993, his widow offered the Duke of Edinburgh the buttons. He asked her for the jacket and told her he would like to wear it on occasion to remember his old friend. Whenever I met him for a National Playing Fields Association event, he was always wearing the NPFA tie.

I told Prince Philip that, in my experience, readers like some human detail alongside the facts. He was not convinced. 'People misremember things,' he said. In 2005 I sent on to him a letter I had received from a Commander Colin F. Douglas RN, who had served on the Royal Yacht *Britannia*. Commander Douglas shared with me a delightful recollection of seeing Prince Philip and the Queen on deck together and in nostalgic and romantic mood on a return visit to Malta, and an anecdote about the naval review marking the fiftieth anniversary of the Battle of the Atlantic during which Prince Philip had kept his hands warm while taking the salute by plunging them into a bowl of hot water. From Sandringham House on 22 January 2005, His Royal Highness wrote to me: 'I think Douglas would have made a good journalist. He can't resist elaborating on a story. We most certainly did not fall into each other's arms on sailing into Malta, neither did the Queen burst into tears! As to the story of the Battle of the Atlantic Review, most of it is accurate, but I have no recollection of plunging my hands into a bowl of hot water. It may be a good idea, but it never occurred to me! In any case, although it was blowing a real gale, I don't think it can have been as cold as all that as I can't remember wearing a greatcoat.'

On another occasion, when I asked the Duke to elaborate on his own experience of the Battle of Cape Matapan, 'just sticking to the facts', he was reluctant. 'I don't remember the detail. I really don't.' He was not being difficult. Later, in 2012, he provided a foreword to a history of the battle published by the University of Plymouth Press and confessed, 'All these events took place seventy years ago, and, as most elderly people have discovered, memories tend to fade.'

Knowing that I was writing about him, more than once the Duke warned me to beware of 'faction' – that dangerous mix of facts and fiction. He allowed me to ask him anything I liked and if it was a 'matter of record' he would do his best to provide a detailed answer; if it was a matter of 'mere recollection' or me hoping for 'a bit of colour to spice up your book', he would just look at me balefully and say nothing. He did not like talking about himself. It was as simple as that. Prince Edward summed it up when he said, 'My father plain and simply is very modest about himself and doesn't believe in talking about himself. One of his best pieces of advice he gives to everybody is talk about everything else, don't talk about yourself, nobody's interested in you.'

In 2012, in the lead-up to the Queen's Diamond Jubilee, the National Portrait Gallery commissioned a portrait of the Queen and the Duke from the 'cutting edge' German photographer Thomas Struth. His experience of meeting Prince Philip was typical. 'I felt very nervous,' he recalled of his session with the couple at Buckingham Palace. He asked them to sit side by side on a sofa. 'I knew the Queen was much smaller than him, and since she was the main person in the portrait, I tilted the sofa just slightly so that she would seem bigger in the picture than she actually is. The Duke went, "Oh, really?" – he seemed a bit irritated that they would be positioned like this. He is like an old eagle: he has very sharp eyes. I was surprised by how much energy he has, and how alert he is. People

431

says he's bizarre or awkward, but I found him quite impressive – though I was surprised when I asked him to move his hand and he reacted a little grumpily. He is eccentric – he tried to crack a few jokes during the sitting. But I felt they have a good relationship.'

There is no question: the Queen and Prince Philip enjoyed an outstanding partnership that certainly worked to the nation's benefit and appeared to work to their own. But were they truly happy – whatever happiness means?

I once asked the eminent Irish psychiatrist Dr Anthony Clare, Professor of Clinical Psychiatry at Trinity College, Dublin, to define happiness for me. He laughed, but, obligingly, had a go. 'I would say happiness is a cognitive state, an intellectual perception or under-standing of you, the person, and your relationship with your envi-ronment. It does have pleasurable components, but that's not the essence of happiness. The essence of happiness is a conscious appre-ciation of the rightness of being. And it's a state. It's not a permanent trait. People aren't "happy" – they have experiences of happiness. Most people's customary state is one of balance between conflicting needs and desires and emotions, and happiness comes into play as one of those experiences which people from time to time describe and clearly aim for.'

I then asked Professor Clare to go further, to forget his caveats, throw caution to the wind, and give me a prescription for happiness – tell me what it takes, in his experience, to be 'happy' in the way most of us understand the word. He laughed again, but, again, sitting in his consulting room at St Patrick's Hospital in Dublin, he did his best to oblige. 'OK,' he said. 'Here goes. Number one: cultivate a passion. How important it seems to me in my model of happiness is having something that you enjoy doing. Next, be a leaf on a tree. You have to be both an individual – you have to have a sense that you are unique and you matter – and at the same time you need to be connected to a bigger organism, a family, a community. Some very interesting stuff has been done over the years on the issue of networks. The people who are best protected against certain physical diseases – cancer and heart disease, for example – in addition to doing all the other things they should do, seem to be much more likely to be part of a community, socially involved. If you ask them to enumerate the people that they feel close to and would connect and communicate with, those who name most seem to be happiest and those with least unhappiest. Of course, there may be a circular argument here. If you are a rather complicated person, people may avoid you. If, on the other hand, you are a centre of good feeling people will come to you. I see the tragedy here in this room where some people may sit in that chair and say they don't think they've got very many friends and they're quite isolated and unhappy, and the truth is they are so introspective they've become difficult to make friends with. So that's my third rule: avoid introspection. Next, don't resist change. Change is important. People who are fearful of change are rarely happy. I don't mean massive change, but enough to keep your life stimulated. And finally, live in the moment. Live now.'

On the basis of Professor Clare's 'happiness index', I reckon we can regard the Queen and Prince Philip as happy individuals. The Queen is much more resistant to change than her husband was, but a score of four out of five isn't bad. Even in their eighties and nineties both of them lived in the moment, neither was introspective, each could be described as 'a leaf on a tree', both were undoubtedly community-orientated and socially involved. Each had a consuming passion: the Duke had his carriage driving, the Queen has her horses and her dogs.

But were they happy together? Off and on, and particularly when they were young and middle-aged, they seemed to spend quite a lot of time apart. Even when they were in their sixties and seventies, the Queen was frequently on her own, walking the dogs, riding her horses, playing Patience, completing a jigsaw, sorting her photograph albums, watching television, phoning friends. Was she neglected? Did she mind? Or did she simply take it in her stride because she understood the nature of her man?

Robin Dalton, his cousin David Milford Haven's girlfriend, said to me, 'Philip's a cold fish.' Reginald Bennett, once an MP, a member of the Thursday Club, and a sailing companion of the Duke's, said, 'Philip is the coolest man I know.' But talk with Lord Buxton or Lord Brabourne and the impression you got was a quite different one. They had stories to tell of Philip holding his wife's hand, gently stroking her hair, coming into the room at the end of the day and saying simply, 'Lovely to see you' and watching her face light up with happiness. 'Philip is not sentimental,' Lord Brabourne said to me, 'but he is sensitive, profoundly so. When our son was killed [by the IRA bomb that killed Lord Mountbatten] the first letter that arrived was from Philip. It was wonderful. You can talk to him about matters of the heart.'

Countess Mountbatten said to me, 'The Queen and Prince Philip have a mutual understanding that's profound. And they get on. They are good together – anyone who knows them well will tell you that.'

Archbishop Carey told me, 'I had the great joy of presiding over the Queen and Prince Philip's fiftieth wedding anniversary service in Westminster Abbey. And you know it was so moving for me to lay hands on both of them – that was at their request. They wanted me to lay hands on them and to pray for them.'

But what about Philip's testiness, his grumbling and his grouches? Lord Charteris said to me, 'Prince Philip is the only man in the world who treats the Queen simply as another human being. He's the only man who can. Strange as it may seem, I believe she values that. And, of course, it's not unknown for the Queen to tell Prince Philip to shut up. Because she's Queen, that's not something she can easily say to anybody else.'

Lord Charteris also pointed me in the direction of this line from *The Unquiet Grave* by Cyril Connolly: 'The true index of a man's character is the health of his wife.' This was more than twenty years ago and, by implication, the Queen's longest-serving secretary was inviting me to compare and contrast Her Majesty's robust and life-long good health with the frailty of the then Princess of Wales.

Countess Mountbatten said to me, 'They're good together. They're good for one another. They always have been. Make no mistake.' 'Oh, yes,' said Gina Kennard, who knew them, individually and as a couple, for something like seventy-five years, 'They own each other. Nothing could come between them. What they have for one another is the greatest respect – which counts for so much – and deep love. Deep love that goes back a long, long way.'

'After all,' as Lord Mountbatten reminded Prince Charles, 'Mummy never seriously thought of anyone else after the Dartmouth encounter when she was 13!' Mountbatten's son-in-law, John Brabourne, said to me, 'Philip learnt singularity of purpose from Mountbatten. The course that's set is the course that's followed. Philip is not a man to be deflected. When he gave Elizabeth his love and his loyalty, he gave them to her for life. He has not deviated from that.'

On 3 December 1947 the Duke of Edinburgh, aged twenty-six and just married, wrote to his mother-in-law and outlined for her the course he had set himself: 'Lilibet is the only "thing" in the world which is absolutely real to me and my ambition is to weld the two of us into a new combined existence that will not only be able to withstand the shocks directed at us but will also have a positive existence for good.'

I think that Lilibet would tell you that he achieved his ambition. Their marriage was not a fairy tale: it was 'absolutely real' to them both. Welded together, they withstood all the shocks and, between them, theirs was indeed 'a positive existence for good'. The Duke of Edinburgh gave the Queen a lifetime of unwavering support – and it was support that was personal, specific, intelligent, consistent, and thought through. And what did Lilibet give Philip? Beyond the obvious (her beauty, her integrity, her sense of fun, her transparent worth), she gave him security, a settled place in an uncertain world, and a love that he knew that he could depend upon – always.

Whenever I challenged Prince Philip about the traumatic nature of his childhood, he brushed away the subject. But he knew the truth. When once I asked him how he thought he was perceived, he said, 'Refugee husband.' When he was a boy, if you asked for his address, he answered, 'No fixed abode.' From the chaos of his childhood, he sought – and found – order in his life as the Queen's consort. In 1991 he began working on a personal project that he called 'The Edinburgh Tables'. Essentially, it was an updated version of a family tree that his uncle, Earl Mountbatten of Burma, had begun to compile before the war, based on both research and the recollections of Prince Philip's grandmother, Victoria, Marchioness of Milford Haven. The Duke of Edinburgh brought it right up to date, tracing every one of the many descendants of the grandfathers of both the Queen and of himself – namely the descendants of George V and the 14th Earl of Strathmore and George I of Greece and Prince Louis of Battenberg (later Marquess of Milford Haven). The project was very important to him. As a boy Philip had been a prince without a country, a son without a home. As Lilibet's husband, Philip was a refugee who found a refuge – a nationality, a wife, and a home. In 'The Edinburgh Tables' everything is well ordered and HRH The Duke of Edinburgh KG KT is there alongside HM Queen Elizabeth II, each in their proper place.

Philip and Elizabeth were two very different human beings. Their childhoods were so different. Each was royal, they had shared values, a joint heritage and a common purpose, but as characters, as personalities, they were not at all alike. They had different attributes and different interests. Philip was more adventurous, more assertive, and more intellectual than his wife. She was more placid, more cautious, more conventional, less changeable in mood. They were different people. Yet they understood each other – and they got on so well. Once I travelled in the car behind theirs and watched them chatting. For half an hour I saw them telling each other stories, listening to each other, laughing repeatedly. These two were good companions: the chattering never stopped. And they were allies. I saw that, one November night, in the interval at the Royal Variety Performance, as they looked at each other across a crowded room, and smiled. I caught then a glimpse of the conspiracy – the shared secret – that sustained them in their marriage over more than seventy years. You will recall that it was seeing them in that brief moment, apart yet together, that made me want to write this book.

Life is complicated. Marriage is not easy. But, somehow, these two distinct, unusual, profoundly impressive people made it work. They gave each other respect and freedom. They accepted each other – completely. He was active, she was passive, but both were strong. As I heard a Jungian say once, 'The passive are not necessarily weak or put-upon. Passivity is a kind of control: control by what one doesn't do.' The Queen has always been in command of her own ship – and she knows about the movement of the tides. Her father explained that to her many moons ago.

In 1930, when Philip was nine and Elizabeth was four, Philip's middle sister, Cécile – the one who died in an aeroplane crash in 1937 – was engaged to be married. From her sanatorium, near Lake Tegel, in the north of Berlin, Philip's mother, Princess Alice, sent her daughter a letter of congratulation and advice. 'For you know, dear child,' she wrote, 'each woman manages & directs her married life herself, just as she would control herself in a profession if she had one & so you see when a girl marries a decent boy, she makes

436

her *own* happiness with her *own* judgement and self-control. No marriage entered into, in that spirit, with the most dissimilar characters even, ought to be a failure. A little patience in the first years & one has an enduring happy love & friendship for life & which unlike ordinary friendships will be just as fresh when you are old.'

When they were old, when the tide was in, I sensed that Philip and Elizabeth – as man and wife, as consort and queen, as the best of friends – were closer than they had ever been.

ELIZABETH ALONE

Chapter Fourteen

'Thou know'st 'tis common. All that lives must die,
Passing through nature to eternity.'

William Shakespeare (1564-1616), *Hamlet*

The Duke of Edinburgh formally 'retired' in the summer of 2017, a couple of months after his ninety-sixth birthday. He completed what was reckoned to be his 22,219th official engagement on Wednesday 2 August 2017, stepping out onto the forecourt at Buckingham Palace in his role as Captain General of the Royal Marines, an appointment he had taken on sixty-four years earlier in succession to his father-in-law, the late King George VI.

In the Palace forecourt, Prince Philip, wearing a bowler hat and fawn raincoat (yes, it rained on his final parade), inspected men from the Royal Marines who had taken part in the 1664 Global Challenge, each running 16.64 miles a day over a period of one hundred days, among other tests of endurance.

Typically, he told them, 'You should all be locked up' and asked if the rain was trickling down their backs. Joshing and banter done, the inspection duly completed, the Regimental Sergeant Major called for 'three cheers for the Captain General', to which the Duke responded by raising his bowler. As the Plymouth Band played 'For He's a Jolly Good Fellow', His Royal Highness offered a small wave, turned on his heels and walked back into the palace. And that was that: a simple, unassuming end to a lifetime of public service.

In December 2017, the Queen confirmed that her grandson, Prince Harry, would succeed her husband as Captain General of the Royal Marines. 'It was high time to hand it on,' said Prince Philip. 'Enough's enough.'

Prince Philip retired because the Queen encouraged him to do so. She wanted to stop him 'pushing himself all the time'. She had become anxious about him. A senior courtier told me he had found the Queen in the corridor at Buckingham Palace one day looking for her husband. 'Where's he got to?' she asked. 'Where is he? I can't find him.' In 2017, the Queen decided to let the Prince of Wales take her place laying a wreath at the Cenotaph on Remembrance Sunday – not to spare herself, but to spare her husband. The royal couple sat together watching the ceremony from a balcony in the Foreign Office.

Prince Philip told me that he was ready to retire, glad to be getting some time to himself at last, but he didn't plan to 'disappear completely'. He said he preferred to bow out of solo public engagements 'while I'm still standing, just about'. He had had the occasional health scare – including heart surgery and stenting to deal with a blocked artery when he was ninety – but for a man of his age he was remarkably fit—and steady on his feet. He kept himself active and did daily stretching exercises. He maintained his sensible diet. (According to his tailor, John Kent, who made his suits for half a century, 'He was a 31in waist when I first measured him and that only ever went up to 34in. There wasn't an ounce of fat on him.') For as long as possible the Duke was determined not to be seen using a walking stick. He hoped his retirement would reduce speculation about his health and would 'spare people having to see me falling to pieces in front of them.'

Inevitably, as he moved through his mid-nineties, he was beginning to look his age: his eyes were increasingly red-rimmed, his nose grew beakier, he became more stooped, he shrank a bit. 'I'll soon be dead,' he kept saying. Increasingly, of course, there were reminders of mortality all around him.

Sir Brian McGrath, the wine merchant turned courtier who became his private secretary in 1982 and went on to become one of his closest friends, died in June 2016, aged 90. McGrath had officially retired in 1992, but he continued to serve the Duke thereafter in a variety of capacities, from attending memorial services on his behalf to overseeing his personal finances. He retained an office at Buckingham Palace until the end and, famously, was the only courtier allowed to bring his dog (a black Labrador) with him to work. McGrath's father, it turned out, had been a friend of Prince Andrew of Greece, and one of Sir Brian's principal duties was to deal with Prince Philip's assorted German relations. Philip was generous to his nephews, nieces and cousins, often helping fund their education, and when required McGrath would be drafted in to assist younger members of the family when they got into scrapes. 'I'm just a nanny really,' he used to say. Until their deaths, one of his particular responsibilities was to look after Prince Philip's sister, Princess Sophie, and her husband, Prince George of Hanover, when they came to visit. This could be quite challenging, according to McGrath, because as Prince George grew older he tended to leave his bath overflowing or forget items from his personal luggage when he moved from Windsor Castle to Buckingham Palace.

Gregarious, bluff but beady-eyed, McGrath was Prince Philip's no-nonsense man-of-all-business and good companion for thirty-four years. In March 2017, the Duke lost another key ally with the death of his archivist and librarian, Dame Anne Griffiths, aged 84. She first joined the Duke of Edinburgh's office in 1952, when she was only nineteen, originally employed as a 'temp' to help out with the additional workload in the run-up to the Coronation. She was one of the two lady clerks who accompanied Philip on board *Britannia* on the controversial 1956/57 trip to the South Atlantic and the Melbourne Olympic Games. As a consequence of this trip, she and her colleague, Ione Eadie, became the first British women to cross the Antarctic Circle. Ione went on to marry the commander of the Royal Yacht and, inevitably, some said that Anne and the Duke became quite sweet on each other during that four months at sea. Anne left royal service in 1960 to get married herself, but returned in 1983 and remained part of the Prince's team for ever after. On the day of the announcement of her DCVO in 2005, Prince Philip was heard walking along the corridor at Buckingham Palace towards her office cheerily singing, 'There's nothing like a dame...'

With advancing years, the Queen, too, began to lose many of her closest friends. Her cousin, Margaret Rhodes, died aged 91, in November 2016 and, two weeks later, Elizabeth Longman, another of her childhood friends and bridesmaids at her wedding, died, aged 92. In January 2017, Shirley, the Marchioness of Anglesey died. Until the death of the Marquess in 2013, the Angleseys were the only survivors to have both attended the Coronation, other than the Queen and Prince Philip. A generation was disappearing: an era was coming to a close.

Both at Buckingham Palace and at Clarence House the talk was of a 'gentle succession'. Prince Philip had long been responsible for the management of the royal estates at Windsor, Balmoral and Sandringham. (Take a look at page 469 for a list of some of the specific projects he oversaw on those estates.) In 2014, Philip ceded the management of Sandringham's 20,000 acres to Prince Charles – knowing that his son's approach to land management and farming were very different from his own. 'He has his ideas and I have mine,' said Prince Philip, 'but I won't be here for ever so he'd better get on with it.'

Happily, relations between Philip and his son mellowed with the passing years. In his eighties and nineties I noticed the Duke of Edinburgh make many fewer waspish remarks about the Prince of Wales than he had done in his fifties and sixties. And Prince Charles, so much happier in his second marriage than in his first, stopped bleating about the travails of his childhood. Charles appeared more comfortable talking about his parents, and did so with respect (as ever) but with increasing affection. Prince Philip was especially happy when, in October 2016, Prince Charles visited the grave of his paternal grandmother, Princess Alice, in Jerusalem.

Earlier in same year, for the Queen's ninetieth birthday, Charles organised a private celebration for his mother at Windsor Castle and invited the theatre director Christopher Luscombe to provide the post-dinner entertainment. Knowing the Queen's fondness for the songs of George Formby, I suggested to Christopher that the Ukulele Orchestra of Great Britain might amuse Her Majesty. It did, along with magic (involving Prince Harry) and a ventriloquist (the brilliant Nina Conti). It was not a show that Prince Charles would have chosen for himself (which would have included Shakespeare and an operatic aria): it was a show entirely designed to please his mother. The day after the party Prince Philip called his son to congratulate him on organising a perfect family evening. Charles was touched and delighted to receive the call.

How did the Duke of Edinburgh spend his retirement? He divided his time principally between Wood Farm on the Sandringham estate and Windsor Castle – his two favourite homes – where he read, wrote letters, dabbled with watercolours, harrumphed now and again at stories in the *Daily Telegraph* and invited friends to stay. He continued to make occasional public appearances alongside the Queen – at the Cenotaph on Remembrance Sunday, going to church at Sandringham on Christmas Day – but their 70th wedding anniversary on 20 November 2017 was a low-key affair. In the morning, the Duke took two of his nephews – Ludwig and Max of Baden – out for a carriage drive in Windsor Great Park; in the evening, there was a family dinner at Windsor Castle.

The Queen wanted to honour her husband on their wedding anniversary. On his ninetieth birthday the Queen had made the Duke Lord High Admiral, the titular head of the Royal Navy. It was a title she had held and she handed it over to him, both because it seemed appropriate and because she had already bestowed on him almost every other available honour. In 2015, to mark ANZAC Day and the centenary of the Gallipoli landings, the Queen invested the Duke of Edinburgh with the Insignia of a Knight of the Order of Australia. In 2016, as her anniversary present, she appointed him a Knight Grand Cross of the Royal Victorian Order. Prince Philip wasn't entirely sure about this – most of the recipients of honours within this order are long-serving members of staff who have given personal service to the sovereign and, in any event, he already had the Royal Victorian Chain (given to him in 2007) – but he accepted it with a slightly grudging grace and was amused (and pleased) because it meant that he was the first person to be able to wear four orders of chivalry breast stars – alongside the Order of the Garter, the Order of the Thistle and the Order of the British Empire – since his uncle, Earl Mountbatten of Burma.

In her Christmas broadcast that year, the Queen said she was 'grateful for the blessings of home and family, and in particular for 70 years of marriage.' She went on: 'I don't know that anyone had invented the term "platinum" for a 70th wedding anniversary when I was born. You weren't expected to be around that long. Even Prince Philip has decided it's time to slow down a little – having, as he economically put it, "done his bit". But I know his support and unique sense of humour will remain as strong as ever, as we

445

enjoy spending time this Christmas with our family and look forward to welcoming new members into it next year.'

Both the Queen and her husband accepted that the focus was moving away from them and onto the next generation – and the ones beyond. The Queen scaled down her public appearances, handing over more duties to Prince Charles and Prince William, and spending more time in the company of her daughter, Princess Anne, and her favourite daughter-in-law, Sophie Wessex – the next Duchess of Edinburgh. She spent more time at Windsor and less at Buckingham Palace. Where Prince Philip would once have been at her side for the launching of a ship or a civic lunch, now Prince Andrew or the Princess Royal would be at her side.

The Queen did not retire when her husband did, but she did reduce her workload. She maintained her interests, of course. She continued to ride into her nineties and to walk her corgis after lunch; she continued to phone her racing manager in the evening. (Her racehorses have won her some £7 million in prize money in the past thirty-five years, including £557,650 in a record-breaking 2016.) She and Prince Philip went out for dinner with friends and enjoyed weekends away together. She was often alone in the evenings (she was accustomed to that), watching television and having supper in her rooms, but frequently she saw friends and family – grandchildren and great-grandchildren – for afternoon tea. Her faith remained, her abiding comforter and her solace in times of sadness. (On a Sunday morning, she would often attend church twice – first, privately, for Holy Communion and then, later, dressed in an outfit in which to be photographed, for Matins with other members of the family. The press, as a rule, respected her privacy and photographs and footage were rarely taken of her first church visit of the day.)

The 'quiet succession' became a little noisy in the summer of 2017 when Sir Christopher Geidt, for ten years the Queen's private secretary, took early retirement and Samantha Cohen, number three in the Palace hierarchy, stepped down in support of her boss. The feeling was that Sir Christopher was manoeuvered out by Prince Charles (abetted by Prince Andrew) to improve relations between the secretariats at Buckingham Palace and Clarence House. The Queen, usually averse to unnecessary change, accepted it in this case because it was what her sons wanted. (Prince Andrew felt that Sir

Christopher had not supported him sufficiently when he was under media attack for his role as a UK 'trade ambassador' – and the Queen always had a particularly soft spot for her second son.) Sir Christopher's departure (sweetened by the award of the GCVO – the honour Prince Philip received as an anniversary gift but rather felt was the preserve of staff – and a peerage and then another knighthood in the Order of the Bath a few months later) caused considerable fluttering in the court dovecotes. Prince Philip told me he had 'kept out of all that'. From the time of the Queen's accession in 1952 onward, he had always found internal Palace politics 'frustrating and infuriating'. He was proud of the straightforward, stream-lined way in which he and his small team ran his office and implied that, had he been given the opportunity (as Prince Albert had been), he would have been able to 'run the show with half the staff.'

While, understandably, the spotlight moved away from Philip and Elizabeth and on to William and Catherine and their three children and to Harry and his beautiful bride Meghan (an actress, American, divorced), the Duke of Edinburgh continued to make occasional headlines. Predictably, the Netflix television series *The Crown* reheated some of the rumours of the Prince's alleged extra-marital romances from the 1950s and, more interestingly, a correspondence from 1981 emerged that surprised some people. It was between Fenner Brockway, a Labour peer and long-standing supporter of the Campaign for Nuclear Disarmament, and the Duke. Lord Brockway wrote to Prince Philip presupposing that he was active Cold War warrior and enthusiastic supporter of nuclear might. With his letter, Brockway included a copy of a speech which Earl Mountbatten had delivered just months before his untimely death. It concluded with the statement: 'As a military man who has given half a century of active service, I say in all sincerity that the nuclear arms race has no military purpose. Wars cannot be fought with nuclear weapons. Their existence only adds to our perils of the illusions they have generated.' The Duke replied: 'Dear Lord Brockway, Thank you for the copy of Lord Mountbatten's Stockholm speech. I agree with everything he said. The arms race is ridiculous.' The Duke also stressed he was in favour of 'multilateral disarmament and the Strategic Arms Limitation Talks,' adding, 'Security and peace depend upon being prepared for every eventuality, not in creating conflict where none is needed.' Brockway evidently expected the Duke to adopt a hawkish, gung-ho stance and was taken aback by the thoughtful and measured response that he received. *The Times* got in touch with me to ask, 'Does this accord with your knowledge of Prince Philip as a humane pragmatist, who is pained by the caricature painted of him as gaffe-prone and insensitive?'

In fact, by the time the obituaries of Prince Philip appeared the caricature had been replaced by a fuller, fairer portrait. He was recognized as a remarkable man: as an individual, progressive, challenging, thoughtful, pragmatic, unexpected; as the Queen's consort, uniquely supportive from start to finish. If we regard the Queen's uniquely long reign as a success – and I believe most of us do – the joint author of that success has been the Duke of Edinburgh. In 1997, at the time of her fiftieth wedding anniversary and in the aftermath of the death of Diana, Princess of Wales, in a speech at the Banqueting House in Whitehall the Queen acknowledged that it was sometimes difficult to fully understand 'the message' of the people, 'obscured as it can be by deference, rhetoric or the conflicting currents of public opinion'. She said, 'I have done my best, with Prince Philip's constant love and help, to interpret it correctly through the years of our marriage and of my reign.' Theirs was an extraordinary partnership and the worldwide coverage of the Duke's death acknowledged the fact.

Some myths, of course, were hard to put to rest. Most of the obituaries repeated the line that Princess Elizabeth first met Prince Philip when she was thirteen and, from that moment on, had eyes only for him. Not so, as we know. From the letters she sent to her cousin, Diana, in 1943, we know she regretted that Andrew Elphinstone was also her first cousin because he was 'just the sort of husband any girl would love to have.' In 1945, when Lilibet was nineteen, she wrote to Diana about another young man who took her fancy, describing him as 'a devastatingly attractive young giant (with fair hair and blue eyes, of course) from Skye called Roddy Macleod!' The twenty-six year old 6ft 4ins tall Eton-educated Cameroon Highlander, assigned to the royal guard at Balmoral, danced with the young princess and took her out to the theatre, but the fun evenings did not develop into a full-blown romance.

When I tackled Prince Philip about how and when he came to woo his future wife, he was not particularly forthcoming. He and Princess Elizabeth were cousins; they became friends; they got to know one another better; they became closer; in due course, they became engaged. 'That's about it, really,' he said to me, with a shrug.

Interestingly, the Queen's own account of her engagement to Prince Philip tallies very much with his own – and, surprisingly, I can share it with you. In 1947, in the run-up to the royal wedding in November, an author by the name of Betty Shrew contacted the 21-year old princess with a request for accurate background information for a souvenir book about the royal wedding. Princess Elizabeth was happy to oblige. She said the first time she remembered meeting Philip was at the Royal Naval College in Dartmouth in July 1939. 'I was 13 years of age,' she wrote, 'and he was 18 and a cadet just due for leave. He joined the Navy at the outbreak of war, and I only saw him very occasionally when he was on leave – I suppose about twice in three years. We first started seeing more of each other when Philip went for a two-year job to the RN Petty Officer School at Corsham [after the war] – before that we hardly knew each other. He'd spend weekends with us, and when the school was closed he spent six weeks at Balmoral.'

The young princess was ready to supply the enquiring author with details of her engagement and wedding rings: 'The wedding ring will be made of Welsh gold, but not from the Craigwen mine. The engagement ring was made by Antrobus [jewellers of Bond Street]. Princess Alice took it in as Philip obviously couldn't but he designed the ring.'

Elizabeth told her correspondent: 'We both love dancing – we have danced at Ciro's and Quaglino's as well as at parties. Philip enjoys driving and does it fast! He has his own tiny MG which he is very proud of – he has taken me about in it, once up to London, which was great fun, only it was like sitting in the road, and the wheels are almost as high as one's head. On that one and only occasion we were chased by a photographer which was disappointing.'

The behaviour of photographers continued to be a disappointment to the royal couple as the years went by. Prince Philip did his

449

best to protect the Queen from their excesses, barking ferociously at them when necessary. He always did what he could to safeguard her person and her dignity. He hated to see her taken advantage of in any way. One year, at the Royal Variety Performance, one of the stars performed a routine directly at the Queen. Prince Philip was incandescent and descended on the producer in the interval: 'I've been coming to this for 50 years. It never ends on time. The jokes are lavatorial. And now you insult the Queen!' As Philips's friend, the eccentric baronet Sir Humphry Tyrrell Wakefield (who was at Gordonstoun a few years after Philip) put it not long ago: 'The Queen would have such a miserable time if she didn't have him to play with. And if people try to take advantage of her, he's on them like a whippet.'

That about sums it up. Prince Philip protected the Queen and made her laugh. He was her 'liege man of life and limb' for more than seventy years. He was there when she wanted him – even if he might have preferred to be somewhere else. At Royal Ascot, he would drive with the Queen along the course, help Her Majesty out of her carriage and then discreetly jump into a waiting car to be driven swiftly back to Windsor Castle to watch the cricket or work on correspondence before returning to the race course to be with the Queen again for tea. When the Duchess of Cornwall had difficulty alighting from her carriage at Ascot, she is happy to let a coachman lend her a hand to help her down. The Queen would only accept help from Prince Philip. And now he's gone.

The end began by accident – literally so. On Thursday 17 January 2019, at around three o'clock in the afternoon, Prince Philip was driving his Land Rover near the Queen's Sandringham Estate in Norfolk. Pulling out from a side road onto the A149, he was momentarily blinded by sunlight and involved in a collision with another vehicle. The other car was a Kia, containing two women and a nine-month-old baby boy. The prince's vehicle was overturned in the crash, but he was pulled out alive, 'very shocked' but apparently physically unharmed. Happily the baby was unharmed, too, though both the women travelling in the Kia needed hospital treatment for minor injuries before being discharged.

Had any of those involved in the accident been seriously injured, it might have been a major tragedy. For the prince, in some ways it was. It meant that his driving days were over – though he did not realise it at once. His Royal Highness's immediate response to the collision was typical: he returned to Sandringham and ordered a replacement Land Rover. It arrived the next day and the prince, 97 and defiant, took to the wheel again. But, within days, reality dawned. On the advice of the police (and to avoid the possibility of prosecution) he gave up his driving licence voluntarily.

For many older people their car provides them with their last bit of independence. In your car, you are your own master: you can go where you please, when you please. You are not dependent on others. The Duke of Edinburgh was a realist all his life and a pragmatist to the last. After a few days' consideration, having written to apologise to the driver of the Kia, he accepted that his motoring days were done – on public roads, at least. It was another sign that his world was shrinking and it was not easy. He had been driving for eighty years and was accustomed to living life in the fast lane.

Prince Philip had always enjoyed speed. He began driving in the 1930s. In the mid 1940s, when he was in his twenties and courting the young Princess Elizabeth, he owned the celebrated MG sports car that was his pride and joy – and, yes, had involved him in a couple of minor prangs. Once he became Duke of Edinburgh, he was able to graduate from an MG to an Aston Martin. He had it 'improved' to his own specification, installing an extra vanity mirror so that his wife could more easily check her make-up and adjust her hat. He equipped the car with a radio telephone which he used to make prank calls to the young Prince Charles. (The royals have always been hot on goonish practical joking.)

In 1954 he acquired a Lagonda 3 Litre Drophead Coupé. It was made to order, finished in a shade of Edinburgh Green with grey leather upholstery, and earned Aston Martin its first Royal Warrant. The convertible served as Prince Philip's personal car for seven years. He had it loaded on to the Royal Yacht Britannia so that he could take it to the opening of the 1956 Melbourne Olympics and his controversial tour of the Commonwealth. Its non-standard extras included a power hood and floor-change gearbox. It boasted a 3-litre engine, allowing acceleration from 0-60mph in 12.9 seconds, and a top speed of 104mph. Philip enjoyed fast cars – the Lagonda was succeeded by a 1961 Alvis TD21 Drophead Coupé – and was fascinated by how they worked. He used to drive at speed, but always with due care and attention. In the 1960s, when he was President of the Automobile Association, and my father was the AA's legal adviser, Prince Philip summoned my dad to Buckingham Palace to deal with an alleged motoring offence – but, as I recall, it was a parking issue not a speeding one.

As he grew older, he drove less fast – and became more environmentally aware. A generation before the birth of Greta Thunberg, Prince Philip was travelling around London in his own electric taxi cab.

He always liked to be behind the wheel. He liked to be in command. One of the police officers detailed to look after him told me that, regularly, he would hear the Prince, in his nineties, calling out to the Queen (and anyone else within earshot), 'Where are the fucking car keys?' Memorably, when the Obamas visited the Queen at Windsor in 2016, the Duke, then 95, to the consternation of the presidential security team, drove the US President around the royal estate, with their two wives tucked up in the back.

Inevitably, with age, and without his car, his life became more circumscribed. He ceased to be actively involved in the plans for the restoration of Buckingham Palace. He handed over the management of the Sandringham Estate to Prince Charles ('You can bugger about with it now,' he told him), though he enjoyed a late-life horticultural success when, well into his 98th year, he became the first person in Britain to cultivate a successful crop of black truffles.[120] He went on with his carriage driving for as long as he could. He continued with his exercise routine as best he was able. He watched television, 'without much pleasure', he told me. He went on painting; 'They're not up to much,' he insisted. He always had a book or two on the go: military history and biography in the main ('Napoleon

---

120 He began the exercise in 2006 when he planted more than 300 saplings of hazel and oak impregnated with truffle spores at £15 apiece. He knew that the royal estate in Norfolk was well suited for the fungi because of its abundance of alkaline soil. He was introduced to the truffle-hunting with dogs by his uncle Earl Mountbatten of Burma on a trip to Italy. His attempts to create a 'truffière' in the Royal Fruit Farm at Sandringham, which yields apples, gooseberries and blackcurrants, had become something of a family joke, as year after year truffle-sniffing dogs failed to root out a thing – until 2018.

wasn't very nice, was he?'). He read the obituaries in the *Daily Telegraph*: every week someone died whom he had known. 'Some weeks,' he said, 'it's every day.'

The Queen carried on with her royal duties at Buckingham Palace or at Windsor Castle while he lived out his days at Wood Farm on the Sandringham Estate. She left him to it. They would speak regularly on the phone, but weeks could go by without them seeing one another. That shocked some people, though not those who knew them and who understood how well the Queen understood her husband – understood his wish to be left to his own devices, 'not to be fussed over', to be allowed, after more than seventy years of duty, to see out his days in his own way. For example, on the Friday before Christmas 2019, the prince was being airlifted and driven from Sandringham in Norfolk to the King Edward VII Hospital in London 'as a precautionary measure, for observation and treatment' at exactly the time the Queen was travelling by train from London to Sandringham. He did as the doctor ordered. She did as she had been planning, setting off, as scheduled, for her Christmas break on the Sandringham Estate.

The Duke's world *was* getting smaller, but the royal story was carrying on. The Queen was doing her duty, as assiduously as ever. 2019 proved a busy year: she said goodbye to her thirteenth prime minister (Theresa May) and hello to her fourteenth (Boris Johnson); she opened parliament and read the Queen's Speech, twice; she did all the things she had been doing since 1952, year in, year out, opening this, unveiling that, hosting receptions for ambassadors and diplomats – and the rest. On Remembrance Sunday she was seen with a tear in her eye. Was that the biting wind? Or was she thinking of her absent husband who was undeniably growing frailer by the day? I recall seeing her with a tear in her eye on another occasion, in September 2001, emerging from St Paul's cathedral following a special service held in the immediate aftermath of the terrorist attacks over New York and Washington DC in which 2,977 people were killed. As it happened, '9/11' coincided with the death of the Queen's friend, the Earl of Carnarvon. In her message of condolence to the American people, she wrote: 'These are dark and harrowing times for families and friends of those who are missing or who suffered in the attack.' She ended her message in a quite personal way:

'Nothing that can be said can begin to take away the anguish and the pain of these moments. Grief is the price we pay for love.'

As the end drew nearer, Prince Philip, always his own man, even in crowds always something of a loner, was retreating from the world. He still saw friends and he still turned up for family occasions. At the wedding of his grandson Prince Harry with Meghan Markle in May 2018, he appeared, aged 96, still upright, still without a stick, despite having had a hip operation only a few weeks before and having cracked a rib in a fall in the shower a few days before. At the wedding of his granddaughter, Princess Eugenie in October 2018, he appeared, now aged 97, *still* upright, *still* without a stick, impeccably dressed but looking gaunt and cadaverous. In the official wedding photograph – the last official photograph in which he appeared – he was seated immediately in front of his former daughter-in-law, Sarah, Duchess of York. In May 2019, at Windsor Castle, the Duke joined the Queen for a rare official appearance together when they hosted a lunch for members of the Order of Merit. It was the week of the arrival of Harry and Meghan's firstborn and Philip was photographed admiring his eighth great-grandchild, Archie Harrison Mountbatten-Windsor, alongside the Queen and Meghan's mother, Doria Ragland. In the same month he was on parade again for another family wedding at St George's Chapel, Windsor, when Lady Gabriela Windsor, daughter of the Queen's first cousin, Prince Michael of Kent, married her long-time boyfriend, Thomas Kingston. 'I don't know who half these people are,' said the Duke of Edinburgh, laughing.

There was no laughter later in the year when the Queen, having consulted both her husband and the Prince of Wales, decided that the time had come for her second son, Prince Andrew, to give up all his royal duties and step back from public life. The Duke of York had given a disastrous television interview about his friendship with the convicted paedophile, Jeffrey Epstein, and the accusation that he, Andrew, had slept with an American girl, 'trafficked' by Epstein, when she was just seventeen. In the interview, Andrew protested his innocence, but appeared to show no empathy for Epstein's victims nor to regret his friendship with the man. The backlash that followed forced the Queen's hand. On 20 November 2019, HRH The Duke of York KG issued a statement:

It has become clear to me over the last few days that the circumstances relating to my former association with Jeffrey Epstein has become a major disruption to my family's work and the valuable work going on in the many organisations and charities that I am proud to support.

Therefore, I have asked Her Majesty if I may step back from public duties for the foreseeable future, and she has given her permission.

The Queen essentially fired her own son, but the following day showed us how much she loved him by taking him riding with her through Winsdor Great Park in the rain and ensuring that there were photographers on hand to capture the shot. A senior courtier said to me, 'There was a lot of nonsense talked about noone being at the helm, but the Queen took a firm grip of things. To use the military jargon, there was only a few days between flash and bang. Action was called for and the Queen took it.'

The Queen took further firm action in January 2020, when Harry and Meghan, the Duke and Duchess of Sussex, announced their desire to 'step back' from their lives as 'senior Royals'. They planned to divide their time between the United Kingdom and North America; they wanted financial independence; they hoped to be able to continue to serve Queen and Commonwealth, but on their own terms. It was a naïve hope and not to be. The Queen convened a family meeting at Sandringham – attended by her immediate heirs, the Prince of Wales and the Duke of Cambridge, as well as the Duke of Sussex – and a way forward was agreed. Harry and Meghan could do as they pleased, but they could not represent the Queen while doing so. Their HRH titles would be put in abeyance and Harry, to his dismay, was required to give up his royal patronages and military appointments. Harry was distressed, as he put it, 'that it should come to this'. So was his grandmother. In a personal statement, she made it clear that Harry and Meghan would always be close members of her family, and she went out of her way to praise her American granddaughter-in-law, but, so far as the Crown was concerned, she was equally clear: she wasn't going to have a couple of freelance royals roaming the world doing their own thing in any sense in her name.

The Duke of Edinburgh was equally sorry 'that it should come to this'. Harry had only succeeded his grandfather as Captain General of the Royal Marines in 2017. Philip had done the job for sixty-four years. Harry had barely managed thirty months. The Duke of Edinburgh was not pleased, nor did he believe that Harry and Meghan were doing the right thing, either for the country or for themselves. I am reminded of something wise he told me more than once, something worth repeating here. 'It's a big mistake to think about yourself. No one is interested in you in the long run. Don't court popularity. It doesn't last. Remember that the attention comes because of the position you are privileged to hold, not because of who you are. If you think it's all about you you'll never be happy.'

Prince Philip regretted Harry's decision, but did not get involved in its aftermath. On the day the Queen held her Sandringham 'summit' with Charles, William and Harry, he made himself scarce, deliberately leaving the main house and retreating to Wood Farm. 'I'll soon be out of it,' he said, 'and not before time.'

Prince Philip of Greece was born in the aftermath of the influenza pandemic that swept the world between 1918 and 1920, infecting around 500 million people – about a third of the world's population at the time – in four successive waves. As Prince Philip, Duke of Edinburgh, he was still alive a century later, as the Covid 19 pandemic swept the world in 2020. He spent 'lockdown' with the Queen, and a small retinue of staff, at Windsor Castle. In what turned out to be his final public statement in April 2020, he issued a message that reminded us that he had always been the pragmatic prince, properly interested in science, engineering and technology, and committed to the people who, as he liked to put it, 'get their hands dirty and get things done'. 'As we approach World Immunisation Week,' he said, 'I wanted to recognise the vital and urgent work being done by so many to tackle the pandemic; by those in the medical and scientific professions, at universities and research institutions, all united in working to protect us from Covid-19. On behalf of those of us who remain safe and at home, I also wanted to thank all key workers who ensure the infrastructure of our life continues; the staff and volunteers working in food production and distribution, those keeping postal and delivery services going, and those ensuring the rubbish continues to be collected.' He saw the headline 'Philip praises bin men' and, for once, didn't complain about the press.

He made his last parade-ground appearance aged 99, in July 2020, handing over his role as Colonel-in-Chief of The Rifles to his daughter-in-law, the Duchess of Cornwall. He was in the quadrangle at Windsor Castle. She was 'socially distanced' at Highgrove House, a hundred miles away. The hand-over happened on-line. The world had changed in so many ways in the one hundred years of Philip's extraordinary lifetime. The Queen was taking part in Zoom conference calls. Her father had only become king because her uncle had married a divorced American. Now three of her children had been divorced and her grandson, Harry, had not only married a divorced American, but gone to live in America as well. The Duke of Edinburgh accepted all this with a shrug – and the occasional exasperated sigh. His cousin, Ivar Mountbatten – the son of Philip's friend and contemporary, his first choice as best man, David Milford Haven – became the first member of the royal family to marry someone of the same sex. 'Whatever makes them happy,' said Prince Philip.

Because he lived so long, Philip saw so much. He knew the royal road had always been a rocky one. 'My grandfather was assassinated,' he reminded me, 'my father was sent into exile, my parents separated, my sister was killed in that aeroplane crash, my uncle was murdered by the IRA . . . things happen, but life goes on.' Life went on into 2021 with Princess Eugenie and her husband, Jack Brooksbank, having their first baby: the Queen and Prince Philip's ninth great-grandchild. The Duke wouldn't be drawn on the future of the Royal Family. 'There'll be ups and there'll be downs, but beyond that I've no idea what the future holds. There's no point in speculating about it. All I'll say is that I've tried to help keep it going while I've been here.'

When lockdown was lifted, Philip and Elizabeth, having spent more time close together than they had done in years, decided it rather suited them. They left Windsor together and travelled up to Balmoral for their traditional summer break. When it was over, they went back to Sandringham – but not the big house. Instead, together they went to live at Wood Farm, Philip's favourite bolt-hole, the ungrand, unpretentious place he regarded as his home on the Sandringham estate.

Then, for the last time, they returned together to Windsor Castle, where Philip's mother had been born way back in 1885 and where, on the morning of Friday 9 April 2021, Philip ended his days.

In mid-February, he had felt unwell and was taken to the King Edward VII Hospital in London. On 1 March he was transferred to St Bartholomew's Hospital for a heart procedure. On 16 March, after four weeks, his longest ever confinement in hospital, he was driven home.

Twenty years before, he had told me he had no desire to live to be 100. 'I can't imagine anything worse,' he said then. As his centenary approached, he changed his tune, acknowledging that it would be 'a bit of a milestone, I suppose', though he was 'dreading all the fuss'. When he became ill in February, he said 'I'm on the way out,' – but he had been saying that for years. His final month in hospital was 'pretty ghastly', principally because he no longer had the energy and concentration to read – and reading was one of the sustaining pleasures of his retirement. 'Staring at the ceiling is bloody boring.' He took phone calls from his family, but because of the lockdown restrictions his only visitor was the Prince of Wales.

The news of his death came in an announcement posted, according to custom, on the gates of Buckingham Palace: 'It is with deep sorrow that Her Majesty The Queen announces the death of her beloved husband, His Royal Highness, The Prince Philip, Duke of Edinburgh.' Within hours fulsome tributes to the Duke and heartfelt condolences to the Queen were pouring in from across the world. Even Donald Trump and Vladimir Putin sent messages. 'My dear Papa was a very special person,' said Prince Charles, 'who I think above all else would have been amazed by the reaction and the touching things that have been said about him.' The outpouring was much greater than most commentators had expected. People, young and old, acknowledged the Duke's remarkable character and recognized his extraordinary contribution – and they felt for the Queen.

Prince Philip had never wanted a state funeral. He was all for a quiet send-off and by royal standards, thanks to the pandemic, he got one, at the St George's Chapel, Windsor, on Saturday 17 April. Given his frustration two years before at having to give up driving his cherished Land Rover, as if to get the last laugh, he designed his own hearse to carry his own body to his own funeral – a Land

Rover modified to His Royal Highness's personal specification. He was a pragmatist with a sense of humour to the last. And at the last, because of the Covid restrictions, the funeral itself was attended by just thirty mourners – members of his immediate family who followed his coffin into the Chapel to bid their final farewell.

The only mourner who did not walk with the others was the Queen, a few days short of her ninety-fifth birthday, still there, still driven by duty and sustained by faith, but now, for the first time in more than seventy-three years, alone. Philip gave Elizabeth a lifetime of unstinting support. He made her laugh. He understood her. She understood him. It was a unique marriage – the longest in all royal history – and it worked.

APPENDICES

Prince Philip's Achievements and Appointments

I think this final section of my book is the only one of which Prince Philip would have approved wholeheartedly. It deals in facts and nothing else. I showed him the material and he said, 'It seems to cover the ground, more or less.'

From the time of his marriage to Princess Elizabeth, the Duke of Edinburgh began to acquire honours, awards, and decorations – and plenty of them: Knight of the Garter, 1947; Privy Counsellor, 1951; Knight of the Thistle, 1952; Knight Grand Cross of the Order of the British Empire, 1953 (he also served as Grand Master of the OBE); the Order of Merit, 1968; plus at least fifty-two foreign orders and decorations, from the Danish Order of the Elephant to the Moroccan Order of Muhammed (First Class). Under the circumstances, these distinctions were relatively easily come by. As he said to me, 'The foreign decorations came as a result of visits abroad. They came with the territory – literally.' The real challenge for him, of course, was not to acquire honours, awards, and decorations, but to carve out for himself some sort of worthwhile role.

The first charity in which the Duke became involved, in 1947, was the London Federation of Boys' Clubs; the next, in 1948, was the National Playing Fields Association; both reflected what would become a lifelong commitment to the healthy, active, challenging development of young people and to the value of competitive sport and team games. He was President of the Central Council for Physical Recreation from 1951; President of the Commonwealth Games Federation from 1955 to 1990; President of the British Sports Trust from 1989.

In 1953 he became Patron of the Outward Bound Trust (between 1995 and 2000 he was also Chairman of the Trustees), another organisation that reflected his core concerns. Here is his account of the origins of Outward Bound and the philosophy behind it: '"Outward Bound" is the meaning of the "Blue Peter" signal flag hoisted by merchant ships as they leave harbour for foreign ports. The combined experience and skills of the navigator, the seaman and the engineer are needed to ensure that a ship makes a safe journey. Outward Bound was therefore an apt choice as the name for an organisation designed to help young men about to start their careers in the British Merchant Navy at the height of the Second World War. It is easy enough to teach technical skills; it is quite another matter to exercise those skills in the stress of Atlantic gales and in the face of submarine attacks. Outward Bound had been the brainchild of Laurence Holt, of the Blue Funnel Line, and Kurt Hahn, the Headmaster of Gordonstoun . . . It all began in a small way in Aberdovey in North Wales in 1941. The idea has since spread through eighteen countries in five continents, and there is plenty of scope for further expansion. From the very beginning, Outward Bound was intended to develop self-confidence and self-awareness through self-discovery. Every individual needs the inner capacity to cope with the vicissitudes of life; this could be said to involve using the art of a navigator to avoid hazards, the craft of a seaman to avoid storms, and the skill of an engineer to maintain the will to go on.'

Over a long life the Duke's public offices and involvements were many and varied. In 1952, at the time of the Queen's Accession, he became Admiral of the Sea Cadet Corps, Colonel-in-Chief of the Army Cadet Force, and Air-Commodore-in-Chief of the Air Training Corps. In 1953, Coronation Year, he was elevated to the rank of Admiral of the Fleet, Field Marshal and Marshal of the Royal Air Force. Subsequently he became Colonel or Colonel-in-Chief, Captain-General, and Air Commodore forty-two times over. Away from the services, he was founder, fellow, patron, president, chairman, or member of at least 837 different organisations.

In 1948 he became a Trustee of the National Maritime Museum, an active involvement that continued until 1998. Also in 1948, he became an honorary member of the Royal Yachting Association, and was twice President, 1956–70 and 1975–80. Between 1951 and 1954 he was closely involved in the design and fitting out of the interior of the new Royal Yacht, *Britannia*. In 1951 he co-founded (with Frank Carr) the Cutty Sark Preservation Society, later Trust. In 1952 he became an Elder Brother of Trinity House and, subsequently, Master. In 1953 he joined the Royal Yacht Squadron: he was Admiral and Commodore, 1962–8, and rewrote the statutes. In 1955 he became Patron of the Sail Training Association. In 1969, again with Frank Carr, he was co-founder of the Maritime Trust.

From 1948 to 1976, he was Chancellor of the University of Wales. He became Chancellor of Edinburgh University in 1952, was Chancellor of Salford University 1967–91, and became Chancellor of Cambridge University in 1976. He became President of the City & Guilds of London Institute in 1951 and, in 1962, instituted the Institute's Prince Philip Medal. In 1951–2 he was President of the British Association for the Advancement of Science. In 1952 he became President of the English-Speaking Union. Again in 1952, with the Design Council he initiated the Designers' Prize, and in 1959 initiated the Prize for Elegant Design, later known as Designer of the Year Award. From 1952 he was President of the Royal Society of Arts. From 1965 to 1975 he was President of the Council of Engineering Institutions. In 1976 he initiated the Fellowship of Engineering and became Senior Fellow of what was to become the Royal Academy of Engineering. In 1965 he was chairman of the originating committee of the Queen's Award for Industry.

The list of his involvements, initiatives, and chairmanships is a long one: Variety Club (Life Member from 1949), MCC (Life Member from 1948, President 1949–50, 1974–5), Lord's Taverners (Patron and Twelfth Man from 1950), Automobile Association (President, 1951–61), the Coronation Commission (Chairman, 1952–3), Royal Mint Advisory Committee on the Design of Coins, Seals and Medals (1952–99), Air League (Patron from 1950), Guild of Air Pilots and Air Navigators (Grand Master from 1952 and initiator of the Prince Philip Prize for Helicopter Rescue), Guards Polo Club (Founder, 1955), Royal Agricultural Society of the Commonwealth (President and co-founder, with Sam Hordern, 1956), Commonwealth Technical Training Week (initiator, 1957), Voluntary Service Overseas (Patron from 1961), National Federation of Housing Associations (President, 1975–80, Patron from 1981), St George's House (Co-founder with the Dean of Windsor, Robin Woods, 1965), Westminster Abbey Trust (President, 1972–97: the Trust raised some £22 million and oversaw major repairs to the exterior of the Abbey),

British Commonwealth Ex-Service League (Grand President from 1974), Prince Philip Trust for Windsor and Maidenhead (Co-founder with Sir Kit Aston, 1976, and chairman of Trustees).

The significant prizes and medals that he initiated or that bear his name (there are at least seventy-five) reflect a cross-section of his interests: yachting, sailing, rowing, riding, carriage driving, dressage, flying, design, engineering, education, conservation, agriculture, even tiddlywinks (the inter-university championship), greyhound racing, and the Pakistan Army Pipe Band Trophy.

When I first showed Prince Philip this list of 'achievements' he made some factual corrections which I have incorporated and reminded me that 'getting the details right' matters. For example, while he acknowledged that it was reasonable to describe him as a founder of the Guards Polo Club in 1955, 'To be strictly accurate, I organised for, what was then, the Household Brigade Polo Club, to play on Smith's Lawn [at Windsor]. The club was founded by officers of the Brigade. It later became the Guards Club.'

If I had to highlight just three of the organisations in which Prince Philip was involved, I would choose these:

1. The Duke of Edinburgh's Award Scheme. Started from scratch in 1956, the concept has spread to 132 countries. More than eight million young people have taken part. In terms of a legacy, this is, to me, the Great Achievement, both because of its impact on so many individual lives and because the qualities the Award encourages – self-reliance, compassion, fitness, skill, endeavour – are among those Prince Philip valued most.

2. The International Equestrian Federation. Outside the horse-orientated world, this means very little, but it features on the list because the Duke was the active (some felt hyper-active) President for twenty-two years. He introduced international rules for carriage driving, long-distance riding and vaulting; he added international competitions for ponies, juniors and young riders; he steered the veterinary committee; he ran the show. In 1971 he initiated the International Carriage Driving Grand Prix at the Royal Windsor Horse Show. In 1972 he founded the Windsor Park Equestrian Club.

3. The World Wide Fund for Nature. Ornithology was a lifelong enthusiasm (800 books on birds on his shelves, President of the British Trust for Ornithology since 1987) and he was President of

the London Zoological Society from 1960 to 1977, but his close involvement with WWF (UK President since 1961, International President from 1981, President Emeritus from 1996) saw his interest in wildlife broaden from a commitment to the conservation of natural habitats to a passionate and tireless championing of global environmental issues. (He was President of the Game Research Association, 1964–70; President of Game Conservancy, 1970–73, and subsequently Patron and Life Member; he was Patron of the British Association for Shooting and Conservation from 1967 and Patron of the British Trust for Conservation Volunteers from 1970.)

For the record, and because I have not seen the information given elsewhere, here is the note Prince Philip sent to me about his involvement in the World Wide Fund for Nature. It is typical of HRH's style in several ways – not least because it manages to include a side-swipe at the press! 'The exact story of my involvement in WWF started when Peter Scott [ornithologist and conservationist, 1909–89] came to me to invite me to become President of the newly founded international organisation. I had already been attacked by the *Daily Mirror* for shooting, so I thought it might be counter-productive to take a high-profile position in a conservation organisation. In any case I was already committed to the FEI [International Equestrian Federation] and I did not think that I could do two international jobs at the same time. However, I happened to know that P Bernhard [Prince Bernhard of the Netherlands] was staying at Claridge's. I knew he was very interested in the African Game Parks, so I suggested that Peter should approach him. However, I agreed to become a Trustee of the international body and I also agreed to become President of the UK National Appeal while I was President of the London Zoo. That was later conveniently forgotten and I stayed on the Board. I eventually became International President in – I think – 1981 till 1995.'

Finally, here is a list of the Duke's 'offices and involvements' kindly prepared by Dame Anne Griffiths, Prince Philip's archivist and librarian:

Offices and Involvements

1947	Patron, London Federation of Boys' Clubs (later London Federation of Clubs for Young People, then Federation of London Youth Clubs and now London Youth)
1948	President, National Playing Fields Association
1948–2000	Trustee, National Maritime Museum Patron from 2000
1948	Hon. Member, Royal Yachting Association Hon. Member of Council from 1980 President, 1956–70 and 1975–80
1948	Member, Royal Yacht Squadron Admiral from 1953 1962–8 Commodore and rewrote Statutes
1948	Hon. Life Member, Marylebone Cricket Club (MCC) President, 1949–50 and 1974–5
1948–76	Chancellor, University of Wales
1949	Life Member, Variety Club of Great Britain
1950	Patron and Twelfth Man, Lords Taverners President 1960–61
1951–61	President, Automobile Association Hon. Life Member from 1947 Ex-officio Member of the Committee from 1961
1951	President, Central Council of Physical Recreation and saved it from extinction
1951	Co-founder, with Frank Carr, the Cutty Sark Preservation Society (now Cutty Sark Trust), Patron 1952–2000 President from 2000

1951	President, City and Guilds of London Institute 1962 initiated Prince Philip Medal
1951–2	President, British Association for the Advancement of Science
1951–4	HM Yacht *Britannia* – involved in design until commissioned
1952–99	President, Royal Mint Advisory Committee on the design of coins, seals and medals
1952	President, English-speaking Union of the Commonwealth. Chairman, English Language Committee from 1977
1952	Chancellor, University of Edinburgh
1952–2002	Grand Master, Guild of Air Pilots and Air Navigators 1979 Prince Philip Prize for Helicopter Rescue Patron from 2002
1952	Elder Brother, Trinity House Master from 1969
1952	Patron, Air League President in 1969
1952–2000	President, British Amateur Athletic Board (later British Athletic Federation and now UK Athletics) Patron from 2000
1952	First flight on 12 November – Chipmunk from White Waltham
1952	President and Hon. Life Fellow, Royal Society for the Encouragement of Arts, Manufactures and Commerce
1953	Patron, Outward Bound Trust 1995–2000, Chairman of Trustees
1955	Founder and President, Guards Polo Club (originally Household Brigade Polo Club)
1955–90	President, Commonwealth Games Federation
1956	Founder, Commonwealth Study Conferences, held every six years – 1956, 1962, 1968, 1974, 1980, 1986, 1992, 1998, 2003
1956	Co-founder with Kurt Hahn and Chairman of Trustees, the Duke of Edinburgh Award Scheme Patron and Trustee 1961–2001 Patron from 2001
1956	Initiator, Lunches at Buckingham Palace
1956–92	Patron, Sail Training Association

1957	Co-founder with Sam Hordern, Royal Agricultural Society of the Commonwealth, President from 1958
1957	Patron and co-founder with Michael Ansell, Pony Club Mounted Games Championship – Prince Philip Cup President, the Pony Club 1997–2002
1957	Initiator, Commonwealth Technical Training Week, held in 1961
1959	Initiated Designer's Prize with the Design Council (formerly the Duke of Edinburgh's Prize for Elegant Design (1959), the Duke of Edinburgh's Design Prize (1971) and the Duke of Edinburgh's Prize for Industrial Design (1976–89). Since 1990 the Prince Philip Designer's Prize for the Designer of the Year)
1960–77	President, Zoological Society of London Life Fellow 1959–77 Hon. Fellow from 1977
1960	Founder with Lord Buxton of Alsa, Countryside in 1970 Conferences, 1963, 1965 and 1970
1961	Patron, Voluntary Service Overseas
1961–81	UK President and International Trustee, World Wildlife Fund (now World Wide Fund for Nature) 1981–96 International President 1996– President Emeritus
1964–70	President, Game Research Association 1970–73 President, the Game Conservancy 1973– Patron and Life Member
1964–86	President, International Equestrian Federation (FEI) *Introduced International Rules for Carriage-Driving, Long-Distance Riding, Vaulting and initiated Veterinary Committee and Veterinary Regulations* Added International Competitions for Pony Riders, Jumons and Young Riders
1965	President, Royal Commission for the Exhibition of 1851
1965	Co-founder with Robin Woods, Dean of Windsor, and Trustre of the Council, St George's House, Windsor Castle

1965	Chairman, Originating Committee, Queen's Award for Industry, now the Queen's Awards for Export & Technology
1965–75	President, Council of Engineering Institutions 1976 Initiator, Fellowship of Engineering 1976– Senior Fellow From 1992 Royal Academy of Engineering
1966	Chairman and President Panel of Judges, Tiger Club 'Dawn to Dusk' (flying) Competition for the Duke of Edinburgh Trophy
1967	Patron, British Association for Shooting & Conservation (formerly WAGBI)
1967–91	First Chancellor, University of Salford
1968	Initiator, Standing Conference on Schools Science and Technology (SCSSI), subsequently Patron, Association for Schools' Science Engineering and Technology From 1961 Patron, Association for Science Education
1969	Co-founder with Frank Carr and President, the Maritime Trust
1970	Patron, British Trust for Conservation Volunteers
1971	Initiator, International Carriage-driving Grand Prix, Royal Windsor Horse Show
1971	Founder and Life Member, Windsor Park Equestrian Club, Patron 1971–84 President from 1984
1972	Initiator, Private Dinners at Buckingham Palace
1973–97	Chairman, Westminster Abbey Trust
1974	Grand President, British Commonwealth Ex-Services League and known from 2003 as the Royal Commonwealth Ex-Services League
1975–80	President, National Federation of Housing Associations Patron from 1981
1976	Chancellor of the University of Cambridge
1976	Co-founder with Sir Kit Aston, then Mayor of Windsor, and Chairman of Trustees, Prince Philip Trust for the Royal Borough of Windsor and Maidenhead

1977–8	Promoter, Degrees in Military Studies for Service Officers
1978	Co-founder with Colonel Anderton of Standing Conference on Countryside Sports
1978	Member of the British Team at the Four-in-Hand World Driving Championships which won the Team Bronze Medal at Kecskemet, Hungary
1980	Member of the British Team at the Four-in-Hand World Driving Championships which won the Team Gold Medal at Windsor
1981	Member of the British Team at the Four-in-Hand European Driving Championships which won the Team Bronze Medal at Zug, Switzerland
1982	Member of the British Team at the Four-in-Hand World Driving Championships which won the Team Bronze Medal at Apeldoorn, Netherlands
1984	Member of the British Team at the Four-in-Hand World Driving Championships which won the Team Bronze Medal at Szilvasvarad, Hungary
1984–91	Chairman of Inquiry into British Housing as Patron of the National Federation of Housing Associations (1st Report 1985, 2nd Report 1991)
1987	Patron, British Trust for Ornithology
1989	President, British Sports Trust
1991	President, Royal Windsor Horse Show
1992–7	Chairman, Restoration Committee following Windsor Castle Fire
1997	Last flight on 11 August – Carlisle to Islay in BAe 146 after 5,986 hours in fifty-nine types including nine helicopters

Prizes and Medals Donated by the Duke of Edinburgh

1949–	Edinburgh Cup for Yachts of the International Dragon Class
1955–	'Royal Windsor Cup' for Ascot Week Polo Tournament
1957–	Prince Philip Cup for Isle of Wight inter-club racing
1957–	Prince Philip Cup for Pony Club Mounted Games

1959–	Prince Philip Designer's Prize for the Designer of the Year
1961–	Silver Wink for Inter-University Tiddlywinks Championships
1962	Coweslip Trophy for Championships held by the Australian Flying Fifteen Association
1962–	Prince Philip Medal for outstanding achievement in work with Science or Technology, City and Guilds of London Institute
1962–	Silver collar for Greyhound Racing
1962–	Grand Master's Medal, Guild of Air Pilots and Air Navigators
1963–	Bagpiping trophy for the Pakistan Army
1963–	President's Prize for Design Management, Royal Society of Arts
1964–	Prince Philip Challenge Cup for coxed fours, Henley Regatta
1972–	Trophy for World Individual Team Driving Champion
1991–	Duke of Edinburgh's Trophy for the Royal Windsor Horse Show
1993–	Prince Philip Cup for Modern Horse-drawn Machinery
1997–	Duke of Edinburgh Conservation Medal, World Wide Fund for Nature

Houses and Gardens

Buckingham Palace

1962	Conversion of chapel to the Queen's Gallery

Windsor	South slopes, moved road and laid out border and beds
	East terrace beds and fountain
	'Coronation' Oak Avenue from Golf Course Cottage
	'Hurricane' Lime Avenue
	'Grenadier' Avenue
	Budgerigars and pigeons
	Queen Anne's Ride – replanting

Balmoral	North side, fountain court, kitchen garden, water garden, 'heath' beds
	Oak bank
	Log cabin, conversation of Gelder Shiel and Inchnabobart
	Demolition of dry-rotten Victorian addition to Abergeldie Castle
Birkhall	Replacement of the 'tin wing'
Sandringham	Wood Farm – conversion
	Coronation Lime Avenue from Appleton to Gatton Water
	Copper Beach Avenue – Norwich Gates, Dersingham Hill
	Game coverts, marsh 'sanctuary', new hedgerows
	Construction of the two log cabins
	Conversion of new lunch room
Collections	Books on carriage-driving
	Bird books
	Pictures of birds and animals
	Coach and carriage driving books
	Contemporary Scottish pictures (mostly at Holyrood)
	Contemporary watercolours
	Sixty oil paintings by Edward Seago from World Tour 1956–7
	Competition carriage-driving scrapbooks and videos
	Photographs – 150 albums of Minox from foreign visits 100 albums of conventional photographs

Books

1957	*Selected Speeches – 1948–55*
1960	*Selected Speeches – 1956–59*
1962	*Birds from Britannia*; American edition, *Seabirds from Southern Waters*
1970	*Wildlife Crisis* (with James Fisher)

1978	*The Environmental Revolution – Speeches on Conservation 1962–1977*
1982	*Competition Carriage Driving*, French edition 1984, second edition 1984
1982	*A Question of Balance*
1984	*Men, Machines and Sacred Cows*
1984	*A Windsor Correspondence* (with Michael Mann)
1988	*Down to Earth – Collected Writings and Speeches on Man and the Natural World*, 1961–87, paperback edition 1989, Japanese edition 1992
1989	*Survival or Extinction: A Christian Attitude to the Environment* (with Michael Mann)
1994	*Competition Carriage Driving*, revised edition
1996	*Driving and Judging Dressage*
2004	*Thirty Years On, and Off, the Box Seat*

Service Appointments Held by the Duke of Edinburgh between 1952 and 2017

1952–92	Admiral, Sea Cadet Corps
1953	Admiral of the Fleet (15/1/53)
	Field Marshal (15/1/53)
	Marshal of the Royal Air Force (15/1/53)
	Captain-General, Royal Marines (1/6/53)
	Colonel-in-Chief
	The Queen's Own Cameron Highlanders until February 1961
	The Queen's Own Highlanders (Seaforths and Camerons) until September 1994
	The Highlanders (Seaforth, Gordons and Camerons) from September 1994
	Colonel-in-Chief
	The Wiltshire Regiment until June 1959
	The Duke of Edinburgh's Royal Regiment (Berkshire and Wiltshire) until 1994
	The Royal Gloucestershire, Berkshire and Wiltshire Regiment from April 1994
	Colonel-in-Chief
	The 8th King's Royal Irish Hussars until October 1958

The Queen's Royal Irish Hussars until
September 1993
Deputy Colonel-in-Chief from September, 1993
and Colonel-in-Chief from 2002
The Queen's Royal Hussars (The Queen's Own
and Royal Irish)
Colonel-in-Chief, Royal Canadian Regiment
Air Commodore-in-Chief, Air Training Corps
(15/1/53)
Colonel-in-Chief, Army Cadet Force (15/1/53)
Air Commodore-in-Chief, Royal Canadian Air
Cadets
Colonel-in-Chief, Royal Canadian Army Cadets
Admiral, Royal Canadian Sea Cadets (15/1/53)
Royal Hon. Colonel, University of Edinburgh and
Heriot Watt
Officer Training Corps and from 1994 City of
Edinburgh
Universities Officers' Training Corps

1953–75	Colonel, Welsh Guards
1954	Field Marshal, Australian Military Forces (1/4/54)
	Marshal, Royal Australian Air Force (1/4/54)
	Admiral of the Fleet, Royal Australian Navy (1/4/54)
	Extra Master, Merchant Navy
1957	Member, Honourable Artillery Company
1958	Admiral of the Fleet, Royal New Zealand Navy (21/4) (seniority backdated to 15/1/53)
	Colonel-in-Chief, the Queen's Royal Irish Hussars (see above)
1959	Colonel-in-Chief, The Duke of Edinburgh's Royal Regiment (Berkshire and Wiltshire) (see above)
	Colonel-in-Chief, Royal Australian Corps of Electrical and Mechanical Engineers
1961	Colonel-in-Chief, The Queen's Own Highlanders (Seaforth and Camerons) (see above)
1963	Colonel-in-Chief, Australian Cadet Corps

Family Trees

The British Royal Family: A select family tree (I)

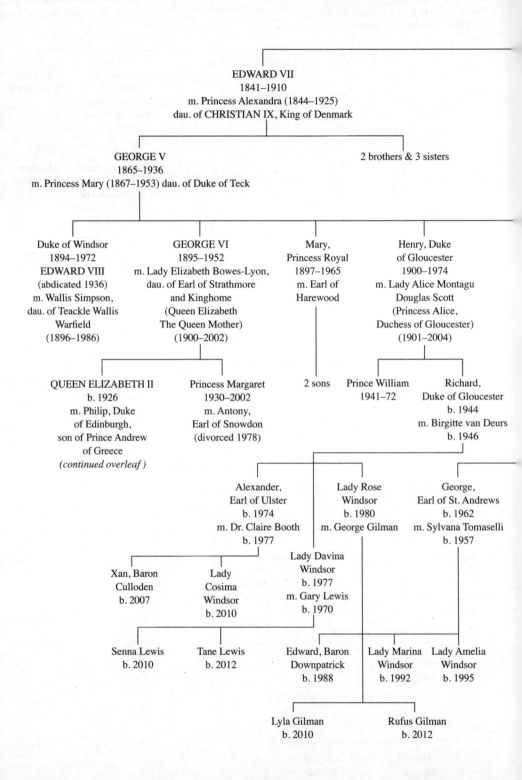

VICTORIA
1819–1901
m. Prince Albert of Saxe-Coburg & Gotha
(Prince Consort) (1819–61)

Princess Alice
1843–78
m. Grand Duke
Louis of Hesse
(1837–92)

3 brothers
& 4 sisters

Princess Victoria
1863–1950
m. Marquess of
Milford Haven
(1854–1921)

2 brothers
& 4 sisters

George, Duke of Kent
1902–42
m. Princess Marina
of Greece
(1906–68)

Prince John
1905–19

Princess Alice
1885–1969
m. Prince Andrew
of Greece
(1882–1944)

2 brothers
& 1 sister

Edward,
Duke of Kent
b. 1935
m. Katharine
Worsley
b. 1933

Princess Alexandra
b. 1936
m. Rt Hon Sir Angus
Ogilvy
(1928–2004)

Prince Michael
b. 1942
m. Baroness
Marie-Christine von
Reibnitz
b. 1945

Philip,
Duke of Edinburgh
b. 1921
m. Princess Elizabeth
(QUEEN ELIZABETH II)

4 sisters

Lord Nicholas
Windsor
b. 1970
m. Paola de Frankopan
b. 1969

James Ogilvy
b. 1964
m. Julia
Rawlinson

Lord Frederick
Windsor
b. 1979

Lady Helen
Windsor
b. 1964
n. Timothy Taylor
b. 1963

Marina Ogilvy
b. 1966
m. Paul Mowatt
(divorced 1997)

Lady Gabriella
Windsor
b. 1981

Columbus
Taylor
b. 1994

Eloise
Taylor
b. 2003

Flora Ogilvy
b. 1994

Zenouska
Mowatt
b. 1990

Christian
Mowatt
b. 1993

m. Sophie
Winkleman
b. 1980

Cassius
Taylor
b. 1996

Estella
Taylor
b. 2004

Alexander
Ogilvy
b. 1996

Albert
Windsor
b. 2007

Leopold
Windsor
b. 2009

The British Royal Family: A select family tree (II)

GEORGE VI
1895–1952
m. Lady Elizabeth Bowes-Lyon,
dau. of Earl of Strathmore and Kinghorn
(Queen Elizabeth The Queen Mother)
(1900–2002)

QUEEN ELIZABETH II
(b. 1926)
m. Philip, Duke of Edinburgh,
son of Prince Andrew of Greece

Charles,
Prince of Wales
(b. 1948)
m. 1 Lady Diana Spencer,
dau. of Earl Spencer
(divorced 1996) (1961–97)

Anne,
Princess Royal
(b. 1950)
m. 1 Captain Mark Phillips
(b. 1948)
(divorced 1992)

Andrew,
Duke of York
b. 1960
m. Sarah Ferguson
(b. 1959)
(divorced 1996)

William,
Duke
of Cambridge
(b. 1982)
m. Catherine
Middleton
(b. 1982)

Prince Henry
of Wales
(b. 1984)
m. Meghan
Markle
(b. 1981)

Peter Phillips
(b. 1977)
m. Autumn Kelly
(b 1978)

Princess Beatrice
of York
b. 1988

m. 2 Vice-Admiral Sir
Timothy Laurence
(b. 1955)

Zara Phillips
(b. 1981)
m. Michael Tindall
(b. 1978)

Princess Eugenie
of York
b. 1990
m. Jack Brooksbank
(b. 1986)

Archie Harrison
Mountbatten-
Windsor
(b. 2019)

Mia Tindall
(b. 2014)

Lena Tindall
(b. 2018)

m. 2 Mrs Camilla
Parker Bowles
(b. 1947)

Savannah Phillips
(b. 2010)

Isla Phillips
(b. 2012)

Prince George of
Cambridge
(b. 2013)

Princess Charlotte
of Cambridge
(b. 2015)

Prince Louis
of Cambridge
(b. 2018)

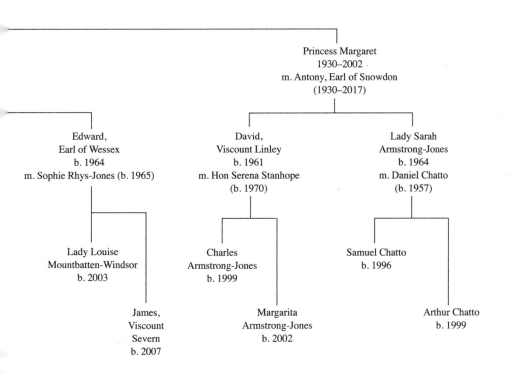

Princess Margaret
1930–2002
m. Antony, Earl of Snowdon
(1930–2017)

Edward,
Earl of Wessex
b. 1964
m. Sophie Rhys-Jones (b. 1965)

David,
Viscount Linley
b. 1961
m. Hon Serena Stanhope
(b. 1970)

Lady Sarah
Armstrong-Jones
b. 1964
m. Daniel Chatto
(b. 1957)

Lady Louise
Mountbatten-Windsor
b. 2003

Charles
Armstrong-Jones
b. 1999

Samuel Chatto
b. 1996

James,
Viscount
Severn
b. 2007

Margarita
Armstrong-Jones
b. 2002

Arthur Chatto
b. 1999

The Greek Royal Family: A select family tree

CHRISTIAN IX
King of Denmark
(1818–1906)
m. Princess Louise
of Hessel-Cassel
(1817–1898)

FREDERIK VIII
King of Denmark
(1843–1912)

William
(GEORGE I King of Greece)
(1845–1913)
m. Grand Duchess Olga of Russia
(1851–1926)

CONSTANTINE I
King of Greece
(1868–1923)
m. Princess Sophie
of Prussia
(1870–1932)

(Big) George
(1869–1957)
m. Princess Marie
Bonaparte
(1882–1962)

Alexandra
(1870–1891)
m. Grand Duke
Paul of Russia
(1860–1919)

Nicholas
(1872–1938)
m. Grand Duchess
Ellen of Russia
(1882–1957)

Peter
(1908–1980)

Eugénie
(1910–1989)

Olga
(1903–1997)
m. Prince Paul
of Yugoslavia
(1893–1976)

Elizabeth
(1904–1955)
m. Count Toering
(1900–67)

GEORGE II
King of Greece
(1890–1947)
m. Prince Elizabeth
of Romania
(1894–1956)

ALEXANDER
King of Greece
(1893–1920)
m. Aspasia Manos
(1896–1972)

Helen
(1896–1982)
m. CAROL II
King of Romania
(1893–1953)

Alexandra
(1921–1993)
m. PETER
King of Yugoslavia
(1923–1970)

MICHAEL
King of Romania
(1921–2017)

Alexandra
(1844–1925)
m. EDWARD VII
(1841–1910)

Marie
(1847–1928)
m. ALEXANDER III
Emperor of Russia
(1845–1894)

Marie
(1876–1940)
m. 1. Grand Duke
George of Russia
(1863–1919)

m. 2. Vice-Admiral Joannides
(1881–1965)

Olga
(b. and d. 1880)

Andrew
(1882–1944)
m. Princess Alice of
Battenberg
(1885–1969)

Christopher
(1888–1940)
m. 1. Mrs Nancy Leeds
(1873–1923)

m. 2. Princess Françoise
of France
(1902–1953)

Marina
(1906–1968)
m. George
Duke of Kent
(1902–1942)

4 daughters

Philip, Duke of Edinburgh
(b. 1921)
m. Princess Elizabeth
(QUEEN ELIZABETH II)

Michael
(b. 1939)

PAUL
King of Greece
(1901–1964)
m. Princess Frederika
of Hanover
(1917–1981)

Irene
(1904–1974)
m. Duke of Aosta
(1900–1948)

Katherine
(1913–2007)
m. Major Richard Brandram
(1911–1994)

CONSTANTINE II
King of Greece
(b. 1940)

Sofia
Queen of Spain
(b. 1938)

Irene
(b. 1942)

The Battenbergs and Mountbattens: A select family tree

| Margarita (1905–1981) m. Prince Gottfried of Hohenlohe-Langenburg (1897–1960) | Thedora (1906–1969) m. Bertold Margrave of Baden (1906–1963) | Cécile (1911–1937) m. Georg Donatus Hereditary Grand Duke of Hesse (1906–1937) | Sophie (1914–2001) m. 1. Prince Christoph of Hesse (1901–1943) | m. 2. Princ George of Hanover (1915–200(|

Prince Kraft of Hohenlohe-Langenburg (1935–2004)

Max Duke of Baden (b. 1933)

Margarita (1932–2013) m. Prince Tomislav of Yugoslavia (1928–2000)

Ludwig (1931–1937)

Johanna (1936–1939)

2 sons & 3 daughters

2 sons & 1 daughter

3 sons & 2 daughters

Ludwig (b. 1937)

Alexander (1933–1937)

Louis
1st Marquess of
Hilford Haven
(1854–1921)
m. Princess Victoria
of Hesse
(1836–1953)

Alice
(1885–1969)
m. Prince Andrew
of Greece
(1882–1944)

Louise
(1889–1965)
m. GUSTAF VI ADOLF
King of Sweden
(1882–1973)

George
2nd Marquess
of Milford Haven
(1892–1938)
m. Countess Nada
Torby
(1896–1963)

Louis, Admiral
of the Fleet
Earl
Mountbatten of Burma
(1900–1979)
m. Hon. Edwina
Ashley
(1901–1960)

Philip, Duke of
Edinburgh
(b. 1921)
m. ELIZABETH II
(b. 1926)

Lady Tatiana
Mountbatten
(1917–1988)

Patricia
Countess Mountbatten
of Burma
(1924–2017)

David
3rd Marquess of
Milford Haven
(1919–1970)

Lady Pamela Hicks
(b. 1929)

Charles,
Prince of Wales
(b. 1948)

Andrew,
Duke of York
(b. 1960)

Anne
Princess Royal
(b. 1950)

Edward
Earl of Wessex
(b. 1964)

Sources and Acknowledgements

I hope this book is accurate. It has been informed by my encounters – some brief, some extended – with all of the principal characters in the story. It has also been informed by my reading of the work of a range of royal biographers and historians to whom I am indebted, most notably my friend Hugo Vickers, whose meticulously researched authorised biography of Prince Philip's mother, *Alice: Princess Andrew of Greece* (2000), I have drawn on extensively. The family trees of the Greek royal family and of the Battenbergs were kindly prepared by Hugo Vickers.

Many people have been involved in the creation of this book. I want especially to thank my literary agent, the late Ed Victor, for suggesting it, and my publisher, Mark Booth, for making it happen.

I began work on the first version of this book more than a decade ago. I remain grateful to the Queen's private secretary at the time, Sir Robin Janvrin, and Her Majesty's then press secretary, Penny Russell-Smith, for their kindness and for enabling me to spend time with the Queen as she went about her royal duties. I am grateful to the Duke of Edinburgh's final private secretary, Brigadier Archie Miller-Bakewell, and to his predecessors, Sir Miles Hunt-Davis and Sir Brian McGrath, as well as His Royal Highness's librarian and archivist, Dame Anne Griffiths, for their kindness and practical assistance over several years. Prince Philip generously gave me permission for the use of his family photographs and I am also indebted to the Queen for the use of photographs from the Royal Collection, notably pictures from her grandmother, Queen Mary's, photograph albums.

Below I have listed the principal conversations and books I have relied on for each chapter. Of course, the blame for any errors of commission or omission should be laid at my door and no one else's.

Chapters 1 and 2

Conversations with Prince Philip, the Queen of Denmark, King Constantine of Greece, Brett Kahr, Lady Kennard, Countess Mountbatten of Burma, Hugo Vickers

Alice: Princess Andrew of Greece by Hugo Vickers, 2000

An Appreciation of Kurt Hahn, with a foreword by HRH The Duke of Edinburgh, 1975

Cheam School from 1645 by Edward Peel, with a foreword by HRH The Duke of Edinburgh, 1974

The Duke: A Portrait of Prince Philip by Tim Heald, 1991

Elizabeth: Grand Duchess of Russia by Hugo Mager, 1998

Hessian Tapestry by David Duff, 1967

Ionian Vision by Michael Llewellyn Smith, 1973

Lillie Langtry: Manners, Masks and Morals by Laura Beatty, 1999

Marie Bonaparte by Celia Bertin, 1982

Memoirs 1849–1897 by Prince von Bülow, 1931

Mountbatten by Philip Ziegler, 1985

Prince Philip: A Family Portrait by Queen Alexandra of Yugoslavia, 1959

Queen Victoria's Relations by Meriel Buchanan, 1954

The Royal House of Windsor by Elizabeth Longford, 1974

Schoolmaster of Kings – Donald MacJannet: 65 Years as an International Educator by Howard Jacobs, 1982

Towards Disaster by Prince Andrew of Greece, 1930

Chapters 3 and 4

Conversations with Prince Philip, Sonia Berry, Lord David Cecil, Lady Longford, Sir John Mills, Countess Mountbatten of Burma, Nigel Nicolson, Graham Payn, the Hon. Margaret Rhodes, Lord Snowdon, Woodrow Wyatt

Among the Bohemians by Virginia Nicholson, 2002

The Asquiths by Colin Clifford, 2002

Chips: The Diaries of Sir Henry Channon, edited by Robert Rhodes James, 1967

Dearest Child: Private Correspondence of Queen Victoria and the Crown Princess of Prussia, 1858–61, edited by Roger Fulford, 1964

Edward VII by Christopher Hibbert, 1976

Elizabeth by Sarah Bradford, 1996

Elizabeth the Queen Mother by Grania Forbes, 2002

George VI by Sarah Bradford, 1989

Harold Nicolson: Diaries and Letters 1930–39, edited by Nigel Nicolson, 1966

A King's Story by the Duke of Windsor, 1951

King Edward the Seventh by Philip Magnus, 1964

Kings, Queens and Courtiers by Kenneth Rose, 1986

Letters from a Prince: Edward Prince of Wales to Mrs Freda Dudley Ward, March 1918–January 1921, edited by Rupert Godfrey, 1999

The Little Princesses by Marion Crawford, 1950

The Lyttleton Hart-Davis Letters, Vol. III: *Correspondence of George Lyttleton and Rupert Hart-Davis*, 1979

A Moment's Liberty: The Shorter Diary by Virginia Woolf, abridged and edited by Anne Olivier Bell, 1990

Queen Mary and Others by Osbert Sitwell, 1974

Recollections of Three Reigns by Frederick Ponsonby, 1951

Thatched with Gold by Mabell, Countess of Airlie, 1962

The Tongs and the Bones by the Earl of Harewood, 1981

The Wheel of Life: The Diary of Beatrice Webb, Vol. 4: 1924–43, edited by B. and J. Mackenzie, 1985

Victoria R.I. by Elizabeth Longford, 1964

Chapters 5 and 6

Conversations with Prince Philip, Sonia Berry, Professor Anthony Clare, Tim Heald, Elizabeth Longford, Countess Mountbatten of Burma, the Hon. Margaret Rhodes

Alice: Princess Andrew of Greece by Hugo Vickers, 2000

Cabbages to Kings by Lisa Sheridan, 1955

The Duke: A Portrait of Prince Philip by Tim Heald, 1991

Elizabeth by Sarah Bradford, 1996

Elizabeth R by Elizabeth Longford, 1983

The Fringes of Power: Downing Street Diaries 1939–1955 by John Colville, 1985

George VI by Sarah Bradford, 1989

George VI: His Life and Reign by John Wheeler-Bennett, 1958

Harold Nicolson: Diaries and Letters 1930–39, edited by Nigel Nicolson, 1966

A Horseman through Six Reigns: Reminiscences of a Royal Riding Master by Horace Smith, 1955

It Wasn't All Mayhem by Harry Hargreaves, 2004

John Buchan by Andrew Lownie, 1995

The Killearn Diaries, edited by Trefor Evans, 1972

The Little Princesses by Marion Crawford, 1950

Mountbatten by Philip Ziegler, 1985

The Noël Coward Diaries, edited by Graham Payn and Sheridan Morley, 1982

Prince Philip: A Family Portrait by Queen Alexandra of Yugoslavia, 1959

The Queen by Ben Pimlott, 1996

Royal: Her Majesty Queen Elizabeth II by Robert Lacey, 2002

To Be a King: A Biography of HRH Prince Charles by Dermot Morrah, 1989

Wallis and Edward: Letters 1931–1937, edited by Michael Bloch, 1986

Chapters 7 and 8

Conversations with Prince Philip, Prince Edward, Larry Adler, Sonia Berry, Cherie Booth, Henry, 7th Earl of Carnarvon, Geordie, 8th Earl of Carnarvon, Robin Dalton, Sir Edward Ford, Michael Foot, Tim Heald, Lady Kennard, Sir Roderic Llewellyn, Countess Mountbatten of Burma and Lord Brabourne, Commander Mike Parker, the Hon. Margaret Rhodes

Alice: Princess Andrew of Greece by Hugo Vickers, 2000

Chips: The Diaries of Sir Henry Channon, edited by Robert Rhodes James, 1967

Counting One's Blessings: The Selected Letters of Queen Elizabeth The Queen Mother, edited by William Shawcross, 2012

The Daily Telegraph Book of Military Obituaries by David Twiston Davies, 2003

The Duke: A Portrait of Prince Philip by Tim Heald, 1991

Elizabeth by Sarah Bradford, 1996

Elizabeth R by Elizabeth Longford, 1983

Footprints in Time by John Colville, 1976

Friends, Enemies and Sovereigns by Sir John Wheeler-Bennett, 1976

The Fringes of Power: Downing Street Diaries 1939–1955 by John Colville, 1985

Harold Nicolson: Diaries and Letters 1930–39, edited by Nigel Nicolson, 1966

A Horseman through Six Reigns: Reminiscences of a Royal Riding Master by Horace Smith, 1955

An Incidental Memoir by Robin Dalton, 1998

King George VI by Sir John Wheeler-Bennett, 1958

The Little Princesses by Marion Crawford, 1950

Long Walk to Freedom by Nelson Mandela, 1994

A Mingled Measure: Diaries 1953–1972 by James Lees-Milne, 1974

Mountbatten by Philip Ziegler, 1985

The Noël Coward Diaries, edited by Graham Payn and Sheridan Morley, 1982

Philip: An Informal Biography by Basil Boothroyd, 1971

Prince Philip: A Family Portrait by Queen Alexandra of Yugoslavia, 1959

The Queen by Ann Morrow, 1983

The Queen by Ben Pimlott, 1996

The Road to Station X by Sarah Baring, 2000

Royal: Her Majesty Queen Elizabeth II by Robert Lacey, 2002

Silver Spoon by Richard Norton, 1954

Step Aside for Royalty by Eileen Parker, 1982

Time and Chance by Peter Townsend, 1978

To Be a King: A Biography of HRH Prince Charles by Dermot Morrah, 1989

Young Prince Philip: His Turbulent Early Life by Philip Eade, 2011

Wallis and Edward: Letters 1931–37, edited by Michael Bloch, 1986

Chapters 9 and 10

Conversations with Prince Philip, Sarah Bradford, Lord Charteris of Amisfield, Sir Edward Ford, John Gibson, Sir Robin Janvrin, Commander Mike Parker, the Hon. Margaret Rhodes

Alice: Princess Andrew of Greece by Hugo Vickers, 2000

Charles by Anthony Holden, 1998

Chips: The Diaries of Sir Henry Channon, edited by Robert Rhodes James, 1967

Counting One's Blessings: The Selected Letters of Queen Elizabeth The Queen Mother, edited by William Shawcross, 2012

Daily Telegraph interview with Sonia Berry by Cassandra Jardine, 2002

The Duke: A Portrait of Prince Philip by Tim Heald, 1991

Elizabeth by Sarah Bradford, 1996

Elizabeth R by Elizabeth Longford, 1983

Footprints in Time by John Colville, 1976

The Fringes of Power: Downing Street Diaries 1939–1955 by John Colville, 1985

Harold Nicolson: Diaries and Letters 1930–39, edited by Nigel Nicolson, 1966

HRH Prince Philip, Duke of Edinburgh: A Portrait by John Dean, 1954

King George VI by Sir John Wheeler-Bennett, 1958

Kings, Queens and Courtiers by Kenneth Rose, 1986

The Little Princesses by Marion Crawford, 1950

The Macmillan Diaries: The Cabinet Years 1950–57, edited by Peter Catterall, 2004

Mountbatten by Philip Ziegler, 1985

The Noël Coward Diaries, edited by Graham Payn and Sheridan Morley, 1982

Philip: An Informal Biography by Basil Boothroyd, 1971

Prince Philip: A Family Portrait by Queen Alexandra of Yugoslavia, 1959

The Queen by Ann Morrow, 1983

The Queen by Ben Pimlott, 1996

Royal: Her Majesty Queen Elizabeth II by Robert Lacey, 2002

Royal Secrets by Stephen Barry, 1985

Time and Chance by Peter Townsend, 1978

To Be a King: A Biography of HRH Prince Charles by Dermot Morrah, 1989

Chapters 11 and 12

Conversations with Prince Philip, the Duchess of Abercorn, Katie Boyle, Lord Brabourne, Sarah Bradford, Archbishop Lord Carey, Geordie, 8th Earl of Carnarvon, Lord Charteris of Amisfield, Robin Dalton, Andrew, 11th Duke of Devonshire, Sir Miles Hunt-Davis, Lord Jenkins of Hillhead, Lady Kennard, Pat Kirkwood, Countess Mountbatten of Burma, Martin Palmer, Commander Mike Parker, the Hon. Margaret Rhodes, Baroness Thatcher, Sarah, Duchess of York

Alice: Princess Andrew of Greece by Hugo Vickers, 2000

Baron by Baron, with a foreword by Peter Ustinov, 1957

Born Bewildered by Hélène Cordet, 1961

Charles: Prince of Wales by Anthony Holden, 1979

Charles: A Biography by Anthony Holden, 1998

Counting One's Blessings: The Selected Letters of Queen Elizabeth The Queen Mother, edited by William Shawcross, 2012

Daily Mirror interview with Norman Barson, 1996

Daily Telegraph interview with Sonia Berry by Cassandra Jardine, 2002

The Diaries of Kenneth Tynan, edited by John Lahr, 2001

The Duke: A Portrait of Prince Philip by Tim Heald, 1991

Elizabeth by Sarah Bradford, 1996

Elizabeth: The Woman and The Queen by Graham Turner, 2002

Feather from the Firebird by Sacha Abercorn, 2003

George V by Kenneth Rose, 1984

George VI by Sarah Bradford, 1989

The Heart Has Its Reasons by the Duchess of Windsor, 1956

An Incidental Memoir by Robin Dalton, 1998

Kings, Queens and Courtiers by Kenneth Rose, 1986

Khrushchev Remembers, edited by Edward Crankshaw, 1971

Mountbatten by Philip Ziegler, 1985

Niv: The Authorised Biography of David Niven by Graham Lord, 2003

Philip: The Man behind the Monarchy by Unity Hall, 1987

The Prince of Wales by Jonathan Dimbleby, 1995

The Queen by Ben Pimlott, 1996

The Queen: 50 Years – A Celebration by Ronald Allison, 2001

Reagan: A Life in Letters by Ronald Reagan, edited by Kiron K. Skinner, Annelise Anderson, and Martin Anderson, 2003

A Royal Duty by Paul Burrell, 2003

Royal: Her Majesty Queen Elizabeth II by Robert Lacey, 2002

Royal Orders: The Honours and the Honoured by Hugo Vickers, 1994

Royal Yacht Britannia: The Official History by Richard Johnstone-Bryden, 2003

Step Aside for Royalty by Eileen Parker, 1982

Picture Credits

Section one
ILN/Camera Press London, Photography by Spice/Camera Press London, Private Collection, Private Collection, Private Collection, Private Collection, Private Collection, Private Collection, Private Collection, Private Collection, Private Collection, Getty Images-Hulton, Getty Images-Hulton, Private Collection, Topham Picturepoint, Sir William Peek, ILN/Camera Press London, Getty Images-Hulton, ©Bettman/Corbis, Private Collection, Topham Picturepoint, Topham Picturepoint.

Section two
Getty Images-Hulton, Private Collection, Private Collection, Royal Archives ©2004 HM Queen Elizabeth II, Getty Images-Hulton, Photography by Bassano/Camera Press London, Getty Images-Hulton, Private Collection, Private Collection, B/S/Camera Press London, Photograph by Baron/Camera Press London, Private Collection, The Royal Archives ©2004 HM Queen Elizabeth II, Getty Images-Hulton, ©Bettman/Corbis, *The Times*/Camera Press London, Getty Images-Hulton, Getty Images-Hulton.

Section three
The Times/Camera Press London, Photograph by James Reid/Camera Press London, Topham Picturepoint, Topham Picturepoint, Camera Press London, Private Collection, Private Collection, Private Collection, Topham Picturepoint, Private Collection, Private Collection, Getty Images-Hulton, Getty Images-Hulton, Topham Picturepoint, Getty Images-Hulton, Rex Features, Photograph by Lichfield/Camera Press London, Photograph by Lichfield/Camera Press London.

Index